OXFORD READINGS IN FEMINISM

FEMINISM & FILM

E. ANN KAPLAN

OXFORD READINGS IN FEMINISM

FEMINISM AND FILM

PUBLISHED IN THIS SERIES:

Feminism and Renaissance Studies
edited by Lorna Hutson

Feminism and Science
edited by Evelyn Fox Keller and Helen E. Longino

Feminism, the Public and the Private
edited by Joan Landes

Feminism and Politics
edited by Anne Phillips

Feminism and History
edited by Joan Wallach Scott

Feminism and Cultural Studies
edited by Morag Shiach

Feminism and Pornography
edited by Drucilla Cornell

Feminism and the Body
edited by Londa Schiebinger

Econ

OXFORD READINGS IN FEMINISM

Feminism and Film

Edited by

E. Ann Kaplan

OXFORD
UNIVERSITY PRESS

OXFORD
UNIVERSITY PRESS

Great Clarendon Street, Oxford OX2 6DP

Oxford University Press is a department of the University of Oxford.
It furthers the University's objective of excellence in research, scholarship,
and education by publishing worldwide in

Oxford New York

Athens Auckland Bangkok Bogotá Buenos Aires Calcutta
Cape Town Chennai Dar es Salaam Delhi Florence Hong Kong Istanbul
Karachi Kuala Lumpur Madrid Melbourne Mexico City Mumbai
Nairobi Paris São Paulo Singapore Taipei Tokyo Toronto Warsaw

with associated companies in Berlin Ibadan

Oxford is a registered trade mark of Oxford University Press
in the UK and in certain other countries

Published in the United States
by Oxford University Press Inc., New York

First published 2000

British Library Cataloguing in Publication Data
Data available

British Library Cataloging in Publication Data
(Data applied for)

ISBN 0–19–878234–9

1 3 5 7 9 10 8 6 4 2

Typeset in Minion
by RefineCatch Limited, Bungay, Suffolk
Printed in Great Britain by
Biddles Ltd, Guildford and King's Lynn, Surrey

Preface

It was an all but impossible task to select which of the abundant excellent essays written on feminism and film since 1970 to put in this volume. Originally, I had chosen twice as many as appear here, only to be forced to cut drastically. Faced with that prospect, I decided to focus on one major strand of thought in the field produced by Laura Mulvey's polemical and influential 1975 essay on 'Visual Pleasure and Narrative Cinema.' Mulvey's work struck a cord so pertinent and provocative that it has remained to this day a site of both appreciation for the insights and contestation and debate about their validity or utility. Many of the major essays in the field responded in one way or another—including outright rejection—to Mulvey's theoretical positions, so I could produce a book of coherent essays by printing work that debated, argued against, or built out from 'Visual Pleasure and Narrative Cinema.'

But re-reading the entire book as I proofed it, I realized something else. A central set of concepts worked and reworked by scholars is that of *difference*: in the early days, it is male/female sexual difference; later on gay/straight difference—that is, the differences *within* female sexuality; still later the difference of 'gender' (as distinct from 'sexuality'); and finally, differences between women produced by race and ethnicity. In reading our varying and complex theorizing about all these differences, I realized how feminist film research was very much at the forefront of questioning and analyzing differences across all these territories, across all these borders. Off hand, I cannot think of any discipline that focussed so closely on difference. Anthropology, on which feminist film theory drew, is perhaps the exception, but in using psychoanalysis, feminist research went in other directions than did most Anthropology.

The question of difference is an important point as we think about the future. I would argue that the tools feminist film theorists have produced will prove extremely important as we move into the 21st century—perhaps the first truly global one because of digital communications technologies. Sexual and ethnic differences in many parts of the world remain entrenched—often in ways with long traditions and histories. It will be interesting to see how and if the tools for analyzing difference that feminist film theorists developed may be useful elsewhere than in the west.

It seems to me that humans' incredibly sophisticated digital and other technologies throw into relief the limitations of human nature. Differences of all kinds remain a key stumbling block to humans' ability to bring about justice, equality, equal distribution of wealth, food, and consumer items. I hope that this volume will be viewed as providing essential background knowledge for understanding current debates, and also for moving feminist film studies forward into new terrain, such as joining hands with Queer Studies. Some premises of Queer Studies challenge positions—even those taken by lesbian film scholars included here—in feminist film theory. It is exciting to think of a companion volume to this one where we could bring together feminist film theorists' discussions of difference with Queer Studies' interest in questions of sexual indeterminacy, transvestism, and transsexuality. But above all, I hope this volume will be useful for thinking of how to move beyond difference to imagine new modes of being.

Let me take this opportunity to thank Teresa Brennan for her support and advice in the process of selecting essays for the volume. I would also like to thank the Humanities Institute staff assistants, Chris Nagle and Theo Cateforis, for their research help. Finally, thanks to the OUP staff, especially Lesley Wilson, for their patience with a taxing text.

E. Ann Kaplan March 2000

Contents

Notes on Contributors xi

Introduction 1
E. ANN KAPLAN

Phase I. Pioneers and Classics: The Modernist Mode

Introductory Notes 19

1. Women's Cinema as Counter-Cinema 22
CLAIRE JOHNSTON

2. Visual Pleasure and Narrative Cinema 34
LAURA MULVEY

3. 'Woman as Sign' 48
ELIZABETH COWIE

4. *Klute* 1: A Contemporary Film Noir and Feminist Criticism 66
CHRISTINE GLEDHILL

5. Woman's Stake: Filming the Female Body 86
MARY ANN DOANE

6. Male Subjectivity and the Celestial Suture: *It's a Wonderful Life* 100
KAJA SILVERMAN

7. Is the Gaze Male? 119
E. ANN KAPLAN

8. Dorothy Arzner: Critical Strategies 139
CLAIRE JOHNSTON

Phase II. Critiques of Phase I Theories: New Methods

Introductory Notes 151

9. Lesbian Looks: Dorothy Arzner and Female Authorship 159
JUDITH MAYNE

10. The Difficulty of Difference 181
DAVID N. RODOWICK

11. Masochism and the Perverse Pleasures of the Cinema 203
GAYLYN STUDLAR

12. Pleasure, Ambivalence, Identification: Valentino and Female Spectatorship 226
MIRIAM HANSEN

13. Masculinity as Spectacle: Reflections on Men and Mainstream Cinema 253
STEVE NEALE

14. Strategies of Coherence: Narrative Cinema, Feminist Poetics, and Yvonne Rainer 265
TERESA DE LAURETIS

15. The Orthopsychic Subject: Film Theory and the Reception of Lacan 287
JOAN COPJEC

Phase III. Race, Sexuality, and Postmodernism in Feminist Film Theory

Introductory Notes 309

16. Speaking Nearby 317
TRINH T. MINH-HA AND NANCY N. CHEN

17. White Privilege and Looking Relations: Race and Gender in Feminist Film Theory 336
JANE GAINES

18. Racism, Representation, Psychoanalysis 356
CLAIRE PAJACZKOWSKA AND LOLA YOUNG

19. That Moment of Emergence 375
PRATIBHA PARMAR

20. Sexual Indifference and Lesbian Representation 384
TERESA DE LAURETIS

Phase IV. Spectatorship, Ethnicity, and Melodrama

Introductory Notes 409

21. Film and the Masquerade: Theorising the Female Spectator 418
MARY ANN DOANE

22. Women's Genres 437
ANNETTE KUHN

23. Desperately Seeking Difference 450
JACKIE STACEY

24. The Case of the Missing Mother: Maternal Issues in Vidor's *Stella Dallas* 466
E. ANN KAPLAN

25. 'Something Else Besides a Mother': *Stella Dallas* and the Maternal Melodrama 479
LINDA WILLIAMS

26. Tears and Desire: Women and Melodrama in the 'Old' Mexican Cinema 505
ANA M. LÓPEZ

27. Three Men and Baby M 521
TANIA MODLESKI

28. The Carapace that Failed: Ousmane Sembene's *Xala* 535
LAURA MULVEY

Further Reading 554

Index 561

Notes on Contributors

NANCY N. CHEN is currently Assistant Professor of Anthropology at UC Santa Cruz where she teaches visual anthropology and medical anthropology.

JOAN COPJEC is Professor of English, Comparative Literature, and Media Study at the University of Buffalo, where she is also Director of the Center for the Study of Psychoanalysis and Culture. She is the author of *Read My Desire: Lacan against the Historicists* and editor of several volumes, including those in her *S* series, published by Verso.

ELIZABETH COWIE is Reader in Film Studies at the University of Kent at Canterbury. She is a founding editor of *m/f*, a journal of feminist theory, and coedited *The Woman in Question*. She has published on psychoanalysis, film noir, classical Hollywood, narrative, and documentary, and is the author of *Representing the Woman* (1997).

MARY ANN DOANE is George Hazard Crooker University Professor of Modern Culture and Media at Brown University. She is the author of *The Desire to Desire: The Woman's Film of the 1940s* and *Femme Fatales: Feminism, Film Theory, Psychoanalysis.* She is currently completing a book on time, contingency and the cinema.

JANE GAINES is Associate Professor of Literature and English and Director of the Program in Film and Video at Duke University. She has recently completed *Other/Race/Desire: Mixed Blood Relations in Early Cinema* (University of Chicago Press, forthcoming), and co-edited *Collecting Visible Evidence* with Michael Renov (University of Minnesota). In addition to writing on feminist film theory over the years, she has written on entertainment law (*Contested Culture: The Image, the Voice and the Law*) and motion picture fashions (*Fabrications: Costume and the Female Body*, co-edited with Charlotte Herzog).

CHRISTINE GLEDHILL is Professor of Cinema Studies at Staffordshire University. She is editor of *Home Is Where the Heart Is: Studies in Melodrama and the Woman's Film* (British Film Institute, 1987), *Stardom: Industry of Desire* (Routledge, 1991), and co-editor of *Reinventing Film Studies* (Edward Arnold, 2000). She has published widely on feminist film criticism, melodrama, and British cinema. She is currently working on a study of 1920s British cinema for the British Film Institute, due for publication in 2000.

MIRIAM HANSEN is Ferdinand Schevill Distinguished Service Professor in the Humanities and Chair of the Committee on Cinema and Media Studies at the University of Chicago. Her most recent book is *Babel and Babylon: Spectatorship in American Silent Film* (Harvard UP, 1991: 1994). She is a co-editor of *New German Critique* and has published widely on American and German Cinema, feminist film theory, and concepts of the public sphere. She is currently completing a study on the Frankfurt School's debates on film and mass culture.

Claire Johnston (1940–1987) was one of the pioneers of feminist film theory and a tireless activist on behalf of intellectually independent cinemas. She co-organized the first ever women's film festival (Edinburgh, 1972), published *Notes on Women's Cinema* (1973), co-edited a book on Jacques Tourneur (1975) and published the first main study of Dorothy Arzner (1975). She committed suicide in 1987.

E. Ann Kaplan is Professor of English and Comparative Literature at The State University of New York at Stony Brook, where she also founded and directs The Humanities Institute. Kaplan has written many books and numerous essays on topics in literary and media theory, practices and politics, with special focus on issues in gender and race. Her most recent book is *Looking for the Other: Feminism, Film and the Imperial Gaze* (1997). Her new project is on *Performing Age: Bodies, Images, Fictions.*

Annette Kuhn is Professor of Film Studies at Lancaster University (UK), and an editor of *Screen.* Her publications include *Women's Pictures: Feminism And Cinema*; *The Power Of The Image: Essays On Representation And Sexuality*; and *Family Secrets: Acts Of Memory And Imagination.*

Teresa de Lauretis is Professor of the History of Consciousness at the University of California, Santa Cruz. The author of numerous essays and books, including *Alice Doesn't* (1984), *Technologies of Gender* (1987), and *The Practice of Love* (1994), she has written on film, literature, semiotics, psychoanalysis, and feminist theory.

Ana M. López teaches film and Latin American studies at Tulane University. She has published widely on Latin American film and media, including the co-edited anthologies *Mediating Two Worlds* (BFI, 1993) and *The Ethnic Eye: Latino Media Arts* (University of Minnesota Press, 1996). Her *Third and Imperfect: The New Latin American Cinema* is forthcoming from the University of Minnesota Press.

Judith Mayne is Professor of French and Women's Studies at Ohio State University (Columbus). She is the author of several books, including *The Woman at the Keyhole* (1990); *Cinema and Spectatorship* (1993); and *Directed by Dorothy Arzner* (1994).

Trinh T. Minh-Ha is a writer, filmmaker and composer. Her more recent works include the books: *Drawn From African Dwellings* (in coll. with Jean Paul Bourdier, 1996), *Framer Framed* (1962), *When The Moon Waxes Red* (1991), *Woman, Native, Other* (1989), *En miniscules* (book of poems, 1987); and the films: *A Tale of Love* (1995), *Shoot for the Contents* (1991), *Surname*

Viet Given Name Nam (1989), *Naked Spaces* (1985), and *Reassemblage* (1982). She taught at the Dakar Conservatory of Music in Senegal, and at universities such as Cornell, San Francisco State, Smith and Harvard, and is Professor of Women's Studies and Film at the University of California, Berkeley. She is now working on a multi-media installation project ('Nothing But Ways') to open at the Yerba Buena Center for the Arts on June 4, 1999, and on a feature film project to be shot partly in Japan.

TANIA MODLESKI is the author of several books including *Loving With a Vengeance: Mass-Produced Fantasies for Women, The Women Who Knew Too Much: Hitchcock and Feminist Theory*, and most recently *Old Wives Tales, and Other Women's Stories.* She teaches in the English Department at the University of Southern California.

LAURA MULVEY has been writing about film and film theory since the mid-1970s and her essays have been published in *Visual and Other Pleasures* (Macmillan, 1989) and *Fetishism and Curiosity* (British Film Institute, 1966). She is also the author of the BFI Film Classic *Citizen Kane.* Laura Mulvey co-directed six films with Peter Wollen including *Riddles of the Sphinx* (BFI, 1978) and *Frida Kahlo and Tina Modotti* (Arts Council, 1980) as well as *Disgraced Monuments* with Mark Lewis (Channel Four, 1994). She is now Professor of Film and Media Studies at Birkbeck College, University of London.

STEVE NEALE is Research Professor in Film, Media and Communication Studies. He is the author of *Genre* (1980), *Cinema and Technology* (1985) and *Genre and Hollywood* (2000), co-author of *Popular Film and Television Comedy* (1990) and co-editor of *Contemporary Hollywood Cinema* (1998).

CLAIRE PAJACZKOWSKA worked as a filmmaker in New York whilst being part of the 'Heresies Six' collective on feminism and art. She then worked in London as a lecturer in film and visual culture. Her doctoral thesis 'Before Language' explored the uses of psychoanalysis as a theory of visual culture. She has translated several books on psychoanalytic theory and lectured in Paris, Naples, Florence, Krakow, Berlin and the USA. Her most recent publications are *Feminist Visual Culture* (edited with Fiona Carson, 2000) and *Perversion* (2000). She is Senior Lecturer in Visual Culture at Middlesex University.

PRATIBHA PARMAR is an award-winning filmmaker whose films and videos have been shown internationally on television, at film festivals and in theatres. She has written and edited several books including *Warrior Marks: Female Genital Mutilation and the Sexual Blinding of Woman*, co-authored with Alice Walker and published in the U.K. and U.S.

DAVID N. RODOWICK is Professor of Visual and Cultural Studies at the University of Rochester and the author of *The Crisis of Political Modernism, The Difficulty of Difference*, and *Gilles Deleuze's Time Machine.* His latest book,

Reading the Figural, or the Ends of Aesthetic in Film, Philosophy, and the New Media will be published by Duke University Press in 2000.

KAJA SILVERMAN is Chancellor's Professor of Rhetoric and Film at the University of California at Berkeley, and the author of *The Subject of Semiotics* (1982); *The Acoustic Mirror: The Female Voice in Psychoanalysis and Cinema* (1988); *Male Subjectivity at the Margins* (1992); *The Threshold of the Visible World* (1996); and (with Harun Farocki) *Speaking About Godard* (1998).

JACKIE STACEY is Reader in Women's Studies and Sociology at Lancaster University in England. She is a co-editor of *Screen* and author of *Star Gazing: Hollywood Cinema and Female Spectatorship* (1994) and *Teratologies: A Cultural Study of Cancer* (1997).

GAYLYN STUDLAR is Professor of Film Studies and English at the University of Michigan-Ann Arbor, where she also directs the Program in Film and Video Studies. She is the author of *This Mad Masquerade: Stardom and Masculinity in the Jazz Age* and *In the Realm of Pleasure: Von Sternberg, Dietrich, and the Masochistic Aesthetic.* Her most recent publication is the co-edited volume, *Titanic: Anatomy of a Blockbuster* (Rutgers, 1999). She is currently working on a social history of women and the American cinema and completing a co-edited volume, *John Ford Made Westerns,* with Matthew Bernstein.

LINDA WILLIAMS teaches film studies and rhetoric at the University of California, Berkeley. She is the author of *Hard Core: Power, Pleasure and the Frenzy of the Visible* and of *Melodramas of Black and White* (forthcoming, Princeton U.P.).

LOLA YOUNG is Professor of Cultural Studies at Middlesex University. Before becoming an academic Professor Young worked in arts development, promoting black arts and culture. She has written widely in issues of 'race', gender and representation, black British culture, and film. Her book, *Fear of the Dark: Race, Gender and Sexuality in Cinema* was published by Routledge in 1996, and she is currently working on an edited collection of her own essays.

Introduction

E. Ann Kaplan

Feminist perspectives on film developed in the context of the various womens' liberation movements that emerged in the United States in the late 1960s and early 1970s. As many historians have shown, women in different nations have periodically over the centuries resisted their social, political, and intellectual marginalizing, their silencing in patriarchal cultures,[1] and set about producing new knowledge. What differing kinds of knowledge about women's film study can offer is partly answered in the rest of this introduction, for the knowledge produced in feminist film study has varied with the goals, methods, and interests of different feminist film scholars. Knowledge produced varied also with the disciplinary basis of scholars taking up feminist film research. But studying images of women, from whatever perspective or within whatever research method, problematizes and raises questions about the relationship of aesthetics to politics and to cultures.

Film study is enhanced by feminist perspectives because the word 'feminist' implies a particular stance vis-à-vis women: it implies a concern with gender difference in general, but taking up the perspective of women specifically. It implies identification with women's concerns, even if, logically, such concerns cannot be dealt with without also considering men. Indeed, as reflected in selections in the volume, feminist film theory includes study of masculinity in cinema—an area first begun in the early 1980s in Britain and being pursued actively in America today.

A feminist perspective should not be confused with the literal gender of the scholar: males can write feminist criticism, and women can write criticism that is not feminist.[2] Looking at women in film pushes feminist theory to a different set of issues than those aspects of films that male scholars traditionally study. The feminist film theorist—whether implicitly or explicitly—asks: what is the relationship between images on film and the context for their production?

S/he may do this through asking: What is the relationship between images of women on film (their social and sexual roles) and what scholars can discover about women's lives in any particular context within which a film is produced? Included here may be questions such as: why are some groups (e.g. white women) featured more frequently than other groups in Hollywood film? Is the same predominance of white women found in other national cinemas? Why? Study of the material conditions for a film's production may serve to answer questions involving gender and race.

Or the scholar may ask how meanings about women are produced on film as these relate to meanings about women produced elsewhere, i.e. socially, politically, and culturally, in different national contexts. Humanities disciplines have traditionally focused on questions of how 'signs' (the materials and symbols used to make any art form) 'signify' (convey meanings). Since art is a deliberate construction by someone (or some groups of people) making art or entertainment for an imagined audience or receiver, what signs have been used to produce meanings about women? Why these signs rather than others? How have signifiers in relation to women changed over time? How do they differ from one Hollywood genre to another, or one kind of film to another?

A third question some feminist theorists ask is: what are the relationships between images of women on film and the level of fantasy, desire, unconscious wishes and fears that has both individual and social/historical formation? Whose desire is at work in a particular film? Whose unconscious is being addressed? How and why? *Film offers a meta-terrain where questions about women, the unconscious, the social imaginary and women's discursive construction can take on different valences than they may take in either the social or natural sciences, or in medicine.* In this way, film pushes feminist studies to develop new theories, or to challenge accepted male theories of aesthetics and entertainment. Film is an important object for feminist practice, since creating art or entertainment with feminist perspectives may help to change entrenched male stances towards women that can be found in commercial or avant-garde entertainment and art. *In so doing, feminist film study may change cultural attitudes towards women, and may deepen our understanding of meanings women have traditionally born in patriarchal cultures.*

Some of the earliest feminist academic work was done by women in history and literary studies: scholars began to investigate women's neglected roles in, and contributions to, various cultures and, in literary studies, to explore neglected women writers and feminist themes in fiction and drama.[3] They also studied how women have been represented in literature across the centuries. Pioneering research in literature was done in the 1970s by Kate Millett, Mary Ferguson, and Susan Koppelman-Cornillon in America; and by Germaine Greer in Britain. In literary studies, early feminist work basically followed New Critical research methods—that is, scholars studied formal aspects of texts, such as motifs, symbols, characters, narrative style, language. But feminists diverged in focusing specifically on images of female characters in fiction. Typically, scholars created categories of female social roles that they found in Western literature, and discussed their limiting of women to the conventional domestic sphere, or, in some cases, analysed the resistances of certain characters to social female constraints.[4]

In contrast to feminist literary perspectives—which emerged at the tail end of decades of academic literary studies—feminist approaches to film came about as Cinema Studies, as a disciplinary area, was in its foundational stage. In this way, feminist approaches gained a place in Cinema Studies more readily and earlier than in other fields. Since feminist perspectives on film developed in several places in the late 1960s and early 1970s, let me name the following founding texts as examples, without claiming to be exhaustive.[5]

- In the USA, the journal originally called *Women and Film* (later to become *Camera Obscura*) started in 1970 by a feminist collective on the West coast; Molly Haskells's 1973 *From Reverence to Rape: The Treatment of Women in the Movies*; another book, *Women and the Cinema: A Critical Anthology*, edited by Karyn Kay and Gerald Peary in 1977; and the journal *Jump Cut*, started in the early 1970s and edited by Julia LeSage, Chuck Kleinhans, and John Hess.
- In Britain, the journals *Screen* (where Laura Mulvey's influential 1975 essay 'Visual Pleasure and Narrative Cinema' was first printed) and *Screen Education*, together with *Working Papers in Cultural Studies* (published by the Centre for Cultural Studies, Birmingham); Claire Johnston's 1973 edited *Notes on Women's Cinema*, together with her booklet on Dorothy Arzner edited with Pam Cook in 1974; Richard Dyer's 1977 edited volume on *Gays and Film*; and E. Ann Kaplan's 1978 edited volume, *Women in Film Noir*.
- In Germany, the periodical *Frauen und Film*, which started in 1974.

- In France, *Cahiers du Cinéma* produced little feminist analysis, but its articles had an influence on feminist theories outside of France.

Taken together, essays in these journals and books laid the groundwork for the emergence of an entirely new research area, namely, feminism and film, which was to play a powerful if often controversial role in the emergence of Film Studies itself, as a now major discipline. It is partly because by the 1990s feminist film criticism has become such a large area within film studies that selecting texts for this volume was so difficult. I bore in mind the edited collections on feminist film theory already in press. Where possible, I tried not to reprint essays already anthologized, preferring to refer students and teachers in the section introductions to pertinent essays not printed in this volume, and to related books. Sometimes a reprinting seemed unavoidable if I was to fulfil my mandate from Oxford University Press to gather together 'classic' essays into this reader. Students need to have these materials in one place if they are to follow the twists and turns of developments in feminist film theory from 1970 to 1997.[6]

Some of the earliest feminist film criticism, illustrated in the 'founding' texts, used social-role methods similar to those in the first feminist literary studies, and such analysis continues in television studies in Schools of Communication. Inspired by the glaring neglect of women directors in *auteur* studies, scholars also undertook archival research on early and neglected women directors,[7] as they tried to understand women's roles in the Hollywood institution.[8] An early feminist film activity was organizing Women's Film Festivals to showcase silent, classical, or foreign 'lost' women directors as well as, importantly, experimental and documentary film-makers struggling to produce work in the 1970s. I take up debates about this kind of research in my 'Notes' to Phase I essays.

But other methods and foci were present within the same founding texts: different methods include Marxist-Feminist perspectives—e.g. a social-role analysis of working class and ethnic women in the American journal *Jump Cut* (see especially Julia LeSage's work and that which she encouraged); or the Althusserian Marxism combined with Saussurian semiotics developed by Claire Johnston and, in E. Ann Kaplan's 1978 volume, Christine Gledhill and Sylvia Harvey; Frankfurt School methods appeared at times in the German periodical, *Frauen und Film*, along with radical feminist perspectives (especially in the early issues) focusing on oppressive depictions of female sexuality and bodies in pornography and elsewhere. Other foci include study of gender and genre (e.g. Kaplan's 1978 and 1992 volumes) and Dyer's focus on homosexuality (male and female) as a neglected stereotype in studying film. As I will clarify in the 'Notes' to sections, a 'focus' or perspective may be pursued using differing research methods. A Marxist scholar, for example, may be drawn to study working-class women, but s/he may use New Critical, sociological, or French Lacanian/Althusserian methods in her analysis; a feminist interested in women's unconscious processes may, for example, study female characters who undergo a film psychoanalysis; or they may analyse psychoanalytic processes as these relate to the construction of gendered subjects basic to the 'language' of film or to the filmic apparatus as a whole, as I explain more below.

If all these methods were present from the start, and if they all continued to be taught and published, how does one account for the apparent special fascination with French theory in the 1980s? Why the lag in following through on Richard Dyer's engagement with gay perspectives? Why the absence of racial, ethnic, and postcolonial theorizing in feminist film theory until the 1990s?

Let me address first the fascination with post-structuralism and things French: perhaps one reason, similar to that found in literary and other disciplines, was reaction against the formalism of an entrenched New Criticism in the humanities still prevalent in the 1970s. The deliberate New Critical confinement to the text and its meanings within a generally humanist framework had coincided with 1950s McCarthyism and the terrorizing within the academy of professors with leftist political views. New Criticism provided a 'safe' literary method in omitting larger cultural formations. With the waning of anti-communism in the 1960s and the emergence of various Anti-Nuclear, Civil Rights, Student and Women's Movements, New Criticism seemed inadequate to the times. In Britain, the focus on the text continued the Arnoldian tradition of stress on morality, and teaching 'the best that has been thought and known', through the influence of F. R. Leavis.

Some faculties within US French Departments eagerly promoted French female theorists such as Simone de Beauvoir, Luce Irigaray, Hélène Cixous, and Julia Kristeva, along with eminent philosophers such as Jacques Derrida and Jean-François Lyotard. Scholars began translating French works in the early 1970s. Partly because Cinema Studies were just forming within academia and did not have entrenched traditions, some feminist film scholars were among the first to turn to French structuralism and post-structuralism, mixed with traces of the German Marxist-influenced Frankfurt School.

The development of links between North American universities and the Paris Cinémathèque added to the French influence on some graduate students in Cinema Studies. Meanwhile, the journals *Screen* (UK), *m/f* (UK), and *Camera Obscura* (USA) (which in the 1980s replaced the earlier West Coast *Women in Film* journal) took a decidedly French turn: British scholars took a natural lead—they were close to France and adept in French culture and language. Members of the *Camera Obscura* collective had participated in the Paris Cinémathèque, sitting in on lectures by Lacan, Roland Barthes, Raymond Bellour, and others. They brought French theories back to North America, while E. Ann Kaplan's British links added to the cross-influencing between the USA and Britain in Cinema Studies.

Partly as a result of all this, feminist structuralist and post-structuralist methods dominated the influential British journal *Screen*, research published in *m/f*, and the early issues of *Camera Obsura*. The first materials bringing French and Frankfurt School theories to anglophone nations were written by white male scholars, but some feminists quickly saw the usefulness of these theories even as they directed them towards different ends. For instance, feminist film research on the so-called 'classical Hollywood film' emerged in response to male film scholars' excitement about *auteur* theory, and about classical genres—the Western, the Gangster film, *film noir*.[9] The male research entirely omitted discussion of women's images or positions within narratives. In their different ways, in essays included in the first section of this volume, 'Phase I. Pioneers and Classics: The Modernist Mode', Claire Johnston and Laura Mulvey intervened in ongoing male theories, as I show in the 'Introductory Notes' to this section. These deliberately polemical and dense essays contained a wealth of ideas (including critique of Hollywood's realist-style as ideologically complicit with sexism) that were to be pursued (either positively or negatively) as feminist film theory got underway. Eileen McGarry's influential 1975 essay (not included) on 'Documentary Realism and Women's Cinema' also argued that realism limited what could be expressed in the documentary film. Meanwhile, essays in the first version of *Women in Film Noir*[10]—a deliberately eclectic anthology containing essays using varied critical methods—argued for both the potentially empowering aspects of the femme fatale as well as for her status as a figment of the male unconscious, the male imaginary, offering women little to identify with (see Gledhill's essay on *Klute* included here).

A start to the other questions about gay/lesbian perspectives and theorizing race and ethnicity along with gender might be to reflect on feminist structuralist and post-structuralist methods: these methods address aesthetic questions, especially how meaning is produced in film, and rely on semiotics (see Cowie's 'Woman as Sign' included here). While some attention is paid to social context, in general the method relies on seeing how far the theories can be supported in a film analysis, using as evidence for arguments the filmic techniques themselves. Theories about unconscious processes account for certain ways 'women' are used as signs within a film. Post-structuralist theories often relied on Lacanian notions of subject-formation in the so-called infantile 'mirror stage'—assumed to be the moment for establishing a split-subject (that is, a subject divided within itself). Theories also assumed that gendered subjectivity was inscribed in the child as it acquired language. In dwelling so heavily on these primitive human beginnings, scholars tended to neglect what they saw as later social formations—namely those of class, ethnicity, sexual preference, nationality, and race. The method also entailed little attention to spectatorship in its first phases, since it basically assumed that at least commercial Hollywood films addressed a male spectator. Often schooled in literary or other humanist disciplines, scholars using these methods were not trained to undertake sociological or psychological studies of actual spectators.

Reaction to post-structuralist and psychoanalytic theories determined much of the succeeding work in feminist film theory, as evidenced in essays in 'Phase II. Critiques of Phase I Theories: New Methods'. In her early, deliberately polemical critique (not included here) of the *Screen* scholars' use of psychoanalysis (*Jump Cut*, 1974), Julie LeSage (writing before Laura Mulvey's intervention in 'Visual Pleasure and Narrative Cinema') objected to what she saw as 'reducing the human norm to the male', among other things. *Screen* editors reprinted and replied to the polemic in 1975. In the very next issue, Laura Mulvey's influential essay took up the issue of cinema as a predominantly male symbolic and psychoanalytic system. Later, her positions were usefully critiqued in differing ways by D. N. Rodowick, Miriam Hansen, Gaylyn Studlar, Jackie Stacey (whose essays are included in the volume if not all in this section), as well as by others, initiating further debates (including Kaja Silverman's reaction to Studlar's critique) that continue today. Still later on—around the mid-1980s—feminists further debated issues of research methodologies in feminist film criticism, this time unfortunately becoming entangled around the unhappy term 'essentialism'. Only in the 1990s, as I explain below, did issues of race, ethnicity, and postcolonialism become central in feminist film research.

Since it took on such importance in the mid-1980s, let me briefly focus on debates between so-called essentializing and non-essentializing feminist film theorists. These terms refer to a difference between scholars supposedly taking femininity or female social roles as 'given', and charting the various fates of women in society and in filmic texts; and those challenging the very category of any 'feminine', seeking to discover how categories such as 'male' and 'female' came into being in the first place, and then were made to function in film. Emerging postmodern theories of subjectivity as produced discursively rather than socially or biologically—a logical development of engaging with French post-structuralist positions—conflicted with feminist scholars interested in historical, sociological, and class-based perspectives. As Teresa Brennan put it lucidly, non-essentialist feminists claim that essentialism involves reducing psychical reality to social reality: 'It is to make sexual difference the result of the social order rather than the foundation of the symbolic order'.[11] While essentialist feminists focused on how social relations and sexual stereotypes are internalized, Lacan's symbolic is the very ground for sanity and any social order. Brennan argues persuasively for a productive tension between psychical and social realities.

Teresa de Lauretis similarly pointed out that some rigid bifurcation of views was a red herring. In her 'Strategies of Coherence' essay, included here, De Lauretis charts a line between claiming something definitive about sexual identification on the part of actual spectators, as some feminists reacting to post-structuralist theories were inclined to do, and being satisfied with analysis of forms of enunciation and the so-called 'hypothetical' spectator psychoanalytic feminist film theorists claimed was the only possible position. Using Yvonne Rainer's *The Man Who Envied Women* as her example, De Lauretis argues that the film does not move her along 'bound in the regulated coherence of a master plot, to the closure of a framed narrative image of Woman as spectacle and object of a controlling gaze—my (master's) gaze. Nor does it, however, repel my woman's gaze, such as it is, or my feminist understanding of the female subject's history of a-womanness, contradiction, and self-subverting coherence. Instead, the film constructs the filmic terms, the filmic conditions of possibility, for women spectators to be asking the question, even as it denies the certainty of an answer' (see below, p. 283).

Parallel debates were going on in history, only with a slightly different slant that reflected the differing disciplinary terrains. In history, it was not so much a question of sexual difference—of how the category 'woman' came into being in the first place—as a problem of what constituted female 'identity'. As Joan Scott put it, the struggle was between 'desire to legitimize feminist claims about women in order to consolidate an effective feminist political movement', and recognition of the irreducible differences—e.g. of class, race, and sexuality— between women.[12] Further, however, feminists use different philosophies of history, so that there are 'those with a more or less positivist outlook who want to . . . correct the biases that masculinist views have imposed on our knowledge of the past', and 'those who insist that history cannot recover an unmediated past, but rather actively produces visions of the past'.[13] This group of historians comes close to the post-structuralist feminist film scholar, in that, as Scott puts it, 'this interpretation often uses "difference" as an analytic category to explore the ways in which identities have been produced'.[14]

Feminists involved in film analyses in fact all drew on a broad spectrum of available theories. But some kind of division emerged between women who turned heavily to French feminist and post-structuralist theories to illuminate female representations and those who focused more on neo-Marxist, sociological, and historical paradigms. It was a matter of emphasis rather than of complete difference, since many of the post-structuralists considered themselves Marxists of a kind, and saw their work as linked to activist practices. But disciplinary affiliation sometimes contributed to preference for one or another methodology, with scholars trained in literature and the arts more favourable to psychoanalysis and post-structuralism, and those with backgrounds closer to the social sciences preferring historical or sociological methods.

In this connection, the influence of the Centre for Cultural Studies in Birmingham (started in 1964) on film studies needs mention because it highlights the importance of the disciplinary formation of feminist film scholars. The CCS was a research institute linked to a Department of Sociology.[15] Much of its research, then, was of a sociological nature, and thus had a certain empirical base. In British Television Studies, sociologists—some of whom had been trained at the CCS—pioneered intensive audience research through in-depth interviews and surveys on audiences for specific TV shows.[16] Other sociological scholars trained at CCS (like Richard Dyer) began to study homosexuality in film, and, a bit later on, another pioneering group challenged the absence of attention to race in much of British media study.[17] The discovery of widely diverging empirical responses to television and film texts seemed to imply that post-structuralist theories were off base in generalizing about unconscious processes that were necessarily at work for all spectators; they also were wrong in not attending to different ethnic groups as images or audiences.

In challenging some of the post-structuralist assumptions, work included in Phase II opened up new questions. The next section, 'Phase III. Race, Sexuality, and Postmodernism in Feminist Film Theory,' offers some examples of new directions. Debates stimulated feminist film theorists to think more about female identities, identifications, and ways of relating to the screen, and several important new directions emerged as a result of debates about both essentialism and postmodernism, especially by scholars noting absence of attention to homosexuality and race. These turned to various methods to begin remedying such gaps. The work first published by Caroline Sheldon in Richard Dyer's 1977 anthology on *Gays and Film* (not included here) began to be followed up finally as feminists in the academy developed perspectives on lesbians in film. Judith Mayne pioneered in this area (the piece reprinted here provides a contrast with Claire Johnston's on film director Dorothy Arnzer included in Phase I). In a brave and provocative book, Teresa de Lauretis returned to Freud to press the limits of his texts so that she could reveal Freud's underlying understanding of a psychic 'path' for *gay/lesbian* desire, albeit he named it 'perverse'. In the USA Patricia White's and in Britain Mandy Merck's and Jackie Stacey's important contributions to this area show the kinds of case studies being researched at the time of writing. Since it combines North American and British perspectives I include Pratibha Parmar's useful essay about black gay women in Britain, from the important 1995 volume, *Queer Looks*, as an example of an important new direction film studies is taking in the 1990s.

For, as the 1990s got underway, with increasing interest in both minority and postcolonial studies, it became clear that feminist film theory had to address its lack of attention to race as well as to gay/lesbian perspectives. As early as 1982, Pratibha Parmar, Paul Gilroy, and others at CCS had pointed to the serious neglect of attention to race and gender in the work of the Centre. In the USA in 1988, Jane Gaines too pointed out the absence of attention to minority perspectives in her influential essay (reprinted here) on 'White Privilege and

Looking Relations', and in the same year, Richard Dyer's essay 'White' illuminated the naturalizing of whiteness as 'not a color', in a study of whiteness in select films as an 'ethnicity'. Ethnic scholars had already developed their own analyses of ethnicity in film, but Gaines's and Dyer's pieces functioned as a kind of 'wake-up-call' to white feminists in film studies. The reasons for the neglect of minority issues in North American research are multi-determined and complex, as both Mary Ann Doane and I have noted in essays not included here. Nevertheless, everyone saw the need to remedy such neglect and to work at theorizing race and gender in film. In Britain, Lola Young's *Fear of the Dark* carefully critiques many prior approaches by scholars working on feminist and ethnic research, and makes valuable contributions of its own. The essay Young wrote with Claire Pajaczkowska (included in Phase III) usefully analyses ways in which psychoanalytic tools can contribute to understanding racism and to illuminating how race is produced in specific films. Michele Wallace and bell hooks (whose books are widely known and read) are two American scholars who eagerly developed an interest in African American representations in cinema, as did Pearl Browser in her pioneering study of a long-ignored pioneering black film-maker, Oscar Micheaux. White feminists began to take up issues of race and gender, and debates among black and white women continue around race issues. Laura Mulvey's essay on Ousmane Sembene's film *Xala* (included here) begins to link some of this new work to African cinema.

Trinh T. Minh-Ha's innovative postmodern film-making and theorizing about hybrid subjects, problems of 'speaking' the Other, and about how to link the specificity of one's unique context and struggles with those of women in different national, cultural, and geographical locations has been influential in furthering connections between feminist theories and practices, and postmodernism. Readers will get an inkling of Trinh's ideas in the interview included here.

Although I could not include in Phase III Australian Barbara Creed's 1986 essay on feminism and postmodernism, Creed also opened up new directions. For the most part, feminist film theory in England and America did not at first engage actively or explicitly with the complicated 1970s debates about modernism and postmodernism that, especially in the USA, were carried on largely by white male theorists in philosophy and the arts. Debates did emerge in relation to popular culture other than film, especially around popular music and television.[18] Literary feminists—those who had studied French feminists Julia Kristeva, Hélène Cixous, and Luce Irigaray—involved themselves in theorizing the virtues of postmodern aesthetics, but Creed, along with also Australian Meaghan Morris, was one of the first to bring these issues to bear on film. While postmodern theorists of popular music and television tended to turn towards Jean Baudrillard, Creed (like Alice Jardine on whom she draws) rather looks toward Jean-François Lyotard and his theory about the end of master narratives. Creed builds on Jardine's analysis of 'gynesis' by which she means that 'the feminine signifies not woman herself, but those "spaces" which could be said to conceptualize the master narrative's own "non-knowledge", that area over which the narrative has lost control'.[19] Creed proceeds to explore the sci-fi horror film in relation to these ideas. It seems to me that Creed's essay opened up space for research that was not really followed up in film study per se.

Debates raged in relation to MTV and other television shows like *Twin Peaks*. Research by Giuliana Bruno and Anne Friedberg on links between cinema and other sites, such as the shopping mall or the street, pursued postmodern issues. As of writing, theorists of internet and cyberspace continue in these directions,[20] but these lie beyond my mandate here.

The last section in this volume, on 'Spectatorship, Ethnicity, and Melodrama', focuses first on studies of the Hollywood woman's melodrama—a logical step in the wake of feminist studies of Hollywood genres addressing male viewers. The sociological television audience work had stimulated feminist theorists to think about spectators. Annette Kuhn's essay included here usefully suggests a need to distinguish the category of 'audience' from that of 'spectator'. The issue of female spectatorship was, implicitly, present in feminist film theory from the start. The research on 'lost' women directors arose because women (whether as film-makers or teachers) wanted to look at women's films, at what women had to say on film. But, as Jackie Stacey points out in her essay in this section, feminist film theorists trained in literary or historical studies were slightly awed by the idea of empirical research with viewers, and also the theoretical apparatus (focused as it was on unconscious filmic processes) rendered such work less central. Thus research (often by social science feminists) which combined in-depth interviews with psychoanalytic insights contributed new ideas about female spectators. The challenges stimulated more work on genres, like melodrama, that addressed women. This, in turn produced more examination of female and male spectatorship, explicitly instead of implicitly.

Less about the problem of 'essentializing' women figures in film, melodrama debates turned rather on what it means to be a female spectator of films with female (not male) protagonists. Differences arose between scholars focusing on literal audiences or on a theoretical 'spectatorship' position in a film. In order to provide an idea of these debates, I include my own and Linda Williams's essays on the 1937 film, *Stella Dallas*, and refer students to the ensuing debates that continued in *Cinema Journal* between 1984 and 1985. Second, the section looks at varied approaches to the problem of spectatorship (raised in earlier sections), through juxtaposing Mary Ann Doane's revision of the abstract female spectator of psychoanalytic theory in her 'Film and the Masquerade' with Jackie Stacey's critique of Doane's (and other prior feminists') positions. Jacqueline Bobo's sociological and cultural study of black women as readers of texts (which I could not unfortunately include here), importantly takes up the specificity of black women's spectatorship. While Mary Ann Doane's intervention was important in making a space for the female spectator, it arguably entailed either that spectator's collusion with the dominant male visual regime, or woman being situated outside the system and unable to take pleasure in seeing cinema. By contrast, Bobo aims to combine 'theoretical concerns with information gleaned from contact with actual audience members'. Constructing what, following Janice Radway, she calls 'an interpretive community', Bobo brings black women together to explore 'not only . . . ways black women make sense of media texts but also . . . their battles against systematic inequities in all areas of their lives, socially as well as culturally'.[21] Christine Gledhill, meanwhile, in her essay 'Women Reading Men' (which I could also not include here) poses a neglected question about female spectators looking at men in cinema. Gledhill aims to move beyond thinking about actual women in the cinema: using melodrama's triangular structure and special strategies of negotiation, Gledhill offers a model alternate to prevailing psychoanalytic ones of woman as image and object of the male gaze. For Gledhill, 'reading' 'includes looking, emotional and visceral response, fantasizing, as well as reflection and reminiscence'.[22]

The volume closes with a necessarily brief look at the burgeoning melodrama studies now being done by scholars working on national cinemas other than Hollywood. I wanted to give students a sense of this important new research: Yan Wei Mei's interesting discussion of the melodramatic importance of music in Zhang Yimou's films (not included here) takes Western melodrama research in new directions, while Ana López' essay (included here) has very interesting things to say about different figurations of mothers, performers, and prostitutes in Mexican melodrama.

It is difficult to say which methodologies and centres of interest will be pursued by the next generations of feminist film scholars. There is much still to be researched about gay/lesbian perspectives, about spectatorship, about feminism, race, and psychoanalysis, or issues in the many national cinemas other than North America's Hollywood. Some of the women prominent in feminist criticism, like Mary Ann Doane and Laura Mulvey, are currently engaged in new kinds of philosophical and technical investigations pertaining to cinema. Others, including myself, are interested in thinking about trauma and cinema, especially in relation to multicultural and multinational cinemas, cultures and political formations; others yet are interested in returning to questions of feminism and postmodernism, as postmodernism possibly cedes to the millennium. Film Studies is itself in a period of transition: Bordwellian formalism is taking Cinema Studies in one direction, while the increasing interest in Cultural Studies is encouraging research that includes film as one amongst a number of related practices, institutions, and discourses a scholar may be examining within a specific cultural matrix. Specifically 'feminist' research is less urgent in an era when feminist perspectives are regularly included as essential to many kinds of investigations. Meanwhile, as new digital and computer-linked technologies grow apace, feminist research into these terrains of the visual are needed. It is in the hopes of stimulating ideas and new directions of thought that I have gathered together these 'classic' and 'significant' essays; but also because I believe knowledge of what feminist film scholars have produced—of the questions and areas our research has opened up—is crucial for continuing film research as well as for venturing into studying gendered and racial aspects of new visual practices and institutions.

Notes

1. See e.g. Sheila Rowbotham, *Hidden from History: 300 Years of Women's Oppression and the Fight Against it* (London: Pluto Press, 1973); Juliet Mitchell and Ann Oakley, *The Rights and Wrongs of Women* (New York: Penguin Books, 1976); Ellen C. Dubois, *Feminism and Suffrage: The Emergence of an Independent Women's Movement in America, 1848–1869* (Ithaca, NY: Cornell University Press, 1978). For more about feminism and history, see Joan Wallach Scott (ed.), *Feminism and History* (Oxford and New York: Oxford University Press, 1996). Also Peter Filene, *Him/Herself: Gender Identities in Modern America*

(Baltimore: Johns Hopkins University Press, 1993); and Gerda Lerner, *The Majority Finds Its Past: Placing Women in History* (New York and Oxford: Oxford University Press, 1979).

2. For example, prior to the 1970s, there were brilliant female cinema critics, such as Pauline Kael, Dilys Powell, and Molly Haskell, who wrote regularly for the top film journals and had columns in top newspapers as well. But they did not focus specifically on issues to do with women in the way that later feminist critics and scholars did. Molly Haskell went on to write one of the founding texts of feminist film criticism as I mention below. Meanwhile, British male scholars such as Stephen Heath and Paul Willemen early on participated in developing feminist film theory. At the present time, most male scholars take for granted in their work feminist perspectives. In America, study of masculinity (which I take as a 'feminist' concern and which Steve Neale from Britain pioneered) has been developed by Peter Lehman and Krin Gabbard, amongst others.
3. It is interesting to note how pervasive across disciplines was the common denominator, as Evelyn Fox Keller and Helen Longino call it, of the 1970s women's movement and 'its insistence that sexual equity in any domain, political or intellectual, depended on first incorporating into these domains the experiences and perspectives of women's social realities'. *Feminism and Science* (Oxford and New York: Oxford University Press, 1996),
4. See e.g. Susan Koppelman-Cornillon's *Images of Women in Fiction: Feminist Perspectives* (Bowling Green, Ohio: Bowling Green Popular University Press, 1973); or Mary Ferguson's *Images of Women in Literature* (Boston: Houghton Mifflin, 1977). These followed upon Kate Millett's searing 1970 *Sexual Politics* (New York: Doubleday, 1970)—a deliberately polemical attack on the patriarchal domination of literature as practice and institution as well as in its themes. Millett also famously condemns Freud as justifying for patriarchy.
5. This is not meant to be an exhaustive list. These materials are relevant to the selections that follow.
6. I have in mind volumes such as *Feminism and Film Theory*, ed. Constance Penley (London and New York: Routledge, 1988); *Issues in Feminist Film Criticism*, ed. Patricia Erens (Bloomington: Indiana University Press, 1990); *The Sexual Subject: A Screen Reader in Sexuality*, ed. Mandy Merck (London and New York: Routledge, 1992); *Visual and Other Pleasures*, ed. Laura Mulvey (Bloomington and Indianapolis: Indiana University Press, 1989); *Multiple Voices in Feminist Film Criticism*, ed. Diane Carson, Linda Dittmar, and Janice R. Welsch (Minneapolis: University of Minnesota Press, 1993); *Feminisms in the Cinema*, ed. Laura Pietropaolo and Ada Testaferri (Bloomington and Indianapolis: Indiana University Press, 1995).
7. Andrew Sarris did eventually add a 'Ladies Pantheon', which included Dorothy Arzner and Ida Lupino.
8. See e.g. essays included in Karyn Kay and Gerald Peary's pioneering volume, *Women and the Cinema* (New York: Dutton, 1977), such as those by Jeanine Basinger, Molly Haskell, Janice Welsch; and books by Molly Haskell, *From Reverence to Rape: The Treatment of Women in the Movies* (1973; 2nd edn. Chicago: University of Chicago Press, 1987); and Marjorie Rosen, *Popcorn Venus: Women, Movies, and the American Dream* (New York: Avon Books, 1973).

9. See E. Ann Kaplan, 'Classical Cinema', in John Hill (ed.), *Film: An Encyclopedia* (Oxford and New York: Oxford University Press, 1998), 272–88.
10. A new revised and expanded version was published by The British Film Institute in 1998.
11. Readers are encouraged to look at Teresa Brennan's 'Introduction' to her edited volume, *Between Feminism and Psychoanalysis* (New York and London: Routledge, 1989), from which I am quoting here (p. 8). It is impossible to do justice to the complexities of her arguments in this context.
12. Joan Scott (ed.), *Feminism and History* (Oxford University Press, 1996).
13. Ibid. 9.
14. Ibid.
15. Indeed, in the early 1990s, the Centre was incorporated into the Department of Sociology at the University of Birmingham.
16. See ground-breaking work by David Morley and Charlotte Brunsdon.
17. See volume, *The Empire Strikes Back: Race and Racism in the 1970s*, ed. Paul Gilroy, Pratibha Parmar, et al., for The Britain Centre for Contemporary Cultural Studies (London: Hutchinson in Association with the Centre for Contemporary Cultural Studies, University of Birmingham, 1982).
18. See esp. E. Ann Kaplan's essays and later volume on MTV, and her work on rock star Madonna, which sparked considerable discussion and debate. See also her edited collection *Postmodernism and Its Discontents: Theories, Practices* (London: Verso, 1988), in which she has an essay also discussing feminism and postmodernism in relation to MTV and alternative women's videos.
19. Barbara Creed, 'From here to Modernity: Feminism and Postmodernism', *Screen*, 28: 2 (1987), 49,
20. See Sue-Ellen Case, *The Domain-Matrix: Performing Lesbian at the End of Print Culture* (Bloomington: Indiana University Press, 1997) and Dale Spender, *Nattering on the Net: Women, Power and Cyberspace* (London: Spinifex Press, 1996).
21. Jacqueline Bobo, *Black Women as Cultural Readers* (New York: Columbia University Press, 1995), 22.
22. Christine Gledhill, 'Women Reading Men', in P. Kirkham and J. Thumin (eds.), *Me Jane: Masculinity, Movies and Women* (New York: St Martin's Press, 1995), 78.

Phase I. Pioneers and Classics: The Modernist Mode

Introductory Notes

This opening section reprints select essays from 1970s British and 1980s North American feminist film criticism, largely in its 'modernist' (i.e. post-structuralist) mode. While, as described in the 'Introduction', several methods were already being developed in the 1970s (and are reflected in the 'Further Reading' for Phase I), I deliberately focus on the poststructuralist strand because its methods were at once fiercely resisted and influential in following research. Claire Johnston's aggressively anti-realist polemic, 'Woman's Cinema as Counter-Cinema', with its heady mix of Lacan, Althusser, Barthes, and Foucault, seized the imagination of many scholars in its brilliant, perhaps reductive, clarity. Much the same happened with Laura Mulvey's 'Visual Pleasure and Narrative Cinema'—the equally passionate polemic which was to shape debates in feminist film criticism for two decades. Even now, Mulvey's theses are often referred to as a place from which to stake out a new position. I include Elizabeth Cowie's 'Woman as Sign' because it lays out so clearly feminist Saussurian/Barthesian semiotic theories. Gledhill's well-known essay on *Klute* is useful in articulating differences between sociological and semiotic/psychoanalytic feminist approaches and in explaining far more fully than Johnston had done the problems with classical Hollywood realist texts vis-à-vis woman's image. Mary Ann Doane's 'Woman's Stake: Filming the Female Body' shifted the discussion by introducing the concept of the female body in its relation to psyche, as against prior focus on image and psyche. She examines how the female body is represented in contrasting ways in Hollywood and in feminist avant-garde cinema. Doane's shift to woman's different relation to language and the unconscious influenced later work.

I reprint Kaja Silverman's essay on 'Male Subjectivity and Celestial Suture' to mark not only how feminist interest in masculinity in the cinema started as early as 1981, but how productive for feminist analysis such a focus can be. My own 'Is the Gaze Male?', originally published as a longer piece in a much-used interdisciplinary volume, *Powers of Desire*, examines assumptions behind both psychoanalytic/semiotic and sociological feminist approaches to cinema: the essay raises questions about gender and genre, and about prior post-structuralist methods, while tending to agree that sociological analysis cannot take issues far enough.

A main methodological question for feminist film criticism in Phases I and II is raised in a second essay by Claire Johnston with which this section ends. The question—one that has haunted and perhaps still does haunt feminist film theory—is whether it is possible at once to retain a category of woman which has political and social reality, and force, while simultaneously avoiding biological essentialism and reinscribing a set of patriarchal values. This double-bind provoked particularly difficult questions in research that involved claiming 'lost' women directors, actresses, and other female Hollywood workers. On what basis were feminist film theorists selecting their directors? Obviously, on the basis of their gender. But wasn't this then to make gender into a defining, and (given current social roles) a limiting signification? How could feminists at once decry a system of gender difference and then do research in accord with it?

Further questions emerged, such as: Did women directors make films that were obviously different from those of male directors? Was gender a governing category in film production? Should feminists be using the category in their theorizing? Other, sociological questions included: Must films by women actually be more 'progressive' than those by males? Did female directors necessarily image women in roles that challenged the status quo? Or was the gender of the film-maker not the main issue?

Claire Johnston's essay appeared in Johnston's 1975 edited volume on Dorothy Arzner. This booklet was an early attempt to bring attention to at least one neglected American woman film-maker while at the same time confronting issues of 'authorship' that were subsequently hotly debated. As Johnston puts it in the essay reprinted here, referring to her aim to explore in what ways Arzner's films are relevant to feminists, 'Feminist film critics are not attempting to establish Arzner as some cult figure in a pantheon of women directors. To see analyses of work by women directors in these terms is to misunderstand the crucial issues which the study of the woman director in the Hollywood system inevitably raises for feminist criticism' (p. 140). Johnston rejects the historicism and pseudo-objectivism of the construction of chronologies, and argues that 'women and film can only become meaningful in terms of a theory, in the attempt to create a structure in which films such as Arzner's can be studied in retrospect' (p. 140).

Later, Sandy Flitterman-Lewis (in her 1990 volume, *To Desire Differently*) noted how complicated issues became when she wished to apply her enunciative model of authorship to Germaine Dulac's work. She noted the paradox that arises in regard to feminist film-makers and elaborating a counter-tradition because 'the power of [enunciative, ed.] . . . theories shifts the discussion of authorship away from the actual individuals and toward relations of unconscious desire generated by the text'.[1] She insists however that cinema production is not gender-neutral, and that sexuality in authorship must be addressed.

Regardless of the theoretical and knotty problems of researching by gender, similar studies of other women directors internationally have followed. By the late 1990s, indeed at the time of this volume, a group of women in North America and Britain are currently engaged in a long-range and ambitious project on 'Women Pioneers in Cinema', aiming to research and develop knowledge about a huge number of women internationally from the silent era to the present who have been involved in all aspects of film production and exhibition. Archival feminist film research is one central strand of feminism and film studies.

But feminists have always also been interested in the experimental films that women have made whenever they could manage to get funding. Maya Deren's extraordinary films have been the object of intense studies (e.g. *The Legend of Maya Deren*, 1984), as have the films of Yvonne Rainer, Laura Mulvey and Peter Wollen, Sally Potter, HD., Dulac, and other avant-garde film artists. Jacqueline Bobo's recent anthology, *Black Video and Film makers*, meanwhile, usefully introduces new and neglected artistic production by African American and other minority women. (Pertinent research on early, independent and avant-garde women directors may be found in 'Further Reading' for all sections.)

Notes

1. Sandy Flitterman-Lewis, *To Desire Differently: Feminisn and the French Cinema* (Urbana and Chicago: University of Illinois Press, 1990), 21.

1 Women's Cinema as Counter-Cinema

Claire Johnston*

MYTHS OF WOMEN IN THE CINEMA

> . . . there arose, identifiable by standard appearance, behaviour and attributes, the well-remembered types of the Vamp and the Straight Girl (perhaps the most convincing modern equivalents of the medieval personifications of the Vices and Virtues), the Family Man and the Villain, the latter marked by a black moustache and walking stick. Nocturnal scenes were printed on blue or green film. A checkered table-cloth meant, once for all, a 'poor but honest' milieu; a happy marriage, soon to be endangered by the shadows from the past symbolised by the young wife's pouring of the breakfast coffee for her husband; the first kiss was invariably announced by the lady's gently playing with her partner's necktie and was invariably accompanied by her kicking out with her left foot. The conduct of the characters was predetermined accordingly.
>
> Erwin Panofsky in *Style and Medium in the Motion Pictures*, 1934, and in *Film: An Anthology*, ed. Dan Talbot, New York, 1959)

Panofsky's detection of the primitive stereotyping which characterised the early cinema could prove useful for discerning the way myths of women have operated in the cinema: why the image of man underwent rapid differentiation, while the primitive stereotyping of women remained with some modifications. Much writing on the stereotyping of women in the cinema takes as its starting point a monolithic view of the media as repressive and manipulative: in this way, Hollywood has

* Claire Johnston, 'Woman's Cinema as Counter-Cinema' from *Notes on Women's Cinema* edited by Claire Johnston (BFI Publishing, 1973), reprinted by permission of Mike Hughes.

been viewed as a dream factory producing an oppressive cultural product. This over-politicised view bears little relation to the ideas on art expressed either by Marx or Lenin, who both pointed to there being no direct connection between the development of art and the material basis of society. The idea of the intentionality of art which this view implies is extremely misleading and retrograde, and short-circuits the possibility of a critique which could prove useful for developing a strategy for women's cinema. If we accept that the developing of female stereotypes was not a conscious strategy of the Hollywood dream machine, what are we left with? Panofsky locates the origins of iconography and stereotype in the cinema in terms of practical necessity; he suggests that in the early cinema the audience had much difficulty deciphering what appeared on the screen. Fixed iconography, then, was introduced to aid understanding and provide the audience with basic facts with which to comprehend the narrative. Iconography as a specific kind of sign or cluster of signs based on certain conventions within the Hollywood genres has been partly responsible for the stereotyping of women within the commercial cinema in general, but the fact that there is a far greater differentiation of men's roles than of women's roles in the history of the cinema relates to sexist ideology itself, and the basic opposition which places man inside history, and woman as ahistoric and eternal. As the cinema developed, the stereotyping of man was increasingly interpreted as contravening the realisation of the notion of 'character'; in the case of women, this was not the case; the dominant ideology presented her as eternal and unchanging, except for modifications in terms of fashion etc. In general, the myths governing the cinema are no different from those governing other cultural products: they relate to a standard value system informing all cultural systems in a given society. Myth uses icons, but the icon is its weakest point. Furthermore, it is possible to use icons (i.e. conventional configurations) in the face of and against the mythology usually associated with them. In his magisterial work on myth (*Mythologies*, Jonathan Cape, London, 1971), the critic Roland Barthes examines how myth, as the signifier of an ideology, operates, by analysing a whole range of items: a national dish, a society wedding, a photograph from *Paris Match*. In his book he analyses how a sign can be emptied of its original denotative meaning and a new connotative meaning superimposed on it. What was a complete sign consisting of a signifier plus a signified, becomes merely the signifier of a new signified, which subtly usurps the place of the original denotation. In this way, the new connotation is mistaken for the natural, obvious and evident denotation: this is what makes it the signifier of the ideology of the society in which it is used.

Myth then, as a form of speech or discourse, represents the major means in which women have been used in the cinema: myth transmits and transforms the ideology of sexism and renders it invisible—when it is made visible it evaporates—and therefore natural. This process puts the question of the stereotyping of women in a somewhat different light. In the first place, such a view of the way cinema operates challenges the notion that the commercial cinema is more manipulative of the image of woman than the art cinema. It could be argued that precisely because of the iconography of Hollywood, the system offers some resistance to the unconscious workings of myth. Sexist ideology is no less present in the European art cinema because stereotyping appears less obvious; it is in the nature of myth to drain the sign (the image of woman/the function of woman in the narrative) of its meaning and superimpose another which thus appears natural: in fact, a strong argument could be made for the art film inviting a greater invasion from myth. This point assumes considerable importance when considering the emerging women's cinema. The conventional view about women working in Hollywood (Arzner, Weber, Lupino etc.) is that they had little opportunity for real expression within the dominant sexist ideology; they were token women and little more. In fact, because iconography offers in some ways a greater resistance to the realist characterisations, the mythic qualities of certain stereotypes become far more easily detachable and can be used as a short-hand for referring to an ideological tradition in order to provide a critique of it. It is possible to disengage the icons from the myth and thus bring about reverberations within the sexist ideology in which the film is made. Dorothy Arzner certainly made use of such techniques and the work of Nelly Kaplan is particularly important in this respect. As a European director she understands the dangers of myth invading the sign in the art film, and deliberately makes use of Hollywood iconography to counteract this. The use of crazy comedy by some women directors (e.g. Stephanie Rothman) also derives from this insight.

In rejecting a sociological analysis of woman in the cinema we reject any view in terms of realism, for this would involve an acceptance of the apparent natural denotation of the sign and would involve a denial of the reality of myth in operation. Within a sexist ideology and a male-dominated cinema, woman is presented as what she represents for man. Laura Mulvey in her most useful essay on the pop artist Allen

Jones ('You Don't Know What You're Doing Do You, Mr. Jones?', Laura Mulvey in *Spare Rib*, February 1973), points out that woman as woman is totally absent in Jones' work. The fetishistic image portrayed relates only to male narcissism: woman represents not herself, but by a process of displacement, the male phallus. It is probably true to say that despite the enormous emphasis placed on woman as spectacle in the cinema, woman as woman is largely absent. A sociological analysis based on the empirical study of recurring roles and motifs would lead to a critique in terms of an enumeration of the notion of career/home/motherhood/sexuality, an examination of women as the central figures in the narrative etc. If we view the image of woman as sign within the sexist ideology, we see that the portrayal of woman is merely one item subject to the law of verisimilitude, a law which directors worked with or reacted against. The law of verisimilitude (that which determines the impression of realism) in the cinema is precisely responsible for the repression of the image of woman as woman and the celebration of her non-existence.

This point becomes clearer when we look at a film which revolves around a woman entirely and the idea of the female star. In their analysis of Sternberg's *Morocco*, the critics of *Cahiers du Cinéma* delineate the system which is in operation: in order that the man remain within the centre of the universe in a text which focuses on the image of woman, the auteur is forced to repress the idea of woman as a social and sexual being (her Otherness) and to deny the opposition man/woman altogether. The woman as sign, then, becomes the pseudo-centre of the filmic discourse. The real opposition posed by the sign is male/non-male, which Sternberg establishes by his use of masculine clothing enveloping the image of Dietrich. This masquerade indicates the absence of man, an absence which is simultaneously negated and recuperated by man. The image of the woman becomes merely the trace of the exclusion and repression of Woman. All fetishism, as Freud has observed, is a phallic replacement, a projection of male narcissistic fantasy. The star system as a whole depended on the fetishisation of woman. Much of the work done on the star system concentrates on the star as the focus for false and alienating dreams. This empirical approach is essentially concerned with the effects of the star system and audience reaction. What the fetishisation of the star does indicate is the collective fantasy of phallocentrism. This is particularly interesting when we look at the persona of Mae West. Many women have read into her parody of the star system and her verbal aggression an attempt at the subversion of male domination in the cinema. If we look more closely there are many traces of phallic replacement in her persona which suggest quite the opposite. The voice itself is strongly masculine, suggesting the absence of the male, and establishes a male/non-male dichotomy. The characteristic phallic dress possesses elements of the fetish. The female element which is introduced, the mother image, expresses male oedipal fantasy. In other words, at the unconscious level, the persona of Mae West is entirely consistent with sexist ideology; it in no way subverts existing myths, but reinforces them.

In their first editorial, the editors of *Women and Film* attack the notion of auteur theory, describing it as 'an oppressive theory making the director a superstar as if film-making were a one-man show'. This is to miss the point. Quite clearly, some developments of the auteur theory have led to a tendency to deify the personality of the (male) director, and Andrew Sarris (the major target for attack in the editorial) is one of the worst offenders in this respect. His derogatory treatment of women directors in *The American Cinema* gives a clear indication of his sexism. Nevertheless, the development of the auteur theory marked an important intervention in film criticism: its polemics challenged the entrenched view of Hollywood as monolithic, and stripped of its normative aspects the classification of films by director has proved an extremely productive way of ordering our experience of the cinema. In demonstrating that Hollywood was at least as interesting as the art cinema, it marked an important step forward. The test of any theory should be the degree to which it produces new knowledge: the auteur theory has certainly achieved this. Further elaborations of the auteur theory (cf. Peter Wollen, *Signs and Meanings in the Cinema*, Secker & Warburg, Cinema One Series, London, 1972) have stressed the use of the theory to delineate the unconscious structure of the film. As Peter Wollen says, 'the structure is associated with a single director, an individual, not because he has played the role of artist, expressing himself or his vision in the film, but it is through the force of his preoccupations that an unconscious, unintended meaning can be decoded in the film, usually to the surprise of the individual concerned.' In this way, Wollen disengages both from the notion of creativity which dominates the notion of 'art', and from the idea of intentionality.

In briefly examining the myths of woman which underlie the work of two Hollywood directors, Ford and Hawks, making use of findings and insights derived from auteur analysis, it is possible to see that the image of woman assumes very different meanings within the different texts of each author's work. An analysis in terms of the presence or absence of 'positive' heroine figures within the same directors' *oeuvre* would produce a very different view. What Peter Wollen refers to as the 'force of the author's preoccupations' (including the obsessions about woman), is generated by the psychoanalytic history of the author. This organised network of obsessions is outside the scope of the author's choice.

Hawks vs Ford

Hawks' films celebrate the solidarity and validity of the exclusive all-male group, dedicated to the life of action and adventure, and a rigid professional ethic. When women intrude into their world, they represent a threat to the very existence of the group. However, women appear to possess 'positive' qualities in Hawks' films: they are often career women and show signs of independence and aggression in the face of the male, particularly in his crazy comedies. Robin Wood has pointed out quite correctly that the crazy comedies portray an inverted version of Hawks' universe. The male is often humiliated or depicted as infantile or regressed. Such films as *Bringing Up Baby*, *His Girl Friday* and *Gentlemen Prefer Blondes* combine, as Robin Wood has said, 'farce and horror'; they are 'disturbing'. For Hawks, there is only the male and the non-male: in order to be accepted into the male universe, the woman must *become* a man; alternatively she becomes woman-as-phallus (Marilyn Monroe in *Gentlemen Prefer Blondes*). This disturbing quality in Hawks' films relates directly to the presence of woman; she is a traumatic presence which must be negated. Ford's is a very different universe, in which women play a pivotal role: it is around their presence that the tensions between the desire for the wandering existence and the desire for settlement/the idea of the wilderness and the idea of the garden revolve. For Ford woman represents the home, and with it the possibility of culture: she becomes a cipher onto which Ford projects his profoundly ambivalent attitude to the concepts of civilisation and psychological 'wholeness'.

While the depiction of women in Hawks involves a direct confrontation with the problematic (traumatic) presence of Woman, a confrontation which results in his need to repress her, Ford's use of woman as a symbol for civilisation considerably complicates the whole question of the repression of woman in his work and leaves room for more progressive elements to emerge (e.g. *Seven Women* and *Cheyenne Autumn*).

TOWARDS A COUNTER-CINEMA

There is no such thing as unmanipulated writing, filming or broadcasting.

> The question is therefore not whether the media are manipulated, but who manipulates them. A revolutionary plan should not require the manipulators to disappear; on the contrary, it must make everyone a manipulator.
>
> (Hans Magnus Enzensberger in *Constituents of a Theory of Media*, New Left Review, No. 64)

Enzensberger suggests the major contradiction operating in the media is that between their present constitution and their revolutionary potential. Quite clearly, a strategic use of the media, and film in particular, is essential for disseminating our ideas. At the moment the possibility of feedback is low, though the potential already exists. In the light of such possibilities, it is particularly important to analyse what the nature of cinema is and what strategic use can be made of it in all its forms: the political film/the commercial entertainment film. Polemics for women's creativity are fine as long as we realise they are polemics. The notion of women's creativity *per se* is as limited as the notion of men's creativity. It is basically an idealist conception which elevates the idea of the 'artist' (involving the pitfall of elitism), and undermines any view of art as a material thing within a cultural context which forms it and is formed by it. All films or works of art are products: products of an existing system of economic relations, in the final analysis. This applies equally to experimental films, political films and commercial entertainment cinema. Film is also an ideological product—the product of bourgeois ideology. The idea that art is universal and thus potentially androgynous is basically an idealist notion: art can only be defined as a discourse within a particular conjuncture—for the purpose of woman's cinema, the bourgeois, sexist ideology of male dominated capitalism. It is important to point out that the workings of ideology do not involve a process of deception/intentionality. For Marx, ideology is a reality, it is not a lie. Such a misapprehension can prove extremely misleading; there is no way in which we can eliminate ideology as if by an effort of will. This is extremely important when it comes to discussing women's cinema. The tools and techniques of cinema themselves, as part of reality, are an expression of the prevailing ideology: they are not neutral, as many 'revolutionary' film-makers appear to believe. It is idealist mystification to believe that 'truth' can be captured by the camera or that the conditions of a film's production (e.g. a film made collectively by women) can *of itself* reflect the conditions of its production. This is mere utopianism: new meaning has to *be manufactured* within the text of the film. The camera was developed in order to accurately reproduce reality and safeguard the bourgeois notion of realism which was being replaced in painting. An element of sexism governing the technical development of the camera can also be discerned. In fact, the lightweight camera was developed as early as the 1930s in Nazi Germany for propaganda purposes; the reason why it was not until the 1950s that it assumed common usage remains obscure.

Much of the emerging women's cinema has taken its aesthetics from television and cinema verite techniques (e.g. *Three Lives, Women Talking*); Shirley Clarke's *Portrait of Jason* has been cited as an important influence. These films largely depict images of women talking to camera about their experiences, with little or no intervention by the film-maker. Kate Millett sums up the approach in *Three Lives* by saying, 'I did not want to analyse any more, but to express' and 'film is a very powerful way to express oneself.'

Clearly, if we accept that cinema involves the production of signs, the idea of non-intervention is pure mystification. The sign is always a product. What the camera in fact grasps is the 'natural' world of the dominant ideology. Women's cinema cannot afford such idealism; the 'truth' of our oppression cannot be 'captured' on celluloid with the 'innocence' of the camera: it has to be constructed/manufactured. New meanings have to be created by disrupting the fabric of the male bourgeois cinema within the text of the film. As Peter Wollen points out, 'reality is always adaptive.' Eisenstein's method is instructive here. In his use of fragmentation as a revolutionary strategy, a concept is generated by the clash of two specific images, so that it serves as an abstract concept in the filmic discourse. This idea of fragmentation as an analytical tool is quite different from the use of fragmentation suggested by Barbara Martineau in her essay. She sees fragmentation as the juxtaposition of disparate elements (cf. *Lion's Love*) to bring about emotional reverberations, but these reverberations do not provide a means of understanding within them. In the context of women's cinema such a strategy would be totally recuperable by the dominant ideology: indeed, in that it depends on emotionality and mystery, it invites the invasion of ideology. The ultimate logic of this method is automatic writing developed by the surrealists. Romanticism will not provide us with the necessary tools to construct a women's cinema: our objectification cannot be overcome simply by examining it artistically. It can only be challenged by developing the means to interrogate the male, bourgeois cinema. Furthermore, a desire for change can only come about by drawing on fantasy. The danger of developing a cinema of non-intervention is that it promotes a passive subjectivity at the expense of analysis. Any revolutionary strategy must challenge the depiction of reality; it is not enough to discuss the oppression of women within the text of the film; the language of the cinema/the depiction of reality must also be interrogated, so that a break between ideology and text is effected. In this respect, it is instructive to look at films made by women within the Hollywood system which attempted by formal means to bring about a dislocation between sexist ideology and the text of the film; such insights could provide useful guidelines for the emerging women's cinema to draw on.

Dorothy Arzner and Ida Lupino

Dorothy Arzner and Lois Weber were virtually the only women working in Hollywood during the 1920s and 1930s who managed to build up a consistent body of work in the cinema: unfortunately, very little is known of their work, as yet. An analysis of one of Dorothy Arzner's later films, *Dance, Girl, Dance*, made in 1940 gives some idea of her approach to women's cinema within the sexist ideology of Hollywood. A conventional vaudeville story, *Dance, Girl, Dance* centres on the lives of a troupe of dancing girls down on their luck. The main characters, Bubbles and Judy are representative of the primitive iconographic depiction of woman—vamp and straight-girl—described by Panofsky. Working from this crude stereotyping, Arzner succeeds in generating within the text of the film, an internal criticism of it. Bubbles manages to land a job, and Judy becomes the stooge in her act, performing ballet for the amusement of the all-male audience. Arzner's critique centres round the notion of woman as spectacle, as performer within the male universe. The central figures appear in a parody form of the performance, representing opposing poles of the myths of femininity—sexuality vs. grace & innocence. The central contradiction articulating their existence as performers for the pleasure of men is one with which most women would identify: the contradiction between the desire to please and self-expression: Bubbles needs to please the male, while Judy seeks self-expression as a ballet dancer. As the film progresses, a one-way process of the performance is firmly established, involving the humiliation of Judy as the stooge. Towards the end of the film Arzner brings about her tour de force, cracking open the entire fabric of the film and exposing the workings of ideology in the construction of the stereotype of woman. Judy, in a fit of anger, turns on her audience and tells them *how she sees them.* This return of scrutiny in what within the film is assumed as a one-way process constitutes a direct assault on the audience within the film and the audience of the film, and has the effect of directly challenging the entire notion of woman as spectacle.

Ida Lupino's approach to women's cinema is somewhat different. As an independent producer and director working in Hollywood in the 1950s, Lupino chose to work largely within the melodrama, a genre which, more than any other, has presented a less reified view of women, and as Sirk's work indicates, is adaptable for expressing rather than embodying the idea of the oppression of women. An analysis of *Not Wanted,* Lupino's first feature film gives some idea of the disturbing ambiguity of her films and their relationship to the sexist ideology. Unlike Arzner, Lupino is not concerned with employing purely formal means to obtain her objective; in fact, it is doubtful whether she operates at a conscious level at all in subverting the sexist ideology. The film tells the story of a young girl, Sally Kelton, and is told from her subjective viewpoint and filtered through her imagination. She has an illegitimate child which is eventually adopted; unable to come to terms with losing the child, she snatches one from a pram and ends up in the hands of the authorities. Finally, she finds a substitute for the child in the person of a crippled young man, who, through a process of symbolic castration—in which he is forced to chase her until he can no longer stand, whereupon she takes him up in her arms as he performs child-like gestures,—provides the 'happy ending'. Though Lupino's films in no way explicitly attack or expose the workings of sexist ideology, reverberations within the narrative, produced by the convergence of two irreconcileable strands—Hollywood myths of woman *v* the female perspective—cause a series of distortions within the very structure of the narrative; the mark of disablement puts the film under the sign of disease and frustration. An example of this process is, for instance, the inverted 'happy ending' of the film.

The intention behind pointing to the interest of Hollywood directors like Dorothy Arzner and Ida Lupino is twofold. In the first place it is a polemical attempt to restore the interest of Hollywood from attacks that have been made on it. Secondly, an analysis of the workings of myth and the possibilities of subverting it in the Hollywood system could prove of use in determining a strategy for the subversion of ideology in general.

Perhaps something should be said about the European art film; undoubtedly, it is more open to the invasion of myth than the Hollywood film. This point becomes quite clear when we scrutinise the work of Riefenstahl, Companeez, Trintignant, Varda and others. The films of Agnès Varda are a particularly good example of an *oeuvre* which celebrates bourgeois myths of women, and with it the apparent innocence of the sign. *Le Bonheur* in particular, almost invites a Barthesian analysis! Varda's portrayal of female fantasy constitutes one of the nearest approximations to the facile day-dreams perpetuated by advertising that probably exists in the cinema. Her films appear totally innocent to the workings of myth; indeed, it is the purpose of myth to fabricate an impression of innocence, in which all becomes 'natural': Varda's concern for nature is a direct expression of this retreat from history: history is transmuted into nature, involving the elimination of all questions, because all appears 'natural.' There is no doubt that Varda's work is reactionary: in her rejection of culture and her placement of woman outside history her films mark a retrograde step in women's cinema.

CONCLUSION

What kind of strategy, then, is appropriate at this particular point in time? The development of collective work is obviously a major step forward; as a means of acquiring and sharing skills it constitutes a formidable challenge to male privilege in the film industry; as an expression of sisterhood, it suggests a viable alternative to the rigid hierarchical structures of male-dominated cinema and offers real opportunities for a dialogue about the nature of women's cinema within it. At this point in time, a strategy should be developed which embraces both the notion of film as a political tool and film as entertainment. For too long these have been regarded as two opposing poles with little common ground. In order to counter our objectification in the cinema, our collective fantasies must be released: women's cinema must embody the working through of desire: such an objective demands the use of the entertainment film. Ideas derived from the entertainment film, then, should inform the political film, and political ideas should inform the entertainment cinema: a two way process. Finally, a repressive, moralistic assertion that women's cinema *is* collective film-making is misleading and unnecessary; we should seek to operate at all levels: within the male-dominated cinema and outside it. This essay has attempted to demonstrate the interest of women's films made within the system. Voluntarism and utopianism must be avoided if any revolutionary strategy is to emerge. A collective film *of itself* cannot reflect the conditions of its production. What collective methods do provide is the real possibility of examining how cinema works and how we can best interrogate and demystify the workings of ideology: it will be from these insights that a genuinely revolutionary conception of counter-cinema for the women's struggle will come.

2 Visual Pleasure and Narrative Cinema

Laura Mulvey*

I INTRODUCTION

(a) A Political Use of Psychoanalysis

This paper intends to use psychoanalysis to discover where and how the fascination of film is reinforced by pre-existing patterns of fascination already at work within the individual subject and the social formations that have moulded him. It takes as its starting-point the way film reflects, reveals and even plays on the straight, socially established interpretation of sexual difference which controls images, erotic ways of looking and spectacle. It is helpful to understand what the cinema has been, how its magic has worked in the past, while attempting a theory and a practice which will challenge this cinema of the past. Psychoanalytic theory is thus appropriated here as a political weapon, demonstrating the way the unconscious of patriarchal society has structured film form.

The paradox of phallocentrism in all its manifestations is that it depends on the image of the castrated women to give order and meaning to its world. An idea of woman stands as linchpin to the system: it is her lack that produces the phallus as a symbolic presence, it is her desire to make good the lack that the phallus signifies. Recent writing in *Screen* about psychoanalysis and the cinema has not sufficiently brought out the importance of the representation of the female form in a symbolic order in which, in the last resort, it speaks castration and nothing else. To summarise briefly: the function of woman in forming the patriarchal unconscious is twofold: she firstly symbolises the

* Laura Mulvey, 'Visual Pleasure and Narrative Cinema' from *Screen*, Vol. 16, no. 3 (1975), reprinted by permission of The John Logie Baird Centre and the author.

castration threat by her real lack of a penis and secondly thereby raises her child into the symbolic. Once this has been achieved, her meaning in the process is at an end. It does not last into the world of law and language except as a memory, which oscillates between memory of maternal plenitude and memory of lack. Both are posited on nature (or on anatomy in Freud's famous phrase). Woman's desire is subjugated to her image as bearer of the bleeding wound; she can exist only in relation to castration and cannot transcend it. She turns her child into the signifier of her own desire to possess a penis (the condition, she imagines, of entry into the symbolic). Either she must gracefully give way to the word, the name of the father and the law, or else struggle to keep her child down with her in the half-light of the imaginary. Woman then stands in patriarchal culture as a signifier for the male other, bound by a symbolic order in which man can live out his fantasies and obsessions through linguistic command by imposing them on the silent image of woman still tied to her place as bearer, not maker, of meaning.

There is an obvious interest in this analysis for feminists, a beauty in its exact rendering of the frustration experienced under the phallocentric order. It gets us nearer to the roots of our oppression, it brings closer an articulation of the problem, it faces us with the ultimate challenge: how to fight the unconscious structured like a language (formed critically at the moment of arrival of language) while still caught within the language of the patriarchy? There is no way in which we can produce an alternative out of the blue, but we can begin to make a break by examining patriarchy with the tools it provides, of which psychoanalysis is not the only but an important one. We are still separated by a great gap from important issues for the female unconscious which are scarcely relevant to phallocentric theory: the sexing of the female infant and her relationship to the symbolic, the sexually mature woman as non-mother, maternity outside the signification of the phallus, the vagina. But, at this point, psychoanalytic theory as it now stands can at least advance our understanding of the *status quo*, of the patriarchal order in which we are caught.

(b) Destruction of Pleasure as a Radical Weapon

As an advanced representation system, the cinema poses questions about the ways the unconscious (formed by the dominant order) structures ways of seeing and pleasure in looking. Cinema has changed over the last few decades. It is no longer the monolithic system based on large capital investment exemplified at its best by Hollywood in the 1930s, 1940s and 1950s. Technological advances (16mm and so on) have changed the economic conditions of cinematic production, which can now be artisanal as well as capitalist. Thus it has been possible for an alternative cinema to develop. However self-conscious and ironic Hollywood managed to be, it always restricted itself to a formal *mise en scène* reflecting the dominant ideological concept of the cinema. The alternative cinema provides a space for the birth of a cinema which is radical in both a political and an aesthetic sense and challenges the basic assumptions of the mainstream film. This is not to reject the latter moralistically, but to highlight the ways in which its formal preoccupations reflect the psychical obsessions of the society which produced it and, further, to stress that the alternative cinema must start specifically by reacting against these obsessions and assumptions. A politically and aesthetically avant-garde cinema is now possible, but it can still only exist as a counterpoint.

The magic of the Hollywood style at its best (and of all the cinema which fell within its sphere of influence) arose, not exclusively, but in one important aspect, from its skilled and satisfying manipulation of visual pleasure. Unchallenged, mainstream film coded the erotic into the language of the dominant patriarchal order. In the highly developed Hollywood cinema it was only through these codes that the alienated subject, torn in his imaginary memory by a sense of loss, by the terror of potential lack in fantasy, came near to finding a glimpse of satisfaction: through its formal beauty and its play on his own formative obsessions. This article will discuss the interweaving of that erotic pleasure in film, its meaning and, in particular, the central place of the image of woman. It is said that analysing pleasure, or beauty, destroys it. That is the intention of this article. The satisfaction and reinforcement of the ego that represent the high point of film history hitherto must be attacked. Not in favour of a reconstructed new pleasure, which cannot exist in the abstract, nor of intellectualised unpleasure, but to make way for a total negation of the ease and plenitude of the narrative fiction film. The alternative is the thrill that comes from leaving the past behind without simply rejecting it, transcending outworn or oppressive forms, and daring to break with normal pleasurable expectations in order to conceive a new language of desire.

II PLEASURE IN LOOKING/FASCINATION WITH THE HUMAN FORM

A. The cinema offers a number of possible pleasures. One is scopophilia (pleasure in looking). There are circumstances in which looking itself is a source of pleasure, just as, in the reverse formation, there is pleasure in being looked at. Originally, in his *Three Essays on Sexuality*, Freud isolated scopophilia as one of the component instincts of sexuality which exist as drives quite independently of the erotogenic zones. At this point he associated scopophilia with taking other people as objects, subjecting them to a controlling and curious gaze. His particular examples centre on the voyeuristic activities of children, their desire to see and make sure of the private and forbidden (curiosity about other people's genital and bodily functions, about the presence or absence of the penis and, retrospectively, about the primal scene). In this analysis scopophilia is essentially active. (Later, in 'Instincts and Their Vicissitudes', Freud developed his theory of scopophilia further, attaching it initially to pre-genital auto-eroticism, after which, by analogy, the pleasure of the look is transferred to others. There is a close working here of the relationship between the active instinct and its further development in a narcissistic form.) Although the instinct is modified by other factors, in particular the constitution of the ego, it continues to exist as the erotic basis for pleasure in looking at another person as object. At the extreme, it can become fixated into a perversion, producing obsessive voyeurs and Peeping Toms whose only sexual satisfaction can come from watching, in an active controlling sense, an objectified other.

At first glance, the cinema would seem to be remote from the undercover world of the surreptitious observation of an unknowing and unwilling victim. What is seen on the screen is so manifestly shown. But the mass of mainstream film, and the conventions within which it has consciously evolved, portray a hermetically sealed world which unwinds magically, indifferent to the presence of the audience, producing for them a sense of separation and playing on their voyeuristic fantasy. Moreover the extreme contrast between the darkness in the auditorium (which also isolates the spectators from one another) and the brilliance of the shifting patterns of light and shade on the screen helps to promote the illusion of voyeuristic separation. Although the film is really being shown, is there to be seen, conditions of screening and narrative conventions give the spectator an illusion of looking in on a private world. Among other things, the position of the spectators in the cinema is blatantly one of repression of their exhibitionism and projection of the repressed desire onto the performer.

B. The cinema satisfies a primordial wish for pleasurable looking, but it also goes further, developing scopophilia in its narcissistic aspect. The conventions of mainstream film focus attention on the human form. Scale, space, stories are all anthropomorphic. Here, curiosity and the wish to look intermingle with a fascination with likeness and recognition: the human face, the human body, the relationship between the human form and its surroundings, the visible presence of the person in the world. Jacques Lacan has described how the moment when a child recognises its own image in the mirror is crucial for the constitution of the ego. Several aspects of this analysis are relevant here. The mirror phase occurs at a time when children's physical ambitions outstrip their motor capacity, with the result that their recognition of themselves is joyous in that they imagine their mirror image to be more complete, more perfect than they experience in their own body. Recognition is thus overlaid with misrecognition: the image recognised is conceived as the reflected body of the self, but its misrecognition as superior projects this body outside itself as an ideal ego, the alienated subject which, reintrojected as an ego ideal, prepares the way for identification with others in the future. This mirror moment predates language for the child.

Important for this article is the fact that it is an image that constitutes the matrix of the imaginary, of recognition/misrecognition and identification, and hence of the first articulation of the I, of subjectivity. This is a moment when an older fascination with looking (at the mother's face, for an obvious example) collides with the initial inklings of self-awareness. Hence it is the birth of the long love affair/despair between image and self-image which has found such intensity of expression in film and such joyous recognition in the cinema audience. Quite apart from the extraneous similarities between screen and mirror (the framing of the human form in its surroundings, for instance), the cinema has structures of fascination strong enough to allow temporary loss of ego while simultaneously reinforcing it. The sense of forgetting the world as the ego has come to perceive it (I forgot who I am and where I was) is nostalgically reminiscent of that pre-subjective moment of image recognition. While at the same time, the cinema has distinguished itself in the production of ego ideals, through the star system for instance. Stars provide a focus or centre both to screen space and screen story where they act out a complex process of likeness and difference (the glamorous impersonates the ordinary).

C. Sections A and B have set out two contradictory aspects of the pleasurable structures of looking in the conventional cinematic situation. The first, scopophilic, arises from pleasure in using another person as an object of sexual stimulation through sight. The second, developed through narcissism and the constitution of the ego, comes from identification with the image seen. Thus, in film terms, one implies a separation of the erotic identity of the subject from the object on the screen (active scopophilia), the other demands identification of the ego with the object on the screen through the spectator's fascination with and recognition of his like. The first is a function of the sexual instincts, the second of ego libido. This dichotomy was crucial for Freud. Although he saw the two as interacting and overlaying each other, the tension between instinctual drives and self-preservation polarises in terms of pleasure. But both are formative structures, mechanisms without intrinsic meaning. In themselves they have no signification, unless attached to an idealisation. Both pursue aims in indifference to perceptual reality, and motivate eroticised phantasmagoria that affect the subject's perception of the world to make a mockery of empirical objectivity.

During its history, the cinema seems to have evolved a particular illusion of reality in which this contradiction between libido and ego has found a beautifully complementary fantasy world. In *reality* the fantasy world of the screen is subject to the law which produces it. Sexual instincts and identification processes have a meaning within the symbolic order which articulates desire. Desire, born with language, allows the possibility of transcending the instinctual and the imaginary, but its point of reference continually returns to the traumatic moment of its birth: the castration complex. Hence the look, pleasurable in form, can be threatening in content, and it is woman as representation/image that crystallises this paradox.

III: WOMAN AS IMAGE, MAN AS BEARER OF THE LOOK

A. In a world ordered by sexual imbalance, pleasure in looking has been split between active/male and passive/female. The determining male gaze projects its fantasy onto the female figure, which is styled accordingly. In their traditional exhibitionist role women are simultaneously looked at and displayed, with their appearance coded for strong visual and erotic impact so that they can be said to connote *to-be-looked-at-ness.* Woman displayed as sexual object is the *leitmotif* of erotic spectacle: from pin-ups to strip-tease, from Ziegfeld to Busby Berkeley, she holds the look, and plays to and signifies male desire. Mainstream film neatly combines spectacle and narrative. (Note, however, how in the musical song-and-dance numbers interrupt the flow of the diegesis.) The presence of woman is an indispensable element of spectacle in normal narrative film, yet her visual presence tends to work against the development of a story-line, to freeze the flow of action in moments of erotic contemplation. This alien presence then has to be integrated into cohesion with the narrative. As Budd Boetticher has put it:

> What counts is what the heroine provokes, or rather what she represents. She is the one, or rather the love or fear she inspires in the hero, or else the concern he feels for her, who makes him act the way he does. In herself the woman has not the slightest importance.

(A recent tendency in narrative film has been to dispense with this problem altogether; hence the development of what Molly Haskell has called the 'buddy movie', in which the active homosexual eroticism of the central male figures can carry the story without distraction.) Traditionally, the woman displayed has functioned on two levels: as erotic object for the characters within the screen story, and as erotic object for the spectator within the auditorium, with a shifting tension between the looks on either side of the screen. For instance, the device of the show-girl allows the two looks to be unified technically without any apparent break in the diegesis. A woman performs within the narrative; the gaze of the spectator and that of the male characters in the film are neatly combined without breaking narrative verisimilitude. For a moment the sexual impact of the performing woman takes the film into a no man's land outside its own time and space. Thus Marilyn Monroe's first appearance in *The River of No Return* and Lauren Bacall's songs in *To Have and Have Not.* Similarly, conventional close-ups of legs (Dietrich, for instance) or a face (Garbo) integrate into the narrative a different mode of eroticism. One part of a fragmented body destroys the Renaissance space, the illusion of depth demanded by the narrative; it gives flatness, the quality of a cut-out or icon, rather than verisimilitude, to the screen.

*

B. An active/passive heterosexual division of labour has similarly controlled narrative structure. According to the principles of the ruling ideology and the psychical structures that back it up, the male figure cannot bear the burden of sexual objectification. Man is reluctant to gaze at his exhibitionist like. Hence the split between spectacle and narrative supports the man's role as the active one of advancing the story, making things happen. The man controls the film fantasy and also emerges as the representative of power in a further sense: as the bearer of the look of the spectator, transferring it behind the screen to neutralise the extra-diegetic tendencies represented by woman as spectacle. This is made possible through the processes set in motion by structuring the film around a main controlling figure with whom the spectator can identify. As the spectator identifies with the main male protagonist, he projects his look onto that of his like, his screen surrogate, so that the power of the male protagonist as he controls events coincides with the active power of the erotic look, both giving a satisfying sense of omnipotence. A male movie star's glamorous characteristics are thus not those of the erotic object of the gaze, but those of the more perfect, more complete, more powerful ideal ego conceived in the original moment of recognition in front of the mirror. The character in the story can make things happen and control events better than the subject/spectator, just as the image in the mirror was more in control of motor co-ordination.

In contrast to woman as icon, the active male figure (the ego ideal of the identification process) demands a three-dimensional space corresponding to that of the mirror recognition, in which the alienated subject internalised his own representation of his imaginary existence. He is a figure in a landscape. Here the function of film is to reproduce as accurately as possible the so-called natural conditions of human perception. Camera technology (as exemplified by deep focus in particular) and camera movements (determined by the action of the protagonist), combined with invisible editing (demanded by realism), all tend to blur the limits of screen space. The male protagonist is free to command the stage, a stage of spatial illusion in which he articulates the look and creates the action. (There are films with a woman as main protagonist, of course. To analyse this phenomenon seriously here would take me too far afield. Pam Cook and Claire Johnston's study of *The Revolt of Mamie Stover* in Phil Hardy (ed.), *Raoul Walsh* (Edinburgh, 1974), shows in a striking case how the strength of this female protagonist is more apparent than real.)

*

C1. Sections III A and B have set out a tension between a mode of representation of woman in film and conventions surrounding the diegesis. Each is associated with a look: that of the spectator in direct scopophilic contact with the female form displayed for his enjoyment (connoting male fantasy) and that of the spectator fascinated with the image of his like set in an illusion of natural space, and through him gaining control and possession of the woman within the diegesis. (This tension and the shift from one pole to the other can structure a single text. Thus both in *Only Angels Have Wings* and in *To Have and Have Not*, the film opens with the woman as object of the combined gaze of spectator and all the male protagonists in the film. She is isolated, glamorous, on display, sexualised. But as the narrative progresses she falls in love with the main male protagonist and becomes his property, losing her outward glamorous characteristics, her generalised sexuality, her show-girl connotations; her eroticism is subjected to the male star alone. By means of identification with him, through participation in his power, the spectator can indirectly possess her too.)

But in psychoanalytic terms, the female figure poses a deeper problem. She also connotes something that the look continually circles around but disavows: her lack of a penis, implying a threat of castration and hence unpleasure. Ultimately, the meaning of woman is sexual difference, the visually ascertainable absence of the penis, the material evidence on which is based the castration complex essential for the organisation of entrance to the symbolic order and the law of the father. Thus the woman as icon, displayed for the gaze and enjoyment of men, the active controllers of the look, always threatens to evoke the anxiety it originally signified. The male unconscious has two avenues of escape from this castration anxiety: preoccupation with the re-enactment of the original trauma (investigating the woman, demystifying her mystery), counterbalanced by the devaluation, punishment or saving of the guilty object (an avenue typified by the concerns of the *film noir*); or else complete disavowal of castration by the substitution of a fetish object or turning the represented figure itself into a fetish so that it becomes reassuring rather than dangerous (hence overvaluation, the cult of the female star).

This second avenue, fetishistic scopophilia, builds up the physical beauty of the object, transforming it into something satisfying in itself. The first avenue, voyeurism, on the contrary, has associations with sadism: pleasure lies in ascertaining guilt (immediately associated with castration), asserting control and subjugating the guilty person through punishment or forgiveness. This sadistic side fits in well with narrative. Sadism demands a story, depends on making something happen, forcing a change in another person, a battle of will and strength, victory/defeat, all occurring in a linear time with a beginning and an end. Fetishistic scopophilia, on the other hand, can exist outside linear time as the erotic instinct is focused on the look alone. These contradictions and ambiguities can be illustrated more simply by using works by Hitchcock and Sternberg, both of whom take the look almost as the content or subject matter of many of their films. Hitchcock is the more complex, as he uses both mechanisms. Sternberg's work, on the other hand, provides many pure examples of fetishistic scopophilia.

C2. Sternberg once said he would welcome his films being projected upside-down so that story and character involvement would not interfere with the spectator's undiluted appreciation of the screen image. This statement is revealing but ingenuous: ingenuous in that his films do demand that the figure of the woman (Dietrich, in the cycle of films with her, as the ultimate example) should be identifiable; but revealing in that it emphasises the fact that for him the pictorial space enclosed by the frame is paramount, rather than narrative or identification processes. While Hitchcock goes into the investigative side of voyeurism, Sternberg produces the ultimate fetish, taking it to the point where the powerful look of the male protagonist (characteristic of traditional narrative film) is broken in favour of the image in direct erotic rapport with the spectator. The beauty of the woman as object and the screen space coalesce; she is no longer the bearer of guilt but a perfect product, whose body, stylised and fragmented by close-ups, is the content of the film and the direct recipient of the spectator's look.

Sternberg plays down the illusion of screen depth; his screen tends to be one-dimensional, as light and shade, lace, steam, foliage, net, streamers and so on reduce the visual field. There is little or no mediation of the look through the eyes of the main male protagonist. On the contrary, shadowy presences like La Bessière in *Morocco* act as surrogates for the director, detached as they are from audience identification. Despite Sternberg's insistence that his stories are irrelevant, it is significant that they are concerned with situation, not suspense, and cyclical rather than linear time, while plot complications revolve around misunderstanding rather than conflict. The most important absence is that of the controlling male gaze within the screen scene. The high point of emotional drama in the most typical Dietrich films, her supreme moments of erotic meaning, take place in the absence of the man she loves in the fiction. There are other witnesses, other spectators watching her on the screen, their gaze is one with, not standing in for, that of the audience. At the end of *Morocco*, Tom Brown has already disappeared into the desert when Amy Jolly kicks off her gold sandals and walks after him. At the end of *Dishonoured*, Kranau is indifferent to the fate of Magda. In both cases, the erotic impact, sanctified by death, is displayed as a spectacle for the audience. The male hero misunderstands and, above all, does not see.

In Hitchcock, by contrast, the male hero does see precisely what the audience sees. However, although fascination with an image through scopophilic eroticism can be the subject of the film, it is the role of the hero to portray the contradictions and tensions experienced by the spectator. In *Vertigo* in particular, but also in *Marnie* and *Rear Window*, the look is central to the plot, oscillating between voyeurism and fetishistic fascination. Hitchcock has never concealed his interest in voyeurism, cinematic and non-cinematic. His heroes are exemplary of the symbolic order and the law—a policeman (*Vertigo*), a dominant male possessing money and power (*Marnie*)—but their erotic drives lead them into compromised situations. The power to subject another person to the will sadistically or to the gaze voyeuristically is turned onto the woman as the object of both. Power is backed by a certainty of legal right and the established guilt of the woman (evoking castration, psychoanalytically speaking). True perversion is barely concealed under a shallow mask of ideological correctness—the man is on the right side of the law, the woman on the wrong. Hitchcock's skilful use of identification processes and liberal use of subjective camera from the point of view of the male protagonist draw the spectators deeply into his position, making them share his uneasy gaze. The spectator is absorbed into a voyeuristic situation within the screen scene and diegesis, which parodies his own in the cinema.

In an analysis of *Rear Window*, Douchet takes the film as a metaphor for the cinema. Jeffries is the audience, the events in the apartment block opposite correspond to the screen. As he watches, an erotic dimension is added to his look, a central image to the drama. His girlfriend Lisa had been of little sexual interest to him, more or less a drag, so long as she remained on the spectator side. When she crosses the barrier between his room and the block opposite, their relationship is reborn erotically. He does not merely watch her through his lens, as a distant meaningful image, he also sees her as a guilty intruder exposed by a dangerous man threatening her with punishment, and thus finally giving him the opportunity to save her. Lisa's exhibitionism has already been established by her obsessive interest in dress and style, in being a passive image of visual perfection; Jeffries's voyeurism and activity have also been established through his work as a photojournalist, a maker of stories and captor of images. However, his enforced inactivity, binding him to his seat as a spectator, puts him squarely in the fantasy position of the cinema audience.

In *Vertigo*, subjective camera predominates. Apart from one flashback from Judy's point of view, the narrative is woven around what Scottie sees or fails to see. The audience follows the growth of his erotic obsession and subsequent despair precisely from his point of view. Scottie's voyeurism is blatant: he falls in love with a woman he follows and spies on without speaking to. Its sadistic side is equally blatant: he has chosen (and freely chosen, for he had been a successful lawyer) to be a policeman, with all the attendant possibilities of pursuit and investigation. As a result, he follows, watches and falls in love with a perfect image of female beauty and mystery. Once he actually confronts her, his erotic drive is to break her down and force her *to tell* by persistent cross-questioning.

In the second part of the film, he re-enacts his obsessive involvement with the image he loved to watch secretly. He reconstructs Judy as Madeleine, forces her to conform in every detail to the actual physical appearance of his fetish. Her exhibitionism, her masochism, make her an ideal passive counterpart to Scottie's active sadistic voyeurism. She knows her part is to perform, and only by playing it through and then replaying it can she keep Scottie's erotic interest. But in the repetition he does break her down and succeeds in exposing her guilt. His curiosity wins through; she is punished.

Thus, in *Vertigo*, erotic involvement with the look boomerangs: the spectator's own fascination is revealed as illicit voyeurism as the narrative content enacts the processes and pleasures that he is himself exercising and enjoying. The Hitchcock hero here is firmly placed within the symbolic order, in narrative terms. He has all the attributes of the patriarchal superego. Hence the spectator, lulled into a false sense of security by the apparent legality of his surrogate, sees through his look and finds himself exposed as complicit, caught in the moral ambiguity of looking. Far from being simply an aside on the perversion of the police, *Vertigo* focuses on the implications of the active/looking, passive/looked-at split in terms of sexual difference and the power of the male symbolic encapsulated in the hero. Marnie, too, performs for Mark Rutland's gaze and masquerades as the perfect to-be-looked-at image. He, too, is on the side of the law until, drawn in by obsession with her guilt, her secret, he longs to see her in the act of committing a crime, make her confess and thus save her. So he, too, becomes complicit as he acts out the implications of his power. He controls money and words; he can have his cake and eat it.

IV SUMMARY

The psychoanalytic background that has been discussed in this article is relevant to the pleasure and unpleasure offered by traditional narrative film. The scopophilic instinct (pleasure in looking at another person as an erotic object) and, in contradistinction, ego libido (forming identification processes) act as formations, mechanisms, which mould this cinema's formal attributes. The actual image of woman as (passive) raw material for the (active) gaze of man takes the argument a step further into the content and structure of representation, adding a further layer of ideological significance demanded by the patriarchal order in its favourite cinematic form—illusionistic narrative film. The argument must return again to the psychoanalytic background: women in representation can signify castration, and activate voyeuristic or fetishistic mechanisms to circumvent this threat. Although none of these interacting layers is intrinsic to film, it is only in the film form that they can reach a perfect and beautiful contradiction, thanks to the possibility in the cinema of shifting the emphasis of the look. The place of the look defines cinema, the possibility of varying it and exposing it. This is what makes cinema quite different in its voyeuristic potential from, say, strip-tease, theatre, shows and so on. Going far beyond highlighting a woman's to-be-looked-at-ness, cinema builds the way she is to be looked at into the spectacle itself. Playing on the tension between film as controlling the dimension of time (editing, narrative) and film as controlling the dimension of space (changes in distance, editing), cinematic codes create a gaze, a world and an object, thereby producing an illusion cut to the measure of desire. It is these cinematic codes and their relationship to formative external structures that must be broken down before mainstream film and the pleasure it provides can be challenged.

To begin with (as an ending), the voyeuristic–scopophilic look that is a crucial part of traditional filmic pleasure can itself be broken down. There are three different looks associated with cinema: that of the camera as it records the pro-filmic event, that of the audience as it watches the final product, and that of the characters at each other within the screen illusion. The conventions of narrative film deny the first two and subordinate them to the third, the conscious aim being always to eliminate intrusive camera presence and prevent a distancing awareness in the audience. Without these two absences (the material existence of the recording process, the critical reading of the spectator), fictional drama cannot achieve reality, obviousness and truth. Nevertheless, as this article has argued, the structure of looking in narrative fiction film contains a contradiction in its own premises: the female image as a castration threat constantly endangers the unity of the diegesis and bursts through the world of illusion as an intrusive, static, one-dimentional fetish. Thus the two looks materially present in time and space are obsessively subordinated to the neurotic needs of the male ego. The camera becomes the mechanism for producing an illusion of Renaissance space, flowing movements compatible with the human eye, an ideology of representation that revolves around the perception of the subject; the camera's look is disavowed in order to create a convincing world in which the spectator's surrogate can perform with verisimilitude. Simultaneously, the look of the audience is denied an intrinsic force: as soon as fetishistic representation of the female image threatens to break the spell of illusion, and the erotic image on the screen appears directly (without mediation) to the spectator, the fact of fetishisation, concealing as it does castration fear, freezes the look, fixates the spectator and prevents him from achieving any distance from the image in front of him.

This complex interaction of looks is specific to film. The first blow against the monolithic accumulation of traditional film conventions (already undertaken by radical film-makers) is to free the look of the camera into its materiality in time and space and the look of the audience into dialectics and passionate detachment. There is no doubt that this destroys the satisfaction, pleasure and privilege of the 'invisible guest', and highlights the way film has depended on voyeuristic active/passive mechanisms. Women, whose image has continually been stolen and used for this end, cannot view the decline of the traditional film form with anything much more than sentimental regret.

3 Woman as Sign

Elizabeth Cowie*

Most work on film by feminists has been in terms of the kinds of images of women represented in films: the stereotypes presented of women, the types of parts women play and the kinds of stories told about women in films. A typical conclusion is that:

> Women, as a fully human form, have almost completely been left out of film . . . That is, from its very beginning they were present but not in characterisations any self-respecting person could identify with. (Sharon Smith, p. 13)

Yet what must be grasped in addressing 'women and film' is the double problem of the production of woman as a category and of film as a signifying system. Feminist analysis of film assumes 'woman' as an unproblematic category constituted through the definitions already produced in society—as mother, housewife, worker, sexual partner and reflected in film. Women are taken as inscribed in a particular position as women, which then determines all representations of women. Film as a practice is posited as secondary to other practices within society. Social definitions of women's roles are seen as the 'lived relations' of women whereas film is merely a 'representation', powerful as ideology yet without the material effectivity of, for instance, employment structures. That is, the material effects of a definition of women as second-class workers suited by virtue of this definition to certain types of work and thereby requiring a lower reward for that work than men.

Woman as a category, as the effect of definitions produced by political and economic practices, is posited as prior to filmic practices, which is then simply reproduced, reflected or distorted by film. Film itself is asserted as an ideological practice and therefore is assumed to

* Elizabeth Cowie, 'Woman as Sign' from *m/f*, vol. 1 (1978). Reprinted with permission of the author.

have ideological effects, in particular on the definitions of women in society, the images of women, masking or reinforcing those definitions. It is these effects which feminists have usually addressed. However these are then seen as part of a problem of ideology, which is defined and theorised outside of the specificity of film.

On the other hand there has been a development within the theory of cinema which argues that film is not simply a reflection of other practices. Instead it defines film as a system which produces meaning through the articulation of signifying elements. That is, the work of film is the definition of meaning produced in the combination of elements within that specific film. The *film* produces the definitions of its elements by which they have meaning and are understood (see especially *Screen* special issue, vol. 14 no. 1/2) But when the political project of feminism—to question the representation of women as against men—is brought to bear on film, the object, woman, is assumed already to have a definition, to have meaning, which is produced outside of the system of representation of the film. Thus the same problem emerges: the category 'woman' is not seen as produced within the film but drawn from a general placing of women outside the film, in society. Films are criticised for not showing 'women as women', or 'as fully human'. The image is criticised as inadequate, as partial and one-sided in relation to a possible definition of women elsewhere, or else it is seen as a negation of that definition. Film is therefore precisely denied as a process of production when it comes to definitions of women, of woman as signifier and signified in the system of the film.

Hence the struggle for definitions of women is placed elsewhere, and film becomes simply the site of the struggle of the *representations* of those definitions, to be replaced or subverted by other, progressive representations. I want to argue however that film as a system of representation is a point of production of definitions. But it is neither unique and independent of, nor simply reducible to other practices defining the position of women in society.

What is at issue is whether it is possible or useful to presuppose a generalised notion woman, whose consistent degradation across all practices justifies the assertion that there is a consistent category of woman produced by film. Lévi-Strauss' ideas are particularly relevant in this context. This is because he has put forward ideas which engage both with the question of the position of women in general, and also with the question of the production of women as a category within a particular signifying system, in his case, kinship. Feminists have recognised his importance but have often fallen into the traps which are implicit in Lévi-Strauss' own work.

It is from this position that I want to look at the notion of 'woman as sign'—a sign which is communicated by men. This concept originates from the work of Lévi-Strauss on forms of kinship, as a result of which he argues that the exchange of women is the constant term in all kinship structures. Lévi-Strauss is important to consider here because he offers not simply a description of kinship structures but also a theory: that kinship structures are a system of exchange—the exchange of women— which is a system of communication.

> These results [in the understanding of kinship structures] can be achieved only by treating marriage regulations and kinship systems as a kind of language, a set of processes permitting the establishment, between individuals and groups, of a certain type of communication. That the mediating factor, in this case, should be the *women of the group*, who are circulated between clans, lineages, or families, in place of the *words of the group*, which are circulated between individuals, does not at all change the fact that the essential aspect of the phenomenon is identical in both cases. (Lévi-Strauss, *Structural Anthropology*, p. 61)

Kinship is a structure through which men and women are put into place, through the complex rules of familial affiliation and the implications of these for a group in terms of duties and rituals to be performed by each sex as a result of that placing—as father, son, husband and brother/uncle, and as mother, daughter, wife, sister/aunt. Kinship is also a system of communication, the production of meaning between members of the system, a signifying system, in which women are produced as a sign, which is circulated in an identical way to words.

I want to examine Lévi-Strauss' notion of kinship, in terms of his theory of communication and in terms of his presentation of women as the term of exchange and some of its implications. I want to argue that though these two theses are linked within Lévi-Strauss' argument, it is important to disengage them in order to open up questions about women's subordinate position, on the one hand, and the representation of women in signifying systems, on the other. This is precisely made possible by Lévi-Strauss' work, although he himself closes off such questions. Further I want to look at the way this work has been taken up by feminists, in particular by Juliet Mitchell in her book *Psychoanalysis and Feminism*, which remains one of the most important contributions to feminist theory; and by Pam Cook and Claire Johnston in their article, 'The Place of Women in the Cinema of Raoul Walsh' which is one of the first attempts to theorise women in the cinema. Nevertheless in both texts similar problems emerge in relation to their use of Lévi-Strauss: first, the uncritical acceptance of Lévi-Strauss' elaboration of woman as sign; and second, the too literal use of the concept of woman as sign.

For Lévi-Strauss exogamy is fundamental to social life; in discussing structures of reciprocity he states:

> The law of exogamy, by contrast, is omnipresent, acting permanently and continually; moreover, it applies to valuables—viz, women—valuables *par excellence* from both the biological and social points of view, without which life is impossible, or, at best, is reduced to the worst forms of abjection. It is no exaggeration, then, to say that exogamy is the archetype of all other manifestations based upon reciprocity, and that it provides the fundamental and immutable rule ensuring the existence of the group as a group. (*Elementary Structures of Kinship*, p. 481)

Exogamy is the foremost mode of exchange and for Lévi-Strauss exchange is the giving and receiving of equivalent but different items. It creates 'social bonds' which are reflected, for instance, in feasts, where food is distributed on the basis of marriage relationships. For Lévi-Strauss, then, exchange is a principle of culture, and hence exogamy, together with its corollary, the incest taboo, insofar as it is the rule ensuring the exchange of women through marriage outside the group, is the pre-eminent mode or structure ensuring social life—the rules of kinship *are* the society.

In the kinship structures which Lévi-Strauss has analysed it is women, and only women, who are exchanged under the rules of exogamy. Lévi-Strauss states that there is no theoretical reason why women should not exchange men, but that empirically this has never taken place in any human society. Yet in establishing his thesis of exogamy as the consequence of the rule of reciprocity the implications of Lévi-Strauss' argument are very different, i.e. he asserts that women have a fundamental *value* for the community: '. . . women are held by the group to be values of the most essential kind' (*Structures of Kinship*, p. 61). In his discussion of the universe of rules and the system of exchange in primitive groups, Lévi-Strauss places women with food as the most valuable commodities to the community: under the 'system of the scarce product', 'The group controls the distribution not only of women, but of a whole collection of valuables', and 'The methods for distributing meat in this part of the world [by the Eskimo hunters of Hudson bay] are no less ingenious than for the distribution of women.' Later, as an example of the 'value' of women, he quotes the Pygmies as saying 'the more women available the more food' because of the importance of their role as gatherers of fruit etc. to the diet of the group. He cites as well a Brazilian village where he saw '. . . in the corner of a hut, dismal, ill-cared for, fearfully thin . . . in complete state of dejection' a young man whose problem, or sin, turned out to be that 'he is a bachelor'. In other words, it is crucial for a man to have a wife. Nowhere does Lévi-Strauss argue why women are constituted as valuable to the group in this way, nor why women are valuable to women—the group may find women 'essential values' but how far does the group here indicate its male members? (Quotations from *Elementary Structures of Kinship*, chapter IV, 'The Universe of Rules'.)

Theoretically it is not required that women rather than men be exchanged, but as Lévi-Strauss himself shows, it is constituted through the principle of reciprocity whose condition of existence is a hierarchy of 'valuables', of exchangeable items (a value defined by the group, a value which is not necessarily a function of the 'usefulness' of the object to the group but is a socially constituted value), different but equivalent, of which women are the 'valuables *par excellence*'. What is important here is that exchange is not itself constitutive of the subordination of women; women are not subordinate because of the fact of exchange but because of the modes of exchange instituted. In arguing the 'neutrality' of exchange as a concept, Lévi-Strauss overlooks the fact that while in his theory the principle of exchange itself does not define or 'value' the items of exchange, which must always be equivalents although different, the terms or items of exchange must *already be* constituted, in a hierarchy of value, in order to be available to a system of exchange. Yet once constituted as terms in exchange, they are then defined by the mode of the structure of exchange.

Lévi-Strauss posits that women become a 'symbol or sign' within exogamy, a sign which is exchanged. There seem to be two aspects to this: first, in relation to prohibitions generally, that the incest taboo, which is the corollary of exogamy, is comparable to other prohibitions:

For several very primitive peoples in the Malay Archipelago the supreme sin, unleashing storm and tempest, comprises a series of superficially incongruous acts which informants list higgledy-piggledy as follows: marriage with near kin; father and daughter or mother and son sleeping too close to one another; incorrect speech between kin; ill-considered conversation; for children, noisy play, and for adults, demonstrative happiness shown at social reunions;

imitating the calls of certain insects or birds; laughing at one's own face in the mirror; and finally, teasing animals and in particular, dressing a monkey as a man, and making fun of him. *(ibid.*, p. 494)

Lévi-Strauss argues that

'all these prohibitions can be reduced to a single common denominator: they all constitute a misuse of language, and on this ground they are grouped together with the incest prohibition, or with acts evocative of incest. What does this mean, except that women themselves are treated as signs, which are *misused* when not put to the use reserved to signs, which is to be communicated?' (*ibid.*, pp. 495–6)

Thus the incest taboo is assimilated to all other prohibitions as a prohibition on the *misuse* of language, a misuse which puts in jeopardy social relations. Hence exchange is defined as a language in as much as the taboo—incest—which is its corollary, is defined as a misuse of language, i.e. a misuse because there is no exchange. And this is the second aspect of the concept of woman as sign, that the exchange of women which is fundamental to all kinship structures is a system of communication: 'In any society, communication operates on three different levels: communication of women, communication of goods and services, communication of messages' (*Structural Anthropology*, p. 296). Lévi-Strauss argues that women are signs in as much as women are 'communicated' that is, because they are exchanged in all kinship structures. Primitive groups themselves recognise this by putting the incest taboo together with other prohibitions that relate, as he says, to a misuse of language. Incest is the 'misuse' of woman as sign since it is not using woman in the way reserved for signs 'which is to be communicated'.

Lévi-Strauss obviously doesn't think exogamy is a system of communication of the same sophistication as language but he strongly associates language and exogamy as two solutions to the same fundamental situation—which could perhaps be loosely put as the necessity for the resolution of the opposition between the self and others in order to make possible social intercourse. This leads to the assertion of universal mental structures, that is:

the exigency of the rule as rule; the notion of reciprocity regarded as the most immediate form of integrating the opposition between the self and others; and finally, the synthetic nature of the gift, i.e. that the agreed transfer of a valuable from one individual to another makes these individuals into partners, and adds a new quality to the valuable transferred. (*op. cit.* p. 84)

It is in terms of these structures that Lévi-Strauss sees myths as well as kinship structures as a synthesis of the oppositions involved. Man still dreams of a time when the law of exchange could be evaded, when one could 'gain without losing, enjoy without sharing' and quotes as examples the way the Sumerian and Andaman myths of future life correspond:

> the former placing the end of primitive happiness at a time when the confusion of languages made words into common property, the latter describing the bliss of the hereafter as a heaven where women will no longer be exchanged, ie removing to an equally unattainable past or future the joys, eternally denied to social man, of a world in which one might *keep to oneself.* (*ibid.*, p. 497)

It is in terms of this necessity to resolve oppositions that Lévi-Strauss earlier states that:

> The emergence of symbolic thought must have required that women, like words, should be things that were exchanged. In this new case, indeed, this was the only means of overcoming the contradiction by which the same woman was seen under two incompatible aspects: on the one hand, as the object of personal desire, thus exciting sexual and proprietorial instincts; and on the other, as the subject of the desire of others, and seen as such, i.e. as the means of binding others through alliance with them. (*ibid.*, p. 496)

I have quoted Lévi-Strauss at length because I think that these passages show most clearly the problems in his argument. By raising a philosophical premise—the necessity of integrating self and other—language and exogamy are reduced to solutions. The primacy of human essence—here represented in the necessity to integrate self and others is asserted, from which language and exogamy become consequences. An appeal to humanism is made, so that women can never be simply a sign since they are persons as well. The human exceeds the sign, which is derivative of it.

> But woman could not become just a sign and nothing more, since even in a man's world she is still a person, and since insofar as she is defined as a sign she must be recognised as a generator of signs . . . In contrast to words, which have wholly become signs, woman has remained at once sign and value. (*ibid.*, p. 496)

Woman as exchange, and hence as sign, is a solution to a contradiction—but the solution is always only partial since Lévi-Strauss poses as part of the same problem of women as sign, the ability of women to be more than a sign, that within marriage and indeed before it woman is more than a term in a signifying system, exchange, because of her 'talent . . . for taking part in a duet'. He qualifies the concept precisely because of that contradiction for which it is a solution. In other words he qualifies the concept of woman as sign because of a humanist notion of woman as already constituted, a position which is also implicit in his notion of the 'value' of women. This has important consequences for Lévi-Strauss' use of the concept of sign, a use which is marked by the same ambiguity that is involved in his relationship to the structural approach in anthropology which he introduced. That is, the dilemma that it is the structures which 'produce' man and yet man is still always posited as prior to those structures. Lévi-Strauss refuses the radical implications of his own concepts, which I want to take up here as being of important use to feminists. That is that his theory can be understood as specifying the production of woman within a particular system—exchange—and that this system is a signifying system producing woman as both object of exchange—positioned by the structure as mother, wife etc.—and as sign within that signifying system.

Lévi-Strauss draws extensively in his work on the theoretical developments of the Swiss linguist Ferdinand de Saussure, and on subsequent structural linguistics; however it is not clear that the sign for Lévi-Strauss is the same as the Saussurean sign. Rather he uses the term interchangeably with 'symbol': 'as producers of signs, women can never be reduced to the status of symbols or tokens' (*Structural Anthropology*, p. 61). Taken in this sense there is a difference between the signs women produce or speak, i.e. linguistic signs, and the sign or symbol woman *is* in the act of exchange within kinship structures. Lévi-Strauss himself is not concerned with this question but it is clearly important if one wishes to develop his notion of the exchange of women for signifying systems other than that of kinship.

Two questions have to be dealt with, one, whether woman is a *symbol* or a *sign*. Two, whether woman as a sign is a function of a cultural reflection of a natural gender-position of women *or* is specific to the position of women in the specific signifying structure, kinship.

In linguistics the difference between a sign and a symbol is clear; for example words are signs (which can also be used symbolically) because their relation to the idea or concept is arbitrary and unmotivated. There is no necessary analogy between the word *ox*, and the image of an *ox*. In non-linguistic signifying systems a confusion of the two notions consistently arises. In the symbol the relation of the form of the symbol, the signifier, to the signified, the concept which is communicated by the symbol, is never wholly arbitrary. Thus the scales as the symbol of justice could not be replaced by just any other symbol such as a chariot, since the scales incorporate the notion of balance which is the embodiment of the concept of justice in a particular social formation.

Within kinship structures of exchange, however, women must be a *sign*, and not a symbol, in as much as 'woman' does not represent any notion intrinsic to what is communicated in exchange, i.e. to what Lévi-Strauss argues as a 'social contract'. The term 'woman' is part of a semiotic chain of communication with a sender and a receiver and an object of exchange—woman—which is the *sign* produced, signifying the 'social contract'. In other words, the agreement to give up a present right (to this woman) for a future right (access to all women, or all women in a certain group) and which Lévi-Strauss argues is the fundamental principle of culture, of the possibility of culture as a social structure.

Thus 'woman' here is not a sign because of any immanent meaning. Meaning is not some substance contained within the sign which might be examined independently of the signs in which it is apprehended; it only exists through the relations in which it takes part' (Tzvetan Todorov, 'Le Signe', in *Dictionnaire encyclopedique des sciences du langage*, pp. 131–8). *Woman* is produced as a sign within exchange systems in as much as she is the signifier of a difference in relation to men, i.e. women are exchanged rather than men. Saussure emphasises in relation to language that 'there are only differences *without positive terms*' (*Course in General Linguistics*, p. 120). Both men and women are positioned in exchange—as husbands or wives etc., but only women are produced as signs. In other words, that women are exchanged rather than men as a sign does not mean that there is a positive difference which determines this, simply that men are not the term of exchange. The position of women *as sign* in exchange therefore has no relation to *why* women are exchanged. In other words, it has no relation to the 'idea' of women in a society—which is what Lévi-Strauss is in fact referring to in his notion of the 'value' of women. The sign woman is produced within a specific signifying system—kinship structures—and hence while the form or rather *signifier* of the sign (which in language would be the sounds making up the word) is the actual person, woman, the substance or meaning of the sign, its signified, is *not* the concept woman. One cannot speak of 'a' sign—woman—without specifying the system in which it has signification—exchange. Signs are only meaningful within the system of signification in which they are produced, and not as discrete units.

The problem of value is explicit in Lévi-Strauss' use of the concept of sign:

It is generally recognised that words are signs; but poets are practically the only ones who know that words were also once values. As against this, women are held by the social group to be values of the most essential kind, though we have difficulty in understanding how these values become integrated in systems endowed with a significant function. (*Structural Anthropology*, p. 61)

It is the same problem indicated earlier in relation to the question of why it is women who are exchanged. In both cases value is left undefined but Lévi-Strauss signals it as determining in signifying systems.

In associating value in the sign or word with the 'cultural' value of women, and posing these as somehow pre-existing but then integrated in 'systems endowed with a significant function' Lévi-Strauss radically undermines the concept of sign as he uses it. Saussure emphasised that value in the sign is only produced once the sign is truly a sign—arbitrary and unmotivated. Value in the sign is produced *by* the signifying system—language—and is not a determinant of it. 'Value' as a notion is unclear in Lévi-Strauss but it seems to be used in the sense of hierarchical values of a society. But then it is a question of certain things being more 'valuable' than others, of a cultural hierarchy being formed. In this sense a term or object only has value *to* or *for* someone or some group.

This returns to the question of how women are constituted as 'values of the most essential kind', and raises a further question of how the social group is constituted since Lévi-Strauss argues that it is through exogamy that culture, and hence the social group, is possible. Yet exogamy is characterised by the term of exchange involved being uniquely women; women are *already* marked as of value by exchange itself. If however women are exchanged in kinship structures because they have value for the group, then the group must have already entered culture to the extent of recognising women as socially valuable. In ascribing 'origins' the trap is set for the inscription of a fundamental sexual difference into the social, even though he appears to be claiming that the mode of inscription is cultural. The exchange of women defines society as human. The act of exogamy transforms 'natural' families into a cultural kinship system, thereby ensuring the rights and obligations between groups as kin which incest, i.e. sexual relations contained within the biological family unit, can never produce. But sexual division as social must already exist in order for women to be available for men to exchange in an organised way, and for women to be 'valued' as an object of exchange. What remains problematic therefore is that the exchange of women, on which culture is based, is itself predicated on a pre-given *sexual division* which must already be social. The exchange of women is thus presented as the necessity for culture, because man is inherently unsocial, desiring without giving, inherently incestuous and engaged in permament warfare over 'possessions', including women.

Yet it is not the question of origins, of 'what came first', which is important here, although this is clearly a problem with Lévi-Strauss' use of the notion of value in his thesis of exchange. Rather, it is a problem of the limits it sets on his notion of exchange as a system of communication, of signification. Once exchange is established in practice and theoretically, as constituted in Lévi-Strauss' work, the questions then raised are ones about the place of women in certain social structures. The question of the *necessity* of the *exchange* of *women* may not be determinant *of* the position of women within exchange. Here what is important is not why but how women are placed in exchange, for which Lévi-Strauss himself gives two answers: as objects and as signs.

Therefore work should be undertaken not simply around the empirical reality of women as exchange objects, i.e. placed as wives, mothers and sisters within families, but also in terms of the exchange of women in a signifying system in which woman is produced as a sign. It is here that the notion of value can be taken up again, in the sense Saussure established:

> Language is a system of interdependent terms in which the value of each term results solely from the simultaneous presence of the others. (*Course in General Linguistics*, p. 114)

The value of words does not lie in their 'exchangeability'; in any case words can only be interchanged with each other, and exchanged with a concept or idea:

> Its value is therefore not fixed so long as one simply states that it can be exchanged for a given concept, i.e. that it has this or that signification: one must also compare it with similar values, with other words that stand in opposition to it. Its content is really fixed only by the concurrence of everything that exists outside it. Being part of a system, it is endowed not only with

signification but also and especially with a value, and this is something quite different. (*ibid.*, p. 115)

Value is the measure of difference; a term has value only relative to other terms in the same system, for instance numbers, where '8' is more than '6', yet the higher value does not indicate that 8 is necessarily preferred to 6, simply that its value in the numerical system is different and higher than that relatively of 6.

The value of a word is produced by the system of language—Saussure gives the example of the word sheep which he says in French, as *mouton*, has a different value because it serves for two meanings, than in English, which uses two distinct words for those meanings: mutton and sheep. Further, the value of a word is conditional on all other words which surround it, rather than on its signification. For Saussure the value of words is not intrinsic, nor a function of signification, but is a property of the system, thus

The Community is necessary if values that owe their existence solely to usage and general acceptance, are to be set up; by himself the individual is incapable of fixing a single value. (*op. cit.*, p. 113)

Why bother then to suggest that women are signs in exchange systems? What does it add to Lévi-Strauss' argument that women are exchanged and that this is the basis of kinship structures and society? Its importance lies in that exchange is not just an operation—the bodily movement of women from one place to another via a matrimonial ceremony, but a system of communication (Lévi-Strauss), or, more precisely, of signification. I use signification here rather than communication because what is crucial is the notion of a system which posits the sender as well as the receiver of the signified as *part of the system*, rather than as *operators* of the system.

The fundamental problem with the conception of language as communication is that it tends to obscure the way in which language sets up the positions of 'I' and 'You' that are necessary for communication to take place at all. Communication involves more than just a message being transmitted from the speaker to the destinee . . . [it] involves not just the transfer of information to another, but the very constitution of the speaking subject in relation to its other. (Coward and Ellis, pp. 79–80)

Thus exchange is not simply the 'communication of women', which for Lévi-Strauss is always the act of exchange, of goods, words or women, without attention to the specificity of the system in which this occurs, and hence representing it as neutral or passive vis-à-vis the terms communicated. But rather a putting into place—of culture, and crucially, of sexual relations. Jacques Lacan, writing from within psychoanalysis, has taken this up, relating the exchange of women, as Lévi-Strauss elaborates it, to the Oedipus complex which together function to institute 'subjectivity' in the human animal.

The primordial law is therefore that which in regulating marriage ties superimposes the kingdom of culture on that of a nature abandoned to the law of mating. The prohibition of incest is merely its subjective pivot . . . This law, then, is revealed clearly enough as identical with an order of language. For without kinship nominations, no power is capable of instituting the order of preferences and taboos that bind and weave the yarn of lineage through succeeding generations. And it is indeed the confusion of generations which, in the Bible, as in all traditional laws, is accused of being the abomination of the Word *(verbe)* and the desolation of the sinner. (*Ecrits*, p. 66)

That woman is a sign in exchange and not only an object of exchange has important consequences. Exchange becomes not just a series of acts but a structure which makes possible all particular acts of exchange within a group. The structure, its rules, prescribes the kinship relations of a group, producing the positions of men and women in the group in terms of their marriage relations:

. . . from a social viewpoint, these terms cannot be regarded as defining isolated individuals, but relationships between these individuals and everyone else. Motherhood is not only a mother's relationship to her children, but her relationship to other members of the group, not as a mother, but as a sister, wife, cousin or simply a stranger as far as kinship is concerned. (Lévi-Strauss, *ibid.*, p. 482)

As a result

Every family relationship defines a certain group of rights and duties, while the lack of family relationship does not define anything; it defines enmity . . . (p. 482)

For primitive groups kinship is *the* structure which defines relationships, produces its members in the position of mother, sister etc., so that for the Australian Aboriginal group the most important question put to a stranger is 'Who is your *maeli* (father's father)' in order to establish kinship relations; to have no such relations is to be an enemy, one to whom the group has no obligations. Kinship is thus part of a system which produces women as object of exchange, which on one side becomes a sign, of the institution of culture through reciprocity:

the inviolable debt . . . guarantee that the voyage on which wives and goods are embarked will bring back to their point of departure in a never-failing cycle other women and other goods, all carrying an identical identity. (Lacan, *op. cit.*, p. 68)

And on the other side exchange becomes the mode by which women are defined, are placed. Once posited within kinship structures, i.e. as a category which is not-men, women are 'produced' as mother, daughter, wife, sister.

A number of complex and different points come together here: that of woman as sign, through a 'negative' difference, as the term of exchange; that of the institution of culture through the establishing of reciprocity—primarily through the exchange of women; that of the institution of and social/symbolic inscription of difference through the castration complex. It is exogamy with its corollary, the incest taboo, which enables man to locate himself—and his goods—in relation to others; it produces a *difference* socially secured/secure through the rule of reciprocity. Paternity is therefore a crucial term here. In the realm of the psyche it is the castration complex—the unconscious counter-part of the incest taboo—which establishes difference, sexual and hence also social, in the human animal. It is therefore possible to see 'woman' not as a given, biologically or psychologically, but as a category produced in signifying practices—whether through exogamy and kinship structures, or through signification at the level of the unconscious. To talk of 'woman as sign' in exchange systems is to no longer talk of woman as the signified, but of a different signified, that of: establishment/re-establishment of kinship structures or culture. The form of the sign—the signifier in linguistic terms—may empirically be woman, but the signified is not 'woman'.

The question of the nature of the operation of Lévi-Strauss' concept of woman as a sign in exchange systems has thus seemed to me to be of fundamental importance, on the one hand, for work on the constitution of the place of women within kinship structures which produces both an inscription of sexual difference within a practice, kinship, and has effects within for example economic practices, in terms of the structure of ownership of property within the family and by the family. On the other hand, it has importance in relation to questions of how woman as a sign is produced in other signifying systems.

It is this role of exogamy in establishing sexual difference that Juliet Mitchell draws attention to in her book *Psychoanalysis and Feminism*. In that book she is concerned to show how exogamy corresponds to

Freud's theory of the incest taboo and Oedipus complex. She points to the way in which Lévi-Strauss argues that kinship structures are not based on the biological family but on the principle of the reciprocal exchange of women. It is this exchange which organises difference and thereby inscribes it within men and women.

At the same time Juliet Mitchell seeks to secure her use of Lévi-Strauss from an accusation of sexism by using Lévi-Strauss' own defence. Thus she says:

> Lévi-Strauss is correct to stress that the given place in a system of communication is no index of inferiority or superiority and that we must not be led astray by the false derogatory connotations of the word 'object' . . . (p. 372)

I have tried to show however that this defence—that women are more than objects and signs in exchange because they are also producers of signs, and because of their inherent value over and above their participation in the act of exchange—is highly problematic. Thus Juliet Mitchell accepts the construction of woman as object of exchange as not itself sexist, while noting that Lévi-Strauss' repudiation of anti-feminism is inadequate although correct (see here her quote from Lévi-Strauss, p. 371). However the problem is then left as

> Nevertheless this primary sexual division is an important indicator of difference and a difference that may well be historically exploited to establish a system of deference. (p. 372)

However, in emphasising the role of exogamy in establishing difference kinship is reduced to a more or less fixed structure which has already produced sexual difference and culture. The implications of the notion that 'woman thus becomes the equivalent of a sign which is being communicated' are not addressed by her. Rather, kinship is taken as a given structure whose description will expose the situation of women generally: 'What we need is kinship analysis of contemporary capitalist society, for it is within kinship structures that women as women are situated'.

Yet it is not just as structure but also as process that kinship is important. What Lévi-Strauss' emphasis on kinship as communication has marked, although in an inadequate way, is that the work of kinship, i.e. of exogamy, is a production, of woman as sign and of men and women 'in position' in society. That is, of placing rather than placed. It is not that women as women are *situated* in the family. But that it is in the family—as the effect of kinship structures—that women as women are produced, are defined within and by the group.

Thus kinship structures should in no way be seen as neutral or non-sexist, as effectively a-political; exogamy must instead be seen as a practice as well as a structure which signifies men and women as mother, father, wife and husband etc.

Juliet Mitchell reproduces problems within Lévi-Strauss' work by failing to consider the implications of his theory of women as sign. Pam Cook and Claire Johnson use this notion directly in their article 'The Place of Women in the Cinema of Raoul Walsh' and therefore reinscribe the problems already outlined in relation to Lévi-Strauss. They seek to translate his concept of women as object of exchange in kinship structures into a parallel operation in film structures. It assumes that Lévi-Strauss is adequately talking of a system of signification and that a comparable exchange of women in another system can be posited which then also produces women as signs.

They refer in their article specifically to those films produced by the director Raoul Walsh, but see their argument as applying beyond the Walsh oeuvre in as much as 'Woman as signifier of woman under patriarchy is totally absent in most image-producing systems, but particularly in Hollywood' (pp. 107–9). What is important in their article is that they take up Lévi-Strauss' point that woman is a sign in exchange systems, rather than woman simply being the object of exchange. However the structure of exchange is simply seen as taken up by the filmic system: 'As an object of exchange between men, a sign oscillating between the images of prostitute and mother-figure, she represents the means by which men express their relationships with each other . . . (p. 95). Further they continue Lévi-Strauss' confusion about the nature of this sign, hence arguing that woman as sign remains a token of exchange in the patriarchal order of a Walsh film. But in fact in kinship structures the sign is much more than a token of exchange, since its signification *exceeds* simply that of 'exchange' or the system of marriage rules, signifying the possibility of culture organised on the basis of kinship structures. The sign 'woman' in exogamy is not exchanged but produced in the exchange of actual women. What is raised is indeed the relationship of actual women to the signification constituted within kinship structures, but this cannot be in terms of a 'real' signified, woman, in contrast to a distorted or inadequate signified, woman as exchange. As soon as a system of representation is posited—as with film—it is no longer possible to talk, as above, of 'woman as signifier of woman' since this poses the system of representation over and against a true signified woman, or, presumably, actual women. What is important is not that film falsely signifies women, or appropriates the signifier (image) woman to another signification, but the particular mode of constituting woman as sign within film. What is of concern is the specific consequences of that mode of constitution both within film and in relationship to other signifying systems and discourses.

In fact this is the implication of the analysis of the film *The Revolt of Mamie Stover* (1956) where they 'attempt to demonstrate that women (e.g Mamie Stover) in fact function as a signifier in a circuit of exchange where the values exchanged have been fixed by/in a patriarchal culture' (Introduction, p. 94). That the system of the film produces the main protagonist, Mamie Stover, as signifier of lack—castration—around which male desire, and patriarchal law, are organised:

> The male protagonist's castration fears, his search for self-knowledge all converge on woman: it is in her that he is finally faced with the recognition of 'lack'. Woman is therefore the locus of emptiness . . . (p. 97)

However this does not make 'Mamie Stover' an *empty sign* as they claim: 'woman is not only a sign in a system of exchange, but an empty sign' (p. 96). The term 'empty' is problematic because it suggests a 'fullness' somewhere else. Rather the sign always has signification; on the other hand the signifier is necessarily 'empty' inasmuch as it is unmotivated and arbitrary, i.e. without an already given meaning. Nevertheless this does not mean that women *are* lack or anything else, but that in a certain signifying system, here in *Mamie Stover* woman signifies lack in a circulation of desire organised around the male dilemma/fear of castration

It is precisely this circuit of desire, of signifiers, by which the meaning of the film is organised. However the 'values' of the terms in circulation are not simply already fixed 'by/in a patriarchal culture' which is outside of the film. The film itself is part of the operation of the 'fixing' of the 'values'. Therefore it is crucial to keep separate the question of the representation of women and woman as a sign, to avoid any simple denunciation of the sign as inadequate representation/signification of the 'real' object woman, and rather to take up the implications of certain modes of representations of women for the position of women constructed within society.

References

Rosalind Coward and John Ellis, *Language and Materialism* (London, 1977: Routledge & Kegan Paul).

Pam Cook and Claire Johnston, 'The Place of Women in the Cinema of Raoul Walsh', in *Raoul Walsh*, ed. Phil Hardy (Edinburgh Film Festival, 1974).

Jacques Lacan, 'The Function and Field of Speech and Language in Psychoanalysis', in *Ecrits*, trans. Alan Sheridan (Tavistock, 1977).

Claude Lévi-Strauss, *The Elementary Structures of Kinship* (London, 1969: Eyre & Spottiswoode).

—— *Structural Anthropology* (London, 1972: Penguin).

Juliet Mitchell, *Psychoanalysis and Feminism* (London 1974: Allen Lane).

Ferdinand de Saussure, *Course in General Linguistics* (New York, 1966: McGraw-Hill).

Screen, vol. 14, no. 1/2, published by Society for Education in Film and Television. Sharon Smith, 'The Image of Women in Film: Some Suggestions for Future Research', in *Women & Film*, no. 1, 1972.

Tzvetan Todorov, 'The Sign', in Oswald Ducrot and Tzvetan Todorov, *Dictionaire encyclopedique des sciences du langage* (Paris, 1972: Editions du Seuil).

4 *Klute* 1: A Contemporary Film Noir and Feminist Criticism

Christine Gledhill*

In the second part of this book [*Ed.'s note*: This is the first of 2 chapters that discuss *Klute* in E. Ann Kaplan (ed.), *Women in Film Noir*, revised and expanded edn. (London: BFI, 1998).] I have attempted an analysis of *Klute*—a 'new American cinema'[1] production starring Jane Fonda and supporting a reputedly 'liberated' heroine within a thriller plot structure—in terms of film noir. What my analysis attempts to describe is the ideological effect of the structural interaction between the two apparently contradictory film-making traditions implied in this description. On the one hand, the film's modernity and seriousness of theme, linking prostitution, psychotherapy and the problem of woman, places it within a humanist realist tradition of European art cinema. On the other hand, the film's themes are cast within the plot structure and stylistic appeal of the noir thriller—an invocation of this period of the genre characteristic of the 1970s—for example, *Chinatown* (Polanski, 1974), *The Long Goodbye* (Altman, 1973), *Farewell My Lovely* (Richards, 1975), *Marlowe* (Bogart, 1969).

As film noir has been largely discussed in terms of a highly elaborated visual style; of baroque stereotypes—among which a particularly virulent form of the *femme fatale* stands out—and of tangibly artificial, often incomprehensible plot structure, the capacity for *Klute* to make claims for the authenticity and progressiveness of what it says about women is worth investigating. Since my analysis is largely descriptive, what I want to do here is reflect on some of the problems such a film poses for feminist film theory. These problems turn on the different ways the critical notions 'realism' and 'genre' have been taken up by ideological analysis both in film theory and feminist criticism.

* Christine Gledhill, 'Klute: A Contemporary Film Noir and Feminist Criticism' from *Women in Film Noir* edited by Ann Kaplan (BFI Publishing, 1998), reprinted by permission of the publisher.

THE REAL WORLD AND FICTIONAL PRODUCTION

For much feminist criticism of the cinema—especially that coming from the Women's Movement rather than from a background of film study—the notions of realism and genre are totally opposed. While realism embraces such cultural values as 'real life' 'truth' or 'credibility', genre production holds negative connotations such as 'illusion', 'myth', 'conventionality', 'stereotypes'. The Hollywood genres represent the fictional elaboration of a patriarchal culture which produces macho heroes and a subordinate, demeaning and objectified place for women.[2]

In the first instance then, if feminist criticism is not simply to set generic convention against 'reality', yet at the same time is to avoid a formalism that evades the issue of society with the edict 'films refer to films', the problem it faces is how the operation of such conventions and stereotypes are to be understood in feminist terms—at what level their meanings and ideological effect are located.

At this point two different approaches emerge, the one deriving from a humanist literary tradition, the other arising from a more recent revival of Marxist aesthetics. Criticism deriving from liberal approaches to the humanities tends to treat an art product's fictional structures as providing aesthetic access to the work's truth which is then evaluated in terms of how it illuminates the world. In these terms conventions and stereotypes can be read metaphorically for their immanent meaning. In the second part of my discussion of *Klute*, I see Diane Giddis' analysis of the film[3] as an example of such a metaphoric treatment of genre. However, recent neo-Marxist developments in feminist film theory effectively reverse the values of 'real life' and stereotype, *changing the project of criticism from the discovery of meaning to that of uncovering the means of its production.* This change in direction is set out in Claire Johnston's seminal 'Women's Cinema as Counter-Cinema'[4] and informs much of the writing in this contribution.

In the first instance the aim of this new critical project is greater rigour and demands that closer attention be paid to the specificities of artistic production, and particularly how character is produced by other textual operations such as narration, plot, *mise en scène* etc. But it also implies investigation of a different order of meaning, something I will discuss in more detail shortly.

Behind this new perspective lies a change in the epistemological status of reality and fictional production respectively. In

Marxist-feminist terms reality is understood not as phenomenal forms that present themselves to our immediate perceptions but as the historical product of socio-economic forces; it is a social product of which we, as feminists, our knowledge and ideas are an equally constructed part. To understand the real world, then, it is not enough to observe life as it is lived on a day-to-day basis; nor can we call on the values preserved by human civilisation to penetrate phenomenal appearances. What we need is to conceptualise from a feminist standpoint the historical forces at work in the social formation which have produced and are continuing to produce both our material world and those phenomenal forms which appear to constitute reality.

Individual, concrete experience of oppression leads us to resist aspects of our world and provides the motive to interrogate it; but only the developing conceptual framework of feminism will enable us to locate the sources and assess the nature of patriarchy and so formulate the conditions necessary for change. In this sense feminist meaning is not immanent in the world waiting to be revealed. It is a social-sexual dynamic being produced by history.

Thus a change in the status of the real requires a corresponding change in conception of the aesthetic practice which seeks to represent the real. Language and signifying systems in general as part of a socially produced reality are similarly conceived as social products. Language, fiction and film are no longer treated as expressive tools reflecting a transparent reality, or a personal world view, or truths about the human condition; they are seen instead as socially-produced systems for signifying and organising reality, with their own specific histories and structures and so with their own capacity to produce the effects of meaning and values. Thus the 'convincing' character, the 'revealing' episode, or 'realistic' image of the world is not a simple reflection of 'real life', but a highly mediated production of fictional practice.

A critical practice for which meaning is already constituted in the world, stored up in 'the highest achievements of mankind', is clearly dangerous for feminism, which understands such achievements as posited on the oppressive location of woman as the unknowable other, outside history, in the realm of nature and eternal truth, man's mysterious *alter ego* against whom he achieves his definition, and symbolically controls in artistic production. Thus it is arguably more important for feminist film criticism to analyse not what a film means in terms of its 'image of women'—measured against some supposedly objective reality or the critic's personal predilections—but rather those mediations which produce and place that image within the total fictional structure of the film with particular ideological effects.

In other words there are two levels at which meaning can be located: one as revelation read off metaphorically as the immanent content of the film's devices and style—of which I argue Diane Giddis' article is an example—the second as the set of structured effects produced by the dynamic interplay of the various aesthetic, semiotic and semantic processes which constitute the 'work' of the film. The second level of analysis asks, according to the now familiar phrase, not 'what is this film's meaning?', but 'how is its meaning produced?'

Whereas the first approach tends towards the validation of ideology in giving meaning the status of a 'truth', the latter attempts to locate behind the manifest themes of a film a second order of meaning which lies not in thematic coherence but rather in the implications the structural relationships of the text have for the place of woman in patriarchy. In other words the critic does not examine the relation between a narrative device, such as male voice-over, and the heroine for its equivalence to some symbolic meaning, but rather for the way it organises the female image into a patriarchal location. What this shows us is not the expression of a truth individual women can translate in terms of an inner world, but rather an aspect of how patriarchy works. It is under this rubric that I have attempted my analysis of *Klute.*

The second point which emerges from the foregoing is the refusal to conceive of meaning as a static quantity residing inside the art work, waiting to be revealed by the ultimate, 'correct' interpretation. If meaning is a production, then the reader/critic plays a part in this production by bringing to bear on the work her/his own cultural knowledge and ideological perspective. A feminist reading reworks the text and produces meanings that would have been impossible prior to the development of the conceptual framework of feminism.

Within this context of a broad change in feminist film criticism, from the interpretation of immanent meaning to the interrogation of the production of meaning, I want now to look more closely at the way the opposition between realism and genre has been reworked in neo-Marxist feminist aesthetics.

BOURGEOIS IDEOLOGY, ARTISTIC PRACTICE AND REALISM

In much 1970s theoretical work on cultural production,[5] the task of bourgeois ideology in western capitalist society is seen as that of masking those socio-economic contradictions which are the driving force of history—the contradictions between the forces and relations of production and consequent division of the social formation into opposing class interests. The result of such masking is to obscure the fact of society as an interrelated totality grounded on contradiction, and as a historical and social production. In bourgeois ideology the members of the social formation find themselves as isolated individuals who confront over and against them society as a preconstituted given which appears to derive from nature. The bourgeois concept of the human condition or of human nature thus serves to 'naturalise' and so put beyond human control those socio-economic forces which produce the social formation, and its contradictions. Besides masking the social origins of those contradictions, bourgeois ideology finds means to produce their illusory unification through such notions as the 'common interest'; or fundamentally antagonistic material contradictions are displaced on to idealist contradictions within bourgeois ideology which are amenable to resolution—such as the conflict between love and honour in neo-classical drama.

Having proposed the function of bourgeois ideology it is necessary to ask how this takes place in practice.

Ideology, in much recent cultural analysis, is understood in Althusser's terms as 'a system (with its own logic and rigour) of representations (images, myths, ideas or concepts, depending on the case) endowed with a historical existence and role within a given society'.[6] In other words, the work of masking, unifying or displacing contradiction goes on at one level in the circulation of pre-formed ideas, common-sense understandings, the conventional wisdom of a given social group or society. On another level, according to Althusser's arguments, this conventional wisdom is materialised in the way we live our daily lives. If ideology is to be defined as a system of representations that have a material organisational force in society, the issue for film theory is the role in this of art as a practice specifically developed for the purposes of aesthetic representation and distinct from other forms of signifying practice.

In this context, the notion of a realist practice takes on a sinister aspect. On one level the issue is: what is the epistemological status of the 'reality' that the realist artist represents? Given that the 'representations' of bourgeois ideology attempt to present reality as a phenomenal, unified, naturalised entity to which the individual must adapt, there is clearly an ideological pressure on the artistic producer to identify reality with the *status quo.* On another level, if we grant that this is frequently the case in so-called realist production, our task is to identify in particular realist practices those conventions and devices which serve both to reproduce an ideological sense of reality—masking and naturalising contradiction—and to mask their own work of artistic production. Current film theory has developed an analysis of the so-called classic text constituted in a monolithically conceived realism embracing Hollywood genres, European art cinema and TV naturalism, which claims to demonstrate how this inevitably and always takes place in any attempt to represent reality. In the end the project of representation itself is said to be based on the denial of contradiction.[7]

This is not the place to argue the pros and cons of a potential progressive realist practice—something I feel needs urgently to be done. But what anti-realist theory rightly draws attention to is that traditional humanist criticism, which reads artistic texts in terms of their immanent revelation of the meaning of life and the human condition, is reactionary in that it posits a reality outside the action of social forces and so outside human control and the possibility of change; and that the iconic media of the twentieth century perpetuate this epistemology in the interests of the dominant ideology by promulgating a natural view of themselves as a 'window on the world', or as an expression of human life. It is in these terms that contemporary Hollywood's European look can be approached and similarly its need to take account of the contemporary phenomenon of Women's Liberation.

IDEOLOGY, GENRE AND SUBVERSION

What has been described above is in a sense the *ideal project* of the dominant ideology in its attempt to turn artistic practice to its own ends. Realist artistic practice clearly can provide ample ground for bourgeois ideology to seed itself in because of the epistemological ambiguity surrounding the concept of 'reality' However, due to a complex of contradictions in the socio-economic and cultural conditions of the mass media and aesthetic production, the hegemony of the dominant ideology is always in question. Despite the claim that all mainstream production is tainted with realist reaction, genre has been seized on by radical cultural analysts as the ground on which 'progressive' appropriations may be made of bourgeois and patriarchal products. It is here that neo-Marxist aesthetic theory can make use of the specificities of fictional production which get lost in the description of the realist text as a form of production whose aim is precisely to disguise that fact.

The economic rationale of this compromise with the ideological requirements of 'realism' is found in the studio system. The formulaic plots, stereotypes and stylistic conventions of the different genres were developed in response to the needs of a mass industry to predict market demand in order to standardise and so stabilise production. A contradictory demand of the market, however, is for novelty, innovation. So, unlike the concern with artistic exploration of the human condition which became the dominant themes of the European art cinema, Hollywood genre production tended both to foreground convention and stereotypicality in order to gain instant audience recognition of its type—this is a Western, a Gangster, a Woman's Picture, etc.—and to institute a type of aesthetic play among the conventions in order to pose the audience with a question that would keep them coming back—not 'what is going to happen next?' to which they would already have the answer, but 'how?'[8]

Thus genre provides neo-Marxist criticism with suitable territory on which to develop the more progressive possibilities of the notion of fictional production. Behind this approach lies the Russian formalist Victor Shklovsky's theory of 'art as device', in which he proposed that the function of aesthetic form should be to distort or 'make strange' everyday, 'normal' appearances, in order to impede our automatic perception of them, and so return them to our vision anew.[9] For Marxist aesthetics, because the means of artistic production are not simply formal devices any more than they are mere expressive devices, but rather determinate and determining structuring principles, Shklovsky's notion of 'making strange' is located in the contradictions that may arise between the structuring activity of art—which may produce its own effects of meaning—and the ideological themes of its subject matter. This is more likely to happen, however, where form is foregrounded rather than transparent.

In these terms the generic conventions and stereotypes of classic Hollywood can be seen as offering highly formalised and foregrounded sets of codes which can be set into play one against another, or against the grain of the film's thematic material, to expose the contradiction it is the film's project to unify, in a kind of *aesthetic subversion.*[10] Thus a criticism operating according to a perspective at odds with the ideology privileged as the film's 'message' or 'world-view' may be able to animate these effects to produce a progressive reading of an apparently reactionary film, or (as I attempt with *Klute)* an ideological reading of an apparently radical film.

FEMINIST READINGS OF HOLLYWOOD GENRE

Claire Johnston and Pam Cook[11] have developed progressive feminist readings of this kind for the classic decades of Hollywood in the 1940s and 1950s—the period of film noir. Possibly this period is particularly amenable to subversive analysis in that what has been called the cinema's recapitulation of the embourgeoisement of the novel had reached the stage of discarding a purely emblematic and heroic mode of characterisation and event and was grappling with contemporary issues and larger themes in the interests of a more mature and demanding realism, but still within the confines of a highly codified studio-based mode of generic production.

For feminists such a formulation has interesting possibilities for analysis of patriarchal ideology in cultural production. The twentieth century has seen an acceleration in the process of the emancipation of women and an intensification of the contradictions surrounding the sexual division of labour and reproduction, so that women perhaps more crucially than before constitute a consciously perceived social problem. At the same time feminists have discerned how women occupy a tangential position in relation to production and culture, and, as guardians of reproduction, or a reserve labour force, or the mythical 'other' against which man takes his definition, are defined as constitutive functions in society rather than among its producers.

In such terms the attempt of much Hollywood production in its classic decades to handle the issue of women as a growing social force can be read as foregrounding the problem of the 'image' of woman not simply as a reflection of an economically constituted problem—the post-war impulse, for instance, to punish the independent female image as a reflex of the economy's need to push women out of production and back into the home—but also as a crisis in the function of that image of defining male identity. Thus the analyses of Pam Cook and Claire Johnston seek to demonstrate how the attempt of the 1940s and 1950s to produce the independent woman stereotype repeatedly founders against the role of the female image in the fictional and iconic systems of the cinema.

CHARACTER, DISCOURSE

The *progressive or subversive reading*, which shifts the focus of criticism from the interpretation of immanent meaning to analysis of the means of its production, seeks to locate not the 'image of woman' centred in character, but the woman's voice heard intermittently in the female discourse of the film.[12]

The problem for feminist analysis of the impulse of traditional criticism to locate meaning in character is first that it leads the critic into moralistic assessment of the heroine and her subjectivity in terms of its truth to the actual condition of women, or to supposed female aspiration, or to a feminist perspective on either. The problem with this is that ideological myths about women are as much a part of the real world as any other construct. Thus to use a particular individual's notion of 'the realistic' as a criterion of truth can only lead to disagreement, and if used simply to dismiss what is defined as stereotypical, to the elimination of the chance to examine the power of recognition which certain character structures or stereotypes may invoke.[13]

Second, as I have already suggested, the character becomes the dominant element in the text, the focus of its 'truth' in terms of which all other aesthetic structures are read. Such a procedure ignores the fact of character as a production of these mechanisms and of its structural location within the narrative.[14] As I hope to show in terms of film noir, these structural determinants can be crucial in affecting the degree or otherwise of ideological control over the character. If a positive heroine is to be created, who can speak from and for the woman's point of view, then there has to be a change in the structures of fictional production and these have first to be identified for their patriarchal determinations.

The concept of the *woman's discourse* avoids this collapse of text into character; it is equally valuable in that it cuts across the form/content division and similarly the division fiction/society. A discourse is shared by a socially constituted group of speakers or particular social practice, provides the terms of what can or cannot be said and includes all those items, aesthetic, semantic, ideological, social which can be said to speak for or refer to those whose discourse it is. It is to be distinguished from point of view in that the latter is attached to a particular character or authorial position, while a discourse stretches across the text through a variety of different articulations of which character is only one; it need not be coherent but can be broken by a number of shorter or longer gaps or silences.

A filmic text is composed of a variety of different discourses which may be organised along class, racial or gender lines, to name a few. The structural coherence of the text arises from the interrelations of its discourses while ideological hegemony is gained by the power of the discourse carrying the dominant ideology to place and define the 'truth' of the others. Within patriarchal culture the various discourses that interweave through a specific text are so organised along gender lines as to give priority to the 'male discourse'. One form of subversion that feminists will look for, then, are those moments when in the generic play of convention and stereotype the male discourse loses control and the woman's voice disrupts it, making its assumptions seem 'strange'. From this perspective the question the feminist critic asks is not 'does this image of woman please me or not, do I identify with it or not?'[15] but rather of a particular conjuncture of plot device, character, dialogue or visual style: '*what is being said about women here, who is speaking, for whom?*'

WOMEN AND FILM NOIR

In this context film noir stands out as a phase in the development of the gangster/thriller of particular interest to feminist film criticism, which seeks to make progressive or subversive readings of Hollywood genre films. Film noir is a purely critical term (as opposed to an industrial category of studio production) and interest in the films it designates is itself fairly recent, arising as part of the 1960s revaluation of classic Hollywood genres and concern with *mise en scène* as opposed to auteurs and thematic analysis.

Film noir is commonly identified as a particular period in the development of the thriller in the 1940s and 1950s during which certain highly formalised inflections of plot, character and visual style dominated at the expense of narrative coherence and comprehensible solution of a crime, the usual goal of the thriller/detective film. *Mise en scène* criticism has tended to interpret the aberrant style of film noir metaphorically, as aiming at the production of a certain mood—angst, despair, nihilism—within which are rearticulated perennial myths and motifs such as the deceptive play of appearance and reality, the eternal fascination and destructiveness of the *femme fatale*, the play of salvation and damnation.

However, my analysis, which follows, of the location of women in film noir will not attempt to interpret the genre's themes but rather to identify some of those devices, the effects of which structure, in an intermittent commentary, a discourse about women and sometimes, perhaps subversively, for women.

FIVE FEATURES OF FILM NOIR

In my viewing experience there are five main structural features of film noir that together produce a specific location for women and somewhat ambiguous ideological effects. These are:

(1) the investigative structure of the narrative;
(2) plot devices such as voice-over or flashback, or frequently both;
(3) proliferation of points of view;
(4) frequent unstable characterisation of the heroine;
(5) an 'expressionist' visual style and emphasis on sexuality in the photographing of women.

Investigative Narrative Structure

In the mainstream thriller the investigative structure presupposes a male hero in search of the truth about an event that either has already happened or is about to come to completion. This premiss has two consequences. The plots of the thriller/detective story offer a world of action defined in male terms; the locales, situations, iconography, violence are conventions connoting the male sphere. Women in this world tend to split into two categories: there are those who work on the fringes of the underworld and are defined by the male criminal ambience of the thriller—barflies, nightclub singers, expensive mistresses, *femmes fatales*, and ruthless gold-diggers who marry and murder rich old men for their money; and then there are on the outer margins of this world, wives, long-suffering girlfriends, would-be fiancées who are victims of male crime, sometimes the objects of the hero's protection, and often points of vulnerability in his masculine armour. The second consequence is an epistemological one in so far as the investigation assumes truth to be a goal attainable by tracing a logical process of cause and effect, and that to every puzzle there is a key through which a complex but coherent pattern will emerge within seemingly anarchic events.

In the film noir cycle of thrillers both these features are inflected through the intervention of its other defining characteristics. To take the second first: the plots of noir thrillers are frequently impossible to fit together even when the criminal secret is discovered, partly through the interruptions to plot linearity and the breaks and frequent gaps in plot produced by the sometimes multiple use of flashback, and partly because the processes of detection are for the most part displaced from the centre of the film by other features.

This brings us to the roles of women in the male world of the thriller, and to a kind of dual inflection of these roles, in which the norm of the bourgeois family becomes markedly absent and unattainable, at the same time as the female figure becomes more central in the plot than usual.[16] Frequently the female figure exists as a crucial feature within the dangerous criminal world which the hero struggles with in the course of his investigation, and as often as not constitutes the central problem in the unravelling of truth. Woman becomes the object of the hero's investigation. Thus the place of the female figure in the puzzle which the hero has to solve often displaces solution of the crime as the object of the plot; the processes of detection—following clues and deductive intellection—are submerged by the hero's relations with the women he meets, and it is the vagaries of this relationship that determine the twists and turns of the plot.

Rather than the revelation of socio-economic patterns of political and financial power and corruption which mark the gangster/thriller, film noir probes the secrets of female sexuality and male desire within patterns of submission and dominance. Thus the enquiries of the police or private detective come eventually to concentrate on the state of the hero's, and more frequently, the heroine's, heart.

These inflections set up a conflict in the treatment of women in film noir. On the one hand their image is produced in the course of male investigation and moral judgment. On the other the suppression of the bourgeois family and centrality of women in the male world of action produces female representations outside family definition and dependency. This means that questions of economic survival have to be broached. Two options are available to women—work or living off a man. In film noir both options emphasise the sexual objectification of women, for its criminal ambience situates working women in bars and nightclubs rather than in professions or factories. But sexuality and money are brought into explicit juxtaposition—a contradiction for bourgeois morality in that female sexuality is supposed to be sanctified by love given freely, which is hidden within marriage and the family. Moreover, the heroine often shares the hard-boiled cynicism of the hero, which further undermines conventional sexual ideology. But this does not imply an unambiguously progressive approach in the noir treatment of women, for female sexuality is also juxtaposed within the investigative structure to the law and the voice of male judgment, and in many ways it is the underside of the bourgeois family that is brought to the surface for investigation.

One final feature of the investigatory structure of film noir consequent on its almost consistent use of flashback is that the investigation need not necessarily be carried through the agency of police or private detective, but often takes the form of a confession either to another person (*Out of the Past*, *Double Indemnity*) or to oneself/the audience (*Detour*, *The Postman Always Rings Twice*).

Flashback and Voice-Over

These two plot devices frequently work together in film noir, though their effects seem to remain the same even if they are used separately. The voice-over technique is usually an authoritative mode, either invoking the authority of the nineteenth-century, omniscient story-teller (see *The Magnificent Ambersons*) or pronouncing with a documentary 'voice-of-God' (see *The House on 92nd Street*). However, within an investigative narrative with a flashback—and sometimes multiple flashback—structure, the voice-over loses some of its control over events which are locked in the past and which the investigative or confessional voice-over seeks to unravel.

Two consequences arise from this. First, the story-teller is put on much more of an equal footing with the audience, the temporal separation of the moment of telling and the event told leading to something of a dislocation between sound and image and leaving a gap within which an audience can judge between what they observe and the story-teller's account of it. This aspect is intensified in that the story-teller is often proved wrong by subsequent events and may even be lying (see, for example, *Gilda, Crossfire).* Second, the whole process of story-telling is itself foregrounded in the noir thriller in that the investigation proceeds through a complex web of stories told by the characters to each other or by the narrator to the audience.

Both these consequences are intensified by the fact that the centre of the plot is dominated by questions about female sexuality, and sexual relationships involving patterns of deception, seduction and unrecognised revelations rather than by deductions of criminal activity from a web of clues. An extreme version of the story-telling structure of the film noir narrative is found in *Crossfire*, where three accounts of the same event are given, only one of which is true, and where, in a purely gratuitous scene, a mysterious and unidentified stranger offers to the hero three different versions of his relationship to the bar hostess they are apparently both involved with, without ever confirming which if any of the stories is true.

One way of looking at the plot of the typical film noir is to see it as a struggle between different voices for control over the telling of the story. This feature of the noir thriller is important to feminist criticism and perhaps offers the key to a feminist analysis of this cycle of films.

In film noir the voice-over is generally male—(*Mildred Pierce* is a notable exception and very interesting for this reason, but it also represents an attempt to fuse two genres; the Woman's Film and the noir thriller)—something Molly Haskell sees as the ultimate sexist structure,[17] and it is true that in some versions of the cycle the heroine is almost totally robbed of a speaking voice (see *Laura*, where the possessor of the voice-over, Lydecker, struggles to retain control over his protégée's story against the investigations of the detective, McPhearson, who silences his controlling voice halfway through the film when he reveals the mistake on which Lydecker's version of Laura's story is based). However, the tendency of the flashback structure to put a distance between the narrating voice-over and the story narrated also means that a distance sometimes appears between the expressed male judgment and the woman who is being investigated and judged—leaving room for the audience to experience at least an ambiguous response to the female image and what is said about her. A good example of this is Gilda's strip routine song 'Put the Blame on Mame, Boys' (in the film which is named after her).

Thus the woman's discourse may realise itself in a heroine's resistance to the male control of her story, in the course of the film's narration. To be clear, this has little to do with a conscious struggle on the part of the film's *characters* but is to do with effects structured in by the interaction of different generic and narrative conventions.

Point of View

Point of view may be a visual or a fictional factor in the cinema. In fiction the term refers to the subjective perspective within which the story and its meaning is being conceived and from which the viewer should ideally interpret it. This perspective may belong to the narrator, more difficult to identify in films than in novels, to the consciousness of a particular character, or it may be divided across several characters. In fiction, where there are several different points of view operating, coherence and harmony are usually maintained by one point of view carrying more weight than the others—often, in the nineteenth-century novel, the omniscient author's.

As was evident in the preceding discussion of voice-over, in film noir there is a proliferation of points of view and a struggle within the text for one viewpoint to gain hegemony. For the image of women in these films this may have a number of different implications. Where a single woman is seen from several viewpoints—either by different characters (*Laura*) or at different moments in time (*Double Indemnity*, *Out of the Past*), what is produced is a fractured, incoherent image. This is taken up again in terms of characterisation below.

The struggle between different viewpoints may be between men for control of the image (*Laura*) or, more usually in the 1940s noir thriller, between the man and the woman (*Gilda*). The generic features of the noir thriller which locate strong women in image-producing roles—nightclub singers, hostesses, models etc.—encourage the creation of heroines whose means of struggle is precisely the manipulation of the image which centuries of female representations have provided.

Thus, though the heroines of film noir, by virtue of male control of the voice-over, flashback structure, are rarely accorded the full subjectivity and fully expressed point of view of psychologically realist fiction, yet their *performance* of the roles accorded them in this form of male story-telling foregrounds the fact of their image as an artifice and suggests another place behind the image where the woman might be. So when in *Double Indemnity*, Phyllis Dietrichson comes to Walter Neff's flat there is at least a sense of discrepancy between his vilification of her duplicity and the power of her sexual appeal to him. In reverse, in *Out of the Past* a similar discrepancy might seem to arise between Jeff's sentimental romanticising of his first meeting with

Kathie—'She walked out of the moonlight'—and her 'playing' of the role.

Characterisation of the Heroine

The material for the film noir heroine is drawn from the stereotypes of the *femme fatale* or evil woman and the good–bad girl, and generally contrasted in the film with a marginal female figure representing the good woman, who is worthy of being a wife, and often the victim. But the processes of narration in film noir described above modify this stereotypical material and the conventions of characterisation, particularly in terms of coherence and motivated development. The *femme fatale* is noted for changeability and treachery (see Sternberg's films with Marlene Dietrich). But in the noir thriller, where the male voice-over is not in control of the plot, and on the contrary represents a hero on a quest for truth, not only is the hero frequently not sure whether the woman is honest or a deceiver, but the heroine's characterisation is itself fractured so that it is not evident to the audience whether she fills the stereotype or not.

Rather than a coherent realisation of the unstable, treacherous woman, we tend to find in film noir a series of partial characterisations juxtaposed, not necessarily in continuity but separated by gaps in time (see *Out of the Past*) and often in blunt contradiction with each other. So, for instance, in *The Postman Always Rings Twice* Cora exhibits a remarkable series of unmotivated character switches and roles something as follows: (1) sex-bomb; (2) hardworking, ambitious woman; (3) loving playmate in an adulterous relationship; (4) fearful girl in need of protection; (5) victim of male power; (6) hard, ruthless murderess; (7) mother-to-be; (8) sacrifice to law.[18] Such a mode of characterisation, needless to say, is in marked contrast to the consistent moral trajectory of the male, who, although he may be confused or uncertain as to the relation of appearances and reality, at least maintains a consistency of values.

The ultimate ideological effect of this unstable and fractured characterisation of women depends on the organisation of each particular film. As an aspect of the genre's theatricality such characterisations contribute to the instability and uncertainty of the hero's world, to the ever-deceiving flux of appearance and reality. In this sense they express a male existential anguish at the failure of masculine desire. But in the course of this, noir female characterisations, while they superficially confirm popular stereotypes about women, in their stylisation and play with the surfaces of the cinematic image they arguably foreground some of the features of that image. This is not to claim the progressiveness of the cycle but merely to assert its ideological interest for feminists.

Visual Style

The visual style of film noir is commonly seen as its defining characteristic through which its formal excesses carry and submerge the incomprehensibility of plot and contradictoriness of characterisation —or rather turn these features into a further expression of the existential angst carried by the films' 'expressionist' lighting schemes and camera angles.

Within this context the female image is frequently part of this visual environment, just as she is part of the hostile world of the plot in which the hero is enmeshed. The noir heroine frequently emerges from shadows, her harsh white face, photographed without softening filters, part of the abstract lighting schemes. More crucially, of course, she is filmed for her sexuality. Introductory shots, which catch the hero's gaze, frequently place her at an angle above the onlooker, and sexuality is often signalled by a long, elegant leg (*The Postman Always Rings Twice, Double Indemnity, Deadlier Than the Male*). Dress either emphasises sexuality—long besequined sheath dresses—or masculine independence and aggression—square, padded shoulders, bold striped suits.

FILM NOIR—A SUBVERSIVE GENRE?

From this account of film noir we see that it exists in highly foregrounded generic terms, exhibiting as its principal features conventionalisation, stylisation, theatricality, stereotypicality. As a sub-genre its mode has been described as determinedly anti-realist. To understand what produced this and its significance for women, it would be necessary to analyse the conjuncture of specific aesthetic, cultural and economic forces; on one hand the ongoing production of the private eye/thriller form of detective fiction; on the other the post-war drive to get women out of the workforce and return them to the domestic sphere; and finally the perennial myth of woman as threat to male control of the world and destroyer of male aspiration—forces which in cinematic terms interlock to form what we now think of as the aberrant style and world of film noir. What this means for women is the focusing of a number of contradictions, for the films both challenge the ideological hegemony of the family and in the end locate an oppressive and outcast place for women.

KLUTE AND FILM NOIR

The issue, then, that my analysis of *Klute* will try to explore, is the relation between the claims made for the film in terms of a so-called progressive realism, and the potentially subversive elements it might incorporate in its recourse to the generic features of film noir. In fact the 'realism' of *Klute* is derived from a Europeanised Hollywood which, while it seeks stylishness—a certain cinematic elaboration on the surfaces of the contemporary world—also eschews the notion of the conventional, the stereotype, and looks for a contemporary authenticity and psychological truth.

It is perhaps significant that its explicit generic affiliations are to a phase of the thriller that is firmly locked away in history. Their distance in time enables the noir conventions to be used less conventionally and more as metaphor, and so to comply with the aesthetic needs of the European tradition which the film is assimilating. In this respect *Klute* joins other examples of the 1970s noir revival such as *Chinatown* or *The Long Goodbye* whose Europeanised mode distinguishes them from the more orthodox line of development of the gangster/thriller into the Clint Eastwood police movie such as *Dirty Harry* or *Magnum Force.*

Such a view of the film's generic affiliation is supported by Alan Pakula's account of his aims:

> At the outset *Klute* has all the characteristics of a forties thriller. For me, starting to direct quite late, the attraction was in using a genre for my own ends; it wasn't pastiche which interested me but, on the contrary, making a contemporary exploration through the slant of a classic form. What's also marvellous about the suspense film is it allows for stylisation or theatricalisation, which is not possible in more simple films like *The Sterile Cuckoo* (*Pookie*).[19]

Thus the conventions, which in the classic film noir affect a structural distortion to plot and character and present a dislocated world, are now used consciously to offer a metaphoric revelation of a modern social and psychic malaise. What I will want to argue in my analysis of the significance of this for women is that, under pressure of the psychologism of the European tradition, the contradictions around woman animated by the dislocated world of film noir are thematically relocated and made amenable to resolution in the name of contemporary authenticity.

Notes

1. For a discussion of this notion, see Steve Neale, 'New Hollywood Cinema' *Screen*, 17: 2 (Summer 1976), 117–122.
2. For examples of early film criticism close to the Women's Movement and concerned with the opposition of generic stereotype and realism, see the first issues of *Women and Film* (now discontinued). For instance, in the first issue, Christine Mohanna, in her article 'A One-Sided Story: Women in the Movies', poses against the stereotypes of male-dominated mass cinema—mostly Hollywood—individual 'works of art'—mostly European cinema—which support heroines, defined not in 'romantic or sexual terms' but in their own terms, as people. Thus Dreyer's '*The Passion of Joan of Arc*', she says, 'evokes an image of woman so powerful it evades all stereotypes.'
3. Diane Giddis, 'The Divided Woman: Bree Daniel in *Klute*', *Women and Film*, 1: 3/4 (1973), 57–61; anthologised in Bill Nichols (ed.), *Movies and Methods* (Berkeley: University of California Press, 1976).
4. Claire Johnston, 'Women's Cinema as Counter-Cinema', in *Notes on Women's Cinema, Screen*, Pamphlet No. 2, SEFT (London, 1973).
5. The account of bourgeois ideology given here is largely drawn from Stuart Hall, 'Culture, the Media and the "Ideological Effect"', in James Curran et al. (eds.), *Mass Communication and Society* (London: Edward Arnold, 1977).
6. Louis Althusser, 'Marxism and Humanism', *For Marx* (Harmondsworth: Penguin, 1969), 231.
7. For different examples of the anti-realist polemic, see Paul Willemen, 'On Realism in the Cinema', *Screen*, 13: 1 (Spring 1972); Colin MacCabe, 'Realism and the Cinema: Notes on some Brechtian Theses', *Screen*, 15: 2 (Summer 1974); and Peter Wollen, '*Vent d'est*: Counter-Cinema' in *Afterimage*, 4 (Autumn 1972). For a feminist development of this position, see Eileen McGarry, 'Documentary, Realism and Women's Cinema; *Women and Film*, 2: 7 (Summer 1975); and *Camera Obscura*, 1 (Fall 1976).
8. For seminal accounts of the function of convention and stereotyping in the cinema, see Erwin Panofsky, 'Style and Medium in the Moving Pictures', in Daniel Talbot (ed.), *Film: An Anthology* (Berkeley: University of California Press, 1969); Robert Warshow, 'The Gangster as Tragic Hero; *The Immediate Experience* (New York: Atheneum, 1970); and Lawrence Alloway, 'The Iconography of the Movies', in Ian Cameron (ed.), *Movie Reader* (London: November Books, 1972).
9. Victor Shklovsky 'Art as Technique', in Lee T. Lemon and Marion J. Reis (eds.), *Russian Formalist Criticism* (Lincoln: University of Nebraska Press, 1965).

10. For an early elaboration of a theory of ideological subversion in the cinema, see Jean-Louis Comolli and Jean Narboni, 'Cinema/Ideology/Criticism', translated in *Screen*, 12: 1 (Spring 1971), and reprinted in *Screen Reader*, 1. For a feminist adaptation, see Claire Johnston, 'Women's Cinema as Counter-Cinema', in Claire Johnston (ed.), *Notes on Women's Cinema*, op. cit.
11. See Claire Johnston and Pam Cook's essays in Claire Johnston (ed.), *The Work of Dorothy Arzner: Towards a Feminist Cinema* (London: BFI, 1975); and Pam Cook, '"Exploitation" Films and Feminism', *Screen*, 17: 2 (Summer 1976).
12. See, for example, Claire Johnston's discussion of Dorothy Arzner in *The Work of Dorothy Arzner*, op. cit.
13. For discussion of the function and value of stereotypes for oppressed groups, see Richard Dyer, 'Stereotyping', in Richard Dyer (ed.), *Gays and Film* (London: BFI, 1977).
14. See Richard Dyer, *Stars: New Edition* (London: BFI, 1998), which includes an account of the star image of Jane Fonda.
15. Julia Lesage comments on Joan Mellen's *Women and their Sexuality in the New Film*: 'Mellen rejects women characters she finds "unpleasant". Thus Chloe in Rohmer's *Chloe in the Afternoon* is "plain, with shaggy. unwashed hair falling in her eyes. Her complexion is sallow and unaided by make up. Her sloppiness is intensified by a decrepit raincoat without style."', 'Whose Heroines', *Jump Cut*, 1 (May–June 1974) 22–24.
16. See Sylvia Harvey, 'Woman's Place: The Absent Family of Film Noir' in E. Ann Kaplan (ed.), *Women in Film Noir* (London: BFI, 1978).
17. Molly Haskell, *From Reverence to Rape* (New York: Holt, Rinehart and Winston, 1974), 198: 'The guilt for sexual initiative, and faithlessness was projected on to woman; she became the aggressor by male design and in male terms, and as seen by the male in highly subjective narratives, often recounted in the first person and using interior monologue, by which she was deprived of her point of view.'
18. Richard Dyer has analysed in detail the role of Lana Turner as Cora in *The Postman Alway's Rings Twice*, in 'Four Films of Lana Turner', *Movie*, 25 (Winter 1977/8).
19. Pakula, in 'Entretien avec Alan J. Pakula' by Michel Ciment in *Positif* 36 (March 1972), 36.

5 Woman's Stake: Filming the Female Body

Mary Ann Doane*

> We know that, for want of a stake, representation is not worth anything.
>
> (Michèle Montrelay)

To those who still ask, ' What do women want?' the cinema seems to provide no answer. For the cinema, in its alignment with the fantasies of the voyeur, has historically articulated its stories through a conflation of its central axis of seeing/being seen with the opposition male/female. So much so that in a classical instance such as *Humoresque*, when Joan Crawford almost violently attempts to appropriate the gaze for herself, she must be represented as myopic (the moments of her transformation from spectacle to spectator thus captured and constrained through their visualization as the act of putting on glasses) and eventually eliminated from the text, her death equated with that of a point of view. Cinematic images of woman have been so consistently oppressive and repressive that the very idea of a feminist filmmaking practice seems an impossibility. The simple gesture of directing a camera toward a woman has become equivalent to a terrorist act.

This state of affairs—the result of a history which inscribes woman as subordinate—is not simply to be overturned by a contemporary practice that is more aware, more self-conscious. The impasse confronting feminist filmmakers today is linked to the force of a certain theoretical discourse which denies the neutrality of the cinematic apparatus itself. A machine for the production of images and sounds, the cinema generates and guarantees pleasure by a corroboration of the spectator's identity. Because that identity is bound up with that of

* Mary Ann Doane, 'Woman's Stake: Filming the Female Body' from *October*, vol. 17, Summer 1981, reprinted by permission of the author.

the voyeur and the fetishist, because it requires for its support the attributes of the 'noncastrated', the potential for illusory mastery of the signifier, it is not accessible to the female spectator, who, in buying her ticket, must deny her sex. There are no images either *for* her or *of* her. There is a sense in which Peter Gidal, in attempting to articulate the relationship between his own filmmaking practice and feminist concerns, draws the most logical conclusion from this tendency in theory:

> In terms of the feminist struggle specifically, I have had a vehement refusal over the last decade, with one or two minor aberrations, to allow images of women into my films at all, since I do not see how those images can be separated from the dominant meanings. The ultra-left aspect of this may be nihilistic as well, which may be a critique of my position because it does not see much hope for representations for women, but I do not see how, to take the main example I gave round about 1969 before any knowledge on my part of, say, semiotics, there is any possibility of using the image of a naked woman—at that time I did not have it clarified to the point of any image of a woman—other than in an absolutely sexist and politically repressive patriarchal way in this conjuncture.[1]

This is the extreme formulation of a project which can define itself only in terms of negativity. If the female body is not necessarily always excluded within this problematic, it must always be placed within quotation marks. For it is precisely the massive reading, writing, filming of the female body which constructs and maintains a hierarchy along the lines of a sexual difference assumed as natural. The ideological complicity of the concept of the natural dictates the impossibility of a nostalgic return to an unwritten body.

Thus, contemporary filmmaking addresses itself to the activity of uncoding, de-coding, deconstructing the given images. It is a project of de-familiarization whose aim is not necessarily that of seeing the female body differently, but of exposing the habitual meanings/values attached to femininity as cultural constructions. Sally Potter's *Thriller*, for instance, is a rereading of the woman's role in opera, specifically in Puccini's *La Bohème*, in terms of its ideological function. Mimi's death, depicted in the opera as tragedy, is rewritten as a murder, the film itself invoking the conventions of the suspense thriller. In Babette Mangolte's *The Camera: Je/La Caméra: Eye*, what is at stake are the relations of power sustained within the camera–subject nexus. The discomfort of the subjects posing for the camera, together with the authority of the off-screen voice giving instructions ('Smile', 'Don't smile', 'Look to the left', etc.), challenge the photographic image's claim to naturalism and spontaneity. And, most interestingly, the subjects, whether male or female, inevitably appear to assume a mask of 'femininity' in order to become photographable (filmable)—as though femininity were synonymous with the *pose*. This may explain the feminist film's frequent obsession with the pose as position—the importance accorded to dance positions in *Thriller* or those assumed by the hysteric in Terrel Seltzer's *The Story of Anna O*—which we may see as the arrangements of the body in the interests of aesthetics and science. In their rigidity (the recurrent use of the tableau in these films) or excessive repetition (the multiple, seemingly unending caresses of the woman's breasts in Mangolte's *What Maisie Knew*), positions and gestures are isolated, deprived of the syntagmatic rationalization which, in the more classical text, conduces to their naturalization. These strategies of demystification are attempts to strip the body of its readings. The inadequacy of this formulation of the problem is obvious, however, in that the gesture of stripping in relation to a female body is already the property of patriarchy. More importantly, perhaps, the question to be addressed is this: what is left after the stripping, the uncoding, the deconstruction? For an uncoded body is clearly an impossibility.

Attempts to answer this question by invoking the positivity or specificity of a definition have been severely criticized on the grounds that the particular definition claims a 'nature' proper to the woman and is hence complicit with those discourses which set woman outside the social order. Since the patriarchy has always already said everything (everything and nothing) about woman, efforts to give those phrases a different intonation, to mumble, to stutter, to slur them, to articulate them differently, must be doomed to failure. Laura Mulvey and Peter Wollen's *Riddles of the Sphinx*, for instance, has been repeatedly criticized for its invocation of the sphinx as the figure of a femininity repressed by the Oedipal mythos. Femininity is something which has been forgotten or repressed, left outside the gates of the city; hence, what is called for is a radical act of remembering. The radicality of that act, however, has been subject to debate. As Stephen Heath points out,

> The line in the figure of the sphinx-woman between the posing of a question and the idea that women are the question is very thin; female sexuality is dark and unexplorable, women, as Freud put it, are that half of the audience which is the enigma, the great enigma. This is the problem and the difficulty—the area of debate and criticism—of Mulvey and Wollen's film *Riddles of the Sphinx* where the sphinx is produced as a point of resistance that seems

nevertheless to repeat, in its very terms, the relations of women made within patriarchy, their representation in the conjunction of such elements as motherhood as mystery, the unconscious, a voice that speaks far off from the past through dream or forgotten language. The film is as though poised on the edge of a politics of the unconscious, of the imagination of a politics of the unconscious ('what would the politics of the unconscious be like?'), with a simultaneous falling short, that politics and imagination not yet there, coming back with old definitions, the given images.[3]

What is forgotten is the critical judgment, but retrieved in Heath's claim that 'the force remains in the risk'— the risk, that is, of recapitulating the terms of patriarchy—is the fact that the sphinx is also, and crucially, subject to a kind of filmic disintegration. In the section entitled 'Stones', the refilming of found footage of the Egyptian sphinx problematizes any notion of perceptual immediacy in refinding an 'innocent' image of femininity. In fact, as the camera appears to get closer to its object, the graininess of the film is marked, thus indicating the limit of the material basis of its representation.

Most of this essay will be a lengthy digression, a prolegomenon to a much needed investigation of the material specificity of film in relation to the female body and its syntax. Given the power of a certain form of feminist theory which has successfully blocked attempts to provide a conceptualization of this body, the digression is, nevertheless, crucial.

The resistance to filmic and theoretical descriptions of femininity is linked to the strength of the feminist critique of essentialism—of ideas concerning an essential femininity, or of the 'real' woman not yet disfigured by patriarchal social relations. The force of this critique lies in its exposure of the inevitable alliance between 'feminine essence' and the natural, the given, or precisely what is outside the range of political action and thus not amenable to change. This unchangeable 'order of things' in relation to sexual difference is an exact formulation of patriarchy's strongest rationalization of itself. And since the essence of femininity is most frequently attached to the natural body as an immediate indicator of sexual difference, it is this body which must be refused. The body is always a function of discourse.

Feminist theory which grounds itself in anti-essentialism frequently turns to psychoanalysis for its description of sexuality because psychoanalysis assumes a necessary gap between the body and the psyche, so that sexuality is not reducible to the physical. Sexuality is constructed within social and symbolic relations; it is most *un*natural and achieved only after an arduous struggle. One is not born with a sexual identity (hence the significance of the concept of bisexuality in psychoanalysis). The terms of this argument demand that charges of phallocentrism be met with statements that the phallus is not equal to the penis, castration is bloodless, and the father is, in any case, dead and only symbolic.

Nevertheless, the gap between body and psyche is not absolute; an image or symbolization of the body (which is not necessarily the body of biological science) is fundamental to the construction of the psychoanalytical discourse. Brief references to two different aspects of psychoanalytic theory will suffice to illustrate my point. Jean Laplanche explains the emergence of sexuality by means of the concept of propping or *anaclisis.* The drive, which is always sexual, leans or props itself upon the nonsexual or presexual instinct of self-preservation. His major example is the relation of the oral drive to the instinct of hunger whose object is the milk obtained from the mother's breast. The object of the oral drive (prompted by the sucking which activates the lips as an erotogenic zone) is necessarily displaced in relation to the first object of the instinct. The fantasmatic breast (henceforth the object of the oral drive) is a metonymic derivation, a symbol, of the milk: 'The object to be rediscovered is not the lost object, but its substitute by displacement; the lost object is the object of self-preservation, of hunger, and the object one seeks to refind is an object displaced in relation to that first object.'[4] Sexuality can only take form in a dissociation of subjectivity from the bodily function, but the concept of a bodily function is necessary in the explanation as, precisely a support. We will see later how Laplanche de-naturalizes this body (which is simply a distribution of erotogenic zones) while retaining it as a cipher. Still, the body is there, as a prop.

The second aspect of psychoanalysis which suggests the necessity of a certain conceptualization of the body is perhaps more pertinent, and certainly more notorious, in relation to a discussion of feminism: the place of the phallus in Lacanian theory. Lacan and feminist theorists who subscribe to his formulations persistently claim that the phallus is not the penis; the phallus is a signifier (the signifier of lack). It does not *belong* to the male. The phallus is only important insofar as it can be put in circulation as a signifier. Both sexes define themselves in relation to this 'third term'. What is ultimately stressed here is the absolute necessity of positing only one libido (which Freud labels masculine) in relation to only one term, the phallus. Initially, both sexes, in desiring to conform to the desire of the other (the mother), define themselves in relation to the phallus in the mode of 'being'.

Sexual difference, then, is inaugurated at the moment of the Oedipal complex when the girl continues to 'be' the phallus while the boy situates himself in the mode of 'having'. Positing two terms, in relation to two fully defined sexualities, as Jones and Horney do, binds the concept of sexuality more immediately, more directly, to the body as it expresses itself at birth. For Jones and Horney, there is an essential femininity which is linked to an expression of the vagina. And for Horney at least, there is a sense in which the little girl experiences an empirical, not a psychic, inferiority.[5]

But does the phallus really have nothing to do with the penis, no commerce with it at all? The ease of the description by means of which the boy situates himself in the mode of 'having' one would seem to indicate that this is not the case. And Lacan's justification for the privilege accorded to the phallus as signifier appears to guarantee its derivation from a certain representation of the bodily organ:

> The phallus is the privileged signifier of that mark in which the role of the logos is joined with the advent of desire. It can be said that this signifier is chosen because it is the most tangible element in the real of sexual copulation, and also the most symbolic in the literal (typographical) sense of the term, since it is equivalent there to the (logical) copula. It might also be said that, by virtue of its turgidity, it is the image of the vital flow as it is transmitted in generation.[6]

There is a sense in which all attempts to deny the relation between the phallus and the penis are feints, veils, illusions. The phallus, as signifier, may no longer *be* the penis, but any effort to conceptualize its function is inseparable from an imaging of the body. The difficulty in conceptualizing the relation between the phallus and the penis is evident in Parveen Adams's explanation of the different psychic trajectories of the girl and the boy.

> Sexuality can only be considered at the level of the symbolic processes. This lack is undifferentiated for both sexes and has nothing to do with the absence of a penis, a physical lack.
>
> Nonetheless, the anatomical difference between the sexes does permit a differentiation within the symbolic process.... The phallus represents lack for both boys and girls. But the boy in having a penis has that which lends itself to the phallic symbol. The girl does not have a penis. What she lacks is not a penis as such, but the means to represent lack.[7]

The sexual differentiation is permitted but not demanded by the body and it is the exact force or import of this 'permitting' which requires an explanation. For it is clear that what is being suggested is that the boy's body provides an access to the processes of representation while the girl's body does not. From this perspective, a certain slippage can then take place by means of which the female body becomes an absolute tabula rasa of sorts: anything and everything can be written on it. Or more accurately, perhaps, the male body comes fully equipped with a binary opposition—penis/no penis, presence/absence, phonemic opposition—while the female body is constituted as 'noise',[8] an undifferentiated presence which always threatens to disrupt representation.

This analysis of the bodily image in psychoanalysis becomes crucial for feminism with the recognition that sexuality is inextricable from discourse, from language. The conjunction of semiotics and psychoanalysis (as exemplified in the work of Lacan and others) has been successful in demonstrating the necessity of a break in an initial plenitude as a fundamental condition for signification. The concept of lack is not arbitrary. The fact that the little girl in the above description has no means to represent lack results in her different relation to language and representation. The work of Michèle Montrelay is most explicit on this issue: '. . . for want of a stake, representation is not worth anything.'[9] The initial relation to the mother, the determinant of the desire of both sexes, is too full, too immediate, too present. This undifferentiated plenitude must be fissured through the introduction of lack before representation can be assured, since representation entails the absence of the desired object. 'Hence the repression that ensures that one does not think, nor see, nor take the desired object, even and above all if it is within reach: this object must remain lost.'[10] The tragedy of Oedipus lies in his refinding of the object. And as Montrelay points out, it is the sphinx as the figure of femininity which heralds this 'ruin of representation'.

In order for representation to be possible then, a stake is essential. Something must be threatened if the paternal prohibition against incest is to take effect, forcing the gap between desire and its object. This theory results in a rather surprising interpretation of the woman's psychic oppression: her different relation to language stems from the fact that she has nothing to lose, nothing at stake. Prohibition, the law of limitation, cannot touch the little girl. For the little boy, on the other hand, there is most definitely something to lose. 'He experiments, not only with chance but also with the law and with his sexual organ: his body itself takes on the value of stake.'[11]

Furthermore, in repeating, doubling the maternal body with her own, the woman recovers the first stake of representation and thus undermines the possibility of losing the object of desire since she has, instead become it.

> From now on, anxiety, tied to the presence of this body, can only be insistent, continuous. This body, so close, which she has to occupy, is an object in excess which must be 'lost,' that is to say, repressed, in order to be symbolised. Hence the symptoms which so often simulate this loss: 'there is no longer anything, only the hole, emptiness . . .' Such is the *leitmotif* of all feminine cure, which it would be a mistake to see as the expression of an alleged 'castration.' On the contrary, it is a defence produced in order to parry the avatars, the deficiencies, of symbolic castration.[12]

There are other types of defense as well, based on the woman's imaginary simulation of lack. Montrelay points to the anorexic, for instance, who diminishes her own body, dissolving the flesh and reducing the body to a cipher.[13] Or the woman can operate a performance of femininity, a masquerade, by means of an accumulation of accessories—jewelry, hats, feathers, etc.—all designed to mask the absence of a lack.[14] These defenses, however, are based on the woman's imaginary simulation of lack and exclude the possibility of an encounter with the symbolic. She can only mime representation.

Montrelay's work is problematic in several respects. In situating the woman's relation to her own body as narcissistic, erotic, and maternal, Montrelay insists that it is the 'real of her own body' which 'imposes itself', prior to any act of construction.[15] Furthermore, she does, eventually, outline a scenario within which the woman has access to symbolic lack, but it is defined in terms of a heterosexual act of intercourse in which the penis, even though it is described as 'scarcely anything', produces the 'purest and most elementary form of signifying articulation'.[16] Nevertheless, Montrelay's work points to the crucial dilemma confronting an anti-essentialist feminist theory which utilizes psychoanalysis. That is, while psychoanalysis does theorize the relative autonomy of psychic processes, the gap between body and psyche, it also requires the body as a prop, a support for its description of sexuality as a discursive function. Too often anti-essentialism is characterized by a paranoia in relation to all discussions of the female body (since ideas about a 'natural' female body or the female body and 'nature' are the linchpins of patriarchal ideology). This results in a position which simply repeats that of classical Freudian psychoanalysis in its focus upon the little boy's psychic development at the expense of that of the little girl. What is repressed here is the fact that psychoanalysis can conceptualize the sexuality of both the boy and the girl *only* by positing gender-specific bodies.

Even more crucially, as Montrelay's work demonstrates, the use of the concepts of the phallus and castration within a semiotically oriented psychoanalysis logically implies that the woman must have a different relation to language from that of the man. And from a semiotic perspective, her relation to language must be deficient since her body does not 'permit' access to what, for the semiotician, is the motor-force of language—the representation of lack. Hence, the greatest masquerade of all is that of the woman speaking (or writing, or filming), appropriating discourse. To take up a discourse for the woman (if not, indeed, by her), that is, the discourse of feminism itself, would thus seem to entail an absolute contradiction. How can she speak?

Yet, we know that women speak, even though it may not be clear exactly how this takes place. And unless we want to accept a formulation by means of which woman can only mimic man's relation to language, that is, assume a position defined by the penis-phallus as the supreme arbitrer of lack, we must try to reconsider the relation between the female body and language, never forgetting that it is a relation between two terms and not two essences. Does woman have a stake in representation or, more appropriately, can we assign one to her? Anatomy is destiny only if the concept of destiny is recognized for what it really is: a concept proper to fiction.

The necessity of assigning to woman a specific stake informs the work of theorists such as Luce Irigaray and Julia Kristeva, and both have been criticized from an anti-essentialist perspective. Beverley Brown and Parveen Adams, for example, distinguish between two orders of argument about the female body which are attributed, respectively, to Irigaray and Kristeva:

> We can demand then: what is this place, this body, from which women speak so mutely?
>
> Two orders of reply to this question can be distinguished. In the first there is an attempt to find a real and natural body which is pre-social in a literal sense. The second, more sophisticated reply, says that the issue at stake is not the actual location of a real body, but that the positing of such a body seems to be a condition of the discursive in general.[17]

Although the second order of argument is described as 'more sophisticated', Brown and Adams ultimately find that both are deficient. I want briefly to address this criticism although it really requires an extended discussion impossible within the limits of this essay. The criticisms of Irigaray are based primarily on her essay, 'That Sex

Which Is Not One',[18] in which she attempts to conceptualize the female body in relation to language/discourse, but independently of the penis/lack dichotomy. Irigaray valorizes certain features of the female body—the two lips (of the labia) which caress each other and define woman's auto-eroticism as a relation to duality, the multiplicity of sexualized zones spread across the body. Furthermore, Irigaray uses this representation of the body to specify a feminine language which is plural, polyvalent, and irreducible to a masculine language based on restrictive notions of unity and identity. Brown and Adams claim that 'her argument turns upon the possibility of discovering that which is already there—it is a case of "making visible" the previously "invisible" of feminine sexuality'.[19] While there are undoubtedly problems with the rather direct relation Irigaray often posits between the body and language, her attempt to provide the woman with an autonomous symbolic representation is not to be easily dismissed. Irigaray herself criticizes the logic which gives privilege to the gaze, thereby questioning the gesture of 'making visible' a previously hidden female sexuality. Her work is a radical rewriting of psychoanalysis which, while foregrounding the process of mimesis by which language represents the body, simultaneously constructs a distinction between a mimesis which is 'productive' and one which is merely 'reproductive' or 'imitative'—a process of 'adequation' and of 'specularization'.[20] An immediate dismissal of her work in the interests of an overwary anti-essentialism involves a premature rejection of 'the force that remains in the risk'.

The criticism addressed to Kristeva, on the other hand, is directed toward her stress on pre-Oedipal sexuality, allying it with a femininity whose repression is the very condition of Western discourse.[21] For Kristeva, the woman's negative relation to the symbolic determines her bond with a polymorphous, prelogical discourse which corresponds to the autonomous and polymorphous sexuality of the pre-Oedipal moment. Brown and Adams formulate their criticism in these terms: 'Setting up this apolitical autonomy of polymorphous sexuality is, in effect, the positing of sexuality as an impossible origin, a state of nature, as simply the eternal presence of sexuality at all.'[22] However, pre-Oedipal sexuality is not synonymous with 'nature'; it already assumes an organized distribution of erotogenic zones over the body and forms of relations to objects which are variable (whether human or nonhuman). Both male and female pass through live pre-Oedipality. Hence, pre-Oedipality can only be equated with femininity retrospectively, *après coup* after the event of the Oedipal complex, of the threat of castration, and the subsequent negative entry into the symbolic attributed to the woman. Insofar as Kristeva's description of pre-Oedipality is dependent upon notions of the drive, it involves displacement of sexuality in relation to the body. As Laplanche points out, the drive is a metonymic derivation from the instinct which is itself attached to an erotogenic zone, a zone of *exchange.*

The drive properly speaking, in the only sense faithful to Freud's discovery, *is* sexuality. Now sexuality, in its entirety, in the human infant, lies in *a movement which deflects the instinct, metaphorizes its aim, displaces and internalizes its object, and concentrates its source on what is ultimately a minimal zone, the erotogenic zone.* . . . This zone of exchange is also a zone for care, namely the particular and attentive care provided by the mother. These zones, then, attract the first erotogenic maneuvers from the adult. An even more significant factor, if we introduce the subjectivity of the first 'partner': these zones *focalize parental fantasies* and above all *maternal fantasies,* so that we may say, in what is barely a metaphor, that they are the points through which is *introduced into the child that alien internal entity* which is, properly speaking, the *sexual excitation.*[23]

The force of this scenario lies in its de-naturalization of the sexualized body. The conceptualization of the erotogenic zone as a zone of exchange demonstrates that the investment of the body with sexuality is always already social. Since it is ultimately *maternal* fantasies which are at issue here, it is apparent that, without an anchoring in the social, psychoanalysis can simply reiterate, reperform in its theorization, the vicious circle of patriarchy.

The rather long digression which structures this essay is motivated by the extreme difficulty of moving beyond the impasse generated by the opposition between essentialism and anti-essentialism. In the context of feminist film theory, both positions are formulated through a repression of the crucial and complex relation between the body and psychic processes, that is, processes of signification. From the point of view of essentialist theory, the goal of a feminist film practice must be the production of images which provide a pure reflection of the real woman, thus returning the real female body to the woman as her rightful property. And this body is accessible to a transparent cinematic discourse. The position is grounded in a mis-recognition of signification as outside of, uninformed by, the psychic. On the other hand, the logical extension of anti-essentialist theory, particularly as it is evidenced in Gidal's description of his filmmaking practice, results in the absolute exclusion of the female body, the refusal of any attempt to figure or represent that body. Both the proposal of a pure access to a natural female body and the rejection of attempts to conceptualize the female body based on their contamination by ideas of 'nature' are inhibiting and misleading. Both positions deny the necessity of posing a complex relation between the body and psychic/signifying processes, of using the body, in effect, as a 'prop'. For Kristeva is right—the positing of a body *is* a condition of discursive practices. It is crucial that feminism move beyond the opposition between essentialism and anti-essentialism. This move will entail the necessary risk taken by theories which attempt to define or construct a feminine specificity (not essence), theories which work to provide the woman with an autonomous symbolic representation.

What this means in terms of the theorization of a feminist filmmaking practice can only be sketched here. But it is clear from the preceding exploration of the theoretical elaboration of the female body that the stake does not simply concern an isolated image of the body. The attempt to 'lean' on the body in order to formulate the woman's different relation to speech, to language, clarifies the fact that what is at stake is, rather, the syntax which constitutes the female body as a term. The most interesting and productive recent films dealing with the feminist problematic are precisely those which elaborate a new syntax, thus 'speaking' the female body differently, even haltingly or inarticulately from the perspective of a classical syntax. For instance, the circular camera movements which carve out the space of the mise-en-scène in *Riddles of the Sphinx* are in a sense more critical to a discussion of the film than the status of the figure of the sphinx as feminine. The film effects a continual displacement of the gaze which 'catches' the woman's body only accidentally, momentarily, refusing to hold or fix her in the frame. The camera consistently transforms its own framing to elide the possibility of a fetishism of the female body. Chantal Akerman's *Jeanne Dielman, 23 Quai du Commerce—1080 Bruxelles* constructs its syntax by linking together scenes which, in the classical text, would be concealed, in effect negated, by temporal ellipses. The specificity of the film lies in the painful duration of that time 'in-between' events, that time which is exactly proper to the woman (in particular, the housewife) within a patriarchal society. The obsessive routine of Jeanne Dielman's daily life, as both housewife and prostitute, is radically broken only by an instance of orgasm (corresponding quite literally to the 'climax' of the narrative) which is immediately followed by her murder of the man. Hence, the narrative structure is a parodic 'mime' that distorts, undoes the structure of the classical narrative through an insistence upon its repressions.

The analysis of the elaboration of a special syntax for a different articulation of the female body can also elucidate the significance of the recourse, in at least two of these films, to the classical codification of suspense. Both *Jeanne Dielman* and Sally Potter's *Thriller* construct a suspense without expectation. *Jeanne Dielman*, although it momentarily 'cites' the mechanism of the narrative climax, articulates an absolute refusal of the phatic function of suspense, its engagement with and constraint of the spectator as consumer, devourer of discourse. *Thriller*, on the other hand, 'quotes' the strategies of the suspense film (as well as individual films of this genre—for example, *Psycho*) in order to undermine radically the way in which the woman is 'spoken' by another genre altogether, that of operatic tragedy. This engagement with the codification of suspense is an encounter with the genre which Roland Barthes defines as the most intense embodiment of the 'generalized distortion' which 'gives the language of narrative its special character':

> 'Suspense' is clearly only a privileged—or 'exacerbated'—form of distortion: on the one hand, by keeping a sequence open (through emphatic procedures of delay and renewal), it reinforces the contact with the reader (the listener), has a manifestly phatic function; while on the other, it offers the threat of an uncompleted sequence, of an open paradigm (if, as we believe, every sequence has two poles), that is to say, of a logical disturbance, it being this disturbance which is consumed with anxiety and pleasure (all the more so because it is always made right in the end) 'Suspense', therefore, is a game with structure, designed to endanger and glorify it, constituting a veritable 'thrilling' of intelligibility: by representing order (and no longer series) in its fragility, 'suspense' accomplishes the very idea of language. . . .[24]

It is precisely this 'idea of language' which is threatened by both *Jeanne Dielman* and *Thriller* in their attempts to construct another syntax which would, perhaps, collapse the fragile order, revealing the ending too soon.

While I have barely approached the question of an exact formulation of the representation of the female body attached to the syntactical constructions of these films, it is apparent that this syntax is an area of intense concern, of reworking, rearticulating the specular imaging of woman, for whom, in the context of a current filmmaking, the formulation of a stake is already in process.

Notes

1. Peter Gidal, transcription of a discussion following 'Technology and Ideology in/through/and Avant-Garde Film: An Instance', in *The Cinematic Apparatus*, ed. Teresa de Lauretis and Stephen Heath (New York: St Martin's Press, 1980), 169.
2. This calls for a more thorough dissection and analysis of the assumptions underlying the cliché that male models are 'effeminate'.
3. Stephen Heath, 'Difference', *Screen*, 19: 3 (Autumn 1978), 73.
4. Jean Laplanche, *Life and Death in Psychoanalysis.* trans. Jeffrey Mehlman (Baltimore: Johns Hopkins, 1976), 20.
5. See, for example, 'The Denial of the Vagina', in *Psychoanalysis and Female Sexuality*, ed. Hendrick M. Ruitenbeek (New Haven: College and University Press, 1966), 73–87; and *Feminine Psychology*, ed. Harold Kelman (New York: W. W. Norton, 1967).
6. Jacques Lacan, *Écris: A Selection*, trans. Alan Sheridan (New York: W. W. Norton, 1977), 287.
7. Parveen Adams, 'Representation and Sexuality', *m/f*, 1 (1978), 66–67. Even if the phallus is defined as logically prior to the penis, in that it is the phallus which bestows significance on the penis, a *relation* between the two is nevertheless posited, and this is my point.
8. I am grateful to Philip Rosen for this 'representation' of the problem.
9. Michèle Montrelay, 'Inquiry into Femininity', *m/f*, 1 (1978), 89.
10. Ibid.
11. Ibid. 90.
12. Ibid. 91–92.
13. Ibid. 92
14. This description is derived from Lacan's conceptualization of masquerade in relation to femininity. *See Écrits: A Selection*, 289–290. Lacan, in turn, borrows the notion of masquerade from Joan Riviere; see 'Womanliness as Masquerade', in *Psychoanalysis and Female Sexuality*, 209–220.
15. Montrelay, 91.
16. Ibid. 98.
17. Beverley Brown and Parveen Adams, 'The Feminine Body and Feminist Politics', *m/f*, 3 (1979), 37.
18. Luce Irigaray, 'That Sex Which Is Not One', trans. R. Albury and P. Foss, in *Language, Sexuality, Subversion*, ed. Paul Foss and Meaghan Morris (Darlington: Feral Publications, 1978), 161–172. This is a translation of the second essay in *Ce sexe qui n'en est pas un* (Paris: Minuit, 1977), 23–32.
19. Brown and Adams, 38.
20. *Ce sexe qui n'en est pas un*, 129–130.
21. The critique of Kristeva is based on *About Chinese Women*, trans. Anita Barrows (New York: Urizen Books, 1977).
22. Brown and Adams, 39.
23. Laplanche, 23–24.
24. Roland Barthes, 'Introduction to the Structural Analysis of Narratives', in *Image–Music–Text*, trans. Stephen Heath (New York: Hill and Wang, 1977), 119.

6 Male Subjectivity and Celestial Suture

It's a Wonderful Life

Kaja Silverman*

> Before its birth, the child is . . . always—already a subject, appointed as a subject . . . by the specific familial ideological configuration in which it is 'expected' once it has been conceived. I hardly need add that this familial ideological configuration is, in its uniqueness, highly structured, and that it is in this implacable and more or less 'pathological' (presupposing that any meaning can be assigned to that term) structure that the former subject-to-be will have to 'find' 'its' place, i.e. 'become' the sexual object (boy or girl) which it already is in advance.
>
> (Louis Althusser)

The scenario of cultural subjectivity, in both its male and female versions, consists of a compulsion to repeat experiences which are instinctually unpleasurable, and involves an ever-increasing accommodation of passivity and masochistic pleasure. Within contemporary Western culture this scenario is usually associated at the manifest level only with the female subject, and is disassociated from the male subject through a series of displacements and denials.[1] Thus within the classical narrative text (a paradigm inherited from the nineteenth century, but still fully operative), the penis is consistently confused with the phallus, and the male subjects who occupy the paternal position are conflated with the symbolic values (knowledge, potency, legal authority, linguistic, monetary, visual and narrative control, etc.) which structure that position. In short, the 'actual' father is passed off as the symbolic father.

However, Frank Capra's *It's a Wonderful Life* makes startlingly evident the necessary cultural subordination of the male subject, as well as his full participation in the passivity and masochism usually

* Kaja Silverman, 'Male Subjectivity and Celestial Satire: It's a Wonderful Life' from *Framework*, vol. 14, Spring 1981. Reprinted with permission of the author.

associated with the female subject. It also emphasizes the distance between the actual father, or the father who actualizes the paternal position, and the symbolic father or paternal position. The film effects the forced identification of the male subject with a 'weak' or 'castrated' father, an identification which would seem to challenge in every respect the normative representations of the Oedipal drama with which mainstream Hollywood cinema provides us. Indeed, it would seem no exaggeration to say that the position which Peter Bailey occupies, and from which George Bailey tries unsuccessfully to escape, more closely resembles that of the female subject than that which is generally connected with the male subject. *It's a Wonderful Life* seems almost to collapse the distinction between male and female subjectivity—to suggest that the only point of view for both subjects is finally that which psychoanalysis associates with the mother.[2]

I am not proposing that Capra's film eliminates the phallus/lack opposition. On the contrary, that opposition proves as central an organizing principle within this text as it does within any classical narrative. However, because the dominant discourse of *It's a Wonderful Life* is Christianity, and because that discourse provides us with a symbolic father who radically and indeed openly transcends all human fathers, the phallus/lack opposition tends to be elaborated more in relation to the terms 'divine' and 'mortal' than 'male' and 'female'. Needless to say, the film does not in any way challenge the ultimate authority and potency of the male subject; it merely shows that authority and potency to be invested in certain earthly institutions and agencies which exceed him, and to have their origin in a heavenly father to whom he stands as son. The authority and potency of the male subject are constantly deferred, like an inheritance into which he will some day come. In the mean time, those things are institutionally secured, like money in the bank, and watched over by the 'real' owner—what Lacan would call the symbolic father, or what the film prefers to designate as 'God'.

In the pages which follow I would like to examine the cultural operations for effecting the identification of the male subject with a 'weak' or 'castrated' father, as well as the precise relationship between that father and the institutional supports which assure his symbolic dominance.

It's a Wonderful Life opens at a moment of extreme crisis, one which threatens to disclose the lethal nature of the Oedipal legacy. George Bailey has been called upon by his family to make so large a self-sacrifice (i.e. to take upon himself responsibility for the $8,000 deficit created by Uncle Billy) that it seems to him synonymous with suicide. However, George must be taught that he cannot 'take' his own life, because it belongs to his culture. (At the very beginning of the film, Joseph the 'senior' angel announces that life is 'God's favourite gift'. In a later scene an inhabitant of Bedford Falls, where George lives, says that 'It's against the law to commit suicide in this town,' and Clarence, a second and more 'junior' angel responds: 'It's against the law where I come from too.')

This potentially very dangerous situation is cinematically contained through a 'celestial' suture;[3] we are given an implied shot/reverse shot between the roofs of the town's houses and the heavens above. This visual formation is supplemented by an equivalent sound formation, in which we first hear the voices of George's family and friends praying for him, and then the voices of the answering angels. The film's immediate recourse to supernatural assistance suggests that without it there would be no possibility of cultural reintegration for George, only one last existential 'cut'.

As this dual formation makes immediately apparent, the film's structuring discourse is Christianity. It is also the discourse chosen by Althusser in the essay quoted above ('Ideology and Ideological State Apparatuses') to illustrate the point that subjects always emerge within ideology. He argues there for a mirror relationship between Christianity's Absolute Subject and its numerous human subjects:

> We observe that the structure of all ideology, interpellating individuals as subjects in the name of a Unique and Absolute subject is speculary, i.e. a minor-structure, and *doubly* speculary: this mirror duplication is constitutive of ideology and ensures its functioning. Which means that all ideology is centred, that the Absolute Centre occupies the place of the Centre, and interpellates around it the infinity of individuals into subjects in a double mirror-connection such that it *subjects* the subjects to the Subject, while giving them in the Subject in which each subject can contemplate its own image (present and future) the *guarantee* that this really concerns them and Him, and that since everything takes place in the Family (the Holy Family: the Family is in essence Holy), 'God will *recognize* his own in it', i.e. those who have recognized God, and have recognized themselves in him, will be saved.[4]

At first glance, *It's a Wonderful Life* conforms with startling precision to the model described by Althusser: it delineates a series of mirror relationships between heaven and earth, all of which take place 'in the Family'. However, on closer examination the situation becomes much more complex, and obliges us to qualify the terms of Althusser's analysis.

At both the film's heavenly and earthly levels a 'father' calls upon a 'son' to undergo a number of trials and tribulations whereby the latter will earn what is jokingly referred to as his 'wings'. This is a familiar Christian paradigm, but it is not elaborated in the usual ways. Here the alignment is not between God the Father and God the Son on the one hand, and Peter and George Bailey on the other, but rather between Joseph and Clarence in heaven, and Peter and George Bailey on earth. The fact that the success of Clarence's mission is closely tied to that of George reinforces the connection between them.

At the same time, the more 'exalted' figures of God the Father and God the Son are constantly invoked by the film, or to be more specific, by the other four characters (Joseph, Clarence, Peter Bailey and George Bailey). The relationship between these three sets warrant careful consideration.

'Joseph' is the name of the New Testament figure who marries an already-pregnant Mary, and thereafter stands in for God as the father of Christ. In other words, he occupies the paternal position, but is never equal to it. Within the Lacanian scheme Joseph would be described as the 'actual' or incarnate father, whereas God would function as the symbolic father. The angel Joseph in *It's a Wonderful Life* enjoys a similar status, and is for all intents and purposes interchangeable with his New Testament counterpart; he stands in textually for God the Father, who as Christian commentators constantly repeat is 'unrepresentable', sending Clarance to earth on a mission of salvation.[5]

The subsequent equation of Peter Bailey with the figure of Joseph serves to distinguish him from the adequate and potent symbolic father, and to associate him instead with a low mimetic version of that father. As I will attempt to demonstrate later in this essay, Capra's film reinforces this view of the character at every point. Indeed, George's own retreat from the Oedipal legacy is primarily motivated by his perception of his father's inadequacy and impotence.

And while details like the temptation scene in Peter's office, or the celebration of Christmas at the end of the film link up the figure of George with that of Christ, their relationship is also mediated, this time through Clarence. The latter parodically re-enacts Christ's incarnation and descent to earth. He too, although on a much smaller scale, performs a divinely-commissioned task. Clarence is the type of the good Christian, who despite tempations like alcohol perseveres in the attempt to accommodate himself within a narrative which always exceeds him. (It should be noted that the film mediates George's relationship to Christ—himself a mediating figure—not only through the 'celestial' Clarence, but the secular Tom Sawyer.)

Christianity contains many such mediations, all of which serve not only to identify but to distance the human subject from the divine or Absolute Subject. That distance, which is often concealed, but never abolished, separates the enunciating or discoursing subject from the subject of the enunciation or discourse. The distinction which I here maintain is of course very similar to that which was first proposed by Benveniste,[6] and later made the general platform of the suture argument—the distinction, that is, between the speaking subject and the grammatical subject, or the gaze of the camera and the gaze of a character within the fiction. The second of these is in fact dramatized by the film, immediately after the 'celestial' suture, and it helps to reinforce the distinction between Christianity's discoursing subject and the subject of its discourse. The episode in question also suggests that the attributes normally associated with the father in the dominant cultural order find their real locus in apparatuses and institutions with which he is allied, but which remain inevitably detached from him.

The moment in question occurs just before the beginning of the film-within-the-film—i.e. the montage sequence which inform both Clarence and the viewer about George's past. Joseph invites Clarence to look through a kind of heavenly view-finder at that past, but when the latter does so all he sees is an out-of-focus field, little better than what he would see with a 'naked' eye. Joseph adjusts the apparatus, bringing that field into focus and giving Clarence a privileged and omniscient point of view of George's life up until the diegetic present. At one juncture he even freezes a frame so that Clarence can get a good look at George.

Clarence is never in control of the cinematic apparatus. That fact is made clear not only when he first attempts to look at George's past, and sees only a blur, but at the end of the 'screening', when he wants to know what happens next and is told he'll have to wait to find out. The apparatus not only controls what Clarence sees, but it gives him a place in the narrative (i.e. it 'speaks' him, provides him with a subject-position).

In other words, the position of the discoursing or Absolute Subject is made temporarily and provisionally available both to Clarence and the viewer. That position never 'belongs' to either but they are permitted to use it as a brief look-out point from which to observe a very different subjectivity—the subjectivity of the suffering and self-renouncing George. An accelerated montage of the latter's life features only these episodes in which he has been called upon to sacrifice some cherished object—first the hearing in one of his ears, then his dreams of travel and education, and finally his hopes of leaving Bedford Falls to become an architect. These sacrifices are required not only by his immediate family, but by the extended family of the town, and the holy family above. Moreover, they are in every respect *exemplary*—i.e. they are projected as an imitative model for the viewing subject. Thus just as Clarence mediates George's relationship with the Christian narrative, George mediates the viewing subject's relationship with the cinematic narrative. This elaborate system of identification assures that both George and the viewing subject will remain isolated from the discursive apparatuses which define them.

Joseph is permitted to participate in the operation of one of those apparatuses, but not to alter its product. His position is analogous to that of a projectionist, in charge of running the machine which delivers the narrative, but unable to interfere in the construction of that narrative. Like Peter Bailey or any 'actual' father, he benefits from his association with the agencies of social reproduction, while at the same time being himself fully coerced by them.

An important episode near the middle of the film-within-the-film dramatizes the distance between Peter Bailey and that ideal paternal representation which Lacan calls the symbolic father—a distance equivalent to that which separates Joseph from God the Father, or the enunciating subject from the subject of the enunciation. It also suggests that the castration crisis proceeds not so much from the son's first glimpse of the mother's genitals, but from his confrontation with the father's inadequacy or lack. In that episode, a drunken pharmacist mistakenly fills a prescription with poison. George, who works for the pharmacist, witnesses the filling of the prescription. He also discovers the reason for his employer's intoxication: the latter has just received a telegram announcing the death of his son. When the pharmacist gives George the poison to take to the patient, the young man is in a quandary as to what he should do. He glances with seeming spontaneity at an advertisement on the wall which encourages him to 'Ask Dad', and which reinforces its verbal message with a drawing of a cigar wielding patriarch. George responds immediately to this cultural command; and goes to find his father. However, when he arrives at his father's office he discovers that the latter is being publicly humiliated by Potter (significantly over a $5,000 deficit). In a frenzy of filial distress, George comes to the rescue not so much of his father as of that father, as the symbolic father. He shouts at Potter: 'My dad's the biggest man in the whole town, not you.' George is thus subjected in quick succession to two reinforcing views of paternal inadequacy.

Despite George's protestations to the contrary, the last of these scenes clearly represents a castration crisis. It conforms to the classic description of that event in every respect except the one which Freud would maintain is the most essential—i.e. the location of lack on the site of the female body:

> . . . when a little boy first catches sight of a girl's genital region, he begins by showing irresolution and lack of interest; he sees nothing, or disavows what he has seen. . . . It is not until later, when some threat of castration has obtained a hold upon him, that the observation becomes important to him. . . .[7]

Like the male subject in Freud's account, George disavows what he sees in the board meeting: Peter Bailey's symbolic deficiency. And like that male subject he acknowledges what he has seen only later, when he feels himself exposed to a similar fate. (The subsequent scene which best dramatizes George's retroactive realization of his father's lack takes place on the eve of the latter's death, immediately prior to the big dance.)

However, unlike Freud's protagonist, George Bailey experiences castration entirely in terms of a cultural inadequacy; his crisis has no anatomical motivation. Indeed, the figure who represents the potency in relation to which Peter Bailey is found to be weak and lacking is himself a cripple. His superiority is monetary rather than anatomical—he is known as 'the richest man in town'.

A final way in which Capra's film differs from Freud's account is that in it the son is obliged to identify not with the strength but rather with the weakness of the father. His fear of castration proceeds not so much from an encounter with female anatomy as a confrontation with male subjectivity. In other words, he retreats from the father's rather than the mother's lack, a lack compounded of passivity, self-sacrifice and above all indebtedness.

The seme of indebtedness attaches itself definitively to Peter Bailey in the board meeting where George is obliged to come to his defence. It ultimately attaches itself to George as well, and provokes his contemplated suicide. However, in the interval before he comes into possession of the full paternal legacy, the agency of indebtedness is shown to be Uncle Billy, whose forgetfulness wreaks havoc not only on the family's finances, but those of the town. We can only assume that the $5,000 which provides Potter with the opportunity to humiliate Peter Bailey was also misplaced by Uncle Billy.

Thus within Capra's film the assumption of other people's debts—i.e. the assumption of a general cultural indebtedness—defines exemplary male subjectivity. That assumption necessarily implies the renunciation of 'personal' desires, a renunciation to which Peter Bailey accommodates himself easily (George says of his dead father during a later board meeting: 'In all the years he had the business he never once thought of himself'), but against which his son rebels.

Potter makes evident the lethal nature of this cultural debt and 'personal' renunciation when he remarks: 'Peter Bailey was not a businessman; that's what killed him. He was a man of high ideals.' And long before the final crisis, George echoes Potter's sentiment; he tells his father 'I feel that if I didn't get away, I'd die.' He is of course referring not only to Bedford Falls, but the family business—the business of managing the collective indebtedness of a large part of the town's inhabitants. Within the context of *It's a Wonderful Life*, to be a businessman is to make a profit, and in so doing to violate the imperative of sacrificing oneself for the common good, i.e. of losing oneself in order to find oneself.

George resists this imperative quite strenuously, although he capitulates to it in the end. The film's narrative consists of the repeated re-enactment of a set scenario: George first voices a set of desires which are not part of the cultural apparatus of Bedford Fails, and which would locate him outside of its purview. A crisis is then engineered which calls those desires into question, and which reaffirms his subject-position within Bedford Falls. George rebels for a time, but eventually renounces his wayward desires for the domesticated values of family and small-town life. However he must be culturally 'hailed' again and again, and ultimately even more extreme strategies must be used for securing him within his pre-ordained place.

It must be stressed that George understands only too clearly what his father's legacy entails: he knows that it is an inheritance of indebtedness and lack. The film makes certain that we understand just as clearly that George has been called upon to sacrifice himself—it is unusually specific on this point. However, in its concluding scenes *It's a Wonderful Life* transforms that debt into a handsome credit, that self-sacrifice into a 'personal' gain, and that lack into a plenitude. These transformations are effected by means of the film's dominant discourse, within which paradox and redemptive reversal function as centrally structuring devices.

I shall then suggest that ideology 'acts' or 'functions' in such a way that it 'recruits' subjects among the individuals (it recruits them all), or 'transforms' the individuals into subjects (it transforms them all) by the very precise operation which I have called interpellation or *hailing*, and which can be imagined along the lines of the most commonplace everyday police (or other) hailing: 'Hey, you there!'

Assuming that the theoretical scene I have imagined takes place in the street, the hailed individual will turn round. By this mere one-hundred-and-eighty-degree physical conversion, he becomes a *subject*. Why? Because he has recognized that the hail was 'really' addressed to him, and that 'it was *really him* who was hailed. . . .'

In one of the scenes from George's early life, he is shown making Mary a sundae in the drugstore where he works. As he leans down to scoop up the ice cream, she reaches over and whispers 'I love you George Bailey', thereby inviting him to take his place in his culture's prescriptive heterosexual narrative. (That narrative receives support from so many of the operative discourses within Western culture that its operations are virtually synonymous with the symbolic order.) This episode constitutes the first of many in which George is 'hailed', in the Althusserean sense of the word. These social invitations are generally issued at moments when his rebellious desires become most manifest, and he invariably declines them. The film consequently resorts to increasingly drastic measures for containing George within his cultural position, dramatizing in the process both the compulsory nature of subjectivity, and the unpleasure which it implies.

In the scene just cited, George flourishes at Mary his travel brochures and announces his intention to see the world, have numerous wives, and treat himself to several harems. These ambitions run absolutely counter to those dictated by Bedford Falls; instead of one wife and many children, they revolve around many wives and no children, and rather than the soap-opera of small-time life, they project adventure on the high seas.

These exploratory and accumulatory desires, to which George returns again and again, have of course been as culturally mediated as the ones to which he ultimately succumbs, even if they are not admissable in Bedford Falls. George even reveals the source of that mediation when he proudly announces to Mary that he has been nominated for a membership in the National Geographic. He has as it were been invited by that magazine to take up a subject-position within its discourse, to permit it to 'speak' him.

The fantasies within which the National Geographic discourse contains its subjects are intensely 'American', even if they rely upon foreign settings—they belong, that is, to the general pool of narratives upon which American popular culture repeatedly draws—safaris, expeditions to the North Pole, mountain climbing, etc. However, Capra's film treats them as if they were almost unpatriotic, deflecting attention away from the home front. It suggests that at best the desire to travel and experiment romantically are the sanctioned fantasies only of a young man, and it thrusts adulthood upon George before he has even come of age. Indeed, when he outlines his plans to his father somewhat later in the film, the latter dryly observes: 'You were born old.' We know at that point, if we didn't know before, that those 'adolescent' fantasies are doomed to extinction. (I will return to the film's censorship of the National Geographic discourse below, but I would like to note here that it is quite extreme.)

When George ignores the imperative of monogamy implied by Mary's romantic cliche, he is forceably inserted into another narrative in which the only possible subject-positions are those of father and son—the narrative in which he discovers Peter Bailey being verbally abused by Potter. That narrative contains two father-and-son relationships, but the son is missing from the first of them, obliging George to stand in as a filial complement not only to Peter Bailey, but the pharmacist. Moreover, because the former has shown himself to be absolutely vulnerable, while the latter is at least for the moment completely unreliable, George is cast as well in the protective, paternal role. He is in the process overdetermined as an Oedipal subject. He is also defined as (i.e. subordinated to the seme of) 'responsible'. Once he has been so defined, that definition can be used as a means of further control, and evoked at times of crisis to constrain him within rigorously maintained limits.

On the eve of George's planned trip around the world, equipped with a suitcase large enough for one thousand and one nights, Peter Bailey 'hails' him to assume the full paternal legacy. George once again rebels, and in the process reveals a very clear perception of what is at stake: indebtedness and restriction. He responds, almost violently: 'I couldn't be cooped up in that shabby office all my life, collecting nickels and dimes and trying to save 3¢ on a length of pipe. . . . I feel that if I didn't get away I'd die.' Of course Peter Bailey does die later that night, and the moral is unavoidable: in rejecting the paternal legacy George has in effect killed his father. Moreover, that death leaves a culturally inadmissable vacuum—i.e. the place of the father—into which George is once again involuntarily interpellated.

Between the paternal invitation and Peter Bailey's death, George is 'hailed' several more times, first by Mary's brother, who asks him to dance with her and won't take no for an answer, and later by an old man sitting on the balcony of the house at which Mary and George are throwing stones. The second of these invitations is issued immediately after George has confided in an adult Mary the same dreams he earlier confessed in the drugstore ('I'll see the world, then I'll go to college and find out what they know, then I'll build airplanes and sky-scrapers and bridges a mile long'). The old man, who overhears the conversation, brings it to an abrupt conclusion by shouting out: 'Shut up and kiss her.'

The death of his father obliges George to renounce his travel plans, and to postpone his college education for four years while his brother goes to school. This second sacrifice is 'called for' by the board members of the Bailey Building and Loan, who threaten to dissolve the business unless George takes over for Peter Bailey. And by the time Harry returns from college with a wife and professional career, George has become so fully defined in relation to that business that it is virtually impossible for him to extricate himself from it.

Mrs. Bailey responds to George's obvious unhappiness on the night of his brother's homecoming—a homecoming which is simultaneously a marriage celebration—by attempting to interpellate him into a marriage of his own. She describes Mary, just home from college herself, as 'the kind that will help you find the answers'. (Actually, as it turns out, Mary helps him find the questions as well.) George jokingly asks his mother to point him in the right direction, which she does. He walks off in the opposite direction, but eventually arrives at the foreordained destination.

Mary 'hails' him from the balcony, in a reprise of the earlier scene where the two of them threw rocks at the old house: 'What are you doing? Picketing? Made up your mind about coming in?' Indeed, she quite painstakingly reconstructs that earlier situation, and with it a subject-position with which George has already identified himself, through strategically chosen props: a drawing of George lassooing the moon, and a recording of the song 'Buffalo Girl'. (These props also represent part of the film's larger project to relocate George's desires within the confines of the family—to convince him that the only frontier worth conquering is that of the home, and that the most celestial of bodies is the one already sitting by his side.)

George gives the impression of not at all liking the position into which he has been interpellated. He squirms unhappily, and when

Mary's mother asks him what he wants he angrily replies: 'Want? Nothing.' This refusal to invest in heterosexual narrative, and to have 'needs' which only the family can satisfy, cannot be tolerated. George's desires are subsequently orchestrated with terrifying precision. Mary tells her mother that 'He's making violent love to me,' and then coerces him into doing just that through an ingenious deployment of triangulation, in which the Althusserean metaphor is nicely literalized.

Sam Wainwright phones, and Mary, feigning a rather exaggerated enthusiasm, calls George to the receiver, which she holds between them. Sam attempts to persuade George to invest in plastics but after a moment or two his voice and the promises it utters become as 'absent' to Mary and George as the man himself. He is present only as a rival through whom George's desire for Mary is forcibly mediated; although he ostensibly calls George to high finance, he in fact interpellates him into the heterosexual scenario which the other has for so long resisted. But for a moment George remains divided from the subjectivity which will thereafter completely subsume him. He throws down the phone, grabs Mary, and shouts his protest against the desires which the others have thrust upon him: 'I don't want to get in on the ground floor of plastics! I don't want to get married! I want to do what I want to do.'

The next shot shows George and Mary becoming man and wife. He has been cut off from a number of what the film insists are wayward ambitions—the adolescent dream of harems and polygamy as well as the more 'mature' dreams of going to college and building massive structures—and integrated into a second familial organization. But Bedford Falls insists on a further renunciation. At the very moment of seeming cultural integration, when George has at last been recruited to a life of responsible heterosexuality he is obliged to relinquish one last unacceptable desire—the desire to see the world. As they drive away from the church, George flourishes a wad of bills and describes to the cab driver how he and Mary plan to spend it—a week in New York and then a week in the Bahamas with 'the most expensive hotels, the best wines and the hottest music.' Later that day the wad of bills has been reduced to a 'papa dollar' and a 'mama dollar', and George retires to the tumble-down building which will thereafter be his home. He and Mary never make it either to New York or the Bahamas since on their way to the airport there is a run on the mortgage company, and he must return to save the situation.

This last sacrifice seems in excess of what even a culture predicated on renunciation could demand of its subjects. However, the film suggests that George's debt is so large that he can never fully repay it. His honeymoon money, like his school money, shows that somehow a personal profit has been made, and that profit is a violation of the paternal imperative. He is therefore 'called' upon to reinvest the money immediately in socially productive (and reproductive) ways. The film also suggests that George is guilty of overvaluing the world beyond Bedford Falls, a mistake which can only be rectified by reinvesting all of his emotional reserves within its perimeters. Thus at the end of his wedding day George is escorted back to the old house against which he and Mary had earlier thrown stones, and he is given to understand that henceforth it will be the locus of his desires. Mary has transformed the interior into a comic condensation of the countries George has dreamed of visiting: travel posters cover the walls, red-checked curtains adorn the windows, and Mary (a veritable incarnation of the Buffalo Girl) is roasting chickens over an open fire. This scene represents the triumph of family values over the National Geographic discourse, a triumph which is consolidated in the accelerated montage which follows. That sequence shows George engaging in various forms of social service connected with the war, most of which revolve in one way or another around salvage. He is in effect struggling to save 3¢ on a length of pipe.

At this juncture in *It's a Wonderful Life*, George has been interpellated into the position of the 'castrated' father, i.e. the exemplary male subject who assumes a larger cultural indebtedness, and whose lack is a gain for those around him. However, he doesn't like that position. He hasn't yet learned to take pleasure in his pain, and that fact threatens to disrupt the entire town. It remains to examine the means whereby the suffering male subject is metamorphosed into the masochistic male subject, means which converge very specifically upon the operations of binary opposition. However, before doing so I want to take account of a detail which, given its further literalization of the Althusserean metaphor, would seem of immediate relevance to any discussion of interpellation in the film: George's deficient hearing.

The first thing we learn about George Bailey is that while saving his brother from drowning in an icy pond he lost the use of one ear. This injury constitutes only one of many subsequent 'splittings' or 'castrations' by means of which George is finally transformed into a 'whole' subject, and which are objectified by the film not only through its major crises (e.g. the negation of George's dreams of travel, education and architectural creativity, or Uncle Billy's loss of the $8,000) but through asserted minor ones, like Zu Zu's broken flower, the cut on

George's lip, or the bannister knob which always comes off in his hand as he goes upstairs. All of these cultural injuries are miraculously healed during the nightmare sequence, during which however George loses his subjectivity, and is no longer even recognized—let alone 'hailed'—by anyone in Bedford Falls. When, at the conclusion of the film, George is re-inserted into his cultural place, he shouts with joy to discover that his face is bleeding once again; searches excitedly for the petals of Zu Zu's flower; and kisses the broken bannister. He even welcomes the consequences of Uncle Billy's negligence ('Isn't it wonderful? I'm going to jail'). He has learned at last that instinctual loss means the gain of subjectivity—that an impairment of physical hearing implies a hypersensitivity to cultural messages.

It's a Wonderful Life resorts obsessively to binary opposition. It pits Violet against Mary, Uncle Billy against Clarence, Pottersville against Bedford Falls, Peter Bailey against Potter, greed against indebtedness. However, many of these oppositions lack the symmetry we normally associate with the binary experience. For instance, Violet embodies the desire to leave Bedford Falls and the related wish not to be part of a stable family, placing her in contrast to Mary (when George asks the latter why she didn't go off to New York after college, she responds: 'I got homesick'). But Violet never does manage to move away, and many of her other functions overlap with those assigned to Mary—she also wants George, and at the end of the film she articulates a desire for small-town closure. And while Clarence has ostensibly been sent by Joseph to get George out of trouble, whereas Billy gets him *into* trouble, the former incorporates the same values of limited intelligence, modest aspirations, good-heartedness and buffoonery as the latter. In addition, Uncle Billy helps to raise the money which finally balances the books. Both oppositions are virtually erased in the last scene of the film; they enact a dichotomy which is really just a matched set. *It's a Wonderful Life* projects an absolutely closed discourse: not only are many of the terms it contrasts quite compatible, but even those terms which are more radically opposed derive their value and meaning from each other.

The most important and intricately worked out of these last oppositions is that between Peter Bailey and Potter. Peter Bailey is defined almost entirely in relation to what he doesn't have—he not only lacks money and power, but the desire of the son; he seems incapable of inspiring in George any wish to become the father, or any pleasure at the prospect of coming into the paternal legacy. (Actually, it is George's refusal to perceive his father as the phallus which exposes the latter's deficiencies; otherwise he would be conspicuous not for what he lacks, but for what he has—a family.)

Potter, on the other hand, possesses enormous wealth and political power. However he has no motor coordination, and must depend on others to move him from place to place. Even more significantly, he lacks a family: no female figure aligns herself with him by means of which his potency can be established, and no son stands by to whom he can pass on his legacy. This last deficiency is dramatized when Potter summons George, and offers him an essentially filial position.

That position includes not only a munificent salary, but travel opportunities. It thus promises to fulfill, at least in part, the dreams which George has been forced to relinquish. He is clearly tempted by Potter's offer, and is in fact about to accept it when he touches the latter's hand and recoils in disgust. The older man would seem to represent a return of the repressed: as George brings himself into a more intimate relationship with that repressed, the cultural censorship is activated and he feels compelled to deny the strength or importance of his own earlier, unfulfilled desires—to insist, indeed, on their subhuman quality. He therefore shouts at Potter: 'In the whole vast configuration of things, I'd say you're no more than a scary spider. You think you're the whole world.'

As George steps back from the desk, we become aware of a portrait of Potter immediately across the room from the man himself, which in effect mirrors him. This shot makes explicit what has been implicit all along, the notion that Potter is locked in a narcissistic relationship with his wealth. The film attempts to discredit Potter, and in the process George's unsatisfied dreams, by connecting him with sterility and motor uncoordination, and by suggesting that these things derive from his refusal to align himself with an Oedipal structure.[8] In fact, what the film communicates through the figure of Potter is a bourgeois fantasy in which money is shown to be impotent to reproduce itself except through the intermediate agency of the family (George's 'papa dollar' and 'mama dollar').[9] Potter is obliged to invite George into his business because ever since the younger man stepped into his father's position his own profits have fallen off. Having declined that invitation—i.e. having repudiated once again his desire to see the 'whole world'—George comes even more fully into the paternal heritage: later that night Mary announces to him that he is about to become a father.

Although Peter Bailey and Potter are systematically opposed throughout *It's a Wonderful Life*, there are a number of interesting points of convergence between them. In effect the two men split between them the privileges of the symbolic order. Peter Bailey enjoys the position of the father, but lacks money, power and—most importantly—the desire of his son. Potter, on the contrary, has money and power but is excluded from the position of the father. Both men attempt to validate their place within the symbolic order through the figure of George. When George comes at last to invest his desires in his father's position, he shows that position to belong to 'the richest man in town'—an extraordinary demonstration given the fact that it actually belongs to the most indebted inhabitant of Bedford Falls. Conversely, his refusal to ally himself with Potter transforms the latter into the 'poorest man in town', despite his evident wealth. These paradoxes are underwritten by the film's dominant discourse; they are made possible only by the positing of a holy family which makes good the insufficiencies of the earthly family—of a symbolic father who rewards the indebtedness of the actual father, and who transforms his lack into a plenitude.

The scene in Potter's office associates George even more fully than before with the position of the suffering and indebted father, but when Uncle Billy loses $8,000 George rebels once again, more violently than before. At this point the film resorts to the most extreme of its binary operations in an attempt to prove both to George and to the viewer that his long-frustrated dream is really a nightmare. As the result of a 'divine intervention', George finds himself abruptly cut off from the subject-position into which he was earlier interpellated, and alienated from all of the objects he has never learned to value: Bedford Falls, the Building and Trust, the children and Mary.

The absence of the last of these objects proves the most definitive. Mary's failure to recognize him, her struggle to escape, and the disequivalence between her appearance and occupation in the nightmare sequence and those in George's 'waking' life prove more terrifying than all of the other disruptions within the geography of Bedford Falls. Lacking Mary, he at last desires her—he discovers his 'moon' in the mother of his children.

But George is not only deprived of Mary, his children, his home, his business and his town; he is deprived of his subjectivity, or so Clarence would have him believe. At a certain juncture in the nightmare sequence George's guardian angel tells him that he has been stripped of all the signifiers which confer identity: 'You're nobody. You have no identity. You have no car, no driver's licence, no 4F card, no insurance policy.' Lacking these signifiers, George can only be designated by the gap his absence leaves behind in the symbolic field ('Each man's life touches so many other people's lives that when he isn't around it leaves an awful hole'). As George moves through Bedford Falls, now renamed Pottersville, no one recognizes him—no one calls out to him or 'hails' him. This form of terrorism proves so effective that he literally begs to be re-interpellated and at whatever cost: 'Get me back . . . to my wife and kids. I don't care what happens to me. I want to live again—please God let me live.' His desire has been reorganized not only around the objects he earlier scorned, but the subject-position which those objects help to define. At the moment of cultural re-entry, George embraces most enthusiastically precisely those objects (his bleeding mouth, the broken bannister knob, Zu Zu's petals, the debt incurred by Uncle Billy) which most directly speak to his cultural subjugation. He has become an exemplary (i.e. masochistic) male subject. The concluding moments of the film dramatize the triumph of Christian paradox, transforming George's pain into pleasure, his lack into plenitude, and his debt into a gain.

Clarence insists that George has no subject-position during the nightmare sequence. Actually, the film carefully orchestrates his movements by inserting him into the subject-position occupied at other times by Potter. This fact is made clear not only by the town's new name (Pottersville), but by George's own acknowledgement that the entire episode surfaces from some place within his unconscious (he tells Clarence 'This is some kind of crazy dream I'm having'). Earlier he attempts to deny any psychic connection with Potter by relegating the latter to the status of a 'scary spider', but now the values represented by him have suffused the entire dreamscape and, as Freud notes, everything within that field corresponds in some way to the ego of the dreamer. George recognizes his own repressed desires in the world of Pottersville, and that recognition frightens him into relocating his emotional investment in Bedford Falls.

The juxtaposition of the two towns is really only an extension of the conflict between Peter Bailey and Potter—the conflict, that is, between self-sacrifice and narcissism, indebtedness and profit, familial closure and sterility (in Pottersville Mary becomes a spinster). The nightmare re-articulates these options as the only ones available to George.

George's final choice is further overdetermined by the constant: evocation of a transcendental point-of-view. He is told that if he aligns himself with Potter instead of Peter Bailey he will not only be exiled from the family and the larger social order but the authenticating vision of God and the angels who stand in for him in the film. Since that vantage is the only one from which we ever look at George, and since it is associated so fully with the cinematic apparatuses, he is in effect threatened with non-representation.

The viewing-subject's relation to the film is a remarkably double one. We are encouraged to identify both with George, the masochistic subject, and with the gaze which simultaneously inflicts pain and pleasure. (It must be added that the various mediating agencies which distance the actual father—Peter Bailey—from the symbolic father—God—also function to alienate us from any real participation in that gaze; our situation is thus analogous to that of Clarence.) This dual interpellation prevents us from ever really calling into question the sacrifices required of George; indeed, it works to eroticize, through its relation to a gaze which cannot be resisted, and which one would not wish to resist since it 'blesses' the position of the victim. This voyeuristic paradigm assures us that everything has been foreseen. It permits us to enter with pleasure into George's pain, to expose ourselves to lack and insufficiency with the confidence that these things will not only be condoned, but will provide the means whereby we too are integrated into a celestial plenitude and sufficiency.

Notes

1. I have advanced this argument elsewhere in relation to Liliana Cavani's *Portiere di Notte.* See 'Masochism and Subjectivity', *Framework*, xii (1980), 2–9.
2. Lacan defines that position as one of lacking, and therefore desiring, the phallus. It is, in fact, the mother's desire for the phallus which determines its centrality within the symbolic order, and it is from her that the son learns the 'way' of his desire. This paradigm is most explicitly articulated by Lacan in his seminar on *Hamlet* ('Desire and the Interpretation of Desire in *Hamlet*', trans. James Hulbert, *Yale French Studies*, 55/56 (1977)).
3. For a variety of approaches to more conventional kinds of suture, see Daniel Dayan, 'Tutor-Code of Classical Cinema', in *Movies and Methods: An Anthology*, ed. Bill Nichols (Berkeley), 438–451; Jacques-Alain Miller, 'Suture (elements of the logic of the signifier)', *Screen*, 18: 4, 24–34; Jean-Pierre Oudart, 'Cinema and Suture', *Screen*, 18: 4, 35–47; and Stephen Heath, *Screen*, 18: 4, 48–76.
4. Thomas Aquinas rehearses a commonplace when he writes in *Summa Theologica*, trans. Fathers of the English Dominican Province (New York: Benziger Brothers, 1947), I: 'We cannot know of the essence of God in this life, as He really is Himself; but we can know Him according as He is represented in the perfection of creatures; and thus the names imposed by us signify Him in that manner only' (p. 61).
5. *Lenin and Philosophy*, trans. Ben Brewster (London: Monthly Review Press, 1971), 180.

6. See *Problems in General Linguistics*, trans. Mary Elizabeth Meek (Coral Gables: University of Miami Press, 1971), 218: '"I" signifies the person who is uttering the present instance of the discourse containing "I" . . . the form of "I" has no linguistic existence except in the act of speaking in which it is uttered. There is thus a combined double instance in this process: the instance "I" as reference and the instance of the discourse containing "I" as the referee. The definition can now be stated precisely as: "I" is the individual who utters present instance of discourse containing the linguistic instance "I".'
7. *The Standard Edition of the Complete Psychological Works* trans. James Strachey (London: Norton Press, 1958), 252.
8. One of the figures through whom the film attempts to neutralize these desires is Sam Wainwright. He periodically appears either *in propria persona* or by telephone or telegram, offering George a chance to become rich by investing in plastics, or inviting him to go on a trip. However the commodity in which he traffics is shown to be absurd (the frivolity of plastics is counterpoised to the meaningful production of babies and houses), and the vacation he suggests is rather scornfully rejected by Mary and George, who have just made a different kind of journey with the Martini family—one away from overpriced rented lodgings to a home of their own. In the scene involving the Martini family Sam is excluded from the rituals of a very important fellowship, rituals involving the totem foods of bread and wine. Once again, if indirectly, his association with artificial substances is stressed.
9. I call this narrative construct a bourgeois fantasy because Gille Deleuze and Felix Guattari have shown that in fact within capitalism money begets money, enters into alliances with money, and effectively signifies money, effectively excluding both family and individual subject from its axiomatic. See *Anti-Oedipus: Capitalism and Schizophrenia*, trans. Robert Hurley, Mark Seem and Helen R. Lane (New York: Viking Press: 1977), 263.

7 Is the Gaze Male?

E. Ann Kaplan*

Since the beginning of the recent women's liberation movement, American feminists have been exploring the representation of female sexuality in the arts—literature, painting, film, and television.[1] The first wave of feminist critics adopted a broadly sociological approach, looking at sex roles women were seen to occupy in all kinds of imaginative works, from high art to mass entertainment. Roles were assessed as 'positive' or 'negative' according to some externally constructed criteria for the fully autonomous, independent woman.

Feminist film critics were the first to object to this prevailing critical approach, largely because of the general developments taking place in film theory at the beginning of the 1970s.[2] They noted the lack of awareness about the way images are constructed through the mechanism of whatever artistic practice is involved; representations, they pointed out, are mediations, embedded through the art form in the dominant ideology. Influenced by the work of Claude Lévi-Strauss, Roland Barthes, Jacques Lacan, Christian Metz, Julia Krîsteva, and others, women began to apply the tools of psychoanalysis, semiology, and structuralism in analyzing the representation of women in film.[3] I will not duplicate the history of these theoretical developments here; let it suffice to note, by way of introduction, that increasing attention has been given first, to cinema as a signifying practice, to *how meaning is produced* in film rather than to something that used to be called its 'content'; and second, to the links between the processes of psychoanalysis and those of cinema.[4] Feminists have been particularly concerned with how sexual difference is constructed psychoanalytically through the Oedipal process, especially as this is read by Lacan. For Lacan, woman cannot enter the world of the symbolic, of language,

* E. Ann Kaplan, 'Is the Gaze Male?' from *Women and Film: Both Sides of the Camera* (Routledge, 1983), reprinted by permission of the author.

because at the very moment of the acquisition of language, she learns that she lacks the phallus, the symbol that sets language going through a recognition of difference; her relation to language is a negative one, a lack. In patriarchal structures, thus, woman is located as other (enigma, mystery), and is thereby viewed as outside of (male) language.[5]

The implications of this for cinema are severe: dominant (Hollywood) cinema is seen as constructed according to the unconscious patriarchy, which means that film narratives are constituted through a phallocentric language and discourse that parallels the language of the unconscious. Women in film, thus, do not function as signifiers for a signified (a real woman) as sociological critics have assumed, but signifier and signified have been elided into a sign that represents something in the male unconscious.[6]

Two basic Freudian concepts—voyeurism and fetishism—have been used to explain what exactly woman represents and the mechanisms that come into play for the male spectator watching a female screen image. (Or, to put it rather differently, voyeurism and fetishism are mechanisms the dominant cinema uses to *construct* the male spectator in accordance with the needs of his unconscious.) The first, voyeurism, is linked to the scopophilic instinct (i.e. the male pleasure in his own sexual organ transferred to pleasure in watching other people having sex). Critics argue that the cinema relies on this instinct, making the spectator essentially a voyeur. The drive that causes little boys to peek through keyholes of parental bedrooms to learn about their sexual activities (or to get sexual gratification by thinking about these activities) comes into play when the male adult watches films, sitting in a dark room. The original eye of the camera, controlling and limiting what can be seen, is reproduced by the projector aperture that lights up one frame at a time; and both processes (camera and projector) duplicate the eye at the keyhole, whose gaze is confined by the keyhole 'frame'. The spectator is obviously in the voyeur position when there are sex scenes on the screen, but screen images of women are sexualized no matter what the women are doing literally, or what kind of plot may be involved.

According to Laura Mulvey (the British filmmaker and critic whose theories are central to new developments), this eroticization of women on the screen comes about through the way the cinema is structured around three explicitly male looks or gazes: there is the look of the camera in the situation where events are being filmed (called the profilmic event)—while technically neutral, this look, as we have seen, is inherently voyeuristic and usually 'male' in the sense of a man doing the filming; there is the look of the men within the narrative, which is structured so as to make women objects of their gaze; and finally there is the look of the male spectator that imitates (or is necessarily in the same position as) the first two looks.[7]

But if women were simply eroticized and objectified, things might not be too bad, since objectification may be an inherent component of both male and female eroticism. (As I will show later on, however, things in this area are not symmetrical.) But two further elements enter in: to begin with, men do not simply look; their gaze carries with it the power of action and of possession that is lacking in the female gaze. Women receive and return a gaze, but cannot act on it. Second, the sexualization and objectification of women is not simply for the purposes of eroticism; from a psychoanalytic point of view, it is designed to annihilate the threat that woman (as castrated, and possessing a sinister genital organ) poses. In her 1932 article 'The Dread of Woman', Karen Horney goes to literature to show that 'men have never tired of fashioning expressions for the violent force by which man feels himself drawn to the woman, and side by side with his longing, the dread that through her he might die and be undone'.[8] Later on, Horney conjectures that even man's glorification of women 'has its source not only in his cravings for love, but also in his desire to conceal his dread. A similar relief, however, is also sought and found in the disparagement of women that men often display ostentatiously in their attitudes.'[9] Horney goes on to explore the basis of the dread of women not only in castration (more related to the father), but in fear of the vagina.

But psychoanalysts agree that, for whatever reason—the fear of castration (Freud), or the attempt to deny the existence of the sinister female genital (Horney)—men endeavor to find the penis in women.[10] Feminist film critics have seen this phenomenon (clinically known as fetishism) operating in the cinema; the camera (unconsciously) fetishizes the female form, rendering it phallus-like so as to mitigate woman's threat. Men, that is, turn 'the represented figure itself into a fetish so that it becomes reassuring rather than dangerous' (hence overvaluation, the cult of the female star).[11]

The apparently contradictory attitudes of glorification and disparagement pointed out by Horney thus turn out to be a reflection of the same ultimate need to annihilate the dread that woman inspires. In the cinema, the twin mechanisms of fetishism and voyeurism represent two different ways of handling this dread. As Mulvey points out, fetishism 'builds up the physical beauty of the object, turning it into something satisfying in itself', while voyeurism, linked to disparagement, has a sadistic side, and is involved with pleasure through control or domination, and with punishing the woman (guilty for being castrated).[12] For Claire Johnston, both mechanisms result in woman's not being presented qua *woman* at all. Extending the *Cahiers du Cinéma* analysis of *Morocco*, Johnston argues that Sternberg represses 'the idea of woman as a social and sexual being', thus replacing the opposition man/woman with male/nonmale.[13]

With this brief look at feminist film theories as background, we can turn to the question of the gaze: as it stands, current work using psychoanalysis and semiology has demonstrated that the dominant cinematic apparatus is constructed by men for a male spectator. Women as women are absent from the screen *and* from the audience. Several questions now arise: first, is the gaze *necessarily* male (i.e. for reasons inherent in the structure of language, the unconscious, all symbolic systems, and thereby all social structures)? Or would it be possible to structure things so that women own the gaze? Second, would women want to own the gaze, if it were possible? Third, in either case, what does it mean to be a female spectator? Women are in fact present in audiences: what is happening to them as they watch a cinematic apparatus that constructs a male viewer? Does a woman spectator of female images have any choice other than either identifying as female object of desire, or if subject of desire, then appropriating the male position? Can there be such a thing as the female subject of desire? Finally, if a female subject is watching images of lesbians, what can this mean to her? How do such images inform women's actual, physical relations with other women?[14]

It is extremely important for feminist film critics to begin to address these questions. First, behind these questions, posed largely in structural terms, lie the larger questions concerning female desire and female subjectivity: Is it possible for there to be a female voice, a female discourse? What can a feminine specificity mean? Second, those of us working within the psychoanalytic system need to find a way out of an apparently overwhelming theoretical problem that has dramatic consequences for the way we are constituted, and constitute ourselves, not just in representation but also in our daily lives. Is there any escape from the overdetermined, phallocentric sign? The whole focus on the materialization of the signifier has again brought daily experience and art close together. Now critics read daily life as structured according to signifying practices (like art, 'constructed;', not naively experienced), rather than the earlier oversimplification of seeing art as a mere reflection/imitation of lived experience (mirroring it, or, better, presenting it as through a transparent pane of glass).

Finally, the growing interest in psychoanalytic and semiological approaches has begun to polarize the feminist film community,[15] and I want to begin by addressing some objections to current theoretical work, since they will lead us back to the larger questions of the female gaze and female desire. In a roundtable discussion in 1979, some women voiced their displeasure with theories that were themselves originally devised by men, and with women's preoccupation with how we have been seen/placed/positioned by the dominant male order. Julia LeSage, for instance, argues that the use of Lacanian criticism has been destructive in reifying women 'in a childlike position that patriarchy has wanted to see them in'; for LeSage, the Lacanian framework establishes 'a discourse which is totally male'.[16] And Ruby Rich objects to theories that rest with the apparent elimination of women from both screen and audience. She asks how we can move beyond our placing, rather than just analysing it.[17]

As if in response to Rich's request, some feminist film critics have begun to take up the challenge of moving beyond the preoccupation with how women have been constructed in patriarchal cinema. In a recent paper on *Gentlemen Prefer Blondes*, Lucie Arbuthnot and Gail Seneca attempt to appropriate for themselves some of the images hitherto defined as repressive. They begin by expressing their dissatisfaction not only with current feminist film theory as outlined above, but also with the new theoretical feminist films, which, they say, 'focus more on denying men their cathexis with women as erotic objects than in connecting women with each other.' In addition, these films, by 'destroying the narrative and the possibility for viewer identification with the characters, destroy both the male viewer's pleasure and our pleasure.'[18] Asserting their need for identification with strong female screen images, they argue that Hollywood films offer many examples of pleasurable identification; in a clever analysis, the relationship between Marilyn Monroe and Jane Russell in *Gentlemen Prefer Blondes* is offered as an example of strong women, who care for one another, providing a model we need.

However, looking at the construction of the film as a whole, rather than simply isolating certain shots, it is clear that Monroe and Russell are positioned, and position themselves, as objects for a specifically male gaze. The men's weakness does not mitigate their diegetic power, leaving to the women merely the limited control they can wield through their sexuality. The film constructs them as 'to-be-looked-at', and their manipulations end up merely comic, since 'capturing' the men involves their 'being captured'. The images of Monroe show her fetishized placement, aimed at reducing her sexual threat, while Russell's stance is a parody of the male position.[19] The result is that the two women repeat, in exaggerated form, dominant gender stereotypes.

Yet Arbuthnot and Seneca begin from important points: first, the need for films that construct *women* as the spectator and yet do not offer *repressive* identifications (as, for example, Hollywood women's films do);[20] and second, the need for feminist films that satisfy our craving for *pleasure.* In introducing the notion of pleasure. Arbuthnot and Seneca pinpoint a central and little-discussed issue. Mulvey was aware of the way feminist films as counter-cinema would deny pleasure, but she argued that this denial was a necessary prerequisite for freedom, and did not go into the problems involved.[21] Arbuthnot and Seneca locate the paradox in which feminist film critics have been caught without realizing it: namely, that we have been analysing Hollywood (rather than, say, avant-garde) films, largely because they bring us pleasure; but we have (rightly) been wary of admitting the degree to which the pleasure comes from identifying with our own objectification. Our positioning as 'to-be-looked-at', as object of the gaze, has, through our positioning, come to be sexually pleasurable.

However, it will not do to simply enjoy our oppression unproblematically; to appropriate Hollywood images to ourselves, taking them out of the context of the total structure in which they appear, will not get us very far. In order to fully understand *how it is* that women take pleasure in the objectification of women, one has to have recourse to psychoanalysis. Since criticisms like those voiced by LeSage, Rich, and Arbuthnot and Seneca are important, and reflect the deepening rift in the feminist film community, it is worth dwelling for a moment on why psychoanalysis is necessary as a feminist tool at this point in our history.

As Christian Metz, Stephen Heath, and others have shown, the processes of cinema mimic in many ways those of the unconscious. The mechanisms Freud distinguishes in relation to dream and the unconscious have been likened to the mechanisms of film.[22] In this analysis, film narratives, like dreams, symbolize a latent, repressed content, only now the 'content' refers not to an individual unconscious but to that of patriarchy in general. If psychoanalysis is a tool that will unlock the meaning of dreams, it should also unlock that of films.

But of course the question still remains as to the ideology of psychoanalysis: is it true, as Talking Lips argues at the start of the film *Sigmund Freud's Dora*, that psychoanalysis is a discourse shot through with bourgeois ideology, functioning 'almost as an Ideological State Apparatus', with its focus on the individual, 'outside of real history and real struggle'?[23] Or is psychoanalysis, although developed at a time when bourgeois capitalism was the dominant form, a theory that applies *across* history rather than being *embedded* in history?

Of these two possibilities, the first seems to me to be true. Psychoanalysis and cinema are inextricably linked both to each other and to capitalism, because both are products of a particular stage of capitalist society. The psychic patterns created by capitalist social and interpersonal structures (especially the nuclear family) required at once a machine for their unconscious release and an analytic tool for understanding and adjusting disturbances caused by the structures confining people. To this extent, both mechanisms support the status quo; but they are not eternal and unchanging, being rather inserted in history and linked to the particular social formation that produced them.

For this very reason. we have to begin by using psychoanalysis if we want to understand how we have been constituted, and the kind of linguistic and cultural universe we live in. Psychoanalysis may indeed have been used to oppress women, in the sense of forcing us to accept a positioning that is inherently antithetical to subjectivity and autonomy; but if that is the case, we need to know exactly *how* this has functioned to repress what we could potentially become. Given our positioning as women raised in a historical period dominated by Oedipal structuring and discourse, we must start by examining the psychoanalytic processes as they have worked to position us as other (enigma, mystery), and as eternal and unchanging, however paradoxical this may appear. For it is only in this way that we can begin to find the gaps and fissures through which we can reinsert woman in history, and begin to change ourselves as a first step toward changing society.

Let us now return to the question of women's pleasure in being objectified and see what we can learn about it through psychoanalysis. We saw earlier that the entry of the father as the third term disrupts the mother/child dyad, causing the child to understand the mother's castration and possession by the father. In the symbolic world the girl now enters she learns not only subject/object positions but the sexed pronouns 'he' and 'she'. Assigned the place of object (since she lacks the phallus, the symbol of the signifier), she is the recipient of male desire, the passive recipient of his gaze. If she is to have sexual pleasure, it can only be constructed around her objectification; it cannot be a pleasure that comes from desire for the other (a subject position)—that is, her desire is to be desired.

Given the male structuring around sadism that I have already discussed, the girl may adopt a corresponding masochism.[24] In practice, this masochism is rarely reflected in more than a tendency for women to be passive in sexual relations; but in the realm of fantasy, masochism is often quite prominent. In an interesting paper, 'The "Woman's Film": Possession and Address', Mary Ann Doane has shown that in the one film genre that constructs a female spectator, that spectator is made to participate in what is essentially a masochistic fantasy. Doane notes that in the major classical genres, the female body *is* sexuality, providing the erotic object for the male spectator. In the woman's film, the gaze must be de-eroticized (since the spectator is now assumed to be female), but in doing this the films effectively disembody their spectator. The repeated masochistic scenarios are designed to immobilize the female viewer, refuse her the imaginary identification that, in uniting body and identity, gives back to the male spectator his idealized (mirror) self, together with a sense of mastery and control.[25]

Later on in her paper, Doane shows that Freud's 'A Child Is Being Beaten' is important in distinguishing the way a common masochistic fantasy works out for boys and for girls. In the male fantasy, 'sexuality remains on the surface' and the man 'retains his own role and his own gratification in the context of the scenario. The "I" of identity remains.' But the female fantasy is, first desexualized, and, second, 'necessitates the woman's assumption of the position of spectator, outside of the event'. In this way, the girl manages, as Freud says, 'to escape from the demands of the erotic side of her life altogether'.[26]

Perhaps we can phrase this a little differently and say that in locating herself in fantasy in the erotic, the woman places herself as either passive recipient of male desire, or, at one remove, positions herself as *watching* a woman who is passive recipient of male desires and sexual actions. Although the evidence we have to go on is slim, it does seem that women's sexual fantasies would confirm the predominance of these positionings. Nancy Friday's volumes, for instance, provide discourses on the level of dream, and, however questionable as scientific evidence, show narratives in which the woman speaker largely arranges the scenario for her sexual pleasure so that things are done to her, or in which she is the object of men's lascivious gaze.[27] Often, there is pleasure in anonymity, or in a strange man approaching her when she is with her husband. Rarely does the dreamer initiate the sexual activity, and the man's large, erect penis usually is central in the fantasy. Nearly all the fantasies have the dominance-submission pattern, with the woman in the latter place.

It is significant that in the lesbian fantasies that Friday has collected women occupy *both* positions, the dreamer excited either by dominating another woman, forcing her to have sex, or enjoying being so dominated. These fantasies suggest either that the female positioning is not as monolithic as critics often imply, or that women occupy the 'male' position when they become dominant. Whichever the case may be, the prevalence of the dominance-submission pattern as a sexual turn-on is clear. At a discussion about pornography organized by Julia LeSage at the Northwestern Conference on Feminist Film Criticism, gay and straight women admitted their pleasure (in both fantasy and actuality) in being 'forced' or 'forcing' someone else. Some women claimed that this was a result of growing up in Victorian-style households where all sexuality was repressed, but others denied that it had anything to do with patriarchy. Women wanted, rightly, to accept themselves sexually, whatever the turn-on mechanism.[28] But to simply celebrate whatever gives us sexual pleasure seems to me both problematic and too easy: we need to analyze how it is that certain things turn us on, how sexuality has been constructed in patriarchy to produce pleasure in the dominance-submission forms, before we advocate these modes.

It was predictable that many of the male fantasies in Friday's book *Men in Love* would show the speaker constructing events so that he is in control: again, the 'I' of identity remains central, as it was not in the female narrations.[29] Many male fantasies focus on the man's excitement arranging for his woman to expose herself (or even give herself) to other men, while he watches. The difference between this male voyeurism and the previous female form is striking: the women do not own the desire, even when they watch; their watching is to place responsibility for sexuality at yet one more remove, to distance themselves from sex; the man, on the other hand, owns the desire and the woman, and gets pleasure from exchanging the woman, as in Lévi-Strauss' kinship system.

Yet some of the fantasies in Friday's book show men's wish to be taken over by an aggressive woman who would force them to become helpless, like the little boy in his mother's hands. The Women Against Pornography guided trip around Times Square corroborated this; after a slide show that focused totally on male sadism and violent sexual exploitation of women, we were taken on a tour that showed literature and film loops expressing as many fantasies of male as of female submission. The situations were the predictable ones, showing young boys (but sometimes men) seduced by women in a form of authority—governesses, nursemaids, nurses, schoolteachers, stepmothers. (Of course, it is significant that the corresponding dominance-submission female fantasies have men in authority positions that carry much more status—professors, doctors, policemen, executives: these men seduce the innocent girls, or young wives, who cross their paths.)

Two interesting things emerge from all this: one is that dominance-submission patterns are apparently a crucial part of both male and female sexuality as constructed in western capitalism. The other is that men have a far wider range of positions available: more readily both dominant and submissive, they vacillate between supreme control and supreme abandonment. Women, meanwhile, are more consistently submissive, but not excessively abandoned. In their own fantasies, women do not position themselves as exchanging men, although a man might find being exchanged an exciting fantasy.

But the important question remains: when women are in the dominant position, are they in the *masculine* position? Can we envisage a female dominant position that would differ qualitatively from the male form of dominance? Or is there merely the possibility for both sex genders to occupy the positions we now know as masculine and feminine?

The experience of recent films of the 1970s and 1980s would support the latter possibility, and explain why many feminists have not been excited by the so-called liberated woman on the screen, or by the fact that some male stars have recently been made to seem the object of the female gaze. Traditionally male stars did not necessarily (or even primarily) derive their glamour from their looks or their sexuality, but from the power they were able to wield within the filmic world in which they functioned (i.e. John Wayne); these men, as Laura Mulvey has shown, became ego ideals for the men in the audience, corresponding to the image in the mirror, who was more in control of motor coordination than the young child looking in. 'The male figure', Mulvey notes, 'is free to command the stage . . . of spatial illusion in which he articulates the look and creates the action.'[30]

Recent films have begun to change this pattern: a star like John Travolta (*Saturday Night Fever, Urban Cowboy, Moment by Moment*) has been rendered the object of woman's gaze and in some of the films (i.e. *Moment by Moment*) placed explicitly as a sexual object to a woman who controlled the film's action. Robert Redford likewise has begun to be used as the object of female desire (i.e. in *Electric Horseman*). But it is significant that in all these films, when the man steps out of his traditional role as the one who controls the whole action, and when he is set up as a sex object, the woman then takes on the masculine role as bearer of the gaze and initiator of the action. She nearly always loses her traditionally feminine characteristics in so doing—not those of attractiveness, but rather of kindness, humaneness, motherliness. She is now often cold, driving, ambitious, manipulating, just like the men whose position she has usurped.

Even in a supposedly feminist film like *My Brilliant Career* the same processes are at work. The film is interesting because it places in the foreground the independent minded heroine's dilemma in a clearly patriarchal culture: in love with a wealthy neighbor, the heroine makes him the object of her gaze, but the problem is that, as female, her desire has no power. Men's desire naturally carries power with it, so when the hero finally concedes his love for her, he comes to get her. However, being able to conceive of 'love' only as 'submission', an end to autonomy and to her life as a creative writer, the heroine now refuses. The film thus plays with established positions, but is unable to work through them to something else.

What we can conclude from the discussion so far is that our culture is deeply committed to clearly demarcated sex differences, called masculine and feminine, that revolve on, first, a complex gaze-apparatus; and, second, dominance-submission patterns. This positioning of the two sex genders clearly privileges the male through the mechanisms of voyeurism and fetishism, which are male operations, and because his desire carries power/action, where woman's usually does not. But as a result of the recent women's movement, women have been permitted in representation to assume (step into) the position defined as masculine, as long as the man then steps into *her* position), so as to keep the whole structure intact.

It is significant, of course, that while this substitution is made to happen relatively easily in the cinema, in real life any such 'swapping' is fraught with the immense psychological difficulties that only psychoanalysis can unravel. In any case, such 'exchanges' do not do much for either sex, since nothing has essentially changed: the roles remain locked into their static boundaries. Showing images of mere reversal may in fact provide a safety valve for the social tensions that the women's movement has created by demanding a more dominant role for women.

We have thus arrived at the point where we must question the necessity for the dominance-submission structure. The gaze is not necessarily male (literally), but to own and activate the gaze, given our language and the structure of the unconscious, is to be in the masculine position. It is for this reason that Julia Kristeva and others have said that it is impossible to know what the feminine might be; while we must reserve the category 'women' for social demands and publicity, Kristeva says that by 'woman' she means 'that which is not represented, that which is unspoken, that which is left out of meanings and ideologies.'[31] For similar reasons, Sandy Flitterman and Judith Barry have argued that feminist artists must avoid claiming a specific female power residing in the body of women that represents 'an inherent feminine artistic essence which could find expression if allowed to be explored freely.' The impulse toward this kind of art is understandable in a culture that denies satisfaction in being a woman, but it results in motherhood's being redefined as the seat of female creativity, while women 'are proposed as the bearers of culture, albeit an alternative one'.[32]

Barry and Flitterman argue that this form of feminist art, along with some others that they outline, is dangerous in not taking into account 'the social contradictions involved in "femininity"'. They suggest that 'a radical feminist art would include an understanding of how women are constituted through social practices in culture', and argue for 'an aesthetics designed to subvert the production of "woman" as commodity', much as Claire Johnston and Laura Mulvey had earlier stated that to be feminist, a cinema had to be a counter-cinema.[33]

The problem with all these arguments is that they leave women trapped in the position of negativity—subverting rather than positing. Although the feminists asserting this point of view are clearly right in placing in the foreground women's repression in representation and culture (and in seeing this work as a necessary first step), it is hard to see how women can move forward from these awarenesses. If certain feminist groups (i.e. Women Against Pornography) err on the side of eliding reality with fantasy (i.e. in treating an image's violating of women on the same level as a literal act of violation on the street), feminist critics err on the side of seeing a world constructed only of signifiers, of losing contact with the 'referred' world of the social formation.

The first error was in positing an unproblematic relationship between art and life in the sense that (1) art was seen as able simply to imitate life, as if through a transparent pane of glass; and (2) that representation was thought to affect social behaviour directly; but the second error is to see art and life as both equally 'constructed' by the signifying practices that define and limit each sphere. The signifier is here made material, in the sense that it is all there is to know. Discussing semiology in relation to Marxism, Terry Eagleton points out the dangers of this way of seeing for a Marxist view of history. History evaporates in the new scheme; since the signified can never be grasped, we cannot talk about our reality as human subjects. But, as he goes on to show, more than the signified (which in Saussure's scheme obediently followed the signifier, despite its being arbitrary) is at stake: 'It is also', he says, 'a question of the referent, which we all long ago bracketed out of being. In re-materializing the sign, we are in imminent danger of de-materializing its referent; a linguistic materialism gradually reverts itself into a linguistic idealism.'[34]

Eagleton no doubt overstates the case when he talks about 'sliding away from the referent', since neither Saussure nor Althusser denied that there *was* a referent. But it is true that while semiologists talk about the eruption of 'the real' (i.e. accidents, death, revolution), on a daily basis they tend to be preoccupied with life as dominated by the prevailing signifying practices of a culture. It may be true that all lived experience is mediated through signifying practices, but we should not therefore pay exclusive attention to this level of things. In attempting to get rid of an unwelcome dualism, inherent in western thought at least since Plato, and rearticulated by Kant on the brink of the modern period, some semiologists run the danger of collapsing levels of things that need to remain distinct if we are to work effectively in the political arena to bring about change.

Thus while it is essential for feminist film critics to examine signifying processes carefully in order to fully understand the way women have been constructed in language and the non-verbal arts, it is equally important not to lose sight of the need to find strategies for changing discourse, since these changes would, in turn, affect the structuring of the social formation.

Some feminist film critics have begun to face this challenge. The directors of *Sigmund Freud's Dora*, for example, suggest that raising questions is the first step toward establishing a female discourse, or, perhaps, that asking questions is the only discourse available to women as a resistance to patriarchal domination. Since questions lead to more questions, a kind of movement is in fact taking place, although it is in a nontraditional mode. Sally Potter structured her film *Thriller* around this very notion, and allowed her heroine's investigation of herself as heroine to lead to some (tentative) conclusions. And Laura Mulvey has suggested that even if one accepts the psychoanalytic positioning of women, all is not lost, since the Oedipus complex is not completed in women; she notes that 'there is some way in which women aren't colonized,' having been 'so specifically excluded from culture and language'.[35]

From this position, psychoanalytic theory allows us to see that there is more possibility for women to change themselves (and perhaps to bring about social change) just because they have not been processed, as have little boys, through a clearly defined, and ultimately simple, set of psychic stages. The girl's relationship to her mother remains forever unresolved, incomplete; in heterosexuality, she is forced to turn away from her primary love object, destined never to return to it, while the boy, through marrying someone like his mother, can regain his original plenitude in another form. The girl must transfer her need for love to the father, who, as Nancy Chodorow has shown, never completely satisfies.[36]

Mulvey thus suggests that patriarchal culture is not monolithic, not cleanly sealed. There are gaps, fissures through which women can begin to ask questions and introduce change. The directors of *Sigmund Freud's Dora* end their film with a series of letters from a daughter (who is sometimes called Dora) read out by her mother, some of which deal with the place of the mother in psychoanalysis. The daughter's comments illuminate the fact that Freud dismisses Dora's mother (in his famous account of the case history), instead of talking about her 'as the site of the intersection of many representations' (of which the historical mother is just one). She suggests that Freud's omission was not merely an oversight, but, given his system, a necessity.

Mulvey and Wollen's earlier film, *Riddles of the Sphinx*, confronted the repression of mothering in patriarchal culture directly; the film argued that women 'live in a society ruled by the father, in which the place of the mother is repressed. Motherhood, and how to live it or not to live it, lies at the root of the dilemma.'[37] In an interview, Mulvey noted the influence of psychoanalysis on her conception of the mother–child exchange ('the identification between the two, and the implications that has for narcissism and recognition of the self in the "other"'), but she went on to say that this is an area rarely read from the mother's point of view.[38]

Motherhood thus becomes one place from which to begin to reformulate our position as women, just because men have not dealt with it theoretically or in the social realm (i.e. by providing free child care, free abortions, maternal leave, after-school child programs, etc.). Motherhood has been repressed on all levels except that of hypostatization, romanticization, and idealization.[39] Yet women have been struggling with lives as mothers—silently, quietly, often in agony, often in bliss, but always on the periphery of a society that tries to make us all, men and women, forget our mothers.

But motherhood, and the fact that we were all mothered, will not be repressed; or, if the attempt is made, there will be effects signaling 'the return of the repressed'. The entire construction of woman in patriarchy as a lack could be viewed as emerging from the need to repress mothering and the painful memory traces it has left in the man. The phallus as signified can be set in motion only given the other with a lack, and this has resulted in the male focus on castration. But is it possible that this focus was designed to mask an even greater threat that mothering poses? And if we look from the position of women, need this lack in reality have the dire implications men would have us believe? The focus on women as (simply) sex object, or (more complexly) as fetishized (narcissistic male desire) that we have been tracing through Hollywood films, may be part of the apparatus that represses mothering. The insistence on rigidly defined sex roles, and the dominance-submission, voyeurism-fetishism mechanisms may be constructed to this end.

In placing the problem of mothering in the foreground in this way one is not necessarily falling into the trap of essentialism. First, I am not denying that motherhood has been constructed in patriarchy by its very place as repressed; nor, second, am I saying that women are inherently mothers; nor, third, that the only ideal relationship that can express female specificity is mothering. I am saying rather, that motherhood is one of the areas that has been left vague, allowing us to reformulate the position as given, rather than discovering a specificity outside the system we are in.[40] It is a place to start rethinking sex-difference, not an end.

Let me review briefly some of the main ways in which motherhood can be thought of within psychoanalysis. First, and most conservatively, motherhood has been analyzed as an essentially narcissistic relationship, and as involved with the problem of castration. In this way, it parallels male fetishism; just as men fetishize women in order to reduce their threat (finding themselves thus in the other), so women fetishize the child, looking in the child for the phallus to 'make up' for castration; second, motherhood can be seen as narcissistic, not in the sense of finding the phallus in the child, but of finding *the self* in the child (this parallels male fetishizing of women in another way); women here do not relate to the child as other, but as an extension of their own egos; third, and most radically (but this is also the position that can lead to essentialism), one could argue that since the law represses mothering, a gap is left through which it may be possible to subvert patriarchy.

The problem with this latter (and most hopeful) position, however, is that of how to express motherhood after the period of the imaginary. One could argue that women are faced with an impossible dilemma: to remain in blissful unity with the child in the imaginary (or to try to hold onto this realm as long as possible), or to enter the symbolic in which mothering is repressed, cannot be 'spoken', cannot represent a position of power. Here the only resistance is silence.[41]

But is this not one of those places where a rigid adherence to the theoretical formulation of imaginary and symbolic betrays the inadequacy of the theory? Is not mothering, in fact, now being 'spoken', even through patriarchal discourse? Both Dorothy Dinnerstein and Nancy Chodorow 'speak' a discourse about mothering that, while remaining within psychoanalysis, breaks new ground.[42] And the feminist films about mothering now appearing begin to investigate and move beyond patriarchal representations.[43]

On the social/historical level, in addition, we are living in a period in which mothers are increasingly living alone with their children, offering the possibility for new psychic patterns to emerge; fathers are increasingly becoming involved with childrearing, and also living alone with their children. Freud's own kind of science (which involved studying the people brought up in strict Victorian, bourgeois households) applied rigorously to people today results in very different conclusions. Single mothers are forced to make themselves subject in relation to their children; they are forced to invent new symbolic roles, which combine positions previously assigned to fathers with traditional female ones. The child cannot position the mother as object to the father's law, since in single-parent households *her* desire sets things in motion.

A methodology is often not *per se* either revolutionary or reactionary, but open to appropriation for a variety of usages. At this point, feminists may have to use psychoanalysis, but in a manner opposite to the traditional one. Other kinds of psychic processes obviously can exist and may stand as models for when we have worked our way through the morass that confronts us as people having grown up in western capitalist culture. Julia Kristeva, for example, suggests that desire functions in a very different manner in China, and urges us to explore Chinese culture, from a very careful psychoanalytic point of view, to see what is possible.[44]

Many of the mechanisms we have found in Hollywood films which echo deeply embedded myths in western capitalist culture are thus not inviolable, eternal, unchanging, or inherently necessary. They rather reflect the unconscious of patriarchy, including a fear of the pre-Oedipal plenitude with the mother. The domination of women by the male gaze is part of men's strategy to contain the threat that the mother embodies, and to control the positive and negative impulses that memory traces of being mothered have left in the male unconscious. Women, in turn, have learned to associate their sexuality with domination by the male gaze, a position involving a degree of masochism in finding their objectification erotic. We have participated in and perpetuated our domination by following the pleasure principle, which leaves us no options, given our positioning.

Everything, thus, revolves around the issue of pleasure, and it is here that patriarchal repression has been most negative. For things have been structured to make us forget the mutual, pleasurable bonding that we all, male and female, enjoyed with our mothers. Some recent experimental (as against psychoanalytic) studies have shown that the gaze is first set in motion in the mother–child relationship.[45] But this is a *mutual* gazing, rather than the subject–object kind that reduces one of the parties to the place of submission. Patriarchy has worked hard to prevent the eruption of a (mythically) feared return of the matriarchy that might take place were the close mother–child bonding returned to dominance, or allowed to stand in place of the law of the father.

This is by no means to argue that a return to matriarchy would be either possible or desirable. What rather has to happen is that we move beyond long-held cultural and linguistic patterns of oppositions: male/female (as these terms currently signify); dominant/submissive; active/passive; nature/civilization; order/chaos; matriarchal/patriarchal. If rigidly defined sex differences have been constructed around fear of the other, we need to think about ways of transcending a polarity that has only brought us all pain.[46]

Notes

The material in this essay appears in another form in E. Ann Kaplan, *Women in Film: Both Sides of the Camera* (London and New York: Methuen, 1983).

1. See works by Kate Millett, Linda Nochlin, Molly Haskell, articles in the few issues of *Women in Film* (1972–1975), and articles in *Screen* and *Screen Education* throughout the 1970s. For a summary of early developments across the arts, see Lucy Arbuthnot's Ph.D diss., New York University, 1982.
2. See especially work by Christian Metz, Jean-Louis Comolli, Raymond Bellour, Roland Barthes, and essays in *Cahiers du Cinéma* in France; in England, the work by Stephen Heath, Colin McCabe, Paul Willemen, and others in *Screen* and elsewhere.
3. See especially the work of Claire Johnston, Pam Cook, and Laura Mulvey from England, and subsequent work by the *Camera Obscura* group.
4. Christine Gledhill, 'Recent Developments in Feminist Film Criticism', *Quarterly Review of Film Studies*, 3: 4 (1978), 458–93; E. Ann Kaplan, 'Aspects of British Feminist Film Criticism', *Jump Cut*, nos. 12–13 (Dec. 1976), 52–56; and Kaplan, 'Integrating Marxist and Psychoanalytic Concepts in Feminist Film Criticism', *Millenium Film Journal*, April 1980, 8–17.
5. Jacques Lacan, 'The Mirror Phase as Formative of the Function of the "I"' (1949), in *New Left Review*, 51 (Sept.–Oct. 1968), 71–77. See also essays on Lacan in Anthony Wilden, *System and Structure: Essays in Communication and Exchange* (London: Tavistock Publications, 1972).
6. For a background to semiological concepts, see work by Roland Barthes, Julia Kristeva, and Umberto Eco among others. Terence Hawkes, *Structuralism and Semiology* (London: Methuen, 1977), and Rosalind Coward and John Ellis, *Language and Materialism* (London: Routledge and Kegan Paul, 1977) provide useful summaries of relevant material.
7. Laura Mulvey, 'Visual Pleasure and Narrative Cinema', *Screen*, 16: 3 (Autumn 1975), 16–18.
8. Karen Horney, 'The Dread of Woman' (1932), in *Feminine Psychology* (New York: W. W. Norton, 1967), 134.
9. Ibid. 136.
10. For a useful discussion of fetishism, see Otto Fenichel, *The Psychoanalytic Theory of Neurosis* (New York: W. W. Norton, 1945), 341–345.
11. Mulvey, 'Visual Pleasure', 14.
12. Ibid.
13. Claire Johnston, 'Woman's Cinema as Counter-Cinema', in *Notes on Women's Cinema*, ed. Claire Johnston (London: Screen Pamphlet, 1973), 26.
14. Some of these questions are raised in the letters read by a mother toward the end of the film *Sigmund Freud's Dora*, made by Anthony McCall, Andrew Tyndall, Claire Pajaczkowska, and Jane Weinstock.
15. This has been evident in feminist film sessions at various conferences, but was particularly clear at the Lolita Rodgers Memorial Conference on Feminist Film Criticism, held at Northwestern University, 14–16 Nov. 1980. For a report of some differences, see Barbara Klinger, 'Conference Report', *Camera Obscura*, 7 (Spring 1981), 137–43.
16. 'Women and Film: A Discussion of Feminist Aesthetics', *New German Critique*, 13 (Winter 1978), 93.

17. Ibid. 87.
18. Lucy Arbuthnot and Gail Seneca, 'Pre-Text and Text in *Gentlemen Prefer Blondes*', paper delivered at the Conference on Feminist Film Criticism, Northwestern University, Nov. 1980.
19. See Maureen Turim, 'Gentlemen Consume Blondes', in *Wideangle*, 1: 1 (1979), 52–59. Carol Rowe also (if somewhat mockingly) shows Monroe's phallicism in her film *Grand Delusion*.
20. See Mary-Anne Doane, 'The Woman's Film: Possession and Address', paper delivered at the Conference on Cinema History, Asilomar, Monterey, May 1981.
21. Mulvey, 'Visual Pleasure', 7–8, 18.
22. See the essays in *Edinburgh Magazine*, 1 (1977), by Coward, Metz, Heath, and Johnston. Also the issue of *Screen*, 16: 2 (Summer 1975), on 'Psychoanalysis and Cinema', especially the piece by Metz.
23. See E. Ann Kaplan, 'Feminist Approaches to History, Psychoanalysis, and Cinema in *Sigmund Freud's Dora*', *Millennium Film Journal*, 7/8/9 (Fall/Winter 1979), 173–85.
24. Charles Brenner offers perhaps the most accessible account of Freud's notion of the Oedipus complex in his *An Elementary Textbook of Psychoanalysis* (New York: Anchor Books, 1957), 108–141.
25. Freud's work is central to any discussion of sadism and masochism. Since I wrote this paper, these issues have been discussed by Kaja Silverman in 'Masochism aud Subjectivity', *Framework*, 12 (1981), 2–9, and by Joel Kovel, *The Age of Desire* (New York: Pantheon, 1981).
26. Doane, 'The Woman's Film', 3–8.
27. Nancy Friday, *My Secret Garden: Women's Sexual Fantasies* (New York: Pocket Books, 1981).
28. Unpublished transcript of a discussion, organized by Julia LeSage, at the Conference on Feminist Criticism, Northwestern University, Nov. 1980. See also for discussion of dominance-submission patterns, Pat Califa, 'Feminism and Sadomasochism', *Heresies 12.* 32ff.
29. Nancy Friday, *Men in Love* (New York: Dell, 1980).
30. Mulvey, 'Visual Pleasure', 12–13.
31. Julia Kristeva, "La femme, ce n'est jamais ça', trans. Marilyn A. August, in *New French Feminisms*, ed. E. Marks and I. de Courtviron (Amherst: University of Massachusetts Press, 1980), 37.
32. Sandy Flitterman and Judith Barry, 'Textual Strategies: The Politics of Art-Making', *Screen*, 2: 3 (Summer 1980), 37.
33. Ibid., 36.
34. Terry Eagleton, 'Aesthetics and Politics', *New Left Review* (1978).
35. 'Women and Representation: A Discussion with Laura Mulvey' (collective project by Jane Clarke, Sue Clayton, Joanna Clelland, Rosie Elliott, and Mandy Merck), *Wedge* (London), 2 (Spring 1979), 49.
36. Nancy Chodorow, 'Psychodynamics of the Family', in *The Reproduction of Mothering* (Berkeley: University of California Press, 1978), 191–209.
37. '*Riddles of the Sphinx*: A Film by Laura Mulvey and Peter Wollen; Script', *Screen*, 18: 2 (Summer 1977), 62.
38. Jacquelyn Suter and Sandy Flitterman, 'Textual Riddles: Woman as Enigma or

Site of Social Meanings? An Interview with Laura Mulvey', *Discourse*, 1 (Fall 1979), 107.

39. Ibid. 109–120.
40. Ibid. 116–19.
41. Mulvey, 'Women and Representation', 49.
42. Dinnerstein, *The Mermaid and the Minotaur* (New York: Harper and Row, 1976) and Chodorow, *The Reproduction of Mothering.*
43. See for example, films by Laura Mulvey and Peter Wollen, Michelle Citron, Marjorie Keller, and Helke Sander.
44. Kristeva, 'Les Chinoises à "contre-courant"', *New French Feminisms*, 240.
45. Eleanor Maccoby and John Martin, 'Parent–Child Interaction', in *Handbook of Child Psychology*, ed. E. M. Hetherington (New York: John Wiley & Sons: in press). One has obviously to be careful here about introducing discourses that work on an entirely different level than the theoretical, psychoanalytic discourse that I have mainly been considering. It may be, however, that the confronting of the psychoanalytic discourse with more empirically based kinds of discourse could lead to an opening up of the theory, to suggestions for a way out of the theoretical impasse in which psychoanalytic frameworks place women.
46. See the important essay by Jessica Benjamin, 'Master and Slave: The Fantasy of Erotic Domination', in Ann Snitow (ed.), *Powers of Desire* (New York: Monthly Review Press, 1983).

other hand, have concentrated on her career as an editor for such directors as James Cruze (see Kevin Brownlow, *The Parade's Gone By* and Lewis Jacobs, *The Rise of the American Film*), or else have cited her as a directorial curiosity specialising in that esoteric commodity 'feminine psychology' (see David Robinson, *Hollywood in the Twenties*).

It is therefore the intention of this pamphlet to suggest some approaches to Dorothy Arzner's work as a Hollywood director and to indicate in what way her films are relevant for feminists today. In so doing feminist film critics are not attempting to establish Arzner as some cult figure in a pantheon of Hollywood directors nor, indeed, in a pantheon of women directors. To see analyses of work by women directors in these terms is to misunderstand the crucial issues which the study of a woman director in the Hollywood system inevitably raises for feminist film criticism. In the first place, there is the question of film history itself. Why do feminist film critics place considerable emphasis on the role women have played, however marginal, in film history? Quite clearly women in the film industry have remained until recently 'unspoken', repressed by film history. But do feminist film critics simply want to introduce women into film history? To answer this question, it is necessary to examine the ideology which has dominated film history up to now. Film historians (as J.-L. Comolli's critique in *Cahiers du Cinéma*[3] makes clear) have until very recently confined themselves to the accumulation of 'facts' and the construction of chronologies. From these, they have attempted by a process of induction to derive an interpretation of historical events closely linked to liberal notions of 'progress' and 'development'. The historicism and pseudo-objectivism of this approach leaves little room for theory of any kind. Indeed, it is commonly believed that the pursuit of theory must inevitably be at the expense of 'facts'. Merely to introduce women into the dominant notion of film history, as yet another series of 'facts' to be assimilated into the existing notions of chronology, would quite clearly be sterile and regressive. 'History' is not some abstract 'thing' which bestows significance on past events in retrospect. Only an attempt to situate Arzner's work in a theoretical way would allow us to comprehend her real contribution to film history. Women and film can only become meaningful in terms of a theory, in the attempt to create a structure in which films such as Arzner's can be examined in retrospect. This is not, however, to ignore the political importance of asserting the real role women have played in the history of the cinema. As the French philosopher Michel Foucault has indicated,[4] the need for oppressed peoples to write their own histories cannot be overstressed. Memory, an understanding of the struggles of the past, and a sense of one's own history constitute a vital dynamic in any struggle. The role of women in film history, then, inevitably raises questions about the nature of film history as such, and it is for this reason that this pamphlet has approached Dorothy Arzner's work from the point of view of feminist politics and film theory, as prerequisite research before any attempt at an insertion into film history can be undertaken.

The second issue raised by Dorothy Arzner's work which arises out of the problems outlined above is discussed in some detail in Pam Cook's essay 'Approaching the Work of Dorothy Arzner'. To understand the real achievement of her work, it is necessary to locate it within the constraints imposed by the Hollywood studio system and in relation to the patriarchal ideology of classic Hollywood cinema. In this context we employ 'ideology' in the sense that the Marxist philosopher Louis Althusser uses the term.[5] Ideology is a system of representations: 'images, myths, ideas or concepts'. Ideology in this sense is not concerned with beliefs which people consciously hold; in fact, as Althusser emphasises, 'it is profoundly unconscious', representing itself as at once transparent, 'natural' and universal to the viewer. In her article Pam Cook stresses the point that the system of representations generated by classic Hollywood cinema fixes the spectator in a specific, closed relationship to it, obliterating for the spectator the possibility of experiencing contradiction. She then proceeds to analyse the ways in which Dorothy Arzner's films, through a displacement of identification, through discontinuity and a process of play, succeed in generating a set of contradictions so that a de-naturalisation of patriarchal ideology is effected, and the fixed relationship of the spectator is disturbed. However, this argument is based on the premise that classic Hollywood cinema locks the spectator in a fixed position. Undoubtedly the cinema, as a popular art which implies a viewing situation analogous in many respects to voyeurism (a position exploited by directors such as Hitchcock), encourages a fetishistic reading. Obviously the question of woman as spectacle is also linked closely to the voyeuristic position of the spectator.

Yet the fetishistic reading is not the only possible reading of a 'progressive' classic film text. In recent years there has been an increased interest in the different strategies of reading which some 'progressive' classic Hollywood films appear to require by virtue of the contradictions which can be found in such films between the specific hierarchy of interrelated discourses[6] which each film text comprises and the discourse of the dominant ideology (which in this case is the ideology of patriarchy). Attention has been drawn to a whole group of classic Hollywood films (for example those of Sirk and Ford) which generate within themselves an internal criticism of the dominant ideology. (For further definition of this group of films, see 'Cinema/Ideology/Criticism' by Comolli and Narboni, translated in *Screen*, 12; 1 (Spring 1971).) This internal criticism facilitates a process of de-naturalisation: behind the film's apparent coherence there exists an 'internal tension' so that the ideology no longer has an independent existence but is 'presented' by the film. The pressure of this tension cracks open the surface of the film; instead of its ideology being simply assumed and therefore virtually invisible, it is revealed and made explicit. It is in these terms that I would like to discuss the work of Dorothy Arzner: as a group of 'progressive' classic film texts which de-naturalise the workings of patriarchal ideology. My approach differs from that of Pam Cook to the extent that I do not consider Arzner's work in terms of revolutionary strategies such as notions of 'pregnant moment' and 'tableaux', but in terms of dislocations and contradictions between the discourses which the film text comprises and that of the ideology of patriarchal culture within which the film is placed.

THE ARZNER OEUVRE

In general, the woman in Arzner's films determines her own identity through transgression and desire[7] in a search for an independent existence beyond and outside the discourse of the male. Unlike most other Hollywood directors who pose 'positive' and 'independent' female protagonists (Walsh,[8] Fuller, Cukor and Hawks, for example), in Arzner's work the discourse of the woman, or rather her attempt to locate it and make it heard, is what gives the system of the text its structural coherence, while at the same time rendering the dominant discourse of the male fragmented and incoherent. The central female protagonists react against and thus transgress the male discourse which entraps them. The form of transgression will depend on the nature of the particular discourse within which they have been caught. These women do not sweep aside the existing order and found a new, female, order of language. Rather, they assert their own discourse in the face of the male one, by breaking it up, subverting it and, in a sense, rewriting it. It is this form of rewriting which then becomes the structuring principle of the text, the particular nature of the rewriting depending on what is being rewritten.

In *Christopher Strong* we are presented with the epitome of this desire for transgression in the character of Cynthia Darrington, world champion aviatrix ('I want to do it because I want to do it'). Cynthia achieves her project through role-reversal: by an over-identification with the male universe, flying planes, breaking records, and living and competing in a male world. ('I want to break records, I want to train hard.') *Wild Party* depicts a situation in which desire and transgression are articulated through an unswerving loyalty to the all-female group, the 'hard-boiled maidens' who arrange nightly raids on local speakeasies and men's colleges. In *First Comes Courage* it is Nicole's perilous masquerade as a counter-espionage agent, living the life of a social outcast in extreme danger because of her marriage to a German commandant, which defines the articulation of desire and transgression. In *Craig's Wife* the project assumes pathological proportions. Harriet Craig's masochistic and obsessional relationship with her house and domesticity drives her to sacrifice everything and everyone for material security, order and cleanliness. Her obsessional desire involves expelling any acknowledgement of the value of family ties, while at the same time she guards with passion the physical integrity of her home. *Nana*, adapted from Zola's novel, follows the same basic preoccupations with the possibility of desire and transgression under partiarchy. Nana is a sexual adventuress who, by becoming the object of desire for men, seeks instead to become the *subject* of desire by exploiting the place in patriarchy assigned to her through the achievement of wealth and social influence. *Merrily We Go To Hell* and *Honor Among Lovers*, in the tradition of sophisticated social comedy of the thirties (e.g. Ernst Lubitsch) generate a play on the central motifs of sex and money, and it is within this discourse that the restructuring intervention of the woman's discourse must be placed. In *Honor Among Lovers*, Julia articulates her desire for transgression by rejecting Jerry, her wealthy playboy boss, precisely because, as he says, 'there's nothing you want that I can't give you', and marries a man without money who gambles everything on the stockmarket. In so doing she destroys the possibility of running Jerry's business, albeit as his secretary (at one point Julia describes hell as a place where women have to 'remain private secretaries through all eternity'), though this is presented as infinitely preferable to a marriage which makes her feel 'unhappy' and 'afraid' and finally leads to bankruptcy and betrayal. In

Merrily We Go To Hell the position is reversed. It is the woman, Joan, who is rich, and it is her father's refusal to relinquish her, and his offer of money to Gerry (the alcoholic news reporter and writer) not to marry his daughter, which forms the framework in which she will articulate her desire for transgression.

Undoubtedly *Dance, Girl, Dance* offers the most complex and far-reaching examination of the discourse of woman in relation to the other discourses in the text, in that it poses two central figures: Bubbles, the burlesque queen, and Judy, the aspiring ballet dancer, and it is only in this film that Arzner examines the question of woman as spectacle in patriarchy. Also, here, desire and transgression are articulated through a systematic presentation of opposites. Bubbles' desire to please, to exploit her sexuality for success and money, to 'get her man', is contrasted with Judy's desire for self-expression, for work and the achievement of physical grace, and for acknowledgement within the terms of bourgeois culture. *Dance, Girl, Dance* also employs an additional element, the self-conscious use of stereotyping; Bubbles as the archetypal vamp and Judy as her naïve and innocent straight girl generate within the text of the film an internal criticism of it and of the function woman has within the narrative. The mythic qualities of this primitive iconography become, in effect, a shorthand for an ideological tradition in order to provide a critique of it, generating a series of reverberations which serve to de-naturalise the ideology of patriarchy in operation. In most Arzner films, however, this crude stereotyping occurs only in minor characters (e.g. Claire Hempstead in *Merrily We Go To Hell* and the Ginger Rogers character in *Honor Among Lovers*) and does not derive from the discourse of the woman, but, rather is a facet of the discourse of the male.

In the Arzner oeuvre, then, the dominant discourse, situated as it is within the constraints of classic Hollywood cinema and the rules of verisimilitude we associate with it—that is, the discourse of the male—is not privileged in any way, nor does it provide us with the knowledge to judge the truth of the discourses within the film as a whole. Structural coherence is provided by the discourse of the woman, and it is this which calls into question the dominant discourse and the nature of patriarchy into which it locks; dislocating it, deforming it in the sense that the Russian Formalist Shklovsky uses the term '*ostranenie*', the device of *making-strange.* In his essay 'Art as a Device'[9] Shklovsky describes the device in relation to Tolstoy's story *Kholstomer*, where the entire story is related by a horse describing its reactions to the notion of 'belonging' to a man, thus viewing property relations from an entirely new perspective; the unfamiliar making us pause and look anew at objects which have always appeared perfectly 'natural' up to this moment. Such a device of *making-strange* would seem to be the key strategy by means of which the discourse of the woman subverts and dislocates the dominant discourse of the man and patriarchal ideology in general.

In Arzner's films it is the universe of the male which invites scrutiny, which is rendered strange. In this way, the discourse of the male can no longer function as the dominant one, the one which speaks the truth of the secondary discourses in the film. It is only the discourse of the woman, and her desire for transgression, which provides the principle of coherence and generates knowledge, and it is in woman that Arzner locates the possibility of truth within the film text. It is also for this reason that the narrative appears disjointed and fragmented; the conventions of plot and development are quite fully in evidence, but the work of the woman's discourse renders the narrative strange, subverting and dislocating it at the level of meaning. *Craig's Wife* offers a sustained example of this strategy. Here the rituals of housework and the obsession with order acquire, as the film progresses, a definite validity, and it is evidence of people living and breathing in the house which is rendered strange. The marks of a trunk having been pulled along the floor or someone having sat on a bed acquire a sinister meaning within the text of the film. Another example is the character of Doris Blake in *Honor Among Lovers* who is likened by her millionaire boy-friend, always depicted shrouded in a massive fur coat, to an animal: 'she's dumb but nice' . . . 'I'm breaking her in'. The marriage sequence in *Merrily We Go To Hell* in which a corkscrew, a token of Gerry's inebriated past and an omen for the future, is hurriedly used as a wedding ring works in a similar fashion. The entire relationship between Jimmie Harris and his estranged wife Elinor in *Dance, Girl, Dance* is another example of this device in operation, as is the love-making scene in *Christopher Strong* in which at the moment of sexual consummation, Strong gently and tenderly exhorts Cynthia to give up flying. Only at one point in Arzner's work, as far as I am aware, is a decisive *break* effected between the dominant discourse and the discourse of the woman—in the momentous scene in *Dance, Girl, Dance* where Judy, in a fit of anger, turns on her audience, and tells them how she sees them. This return of scrutiny in what is assumed within the film to be a one-way process, a spectacle to be consumed by men, constitutes a direct assault on the audience *within* the film and the audience *of* the film, directly challenging the entire notion of spectacle as such. This break, a *tour-de-force* in terms of Arzner's work, is nevertheless directly recuperated by the enthusiastic applause which follows, and the discourse of the woman, although it appears momentarily supreme, is returned to the arena of the spectacle.

The drive towards resolution of the narrative and closure of the dominant discourse in the classic Hollywood film traditionally involves the 'happy ending' or its inversion, both embodying the notion of unification, the completion of the man by the woman and the myth of sexual complementariness. In Arzner's work there is a systematic refusal of such a unification. The subversion of the dominant discourse continues, even though the woman fails to impose her desire upon it. The discourse of the woman is not eliminated, and the endings of Arzner's films, whether 'happy' or 'tragic' in the conventional sense, mark, in the final analysis, the triumph of the discourse of woman in surviving at all. *Dance, Girl, Dance* shows Judy exchanging the humiliation of the spectacle for the defeat of the final embrace with Steve Adams, the patriarchal presence which has haunted her throughout the film ('silly child, you've had your own way long enough'). As she turns to the camera, her face obscured by a large, floppy hat, Judy, half crying, half laughing, exclaims 'when I think how simple things could have been, I just have to laugh'. This irony marks her defeat and final engulfment, but at the same time it is the final mark of subversion of the discourse of the male. *Merrily We Go To Hell* offers a similar strategy of subversion within the 'happy ending', but it takes a different form. Having lost her baby in childbirth Joan takes the recalcitrant Jerry in her arms and murmurs 'my baby'; this ironic, even pathological, gesture of substituting the lover for the dead child facilitates the 'happy ending', but this regression also represents the mark of Joan's desire on the final images of the film text. This type of 'happy ending' is consistent with Douglas Sirk's remark[10] about his own 'happy endings'—'it makes the aporia more transparent'.

The 'tragic' type of ending employed frequently by Arzner represents a similar refusal of unification and closure and a resolution instead to play out the discourse of the woman to the bitter end. In *Christopher Strong* it manifests itself in final suicide on a solo flight, as Cynthia watches her past life and the impossible contradictions between her career and her lover flash before her eyes as her plane hurtles to the ground. For Nana the decision to take her own life in the face of impossible constraints placed on her by her lovers and their codes of gallantry is expressed as a sense of relief, as almost pleasurable: 'I was born all wrong' . . . 'I'm glad I'm going'. The final lonely image of Harriet Craig surrounded by her immaculate, empty home implies that the narrative has been resolved, the solitary, emphatically artificial tear in her eye suggesting a sense of irony: convention demands that the tear be there, but its artificiality underlines the contradictions of her pyrrhic victory. This final image of isolation is paralleled in *First Comes Courage* where Nicole rejects her lover to continue her masquerade to the end, a solitary figure on a burning hill. In all these cases, the discourse of the woman fails to triumph *over* the male discourse and the patriarchal ideology, but its very survival in the form of irony is in itself a kind of triumph, a victory against being expelled or erased: the continued insistence of the woman's discourse is a triumph over non-existence.

In this essay I have not attempted to trace in detail the ways in which the strategies of dislocation, subversion and contradiction operate within the texts of individual films, though a close analysis is quite clearly a necessity at some point. Such an analysis would involve the tracing of these dislocations and contradictions within the film text through which meaning is produced: a process which has a resemblance to the examination of permanent traces left upon the 'Mystic Writing-Pad' described by Freud,[11] although in this case the traces are not linked directly to memory. In this essay I have attempted to situate the system of strategies which Arzner employs within her work as a whole, and have indicated that it would be incorrect to look at her work simply as a coherent structure of themes and motifs, in the *auteurist* manner. Rather, it should be seen in terms of a re-writing process. In this process the discourse of the woman is the principal structuring element which re-writes the dominant discourse of the film text together with the patriarchal ideology into which it locks. Arzner's strategies at this level cannot in any sense be seen as revolutionary ones for feminism. Her position in classic Hollywood cinema in many aspects can be paralleled to Lenin's assessment of Tolstoy's position in Soviet literature. Both are progressive artists who hold a specific and important position in history precisely because they open up an area of contradiction in the text, but at the same time they are unable radically to change these contradictions. For this reason, it is particularly important that films such as those of Arzner should be studied by feminists involved in developing a feminist counter-cinema. Her films pose the problem for all of us: is it possible to sweep aside the existing forms of discourse in order to found a new form of language? The French semiologist Roland Barthes has suggested that all stories are based on the structure of the Oedipus myth.[12] How, then, is it possible to produce feminist art which is not based on such a structure and the repression of the feminine which underpins it? In posing the question in the way she does, and through the working out of her own solution as a process of rewriting, Dorothy Arzner has made one of the most important contributions to the development of a feminist counter-cinema.

Notes

1. See the magazine *Women and Film*, and *Notes on Women's Cinema*, a Screen pamphlet, SEFT, 1973.
2. Articles and interview in *Cinema* (USA), Fall 1974; 'Dorothy Arzner's *Dance, Girl, Dance*' in *The Velvet Light Trap*, Fall 1973.
3. 'Technique and Ideology', *Cahiers du Cinéma*, nos. 229, 230, 231, 233, 235, 241.
4. 'Entretien avec Michel Foucault', *Cahiers du Cinéma*, nos. 251–2.
5. Louis Althusser, *For Marx* (London: Allen Lane, 1969).
6. I use 'discourse' to refer to a particular level of 'speech' within a film attributable to a source (or more precisely a 'subject—not to be confused with a character in the film—and thus answers the question 'Who is speaking here?'). It derives from the manner in which the textual system of the film operates. Thus within a film there may a variety of discourses, each having a different perspective on the action; though in classic Hollywood cinema, a male discourse is almost invariably dominant.
7. The notions of desire and transgression used here do not coincide with the conventional ones, but derive from psychoanalytic usage. Readers are referred to J. Laplanche and J.-B. Pontalis, *The Language of Psychoanalysis* (London: Hogarth Press, 1973).
8. 'The Place of Women in the Cinema of Raoul Walsh', by Pam Cook and Claire Johnston, in *Raoul Walsh*, ed. Phil Hardy (Edinburgh Film Festival 1974).
9. *Théorie de la literature*, ed. Tzvetan Todorov (Paris: Editions du Seuil, 1965).
10. Jon Halliday, *Sirk on Sirk* (London: Cinema One, 1971).
11. 'Note on the Mystic Writing Pad', by Sigmund Freud in *Collected Papers*, vol. 5 (Hogarth Press, l950).
12. Roland Barthes, *Le Plaisir du texte* (Paris: Editions du Seuil, 1973).

Phase II. Critiques of Phase I Theories: New Methods

Introductory Notes

Phase II essays were selected with a view first to providing a representative sampling of the varied critiques of post-structuralist feminist theory that quickly became accepted by many in the field; and second, of introducing examples of new foci and new methods that developed from Phase I contributions. Citations for additional critiques, and recent work that remedies important gaps in Phase I contributions (some of which are mentioned below), may be found in the 'Further Reading' for this section.

Some of the essays in Phase I already challenged what I have called the double-bind of feminism and film, partly produced through post-structuralist theories. But the first three essays here are linked in specifically questioning central tenets in Laura Mulvey's 'Visual Pleasure and Narrative Cinema' article. De Lauretis's essay, meanwhile, loops back to Phase I selections in dealing with an influential avant-garde director, Yvonne Rainer, and also in returning to the essentialism-anti-essentialism problematic that Mary Ann Doane commented on in her 'Women's Stake' intervention. I selected Steve Neale's essay on 'Masculinity as Spectacle' because it continues Kaja Silverman's interest in male subjectivity, and introduces questions of males looking at men, while Miriam Hansen takes up issues of woman's gaze at a male object of desire as well as many other important theoretical issues. I could not, in the end, reprint Christine Geraghty's and Christine Gledhill's very recent work on women looking at men, but students are urged to explore that research, collected in a volume edited by Pat Kirkham and Janet Thumin (see discussion of Geraghty below). Meanwhile, Gaylyn Studlar introduces some of Deleuze's ideas into a field largely dominated by Freudian and Lacanian psychoanalytic models, and Joan Copjec critiques theories of the male gaze.

I start with Judith Mayne's 'Lesbian Looks: Dorothy Arzner and Female Authorship', which picks up where Phase I ended—namely, with the question of women film directors, and specifically, Dorothy Arzner, only now Mayne interrogates feminist film theory's strange neglect of Arzner's seemingly obvious lesbianism. (Readers may want to pursue other lesbian approaches in film studies in Teresa de Lauretis's and Pratibha Parmar's essays in Phase III, and Jackie Stacey's in Phase IV, or explore essays by Caroline Sheldon or Lucy Arbuthnot and Gail Seneca listed in 'Further Reading' for Phase I or that by Patricia White in the reading for Phase II.)

I continue with D. N. Rodowick's reworking of his influential 1982 intervention in Mulvey's Freudian-based theories of the three looks in the cinema and of woman as object of the male gaze. Mulvey's method, like many that followed, was to hypothesize a link between certain Freudian theories of sexual difference which privileged the male order and the way women are represented in Hollywood film. Implicitly, in theorizing the place (i.e absent) of the woman spectator in the system she outlines, Mulvey is relying on her own experience of spectatorship. Rodowick's critique takes Mulvey's essay on its own terms, but exposes its tensions and uncertainties instead of, as so often, taking the argument for granted. His strategy is first to provide a careful analysis and summary of Mulvey's essay, focusing on her reading of specific Freud and Lacan texts relevant to her critique of Hollywood's female images; and then to show where he disagrees. Rodowick aims neither to sustain nor subvert Mulvey's thesis, but to expose its assumptions and the series of binary oppositions it involves. A main objection is Mulvey's not attending to Freud's own complex remarks about the contradictoriness of desire that 'problematizes any strict binary distinction between "maleness/femaleness" and activity/passivity' (p. 192). Rodowick illuminates the ultimately political end of the essay which is based on the structured oppositions of the counter-cinema argument so as to build a theory of identification and distanciation to 'free the look of the camera'. Rodowick argues, however, that this binary logic of the counter-cinema argument still only offers woman a negative place.

Instead of critiquing from within Mulvey's methodology, Gaylyn Studlar rather substitutes Mulvey's Freudian framework and her focus on sadism in film narrative with Gilles Deleuze's study of Sacher-Masoch's novels. Methodologically, then, this essay follows a similar strategy to Mulvey, if differing in the psychoanalytic theory applied to film. In arguing that masochism can also ground narrative, Studlar replaces Oedipal sadism, which Mulvey argued rendered woman object of sadistic voyeurism, with pre-Oedipal pleasure in a symbiotic bond with the mother. For Studlar, following Deleuze, the goal of masochism for the male child is an impossible desire for pre-Oedipal reunion with the mother. Studlar argues that the advantage of the masochistic aesthetic is that it avoids the Freudian model's emphasis on 'the phallic phase and the pleasure of control or mastery . . . that have proven to be a dead end for feminist-psychoanalytic theory' (p. 206). She argues that masochism is 'a "subversive" desire that affirms the compelling power of the pre-Oedipal mother . . . ' (p. 210). Studlar claims that the masochistic aesthetic opens up a wide range of spectatorial pleasures 'divorced from castration, sexual difference, and female lack' (p. 211). These include pleasures in submission for both sexes, which is neglected in Freudian film theory. Studlar exemplifies her thesis through analysis of Von Sternberg's films.

Steve Neale's 'Masculinity as Spectacle' was one of a series of articles around the early 1980s seeking to investigate the male erotic gaze as yet another 'correction' to Mulvey's article. Neale's method remains textual but relies less on questioning points in Freudian theory than in building on arguments by other scholars in order to develop questions about heterosexuality and male eroticism, and to introduce new lines of thought. Neale begins by noting Mulvey's focus on the look of the woman at the erotic hero in cinema; and that of theorists like Richard Dyer on the gay spectator's interest in male heroes as well as on subversive homosexual sub-texts to Hollywood films. Neale is interested in 'how heterosexual masculinity is inscribed and the mechanisms, pressures and contradictions that inscription may involve' (p. 254). Picking up on a point in D. N. Rodowick's critique of Mulvey, Neale notes that for neither male nor female spectator can there be a simple and unproblematic identification with the 'ideal ego' on the screen. The narcissistic male image—the aggressive, sadistic, and powerful image the spectator ideally would like to become—has to be accompanied by masochism because the spectator is aware of the gap between who he is and the idealized hero. Also involved, as Paul Willemen has pointed out, is the disavowal of the eroticism of the hero's body in a heterosexual society. The core of Neale's essay is his discussion of scenes in which male bodies are on display, as in Westerns and epics like *Spartacus*, but in which explicit eroticism is displaced. He compares this to the feminization of a figure Rock Hudson plays in Sirk's melodramas as also of heroes in the musical. Neale concludes that while there are instances of similar mechanisms for males to those Mulvey found for the female spectator—that is, identification, voyeurism and fetishism—these mechanisms work so as to disavow the underlying eroticism. This of course is to prevent mainstream cinema from having to 'openly come to terms with the male homosexuality it so assiduously seeks either to denigrate or deny' (p. 263).

Miriam Hansen's 1986 essay on Valentino nicely re-visits earlier arguments and provides a bridge between critiques of Mulvey like those of Rodowick and Studlar focusing on psychoanalytic theories and models, and that of Steve Neale noting the lack of attention to the male figure as object of the erotic look in Mulvey's theory. However, important in Hansen's method is her inclusion of textual readings of films and other feminist film theorists' study of Valentino as star within a particular historical moment—the 1920s—and within a certain stage of cinema's institutional base.

Readers might turn to Phase IV essays prior to, or along with, reading Hansen's article since I reprint there essays on melodrama and spectatorship which Hansen builds on here. Important and original in Hansen's essay is her focus on Valentino and the question of female spectatorial pleasure in the image of a male hero/performer. Acknowledging feminist worries that role reversal 'allows women the appropriation of the gaze only to confirm the patriarchal logic of vision' (p. 231), Hansen goes on to argue for 'the textual difference of a male erotic object as a figure of over determination, an unstable composite figure that . . . calls into question the very idea of polarity rather than simply reversing its terms.' Like Rodowick, Hansen believes that there is more radical potential in the dialectical notions of regression and subjectivity in Freud than in Lacan. She also worries about the dangers in the feminist binary of counter-cinema and patriarchal classical film because the strategy of counter-cinema too often elides the question of the erotic. After an examination of several scenes in Valentino films so as to explicate the kinds of erotic gaze between hero and heroine, Hansen concludes that the Valentino fantasy does beckon the female spectator into the regressive terrain of polymorphous perversity, and beyond Mulvey's 'devil of phallic identification' (p. 241).

As the term 'polymorphous perversity' implies, however, Hansen does not follow Studlar in setting up Deleuze's masochistic aesthetic in place of Freudian theory. Rather, Hansen emphasizes the complexity of Freud's ideas, which include a pre-Oedipal bisexuality. The problem with Deleuze's masochistic thesis, Hansen argues, is its being basically a male fantasy, while she is interested in dealing with female spectatorial pleasures. Valentino films, however problematically, free women from Victorian double standards, and 'articulate a desire outside of motherhood and family' (p. 242).

I was unable to reprint Christine Geraghty's article from Pat Kirkham and Janet Thumin's British volume *Me Jane: Masculinity, Movies and Women* but I refer readers to this essay (and indeed the entire volume) first because it continues feminist work on masculinity begun by Richard Dyer, Neale, and others noted above as a new focus in the early 1980s, and because, in contrast to both Neale and Hansen, Geraghty uses a sociological rather than psychoanalytic analysis of the male hero. She makes her argument through textual study of a single text—a British film, *Saturday Night and Sunday Morning*—which usefully brings in focus so-called 'Angry Young Man' British movies only too infrequently studied in cinema research. Continuing the pioneering work of Richard Dyer in his 1980 volume, *Stars*, Geraghty is interested in the dual image of Albert Finney as the character Arthur Seaton and as the 'pin-up' actor, Finney. Geraghty takes the four 'sites' noted by the editors of *Me Jane*—that is, '"the body, action, the external world and the internal world"',—as a schema through which to 'show how the figure of Finney/Seaton, a composite created out of the star persona and the fictional character, is mapped across these sites'. Geraghty points out the contradictions that emerge from looking at Finney/Seaton in these four sites: while the star's image dominates the screen, and the character aggressively asserts his superiority to his class and community, by the end of the film he is brought to join the group he so despises and to be trapped into an unpromising married life. Geraghty concludes that this indicates 'a social problem being brought to the audience's attention by a realist film'. Yet, paradoxically, 'the image and soundtrack . . . still insist that Finney/Seaton has remained the same'.[1]

In her 'Strategies of Coherence' intervention, de Lauretis brings to bear her knowledge of semiotics, structuralism, and poetics, as well as of the (short) history of feminist film theorizing and practices (nearly 20 years old as she writes in 1987), on the question of the Oedipality of narrative and therefore of what woman's relationship to narrative should be. De Lauretis's method differs from prior ones in bringing these questions up in connection with a prominent independent woman film-maker Yvonne Rainer, and her films. De Lauretis's project loops back to that of Judith Mayne included in this section, and on to those of Jackie Stacey, Mary Ann Doane, and Annette Kuhn in Phase IV, in making prominent the female spectator's position in the cinema. Jacqueline Bobo's work (discussed in the 'Notes' to Phase IV) marks another important intervention.

De Lauretis's project differs in being concerned with the spectator of avant-garde rather than of commercial cinema. Her contribution to debates about essentialism and anti-essentialism may be seen in her call for 'feminist cinema' as 'a process of reinterpretation and retextualization of cultural images and narratives whose strategies of coherence engage the spectator's identification through narrative and visual pleasure and yet succeed in drawing "the Real" into the film's texture' (p. 277). In the course of doing this, de Lauretis usefully summarizes how feminist film theory (including Mulvey's work, as well as texts by Stephen Heath and Christian Metz listed in 'Further Reading' to Phase I) came to opt for a critique of representation and psychoanalysis with their attendant epistemological assumptions. Drawing on theorists of poetics, semiotics, and narrative (such as Umberto Eco and Charles Peirce), de Lauretis critiques the focus on the structure of narrative in favour of narrativity—'a dynamic, processual view of signification as a working of the codes, a production of meaning which involves a subject in a social field' (p. 277). Both documenting women's lives, on the one hand, and anti-narrative avant-garde independent film-making on the other, each continued in their own spheres, but De Lauretis sees Yvonne Rainer's interesting return to narrative of a sort in *The Man Who Envied Women* as breaking the divide between realist imaging of woman, and anti-narrative strategies that highlight woman's absence in mainstream discourse.

Although I was ultimately unable to include the opening chapter of Lola Young's recent volume, *Fear of the Dark*, let me refer readers to her important critique of Phase I feminist methods while building on them in interesting ways. Young's method avoids overly simplistic sociological analysis of images and purely textual, abstract-theoretical readings. She rather argues that 'a cinematic text cannot be attributed exclusively to those directly involved in its production but should be analyzed as part of a complex web of interrelated experiences, ideas, fantasies and unconscious expressions of desire, anxiety and fear that need to be located in their historical, political and social contexts'. In chapter 1, Young notes that much of the critical writing by black women about gender, race, and sexuality has largely addressed sociological issues rather than film and cultural productions. It is this gap which Young addresses in her book. Noting the importance of Mulvey's 'Visual Pleasure' article despite its not taking up race as an issue, Young finds useful the notion of castration anxiety as explaining partially the absence of black women on the screen. But she critiques Mulvey for omitting a historical perspective and for not differentiating between women in her theory of the male gaze. The implicit assumption in Mulvey's, as in much academic as well as common sense discourse, 'is that white experiences are representative of human experiences'. Young moves from there to note the inadequacy of writing about blacks in North American film in the UK (it mainly remains tied to journalism and to notions of negative images) and then provides interesting critiques of some (mainly white) North American scholars' addressing of race in feminist film theory (readers might move to 'Phase III. Race, Sexuality, and Postmodernism' for Young's co-authored essay on race and psychoanalysis). Significantly, given many black scholars' rejection of psychoanalysis, Young is interested in what psychoanalysis might have to offer in regard to understanding race and racial conflict. She revisits Freudian theories, including Joel Kovel's, Homi Bhabha's, and Frantz Fanon's reworking of Freudian ideas. While Young critiques the male bias in these writer's views, she argues that 'the questions that Fanon posed have direct relevance to the way in which racial positions are conceptualized in British society today'. Young concludes by illuminating ways in which psychoanalysis can aid in conceptualizing difference and otherness: she shows that both individual, institutional, and state racisms, as well as those deployed in science and in racial myths, emerge 'from the cycle of repression and projection'. In order to make sense of stereotypes of black femininity and masculinity, Young argues that a scholar has to 'examine historical instances of the process of racialization of discourses on "woman" and "man" and the complex interaction between these axes'.[2]

Let me mention another essay I was unable to include, namely Deborah Thomas's 'Psychoanalysis and Film Noir', which is useful first, for its opening summary of varying methodological possibilities in film studies; second because it addresses the usefulness and potential pitfalls of psychoanalysis to cinema analysis; and finally, because Thomas explores the problem of the male hero in a film genre that feminists have largely studied for meanings of the *femme fatale.* Thomas interestingly 'tries out' what a study of the *film noir* hero would look like if she deployed a Deleuzian instead of the more usual Freudian model of psychoanalysis in exploring the films. She proposes to adopt the hypothesis that 'the unconscious is not a seething Freudian cauldron but, rather, the home of positive flowings and desirings which the social world seeks to bind and contain'. She asks: 'Does *film noir's* representations of desire cede any space to such free-floating desiring . . . '. Interestingly, Thomas's following close look at several *noir* films focuses on the dialogue, not on images. She is concerned with how the heroes see themselves, what qualities they attribute to themselves in speech, rather than on how meaning is produced through other cinematic techniques usually focused on, such as editing, camera angles, lighting, mise-en-scène, etc. This in itself suggests a new kind of method in film study.[3]

I conclude with a selection from Joan Copjec's *Read My Desire.* Copjec critiques film theory (and especially feminist film scholars' use of film theory) for its formulations of both the cinematic apparatus and of the gaze. Copjec examines the underlying Foucauldian concept of knowledge as ultimate and determining power, and then sets it against the Lacanian view. In the latter, 'that which is produced by a signifying system can never be determinate,' says Copjec, 'for no position defines a resolute identity.' Copjec worries about the apparent Foucauldization of Lacanian theory, without the radical theoretical differences being confronted. Such a confrontation is the aim of Copjec's essay. After moving through a brief account of how film theory arrived at its conception of the gaze (for example, by replacing Gaston Bachelard by Louis Althusser), she shows how the panoptic apparatus is the opposite of psychoanalysis. If the apparatus marks the subject's visibility, Lacan's theory shows how the apparatus splits the subject. In the course of her careful and complex argument, involving close reading of Lacan's Seminar X1, Copjec refutes a common claim that for Lacan, language splits the subject from objects and positions them in a realm of signifiers. Rather, she argues that for Lacan there are only signifiers. Yet the belief in referents beyond language paradoxically founds the subject as a desiring subject. Against the 'stable subject of film theory', we have instead a subject founded on an absence that anchors it.

Notes

1. Christine Geraghty, 'Albert Finney: A Working-Class Hero', in Pat Kirkham and Janet Thumin (eds.), *Me Jane: Masculinity, Movies and Women* (London: Lawrence and Wishart, 1995), 62, 69, 71.
2. Lola Young, *Fear of the Dark: 'Race', Gender and Sexuality in Cinema* (London and New York: Routledge, 1995), 17, 26, 29, 36, 174.
3. Deborah Thomas, 'Psychoanalysis and Film Noir', in Ian Cameron (ed.), *The Book of Film Noir* (New York: Continuum, 1990), 74.

9 Lesbian Looks

Dorothy Arzner and Female Authorship

Judith Mayne*

Some cinematic images have proven to be irresistibly seductive as far as lesbian readings are concerned: Greta Garbo kissing her lady-in-waiting in *Queen Christina* (1933), Marlene Dietrich in drag kissing a female member of her audience in *Morocco* (1930), Katharine Hepburn in male attire being seduced by a woman in *Sylvia Scarlett* (1935)—all these images have been cited and reproduced so frequently in the context of gay and lesbian culture that they have almost acquired lives of their own. By lives of their own, I am referring not only to their visibility, but also to how lesbian readings of them require a convenient forgetfulness or bracketing of what happens to these images, plot and narrative-wise, in the films in which they appear, where heterosexual symmetry is usually restored with a vengeance. Depending upon your point of view, lesbian readings of isolated scenes are successful appropriations and subversions of Hollywood plots, or naive fetishizations of the image. Put another way, there is a striking division between the spectacular lesbian uses to which single, isolated images may be applied and the narratives of classical Hollywood films, which seem to deaden any such possibilities.

Feminist film theory, as it has developed in the last fifteen years, has scorned the subversive potential of such appropriations. Although the narrative of feminist film theory does not exactly follow the plot of a classical Hollywood film, the writings of feminist film theorists have affirmed, in a rather amazingly mimetic fashion, that the Hollywood apparatus is absolute, the codes and conventions of Hollywood narrative only flexible enough to make the conquest of the woman and the affirmation of the heterosexual contract that much more inevitable. In

* Judith Mayne, 'Dorothy Arzner and Lesbian Looks' from *How Do I Look? Queer Film and Video* edited by Bad Object-Choices (Bay Press, 1991), reprinted by permission of the author.

countering 'spectacular' lesbian uses with 'narratives'—those of Hollywood or of feminist film theory—I am, of course, evoking what has become the standard feminist account of the classical Hollywood cinema, where the spectacle of the male gaze and its female object and the narrative of agency and resolution make for a perfect symmetrical fit, with heterosexual authority affirmed.

Although much may be said about the relation between feminism, Hollywood plots, and lesbian images, my purpose here is to explore another cinematic image with unmistakable lesbian contours, one which has attained—at least in feminist film theory and criticism—the kind of visibility more commonly and typically associated with the female star. Dorothy Arzner was one of the few women to have been a successful director in Hollywood, with a career that extended from the late 1920s to the early 1940s. Arzner was one of the early 'rediscoveries' of feminist film theory in the 1970s, and that rediscovery remains the most significant and influential attempt to theorize female authorship in the cinema. As one of the very few women directors who were successful in Hollywood, particularly during the studio years, Arzner has served as an important example of a woman director working within the Hollywood system who managed, in however limited ways, to make films that disturb the conventions of Hollywood narrative.

A division characterizes the way Arzner has been represented in feminist film studies, a division analogous to the tension between the lesbian reading of Dietrich, Garbo, and Hepburn and the textual workings of the films that, if they do not deny the validity of such a reading, at least problematize it. For there is, on the one hand, a textual Arzner, one whose films—as the by-now classic feminist account developed by Claire Johnston would have it—focus on female desire as an ironic inflection of the patriarchal norms of the cinema. On the other hand, there is a very visible Arzner, an image that speaks a kind of desire and suggests a kind of reading that is quite notably absent in discussions of Arzner's films.

Noting that structural coherence in Arzner's films comes from the discourse of the woman, Claire Johnston—whose reading of Arzner has defined the terms of subsequent discussions of her work—relies on the notion of defamiliarization, derived from the Russian formalists' *priem ostrananie*, the device of making strange, to assess the effects of the woman's discourse on patriarchal meaning: 'the work of the woman's discourse renders the narrative strange, subverting and dislocating it at the level of meaning.'[1] In this context Johnston discusses what has become the single most famous scene from Arzner's films, the scene in which Judy (Maureen O'Hara), who has played ballet stooge to the vaudeville performer Bubbles (Lucille Ball) in *Dance, Girl, Dance* (1940), confronts her audience and tells them how *she* sees *them.* This is, Johnston argues, the only real break between dominant discourse and the discourse of the woman in Arzner's work. The moment in *Dance, Girl, Dance* when Judy faces her audience is a privileged moment in feminist film theory and criticism, foregrounding as it does the sexual hierarchy of the gaze, with female agency defined as the return of the male look, problematizing the objectification of woman.[2] The celebrity accorded this particular scene in Arzner's film needs to be seen in the context of feminist film theory in the mid-1970s. Confronted with the persuasive psychoanalytically-based theoretical model according to which women either did not or could not exist on screen, the discovery of Arzner; and especially of Judy's 'return of the gaze', offered some glimmer of historical hope as to the possibility of a female intervention in the cinema. To be sure, the scope of the intervention is limited, for as Johnston herself stresses, Judy's radical act is quickly recuperated within the film when the audience gets up to cheer her on and she and Bubbles begin to fight on stage to the delight of the audience.

Other readings of Arzner's films develop, in different ways, the ambivalence of the female intervention evoked in Johnston's analysis. In responses to Arzner's work, one can read reflections of larger assumptions concerning the Hollywood cinema as an apparatus. At one extreme is Andrew Britton's assessment of Arzner (in his study of Katharine Hepburn) as the unproblematized *auteur* of *Christopher Strong* (1933), the film in which Hepburn appears as an aviatrix who falls in love with an older, married man. That *Christopher Strong* functions as a 'critique of the effect of patriarchal heterosexual relations on relations between women' suggests that the classical cinema lends itself quite readily to a critique of patriarchy, whether as the effect of the woman director or the female star.[3] At the opposite extreme, Jacquelyn Suter's analysis of *Christopher Strong* proceeds from the assumption that whatever 'female discourse' there is in the film is subsumed and neutralized by the patriarchal discourse on monogamy.[4] If the classical cinema described by Britton seems remarkably open to effects of subversion and criticism, the classical cinema described by Suter is just as remarkably closed to any meanings but patriarchal ones; one is left to assume that female authorship, as far as Hollywood cinema is concerned, is either an unproblematic affirmation of agency or virtually an impossibility. That Britton is the only openly gay critic among those I've mentioned thus far suggests, of course, a familiar desire to assert the possibility of lesbian authorship, to identify the conventions of Hollywood cinema as less absolutely consonant with heterosexual and patriarchal desire than other critics have suggested.

Interestingly, however, the appearance of Arzner within the context of lesbian and gay studies is quite literally that—a persona, an image quite obviously readable in lesbian terms. In Vito Russo's *The Celluloid Closet*, a striking photograph of Arzner and her good friend Joan Crawford appears in the text, along with a brief mention by another director concerning Arzner's lesbianism and her closeted status, but none of her films are cited: even by the measure of implicit gay content, Arzner's films seem to offer little.[5] This photograph is adapted in the images included in Tee Corinne's *Women Who Loved Women*, and Corinne's description of Arzner emphasizes again an isolated image that is readable in lesbian terms only when placed within Corinne's narrative sequence: 'Quiet closeted women,' she writes, 'like film director Dorothy Arzner worked in Hollywood near flamboyant and equally closeted bisexuals like Garbo and Dietrich.'[6]

The textual practice that has been central to a feminist theory of female authorship disappears when Arzner is discussed in the context of lesbian and gay culture, suggesting a tension between Arzner as a lesbian image and Arzner as a female signature to a text. This tension is addressed explicitly in the introduction to the *Jump Cut* special section on lesbians and film that appeared in 1981. The editors of the special section note that Arzner's 'style of dress and attention to independent women characters in her films has prompted the search for a lesbian subtext in her work—despite the careful absence of any statements by Arzner herself that could encourage such an undertaking.'[7] It is curious that Arzner's dress is not readable as such a 'statement'; and the term *subtext* seems curiously anachronistic at a time in film criticism when so much attention was being paid to the apparently insignificant detail through which an entire film could be read deconstructively or at least against the grain. Yet the awkwardness of the term suggests the difficulty of not only reconciling but also accounting for any connection between Arzner's image and her films. Despite the supposed absence of lesbian 'subtexts' in Arzner's films, Arzner looms large as an object of visual fascination in the *Jump Cut* text.

It is not only in gay and lesbian studies, however, that Arzner's persona acquires a signifying function seemingly at odds with her film practice. Even though what I've said thus far suggests a gap between

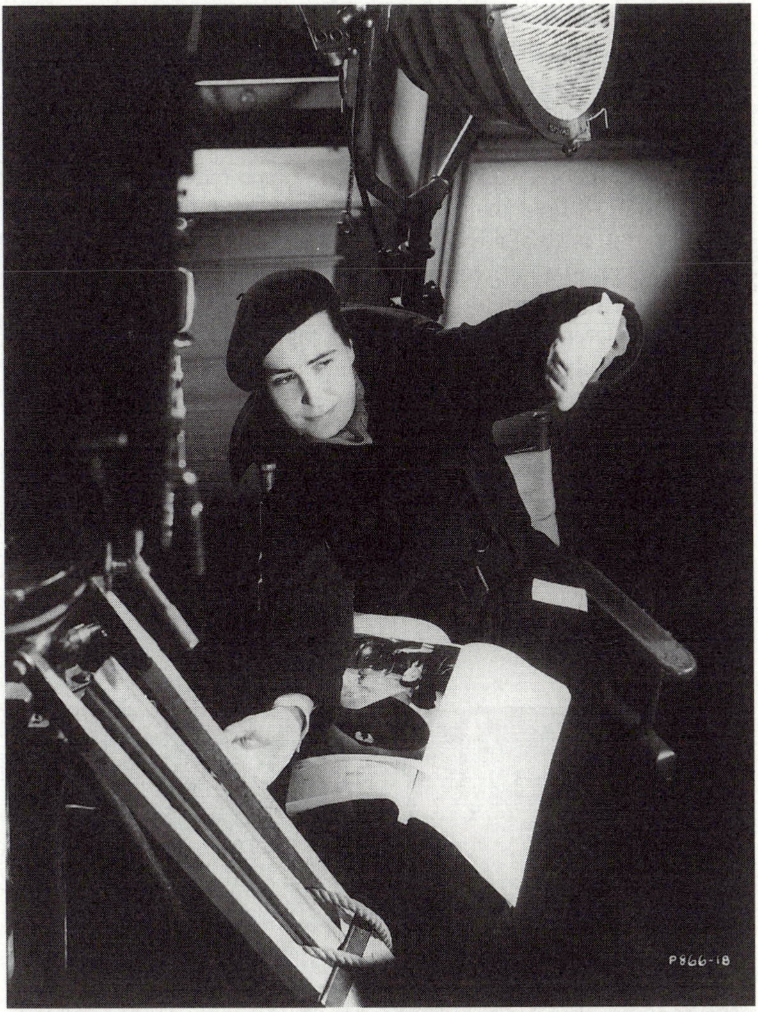

feminist readings of Arzner's films and lesbian and gay readings of her image, Arzner has proven to be a compelling image for feminist film theory and criticism. Although Arzner favored a look and a style that quite clearly connotes lesbian identity, discussions of her work always seem to stop short of any concrete recognition that sexual preference might have something to do with how her films function, particularly concerning the 'discourse of the woman' and female communities, or that the contours of female authorship in her films might be defined in lesbian terms. This marginalization is all the more striking, given how remarkably *visible* Arzner has been as an image in feminist film theory. That Arzner's image and appearance would find a responsive audience in gay and lesbian culture makes obvious sense. But in a field like feminist film theory, which has resolutely bracketed any discussion of lesbianism or of the female homoerotic, such visibility seems curious indeed, and in need of a reading. With the possible exception of Maya Deren, Arzner is more frequently represented visually than any other woman director central to contemporary feminist discussions of film. And unlike Deren, who appeared extensively in her own films, Arzner does not have the reputation of being a particularly self-promoting, visible, or *out* (in several senses of the term) woman director.

Not only has Arzner been consistently present as an image in feminist film studies, but two tropes are obsessively present in images of her as well—tropes that have been equally obsessive points of departure and return in feminist film theory. She is portrayed against the backdrop of the large-scale apparatus of the Hollywood cinema, or she is shown with other women, usually actresses, most of whom are emphatically

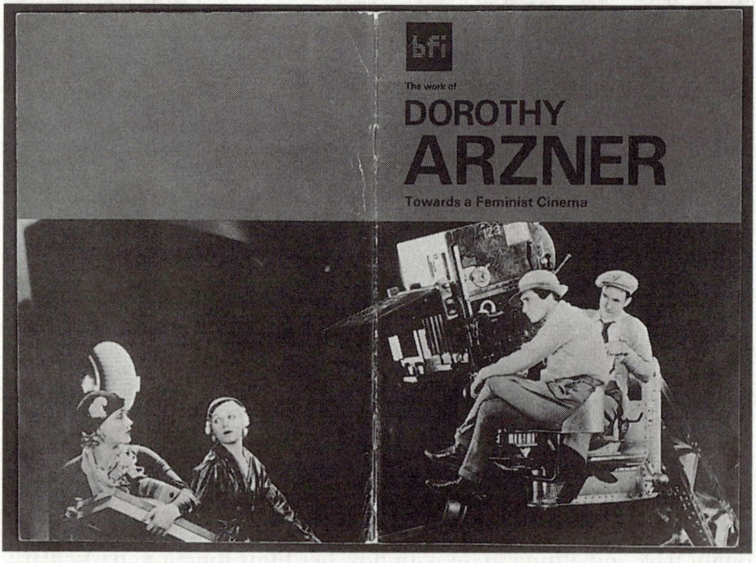

Cover of *The Work of Dorothy Arzner*, 1975.

'feminine', creating a striking contrast indeed. Both of these tropes appear in the photograph on the cover of the British Film Institute (BFI) collection edited by Claire Johnston, *The Work of Dorothy Arzner: Towards a Feminist Cinema.* On the front, we see Arzner in profile, slouching directorially in a perch next to a very large camera; seated next to her is a man. They both look toward what initially appears to be the unidentified field of vision. When the cover is laid out flat, however, we see that the photograph 'continues' on the back: two young women, one holding packages, look at each other, their positions reflecting symmetrically those of Arzner and her male companion.

It is difficult to read precisely the tenor of the scene (from *Working Girls*, 1930) between the two women: some hostility perhaps, or desperation. The camera occupies the center of the photograph, as a large, looming—and predictably phallic—presence. The look on the man's face strongly suggests the clichés of the male gaze that have been central to feminist film theory: from his perspective the two women exist as objects of voyeuristic pleasure. Arzner's look has quite another function, however, one that has received very little critical attention, and that is to decenter the man's look and eroticize the exchange of looks between the two women.[8] Although virtually none of the feminist critics who analyze Arzner's work have discussed her lesbianism or her lesbian persona, a curious syndrome is suggested by this use of 'accompanying illustration'. The photograph on the cover of the pamphlet edited by Claire Johnston teases out another scene of cinematic desire, complete with the devices of delay, framing, and even a version of shot/countershot more properly associated with the articulation of heterosexual desire in the classical narrative cinema.

Conversely, the representation of Arzner with the camera and with more 'feminine' women can be read in relation to one of the most striking preoccupations of feminist film theory, that of the preferred notion of sexual difference, which has consistently displaced marginal desires from the center stage of heterosexual symmetry. Whether blending into a background of the cumbersome and quite literal cinematic apparatus or gazing longingly at another woman, whether assuming the phallic machinery of the classical cinema or the position of spectatorial desire, Arzner's image oscillates between a heterosexual contract assumed by feminist theorists to be absolute, on the one hand, and another scene, another configuration of desire, on the other. Arzner's persona has acquired a rather amazing flexibility as well, if not always with the same teasing play of front and back cover evident in the BFI pamphlet. One of the early, 'classic' anthologies of feminist film theory and criticism (Karyn Kay and Gerald Peary's *Women and the Cinema: A Critical Anthology*, New York: E. P. Dutton, 1977), for instance, features Arzner on its cover along with three other women, all of them well-known actresses, in a rectangle of shifting opposing poles: the good girl (Bardot in wedding dress)/bad girl (Jane Fonda as prostitute in *Klute*) dichotomy characteristic of an 'images of women' approach to film analysis and a classically feminine (Bardot and Fonda) demeanor as opposed to a more androgynous one (Arzner and Dietrich). In a recent collection of essays on feminist film theory, not one of the several reprinted essays on Arzner discusses erotic connections between women. Yet on the cover of the book is a photograph of Arzner and Rosalind Russell exchanging a meaningful look with more than a hint of lesbian desire—enough, certainly, to provide images for the flyer advertising the 'How Do I Look?' conference.

One begins to suspect that the simultaneous evocation and dispelling of an erotic bond between women in Arzner's work is a structuring absence in feminist film theory. Arzner's lesbianism may not be theorized in relation to her films, but her remarkable visibility

Rosalind Russell and Dorothy Arzner on the set of Arzner's *Craig's Wife*, 1936.

in feminist film criticism suggests that feminists replicate the very fetishism they have identified as being 'criticized' in Arzner's films. To be sure, any parallel between a classical, male-centered trajectory like fetishism and the dynamics of feminist theory can only be made tentatively.[9] But there is nonetheless a striking fit between Octave Mannoni's formula for disavowal ('I know very well, but all the same . . . '), adapted by Christian Metz to analyze cinematic fetishism, and the consistent and simultaneous evocation and disavowal of Arzner's lesbian persona.[10] The evidence of lesbianism notwithstanding, feminist critics would speak, rather, through a heterosexual master code, where any and all combinations of 'masculinity', from the male gaze to Arzner's clothing, and 'femininity', from conventional objectification of the female body to the female objects of Arzner's gaze, result in a narrative and visual structure indistinguishable from the dominant Hollywood model. To be sure, Arzner's work is praised for its 'critique' of the Hollywood system, but the critique is so limited that it only affirms the dominance of the object in question.

Some feminist work on Arzner does acknowledge her supposed 'mannish' appearance, and one of the preferred phrases for avoiding any mention of lesbianism—'female bonding'—is fairly common in writing on Arzner. However, the two separate but interconnected questions I am raising here—whether there is any fit to be made between the persona and the films, and why feminist film theorists are so drawn to the dykey image yet so reluctant to utter the word *lesbian*—have not been widely addressed. To my knowledge, the only feminist critic to suggest that Arzner's films cite the persona, and are therefore informed by lesbian desire, is Sarah Halprin. Halprin suggests, fairly generously, that the reason for the omission of any discussion of Arzner's obvious lesbian looks in relation to her films is, in part, the suspicion of any kind of biographical information in analysis of female authorship; and she suggests that a reading of marginal characters in Arzner's films, who resemble Arzner herself, might offer, as she puts it, a 'whole new way of relating' to Arzner's work.[11] As with the term *subtext* mentioned earlier, in relation to the *Jump Cut* essay, there is an acknowledgment here that the wish to read Arzner's films through Arzner's appearance may resurrect a traditional form of auteurism, a form of biographical criticism that would seem to be hopelessly naive in an era of poststructuralist suspicion of any equations between the maker and the text. But the Arzner persona as it circulates in feminist film studies does not seem to me to be a simple case of the 'real woman' versus the 'text', since those illustrations of

Arzner have themselves become so thoroughly a part of the web of both feminist film theory and Arzner's work. More strikingly, the 'illustrations' of Arzner in the company of a female star echo uncannily in the stills from her films that illustrate the discussions of textual practice—like Billie Burke and Rosalind Russell in *Craig's Wife* (1936)

Maureen O'Hara and Maria Ouspenskaya in Dorothy Arzner's *Dance, Girl, Dance*, 1940.

(with Russell now assuming the more Arzneresque position), or Madame Basilova and Judy in *Dance, Girl, Dance*.

Take Madame Basilova, for example. What has been read, in *Dance, Girl, Dance*, as the woman's return of a male gaze she does not possess might be read differently as one part of a process of the exchange of looks between women that begins within the female dance troupe managed by Basilova. Judy's famous scolding of the audience is identified primarily as a communication, not between a female performer and a male audience (the audience is not, in any case, exclusively male) but between the performer and the female member of the audience (secretary to Steven Adams, the man who will eventually become Judy's love interest) who stands up to applaud her.[12] And the catfight that erupts between Judy and Bubbles on stage seems to me less a recuperative move—transforming the potential threat of Judy's confrontation into an even more tantalizing spectacle—than the claiming by the two women of the stage as an extension of their conflicted friendship, not an alienated site of performance. The stage is, in other words, *both* the site of the objectification of the female body *and* the site for the theatricalizing of female friendship.

This 'both/and'—the stage (and by metaphoric implication, the cinema itself) simultaneously serving as an arena of patriarchal exploitation and of female self-representation—contrasts with the more limited view of Arzner's films in Johnston's work, where more of a 'neither/nor' logic is operative—neither patriarchal discourse nor the 'discourse of the woman' allows women a vantage point from which to speak, represent, or imagine themselves. Reading Arzner's films in terms of the 'both/and' suggests an irony more far-reaching than that described by Johnston. Johnston's reading of Arzner is suggestive of Shoshana Felman's definition of irony as 'dragging authority as such into a scene which it cannot master; of which it is not aware and which, for that very reason, is the scene of its own self-destruction. . . .'[13] But the irony in *Dance, Girl, Dance* does not just demonstrate how the patriarchal discourse of the cinema excludes women, but rather how the cinema functions in two radically different ways, both of which are 'true', as it were, and totally incompatible. I am borrowing here from Donna Haraway's definition of irony: 'Irony is about contradictions that do not resolve into larger wholes, even dialectically, about the tension of holding incompatible things together because both or all are necessary and true.'[14] This insistence on two equally compelling and incompatible truths constitutes a form of irony far more complex than Johnston's analysis of defamiliarization.

Johnston's notion of Arzner's irony assumes a patriarchal form of representation that may have its gaps and its weak links, but which remains dominant in every sense of the word. For Johnston, Arzner's irony can only be the irony of negativity puncturing holes in patriarchal assumptions. Such a view of irony has less to do, I would argue, with the limitations of Arzner's career (for example, as a woman director working within the inevitable limitations of the Hollywood system) than with the limitations of the film theory from which it grows. If the cinema is understood as a one-dimensional system of male subjects and female objects, then it is not difficult to understand how the irony in Arzner's films is limited, or at least would be *read* as limited. Although rigid hierarchies of sexual difference are indeed characteristic of dominant cinema, they are not absolute, and Arzner's films represent other kinds of cinematic pleasure and desire.

An assessment of Arzner's importance within the framework of female authorship needs to account not only for how Arzner problematizes the pleasures of the cinematic institution as we understand it—for example, in terms of voyeurism and fetishism reenacted through the power of the male gaze and the objectification of the female body—but also for how, in her films, those pleasures are identified in ways that are not reducible to the theoretical clichés of the omnipotence of the male gaze. The irony of *Dance, Girl, Dance* emerges from the conflicting demands of performance and self-expression, which are linked, in turn, to heterosexual romance and female friendship. Female friendship acquires a resistant function in the way that it exerts a pressure against the supposed 'natural' laws of heterosexual romance. Relations between women and communities of women have a privileged status in Arzner's films. To be sure, Arzner's films offer plots—particularly insofar as resolutions are concerned—compatible with the romantic expectations of the classical Hollywood cinema: communities of women may be important, but boy-still-meets-girl. Yet there is also an erotic charge identified within those communities. If heterosexual initiation is central to Arzner's films, it is precisely in its function as rite of passage (rather than natural destiny) that a marginal presence is felt.

Consider, for instance, *Christopher Strong*. Katharine Hepburn first appears in the film as a prize-winning object in a scavenger hunt, for she can claim that she is over twenty-one and has never had a love affair. Christopher Strong, the man with whom she will eventually become involved, is the male version of this prize-winning object, for he has been married for more than five years and has always been faithful to his wife. As Cynthia Darrington, Hepburn dresses in decidedly unfeminine clothing and walks with a swagger that is masculine, or athletic, depending upon your point of view. Hepburn's jodhpurs and boots may well be, as Beverle Houston puts it, 'that upper-class costume for a woman performing men's activities',[15] but this is also clothing that strongly denotes lesbian identity and (to stress again Sarah Halprin's point) that is evocative of the way Arzner herself, and other lesbians of the time, dressed. Cynthia's 'virginity' becomes a euphemistic catch-all for a variety of margins in which she is situated, both as a woman devoted to her career and as a woman without a sexual identity. The process the film traces is, precisely, that of the acquisition of heterosexual identity.

I am not arguing that *Christopher Strong*, like the dream that says one thing but ostensibly 'really' means its mirror opposite, can be decoded as a coherent 'lesbian film' or that the real subject of the film is the tension between gay and straight identities. The critical attitude toward heterosexuality takes the form of inflections—bits and pieces of tone and gesture and emphasis—that result in the conventions of

heterosexual behavior becoming loosened up, shaken free of some of their identifications with the patriarchal status quo. Most important perhaps, the acquisition of heterosexuality becomes the downfall of Cynthia Darrington.

. . .

The female signature in Arzner's work is marked by that irony of equally compelling and incompatible discourses to which I have referred, and the lesbian inflection articulates the division between female communities that can function, although problematically, within a heterosexual universe, and the eruptions of lesbian marginality that do not. This lesbian irony taps differing and competing views of lesbianism within contemporary feminist and lesbian theory—as the most intense form of female and feminist bonding and as distinctly opposed to and other than heterosexuality (whether practiced by women or men). In Arzner's own time, these competing definitions would be read as the conflict between a desexualized nineteenth-century ideal of romantic friendship among women and the 'mannish lesbian' (exemplified by Radclyffe Hall), defined by herself and her critics as a sexual being.[16] Arzner's continued 'visibility' suggests not only that the tension is far from being resolved, but also that debates about lesbian identity inform, even (and especially!) in unconscious ways, the thinking of feminists who do not identify as lesbians.

I am suggesting, of course, that lesbian irony constitutes one of the pleasures in Arzner's films and that irony is a desirable aim in women's cinema. Irony can, however, misfire.[17] It has been argued that in Jackie Raynal's film *Deux fois* (1970), for instance, the ironic elaboration of woman-as-object-of-spectacle is rendered decidedly problematic by the fact that it is only in offering herself as an object of spectacle that the category of woman-as-object-of-spectacle can be criticized; that is, it is only by affirming the validity of patriarchal representation that any critique is possible.[18] I have in mind here another kind of misfiring, when the ironic reading of patriarchal conventions collides with other coded forms of representation that may serve, quite disturbingly, as a support for that irony. In *Dance, Girl, Dance*, for instance, racial stereotypes emerge at three key moments in the narrative of the film. In the opening scenes of the film, at a nightclub in Akron, Ohio, the camera moves over the heads of the members of the audience as it approaches the stage, where the female dance troupe is performing. Intercut is an image of the black members of the band, who are smiling as the proverbially happy musicians. Although an equivalence seems to be established between women and blacks as objects of spectacle, I see little basis for reading this as a critical use of the racial stereotype.

Later in the film, when Judy longingly watches the rehearsal of the ballet company, another racial stereotype emerges. The performance number portrays the encounter between ballet and other forms of dance and body language within the context of the city. At one point in the performance, the music switches suddenly to imitate a jazzy tune, and a white couple in blackface strut across the stage. During one of the concluding scenes of the film, when Judy and Bubbles resolve their friendship in a court of law, the ostensibly amusing conclusion to the scene is provided when the clerk announces the arrival of a black couple whose names are 'Abraham Lincoln Johnson' and 'Martha Washington Johnson'. However disparate these racial stereotypes, they do emerge at crucial moments in the deployment of irony and performance. In each case, the racial stereotype appears when the sexual hierarchy of the look is deflected or otherwise problematized. The black performers at the beginning of the film are defined securely within the parameters of objectification when it is apparent—much to Bubbles's irritation and eventual attendant desire—that Jimmie Harris, one of the spectators in the audience, is totally unengaged in the spectacle on stage. The appearance of the white couple in blackface occurs when the centrality of Judy's desire, as defined by her longing gaze at the performance, is affirmed. In the courtroom scene, Judy aggressively and enthusiastically assumes the court as her stage, and the racial stereotype of 'Mr. and Mrs. Johnson' appears only when the rivalry between the two women is on the verge of resolution.

In each of these instances, the racial stereotype affirms the distinction between white subject and black object just when the distinction between male subject and female object is being put into question. Though there is nothing in *Dance, Girl, Dance* that approximates a sustained discourse on race, these brief allusions to racial stereotypes are eruptions that cannot be dismissed or disregarded as mere background or as unconscious reflections of a dominant cinematic practice that was racist. The marks of authorship in *Dance, Girl, Dance* include these extremely problematic racist clichés as well as the ironic inflection of the heterosexual contract. I want to stress that female irony is not just a function of sexual hierarchy, but that virtually all forms of narrative and visual opposition are potentially significant. To ignore, in Arzner's case, the intertwining of sexual and racial codes of performance is to claim female authorship as a white preserve. The racial stereotypes that serve as an anchor of distinct otherness in *Dance, Girl, Dance* speak to a more general problem in female authorship. Although Arzner's films suggest other forms of cinematic pleasure that have been relatively untheorized within film studies, these forms cannot be posited in any simple way as 'alternatives'. I think it is a mistake to assume that the racist clichés are symptomatic of the compromises that inevitably occur with any attempt to create different visions within the classical Hollywood cinema. Such clichés are possible within virtually any kind of film practice.

Dorothy Arzner has come to represent both a textual practice (consciously) and an image (less consciously) in feminist film theory. The textual practice has been described as if there were no determinations—such as those in *Dance, Girl, Dance* having to do with race—besides those of gender. In other words, Arzner's reception foregrounds the extent to which feminist film theory has disavowed the significance of race, particularly when racist codes contradict or complicate the disruption of gender hierarchies. The relationship between the textual practice and the image suggests an area of fascination, if not love, that dare not speak its (her) name. The preferred term *sexual difference* in feminist film theory slides from the tension between masculinity and femininity into a crude determinism whereby there is no representation without heterosexuality. Lesbianism raises some crucial questions concerning identification and desire in the cinema, questions with particular relevance to female cinematic authorship. Cinema offers simultaneous affirmation and dissolution of the binary oppositions upon which our most fundamental notions of self and other are based. In feminist film theory, one of the most basic working assumptions has been that in the classical cinema, at least, there is an unproblematic fit between the hierarchies of masculinity and femininity on the one hand, and activity and passivity on the other. If disrupting and disturbing that fit is a major task for filmmakers and theorists, then lesbianism would seem to have a strategically important function. For one of the 'problems' that lesbianism poses, insofar as representation is concerned, is precisely the fit between the paradigms of sex and agency, the alignment of masculinity with activity and femininity with passivity.

It is undoubtedly one of those legendary 'no coincidences' that one discourse in which the 'problem' of lesbianism is thus posed most acutely is psychoanalysis. For reasons both historical and theoretical, the most persuasive, as well as controversial, accounts of cinematic identification and desire have been influenced by psychoanalysis. Laura Mulvey's classic account of sexual hierarchy in narrative cinema established the by-now familiar refrain that the ideal spectator of the classical cinema—whatever his or her biological sex or cultural gender—is male. Many critics have challenged or extended the implications of Mulvey's account, most frequently arguing that for women (and sometimes for men as well), cinematic identification occurs at the very least across gender lines, whether in transvestite or bisexual terms.[19] However complex such accounts, they tend to leave unexamined another basic assumption common both to Mulvey's account and to contemporary psychoanalytic accounts of identification, and that is that cinematic identification not only functions to affirm heterosexual norms, but also finds its most basic condition of possibility in the heterosexual division of the universe. Although feminist film theory and criticism have devoted remarkably extensive attention to the function of the male gaze in film, the accompanying heterosexual scenario has not received much attention, except for the occasional nod to what seems to be more the realm of the obvious than the explorable or questionable.

An impressive body of feminist writing has been devoted to the exploration of how—following Luce Irigaray—heterosexuality functions as a ruse, a decoy relation to mask male homosocial and homosexual bonds. 'Reigning everywhere, although prohibited in practice,' Irigaray writes, 'hom(m)osexuality is played out through the bodies of women, matter, or sign, and heterosexuality has been up to now just an alibi for the smooth workings of man's relations with himself.'[20] Comparatively little attention has been paid to how heterosexual economies work to assure that any exchange between women remains firmly ensconced within that 'hom(m)osexual' economy. To be sure, male and female homosexualities occupy quite different positions, and given the logic of the masculine 'same' that dominates the patriarchal order, female homosexuality cannot be ascribed functions that are similar to male homosexuality. However, the two homosexualities share the potential to disrupt, in however different ways, the reign of the 'hom(m)osexual'. Irigaray speaks of the 'fault, the infraction, the misconduct, and the challenge that female homosexuality entails.' For lesbianism threatens to upset the alignment between masculinity and activity, and femininity and passivity. Hence, writes Irigaray, '[t]he problem can be minimized if female homosexuality is regarded merely as an imitation of male behavior.[21]

. . .

Despite its reputation as a more successful exploration of questions so problematically posed in the case history of Dora, 'The Psychogenesis of a Case of Homosexuality in a Woman' does not read as a particularly convincing narrative in its own right. The 'problem' of the case history centers on the woman's self-representation, on her desire, not simply for the loved object, but for a certain staging of that desire. What is not entirely clear is the extent to which the attempted suicide was an unconscious attempt to put an end to parental—and particularly paternal—disapproval by literal self-annihilation, or rather an equally unconscious attempt to dramatize her conflicting allegiances by creating a scene where she is at once active subject and passive object (Freud notes frequently that the young woman's amorous feelings took a 'masculine' form). The suicide attempt is best described as both of these simultaneously—one, a desire for resolution, the other a desire for another language altogether to represent her conflicted desires.[22]

Put another way, the suicide attempt crystalizes the position of 'homosexuality in a woman' as a problem of representation and of narrative. Freud discusses the young woman's case in ways that suggest quite strongly the pressure of lesbianism against a system of explanation and representation. Throughout the case history, the young woman's 'masculinity' is the inevitable frame of reference. Masculinity acquires a variety of definitions in the course of the essay, at times associated with the biological characteristics of men (the young woman favored her father in appearance) and at others equated with the mere fact of agency or activity (she displayed a preference for being 'lover rather than beloved' [141]). But 'masculinity' never really 'takes' as an explanation, since throughout the case history the woman remains an embodiment of conflicting desires. The suicide attempt turns upon what has become, in the cinema, a classic account of the activation of desire, the folding of spectacle into narrative. However, in the standard account, woman leans more toward the spectacle, with man defined as the active agent. Here, it is the woman's desires to narrate and to be seen that collide, leading her to make quite a spectacle of herself, but without a narrative of her own to contextualize that spectacle. According to the young woman's account, the disapproving gaze from her father led her to tell her female companion of the father's disapproval and her companion then adopted the opinion of the father, saying that they should not see each other again. The sudden collapse, the identity between lover and father; the erasure of tension, seem to precipitate the woman's quite literal fall. The woman's desire for self-annihilation occurs, in other words, when her desire becomes fully representable within conventional terms.

What I am suggesting, then, is that the conditions of the representability of the lesbian scenario in this case history are simultaneously those of a tension, a conflict (which is 'readable' in other than homosexual terms), *and* those of a pressure exerted against the overwhelmingly heterosexual assumptions of the language of psychoanalysis, a desire for *another* representation of desire. Or as Monique Wittig puts it, 'Homosexuality is the desire for one's own sex. But it is also the desire for something else that is not connoted. This desire is resistance to the norm.'[23] Expanding on Irigaray, Teresa de Lauretis writes: 'Lesbian representation, or rather, its condition of possibility, depends on separating out the two contrary undertows that constitute the paradox of sexual (in)difference, on isolating but maintaining the two senses of homosexuality and hommosexuality.'[24] The lesbian irony in Arzner's signature suggests that division to which de Lauretis refers, a division between a representation of female communities and an inscription of marginality. That irony stands in (ironic) contrast to feminist film theory's division of Arzner into a textual hommo-sexual (in print) and a visible homosexual (in pictures).

Given Arzner's career in Hollywood, and the realist plots central to her films, her influence would seem to be most apparent among those filmmakers who have appropriated the forms of Hollywood cinema to feminist or even lesbian ends—for example, Susan Seidelman (*Desperately Seeking Susan*, 1985) and Donna Deitch (*Desert Hearts*, 1985). A more striking connection, however, exists with those contemporary women filmmakers whose films extend the possibilities of lesbian irony, while revising the components of the classical cinema and inventing new cinematic forms simultaneously. Despite the rigid distinction between dominant and alternative film that has remained a foregone conclusion in feminist film theory, the articulation of lesbian authorship in Arzner's work finds a contemporary echo in films that may be more 'obviously' lesbian than *Dance, Girl, Dance* or *Craig's Wife*, but whose authorial strategies have been either unreadable or misread in the terms of feminist film theory. Films like Chantal Akerman's *Je tu il elle* (1974), Ulrike

Ottinger's *Ticket of No Return* [*Portrait of a Woman Drinker*] (1979), or Midi Onodera's *Ten Cents a Dance* (1985) are remarkable explorations of the desire to see and to be seen, to detach and to fuse, to narrate one's own desire and to exceed or otherwise complicate the very terms of that narration.

Less optimistically, the disturbing fit between sexual and racial codes of performance, between different modes of irony, finds a contemporary echo in those women's films in which lesbian desire and race collide. The results may not be so clearly racist as in *Dance, Girl, Dance,* but they raise equally important questions for feminist readings based on the implicit assumption that all women are white and heterosexual. In several films that have become classics of feminist film theory—Sally Potter's *Thriller* (1977) and *The Gold Diggers* (1983), and Laura Mulvey's and Peter Wollen's *Riddles of the Sphinx* (1977)—an attraction between two women is central in visual and narrative terms, and in each case the attraction occurs between a white woman and a black woman. Now, these films do not evoke lesbianism and race in identical ways, and my point is not to conclude with a blanket condemnation of them. Rather I want to suggest that the disturbing questions they raise beyond the staples of feminist theory, like mothering, female friendship, and reading against the grain (whether of psychoanalysis or of opera), have not been discussed. The tensions and contradictions so dear to contemporary feminist theory stop at the point that an investigation of sexual difference would require exploration of the other sexual difference, or that an examination of female identity as the negative of man would require consideration of white privilege.

Lesbian authorship in Arzner's work constantly assumes the irony of incompatible truths. This irony is not, however, necessarily contestatory or free of the rigid dualisms of white patriarchal film practice. Although I think feminist film theory might do well to explore its own investment in the pleasures of irony, Arzner's case is crucial for a history of lesbian desire and film practice. My own desire, in exploring the way in which Arzner and her films have been read in feminist film theory, has been to make a connection between the lesbian image and the narrative text, while resisting the lure of a seamless narrative, in which the spectacular lesbianism of the photographs of Arzner would fit comfortably and unproblematically with her films, in which spectacle and narrative would be as idealistically joined for feminism and lesbianism as they presumably are in patriarchal film practice.

Notes

1. Claire Johnston, 'Dorothy Arzner: Critical Strategies', in *The Work of Dorothy Arzner: Towards a Feminist Cinema*, ed. Claire Johnston (London: British Film Institute, 1975), 6.
2. Lucy Fischer reads *Dance, Girl, Dance* in terms of this 'resistance to fetishism'. See *Shot/Countershot* (Princeton: Princeton University Press, 1989), 148–54.
3. Andrew Britton, *Katharine Hepburn: The Thirties and After* (Newcastle upon Tyne: Tyneside Cinema, 1984), 74.
4. Jacquelyn Suter, 'Feminine Discourse in *Christopher Strong*', *Camera Obscura*, 3–4 (Summer 1979), 135–50.
5. Vito Russo, *The Celluloid Closet: Homosexuality in the Movies* (New York: Harper and Row, 1981), 50.
6. Tee Corinne, *Women Who Loved Women* (Pearlchild, 1984), 7.
7. Edith Becker, Michelle Citron, Julia Lesage, and B. Ruby Rich, 'Special Section: Lesbians and Film: Introduction', *Jump Cut*, 24–25 (March 1981), 18.
8. Jackie Stacey discusses female sexual attraction as a principle of identification in *All About Eve* (1950) and *Desperately Seeking Susan*; see 'Desperately Seeking Difference', *Screen*, 28: (Winter 1987), 48–61.
9. For an excellent discussion of the very possibility of a feminist fetishism, see Jane Marcus, 'The asylums of Antaeus. Women, war and madness: Is there a feminist fetishism?', in *The Difference Within: Feminism and Critical Theory*; ed. Elizabeth Meese and Alice Parker (Amsterdam and Philadelphia: John Benjamins Publishing Co., 1989), 49–83. Marcus examines how feminists in the suffrage movement oscillated 'between denial and recognition of rape as the common denominator of female experience' (76). Naomi Schor has examined the possibility of female fetishism in the writings of George Sand; see 'Female Fetishism: The Case of George Sand', in *The Female Body in Western Culture*, ed. Susan Suleiman (Cambridge, Mass.: Harvard University Press, 1986), 363–72.
10. See Christian Metz, *The Imaginary Signifier*, trans. Ben Brewster (Bloomington: Indiana University Press, 1982), 69–80. A chapter in Octave Mannoni's *Clefs pour l'imaginaire ou l'autre scène* (Paris: Editions du Seuil, 1969) is entitled 'Je sais bien, mais quand même . . .' ('I know very well, but all the same . . .').
11. Sarah Halprin, 'Writing in the Margins (review of E. Ann Kaplan, *Women and Film: Both Sides of the Camera*),' *Jump Cut*, 29 (February 1984), 32.
12. Barbara Koenig Quart stresses the relationship between Judy and the secretary in her reading of the scene. See *Women Directors: The Emergence of a New Cinema* (New York and Westport, Conn.: Praeger, 1988), 25.
13. Shoshana Felman, 'To Open the Question', *Yale French Studies*, 55–56 (1980), 8.
14. Donna Haraway, 'A Manifesto for Cyborgs: Science, Technology, and Socialist Feminism in the 1980s', *Socialist Review*, 80 (1985), 65.
15. Beverle Houston, 'Missing in Action: Notes on Dorothy Arzner', *Wide Angle*, 6: 3 (1984), 27.
16. See Esther Newton, 'The Mythic Mannish Lesbian: Radclyffe Hall and the New Woman', *Signs*, 9: 4 (Summer 1984), 557–75. See also Lillian Faderman, *Surpassing the Love of Men: Romantic Friendship and Love between Women*

from the Renaissance to the Present (New York: William Morrow and Co., 1981), esp. parts II and III.

17. Nancy K. Miller makes this observation about irony: 'To the extent that the ethos (character, disposition) of feminism historically has refused the doubleness of "saying one thing while it tries to do another" (the mark of classical femininity, one might argue), it may be that an ironic feminist discourse finds itself at odds both with itself (its identity to itself) and with the expectations its audience has of its position. If that is true, then irony, in the final analysis, may be a figure of limited effectiveness. On the other hand, since nonironic, single, sincere, hortatory feminism is becoming ineffectual, it may be worth the risk of trying out this kind of duplicity on the road.' See 'Changing the Subject: Authorship, Writing, and the Reader', in *Feminist Studies/Critical Studies*, ed. Teresa de Lauretis (Bloomington: Indiana University Press, 1986), 119 n. 18.
18. See the Camera Obscura Collective, 'An Interrogation of the Cinematic Sign: Woman as Sexual Signifier in Jackie Raynal's *Deux fois*', *Camera Obscura*, 1 (Fall 1976), 11–26.
19. See David Rodowick, 'The Difficulty of Difference', *Wide Angle*, 5: 1 (1982), 4–15; Teresa de Lauretis, *Alice Doesn't: Feminism, Semiotics, Cinema* (Bloomington: Indiana University Press, 1984), ch. 5; Miriam Hansen, 'Pleasure, Ambivalence, Identification: Valentino and Female Spectatorship', *Cinema Journal*, 25: 4 (Summer 1986), 6–32; Gaylyn Studlar, *In the Realm of Pleasure: Von Sternberg, Dietrich, and the Masochistic Aesthetic* (Urbana: University of Illinois Press, 1988). Mulvey herself has contributed to the discussion; see 'Afterthoughts on "Visual Pleasure and Narrative Cinema" inspired by King Vidor's *Duel in the Sun* (1946)', in *Visual and Other Pleasures* (Bloomington: Indiana University Press, 1989), 29–38.
20. Luce Irigaray, 'Women on the Market', *This Sex Which Is Not One*, trans. Catherine Porter with Carolyn Burke (Ithaca, NY: Cornell University Press, 1985), 172.
21. Luce Irigaray, 'Commodities among Themselves', *This Sex Which Is Not One*.
22. I believe what I am describing as the desire for another representation of desire is quite close to Mandy Merck's discussion of the young woman's conflict about 'masculine identification'. See 'The Train of Thought in Freud's "Case of Homosexuality in a Woman"', *m/f*, 11–12 (1986), 40.
23. Monique Wittig, 'Paradigm', in *Homosexualities and French Literature: Cultural Contexts/Critical Texts*, ed. George Stambolian and Elaine Marks (Ithaca, NY: Cornell University Press, 1979), 114.
24. Teresa de Lauretis, 'Sexual Indifference and Lesbian Representation', *Theatre Journal*, 40: 2 (May 1988), 159.

10 The Difficulty of Difference

David N. Rodowick*

BINARY MACHINES

In *Dialogues*, a book cowritten with Gilles Deleuze, Claire Parnet comments on the function of 'the binary machine'.[1] In these interesting pages she resumes an argument begun by Deleuze concerning the relation of philosophy to the State. Every college educator knows well the official version of this story, defined according to the theory of progress that was the nineteenth century's contribution to Enlightenment philosophy. As philosophy becomes more specialized and departmentalized, its role is to contribute in a 'detached' way to the refinement of procedures of thought. Increasingly the 'image' of thought invoked, along with criteria for its perfectibility, is associated with procedures of 'language' but of a special sort: that defined by linguistics and related logico-mathematical protocols.

Deleuze's position and his ongoing practice of reading philosophy is motivated by a different emphasis. Philosophy is confronted as an 'image of thought' that in its historical manifestations all too perfectly prevents people from thinking. And not only because 'thought' is left to specialists, but also because the definitions of thought produced by specialists accord perfectly with the State's image of power and its juridical definitions of identity. As critics and educators, the language we use to describe 'identity'—as a difference from or conforming to an image of gender, class, or race—is intricately tied to the mechanics of power.

What Parnet calls the binary machine perfectly describes this

* David N. Rodowick, 'The Difficulty of Difference' from *The Difficulty of Difference: Psychoanalysis, Sexual Difference and Film Theory* (Routledge, 1991), originally published in *Wide Angle*, vol. 5 (1) (1982), reprinted by permission of the author.

technology of thought and the notions of identity it fabricates. Its components are easily elucidated: divide into two mutually exclusive terms or categories and thus produce two perfectly self-identical 'ideas' that brook no contradiction or invasion from the outside. Hegel's dialectic is the utopia of this technology, dividing and reconciling into ever higher unities and hierarchies until spirit and subject became one in an image of universal rationality. Nowadays binary thought—which has reproduced itself in the discourses of law, economy, medicine, science, and politics no less than epistemology and aesthetics—is content with cellular division and horizontal replication. According to Parnet,

> Dualisms no longer relate to unities, but to successive choices: are you white or black, man or woman, rich or poor, etc.? Do you take the left half or the right half? There is always a binary machine which governs the distribution of roles and which means that all the answers must go through preformed questions, since the questions are already worked out on the basis of the answer assumed to be probable according to the dominant meanings. Thus a grille is constituted such that everything which does not pass through the grille cannot be materially understood. . . .
>
> [The] binary machine is an important component of apparatuses of power. So many dichotomies will be established that there will be enough for everyone to be pinned to the wall, sunk in a hole. Even the divergences of deviancy will be measured according to the degree of binary choice; you are neither white nor black, Arab then? Or half-breed? You are neither man nor woman, transvestite then? (D 19–21)

The binary machine always pretends to totality and universality. And to a certain extent, Parnet sees the working of language by the binary machine to have been imminently successful. In this context, one could ask if the picture of language developed in structural linguistics differs so much from the image of thought in the Hegelian dialectic.[2] The smallest possible unities—phonemic—are integrated into ever higher levels of unity—morphemic, syntactic, syntagmatic, narratological—that are simultaneously equivalent to 'higher' levels of thought. And when grafted on to structural anthropology, these branching divisions and hierarchies become equivalent to the 'meaningful' organization of human collectivities. This is one way of understanding the feminist critique of Lévi-Strauss, for example, where the binary division and hierarchy of the sexes informs the intelligibility of language, labor, and social life. But Parnet's point is that granting linguistics' recognition and exacting description of the dualities that work language and society is to leave untouched its own language—its patterns of logic, rhetoric, and argumentation—which, tautologically, only produce the legibility and intelligibility of that which is already structured by binary division. A similar tautological situation is no less evident in the ways that contemporary film theory has appropriated the logic of structural semiology and psychoanalysis for the formal analysis of films and the spectatorial relations they imply.

If language and linguistics so perfectly replicate one another, the latter reproducing the 'thought' of language as the limit of what language can render 'thinkable', what alternatives can be imagined? Parnet and Deleuze warn that it is futile to propose a thought 'outside' of language. (How many theories of avant-garde literature and art have been wrecked on this utopian island?) Nor can it be said that language deforms identities, concepts, or realities that can be returned to their proper states. 'We must pass through [*passer par*] dualisms,' writes Parnet, 'because they are in language, it's not a question of getting rid of them, but we must fight against language, invent stammering . . . to trace a vocal or written line which will make language flow between these dualisms, and which will define a minority use of language' (D 34). Rather, it is a matter of reconsidering what 'language' is or could be, of understanding what it leaves aside, and of remembering that totality is a pretension that displaces recognition of the multiplicities it covers over. It is a question above all of reading differently.

The question of reading can now be rephrased: how to understand otherwise these schemata of language and thought? How can one recover the 'individuations without "subject"' that fall between the terms of binary division and are de-territorialized by the law of the excluded middle? How can one apprehend the minority languages and the multiple collectivities that are displaced and overcome by the universalizing unity of binary thought? For Parnet, the Achilles' heel of this logic is the term that not only constitutes the middle, but also guarantees the contiguity and multiplication of binary modules:

> And even if there are only two terms, there is an AND between the two, which is neither the one nor the other, nor the one which becomes the other, but which constitutes the multiplicity. This is why it is always possible to undo dualisms from the inside, by tracing the line of flight which passes between the two terms or the two sets, the narrow stream which belongs neither to the one nor to the other, but draws both into a non-parallel evolution, into a heterochronous becoming. At least this does not belong to the dialectic. (D 34–35)

I have left to one side the principal targets of Parnet and Deleuze's criticisms: structural linguistics, psychoanalysis, and more profoundly, the alliance between them represented by the work of Jacques Lacan. There is much to be said for this critique of psychoanalysis which is more complex and compelling in the *Anti-Oedipus* than it is in the pages of *Dialogues.* The questions that interest me, however, are on one hand how contemporary film theory has read and incorporated psychoanalysis, and on the other, to what degree the logic of psychoanalysis, above all the work of Freud, is inflected by the binary machine? In *The Crisis of Political Modernism*, I argued that the most substantial accomplishment of contemporary film theory was its formulation of new practices of reading that profoundly transformed our notions of filmic and literary texts.[3] But blocked by a formal conception of text, spectator, and the relation between them, Anglo-American film theory has been unable to comprehend historically or theoretically the implications of these reading practices. Despite the gains they have enabled, neither semiology, psychoanalysis, nor feminist theory have entirely eluded the logic of the binary machine in their theoretical language and in their formal conceptualization of film text and film spectators.

The consequences of this situation must be addressed. What I question now is the way that Freud has been mobilized in film theory to address questions of textual analysis, on one hand, and sexual difference in spectatorship on the other. Do Freud's writings implicitly propose a model of reading that might erode the version of language and power formulated by the binary machine? Does the work of Freud enable a different way of understanding sexual difference? Rather than following the 'law' of unity and identity, is Freud among the first to understand the possibilities of 'individuations without "subject"' and a minority language of sexuality? Is there in Freud a theory of reading that renders legible otherwise de-territorialized languages, identities, and meanings?

PLEASURE AND ITS DISCONTENTS

'In a world ordered by sexual imbalance, pleasure in looking has been split between active/male and passive/female.' This phrase from Laura Mulvey's 'Visual Pleasure and Narrative Cinema' is undoubtedly and deservedly one of the most well known in contemporary film theory.[4] I begin with Mulvey's essay not because I disagree with what it 'says', but to open up tensions in Mulvey's own reading of Freud, and, more importantly, in how Mulvey's work has been read and appropriated. Without doubt, it is and will remain one of the most important essays in contemporary film theory. 'Visual Pleasure and Narrative Cinema' has indeed been successful in its original, polemical objective: to place questions of sexual difference at the center of the debate concerning film theory's appeal to psychoanalysis. But what was offered as a polemic and a stepping stone to further analysis has instead too often been treated as axiomatic. What is at stake is how film theory has read Freud in order to understand the construction of 'femininity' by audiovisual media and to reconceptualize the value of psychoanalysis for a theory of narration and spectatorship.

Mulvey's early argument, which is still the subject of an ongoing debate in her own work, remains the best and most brilliant exposition of the reading of Freud produced by Anglo-American film theory in the seventies.[5] Mulvey's project and the many essays inspired by it are organized around the question of identification. The first task of this project is to target and examine the codes and mechanisms through which the classical cinema has traditionally exploited sexual difference as a function of its narrative and representational forms. The second task is to ascertain the affects these mechanisms might inspire in the spectatorial experience of sexed individuals as well as their role within the more general ideological machinery of patriarchal culture. The analysis of narrative forms, and the forms of spectatorship implied by them, are thus intimately related. Similarly, the analysis and criticism of patriarchal ideology by film theory has had a historic impact on these questions.

One of the most striking aspects of Mulvey's argument is the association of a fundamental negativity with the figuration of femininity characteristic of the classic, Hollywood cinema. The great strength of Mulvey's analysis is that it is not a simple condemnation of how women are represented on the screen. Instead she identifies a powerful contradiction in the heart of the structure of image and narrative in Hollywood films. In order to begin to define these issues more precisely I have isolated a rather long citation from Mulvey's essay. My motive is neither to completely sustain nor subvert Mulvey's argument, but rather to illuminate a series of assumptions and a system of oppositions that organize her discussion of sexual difference and mechanisms of visual pleasure in film. In a section entitled 'Woman as Image, Man as Bearer of the Look', Mulvey makes the following argument:

> But in psychoanalytic terms, the female figure poses a deeper problem. She also connotes something that the look continually circles around but disavows: her lack of a penis, implying a threat of castration and hence unpleasure. Ultimately, the meaning of woman is sexual difference, the absence of the penis as visually ascertainable, the material evidence on which is based the castration complex essential for the organisation of entrance to the symbolic order and the law of the father. Thus the woman as icon, displayed for the gaze and enjoyment of men, the active controllers of the look, always threatens to evoke the anxiety it originally signified. The male unconscious has two avenues of escape from this castration anxiety: preoccupation with the re-enactment of the original trauma (investigating the woman, demystifying her mystery), counterbalanced by the devaluation, punishment or saving of the guilty object (an avenue typified by the concerns of the *film noir*); or else complete disavowal of castration by the substitution of a fetish object or turning the represented figure itself into a fetish so that it becomes reassuring rather than dangerous (hence over-valuation, the cult of the female star). This second avenue, fetishistic scopophilia, builds up the physical beauty of the object transforming it into something satisfying in itself. The first avenue, voyeurism, on the contrary, has associations with sadism: pleasure lies in ascertaining guilt (immediately associated with castration), asserting control and subjecting the guilty person through punishment or forgiveness. This sadistic side fits in well with narrative. Sadism demands a story, depends on making something happen, forcing a change in another person, a battle of will and strength, victory and defeat, all occurring in linear time with beginning and an end. Fetishistic scopophilia, on the other hand, can exist outside linear time as the erotic instinct is focused on the look alone. (VP 13–14)

Unlike Raymond Bellour, whose work has many affinities with Mulvey's, Mulvey is less concerned with problems of textual analysis than with the definition of structures of identification and the mechanisms of pleasure or unpleasure that accompany them. I am now using the term identification in its strictly psychoanalytic sense: 'Psychological process whereby the subject assimilates an aspect, property or attribute of the other and is transformed, wholly or partially, after the model the other provides. It is by means of a series of identifications that the personality is constituted and specified.'[6] Mulvey herself does not develop the argument in precisely these terms. Her argument does presume, however, a potentially transformative relation between the object (the narrative film and the mechanisms of visual pleasure characterizing it) and the spectatorial subject such that the libidinal economy of the latter is organized and sustained by the signifying economy of the former. In fact all theories of the subject invoked by psychoanalytic film criticism cast signifying processes in film as the 'other' with the power to transform or sustain categories of subjectivity.

For Mulvey these subject/object relations are a product of the point of view mechanisms of Hollywood cinema. This idea is emphasized by the division of gender and labor in the title of this section: 'Woman as Image, Man as Bearer of the Look'. In the interlacing of diegetic looks between the characters, the look of the camera, and that of the spectator, an economy is preserved where set subject-positions are continually reconfirmed and reproduced by avoiding avenues of identification leading to unpleasure and by seeking out avenues leading to pleasure. That the analysis of sexual difference reveals an imbalance in the social system represented in films is of course important. But of greater significance is the suggestion that visual and narrative forms produce pleasure, that this pleasure is produced for someone, and that this production sustains an imaginary situation where real relations of social imbalance are maintained for a given culture. According to Mulvey, the forms of point of view institutionalized by the cinema as mechanisms of pleasure have defined themselves historically in the same manner as the ego forms itself in relation to the objective world: that which promotes pleasure is introjected and that which promotes unpleasure is systematically rejected.[7] The various forms defining cinematic imaging and point of view at a given historical moment are objectively produced and sustained only to the extent that they maintain a pleasurable relation with the subject at whom they are aimed—the cinema consumer. If these mechanisms perform their social and ideological function efficiently, the production of pleasure will sustain and reinforce the place of the subject in a given structure of representation. An imaginary place is created for this subject in and by the film text that he or she may choose to inhabit. As in Marx's suggestive epigram from the *Grundrisse*, 'production not only creates an object for the subject, but also a subject for the object.'

In sum, processes of identification in the cinema and the various forms of looking that organize their functioning in film narratives regulate an economy of exchange where the production of pleasure guarantees the place of the subject both in and for the text. What constitutes this place and the imaginary from which it is derived, as well as how it is placed and for whom, are the central questions and the greatest difficulties of Mulvey's essay.

The terms and the logic evoked by Mulvey in the long citation above should now be sorted out. Mulvey is primarily concerned with the organization of looking by, for, and in the text of the narrative film.

Again, the concept of identification is understood as the linch-pin on which the relations between subject and object turn. Identification also organizes, or attempts to organize, the vision and the libidinal aims of the spectatorial subject. Drawing on terms from Freud's 'Instincts and their Vicissitudes' (1915c), Mulvey undertakes a classification of the forms of visual pleasure characteristic of the narrative cinema.[8] Her primary distinction is:

active:	male
passive:	female

At first glance this polarization of terms seems faithful to Freud's own schema. Later I will examine whether or not Freud's arguments concerning sexual difference are not somewhat more complex.

Nevertheless, Mulvey's discussion of forms of 'pleasure in looking' crystallizes around this schema. To maintain this polarization of terms, she establishes two crucial sets of distinctions. The first involves the following pairing of terms in section II C, where Mulvey describes fundamental structures of identification in the strictly psychoanalytic sense:

sexual instincts	ego-libido
scopophilia	narcissism
[separation of subject and object]	[identity of subject with object]

Mulvey is careful to differentiate the first pair, sexual instincts/ego-libido, while maintaining the intimate link between them. The nature of this linking of opposites is clarified by examining Freud's distinction between ego-libido and object-libido. Although he was not strictly consistent, Freud often used the terms 'libido' and 'sexual instincts' interchangeably. However, in the distinction between object- and ego-libido he refers primarily to the direction in which the libido is channeled; that is, whether it is being directed toward an exterior object or being reinvested in the ego itself. Obviously the concept of ego-libido is indissolubly linked to narcissism which Mulvey correctly points out in her description of the mirror stage and its apparent similarities with cinematic perception. Mulvey understands the economy of the ego-libido as attached fundamentally to the phenomenon of primary narcissism characterizing Lacan's scenario for the mirror stage. In this scenario the formation of the ego, the potential 'I' of the speaking subject, is understood as a splitting—first in a division between the sexual instincts and the ego-instincts through the organization of narcissistic libido, and second in the formation of an image to which this libido is attached. The formation of this image constitutes an economic relationship with the ego that is *imaginary* in the full sense that Lacan gives to the term. The joy of recognition that the child receives through identifying itself in this exterior image is located in a fundamental misperception where the distance between subject and object is simultaneously formed and canceled. The terms for perceiving, knowing, and desiring are thus constituted and verified by the setting in place of this imaginary other who both is and is not the child. The ego is formed through a simultaneous externalization and internalization of an object constituted by a visual and imaginary structure that governs the child's perception of self.

A first caution is in order here. This scenario of the formative moments of the ego is not yet a scenario of sexual difference. And Mulvey, with great care, has not yet introduced the distinction between active:male/passive:female. To be sure, in both Freudian and Lacanian accounts this scenario establishes the 'first' sexual relations: those attached to the imago of the mother and to the autoeroticism associated with narcissism. In addition, this period of development sets the stage for the complicated and fragile set of sexual identifications that are carried through in the formation of the castration and Oedipus complexes. But in this preoedipal phase of psychological development there is no evidence that masculinity or femininity will follow predetermined routes. In fact, Freud himself is adamant that gender difference is a product of a retroactive 'understanding' of Oedipal relations during puberty. For Freud, up until this point any child's relation to sexual difference is fundamentally undetermined, unformed, and unsure; after puberty sexual identifications remain fragile. Moreover, the anxiety produced by the residue of preoedipal relations characterizes all questions of identity that plague the subject for the rest of its psychological life.[9] The complex of Oedipal identifications is only the first attempt to address questions of sexual identity whose indecisiveness is never fully resolved.

Unquestionably, the problem of the persistence of this anxiety is central to Mulvey's argument. For the structures of desire and pleasurable looking perpetuated by the Hollywood cinema demonstrate for Mulvey both the insistent patriarchal bias of cinematic representations and the potential for eroding that bias:

> During its history, the cinema seems to have evolved a particular illusion of reality in which this contradiction between libido and ego has found a beautifully complementary phantasy world. In *reality* the phantasy world of the screen is subject to the law which produces it. Sexual instincts

> and identification processes have a meaning within the symbolic order which articulates desire. Desire, born with language, allows the possibility of transcending the instinctual and the imaginary, but its point of reference continually returns to the traumatic moment of its birth: the castration complex. Hence the look, pleasurable in form, can be threatening in content, and it is woman as representation/image that crystallizes this paradox. (VP 11)

For Mulvey, the imaging of the woman's body evokes a fundamental negativity that always places the pleasure and security of cinematic looking at risk. The fundamental mechanisms of pleasurable looking are meant to displace the castration anxiety suggested to the male spectator by the representation of the woman's body, and the male spectator obsessively requires this representation to alleviate his anxiety. Yet each repetition simultaneously renews a possibility of threat: the potential negation of Hollywood codes of looking and the security of the male ego they support.

This leads to a second point that Mulvey is careful to emphasize: the drives may only be apprehended through their investment in representations. Or, as Mulvey puts it, they 'are formative structures, mechanisms not meaning. In themselves they have no signification, they have to be attached to an idealisation' (VP 10). Indeed in the citation above Mulvey characterizes the formation of the ego as a kind of 'phantasmization' of the subject. Certainly, almost all of Freud's discussions of instinctual vicissitudes rely on the analysis of representations or phantasy scenarios. This is the fundamental link between the 'instinctual' theory and Freud's analytic method concerning manifestations of phantasy life, including dreams, parapraxes, jokes, and the scattered comments on painting and literature. And any concrete discussion of the construction and dissemination of subject-positions must presuppose that there are historically and socially determined mechanisms, both formal and technological, that organize the desire of the subject and account for the structuring of that desire. But it is not Freud, but rather Lacan's account of the relation between the imaginary and the symbolic that Mulvey follows.

The implications of this choice must be addressed at the risk of oversimplifying Lacan's thought. Lacan's account of the processes of identification and subject formation are often more deterministic than Freud's. Each stage of the formation of the ego, from the mirror stage to the dissolution of the castration and Oedipus complexes, is driven by a process of dialectical incorporation. As Miriam Hansen points out, '. . . in Lacanian models of spectatorship scopic desire is conceptually inseparable from voyeurism, fetishism and, thus, the regime of castration. Not that these are unrelated or free of determinism in Freud. The Freudian speculation, however, does not posit earlier stages of psychic development as always already negated by later ones, in a Hegelian sense of "*Aufhebung*" which Lacan assimilated to psychoanalysis.'[10] Alternatively, Freud understands the relation between the drives and their representatives as causally and temporally more complex, fragile, and historically mobile. In sum, terms that Freud develops on the basis of shifting 'polarities' [*Polarität*] are simultaneously divided and linked through the mechanism of Lacan's dialectic. Moreover, Mulvey has specific reasons for preferring Lacan's scenario of negation even if she thereby fixes Freud's polarities in a system of binary division: to preserve an image of the female body as a site of negativity that can erode rather than sustain the security of the male look.

Returning to Mulvey's argument, some of the assumptions characterizing the long citation above can now be reconsidered. The best place to begin is with the following pairs of oppositions:

male	female
active	passive
scopophilia	narcissism

I have already suggested two cautions in my discussion of primary narcissism. First, the strict distinction between what is 'male' and what is 'female' in processes of identification is undoubtedly the trickiest problem in reading Freud and should be approached with great caution. And where film theory wishes to sustain the analogy between Lacan's mirror stage and the 'primary identification' organized by the cinematographic apparatus, additional care is called for. There is no doubt that sexual difference plays an important role in Lacan's account, both explicitly and symptomatically. But the *a priori* alignment of scopophilia and narcissism with active and passive aims on one hand, and maleness and femaleness on the other, is not clear. None of Freud's texts on sexual difference suggests an unequivocal distinctiveness between maleness and femaleness in this relation as I will make more clear in a moment. Second, if primary narcissism formulates an identification whose visual structure supports pleasure in looking, this structure implicitly contains both active and passive components. It is maintained not only in the *act* of the look, but also in the *return* of the look from the imaginary other who verifies the apparent corporeal and psychical integrity of the 'I' of the subject. Pleasure in looking contains both passive *and* active forms. Mulvey implies as much in the passage cited above, especially in the reference to 'fetishistic scopophilia' which in her schema would have both 'active' scopophilic and 'passive' fetishistic components.

Similarly, for Mulvey the avoidance of castration anxiety (unpleasure), is made possible by two distinctive types of looking:

active	passive
voyeurism	fetishistic scopophilia
sadism	?

There is an implicit blind spot here. For example, Mulvey defines fetishism as an overvaluation of the object, a point Freud would support. But he would also add that this phenomenon is one of the fundamental sources of authority defined as passive submission to the object: in sum, *masochism.*[11] Why is the relation of masochism to 'fetishistic scopophilia' elided in Mulvey's essay? Her emphasis considers the structure of the look not only in terms of the pleasure it allows, but also in how it organizes relations of power and control in and through narrative form. This claim, as powerful as it is provocative, deserves greater theoretical elaboration. Within Mulvey's thesis, though, the structure of the look is based on two givens: it is fundamentally a source of control or mastery and as a product of patriarchal society it is fundamentally masculine. The concept of masochism is deferred by the political nature of her argument. She wishes, justly I believe, neither to underestimate the extensiveness of a 'masculinization' of point of view in the cinema, nor does she want to equate femaleness with masochism.

No one will have missed the reference to Freud in naming this section 'pleasure and its discontents'. But the nature of that 'discontent' has yet to be explicitly addressed. In *Civilization and Its Discontents* [*Das Unbehagen in der Kultur*] Freud himself uses the word *Unbehagen*, more aptly translated as discomfort, uneasiness, or restlessness. The idea of pleasure [*Lust*], then, is inseparable from this uneasiness [*Unlust*] as Mulvey herself implies in her discussion of castration anxiety. Nonetheless, Mulvey's account, and in fact most contemporary film theory follows her in this, is relatively unwelcoming to Freud's own complex remarks in the case histories on the restlessness of identification and the contradictoriness of desire that traverses and problematizes any strict binary distinction between 'maleness'/'femaleness' and activity/passivity.[12] My own view is that the most productive area for a turn to Freud in film theory is to derive a theory of signification from the Freudian theory of phantasy. This theory would first have to account for permutations in the signification of the look in relation to the variations and shiftings of the subject and object of enunciation as transactions in sexual difference. Secondly, I would caution that although this theory could describe *possibilities* of cinematic identification, its claims for the positions adopted by any spectator would be purely speculative. Mulvey has undoubtedly helped to lay the groundwork for such a theory but her own considerations are deficient on several points. For example, Mulvey discusses the male star as an object of the look but denies him the function of an erotic object for either the female or male spectator.[13] Because Mulvey considers the look to be essentially active in its aims, identification with the male protagonist is only considered from a point of view that associates it with a sense of omnipotence and of assuming control in the narrative. She makes no distinction between identification and object-choice where active sexual aims may be directed towards the male figure nor does she consider the signification of authority in the male figure from the point of view of an economy of masochism. On the other hand, her discussion of the female figure is restricted only to its function as a male object-choice. In this manner, the place of maleness is discussed as both the subject and the object of the gaze (though only in a restricted fashion) and femaleness is discussed only as an object structuring the male look according to its active (voyeuristic) and passive (fetishistic) forms. In 'Visual Pleasure and Narrative Cinema' the vicissitudes of identification—whether in its pleasurable or anxious forms, or whether it involves taking the other as an object (scopophilia) or identifying with attributes of a more perfect other (narcissism)—is reserved for the male alone, despite the suggestion of distinctive male and female forms. Where is the place of the female subject in this scenario?

In order to unravel this problem, or at least clarify its contours, here again is Mulvey's schema as I have reconsidered it:

male	female
active	passive
object-libido	ego-libido
scopophilia	narcissism
[object-choice	identification]
voyeurism	fetishistic scopophilia
sadism	[masochism]
masculine unconscious	?

In this context Mulvey must be questioned, as she herself questions Freud, as to whether or not 'anatomy is destiny'. In her schema psychological subjects and the libidinal economies that characterize them are typed according to a bodily definition of sexual difference. In other words, when describing the organization and the economy of the scopic drive, the sets of oppositions defining psychological characteristics are implicitly derived from biological difference. However, it would be too easy and undoubtedly unfair to Mulvey's sensitive and powerful reading of Freud to write off her argument as promoting a biological essentialism. Rather her argument is searching to define the specificity of the female body as the locus of a repressed yet articulate being. Recognition of this body and the representations proper to it, would thus enable both the recognition of a subjectivity so far elided under patriarchy and the overthrow of the discursive and social practices that censor this subjectivity.[14] In short, Mulvey discovers in the patriarchal construction of an image of the female body the materials for negation and critique that allow new possibilities of subjectivity and desire.

Freud's own texts, from the *Studies on Hysteria* to *The New Introductory Lectures on Psychoanalysis*, are marked by a certain ambivalence in this respect to which the comment about anatomy and destiny will always bear witness. Similarly, Freud's anthropological and phylogenetic arguments, with their suggestion of a primitive memory of sexual difference and the universality of a patriarchal social life, must be regarded with a high degree of suspicion.[15] Alternatively, Freud's lifelong reflection on femininity and female sexuality led him to profoundly question the idea of a biological or instinctual determination of sexual difference. This is indeed where the theory of 'instincts' and the theory of the drives diverge. Especially in the case histories, questions of sexual difference, femininity and masculinity, and homosexualities, are understood as highly complex yet not the least determined by inherent biological factors. This is after all the same Freud who was hooted by the Vienna society of physicians in 1886 for suggesting the possibility of 'male' hysteria.

Freud was always uncomfortable with the concept of biological determinism in speaking about sexual difference and cautioned against it in several essays. For example, in a footnote to *Civilization and its Discontents*, Freud writes:

> We are accustomed to say that every human being displays both male and female instinctual impulses, needs and attributes; but though anatomy, it is

> true, can point out the characteristic of maleness and femaleness, psychology cannot. For psychology the contrast between the sexes fades away into one between activity and passivity [that is, in describing the organization of the drives], in which we far too readily identify activity with maleness and passivity with femaleness, a view which is by no means universally confirmed. . . . However this may be, if we assume that it is a fact that each individual seeks to satisfy both male and female wishes in his sexual life, we are prepared for the possibility that those [two sets of] demands are not fulfilled by the same object, and that they interfere with each other unless they can be kept apart and each impulse guided into a particular channel that is suited to it.[16]

Above and beyond the inherent complexities of his arguments, the contradictory responses to Freud's views on sexual difference are explained by the variety of the situations referred to in his use of the terms *Männlichkeit* and *Weiblichkeit.* Freud understood at least three different senses of the distinction between 'maleness' and 'femaleness'—biological, psychological and cultural—and accepted that their interrelation was by no means unequivocal or unproblematic. Moreover, these three senses are only profitably understood by identifying how they are inscribed in the material representations that serve patriarchal ideology as its raw materials.

There is a passage in 'Instincts and their Vicissitudes' that illuminates Mulvey's reading of Freud in this respect. Towards the end of the essay, Freud asserts that the fundamental polarities of mental life are subject (ego)-object (external world), pleasure-unpleasure, and active-passive. When describing the interaction between these polarities—which precisely define the economy of identification—Freud warns that relations of activity and passivity must not be confounded with the relation of the subject (ego) and the object (external world). For the psychical life of the ego is always characterized by a complex of active and passive relations motivated by its reception of and reaction to perceptual information. Moreover, the drives are inherently always active in their aims. To the extent that psychological significations are attached to the meaning of masculinity and femininity in relation to activity and passivity, they do not define mutually exclusive sets of oppositions and are always the product of a historical and social variability. Similarly, there could never be a unilateral response between object and subject when identification takes place.

The rigor of Mulvey's binary schema for describing the relation of the drives to the representation of sexual difference therefore belies the complexity of Freud's thought. The density of contradiction in which the *significations* of feminine and masculine are circulated in our culture is thereby confused in Mulvey's analysis with the related but nevertheless separate problem of *identification* in Freud. Similarly, Mulvey's schema collapses when any one of the three senses of sexual distinction in Freud are systematically applied. Why would this be so? The contradictions of Mulvey's argument derive from an implied ontological definition of feminine identity and the feminine body as the requirement for her theory of political modernism. If the possibility of a 'female unconscious' is a question mark in her essay, it is because the potential for a feminine subjectivity and desire will only be defined by a feminist counter-cinema that will arise through the negation of Hollywood codes of looking and visual pleasure. In her essay, that possibility rests in the very representations of the female body formulated in Hollywood cinema as an uncanny, 'alien presence' that must be contained or mastered.

The clearest way of understanding this aspect of Mulvey's essay is to examine her division of film form into narrative and spectacle. The former is aligned with the vicissitude of sadism and the latter with fetishism as exemplified in the films of Alfred Hitchcock and Joseph von Sternberg. Following the counter-cinema argument, if Hollywood narrative relies on conventions of linearity, continuity, and depth illusion no less than pleasurable looking, then for Mulvey the imaging of the female body 'tends to work against the development of a story line, to freeze the flow of action in moments of erotic contemplation. This alien presence then has to be integrated into cohesion with the narrative' (VP 11). The conventions of Hollywood cinema are understood as an agonistic relation between coherence and contradiction, movement and stasis, containment and erosion. The imaging of the female body always threatens to disrupt the linearity, continuity, and cohesion of the narrative. Mulvey refers to it as a momentary 'no-man's land' outside of the temporal and spatial coherence of the narrative. Similarly, the effort to eroticize and fetishize the female star by fragmenting her body in close-up 'destroys the Renaissance space, the illusion of depth demanded by the narrative, it gives flatness, the quality of a cut-out or icon rather than verisimilitude to the screen' (VP 12).

The organization of looking around the female body thus preserves an anti-realist space and the potential for a narrative, political modernism. Moreover, Sternberg and Hitchcock are not 'symptoms' in this respect; instead they are models, straining the envelope of narrative coherence and pointing the way to a possible counter-cinema. Through an overvaluation of the image, Sternberg's films stress pictorial rather than narrative values. He deemphasizes depth illusion, stresses the flatness of the screen, stages non-linear plots, and, most importantly, refuses to mediate the look through the agency of the male protagonist: 'for him the pictorial space enclosed by the frame is paramount rather than narrative or identification processes' (VP 14). Alternatively, the interest of Hitchcock for Mulvey is that he foregrounds erotic looking, making it central to the plot. He portrays the processes of identification associated with the look in a way that reveals their perverse origins. In Hitchcock's films, 'erotic involvement with the look is disorientating: the spectator's fascination is turned against him as the narrative carries him through and entwines him with the processes that he is himself exercising' (VP 16). In sum, for Mulvey the look of the camera and of the spectator are subordinated in Hollywood cinema to the narrative organization of point of view and its requirements of unity, coherence, linearity, depth illusion, and diegetic verisimilitude. On one hand, 'the look of the audience is denied as an intrinsic force', but on the other, 'the female image as a castration threat constantly endangers the unity of the diegesis and bursts through the world of illusion as an intrusive, static one-dimensional fetish' (VP 18). Thus the binary schema of Mulvey's analysis really begins with the structured oppositions of the counter-cinema argument, mapping them back onto Freud to build a theory of identification and distanciation that will 'free the look of the camera into its materiality in time and space and the look of the audience into dialectics, passionate detachment' (VP 18).[17] The entire essay is organized according to the question of the specificity of the female body-image, rather than the specificity of the female look or feminine identification. In turn, questions of signification and identification in film are structured by a system of binary division and exclusion devolving from that body.

In Freudian theory, however, the relation of the body to the drives is not governed by such a straightforward binary logic. Instead, Freud draws a complex picture of the relations that attach the aims of the drives to systems of representation. In 'Instincts and their Vicissitudes', for example, Freud suggests a classification of drive-components that defines their aims and objects according to both active and passive forms. Here masculinity and femininity are defined solely as psychological and cultural distinctions. In addition, the distribution of terms in Freud's instinctual theory is neither static nor immutable. It relies, in fact, on a mobility where given terms exchange places and function within the structure of their division. Thus the fundamental vicissitudes for Freud are the reversal of a component into its opposite and the turning around of a drive upon the subject's own self. The examples he gives are especially apposite to Mulvey's analysis. The paired opposites Freud uses to explain the reversal of a form into its opposite are *voyeurism* (desire in looking)/*exhibitionism* (desire in being looked at); for the turning around of a form upon the subject's own self Freud uses the pair *sadism* (desire in controlling or hurting an other)/*masochism* (desire to be controlled or hurt). Thus Mulvey draws upon Freud's schema only to substitute fetishism for exhibitionism, and to exclude masochism. And where her schema is marked by a logic of binary opposition, Freud characterizes the mutability of his pairs as 'ambivalence'.

Once again the forms that channel the drives are understood to be active and passive by turns rather than being fixed immutably in their oppositions. Paradoxically, despite the power and the suggestiveness of her argument, Mulvey's thesis ultimately falters by imagining the female subject through the binary logic of the counter-cinema argument. And if the female subject becomes somewhat unimaginable in this context, it is not only because of difficulties in Freudian thought. In Mulvey's analysis the spectating subject is forcibly the male subject. When Mulvey defines the look according to its objective and subjective, as well as active and passive, relations, it is a look made for the male subject. Consequently, the only place for the female subject in her scenario is as an object defined in the receiving end of the glance or as the unrealized possibility of a counter-cinema. Her pairing of voyeurism and fetishism is also interesting in this respect because it is inconsistent with Freud's own schema.[18] Unlike exhibitionism, fetishism is not precisely a passive form of looking. Rather, it is better characterized by another vicissitude—repression. In this manner, a contradictory belief is set up within the ego in which the evidence of castration is elided. The ego is split into two epistemological scenes—one where the woman is phallic and undifferentiated and the other where she is understood to be without a penis.[19] The playing down of masochism is also interesting in Mulvey's essay. However, rather than being a misreading, this is better understood as a point necessitated by her political position. She hesitates—and not without justification—to characterize the position of the female subject as masochistic. This would define woman's place in representation solely as an object of aggression. Moreover, if she were to delimit a place for the female subject in this schema her logic would require that woman's relationship to representation, and to desire organized in representation, would of necessity be defined as masochistic economy.

But the question still remains: where is woman's place? Mulvey speaks of a male unconscious but a female unconscious takes place in her analysis only as an absence, a negativity defining castration and the not-masculine, or as a yet unrealized possibility. If the code of the look may be understood as a figure conjoining identification, desire, and the 'phantasmization' of narrative as many theorists have suggested, what is the place and the function of the female subject with respect to this structure? How does this structure condition the possibility and even the knowledge of her desire through the politics of inclusion and exclusion so characteristic of the power relations of the classic, narrative text?

Notes

1. (Paris: Flammarion, 1977) 27–31, 42–43 and passim. Trans. Hugh Tomlinson and Barbara Habberjam (New York: Columbia University Press, 1987), 21–23 and 33–35. Hereafter cited as D.
2. See, for example, Jean-François Lyotard's comments on Hegel and Saussure throughout the first half of *Discourse, figure* (Paris: Editions Klincksieck, 1974). Especially interesting is Lyotard's gloss on Marx's early critique of Hegel's *Philosophy of Right*, which focuses on how the logic of sexual difference comes to be organized in binary terms. See *Discours, figure*, 138–141.
3. (Urbana: University of Illinois Press, 1988). See especially chapters 8 and 9. Needless to say, these reservations apply to writing on film alone and are not *a fortiori* extendable to all of feminist and psychoanalytic theory. Important critical rereadings of Freud are represented in the work of Luce Irigaray and Shoshana Felman, for example, both of whom are sensitive to Freud's complex and contradictory rhetoric, neither of whom imposes a logic of binary division on his thought.
4. *Screen* 16:3 (Autumn 1975), 6–18. Cited as VP.
5. Mulvey has reconsidered the 'Visual Pleasure' argument, which dates from 1975, in several important essays: 'Afterthoughts on "Visual Pleasure and Narrative Cinema" Inspired by "Duel in the Sun" (King Vidor, 1946)', *Framework*, 15/16/17 (Summer 1981), 12–15 and 'Changes', *Discourse*, 7 (Fall 1985), 11–30. These essays have been collected in her book, *Visual and Other Pleasures* (Bloomington: Indiana University Press, 1988). Important and sympathetic critiques of Mulvey include Mary Ann Doane's 'Misrecognition and Identity', *Ciné-Tracts*, 11 (Fall 1980), 25–32; Kaja Silverman's 'Masochism and Subjectivity', *Framework*, 12 (1980), 2–9, Gaylyn Studlar's 'Masochism and the Perverse Pleasures of Cinema', *Quarterly Review of Film Studies*, 9:4 (Fall 1984), 267–282; Teresa de Lauretis's *Alice Doesn't* (Bloomington: Indiana University Press, 1984), 103–157; and Miriam Hansen's 'Pleasure, Ambivalence, Identification: Valentino and Female Spectatorship', *Cinema Journal*, 25:4 (Summer 1986), 6–32. Also see two special journal issues on sexual difference, *Oxford Literary Review*, 8:1/2 (1986) and *Screen*, 28:1 (Winter 1987).

6. J. Laplanche and J.-B. Pontalis, *The Language of Psychoanalysis*, trans. Donald Nicholson-Smith (New York: W. W. Norton and Co., 1973), 205.
7. This logic is only characteristic of Freud's texts before 1920. The theory of the drives was profoundly transformed by Freud's hypotheses concerning the death drive and primary masochism as represented in *Beyond the Pleasure Principle* and 'The Economic Problem of Masochism'.
8. *The Standard Edition of the Complete Psychological Works of Sigmund Freud*, trans. from German under the editorship of James Strachey (London: Hogarth Press, date by volume), 14: 109–140. Cited as SE. The original title of Freud's essay is 'Triebe und Triebschicksale'. Although *Triebe* is usually translated as 'instinct', Freud also uses the term *Instinkt* and seems to distinguish between them in other writings. In *The Language of Psychoanalysis*, Laplanche and Pontalis suggest that a distinction should be made between the drives [*Triebe*] on one hand, and the instincts [*Instinkts*] on the other, on the basis of ideas that begin to be developed more clearly in 'Triebe und Triebschicksale' (214–217). In this case, the term instinct should be preserved for the classical, biological sense of genetically inherited patterns of behavior and response. The term drive [*Trieb*] however, belongs only to psychoanalysis as one of its essential concepts. The fate of the drives is a consequence of the particular history of each individual in their relation to society. While originating in something like a sexual force, the drives are only comprehensible through their organization into components and their attachment to particular unconscious ideas or representations. I will maintain this distinction even though the translations of the Standard Edition are inconsistent on this point.
9. See Jacqueline Rose's interesting argument in 'Paranoia and the Film System', *Screen*, 17:4 (Winter 1976/77), 85–104. Also see Lacan's essays 'The mirror stage as formative of the function of the I' and 'Aggressivity in psychoanalysis' in Jacques Lacan, *Écrits: A Selection*, trans. Alan Sheridan (New York: Norton, 1977), 1–29.
10. 'Pleasure, Ambivalence, Identification', 11. I am deeply indebted to Hansen's reading of Freud and of suggesting ways of understanding his arguments outside of the Lacanian paradigm that is particular to contemporary film theory.
11. Cf. *Three Essays on the Theory of Sexuality*, SE 7: 150. Two important scholars, Gaylyn Studlar and Kaja Silverman, have addressed this problem from divergent points of view, and I must admit that my sympathies reside with Silverman's position. In a critique of Studlar's reading of Gilles Deleuze's *Masochism: An Interpretation of Coldness and Cruelty* (trans. Jean McNeil [New York: George Braziller, 1971]) in the essay 'Masochism and the Perverse Pleasures of Cinema', Silverman notes that 'Studlar conflates Deleuze's oral mother with the pre-Oedipal mother of object relations psychoanalysis, and extrapolates from that conflation a highly dubious argument about the origin of masochism. According to Studlar, that perversion has its basis in the (male) child's relationship with the actual mother prior to the advent of the father, a relationship predicated upon his helpless subordination to her, and the insatiability of his desire for her. Masochistic suffering consequently derives from the pain of separation from the mother, and the impossible desire to fuse with her again, rather than from the categorical imperative of the Oedipus complex and the symbolic law. This is a determinedly political reading of masochism,

which comes close to grounding that perversion in biology' ('Masochism and Male Subjectivity', *Camera Obscura*, 17 [May 1988], 66). By the same token, in opposing masochism to sadism as a model of filmic pleasure, Studlar fundamentally misconstrues my critique of Mulvey in the original version of this chapter (first published in *Wide Angle* 15:1 (1982), 4–15), reinvoking an agonistic logic of binary terms that I insist must be rejected.

12. Of particular interest, among many relevant essays, are Freud's accounts of the case history of the 'Wolf Man', and the analysis of the phantasy of 'A Child is being Beaten'
13. A number of interesting essays have been published on the eroticization of the male body in film and television, especially from the point of view of homosexual desire. Among the most thought-provoking are: Steve Neale's 'Masculinity as Spectacle', *Screen* 24:6 (November–December 1983), 2–116 and 'Sexual Difference in Cinema', *Oxford Literary Review*, 8:1/2 (1986), 123–132; Richard Dyer's 'Don't Look Now—the Male Pin-Up', *Screen* 23:3/4 (September/October 1982), 61–73; and Andrew Ross's 'Masculinity and *Miami Vice*', *Oxford Literary Review*, 8:1/2 (1986), 143–154.
14. Beverly Brown and Parveen Adams have cogently defined and criticized this problem in feminist politics in their essay, 'The Feminine Body and Feminist Politics', *m/f*, 3 (1979), 35–50. Also see my *Crisis of Political Modernism*, 249–262
15. See in particular *Totem and Taboo* (1912–1913), SE 13: 7–161.
16. SE 21: 106. Compare, for example, this footnote from *Three Essays on the Theory of Sexuality*: 'It is essential to understand clearly that the concepts of "masculine" and "feminine" whose meaning seems so unambiguous to ordinary people, are among the most confused that occur in science. It is possible to distinguish at least three uses. "Masculine" and "feminine" are used sometimes in the sense of activity and passivity, sometimes in a biological and sometimes, again, in a sociological sense. The first of these three meanings is the essential one and the most serviceable in psychoanalysis. When, for instance, libido was described in the text above as being "masculine," the word was being used in this sense, for an instinct is always active even when it has a passive aim in view. The second, or biological, meaning of "masculine" and "feminine" is the one whose applicability can be determined most easily. Here "masculine" and "feminine" are characterized by the presence of spermatozoa or ova respectively and by the functions proceeding from them. . . . The third, or sociological meaning, receives its connotation from the observation of actually existing masculine and feminine individuals. Such observation shows that pure masculinity or femininity is not to be found either in a psychological or biological sense. Every individual on the contrary displays a mixture of the character-traits belonging to his own and to the opposite sex; and he shows a combination of activity and passivity whether or not these character-traits tally with his biological ones' (SE 7: 219–220).
17. Compare Mulvey's argument in this respect with Peter Wollen's 'Godard and Counter-Cinema: *Vent d'est*', which is perhaps the most direct and influential manifesto for a 'Brechtian' conception of political modernism in the cinema. Wollen's essay was originally published in *Afterimage*, 4 (1972) and has recently been anthologized, along with 'Visual Pleasure and Narrative

Cinema', in Philip Rosen (ed.), *Narrative, Apparatus, Ideology* (New York: Columbia University Press, 1986), 120–129.

18. Whether a term like 'fetishistic scopophilia' has a precise sense in the context of Freudian theory or whether it must rest as an interesting neologism on Mulvey's part is also uncertain. In Freud's own important essay on 'Fetishism' [SE 21: 152–157] there is no evidence to characterize this perversion as a 'passive' form of looking. On the contrary, it is characterized by a profound degree of psychical activity. Moreover, the point that is most important for Freud, and indeed most important for any theory of ideology, concerns the problem of *Ichspaltung*, or the splitting of the ego where the subject simultaneously holds contradictory and mutually exclusive beliefs. Contrary to the view promoted in contemporary film theory, the splitting of the ego is not a 'result' of the castration complex, nor is this phenomenon peculiar only to fetishism. Fetishism is only the clearest example of this phenomenon. In short, the splitting of the ego is for Freud a more general and widespread condition, representing one of the ego's strongest means of defense against traumatic events of all kinds. See his late essay, 'Splitting of the Ego in the Process of Defense', SE 23: 275–278.
19. For an interesting discussion of this concept in relation to film, see Thierry Kuntzel, *Le Défilement*: A View in Close Up', trans. Bertrand Augst, *Camera Obscura*, 2 (Fall 1977) 51–65.

11 Masochism and the Perverse Pleasures of the Cinema

Gaylyn Studlar*

This study offers an alternative model to the current discourse that emphasizes voyeurism aligned with sadism, the male controlling gaze as the only position of spectatorial pleasure and a polarized notion of sexual difference with the female regarded as 'lack'. In 1978, Christine Gledhill wrote of the need to broaden the focus of feminist film theory, to question guiding theoretical assumptions and to confront the complexity of 'woman's place' within patriarchal culture.[1] In the context of feminist-psychoanalytic approaches to film, the hegemony of the Freudian–Lacanian–Metzian model has, unfortunately, reduced rather than enlarged the field of questions that feminist theory has asked about specific forms of enunciation in classic narrative cinema and the possibilities of subject positioning. While I do not assume to displace the dominant model, there is I believe an obvious call to question some of the assumptions that have shaped current trends.

My alternative model is derived from Gilles Deleuze's *Masochism: An Interpretation of Coldness and Cruelty.*[2] Deleuze employs a psychoanytic-literary approach to the novels of Leopold von Sacher-Masoch, the namesake of masochism, to challenge basic Freudian tenets regarding the sado-masochistic duality and the etiology of masochism as a response to the father and castration fear. If the qualitative differences between sadism and masochism are disregarded and only the pain/pleasure content is considered, then the two perversions might well be considered to be complementary as Freud maintained, but Deleuze shows that only when masochism's formal patterns are recognized as reflections of a unique underlying psychoanalytic structure can the perversion be correctly defined as a distinct clinical entity or as an aesthetic:

* Gaylyn Studlar, 'Masochism and the Perverse Pleasures of the Cinema' from *Quarterly Review of Film and Video Studies* (1984), reprinted by permission of the author.

Masochism is above all formal and dramatic: this means that its peculiar pleasure–pain complex is determined by a particular kind of formalism, and its experience of guilt by a specific story.[3]

Deleuze considers masochism to be a phenomenology of experience that reaches far beyond the limited definition of a perverse sexuality. Similarly, the masochistic aesthetic extends beyond the purely clinical realm into the arena of artistic form, language, and production of pleasure through a text.

Comparing Masoch's and Sade's novels, Deleuze concludes that Sade's intentions, formal techniques, and language are completely at odds with those of Masoch. These differences are but a reflection of differing psychoanalytic determinants. The Sadian discourse—denotative, scientific, unblinkingly direct in its obscene imperatives and descriptions—creates a fantastically cruel heterocosm based exclusively on the rule of reason. The governing sadistic fantasy expressed in Sade's work exalts the father 'beyond all laws', says Deleuze, and negates the mother.[4] In contrast, Masoch's fictive world is mythical, persuasive, aesthetically oriented, and centered around the idealizing, mystical exaltation of love for the punishing woman. In her ideal form as representative of the powerful oral mother, the female in the masochistic scenario is not sadistic, but must inflict cruelty in love to fulfill her role in the mutually agreed upon masochistic scheme. Masoch writes in a typical passage from his most famous novel, 'Venus in Furs':

To love and be loved, what joy! And yet how this splendour pales in comparison with the blissful torment of worshipping a woman who treats one as a plaything, of being the slave of a beautiful tyrant who mercilessly tramples one underfoot.[5]

As Deleuze notes, the paradox of the masochistic alliance as exemplified in Masoch's work is the subversion of the expected patriarchal positions of power/powerlessness, master/slave, with the ultimate paradox being the slave's (the male's) willingness to confer power to the female.[6]

An excerpt from Sade's *One Hundred and Twenty Days of Sodom* illustrates the blatant absurdity of equating sadism and masochism on a literary level, and, as Deleuze shows, on a psychoanalytic level as well:

This libertine requires a dozen women, six young, six old and if 'tis possible, six of them should be mothers and the other six daughters. He pumps out their cunts, asses, and mouths; when applying his lips to the cunt, he wants copious urine; when at the mouth, much saliva; when at the ass, abundant farts.[7]

Even when Sade chooses a woman as 'heroine', she still acts out the criminally misogynistic impulse that is not satisfied with merely objectifying or demystifing women but must destroy them. In the masochistic text, the female is not one of a countless number of discarded objects but an idealized, powerful figure both dangerous and comforting. Fetishization, fantasy, and idealizing disavowal replace the frenzied Sadian destruction of the female. While Sade's incessantly active libertines challenge the limits of human endurance and evil in endlessly repeated cycles of sex and violence, the masochistic world barely suggests sexual activity or violence. Deleuze remarks: 'Of Masoch it can be said, as it cannot be of Sade, that no one has ever been so far with so little offence to decency.'[8] In the masochistic aesthetic, dramatic suspense replaces Sadian accelerating repetition of action, intimacy between mutually chosen partners replaces the impersonality of masses of libertines and victims, idealized eroticism replaces the obscenity that threatens to burst the limits of conventional language in an attempt to match the unattainable, destructive Idea of Evil.[9] If Sade's writing is 'structurally linked to crime and sex' as Roland Barthes has said,[10] then the work of Masoch reveals a formal and narrative pattern structurally linked to self-abasement and pre-Oedipal desire.

The formal structures of the masochistic aesthetic—fantasy, disavowal, fetishism, and suspense—overlap with the primary structures that enable classic narrative cinema to produce visual pleasure. These similarities raise fundamental questions about the relationship of cinematic pleasure to masochism, sexual differentation, processes of identification, the representation of the female in film, and other issues in which a model derived from Deleuze's theory offers a radical alternative to those Freudian assumptions that have been adopted by most of psychoanalytic film theory.

The key question is: Why replace the line of thought represented by Christian Metz and Laura Mulvey, with its stress on the similarity between the structures of sadism and visual pleasure, with an emphasis on masochism's relationship to visual pleasure? What are the advantages?

By focusing on the pregenital period in the development of desire and sexual identity rather than on the phallic phase emphasized in Freud's studies, a consideration of the masochistic aesthetic and film shifts attention to a stage of psycho-sexual life that has been an overlooked determinant in the 'sadistic' model of cinematic spectatorship. The 'masochistic model' rejects a stance that has emphasized the phallic phase and the pleasure of control or mastery and therefore offers an alternative to strict Freudian models that have proven to be a dead end for feminist-psychoanalytic theory. In trying to come to terms with patriarchal society and the cinema as a construct of that society, current theoretical discourse has often inadvertently reduced the psychoanalytic complexity of spectatorship through a regressive phallocentrism that ignores a wider range of psychological influences on visual pleasure.

The approach presented here brings together two lines of theoretical work previously separated: (1) the analogy between the cinematic apparatus and the dream screen of the oral period of infancy pursued by Jean-Louis Baudry and Robert Eberwein,[11] and (2) the consideration of representation of the female, identification, and sexually differentiated spectatorship in the theories of Laura Mulvey, Claire Johnston, Mary Ann Doane, and others.[12] The 'masochistic model' could be viewed as an attempt to use the former approach to address the concerns of the latter.

Freud dealt with the question of masochism in several essays; his views on the perversion changed over the years, but he was consistent in his belief that Oedipal conflict was the cause of the perversion. Guilt and fear of castration by the father led the male child to assume a passive position in order to placate the father and win his love. Being beaten by the father (or the female who provides the father's disguise in the conscious fantasy) was 'not only the punishment for the forbidden genital relation with the mother, but also a regressive substitute for it'. The punishment acquired 'libidinal excitation', and 'here', Freud declared, 'we have the essence of masochism'.[13] Freud developed a theory of masochism as a primary drive expressing the Death Instinct but was continually drawn into reaffirming the complementary status of masochism and sadism. He stated that, in the former, the heightened sadism of the superego was retained in the libido with the ego as 'victim'. In sadism, the Death Instinct was deflected outwards.[14] Deleuze believes the superego/ego activities of sadism and masochism are completely different, but, more important to a study of masochism and film, he makes the mother the primary determinant in the structure of the masochistic fantasy and in the etiology of the perversion.[15] Both love object and controlling agent for the helpless child, the mother is viewed as an ambivalent figure during the oral period. Whether due to the child's experience of real trauma, as Bernhard Berliner asserts, or due to the narcissistic infant's own insatiability of demand, the pleasure associated with the oral mother is joined in masochism with the need for pain.[16] The masochistic fantasy cannot by its very nature fulfill its most primal desire—'dual unity and the complete symbiosis between child and mother'—except in the imagination.[17] As a consequence, death becomes the fantasy solution to masochistic desire.

The mother assumes her authority in masochism on the basis of her own importance to the child, not, as Freud maintained, because the father figure must be 'hidden' behind her in order to deflect the homosexual implications of the male subject's fantasy. Roy Schafer identifies the child's fear of losing the mother as the primary source of her authority.[18] Rooted in the fear of being abandoned by the mother, masochism obsessively recreates the movement between concealment and revelation, disappearance and appearance, seduction and rejection. Posited as 'lacking nothing', the mother is allied with the child in the disavowal of the destruction of the superego. Deleuze maintains that the father's punishing superego and genital sexuality are symbolically punished in the son, who must expiate his likeness to the father. Pain symbolically expels the father and 'fools' the superego. It is not the son who is guilty, as in Freud's theory, but the father who attempts to come between mother and child.[19] In Deleuze's view, fear of the castrating father and Oedipal guilt cannot account for masochism's paradoxical pain/pleasure structure. His denial of the importance of castration anxiety to the perversion's formation constitutes a revision of Freudian theory that stands in agreement with Michael de M'Uzan and Theodore Reik. M'Uzan deduces from clinical observation that the masochist 'fears nothing, not even castration'.[20] In his lengthy study *Masochism in Modern Man*, in which he details the social rather than sexual manifestations of masochism, Reik parallels M'Uzan's assessment: castration anxiety is not of major significance in the etiology of the perversion.[21]

It should be noted that Deleuze positions the male as the fantasizing subject of his construct. In this respect, his model might be regarded as sexist, although he notes that the female child can take the same position in relation to the oral mother.[22] Deleuze's model may also be approached from another perspective that makes it more applicable to a consideration of spectatorial response to film. The masochistic fantasy may be viewed as a situation in which the subject (male or female) assumes the position of the child who desires to be controlled *within* the dynamics of the fantasy. The sadistic fantasy (while not a simple reversal of instinct or aim) is one in which the subject takes the position of the controlling parent, who is not allied with the child (object) in a mutually agreed upon pact of pleasure/pain but who exercises (within the fantasy) a sadistic power over an unwilling victim.[23]

Masochism subverts traditional psychoanalytic notions regarding the origins of human desire and the mother's and father's roles in the child's psychic development. A theory of masochism that emphasizes pre-Oedipal conflicts and pleasures invites consideration of responses to film by spectators of both sexes that may conflict with conscious cultural assumptions about sexual difference, gender identity, and the separation of identification from object cathexis. A theory of masochistic desire also questions the complicity of most psychoanalytic film theory with phallocentrism as a formative instance in structuring identity and scopic pleasure. It also questions the pre-eminence of a pleasure based on a position of control rather than submission. In suggesting that the oral mother could be the primary figure of identification and power in clinical and aesthetic manifestations of masochism, Deleuze's theory of masochistic desire challenges the notion that male scopic pleasure must center around control—never identification with or submission to the female.

This article is derived from a book-length study of the films of Josef Von Sternberg that uses practical criticism to examine the masochistic aesthetic in film and the relationship between the formal elements of the aesthetic, the films' psychodynamics, and the specific forms of visual pleasure. With their submissive male masochist, the oral mother embodied in the ambivalent, alluring presence of Marlene Dietrich, and their ambiguous sexuality that has often been linked to 'sadomasochism' and 'degradation',[24] the Von Sternberg/Dietrich collaborations offer themselves as a prime case study of the masochistic aesthetic in film.

Within the context of the post-modernist critique of realism, Von Sternberg's films have become the center of increasing interest. They are creations of sublime visual beauty and sensuality; dreamlike chiaroscuro and stifling decorative excess form the backdrop for melodrama pervaded by a diffuse sexuality. As many critics have remarked, the films are poetic but not symbolic, melodramatic and even tragic, but marked by a detached, ironic humor. In these narratives dominated by passion, even passion takes on a curiously distancing coldness. The films featuring Marlene Dietrich add the paradox of the dazzling yet androgynous female who is simultaneously moral and amoral, eminently proper yet irredeemably decadent.

As a result of their multiple layers of paradox, fascinating ambiguity of emotion, and almost transcendental visual beauty, Von Sternberg's films have again and again inspired attempts to explain their structure and meaning. They have just as frequently served as examples in theoretical treatises dealing with the representation of the female in narrative cinema or questions concerning the unconscious determinants of visual pleasure. Among the most important of these is Laura Mulvey's use of Von Sternberg's films to illustrate the concept of fetishistic scopophilia in her milestone article, 'Visual Pleasure and Narrative Cinema'. To her, Von Sternberg's *Morocco* typifies the kind of visual style and narrative structure which traps the female into a position of 'to-be-looked-at-ness', of passive exhibitionism that oppresses women for the sake of the patriarchy's fetishistic aims. Mulvey regards such a female fetish as 'reassuring rather than dangerous'.[25] Although subscribing to Mulvey's thesis, Mary Ann Doane has referred to Dietrich's image as exemplifying the 'excess of femininity . . . aligned with the *femme fatale* . . . and . . . necessarily regarded by men as evil incarnate'.[26] Contrary to Doane, it is Dietrich's androgynous quality that is most often noted, and Carole Zucker has argued (with justification) that Dietrich's morality is 'impossibly exalted' in the Von Sternberg films.[27] Adding to the controversy is Robin Wood's attempt to counter Mulvey's analysis of the role of the female in the films' narrative strategy and visual style. He argues that Von Sternberg is 'fully aware' of the female's position as object for the male gaze and uses this as 'an articulated theme' in *Blonde Venus* rather than an end product.[28] He has not, however, countered Mulvey's fundamental premise: that visual pleasure in classic narrative cinema is based on the workings of the castration complex.

Rather than develop a detailed textual analysis, this examination of the masochistic aesthetic and film explores the wider theoretical implications of masochism to cinematic pleasure. I will very briefly examine these implications in regard to five crucial issues: (1) the female defined as lack, (2) the male gaze defined by control, (3) the cause and function of disavowal and fetishism, (4) the dream screen, and (5) identification, particularly identification with the opposite sex.

THE FEMALE AS LACK

The female as cinematic image is often considered to be an ambivalent spectatorial pleasure for the male because she signifies the possibility of castration. She represents difference, nonphallus, lack. Undoubtably, the tension between attraction and fear is an ambivalence underlying much of cinema's representation of the female, but it is an oversimplification to collapse the entire signification of woman to phallic meaning.[29]

Within masochism, the mother is not defined as lack nor as 'phallic' in respect to a simple transference of the male's symbol of power. She is powerful in her own right because she possesses what the male lacks—the breast and the womb.[30] Active nurturer, first source of love and object of desire, first environment and agent of control, the oral mother of masochism assumes all symbolic functions. Parallel to her idealization is a degrading disavowal of the father. 'The father is nothing,' says Deleuze, 'he is deprived of all symbolic function.'[31]

The infant's fantasy goal of re-fusion, of complete symbiosis with the mother is necessarily informed by ambivalence. The promise of blissful reincorporation into the mother's body and re-fusion of the child's narcissistic ego with the mother as ideal ego is also a threat. Only death can hold the final mystical solution to the expiation of the father and symbiotic reunion with the idealized maternal rule. The masochist imagines the final triumph of a parthenogenetic rebirth from the mother.[32]

Deleuze associates the good oral mother of masochism with the 'ideal of coldness, solicitude, and death', the mythic extremes that crystallize her ambivalence.[33] The female reflects the fantasy of the desiring infant who regards the mother as both sacred and profane, loving and rejecting, frustratingly mobile yet the essence of rhythmic stability and stillness. In the masochist's suspension of the final 'gratification' of death, the obsessive return to the moment of separation from the oral mother must be reenacted continuously as the masochistic *fort/da* game of desire that is the meeting point between fantasy and action.[34] Masochistic repetition sustains the paradoxical pain/pleasure structure of the perversion's psychodynamics and reflects the careful control of desire so necessary to sustaining the masochistic scenario even as it expresses the compulsive aspect of the fixation in infantile sexuality. Overriding the demands of the incest taboo, the castration complex, and progress into genital sexuality, masochism is a 'subversive' desire that affirms the compelling power of the pre-Oedipal mother as a stronger attraction than the 'normalizing' force of the father who threatens the alliance of mother and child.

The repetition of loss, of suffering, does not deter or confuse masochistic desire but inflames it, as graphically demonstrated in Von Sternberg's *The Devil Is a Woman.* His health broken, his career ruined by his involvement with 'the most dangerous woman alive', Don Pasquale protests that he gains 'no pleasure' in telling his friend Antonio about his road to ruin. It becomes obvious that he not only enjoys telling his story, but the retelling itself is the impetus for a new round robin in Don Pasquale's masochistic pursuit of Concha Perez. He allows himself to be shot in a duel to satisfy Concha's desire for another man (Antonio). Lying on his deathbed, he attains what he desires most, Concha and Death, one in the same both, still suspended, promised, but withheld. The eternal masochistic attitude of waiting and suspended suffering is maintained in all its tragedy and comic absurdity to the very end of this, the last Von Sternberg/Dietrich collaboration.

The ambivalence of separation/union from the mother, formalized in masochistic repetition and suspension, is an ambivalence shared by all human beings. Contrary to the Freudian view of familial dynamics, in which the mother has little psychological impact on her children's development, Deleuze, Schafer, Robert Stoller, Nancy Chodorow, and Janine Chasseguet-Smirgel regard the mother's influence and her *authority* as major factors in the child's development. The child's view of the powerful, loved, but threatening female during the pre-Oedipal stage is not obliterated by later stages of life—including the male's passage through the castration complex.[35] Hans Loewald suggests that, while the identification with the powerful pre-Oedipal mother is fundamental to the individual's organization of ego-reality, this same identification is the 'source of the deepest dread'.[36] Janine Chasseguet-Smirgel goes so far as to suggest that the contempt for women Freud believed was an inevitable male reaction to the perception of female 'castration' is actually a pathological and defensive response to maternal power.[37]

In returning to the fantasies originating in the oral stage of development, the masochistic aesthetic opens the entirety of film to the existence of spectatorial pleasures divorced from issues of castration, sexual difference, and female lack. Current theory ignores the pleasure in submission that is phylogenetically older than the pleasure of mastery—for both sexes. In masochism, as in the infantile stage of helpless dependence that marks its genesis, pleasure does not involve mastery of the female but submission to her. This pleasure applies to the infant, the masochist, and the film spectator as well. Psychoanalytic film theory must reintegrate the powerful maternal image that is viewed as a complex, pleasurable 'screen memory' by both male and female spectators, even in the patriarchal society.[38] As Janine Chasseguet-Smirgel asserts:

> *Now the woman as she is depicted in Freudian theory is exactly the opposite of the primal maternal imago* as she is revealed in the clinical material of both sexes . . . the contradictions . . . throughout Freud's work on the problem of sexual phallic monism and its consquences, force us to take a closer notice of this opposition between the woman, as she is described by Freud, and the mother as she is known to the Unconscious. . . . If we underestimate the importance of our earliest relations and our cathexis of the maternal image, this means we allow paternal law to predominate and are in flight from our infantile dependence.[39]

Castration fear and the perception of sexual difference have no importance in forming the masochistic desire for complete symbiosis with the mother. The polarities of female lack/male phallus and the narrow view that the female in film can only function as the object of a sadistic male spectatorial possession must yield to other considerations.

The female in the masochistic aesthetic is more than the passive object of the male's desire for possession. She is also a figure of identification, the mother of plenitude whose gaze meets the infant's as it asserts her presence and her power. Von Sternberg's expression of the masochistic aesthetic in film offers a complex image of the female in which she is the object of the look but also the holder of a 'controlling' gaze that turns the male into an object of 'to-be-looked-at-ness'. In *Morocco*, Private Tom Brown (Gary Cooper), a notorious 'ladykiller', is reduced to the passive 'feminine' position as object of Amy Jolly's appraising, steady gaze. Amy throws him a rose, which Brown then wears behind his ear. Operating within the limitations of the patriarchy, the Dietrich character in these films displays her ability to fascinate in confirmation of what Michel Foucault has called 'power asserting itself in the pleasure of showing off, scandalizing, or resisting'.[40] In response to the male gaze, Dietrich looks back or initiates the look. This simple fact contains the potential for questioning her objectification.

THE GAZE

While the pleasures of the cinematic apparatus as dream screen have been associated with oral phase pleasure by Jean-Louis Baudry and Robert Eberwein, the pleasures of viewing the female image in film have consistently been linked to the phallic phase, the castration complex, and the resulting physiological 'needs' of the male spectator.

The structure of the look is one of the most important elements in defining visual pleasure. According to Laura Mulvey, narrative film is made for the pleasure of the male spectator alone, who 'indirectly' possesses the female through the look, or rather the relay of looks created by the camera, the male star's gaze and the spectator's own gaze. The woman is the bearer of the 'burden of male desire', which is 'born with language'. She crystallizes the paradox of 'the traumatic moment' of desire's birth—the castration complex, because she represents sexual difference. The male spectator escapes the castration anxiety the female image evokes either by a sadistic voyeurism (demystifying the female) or through fetishistic scopophilia. The latter, a 'complete disavowal of castration', turns the female into a fetish, the signifier of the absent phallus.[41]

Mulvey's deterministic, polarized model leads to a crucial 'blind spot' in her theory of visual pleasure, which has been noted by D. N. Rodowick. In 'The Difficulty of Difference', Rodowick argues that Mulvey avoids the logical conclusion of her own theory that would necessitate pairing masochism, the passive submission to the object, with fetishistic scopophilia. Because of the 'political nature of her argument', Rodowick concludes, Mulvey cannot admit that the masculine look contains passive elements and can signify *submission to* rather than *possession of* the female.[42]

In eliding a possible male spectatorial position informed by masochism, Mulvey is forced to limit the male gaze to one that only views the female as a signifier of castration and an object for possession. In reducing spectatorial pleasure to the workings of the castration complex, Mulvey also ignores the existence of pre-Oedipal desires and ambivalences that play a part in the genesis of scopophilia and fetishism as well as masochism. In Mulvey's construct of immutable polarities, the female 'can exist only in relation to castration'; she is either the 'bearer of guilt' or the 'perfect product'.[43]

Cinematic pleasure is much closer to masochistic scopic pleasure than to a sadistic, controlling pleasure privileged by Mulvey and also by Christian Metz. In Metz's *The Imaginary Signifier*, the voyeuristic separation of subject/screen object is used to align the spectator with sadism. 'Voyeuristic desire, along with certain forms of sadism,' says Metz, 'is the only desire whose principle of distance symbolically and spatially evokes this fundamental rent.' Metz believes that all voyeurism is sadistic to a degree and compares cinematic voyeurism to 'unauthorized scopophilia' and its prototype, the child viewing the primal scene.[44]

Contrary to Metz, Jean Laplanche has shown how the spectatorial position in the primal gaze is aligned with masochism, not sadism. Laplanche considers masochism to be the 'fundamental fantasy'. He compares the infant's position to that of 'Odysseus tied to the mast or Tantalus, on whom is imposed the spectacle of parental intercourse.' Corresponding to the perturbation of pain is the 'sympathetic excitation . . . the passive position of the child . . . [that] is not simply a passivity in relation to adult activity, but passivity in relation to adult fantasy intruding within him.'[45] Parallel to Laplanche's description of the primal scene is Masoch's 'A Childhood Memory and Reflection on the Novel'. Ten-year-old Leopold von Sacher-Masoch, hiding in his aunt's bedroom closet, hears his aunt welcome her lover: 'I did not understand what they were saying, still less what they were doing, but my heart began to pound, for I was acutely aware of my situation . . . ' The husband interrupts the lovers' rendezvous. Madame Zenobia begins to beat him. She then discovers Leopold and whips *him*. 'I must admit,' Masoch writes, 'while I writhed under my aunt's cruel blows, I experienced acute pleasure.'[46] Not surprisingly, Von Sternberg's films also contain many scenes that evoke the situation of the child witnessing or overhearing parental intercourse. In *Shanghai Express*, Doc Harvey eavesdrops on the 'negotiations' between Lily and the nefarious General Chang. Like the passive child who sees/overhears the primal scene and fantasizes both discovery and punishment, Doc is threatened with punishment for his curiosity and his desire: General Chang decides to blind him. In *The Scarlet Empress*, Alexei loves Catherine but is forced by her to prepare the royal bedchamber for the arrival of her lover, General Orloff. Alexei assumes the role of the child-spectator.

If Sade's novels are taken as the prototype of sadistic object relations, then it is obvious that the sadist is driven to consume or destroy the object in order to bring about the directly experienced pleasure of orgasm for himself. This negation cannot be exercised merely through the sadistic 'look'—the active gaze. Orgasm is not the goal of the masochist, who is bound to the regime of pregenital sexuality. Masoch's heroes are forever swooning into a faint before the blissful moment of consummation. Closing the gap between the desiring masochistic subject and the object actually threatens the narcissistic gratification of the masochist who 'gives nothing' and cannot endure the 'anxiety [of giving] that must accompany orgasm'.[47] Masochistic desire depends on separation to guarantee the structure of its ambivalent desire. To close the gap, to overcome separation from the mother, to fulfill desire, to achieve orgasm means death. The contracted, mutual alliance of the masochistic relationship guarantees distance/separation. Unlike sadism, which depends upon action and immediate gratification, masochism savors suspense and distance.

The spectator at the cinematic dream screen regresses to a similar state of orality as the masochist and also experiences a loss of ego-body boundary. Spectatorial pleasure is a limited one like the infantile extragenital sexual pleasure that defines the masochist. Like the masochist, but unlike the sadist, to remain within the confines of normal spectatorship and not become, as Stephen Heath says, 'a true voyeur',[48] the spectator must avoid the orgasmic release that would effectively destroy the boundaries of disavowal and disrupt the magical thinking that defines his/her oral, infantile, and narcissistic use of the cinematic object. The spectator's narcissistic omnipotence is like the narcissistic, infantile omnipotence of the masochist, who ultimately cannot control the active partner. Immobile, surrounded in darkness, the spectator becomes the passive receiving object who is also subject. The spectator must comprehend the images, but the images cannot be controlled. On this level of pleasure, the spectator receives, but no object-related demands are made.

FETISHISM AND DISAVOWAL

The masochistic aesthetic appears to be a major site for developing a critique of theories of visual pleasure that hinge on the role of castration fear in the formation of male spectatorial pleasure. Masochism is not associated with castration fear yet fetishism is an integral part of its dynamic. Disavowal and fetishism, the two common matrices of masochism and cinematic spectatorial pleasure, do not always reflect the psychic trauma of castration and sexual difference defined as feminine lack.

Recent psychoanalytic research into the pre-Oedipal period indicates that disavowal and fetishism are operative much, much earlier than the phallic stage and are not necessarily used as a defense against castration anxiety. Of particular importance to the visual pleasure and masochism is the view that fetishism and masochism evidence the prolonged need for primary identification with the 'almighty pre-Oedipal mother'.[49] If the mother/infant relationship is disturbed when the child's body boundaries are not well established, fetishism based on the disavowal of her loss may develop as a defensive maneuver to restore the mother's body, permit passive infant satisfaction, and protect primary identification.[50]

In summarizing various findings, Robert Dickes states that most pregenital research stands in direct opposition to Freud, i.e., that 'the fetish represents more than the female phallus'.[51] Dickes believes that the traditional view of the fetish as 'a talisman in relieving phallic castration anxiety' is a 'late stage of the development . . . ordinarily . . . never reached'.[52] Most children, regardless of sex, use transitional objects to soothe the separation from the mother. If the child cannot accommodate itself to this separation, the transitional object may be retained and lead to fetishism. While Socarides believes fetishism 'may have no etiological connection with phallic or genital sexuality', Wulff concludes that the fetish 'represents a substitute for the mother's breast and the mother's body'.[53]

Fetishism and disavowal are not exclusively male psychoanalytic manifestations, but males may be much more likely to develop such perversions because of problems in resolving gender identity (crossing over from primary to same-sex identification) unrelated to the existence of any sexually differentiated scopic drive.[54] Female perversion does exist; however, the extreme forms, in particular, are less 'visible' than the male version because the female can 'hide' impaired sexual function.[55] As a result, females may, as Charles Socarides believes, tend to exhibit 'forms of fetishism not obviously associated with genital functioning', for example, ritualistic preparations for intercourse.[56] Although it is naive to assume that the identification of female scopophilia or fetishism would open a gap for the female spectator within dominant cinema, the pregenital origin of these manifestations calls into question the views that use them to exclude the female from the fundamental structures of cinematic pleasure or even from the possibility of libidinalized looking.

DREAM SCREEN

Masochistic fantasy is dominated by oral pleasure, the desire to return to the nondifferentiated body state of the mother/child, and the fear of abandonment (the state of nonbreast, nonplenitude). In a sense, these same wishes are duplicated by the film spectator who becomes a child again in response to the dream screen of cinema. This dream screen affords spectatorial pleasure in recreating the first fetish—the mother as nurturing environment. The spectator at the cinematic dream screen regresses to a state that Baudry says is analogous to the oral period.[57] Like the fetish objects that follow, the dream screen restores the sense of wholeness of the first symbiotic relationship as it restores the unity of the undifferentiated ego/ego ideal. It functions like a 'good blanket' reuniting the spectator/child with the earliest object of desire that lessens the anxiety of the ego loosened from body boundaries.[58]

In restoring the first sleep environment of the dream screen, the cinematic apparatus re-establishes the fluid boundaries to self. In 'The Unrememberable and the Unforgettable: The Passive Primal Repression', Alvan Frank discusses the psychic benefits of hallucinatory screen/breast experiences that create an absence of ego boundaries and permit the regression to earlier perceptual modes.[59] The cinema may also offer this type of psychic reparation in the re-creation of a screen phenomenon that gives access to the unremembered 'memories' of earliest childhood experience.

The dream screen as the first hallucination of gratification is an essential notion to considering cinematic pleasure. Through imagination the child creates the mother and the breast. Just as the fantasized breast cannot offer real nourishment or interaction with the mother, the cinematic apparatus cannot provide intimacy or fusion with real objects. The spectator must disavow an absence: the dream screen offers only partial gratification of the symbiotic wish. The object/screen/images cannot be physically possessed or controlled by the spectator. The spectator's 'misapprehension' of control over cinematic images is less a misapprehension than it is a disavowal of the loss of ego autonomy over image formation.

IDENTIFICATION

In restoring the pre-ego of primary narcissism, the cinema encourages a regression characterized by all the possibilities of identification and projection resembling the infantile mechanisms operative in perversions. The pleasures of perversion depend directly on a splitting kind of ego defense to solidify identity.[60] By satisfying the compulsion to repeat archaic stages of life, the artificial regression of the cinema enlarges and reintegrates the ego through different forms of ego-reality.[61] The cinematic spectator experiences infantile forms of object cathexis and identification normally repressed. Among the most important aspects of the release of repressed material are the pleasures of re-experiencing the primary identification with the mother and the pleasurable possibilities of gender mobility through identification. Loewald regards identification with the mother as essential to ego formation and the structuring of the personality:

> . . . the primary narcissistic identity with the mother forever constitutes the deepest unconscious origin and structural layer of the ego and reality, and the motive force for the ego's 'remarkable striving toward unification, synthesis'.[62]

While the male's pre-Oedipal identification with the mother is repressed in adult life, for both male and female, same-sex identification does not totally exclude opposite-sex identification.[63] The wish to be both sexes—to *overcome* sexual difference—remains.

Although Freud recognized the bisexuality of every human being, he continually returned to an emphasis on the polarity between masculine and feminine—a polarity that has infiltrated feminist-psychoanalytic approaches to film. Recent research has revealed the vital importance of psychic androgyny (bisexuality) to understanding sexuality, identity, and the search for pleasure. In his study, 'The Drive to Become Both sexes', Lawrence Kubie details two prominent aspects of bisexuality: (1) the reverse of penis envy, and (2) the urge to become both sexes:

> Overlooked is the importance of the reverse and complementary envy of the male for the woman's breast, for nursing as well as his envy for the woman's ability to conceive and to bring forth babies . . . from childhood and throughout life, on conscious, preconscious, and unconscious levels, in varying proportions and emphases, the human goal seems almost invariably to be *both* sexes with the inescapable consequence that we are always attempting in every moment and every act both to affirm and deny our gender identities.[64]

Socarides, Zilboorg, and others have linked the male's fetishization of the female to this same urge to restore the wholeness of bisexuality—of having both male and female sexual characteristics. In Socarides's view, the male's identification with the pre-Oedipal mother expresses itself in 'the wish for female genitalia, the wish for a child, and the wish to undo the separation from the mother'.[65] Cathexis and identification are simultaneous in the dual aim of the bisexual urge.[66] The ability to simultaneously desire and also identify with the opposite sex has important implications for film spectatorship. When opposite-sex identification has been considered, it has most often been regarded as a problem for the female spectator rather than as a potential pleasure available to both sexes. The 'masculinization' of the feminine spectator has been discussed by Mary Ann Doane and Laura Mulvey in terms of the female spectator's identification with the male position. In their view, this trans-sex identification is the result of the female's lack of a spectatorial position of her own other than a masochistic-female/object identification.[67] Neglected are the possibilities of male identification with the female (even as an ideal ego) or his identification with a 'feminized' masculine character.

Like the wish and counterwish for fusion with and separation from the mother the wish to change gender identity, the 'attempt to identify with and to become both parents', cannot be fulfilled in reality'.[68] Laplanche has stated that fantasy is one means of achieving the goal of reintegrating opposite-sex identification.[69] Otto Fenichel believed that scopophilic pleasure was dependent on taking the position, not of the observed same-sex participant in intercourse, but the opposite sex.[70] Through the mobility of multiple, fluid identifications, the cinema provides an enunciative apparatus that functions as a protective guise like fantasy or dream to permit the temporary satisfaction of what Kubie regards as 'one of the deepest tendencies in human nature'.[71]

Because pleasure in looking and, especially, looking at the dream screen of cinema and the female involves pregenital pleasures and ambivalences, the role and reaction of the sexually differentiated spectator must be approached in a completely different light. The pregenital pleasures of perversion are not limited to the enjoyment of the male spectator, nor available to the female only if she abandons masochistic identification with the 'female object' and then identifies with a male spectatorial position defined only by control.

Prompted by the need to delineate the relationship of masochism and its formal structures to current psychoanalysis, a reconsideration of the role of pregenital states of psychic development holds great promise for opening new areas of exploration in the study of spectatorial pleasure. Many of the assumptions adopted by film theorists from Freudian metapsychology or Lacan seem inadequate in accounting for cinematic pleasure. To understand the structure of looking, visual pleasure must be connected to its earliest manifestations in infancy. As Edith Jacobson's work implies, as well as that of Stoller, Bak, Loewald, and others, the visual pleasure experienced in archaic stages is not automatically negated by later stages of the child's development.[72] The close resemblance of the cinematic apparatus to the structures of perversion and, specifically, to masochism warrants further investigation beyond the limitations imposed by current theoretical discourse if the nature of cinematic pleasure is to be understood in its full complexity and psychological significance.

Notes

1. Christine Gledhill, 'Recent Developments in Feminist Criticism', *Quarterly Review of Film Studies*, 3 (Fall 1978), 457–93. In her 1984 revision of this article for *Re-Vision: Essays in Feminist Film Criticism* (Frederick, Md.: AFI-University Publications of America, 1984), Gledhill rearticulates her original critique.
2. Gilles Deleuze, *Masochism: An Interpretation of Coldness and Cruelty* (New York: George Braziller, 1971); Leopold von Sacher-Masoch, 'Venus in Furs', trans. Jean McNeil, in Deleuze.
3. Deleuze, 95.
4. Deleuze, 52.
5. Sacher-Masoch, 129.
6. Deleuze, 80.
7. Donatien Alphonse François de Sade, *The 120 Days of Sodom and Other Writings*, trans. and ed. Austryn Wainhouse and Richard Seaver (New York: Grove Press, 1966), 577.
8. Deleuze, 31.
9. Deleuze, 16–19. See also Roland Barthes, *Sade/Loyola/Fourier*, trans. Richard Miller (New York: Hill & Wang, 1976), 31–37.
10. Barthes, 34.
11. Jean-Louis Baudry, 'The Apparatus', *Camera Obscura*, 1 (Fall 1976), 105–26; Robert Eberwein, 'Reflections on the Breast', *Wide Angle*, 4: 3 (1981), 48–53.
12. Laura Mulvey, 'Visual Pleasure and Narrative Cinema', *Screen*, 16 (Autumn 1975), 6–18. Claire Johnston, *Notes on Women's Cinema* (London: Society for Education in Film and Television, 1973), 2–4; Mary Ann Doane, 'Misrecognition and Identity', *Cine-Tracts*, 11 (Fall 1980), 28–30; Doane, 'Film and the Masquerade: Theorising the Female Spectator', *Screen*, 23 (September–October 1982), 74–87.
13. Sigmund Freud, 'A Child is being Beaten' (1919), in *Sex and the Psychology of Love*, ed. Philip Rieff (New York: Macmillan, Collier Books, 1963), 117. See 'The Economic Problem in Masochism', in *General Psychological Theory:*

Papers on Metapsychology, ed. Philip Rieff (New York: Macmillan, Collier Books, 1963), 190–93, for Freud's first essay to use the Death Instinct theory as an approach to the clinical and theoretical dilemmas. See also 'Instincts and their Vicissitudes' (1915) in *General Psychological Theoy*, 25 and 'Three Essays on the Theory of Sexuality', *Standard Edition of the Complete Psychological Works*, ed. James Strachey (London: Hogarth Press, 1953–66), vii. 159–61.

14. Freud, 'The Economic Problem in Masochism', 190–91.
15. Deleuze, 50–54. See also Bernhard Berliner, 'On Some Psychodynamics of Masochism', *Psychoanalytic Quarterly*, 16 (1947), 459–71; Gustav Bychowski, 'Some Aspects of Masochistic Involvement', *Journal of the American Psychoanalytic Association*, 7 (April 1959), 248–73; E. Bergler, *The Basic Neurosis* (New York: Grune and Stratton, 1949) for other views that locate masochism's genesis in the mother/child relationship. See Deleuze, 111–12, on superego/ego.
16. Berliner, 'Libido and Reality in Masochism', *Psychoanalytic Quarterly*, 9 (1940), 323–26, 333. Deleuze believes that the oral mother of masochism is the good mother who takes on the functions of the two 'bad mothers of masochism', the uterine mother and the Oedipal mother. In the process, the functions are idealized and, as Deleuze explains, 'This concentration of functions in the person of the good oral mother is one of the ways in which the father is cancelled out' (p.55).
17. Bychowski, 260. The issue of why pain is necessary to masochism's dynamic of pleasure is still one of the most controversial in psychoanalysis. See Abram Kardiner, Aaron Karush, and Lionel Ovesey, 'A Methodological Study of Freudian Theory III: Narcissism, Bisexuality, and the Dual Instinct Theory', *Journal of Nervous and Mental Disorders*, 129 (1959), 215–22. See also Deleuze, 108–109.
18. Roy Schafer, 'The Idea of Resistance', *International Journal of Psycho-Analysis*, 54 (1973), 278.
19. Deleuze, 95. 'Again, while the sense of guilt has great importance in masochism, it acts only as a cover, as the humorous outcome of a guilt that has already been subverted; for it is no longer the guilt of the child towards the father, but that of the father himself, and of his likeness in the child . . . When guilt is experienced "masochistically," it is already distorted, artificial and ostentatious' (p.95). Deleuze's theory—that the father is the guilty one—is not as unusual as it might first appear. See Claude Lévi-Strauss, *The Raw and the Cooked*, trans. Johan and Doreen Weightman (New York: Harper & Row, 1969), 48.
20. Michael de M'Uzan, 'A Case of Masochistic Perversion and an Outline of a Theory', *International Journal of Psycho-Analysis*, 54(1973), 462.
21. Theodore Reik, *Masochism in Modern Man*, trans. M. H. Beigel and G. M. Kruth (New York: Farrar, Straus, 1941), 428.
22. Deleuze, 59–60.
23. See Victor Smirnoff, 'The Masochistic Contract', *International Journal of Psycho-Analysis*, 50 (1969), 666–71, for an analysis of masochism heavily indebted to Deleuze's work, but which discounts the role of pain and emphasizes the role of the contractual alliance in the perversion. I must acknowledge my own debt to Marsha Kinder for suggesting this expansion of Deleuze's model.

24. Robin Wood, 'Venus de Marlene', *Film Comment*, 14 (March–April 1978), 60.
25. Mulvey, 14.
26. Doane, 'Film and the Masquerade: Theorising the Female Spectator', 82. Doane refers to Dietrich's image as a stage performer. She takes Silvia Bovenschen's comments in 'Is There a Feminine Aesthetic?', *New German Critique*, 11 (Winter 1977), 130, and uses them to support her remarks on excess femininity. Bovenschen actually associates Dietrich with an 'intellectual understatement' and refers to her becoming a 'myth' despite 'her subtle disdain for men'. The complexity of Dietrich's image as discussed by Bovenschen does not support Doane's use of her statements to associate Dietrich with 'an excess of femininity'. David Davidson has placed Dietrich's Lola character in *The Blue Angel* within the tradition of the 'amoral woman'. He makes some interesting remarks on the 'threatening' sexuality of these female characters in relation to Mulvey's theory.
27. Carole Zucker, 'Some Observations on Sternberg and Dietrich', *Cinema Journal*, 19 (Spring 1980), 21. Masochism's ambivalent stance toward the female ensures her alternation between coldness and warmth, sacrifice and torture, but, as Deleuze points out, the female in the masochistic scenario is not sadistic, she 'incarnates instead the element of inflicting pain in an exclusively masochistic situation' (p. 38). It is rarely the sexualized female who is judged guilty in Von Sternberg's films, but the representative of the superego and the father.
28. Wood, 61.
29. Claire Pajaczkowska discusses this point in 'The Heterosexual Presumption: A Contribution to the Debate on Pornography', *Screen*, 22 (1981), 86.
30. Deleuze, 56. Although the mothering agent might be considered to be a socially determined role rather than a strictly biological one, this alternative definition does not seem appropriate to this particular application of Deleuze and pregenital research. Interestingly, it has been suggested that in the pregenital stage, sexual difference is not an issue to the child except in terms of breast/nonbreast.
31. Deleuze, 56.
32. Deleuze, 80–81; Bychowski, 260.
33. Deleuze, 49. The female in the masochistic scenario is a *femme fatale*, but a very specific kind. Her danger supersedes her portrayal as an 'amoral', sexualized female who threatens social control. The 'mystery' of the *femme fatale* of masochism is the mystery of the womb, rebirth, and the child's symbiotic bond with the mother. She represents the dialectical unity between liberation and death, the bonding of Eros with Thanatos that places the former in the service of the latter.
34. See Kaja Silverman, 'Masochism and Subjectivity', *Framework*, 12 (1980), 2. Silverman's discussion of the masochistic use of the *fort/da* game is most valuable; however, I cannot agree with her generalizations about cultural pleasure/instinctual unpleasure or with her reading of Freud (especially concerning transference of drive expression to a contrary drive). She also approaches the idea that fetishism is related to identification (p. 6), a notion worth exploring in detail.
35. Schafer, 278. See also Robert Stoller, *Sexual Excitement* (New York: Simon and Schuster, 1979); Nancy Chodorow, *The Reproduction of Mothering: Psycho-*

analysis and the Sociology of Gender (Berkeley: University of California Press, 1978); *Mothering: Essays in Feminist Theory*, ed. Joyce Trebilcot (Totowa, NJ: Rowman & Allanheld, 1984). While my brief consideration of Freud in this article necessitates a generalization about his stance on women, it should be noted that he did consider the influence of the mother, but, as demonstrated in his theories on masochism and various other symptomatologies, the father, penis envy, castration fear, and the emphasis on the phallic stage (and corresponding disinterest in pre-Oedipal or pregenital stages) effectively displace the mother from his work. See Viola Klein, *The Feminine Character: History of an Ideology* (New York: International Universities Press, 1949).

36. Hans Loewald, *Papers on Psychoanalysis* (New Haven: Yale University Press, 1980), 165.
37. Janine Chasseguet-Smirgel, 'Freud and Female Sexuality: The Consideration of Some Blind Spots in the Exploration of the Dark Continent', *International Journal of Psycho-Analysis*, 57 (1976), 196.
38. Robert Dickes discusses the fetish as 'screen memory' in 'Fetishistic Behavior: A Contribution to Its Complex Development and Significances', *Journal of the American Psychoanalytic Association*, 11 (1963), 324–30. See also Anneliese Riess, 'The Mother's Eye: For Better and for Worse', *The Psychoanalytic Study of the Child*, 33 (1978), 381–405.
39. Chasseguet-Smirgel, 281. Ethel Spector Person has suggested that infantile dependence may be the key to power relations in sexuality: 'the limitations to sexual "liberation", meaning liberation from power contaminants, do not reside in the biological nature of sexuality, or in cultural or political arrangements, and certainly not in the sex difference, but may lie in the universal condition of infantile dependence' (p. 627). See 'Sexuality as the Mainstay of Identity: Psychoanalytic Perspective', *Signs*, 5 (Summer 1980).
40. Michel Foucault, *The History of Sexuality*, Vol. 1. *An Introduction*, trans. Robert Hurley (New York: Pantheon Books, 1978), 108–9.
41. Mulvey, 13–14.
42. D. N. Rodowick, 'The Difficulty of Difference', *Wide Angle*, 5:1 (1982), 7–9.
43. Mulvey, 11, 14.
44. Christian Metz, *The Imaginary Signifier*, trans. Celia Britton, Annwyl Williams, Ben Brewster, Alfred Guzzetti (Bloomington: Indiana University Press, 1982), 59–63.
45. Jean Laplanche, *Life and Death in Psychoanalysis*, trans. Jeffrey Mehlman (Baltimore: Johns Hopkins University Press, 1976), 102.
46. Leopold von Sacher-Masoch, 'A Childhood Memory and Reflection on the Novel', Appendix I in Deleuze, 232–33.
47. Sylvan Keiser, 'Body Ego during Orgasm', *Psychoanalytic Quarterly*, 21 (April 1952), 160, 193.
48. Stephen Heath, *Questions of Cinema* (Bloomington: Indiana University Press, 1981), 189.
49. P. J. Van der Leeuw, 'The Preoedipal Phase of the Male', *The Psychoanalytic Study of the Child*, 13 (1958), 369. See also Robert C. Bak, 'Fetishism', *Journal of the American Psychoanalytic Association*, 1(1953), 291.
50. Van der leeuw, 352–74; Charles Socarides, 'The Development of a Fetishistic Perversion: The Contribution of Preoedipal Phase Conflict', *Journal of the American Psychoanalytic Association*, 8 (April 1960), 307–9; Bak, 291. Bak

maintains that the normal male child thinks it is possible to identify with the mother and emulate her positive power (i.e. bear a child) while also repairing the separation from her (through fetishism) without endangering phallic integrity (p. 286). Joseph Solomon, 'Transitional Phenomena and Obsessive-Compulsive States', in *Between Reality and Fantasy: Transitional Objects and Phenomena*, ed. Simon A. Grolnick, Leonard Barkin, and Werner Muensterberger (New York: Jason Aronson, 1978), 250–51, associates fetishism with the child's sense of body intactness derived from the mother.

51. Dickes, 320.
52. Dickes, 327.
53. M. Wulff, 'Fetishism and Object Choice in Early Childhood', *Psychoanalytic Quarterly*, 15 (1945), 465–70. Socarides, 309. Brunswick, Lampl-de Groot, Jacobson, Kestenberg, Socarides, and a number of others link fetishistic perversion to the pre-Oedipal period. Most conclude that fetishism has little connection to the phallic period or genital sexuality in its formation, but this does not mean that a fetish cannot represent the phallus. Wulff qualifies the link between childhood fetishism and adult fetishism by noting the inconsistences in their relationship and the need for further research. Griselda Pollock has pointed out in 'What's Wrong with Images of Women', *Screen Education*, 24 (Autumn 1977), 25–33, that Freud's theory of fetishism (as adopted by Mulvey in particular) cannot account for vaginal imagery in pornography.
54. Ralph Greenson, 'Dis-Identifying from Mother: Its Special Importance for the Boy', *International Journal of Psycho-Analysis*, 49 (1968), 370–74; see also Nancy Chodorow. 'Family Structure and Feminine Personality', in *Woman, Culture, and Society*, ed. S. Rosaldo and L. Lamphere (Stanford, Calif.: Stanford University Press, 1978), 50; Chasseguet-Smirgel, 281–84. In 'Film and the Masquerade', Doane insists that the female is 'constructed differently in relation to processes of looking' (p. 80).
55. Socarides, 304. See also Stoller, *Sexual Excitement*, 7–13; Freud, 'The Psychogenesis of a Case of Homosexuality in a Woman', in *Sexuality and the Psychology of Love*', 133–59.
56. Socarides, 304.
57. Baudry, 125. 'It may seem peculiar that desire which constituted the cine-effect is rooted in the oral structure of the subject. The conditions of projection do evoke the dialectics internal/external, swallowing/swallowed, eating/being eaten, which is characteristic of what is being structured during the oral phase. . . . The relationship visual orifice/buccal orifice acts at the same time as analogy and differentiation, but also points to the relation of consecution between oral satisfaction, sleep, white screen of the dream on which dream images will be projected, beginning of the dream.'
58. Judith S. Kestenberg and Joan Weinstock, 'Transitional Objects and Body-Image Formation', in *Between Reality and Fantasy*, 82.
59. Alvan Frank, 'The Unrememberable and the Unforgettable', *The Psychoanalytic Study of the Child*, 24 (1969), 56. See also Ernst Kris, 'On Preconscious Mental Processes', in *Organization and Pathology of Thought*, ed. David Rapaport (New York: Columbia University Press, 1951), 493.
60. W. Gillespie, 'Notes on the Analysis of Sexual Perversion', *International Journal of Psychoanalysis* (1952), 397. See also Loewald, 268–69, 401–2. See Chodorow,

Mothering, on the splitting technique of ego defense, primary identification, and the oral stage, 60.
61. Loewald, 16–17.
62. Loewald, 17.
63. Freud, 'A Child is being Beaten', 129; Robert Stoller, 'Facts and Fancies: An Examination of Freud's Concept of Bisexuality', in *Women and Analysis*, ed. Jean Strouse (New York: Grossman, 1974), 357–60.
64. Lawrence Kubie, 'The Drive to Become Both Sexes', in *Symbols and Neurosis*, ed. Herbert J. Schlesinger (New York: International Universities Press, 1978), 195, 202. See also Zilboorg and Kittay.
65. Socarides, 307; Gregory Zilboorg, 'Masculine and Feminine; Some Biological and Cultural Aspects', *Psychiatry*, 7 (1944), 257–96; Eva Feder Kittay, 'Womb Envy: An Explanatory Concept', in Treblicot, 94–128.
66. Bruno Bettelheim, *Symbolic Wounds* (Glencoe, Ill.: The Free Press, 1954), 260.
67. Doane, 'Film and the Masquerade', 74–88; Laura Mulvey 'Afterthoughts on "Visual Pleasure and Narrative Cinema", inspired by *Duel in the Sun*', *Framework*, 15/16/17 (Summer 1981), 12–15.
68. Kubie, 211. See also Loewald, 268–69.
69. Laplanche and J. B. Pontalis, *The Language of Psychoanalysis* (New York: W. W. Norton, 1973), 243–46.
70. Otto Fenichel, 'Scopophilic Instinct and Identification', in *Collected Papers of Otto Fenichel: First Series* (New York: W. W. Norton, 1953), 377.
71. Kubie, 211.
72. Edith Jacobson, *The Self and the Object World* (New York: International Universities Press, 1964).

12 Pleasure, Ambivalence, Identification: Valentino and Female Spectatorship

Miriam Hansen*

> Occasionally the movies go mad. They have terrifying visions; they erupt in images that show the true face of society. Fortunately, however, they are healthy at the core. Their schizophrenic outbursts last only a few moments, then the curtain is lowered again and everything returns to normal.
>
> (Kracauer, 'The Little Salesgirls Go to the Movies' (1927)[1])

In the context of discussions on cinematic spectatorship, the case of Rudolph Valentino demands attention, on historical as well as theoretical grounds. For the first time in film history, women spectators were perceived as a socially and economically significant group; female spectatorship was recognized as a mass phenomenon; and the films were explicitly addressed to a female spectator regardless of the actual composition of the audience. As Hollywood manufactured the Valentino legend, promoting the fusion of real life and screen persona that makes a star, Valentino's female admirers in effect became part of that legend. Never before was the discourse on fan behavior so strongly marked by the terms of sexual difference, and never again was spectatorship so explicitly linked to the discourse on female desire. This conjunction was to inform Valentinian mythology for decades to come—as the following cover prose from various biographies illustrates:

Lean, hot-eyed and Latin, Valentino was every woman's dream. . . .

On screen and off, his smoldering glance ignited fierce sexual fires in millions of hearts. . . .

They breathed the words 'The Sheik' like a prayer on their lips. They tried to tear his clothes off when he left the theater. . . .

* Miriam Hansen, 'Pleasure, Ambivalence, Identification: Valentino and Female Spectatorship' from *Cinema Journal*, vol. 25 (4) (Summer 1986). Reprinted with permission of the author.

> The studio telephones could not handle the thousands of calls from women. They begged for any job that would permit even a momentary glimpse of Valentino. Gladly they offered to work without pay.[2]

While these biographies rarely agree on any facts concerning Valentino's life, they stereotypically relate his personal success and suffering to the ongoing crisis of American cultural and social values.[3] Valentino's body, in more than one sense, became the site of contradictions that had erupted with World War I. His problematic centrality and violence of impact unprecedented for a film star are inextricably linked to the particular historical constellation that made him as well as destroyed him. This constellation I see delineated, tentatively, by developments partly caused by, partly in response to the upheaval of gender relations during the war, such as the massive integration of women into the work force and their emergence as a primary target in the shift to consumer economy; the partial breakdown of gender-specific divisions of labor and a blurring of traditional delimitations of public and private; the need to redefine notions of femininity in terms other than domesticity and motherhood; the image of the New Woman promoted along with a demonstrative liberalization of sexual behavior and lifestyles; the emergence of the companionate marriage.[4]

However one may interpret the dialectics of women's so-called emancipation and their integration into a consumer culture, women did gain a considerable degree of public visibility in those years, and the cinema was one of the places in which this increased social and economic significance was acknowledged, in whatever distorted manner. The orientation of the market towards a female spectator/consumer opened up a potential gap between traditional patriarchal ideology on the one hand and the recognition of female experience, needs, fantasies on the other, albeit for purposes of immediate commercial exploitation and eventual containment.[5] It is in this gap that the Valentino phenomenon deserves to be read, as a significant yet precarious moment in the changing discourse on femininity and sexuality. Precarious, not least, because it sidetracked that discourse to question standards of masculinity, destabilizing them with connotations of sexual ambiguity, social marginality, and ethnic/racial otherness.

Valentino also presents a challenge to feminist film theory; in particular as it developed during the 1970s within the framework of psychoanalysis and semiology. This debate inescapably returns to

Laura Mulvey's essay on 'Visual Pleasure and Narrative Cinema' (1975) which first spelled out the implications of Lacanian–Althusserian models of spectatorship (Metz, Baudry) for a critique of patriarchal cinema. Whatever its limitations and blind spots, the significance of Mulvey's argument lies in her description of the ways in which the classical Hollywood film perpetuates sexual imbalance in the very conventions through which it engages its viewer as subject—its modes of organizing vision and structuring narratives. These conventions, drawing on psychic mechanisms of voyeurism, fetishism, and narcissism, depend upon and reproduce the conventional polarity of the male as the agent of the 'look' and the image of woman as object of both spectacle and narrative. In aligning spectatorial pleasure with a hierarchical system of sexual difference, classical American cinema inevitably entails what Mulvey calls 'a "masculinization" of the spectator position, regardless of the actual sex (or possible deviance) of any real live movie-goer'.[6]

Besides its somewhat monolithic notion of classical cinema and provocatively Manichean stance on visual pleasure, Mulvey's argument has been criticized frequently for the difficulty of conceptualizing a female spectator other than in terms of an absence.[7] In the decade since Mulvey's essay was published, however, feminist critics have attempted to rescue female spectatorship from its 'locus of impossibility', in particular in areas elided by the focus on women's systematic exclusion. One such area is the body of films within the Hollywood tradition which are addressed to female audiences and marketed as such; for example, the 'woman's film' of the 1940s and other variants of melodrama centering on female protagonists and their world. Another area of feminist investigation, less clearly delineated, is the question of pleasure and attendant processes of identification experienced by women spectators (including feminist critics) in the actual reception of mainstream films, even with genres devoted to male heroes and activities, such as the Western or the gangster film.

With regard to the latter, Mulvey, reconsidering her earlier argument, suggests that the female spectator, 'enjoying the freedom of action and control over the diegetic world that identification with the male hero provides,' takes recourse to the repressed residues of her own phallic phase. This type of identification, however, requires putting on transvestite clothes, which confirms the dominant polarity of vision by exchanging the terms of opposition for those of similarity. Like Pearl in Mulvey's reading of *Duel in the Sun*, the female spectator ends up being caught in a conflict 'between the deep blue sea of passive femininity and the devil of regressive masculinity'.[8]

While Mulvey's analysis of spectatorial cross-dressing ultimately upholds the notion of patriarchal cinema as a system of binary opposites, it also demonstrates the necessity to complicate such terms. The female viewer of 'masculine' genres does not fit the mold of the spectator/subject anticipated by these films, and in many of them narcissistic identification with female characters is of marginal interest at best, especially when the spectacle is more dispersed (over landscape and action scenes) than in genres like the musical or romantic comedy which concentrate pleasure around the image of the female body. But neither is reception on the woman's part merely accidental, arbitrary, or individual—failing with regard to the meaning-potential of the film. Rather, one might say that the oscillation and instability which Mulvey and others have observed in female spectatorship constitutes a meaningful deviation—a deviation that has its historical basis in the spectator's experience of belonging to a socially differentiated group called women. As a subdominant and relatively indeterminate collective formation, female spectatorship is certainly contingent upon dominant subject positions, and thus not outside or above ideology, but it cannot be reduced to an either/or modality.

The very figure of the transvestite suggests that the difference of female spectatorship involves more than the opposition of activity and passivity, that it has to be conceptualized in terms of a greater degree of mobility and heterogeneity, including a sense of theatricality and selectivity.[9] As I will argue in the case of Valentino, sexual mobility, the temporary slippage between gender definitions, is crucial to an understanding of his historical impact; that sexual mobility is also 'a distinguishing feature of femininity in its cultural construction' and that hence transvestism '*would be* fully recuperable'[10] does not seem a sufficient reason for simply dismissing it from the arsenal of a feminist countertradition. The heterogeneity of the female spectator position, moreover, extends not only to spatial registers (proximity/distance in relation to the screen as Mary Ann Doane proposes) but to registers of temporality as well. For the figure of the transvestite connotes a discrepancy, a simultaneity of unequal psychic developments. Phallic identification, while officially—in the present tense of the film text, as propelled by the linear flow of the narrative aligned with positions of masculine agency and control, for the woman spectator depends upon a memory (on whatever level of consciousness), and thus may reactivate repressed layers of her own psychic history and socialization.[11]

The structural instability of the female spectator position in mainstream cinema surfaces as a textual instability in films specifically addressed to women, as an effect of the collision between immediate market interests and institutional structures of vision. In her work on the 'woman's film' of the 1940s, Doane shows how the ideological crisis precipitated by a female address is contained in turn by scenarios of masochism which work to distance and de-eroticize the woman's gaze, thus restricting the space of a female reading. Linda Williams and Tania Modleski, on the other hand, emphasize the multiplicity of identificatory positions in female-addressed mainstream films (or, as in Modleski's case, TV soap opera), a textual multiplicity which they relate to the problematic constitution of female identity under patriarchy), from patterns of psychic development to a gender-specific division of labor. This difference in emphasis may partly be due to the choice of films—for example, maternal melodrama as opposed to the films analyzed by Doane which overlap with the gothic or horror genre—but it is also, and perhaps most important, a question of reading.[12]

The analysis of positions of identification available to female spectators is inseparable from positions of critical reading, as the recent debate between Linda Williams and E. Ann Kaplan exemplifies.[13] Does the ending of a film like *Stella Dallas* unify the variety of conflicting subject positions mapped out to this point, as Kaplan argues? Does it close off the contradictions in terms of a patriarchal discourse on motherhood, asking the spectator to accept desexualization, sacrifice, and powerlessness? Or do we, as Williams suggests, grant some degree of alterity to the preceding 108 minutes? Are processes of identification necessarily synchronous with the temporal structures of classical narrative, and to what extent is closure effective? How do films construct what we remember of them? How does this memory change over time in relation to the immediate effects of identification?

These questions urge us to reconsider the hermeneutics involved in the critical enterprise. Who is the subject of reading? Ann Kaplan points out the necessity of distinguishing between the historical spectator, the hypothetical spectator constructed through the film's strategies, and the contemporary female spectator with a feminist consciousness. But the textually constructed spectator/subject does not have any objective existence apart from our reading of the film, which is always partial and, if we choose, partisan. Therefore, the question of hermeneutics is not only one of measuring historical scopes of reception against each other, but also one of the politics of reading,[14] a question of how to establish a usable past for an alternative film practice. If all the time, desire, and money spent by women watching mainstream films should be of any consequence whatsoever for a feminist countertradition, then this activity has to be made available through readings, in full awareness of its complicity and contingency upon the dominant structures of the apparatus, but nonetheless as a potential of resistance to be reappropriated.[15]

The Valentino films add yet another angle to these arguments on female spectatorship and a feminist re-writing of film history. While participating in the general problematic of female-addressed Hollywood films, their distinction lies in focusing spectatorial pleasure on the image of a male hero/performer. If a man is made to occupy the place of erotic object, how does this affect the organization of vision? If the desiring look is aligned with the position of a female viewer, does this open up a space for female subjectivity and, by the same token, an alternative conception of visual pleasure?

Feminist theorists like Doane and Kaplan have cautioned against premature enthusiasm regarding such films, arguing that they merely present an instance of role reversal which allows women the appropriation of the gaze only to confirm the patriarchal logic of vision. 'The male striptease, the gigolo—both inevitably signify the mechanism of reversal itself, constituting themselves as aberrations whose acknowledgment simply reinforces the dominant system of aligning sexual difference with a subject/object dichotomy. And an essential attribute of that dominant system is the matching of male subjectivity with the agency of the look.'[16] Undeniably, the figure of the male as erotic object sets into play fetishistic and voyeuristic mechanisms, accompanied—most strikingly in the case of Valentino—by a feminization of the actor's persona. These mechanisms, however, are not naturalized as they are in the representation of a female body. Rather, they are foregrounded as aspects of a theatricality that encompasses both viewer and performer. The reversal thus constitutes a *textual* difference which has to be considered from case to case and cannot be reduced *a priori* to its symbolic content within a phallocentric economy of signification. It seems more promising tentatively, to approach the textual difference of a male erotic object as a figure of overdetermination, an unstable composite figure that connotes 'the simultaneous presence of two positionalities of desire' (Teresa de Lauretis)[17] and thus calls into question the very idea of polarity rather than simply reversing its terms.

Moreover, as even a cursory comparison of Valentino with more recent stars such as John Travolta and Robert Redford makes obvious, we need to observe historical differences as well. Figures like Travolta and Redford—not to mention performers like Mick Jagger, David Bowie, or Michael Jackson—emerge at the end of an era, if not already in the midst of an altogether different one. Valentino appears at the threshold of what has been termed, for better or for worse, Hollywood's 'classical' period. The process by which American cinema became identified with particular conventions of editing and narrative was well under way during the 1920s. But not all of its crucial codes developed simultaneously; some were lagging behind while others were practiced obsessively and promiscuously.[18] This uneven development might account for a certain quality of excess often attributed to films of the 1920s, a quality which could be described more specifically as an unstable relationship between spectacle and narrative, falling back behind an economy already achieved during the mid and late 1910s. Whether a trace of primitive cinema or a mark of contemporary decadence, the peculiar inscription of the spectator in the Valentino films suggests a dissociation of pleasure and meaning which potentially undermines the classical imbrication of the gaze with masculine control and mastery.

From a theoretical perspective, then, this essay on Valentino is motivated by an interest in forms of visual pleasure that are not totally claimed, absorbed, or functionalized by the conventions of classical narrative. The redemption of scopophilia may require a return to Freud without the detour through Lacan, since in Lacanian models of spectatorship scopic desire is conceptually inseparable from voyeurism, fetishism and, thus, the regime of castration. Not that these are unrelated or free of determinism in Freud. The Freudian speculation, however, does not posit earlier stages of psychic development as always already negated by later ones, in a Hegelian sense of '*Aufhebung*' which Lacan assimilated to psychoanalysis. I would argue that Freud's writings still hold a more radical potential of interpretation,[19] in particular a more dialectical concept of regression and subjectivity. The latter might allow feminist film theory to rearticulate the question of aesthetic experience, in conjunction with the question of the erotic, neither of which we can afford to ignore if a feminist counter-cinema is to go beyond the abstract opposition of patriarchal mainstream film and feminist avant-garde.

Valentino. At first sight, Valentino's films seem to rehearse the classical choreography of the look almost to the point of parody, offering point-of-view constructions that affirm the cultural hierarchy of gender in the visual field. Between 1921 (*The Four Horsemen of the Apocalypse*) and 1926, the year of his premature death, Valentino starred in 14 films, produced by different studios and under different directors.[20] Illustrating the significance of the star as *auteur* as much as the economic viability of vehicles, each of these films reiterates a familiar pattern in staging the exchange of looks between Valentino and the female characters. Whenever Valentino lays eyes on a woman first, we can be sure that she will turn out to be the woman of his dreams, the legitimate partner in the romantic relationship; whenever a woman initiates the look, she is invariably marked as a vamp, to be condemned and defeated in the course of the narrative.

. . .

Valentino's appeal depends, to a large degree, on the manner in which he combines masculine control of the look with the feminine quality of 'to-be-looked-at-ness', to use Mulvey's rather awkward term. When Valentino falls in love—usually at first sight—the close-up of his face clearly surpasses that of the female character in its value as spectacle. In a narcissistic doubling, the subject of the look constitutes itself as object, graphically illustrating Freud's formulation of the autoerotic dilemma: 'Too bad that I cannot kiss myself.'[21] Moreover, in their radiant pictorial quality, such shots temporarily arrest the metonymic drive of the narrative, similar in effect to the visual presence of the woman which, as Mulvey observes, tends 'to freeze the flow of action in moments of erotic contemplation'.[22] In Valentino's case, however, erotic contemplation governs an active as well as passive mode, making both spectator and character the subject of a double game of vision.

To the extent that Valentino occupies the position of primary object of spectacle, this entails a systematic feminization of his persona. Many of the films try to motivate this effect by casting him as a performer (torero, dancer) or by situating him in a historically removed or exotic mise-en-scène; in either case, the connotation of femininity persists through the use of costumes—in particular flared coats and headdress reminiscent of a bridal wardrobe, as well as a general emphasis on dressing and disguises. *Monsieur Beaucaire*, a 1924 Paramount costume drama based on the Booth Tarkington novel, combines both the effect and its disavowal in a delightfully self-reflective manner. Valentino, playing the Duke of Chartres, alias Monsieur Beaucaire, is introduced on a stage playing the lute in an attempt to entertain the jaded king, Louis XV. The courtly mise-en-scene ostensibly legitimizes the desiring female gaze, contained in the alternation of relatively close shots of Valentino and the female members of the audience within the film. Unfailingly, however, this sequence thematizes the paradox of female spectatorship. Seeing one woman *not* focusing her eyes upon him in rapture, he stops midway in indignation and a title redundantly explains: 'the shock of his life: a woman not looking at him'—sure enough, this refers to the leading romantic lady.[23] The partial reversal of the gender economy of vision is prepared by the film's opening shot, a close-up of hands doing needle-point work. As the camera pulls back, those hands are revealed to be the king's. In the effeminate universe of the French court, Valentino succeeds in asserting his masculinity only by comparison, staging it as a difference which ultimately fails to make a difference.

Before considering the possibilities of identification implied in this peculiar choreography of vision, I wish to recapitulate some thoughts on female visual pleasure and its fate under the patriarchal taboo. Particularly interesting in this context are certain aspects of scopophilia that Freud analyzes through its development in infantile sexuality, a period in which the child is still far from having a stable sense of gender identity. Stimulated in the process of mutual gazing between mother and child, the female scopic drive is constituted with a *bisexual* as well as an *autoerotic* component. While these components subsequently succumb to cultural hierarchies of looking which tend to fixate the woman in a passive, narcissistic-exhibitionist role, there remains a basic ambivalence in the structure of vision as a component drive. As Freud argues in 'Instincts and their Vicissitudes' (1915), the passive component of a drive represents a reversal of the active drive into its opposite, redirecting itself to the subject. Such a contradictory constitution of libidinal components may account for the coexistence, in their later fixation as perversion, of diametrically opposed drives within one and the same person, even if one tendency usually predominates. Thus a voyeur is always to some degree an exhibitionist and vice versa, just as the sadist shares the pleasures of masochism.[24]

The notion of ambivalence appears crucial to a theory of female spectatorship, precisely because the cinema, while enforcing patriarchal hierarchies in its organization of the look, also offers women an institutional opportunity to violate the taboo on female scopophilia. The success of a figure like Valentino, himself overdetermined as both object and subject of the look, urges us to insist upon the ambivalent constitution of scopic pleasure. Moreover, as one among a number of the more archaic partial drives whose integration is always and at best precarious, scopophilia could be distinguished from a socially more complicit voyeurism, as defined by the one-sided regime of the keyhole and the norms of genitality.[25]

...

The construction of femininity within patriarchal society, however, contains the promise of being incomplete. Women's exclusion from the mastery of the visual field may have diminished the pressure of the ego instincts towards the component drives, which are probably insufficiently subordinated to begin with. Thus the potential dissociation of the scopic drive from its function for survival may not be that threatening to the female subject, may not necessarily provoke the force of repression that Freud holds responsible for certain cases of psychogenic blindness. If such generalization is at all permissible, women might be more likely to indulge—without immediately repressing—in a sensuality of vision which contrasts with the goal-oriented discipline of the one-eyed masculine look. Christa Karpenstein speaks in this context of 'an unrestrained scopic drive, a swerving and sliding gaze which disregards the meanings and messages of signs and images that socially determine the subject, a gaze that defies the limitations and fixations of the merely visible.'[26]

If I seem to belabor this notion of an undomesticated gaze as a historical aspect of female subjectivity, I certainly don't intend to propose yet another variant of essentialism. To the extent that sexual difference is culturally constructed to begin with, the subversive qualities of a female gaze may just as well be shared by a male character. This is precisely what I want to suggest for the case of Valentino, contrary to the official legend which never ceased to assert the power of his look in terms of aggressive mastery. Hollywood publicity persistently advertised the state of bliss in store for the woman who would be discovered by his magical gaze—in the measure that he himself was becoming an erotic commodity of irrestible cash value for the studios.[27]

The feminine connotation of Valentino's 'to-be-looked-at-ness', however, destabilizes his own glance in its very origin, makes him vulnerable to temptations that jeopardize the sovereignty of the male subject. When Valentino's eyes become riveted on the woman of his choice, he seems paralyzed rather than aggressive or menacing, occupying the position of the rabbit rather than that of the snake.

Struck by the beauty of Carmen, in *Blood and Sand*, his activity seems blocked, suspended; it devolves upon Carmen throwing him a flower to get the narrative back into gear. Later in the film, at the height of his career as a torero, Valentino raises his eyes to the president's box, an individual centered under the benevolent eye of the State, when his gaze is side-tracked, literally decentered, by the sight of Doña Sol in the box to the right. The power of Valentino's gaze depends upon its weakness—enhanced by the fact that he was actually nearsighted and cross-eyed—upon its oscillating between active and passive, between object and ego libido. The erotic appeal of the Valentinian gaze, staged as a look within the look, is one of reciprocity and ambivalence, rather than mastery and objectification.

The peculiar organization of the Valentinian gaze corresponds on the level of narrative, to conflicts between the pleasure and the reality principle. Whenever the hero's amorous interests collide with the standards of male social identity—career, family, paternal authority, or a vow of revenge—the spectator can hope that passion will triumph over pragmatism to the point of self-destruction.[28] As the generating vortex of such narratives, the Valentinian gaze far exceeds its formal functions of providing diegetic coherence and continuity; it assumes an almost figural independence. Thus the films advance an identification with the gaze itself; not with either source or object, but with the gaze as erotic medium which promises to transport the spectator out of the world of means and ends into the realm of passion.

The discussion of gendered patterns of vision inevitably opens up into the larger question of identification as the linchpin between film and spectator, the process that organizes subjectivity in visual and narrative terms. It seems useful at this point to invoke Mary Ann Doane's distinction of at least three instances of identification operating in the viewing process: (1) identification *with* the representation of a person (character/star); (2) recognition of particular objects, persons, or action *as* such (stars, narrative images); (3) identification with the 'look', with oneself as the condition of perception, which Metz, in analogy with Lacan's concept of the mirror phase, has termed 'primary'.[29] These psychical mechanisms and their effects can be traced through the various levels of enunciation which structure cinematic identification, interlacing textual units such as shot, sequence, strategies of narrative, and mise-en-scene.[30]

Most productively, feminist film theorists have taken up the debate by insisting on the centrality of sexual difference, questioning the assumption of a single or neutral spectator position constructed in hierarchically ordered, linear processes of identification. While Mulvey initially reduced cinematic identification to a basically active relationship with a protagonist of the same sex (i.e. male), she subsequently modified this notion with regard to the female viewer who may not only cross but also be divided by gender lines (which in turn deflects identification from the fictive telos of a stable identity). As outlined above, the difficulty of conceptualizing a female spectator has led feminists to recast the problem of identification in terms of instability, mobility, multiplicity, and, I would add, temporality. Likewise, a number of feminist critics are trying to complicate the role of sexual difference in identification with the differences of class and race, with cultural and historical specificity. This might make it possible to rethink the concept of subjectivity implied, beyond the commonplace that subjects are constructed by and within ideology. The question of who is the subject of identification (so eloquently posed by Tonto) is also and not least a question concerning which part of the spectator is engaged and how: which layers of conscious or unconscious memory and fantasy are activated, and how we, both as viewers and as critics, choose to interpret this experience.[31]

I am not claiming that Valentino will answer all or any of these questions, but he might help articulate some of them a little more clearly. The first form of identification discussed by Doane, identification with the integral person filmed (Metz's 'secondary' mode of identification), engages the female viewer transsexually insofar as it extends to the Valentino character; thus, it raises the problem of spectatorial cross-dressing—unless we consider other possibilities of transsexual identification beside the transvestite one. The alternative option for the woman spectator, passive-narcissistic identification with the female star as erotic object, appears to have been a position primarily advertised by the industry,[32] but it appears rather more problematic in view of the specular organization of the films.

If we can isolate an instance of 'primary' identification at all—which is dubious on theoretical grounds[33]—the Valentino films challenge the assumption of perceptual mastery implied in such a concept by their foregrounding of the gaze as an erotic medium, a gaze that fascinates precisely because it transcends the socially imposed subject/object hierarchy of sexual difference. Moreover, the contradictions of the female address are located in the very space where the registers of the look and those of narrative and mise-en-scene intersect. In offering the woman spectator a position which is structurally analogous to that of the vamp within the diegesis (looking at Valentino independently of his initiating of the look) identification with the desiring gaze is both granted and incriminated, or, one might say, granted on the condition of its illegitimacy. This may be why the vamp figures in Valentino films (with the exception of *Blood and Sand*) are never totally condemned, inasmuch as they acknowledge a subliminal complicity between Valentino and the actively desiring female gaze. In *The Eagle*, for instance, the czarina is redeemed by her general's ruse of letting Valentino escape execution under an assumed identity; the closing shot shows Valentino and the czarina waving each other a never-ending farewell, much to the concern of the respective legitimate partners.

The least equivocal instance of identification operating in the Valentino films is that which feeds on recognition, the memory-spectacle rehearsed with each appearance of the overvalued erotic object, the star.[34] The pleasure of recognition involved in the identification of and with a star is dramatized, in many Valentino films, through a recurrent narrative pattern, which in turn revolves around the precarious cultural construction of the persona of the Latin Lover. Often, the Valentino character combines two sides of a melodramatic dualism, which he acts out in a series of disguises and anonymous identities. Thus, in *The Sheik* (1921), the barbaric son of the desert turns out to be of British descent; in *Moran of the Lady Letty* (1922), the San Francisco dandy proves himself a hearty sailor and authentic lover; the Duke of Chartres in exile becomes Monsieur Beaucaire; and the Black Eagle pursues courtship instead of revenge under the assumed identity of Monsieur LeBlanc.[35] The spectator recognizes her star in all his masks and disguises—unlike the female protagonist whose trial of love consists of 'knowing' him regardless of narrative misfortune or social status.

...

The emphasis on the sadistic aspects of the Valentino persona echoes the publicity pitch advertising him to female audiences as the 'he-man', the 'menace', reiterated, as late as 1977, by one of his biographers: 'Women were to find in *The Sheik* a symbol of the omnipotent male who could dominate them as the men in their own lives could not.'[36] And, when in the film of that title the son of the desert forces the blue-eyed Lady Diana on his horse, ostensibly for her own pleasure ('lie still you little fool'), millions of women's hearts were said to have quivered at the prospect of being humiliated by the British-bred barbarian. Despite the display of virility in *The Sheik* (1921; based on the novel by Edith Maude Hull), however, this film initiated the much publicized rejection of Valentino by male moviegoers, which had more to do with the threat he presented to traditional norms of masculinity than with the actual composition of audience.[37] Not only the stigma of effeminacy but also, equally threatening, a masochistic aura was to haunt Valentino to his death and beyond. There were widespread rumors about his private life—homosexuality, impotence, unconsummated marriages with lesbians, dependency on domineering women, the platinum 'slave bracelet' given to him by his second wife, Natasha Rambova. More systematically, the masochistic elements in the Valentino persona were enforced by the sadistic placement of the spectator in the films themselves. There is hardly a Valentino film that does not display a whip, in whatever marginal function, and most of them feature seemingly insignificant subplots in which the spectator is offered a position that entails enjoying the tortures inflicted on Valentino or others.[38]

The oscillation of the Valentino persona between sadistic and masochistic positions is yet another expression of the ambivalence that governs the specular organization of the films. As Freud asserts in the 'Three Essays on the Theory of Sexuality,' 'a sadist is always at the same time a masochist, although in one case the active and in another case the passive aspect of the perversion may be more pronounced and may represent the predominant sexual activity.'[39] But the question of the origin and economy of masochism troubled Freud over decades and led him to revise his views at least once.[40] Among post-Freudian attempts to theorize masochism, that of Gilles Deleuze has recently been put forward as an alternative model of spectatorship.[41] Deleuze challenges the conceptual linkage of masochism with sadism and the Oedipal regime; instead he proposes a distinct origin and aesthetics of masochism located in the relationship with the 'oral mother'. While the revisionist impulse to emphasize pregenital sexuality in spectatorship can only be welcomed, Deleuze's model seems somewhat limited by the parameters of his literary source—the writings of Leopold von Sacher-Masoch—and thus to an elaboration of the masochistic scenario within a basically male fantasy.[42] Therefore, I wish to return to Freud's essay, 'A Child Is Being Beaten' (1919), not only for its focus on female instances of sadomasochistic fantasy, but also because it elucidates a particular aspect of the Valentino figure as fantasmatic object.[43]

The formula, 'a child is being beaten', which, regardless of any actually experienced corporal punishment, may dominate masturbation fantasies of the latency period, is remarkable in that it stereotypically reiterates the mere description of the event, while subject, object, and the role of the person fantasizing remain indeterminate. On the basis of jealousy feelings aroused by the Oedipal constellation, Freud proceeds to reconstruct three different phases with explicit reference to female adolescents: (1) 'My father is beating the child that I hate' (presumably a younger sibling); therefore, 'he loves only me'; (2) 'I am being beaten [therefore loved] by my father' (the regressive substitute for the incestuous relationship); (3) 'a child is being beaten.' While the second, sexually most threatening phase succumbs to repression, the first phase is reduced to its merely descriptive part and thus results in the third, in which the father is usually replaced by a more distant male authority figure. Thus the fantasy is sadistic only in its form—but grants masochistic gratification by way of identification with the anonymous children who are being beaten. This series of transformations reduces the sexual participation of the girl to the status of spectator, desexualizing both content and bearer of the fantasy (which, as Freud remarks, is not the case in male variants of the beating fantasy). Just as important in the present context, however, is the observation that in both male and female versions of the sado-masochistic fantasy the children who are being beaten generally turn out to be male. In the case of the female fantasy, Freud employs the concept of the 'masculinity complex', which makes the girl imagine herself as male and thus allows her to be represented, in her daydreams, by these anonymous whipping boys.

The deepest, most effective layer of the Valentino persona is that of the whipping boy—in which he resembles so many other heroes of popular fiction devoured by adolescent girls (one of the examples Freud cites is *Uncle Tom's Cabin*). Freud's analysis of the sado-masochistic fantasy suggests that we distinguish between the sadistic appeal articulated in point-of-view structures on the one hand, and the masochistic pleasure in the identification with the object on the other. Transsexual identification, instead of being confined to simple cross-dressing, relies here as much on the feminine qualities of the male protagonist as it does on residual ambiguity in the female spectator. This simultaneity of identificatory positions is enabled by an interactional structure, a scenario whose libidinal force, protected by a series of repressive/rhetorical transformations, can be traced back to the nursery. (Given the amount of detail that Freud devotes to reconstructing the various stages of this scenario, it is indeed curious—and here one might concur with Deleuze's critique—how briefly he dismisses the role of the mother, especially in view of his emphasis on sibling rivalry.)[44]

Unlike the one-sided masochistic identification with a female protagonist encouraged by the 'woman's film', female identification in Valentino films could be construed to entail the full range of transformations proposed by Freud. As Valentino slips into and out of the part of the whipping boy, intermittently relegating the woman to the position of both victim and perpetrator, he may succeed in recuperating the middle phase of the female fantasy from repression ('I am being beaten—and therefore loved—by my father') and thus in resexualizing it. This possibility is suggested above all by the unmistakable incestuous aura surrounding the Valentino persona; however, the appeal here is less that of a relationship between father and daughter than one between brother and sister, which turns on the desire of both for an inaccessible mother.[45]

The interchangeability of sadistic and masochistic positions within the diegesis potentially undercuts the *a priori* masochism ascribed by current film theory to the female spectator of classical cinema. In making sadomasochistic rituals an explicit component of the erotic relationship, Valentino's films subvert the socially imposed dominance/submission hierarchy of gender roles, dissolving subject/object dichotomies into erotic reciprocity. The vulnerability Valentino displays in his films, the traces of feminine masochism in his persona, may partly account for the threat he posed to prevalent standards of masculinity—the sublimation of masochistic inclinations after all being the token of the male subject's sexual mastery, his control over pleasure.

...

The appeal of the Valentino fantasy is certainly regressive, beckoning the female spectator (to revise Mulvey) beyond the devil of phallic identification into the deep blue sea of polymorphous perversity. Such an appeal cannot but provoke the connotation of monstrosity—which the films displace onto figures like the vamp or the sadomasochistic dwarf in *The Son of the Sheik*, a vicious caricature of Orientalism. The threat posed by Valentino's complicity with the woman who looks, like the affinity of monster and woman in Linda Williams's reading of the horror film, is not a threat merely of sexual difference but of a different *kind* of sexuality, different from the norm of heterosexual, genital sexuality.[46] While playing along with narrative conventions that assert the latter (e.g. the figure of couple formation), the Valentino films allow their spectators to repeat and acknowledge the more archaic component drives, reminders of the precarious constructedness of sexual identity. Moreover, in locating pleasure in the tension—if not excess—of partial libido in relation to genitality, they project a realm of the erotic as distinct from the socially cultivated ideal of a 'healthy sex life'.[47]

To claim a subversive function for polymorphous perversity as such is highly problematic, as Foucault asserts, given the degree to which disparate sexualities themselves have been appropriated by a discourse binding pleasure and power. It is therefore all the more important to reconsider the historical moment at which Valentino enters that discourse, marking its conjunction with other discourses, in particular those of social mobility and racial otherness. In a liberal gesture, Alexander Walker ponders the paradox of the Valentino craze; that is, that it took place alongside the progressive liberation of American women from traditional roles: 'It was a perverse way of celebrating your sex's emancipation.'[48] Perverse, yes, but not so paradoxical. As revisionist historians have argued, the New Woman was usually not as emancipated as her image suggested, and her access to consumer culture often entailed an underpaid job, loneliness, and social insecurity or, in the case of married women, the multiple burdens of wage labor, housework, and childrearing.[49] The period's demonstrative obsession with sexual reform may well confirm Foucault's argument on sexuality as discourse at large; still, this discourse must have had different implications for women than for men, or for single working women as compared, for instance, to upper-middle-class housewives.

However complicit and recuperable in the long run, the Valentino films articulated the possibility of female desire outside of motherhood and family, absolving it from Victorian double standards;[50] instead, they offered a morality of passion, an ideal of erotic reciprocity. Moreover, unlike the feminine reaction to sexual liberation in the shape of Elinor Glyn (the Edwardian novelist who invented the 'it' girl), Valentino did not render the erotic a matter of social etiquette to be rehearsed by the aspiring female subject.[51] Rather, in focusing pleasure on a male protagonist of ambiguous and deviant identity, he appealed to those who most strongly felt the effects—freedom as well as frustration—of transition and liminality, the precariousness of a social mobility predicated on consumerist ideology.

If the Valentino films had no other critical function, they did present, by way of negation, a powerful challenge to myths of masculinity in American culture between the wars. The heroes of the American screen were men of action, like Douglas Fairbanks or William S. Hart, whose energy and determination was only enhanced by a certain lack of social graces, especially toward women. Even the more romantic stars, like Richard Barthelmess or John Barrymore, seemed to owe their good looks to a transcendent spirituality rather than anything related to their bodies and sexuality. Valentino not only inaugurated an explicitly sexual discourse on male beauty, but he also undercut standards of instrumental rationality that were culturally associated with masculine behavior; his resistance to expectations of everyday pragmatism, his swerving from the matter-of-fact and reasonable, may after all account for his subterranean popularity with male moviegoers, whether homosexual or heterosexual.

But Valentino's otherness cannot be explained exclusively in terms of masculinity and its discontents. Beyond the feminine connotations of his persona, his appeal was that of a 'stranger'. Whatever distinguished previous and contemporary male stars from each other, they were all Americans; that is, they did not display any distinct ethnic features other than those that were already naturalized as American. Valentino, however, bore the stigma of the first-generation, non-Anglo-Saxon immigrant—and was cast accordingly. He began his career as a seducer/villain of dark complexion, male counterpart of the figure of the vamp. When female audiences adopted him, despite the moral/racist injunction, he developed the persona of the Latin Lover, marketed as a blend of sexual vitality and romantic courtship. It is not surprising, then, that the paragons of virility responded to the threat he posed in a strongly nativist tone.[52] Yet more systematically, the films themselves both thematized and contained the scandal of his otherness through a recurrent pattern of the double identity mentioned earlier—a pattern which has to be read as a textual symptom of the repression of racial difference.

Valentino's darker self is ostensibly Southern European, somewhat redeemed by a veneer of French manners; in the context of American cinema and American culture, however, he could not have escaped the discursive economy of race and sex, encapsulated in the fear and repressed desire of miscegenation.[53] Sexual paranoia toward black men, rampant since the mid-1890s, reached a new pitch during the 1920s, precipitated by the imagined effects of women's sexual liberation. In terms of this economy, Valentino would have thrived on the fascination with the mulatto, a figure notoriously inscribed with sexual excess (cf. *The Birth of a Nation*), while historically inseparable from the white masters' abuse of black women. Whether or not Valentino touched upon that particular nerve, the connotation of racial otherness was masked by a discourse of exoticism—the Arab sheik, the Indian rajah, the Latin-American gaucho—allowing the female spectator to indulge in the fantasy at a safe distance. Sure enough, the respective narratives reveal the passionate Arab to be of British descent, like Tarzan, just as the lascivious gaucho in *The Four Horsemen* proves himself worthy of his French blood by dying on the field of honor. In such operations of fascination and disavowal, the Valentino films illustrate the ambivalence and fetishism characteristic of all racial stereotypes, the interdependence of racial and sexual difference.[54] At the same time, they mark a historical shift—if not, considering the force of repression provoked, an accidental leap or lapse—which enforced a transvaluation of the taboo and thus its partial recognition, albeit under the guise of the exotic.

Postscript. Some afterthoughts on the psycho-social enigma posed by the cult of Valentino seem appropriate here. While we may speculate on the appeal of the Valentino persona for both a textually and historically constructed female spectator, the massive impact of this appeal and the social forms it assumed remain quite mysterious. Roland Barthes speaks of the cult of the Valentinian face: 'truly feminine Bacchanalia which all over the world were dedicated to the memory of a collectively revealed beauty.'[55] Inevitably, however, such Dionysian rites are contaminated by the mechanisms of the mass media; the voyeuristic and fetishistic aspects of the Valentino excesses cannot be explained away. How could millions of women have indulged in such specifically male perversions? Barthes may ascribe the cult of Valentino to the aura of his face ('*visage*' vs. '*figure*'); yet for Valentino himself and his female admirers it was certainly no less a cult of his body. In scores of publicity stills Valentino posed working out seminude, and in *Blood and Sand* and *Monsieur Beaucaire* he insisted on dressing scenes that would display individual parts of his body (note the close-up of his foot in *Blood and Sand*). Such exhibitionism, given the mechanisms of the apparatus, cannot escape fetishization: the male body, in its entire beauty, assumes the function of a phallic substitute. The more desperately Valentino himself emphasized attributes of physical prowess and virility, the more perfectly he played the part of the male impersonator, brilliant counterpart to the female 'female' impersonators of the American screen such as Mae West or the vamps of his own films.

For the history of American cinema, on the threshold of its classical period, Valentino represents a unique instance of subversive irony—in that the commodity marketed as an idol of virility should have proven its success in the shape of a phallic fetish, a symbol of the missing penis. Valentino's miraculous career as a male impersonator illuminates the basic discrepancy between the penis and its symbolic representation, the phallus, thus revealing the male subject's position within the symbolic order as based upon a misreading of anatomy.[56] If women's fascination with Valentino, on whatever level of consciousness, expressed a recognition of that discrepancy, their massive and collective identification with this peculiar fetish also, and not least, asserted the claim to share in the reputation and representation of phallic power.

In the interaction with female audiences, moreover, the fetishization of Valentino's body assumed forms of theatricality which tended to subvert the mechanisms of separation intrinsic to cinematic voyeurism and fetishism. His female fans actively assailed the barriers that classical cinema was engaged in reaffirming, taking the star system more literally than the institution might have intended, while the media on their part shortcircuited the dialectics of public and private for the narrative of Valentino's life. Once women had found a fetish of their own, they were not content with merely gazing at it, but strove actually to touch it. Moreover, they expected him to reciprocate their fetishistic devotion: Valentino received intimate garments in the mail with the request to kiss and return them (which he did). The cult of Valentino's body finally extended to his corpse and led to the notorious necrophilic excesses: Valentino's last will specifying that his body be exhibited to his fans provoked a fetishistic run for buttons of his suit, or at least candles and flowers from the funeral home.[57] The collective mise-en-scène of fainting spells, hysterical grief, and, to be accurate, a few suicides, cannot be reduced to a mere spectacle of mass-cultural manipulation. It may be read, among other things, as a kind of rebellion, a desperate protest against the passivity and one-sidedness with which patriarchal cinema supports the subordinate position of women in the gender hierarchy. In such a reading, even the commercially distorted manifestation of female desire might articulate a utopian claim—to have the hollow promises of screen happiness be released into the mutuality of erotic practice.

Notes

1. Siegfried Kracauer, 'Die kleinen Ladenmädchen gehen ins Kino', in *Das Ornament der Masse* (Frankfurt: Suhrkamp, 1977), 293. The following essay is a revised and expanded version of 'S. M. Rodolfo', *Frauen und Film*, 33 (Oct. 1982), 19–33. For critical comments and shared enthusiasm, I would like to thank Serafina Bathrick, Atina Grossman, Gertrud Koch, Sally Stein, Maureen

Turim, and, above all, Sandy Flitterman. All translations mine, unless otherwise indicated.

2. Brad Steiger and Chaw Mank, *Valentino: An Intimate and Shocking Exposé* (New York: MacFadden, 1966); Vincent Tajiri, *Valentino: The True Life Story* (New York: Bantam, 1977); Irving Shulman, *Valentino* (1967; New York: Pocket Books, 1968); also see Noel Botham and Peter Donnelly, *Valentino: The Love God* (New York: Ace Books, 1977). Tajiri's book contains a relatively detailed filmography and bibliography.
3. Valentino came to symbolize the failure of the American Dream, especially to more highbrow critics of culture like H. L. Mencken (*Prejudices, Sixth Series*, 1927) and John Dos Passos (*The Big Money*, 1936). Ken Russell's film, *Valentino* (1977), based on the Steiger/Mank biography and starring Rudolf Nureyev in the title role, articulates this theme through its pervasive references to *Citizen Kane*, such as the use of *post mortem* multiple flashback narration and other corny allusions.
4. Among the many reassessments of the period, see Estelle B. Freedman, 'The New Woman: Changing Views of Women in the 1920s', *Journal of American History*, 56: 2 (Sept. 1974), 372–93; Mary P. Ryan, *Womanhood in America*, second edn. (New York: New Viewpoints, 1979), ch. 5; Julie Matthaei, *An Economic History of Women in America* (New York: Schocken, 1982), especially chaps. 7–9.
5. This hypothesis implies a concept of the public sphere, in particular that of an alternative or counter public sphere as developed by Oskar Negt and Alexander Kluge in *Öffentlichkeit und Erfahrung/Public Sphere and Experience* (Frankfurt: Suhrkamp, 1972). For a review in English, see Eberhard Knödler-Bunte, 'The Proletarian Public Sphere and Political Organization', *New German Critique*, 4 (Winter 1975), 51–75; and my own paraphrase of Negt and Kluge in 'Early Silent Cinema: Whose Public Sphere', *New German Critique*, 29 (Spring/Summer 1983), 155–59. The role of the cinema for women during this period of transition is discussed in Judith Mayne, 'Immigrants and Spectator', *Wide Angle*, 5: 2 (1982), 32–41; Elizabeth Ewen, 'City Lights: Immigrant Women and the Rise of the Movies', *Signs*, 5: 3 (1980), S45–S65; Mary Ryan, 'The Projection of a New Womanhood: The Movie Moderns in the 1920s', in *Our American Sisters: Women in American Life and Thought*, second edn., Jean E. Friedman and William G. Shade, eds. (Boston: Allyn and Bacon, 1976), 366–84.
6. Laura Mulvey, 'Afterthoughts. . . .Inspired by *Duel in the Sun*', *Framework*, 15–17 (1981), 12; 'Visual Pleasure and Narrative Cinema' originally appeared in *Screen*, 16: 3 (Autumn 1975), 6–18.
7. For a still useful discussion of Mulvey in a larger context of directions of recent theory, see Christine Gledhill, 'Developments in Feminist Film Criticism' (1978), rpt. in *Re-Vision: Essays in Feminist Film Criticism*, Mary Ann Doane, Patricia Mellencamp, Linda Williams, eds. (Los Angeles: AFI monograph Series, 1983), 18–48. Among articles devoted primarily to a critique of Mulvey, see David Rodowick 'The Difficulty of Difference', *Wide Angle*, 5: 1 (1982): 4–15; Janet Walker, 'Psychoanalysis and Feminist Film Theory', *Wide Angle*, 6: 3 (1984), 16–23. For discussions challenging the Metzian/Mulveyan paradigm of spectatorship altogether, see Gaylyn Studlar, 'Masochism and the Perverse Pleasures of the Cinema', *Quarterly Review of Film Studies*, 9: 4 (Fall

1984), 267–82; Gertrud Koch, 'Exchanging the Gaze: Re-Visioning Feminist Film Theory', *New German Critique*, 34 (Winter 1985), 139–53.

8. Mulvey, 'Afterthoughts', 12.
9. This theoretical endeavor would greatly benefit from a more historical perspective taking into account the discourse on female reception during the formative decades of the institution, in particular the rejection of mass culture in terms of femininity. For German cinema, see Heide Schlüpmann's suggestive essay, 'Kinosucht [Cinema Addiction]', *Frauen und Film*, 33 (Oct. 1982), 45–52; and my own 'Early Silent Cinema', 173–84. Patrice Petro draws an impressive parallel between the German debates on 'distraction' and American discourse on television in 'Mass Culture and the Feminine: The "Place" of Television in Film Studies', *Cinema Journal*, 25: 2 (Spring 1986), 5–21. Significantly, in both American as well as German sources of the 1910s and 1920s, 'distraction' and 'absorption' are more often perceived in a relationship of affinity and simultaneity, than in one of opposition (as Brechtian film theory of the 1970s would have it). On the trope of transvestism, in particular its different uses by male and female writers, see Sandra M. Gilbert, 'Costumes of the Mind: Transvestism as Metaphor in Modern Literature', *Critical Inquiry*, 7: 2 (Winter 1980), 391–417, especially 404 ff.
10. Mary Ann Doane, 'Film and the Masquerade: Theorising the Female Spectator', *Screen*, 23: 3–4 (Sept./Oct. 1982), 81 (emphasis added).
11. The question of temporality has been raised as a crucial aspect of female spectatorship by Teresa de Lauretis, *Alice Doesn't: Feminism, Semiotics, Cinema* (Bloomington: Indiana University Press, 1984), 96 ff.; also see Tania Modleski, 'Time and Desire in the Woman's Film', *Cinema Journal*, 23: 3 (Spring 1984), 19–30. Modleski refers to Julia Kristeva, 'Women's Time', trans. Alice Jardine and Harry Blake, *Signs*, 7: 1 (Fall 1981), 13–35. For a discussion of the conflicting temporal registers of individual life history and social experience, see Negt/Kluge, *Public Sphere and Experience*, 45–74.
12. Doane, 'The "Woman's Film": Possession and Address', in *Re-Vision*, 67–82; Linda Williams, '"Something Else Besides a Mother": *Stella Dallas* and the Maternal Melodrama', *Cinema Journal*, 24: 1 (Fall 1984), 2–27; Tania Modleski, *Loving with a Vengeance: Mass Produced Fantasies for Women* (1982; New York: Methuen, 1984).
13. Williams's '"Something Else"' in part responds to E. Ann Kaplan, 'The Case of the Missing Mother: Maternal Issues in Vidor's *Stella Dallas*', *Heresies*, 16 (1983), 81–85; Kaplan's reply appeared in *Cinema Journal*, 24: 2 (Winter 1985), 40–43.
14. See Jürgen Habermas's critique of Gadamer, *Zur Logik der Sozialwissenschaften* (Frankfurt: Suhrkamp, 1970), 174 ff.; 'Der Universalitätsanspruch der Hermeneutik', *Kultur und Kritik* (Frankfurt: Suhrkamp, 1973), 264–301.
15. This project obviously involves some 'reading against the grain' but ultimately has a different objective: rather than merely to expose, from film to film, the textual contradictions symptomatic of the repression of female subjectivity under patriarchy, a rewriting of film history, in a feminist sense seeks to discover traces of female subjectivity even in the most repressive and alienated forms of consumer culture. The paradigm I have in mind is Benjamin's huge work on the Paris Arcades which Susan Buck-Morss (in a forthcoming book) reads as a dialectical *Ur*-history of mass culture. Also see Habermas,

'Consciousness-Raising or Redemptive Criticism: The Contemporaneity of Walter Benjamin' (1972), *New German Critique*, 17 (Spring 1979), 30–59.

16. Doane, 'Masquerade', 77; Kaplan, *Women and Film: Both Sides of the Camera* (New York and London: Methuen, 1983), 29. In the context of this problem, a number of critics have recently focused on the representation of the male body and the question of masculinity, among them Pam Cook, 'Masculinity in Crisis?' (on *Raging Bull*), *Screen*, 23: 3–4 (Sept.–Oct. 1982), 39–53; Richard Dyer, 'Don't Look Now: The Male Pin-Up', ibid., 61–73; Steve Neale, 'Masculinity as Spectacle', *Screen*, 24: 6 (Nov.–Dec. 1983), 2–16.
17. Teresa de Lauretis, *Alice Doesn't*, 83.
18. David Bordwell, Janet Staiger, Kristin Thompson, *The Classical Hollywood Cinema: Film Style and Mode of Production to 1960* (New York: Columbia University Press, 1985). Thompson, chap. 18, sees the basic narrative and stylistic premises of the classical system in place by 1917; the technological changes that gave 1920s films their distinct visual texture are described in chap. 21.
19. I feel supported in this contention by Teresa de Lauretis, *Alice Doesn't*, 125, 162; she also shares my skepticism concerning the Hegelian premises of Lacan, 128 ff 189 (n. 31), 205 (n. 32). By the same author, see 'Aesthetic and Feminist Theory', *New German Critique*, 34 (Winter 1985), 154–75.
20. A more consistent trait in Valentino's history with the industry is the high number of women in the production of his films, although this was generally more often the case before 1930. His most important films had scripts written by women, in particular June Mathis who 'discovered' him, but also Frances Marion; *Blood and Sand* was brilliantly edited by Dorothy Arzner; Alla Nazimova and Natacha Rambova, a designer and also his second wife, exerted their artistic and spiritual(ist) influence on many productions, with or without credit.
21. Sigmund Freud, 'Three Essays on the Theory of Sexuality' (1905), *Standard Edition* 7: 182.
22. Mulvey, 'Visual Pleasure', 11.
23. A more misogynist version of the same pattern occurs in *Cobra* (1925) when a friend advises the unhappily courting but as usual much pursued Valentino, 'look at the woman with the torch: she is safe!'—cut to the Statue of Liberty. For an excellent reading of these 'duels' and 'ballets' of the gaze, see Karsten Witte, 'Rudolph Valentino: Erotoman des Augenblicks', in *Die Unsterblichen des Kinos* 1, ed. Adolf Heinzlmeier et al. (Frankfurt: Fischer, 1982), 29–35.
24. 'Instincts and their Vicissitudes', *Standard Edition* 14: 128 ff.: 'Three Essays', *SE* 7: 156 ff., 199 f. and passim.
25. I am much indebted here to the work of Gertrud Koch; for essays available in translation, see 'Why Women Go to the Movies', *Jump Cut*, 27 (July 1982); and 'Female Sensuality: Past Joys and Future Hopes', *Jump Cut*, 30 (March 1985). Also see Christian Metz's distinction between cinematic and theatrical voyeurism, in *The Imaginary Signifier* (Bloomington: Indiana University Press, 1982), 64–66, 91–98.
26. Christa Karpenstein, 'Bald führt der Blick das Wort ein, bald leitet das Wort den Blick', *Kursbuch*, 49 (1977), 62. Also see Jutta Brückner's important essay on pornography, 'Der Blutfleck im Auge der Kamera', *Frauen und Film*, 30 (Dec. 1981), 13–23; Brückner links the historical 'underdevelopment' of

women's vision with the modality of dreams, as a more archaic form of consciousness: 'This female gaze, which is so precise precisely because it is not too precise, because it also has this inward turn, opening itself to fantasy images which it melts with the more literal images on the screen, this gaze is the basis for a kind of identification which women in particular tend to seek in the cinema' (19).

27. The discrepancy between advertising pitch and Valentino's actual lack of orientation and focus is obvious in the promotional short, *Rudolph Valentino and His Eighty-Eight American Beauties* (1923), which shows him as a somewhat half-hearted arbiter in a beauty contest. Even in Roland Barthes's compelling reading of the Valentinian face, the emphasis is on the aggressive aspect of his gaze: 'The face is mysterious, full of exotic splendor, of an inaccessible, Baudelairean beauty, undoubtedly made of exquisite dough; but one knows all too well that this cold glistening of make-up, this delicate, dark line under the animal eye, the black mouth—all this betrays a mineral substance, a cruel statue which comes to life only to thrust forth.' 'Visages et figures,' *Esprit*, 204 (July 1953): 7. ['Le visage est arcane, splendeur exotique, beauté baudelairienne, inaccessible, d'une pâte exquise sans doute, mais on sait bien que cette froid luisance du fard, ce mince trait sombre sous l'oeil d'animal, cette bouche noire, tout cela est d'un être minéral, d'une statue cruelle qui ne s'anime que pour percer.'] The metaphor of piercing or thrusting, however, would only confirm the suspicion that the Valentinian gaze is ultimately a substitute for phallic potency, hence the fetishistic cult surrounding it.
28. Two of Valentino's most popular films, *The Four Horsemen* and *Blood and Sand*, actually culminate in the protagonist's death, bringing into play the deep affinity of eros and death drive which Freud observes in his fascinating paper on 'The Theme of the Three Caskets' (1913), *SE* 12: 289–301. According to Enno Patalas, Valentino himself identified much more strongly with these two roles than with the superficial heroism of the Sheik, *Sozialgeschichte der Stars* (Hamburg: Marion von Schröder Verlag, 1963), 96f.
29. Doane, 'Misrecognition and Identity', *Ciné-Tracts*, 3: (Fall 1980), 25; Metz, *The Imaginary Signifier*, 46ff., 56ff and passim.
30. For example, the work of Stephen Heath, Raymond Bellour, and Thierry Kuntzel; also see the section on point of view in *Film Reader*, no. 4 (1979).
31. See Janet Walker, 'Psychoanalysis and Feminist Film Theory' (note 7), 20ff.; de Lauretis, 'Aesthetic and Feminist Theory' (note 19), 164 ff.
32. This option actually prevails in contemporary statements of female spectators; see Herbert Blumer, *Movies and Conduct* (New York: Macmillan, 1933), 69–70. In retrospect, however, as I frequently found in conversations with women who were in their teens at the time, the female star has faded into oblivion as much as the narrative, whereas Valentino himself is remembered with great enthusiasm and vividness of detail.
33. Doane, 'Misrecognition and Identity', 28 ff.; Doane's major objection to Metz's concept of primary identification is that, based as it is on the analogy with the Lacanian mirror stage and thus the hypothetical constitution of the male subject, the concept perpetuates, on a theoretical level, the patriarchal exclusion of female spectatorship.
34. See Richard Dyer, *Stars* (London: BFI, 1979).

35. This pattern of combining dark and light oppositions in one and the same character must have been perceived as typical of the Valentino text; see the change of Dubrovsky's alias in *The Eagle* from Pushkin's Monsieur Deforge to Valentino's Monsieur LeBlanc.
36. Tajiri (note 2), 63.
37. The male contingent among Valentino fans is not to be underestimated, including Elvis Presley, Kenneth Anger, and other luminaries; see Kenneth Anger, 'Rudy's Rep', in *Hollywood Babylon* (1975; New York: Dell, 1981); and his contribution to a catalogue of the Berlin Film Festival retrospective of Valentino's work, 'Sich an Valentino erinnern heisst Valentino entdecken,' discussed by Karsten Witte, in 'Fetisch-Messen', *Frauen und Film*, 38 (May 1985), 72–78. Ken Russell's film (see note 3) both exploits and disavows Valentino's place in the homosexual tradition. More important than biographical fact is the question of how Valentino challenged dominant standards of masculinity, which is also a question of their social and historical variability and changeability.
38. The sadistic spicing of cinematic pleasure (far from being the exclusive domain of Von Stroheim) is still rather common in pre-Code films, though seldom with such strong effects on the sexual persona of the protagonist. Consider, for instance, a sequence early on in the Pickford vehicle *Sparrows* (1926) in which the villain (Gustav von Seyffertitz) crushes a doll sent, by an absent mother, to one of the children he keeps as slaves; the camera lingers, close-up, on the remnants of the doll as it slowly disappears in the swamp. The fascination deployed in such a shot far exceeds narrative motivation; i.e. its function for establishing Mr. Grimes as irredeemably evil.
39. Freud, 'Three Essays', *SE* 7: 160; also 'Instincts', *SE* 14: 126.
40. Most notably in 'The Economic Problem of Masochism' (1924), *SE* 19: 155–70, where Freud develops the notion of a 'primary' masochism linked to the death instinct; this notion is already present though rejected in 'Instincts and Their Vicissitudes' (1915), 127, but resumed as early as 1920 in *Beyond the Pleasure Principle, SE* 18: 55.
41. Studlar, 'Masochism and the Perverse Pleasures of the Cinema' (note 7); Deleuze, *Masochism: An Interpretation of Coldness and Cruelty* (French orig. 1967; New York: George Braziller, 1971).
42. Deleuze, *Masochism*, 21, 37 f. Studlar acknowledges this problem in passing, 'Masochism and Perverse Pleasures', 270 and her note 27. The reason why Deleuze's model seems to work so surprisingly well for the Sternberg/Dietrich films might have less to do with the validity of the model than with Sternberg's indebtedness to the same cultural background that gave us *Venus in Furs*.
43. The essay has been much discussed in recent film theory; for example, Rodowick, 'The Difficulty of Difference', and Doane, 'The Woman's Film'.
44. Freud, 'A Child Is Being Beaten', *Standard Edition* 17: 186.
45. This incestuous-narcissistic aura is encapsulated in a portrait showing Valentino and Rambova in profile and, obviously, in the nude; rpt. in Walker, 73; and Anger, *Hollywood Babylon*, 160–61.
46. Williams, 'When the Woman Looks', *Re-Vision*, 83–96. The point Williams makes with regard to a number of classic horror films also elucidates the function of the dark/light split in the Valentino character: 'the power and

potency of the monster body. . .should not be interpreted as an eruption of the normally repressed animal sexuality of the civilized male (the monster as double for the male viewer and characters in the film), but as feared power and potency of a different kind of sexuality (the monster as double for the woman)' (87).

47. Adorno, 'Sexualtabus und Recht heute', *Eingriffe* (Frankfurt: Suhrkamp, 1963), 104–5; the phrase is used in English and without quotation marks; also see 'This Side of the Pleasure Principle', *Minima Moralia: Reflections from Damaged Life* (London: New Left Books, 1974). Marcuse's plea for polymorphous perversity in *Eros and Civilization* (1955; Boston: Beacon Press, 1966) is more problematic, especially in light of the Foucauldian analysis of the 'perverse implantation' (*The History of Sexuality* 1), but Marcuse himself takes a more pessimistic view in his 'Political Preface 1966', while maintaining a utopian distinction between sexual liberty and erotic/political freedom (xiv–xv). Already during the 1920s, the prophets of a 'healthy sex life' were numerous, drawing on the essentialist sexual psychology of Havelock Ellis, on the newly discovered 'doctrine' of psychoanalysis, as well as libertarian positions developed among the Greenwich Village boheme although not necessarily all that liberating for women; see writings by Hutchins Hapgood, Max Eastman, V. F. Calverton and—probably the single most repressive instance of sexual hygiene—Floyd Dell, *Love in the Machine Age: A Psychological Study of the Transition from Patriarchal Society* (New York: Farrar & Rinehart, 1930).
48. Walker, *Rudolph Valentino*, 8, 47 and passim.
49. See works cited above, note 4.
50. *Blood and Sand*, closest to the melodramatic matrix, is the only film that makes Valentino's mate a mother; by contrast, most other female characters opposite Valentino have tomboyish qualities (especially Moran in *Moran of the Lady Letty*), an air of independence, owing to either a superior social status or work, and, above all, a certain 'mischievous vivacity' (Ryan) that was associated with the New Woman.
51. Glyn actually endorsed Valentino's sex appeal, and he starred in *Beyond the Rocks* (1922), based on one of her novels. Still, the focus on a male star distinguishes the Valentino films from films that more immediately functioned to train their audiences in 'fashionable femininity'; Ryan, 'Projection' (note 5), 370 f.
52. See the notorious 'Pink Powder Puff' attack in the *Chicago Tribune*, 18 July 1926, reported in *Hollywood Babylon*, 156–58.
53. For this aspect of the Valentino persona I am indebted to Virginia Wright Wexman as well as to Richard Dyer's work on Paul Robeson; Winifred Stewart and Jane Hady, who remember the Valentino cult during their teenage years in Martinsburg, West Virginia, further encouraged the following speculations. Also see Jacqueline Hall, '"The Mind that Burns in Each Body": Women, Rape, and Racial Violence', in *Powers of Desire: The Politics of Sexuality*, ed. Ann Snitow et al. (New York Monthly Review Press, 1983), 337.
54. Homi K. Bhabha 'The Other Question: The Stereotype and Colonial Discourse', *Screen* 24, no. 6 (Nov.–Dec. 1983): 18–36.
55. Barthes, 'Visages et figures' (note 29), 6.
56. Richard Dyer suggests that all representations of the male body, especially however, of male nudity, share this fate, since the actual sight of the penis,

whether limp or erect, is bound to be awkward, thus revealing the discrepancy between it and the symbolic claims made in its name, the hopeless assertion of phallic mastery; 'Don't Look Now' (note 16), 71–72.

57. Any Valentino biography will elaborate on these events with great gusto. For the most detailed account, including an astonishing chapter on Valentino's afterlife ('Act V: Cuckooland'), see Shulman's book (note 2).

13 Masculinity as Spectacle

Reflections on Men and Mainstream Cinema

Steve Neale*

Over the past ten years or so, numerous books and articles have appeared discussing the images of women produced and circulated by the cinematic institution. Motivated politically by the development of the Women's Movement, and concerned therefore with the political and ideological implications of the representations of women offered by the cinema, a number of these books and articles have taken as their basis Laura Mulvey's 'Visual Pleasure and Narrative Cinema', first published in *Screen* in 1975.[1] Mulvey's article was highly influential in its linking together of psychoanalytic perspectives on the cinema with a feminist perspective on the ways in which images of women figure within mainstream film. She sought to demonstrate the extent to which the psychic mechanisms cinema has basically involved are profoundly patriarchal, and the extent to which the images of women mainstream film has produced lie at the heart of those mechanisms.

Inasmuch as there has been discussion of gender, sexuality, representation and the cinema over the past decade then, that discussion has tended overwhelmingly to centre on the representation of women, and to derive many of its basic tenets from Mulvey's article. Only within the Gay Movement have there appeared specific discussions of the representation of men. Most of these, as far as I am aware, have centred on the representations and stereotypes of gay men. Both within the Women's Movement and the Gay Movement, there is an important sense in which the images and functions of heterosexual masculinity within mainstream cinema have been left undiscussed. Heterosexual masculinity has been identified as a structuring norm in relation both to images of women and gay men. It has to that extent been profoundly problematised, rendered visible. But it has rarely been discussed and analysed as such. Outside these movements, it has

* Steve Neale, 'Masculinity as Spectacle' from *Screen*, vol. 24 no. 6 (1983), reprinted by permission of John Logie Baird Centre and the author.

been discussed even less. It is thus very rare to find analyses that seek to specify in detail, in relation to particular films or groups of films, how heterosexual masculinity is inscribed and the mechanisms, pressures and contradictions that inscription may involve. Aside from a number of recent pieces in *Screen*[2] and *Framework*,[3] Raymond Bellour's article on *North by Northwest* is the only example that springs readily to mind. Bellour's article follows in some detail the Oedipal trajectory of Hitchcock's film, tracing the movement of its protagonist, Roger Thornhill (Cary Grant) from a position of infantile dependence on the mother to a position of 'adult', 'male', heterosexual masculinity, sealed by his marriage to Eve Kendall (Eva Marie Saint) and by his acceptance of the role and authority of the father. However, the article is concerned as much with the general workings of a classical Hollywood film as it is with the specifics of a set of images of masculinity.[4]

Although, then, there is a real need for more analyses of individual films, I intend in this article to take another approach to some of the issues involved. Using Laura Mulvey's article as a central, structuring reference point, I want to look in particular at identification, looking and spectacle as she has discussed them and to pose some questions as to how her remarks apply directly or indirectly to images of men, on the one hand, and to the male spectator on the other. The aim is less to challenge fundamentally the theses she puts forward, than to open a space within the framework of her arguments and remarks for a consideration of the representation of masculinity as it can be said to relate to the basic characteristics and conventions of the cinematic institution.

IDENTIFICATION

To start with, I want to quote from John Ellis' book *Visible Fictions*.[5] Written very much in the light of Mulvey's article, Ellis is concerned both to draw on her arguments and to extend and qualify some of the theses she puts forward *vis-à-vis* gender and identification in the cinema. Ellis argues that identification is never simply a matter of men identifying with male figures on the screen and women identifying with female figures. Cinema draws on and involves many desires, many forms of desire. And desire itself is mobile, fluid, constantly transgressing identities, positions and roles. Identifications are multiple, fluid, at points even contradictory. Moreover, there are different forms of identification. Ellis points to two such forms, one associated with narcissism, the other with phantasies and dreams. He sums up as follows:

> Cinematic identification involves two different tendencies. First, there is that of dreaming and phantasy that involve the multiple and contradictory tendencies within the construction of the individual. Second, there is the experience of narcissistic identification with the image of a human figure perceived as other. Both these processes are invoked in the conditions of entertainment cinema. The spectator does not therefore 'identify' with the hero or heroine: an identification that would, if put in its conventional sense, involve socially constructed males identifying with male heroes, and socially constructed females identifying with women heroines. The situation is more complex than this, as identification involves both the recognition of self in the image on the screen, a narcissistic identification, and the identification of self with the various positions that are involved in the fictional narration: those of hero and heroine, villain, bit-part player, active and passive character. Identification is therefore multiple and fractured, a sense of seeing the constituent parts of the spectator's own psyche paraded before her or him. . . .[6]

A series of identifications are involved, then, each shifting and mobile. Equally, though, there is constant work to channel and regulate identification in relation to sexual division, in relation to the orders of gender, sexuality and social identity and authority marking patriarchal society. Every film tends both to assume and actively to work to renew those orders, that division. Every film thus tends to specify identification in accordance with the socially defined and constructed categories of male and female.

In looking specifically at masculinity in this context, I want to examine the process of narcissistic identification in more detail. Inasmuch as films *do* involve gender identification, and inasmuch as current ideologies of masculinity involve so centrally notions and attitudes to do with aggression, power and control, it seems to me that narcissism and narcissistic identification may be especially significant.

Narcissism and narcissistic identification both involve phantasies of power, omnipotence, mastery and control. Laura Mulvey makes the link between such phantasies and patriarchal images of masculinity in the following terms:

> As the spectator identifies with the main male protagonist, he projects his look on to that of his like, his screen surrogate, so that the power of the male protagonist as he controls events coincides with the active power of the erotic

look, both giving a satisfying sense of omnipotence. A male movie star's glamorous characteristics are thus not those of the erotic object of his gaze, but those of the more perfect, more complete, more powerful ideal ego conceived in the original moment of recognition in front of the mirror.[7]

I want to turn to Mulvey's remarks about the glamorous male movie star below. But first it is worth extending and illustrating her point about the male protagonist and the extent to which his image is dependent upon narcissistic phantasies, phantasies of the 'more perfect, more complete, more powerful ideal ego'.

It is easy enough to find examples of films in which these phantasies are heavily prevalent, in which the male hero is powerful and omnipotent to an extraordinary degree: the Clint Eastwood character in *A Fistful of Dollars*, *For a Few Dollars More* and *The Good, the Bad and the Ugly*, the Tom Mix westerns, Charlton Heston in *El Cid*, the *Mad Max* films, the Steve Reeves epics *Superman*, *Flash Gordon* and so on. There is generally, of course, a drama in which that power and omnipotence are tested and qualified (*Superman 2* is a particularly interesting example, as are Howard Hawks' westerns and adventure films), but the Leone trilogy, for example, is marked by the extent to which the hero's powers are rendered almost godlike, hardly qualified at all. Hence, perhaps, the extent to which they are built around ritualised scenes which in many ways are devoid of genuine suspense. A film like Melville's *Le Samourai*, on the other hand, starts with the image of self-possessed, omnipotent masculinity and traces its gradual and eventual disintegration. Alain Delon plays a lone gangster, a hit-man. His own narcissism is stressed in particular through his obsessive concern with his appearance, marked notably by a repeated and ritualised gesture he makes when putting on his hat, a sweep of the hand across the rim. Delon is sent on a job, but is spotted by a black female singer in a club. There is an exchange of looks. From that point on his omnipotence, silence and inviolability are all under threat. He is shot and wounded; his room is broken into and bugged; he is nearly trapped on the Metro. Eventually, he is gunned down, having returned to the club to see the singer again. The film is by no means a critique of the male image it draws upon. On the contrary, it very much identifies (and invites us to identify) with Delon. Nevertheless, the elements both of that image and of that to which the image is vulnerable are clearly laid out. It is no accident that Delon's downfall is symtomatically inaugurated in his encounter with the black woman. Difference (double difference) is the threat. An exchange of looks in which

Delon's cold commanding gaze is troubled, undermined and returned is the mark of that threat.

The kind of image that Delon here embodies, and that Eastwood and the others mentioned earlier embody too, is one marked not only by emotional reticence, but also by silence, a reticence with language. Theoretically, this silence, this absence of language can further be linked to narcissism and to the construction of an ideal ego. The acquisition of language is a process profoundly challenging to the narcissism of early childhood. It is productive of what has been called 'symbolic castration'. Language is a process (or set of processes) involving absence and lack, and these are what threaten any image of the self as totally enclosed, self-sufficient, omnipotent. The construction of an ideal ego, meanwhile, is a process involving profound contradictions. While the ideal ego may be a 'model' with which the subject identifies and to which it aspires, it may also be a source of further images and feelings of castration, inasmuch as that ideal is something to which the subject is never adequate.[8]

If this is the case, there can be no simple and unproblematic identification on the part of the spectator, male or female, with Mulvey's 'ideal ego' on the screen. In an article published in *Wide Angle*, D. N. Rodowick has made a similar point. He goes on to argue both that the narcissistic male image—the image of authority and omnipotence—can entail a concomitant masochism in the relations between the spectator and the image, and further that the male image can involve an eroticism, since there is always a constant oscillation between that image as a source of identification, and as an other, a source of contemplation. The image is a source both of narcissistic processes and drives, and, inasmuch as it is other, of object-oriented processes and drives:

> Mulvey discusses the male star as an object of the look but denies him the function of an erotic object. Because Mulvey conceives the look to be essentially active in its aims, identification with the male protagonist is only considered from a point of view which associates it with a sense of omnipotence, of assuming control of the narrative. She makes no differentiation between identification and object choice in which sexual aims may be directed towards the male figure, nor does she consider the signification of authority in the male figure from the point of view of an economy of masochism.[9]

Given Rodowick's argument, it is not surprising either that 'male' genres and films constantly involve sado-masochistic themes, scenes and phantasies or that male heroes can at times be marked as the object of an erotic gaze. These are both points I wish to discuss below. However, it is worth mentioning here that they have also been discussed in Paul Willemen's article 'Anthony Mann: Looking at the Male'.[10]

Willemen argues that spectacle and drama in Mann's films tend both to be structured around the look at the male figure: 'The viewer's experience is predicated on the pleasure of seeing the male "exist" (that is walk, move, ride, fight) in or through cityscapes, landscapes or, more abstractly, history. And on the unquiet pleasure of seeing the male mutilated (often quite graphically in Mann) and restored through violent brutality.'[11] These pleasures are founded upon a repressed homosexual voyeurism, a voyeurism 'not without its problems: the look at the male produces just as much anxiety as the look at the female, especially when it's presented as directly as in the killing scenes in *T-Men* and *Border Incident*.'[12] The (unstated) thesis behind these comments seems to be that in a heterosexual and patriarchal society, the male body cannot be marked explicitly as the erotic object of another male look: that look must be motivated in some other way, its erotic component repressed. The mutilation and sadism so often involved in Mann's films are marks both of the repression involved and of a means by which the male body may be disqualified, so to speak, as an object of erotic contemplation and desire. The repression and disavowal involved are figured crucially in the scenes in *T-Men* and *Border Incident* to which Willemen refers, in which 'an undercover agent must look on, impassively, while his close (male) friend and partner is being killed'.[13]

There is one final and important contradiction involved in the type of narcissistic images of masculinity discussed above to which I'd like to refer. It is the contradiction between narcissism and the Law, between an image of *narcissistic* authority on the one hand and an image of *social* authority on the other. This tension or contradiction is discussed at some length by Laura Mulvey in an article seeking to reconsider her 'Visual Pleasure' piece with particular reference to *Duel in the Sun*.[14] It is a tension she sees as especially evident in the western. Using a narrative model derived from Vladimir's Propp's analyses of folktales,[15] Mulvey points to two narrative functions, 'marriage' (and hence social integration) and 'not marriage', a refusal by the hero to enter society, a refusal motivated by a nostalgic narcissism:

> In the Proppian tale, an important aspect of narrative closure is 'marriage', a function characterised by the 'princess' or equivalent. This is the only func-

tion that is sex specific and thus essentially relates to the sex of the hero and his marriageability. This function is very commonly reproduced in the Western, where once again 'marriage' makes a crucial contribution to narrative closure. However, the function's presence also has come to allow a complication in the Western, its complementary opposite 'not marriage'. Thus, while the social integration represented by marriage is an essential aspect of the folk-tale, in the Western it can be accepted . . . or not. A hero can gain in stature by refusing the princess and remaining alone (Randolph Scott in the Ranown series of movies). As the resolution of the Proppian tale can be seen to represent the resolution of the Oedipus complex (integration into the symbolic), the rejection of marriage personifies a nostalgic celebration of phallic, narcissistic omnipotence.[16]

There are thus two diverging images of masculinity commonly at play in the western:

The tension between two points of attraction, the symbolic (social integration and marriage) and nostalgic narcissism, generates a common splitting of the Western hero into two, something unknown in the Proppian tale. Here two functions emerge, one celebrating integration into society through marriage, the other celebrating resistance to social standards and responsibilities, above all those of marriage and the family, the sphere represented by women.[17]

Mulvey goes on to discuss John Ford's western *The Man Who Shot Liberty Valance*, noting the split there between Tom Doniphon, played by John Wayne, who incarnates the narcissistic function of the anachronistic social outsider, and Ranse Stoddart, played by James Stewart, who incarnates the civilising functions of marriage, social integration and social responsibility. The film's tone is increasingly nostalgic, in keeping with its mourning for the loss of Doniphon and what he represents. The nostalgia, then, is not just for an historical past, for the Old West, but also for the masculine narcissism that Wayne represents.

Taking a cue from Mulvey's remarks about nostalgia in *Liberty Valance*, one could go on to discuss a number of nostalgic westerns in these terms, in terms of the theme of lost or doomed male narcissism. The clearest examples would be Peckinpah's westerns: *Guns in the Afternoon*, *Major Dundee* (to a lesser extent), *The Wild Bunch* and, especially, *Pat Garrett and Billy the Kid*. These films are shot through with nostalgia, with an obsession with images and definitions of masculinity and masculine codes of behaviour, and with images of male narcissism and the threats posed to it by women, society and the Law. The threat of castration is figured in the wounds and injuries suffered by Joel McCrea in *Guns in the Afternoon*, Charlton Heston in *Major*

Dundee and William Holden in *The Wild Bunch.* The famous slow-motion violence, bodies splintered and torn apart, can be viewed at one level at least as the image of narcissism in its moment of disintegration and destruction. Significantly, Kris Kristofferson as Billy in *Pat Garrett and Billy the Kid*, the ultimate incarnation of omnipotent male narcissism in Peckinpah's films, is spared any bloody and splintered death. Shot by Pat Garrett, his body shows no sign either of wounds or blood: narcissism transfigured (rather than destroyed) by death.

I want now to move on from identification and narcissism to discuss in relation to images of men and masculinity the two modes of looking addressed by Mulvey in 'Visual Pleasure', voyeuristic looking, on the one hand, and fetishistic looking on the other.

LOOKING AND SPECTACLE

In discussing these two types of looking, both fundamental to the cinema, Mulvey locates them solely in relation to a structure of activity/passivity in which the look is male and active and the object of the look female and passive. Both are considered as distinct and variant means by which male castration anxieties may be played out and allayed.

Voyeuristic looking is marked by the extent to which there is a distance between spectator and spectacle, a gulf between the seer and the seen. This structure is one which allows the spectator a degree of power over what is seen. It hence tends constantly to involve sado-masochistic phantasies and themes. Here is Mulvey's description:

> voyeurism . . . has associations with sadism: pleasure lies in ascertaining guilt (immediately associated with castration), asserting control and subjecting the guilty person through punishment and forgiveness. This sadistic side fits in well with narrative. Sadism demands a story, depends on making something happen, forcing a change in another person, a battle of will and strength, victory, and defeat, all occurring in a linear time with a beginning and an end.[18]

Mulvey goes on to discuss these characteristics of voyeuristic looking in terms of the *film noir* and of Hitchcock's movies, where the hero is the bearer of the voyeuristic look, engaged in a narrative in which the woman is the object of its sadistic components. However, if we take some of the terms used in her description—'making something happen', 'forcing a change in another person', 'a battle of will and strength', 'victory and defeat'—they can immediately be applied to 'male' genres, to films concerned largely or solely with the depiction of relations between men, to any film, for example, in which there is a struggle between a hero and a male villain. War films, westerns and gangster movies, for instance, are all marked by 'action', by 'making something happen'. Battles, fights and duels of all kinds are concerned with struggles of 'will and strength', 'victory and defeat', between individual men and/or groups of men. All of which implies that male figures on the screen are subject to voyeuristic looking, both on the part of the spectator and on the part of other male characters.

Paul Willemen's thesis on the films of Anthony Mann is clearly relevant here. The repression of any explicit avowal of eroticism in the act of looking at the male seems structurally linked to a narrative content marked by sado-masochistic phantasies and scenes. Hence both forms of voyeuristic looking, intra- and extra-diegetic, are especially evident in those moments of contest and combat referred to above, in those moments at which a narrative outcome is determined through a fight or gun-battle, at which male struggle becomes pure spectacle. Perhaps the most extreme examples are to be found in Leone's westerns, where the exchange of aggressive looks marking most western gun-duels is taken to the point of fetishistic parody through the use of extreme and repetitive close-ups. At which point the look begins to oscillate between voyeurism and fetishism as the narrative starts to freeze and spectacle takes over. The anxious 'aspects' of the look at the male to which Willemen refers are here both embodied and allayed not just by playing out the sadism inherent in voyeurism through scenes of violence and combat, but also by drawing upon the structures and processes of fetishistic looking, by stopping the narrative in order to recognise the pleasure of display, but displacing it from the male body as such and locating it more generally in the overall components of a highly ritualised scene.

John Ellis has characterised fetishistic looking in the following terms:

> where voyeurism maintains (depends upon) a separation between the seer and the object seen, fetishism tries to abolish the gulf. . . . This process implies a different position and attitude of the spectator to the image. It represents the opposite tendency to that of voyeurism. . . . Fetishistic looking implies the direct acknowledgement and participation of the object viewed . . . with the fetishistic attitude, the look of the character towards the viewer . . . is a central feature. . . . The voyeuristic look is curious, inquiring, demanding to know. The fetishistic gaze is captivated by what it sees, does not wish to inquire

further, to see more, to find out. . . . The fetishistic look has much to do with display and the spectacular.[19]

Mulvey again centrally discusses this form of looking in relation to the female as object: 'This second avenue, fetishistic scopophilia, builds up the physical beauty of the object, transforming it into something satisfying in itself.'[20] 'Physical beauty' is interpreted solely in terms of the female body. It is specified through the example of the films of Sternberg:

While Hitchcock goes into the investigative side of voyeurism, Sternberg produces the ultimate fetish, taking it to the point where the powerful look of the male protagonist is broken in favour of the image in direct erotic rapport with the spectator. The beauty of the woman as object and the screen space coalesce; she is no longer the bearer of guilt but a perfect product, whose body, stylised and fragmented by close-ups, is the content of the film and the direct recipient of the spectator's look.[21]

If we return to Leone's shoot-outs, we can see that some elements of the fetishistic look as here described are present, others not. We are offered the spectacle of male bodies, but bodies unmarked as objects of erotic display. There is no trace of an acknowledgement or recognition of those bodies as displayed solely for the gaze of the spectator. They are on display, certainly, but there is no cultural or cinematic convention which would allow the male body to be presented in the way that Dietrich so often is in Sternberg's films. We see male bodies stylised and fragmented by close-ups, but our look is not direct, it is heavily mediated by the looks of the characters involved. And those looks are marked not by desire, but rather by fear, or hatred, or aggression. The shoot-outs are moments of spectacle, points at which the narrative hesitates, comes to a momentary halt, but they are also points at which the drama is finally resolved, a suspense in the culmination of the narrative drive. They thus involve an imbrication of *both* forms of looking, their intertwining designed to minimise and displace the eroticism they each tend to involve, to disavow any explicitly erotic look at the male body.

There are other instances of male combat which seem to function in this way. Aside from the western, one could point to the epic as a genre, to the gladiatorial combat in *Spartacus*, to the fight between Christopher Plummer and Stephen Boyd at the end of *The Fall of the Roman Empire*, to the chariot race in *Ben Hur*. More direct displays of the male body can be found, though they tend either to be fairly brief or else to occupy the screen during credit sequences and the like (in which case the display is mediated by another textual function). Examples of the former would include the extraordinary shot of Gary Cooper lying under the hut toward the end of *Man of the West*, his body momentarily filling the Cinemascope screen. Or some of the images of Lee Marvin in *Point Blank*, his body draped over a railing or framed in a doorway. Examples of the latter would include the credit sequence of *Man of the West* again (an example to which Willemen refers), and *Junior Bonner*.

The presentation of Rock Hudson in Sirk's melodramas is a particularly interesting case. There are constantly moments in these films in which Hudson is presented quite explicitly as the object of an erotic look. The look is usually marked as female. But Hudson's body is *feminised* in those moments, an indication of the strength of those conventions which dictate that only women can function as the objects of an explicitly erotic gaze. Such instances of 'feminisation' tend also to occur in the musical, the only genre in which the male body has been unashamedly put on display in mainstream cinema in any consistent way. (A particularly clear and interesting example would be the presentation of John Travolta in *Saturday Night Fever*.)

It is a refusal to acknowledge or make explicit an eroticism that marks all three of the psychic functions and processes discussed here in relation to images of men: identification, voyeuristic looking and fetishistic looking. It is this that tends above all to differentiate the cinematic representation of images of men and women. Although I have sought to open up a space within Laura Mulvey's arguments and theses, to argue that the elements she considers in relation to images of women can and should also be considered in relation to images of men, I would certainly concur with her basic premise that the spectatorial look in mainstream cinema is implicitly male: it is one of the fundamental reasons why the erotic elements involved in the relations between the spectator and the male image have constantly to be repressed and disavowed. Were this not the case, mainstream cinema would have openly to come to terms with the male homosexuality it so assiduously seeks either to denigrate or deny. As it is, male homosexuality is constantly present as an undercurrent, as a potentially troubling aspect of many films and genres, but one that is dealt with obliquely, symptomatically, and that has to be repressed. While mainstream cinema, in its assumption of a male norm, perspective and look, can constantly take women and the female image as its object of investigation, it has rarely investigated men and the male image in the same kind of way: women are a problem, a source of anxiety, of

14 Strategies of Coherence

Narrative Cinema, Feminist Poetics, and Yvonne Rainer

Teresa de Lauretis*

> Words are uttered but not possessed by my performers as they operate within the filmic frame but do not propel a filmic plot.
>
> Yvonne Rainer

In the early years of the present decade, speculating upon her own development as an artist and filmmaker, Yvonne Rainer saw herself moving, almost against her will, toward narrative film:

From description of individual feminine experience floating free of both social context and narrative hierarchy, to descriptions of individual feminine experience placed in radical juxtaposition against historical events, to explicitly feminist speculations about feminine experience, I have just formulated an evolution which in becoming more explicitly feminist seems to demand a more solid anchoring in narrative conventions. (I am not sure of the reasons, but I suspect the worst.)[1]

Why this suspicion? Remember Joan Fontaine's suspicion, in Hitchcock's film (*Suspicion*, 1941), about her husband's (Cary Grant's) plot to kill her? Or Mimi's suspicion that she has been murdered by the plot of Puccini's opera *Bohème* in Sally Potter's *Thriller* (1979)? Or Dora's suspicion of Freud's plotting of her case history? Is this suspicion of narrativity on the part of women simply a particular case of paranoia, or is it somehow justified? In other words, are we right in suspecting the worst? And if we are, then how do we account for women's apparently irresistible attraction to narrative, from Anne Radcliffe to Alice Walker, from Germaine Dulac to Yvonne Rainer? Is it simply, again, a case of masochism, of victimism, a gender-specific pathological condition, or is there something else, or something more, at stake?

* Teresa de Lauretis, 'Strategies of Coherence: Narrative, Cinema, Feminist Poetics, Yvonne Rainer' from *Technologies of Gender: Essays on Theory, Film and Fiction* edited by Teresa de Lauretis (Indiana University Press, 1987), reprinted by permission of the publisher and the author.

In a chapter of *Alice Doesn't* entitled 'Desire in Narrative', I have argued that desire is inscribed as well as contained 'in the very *movement* of narrative, the unfolding of the Oedipal scenario as *drama*';[2] and however problematic—doubled and contradictory—the position of a female spectator or reader may be in relation to (pre)oedipal desire, it is nevertheless from there that any possibility of reading, any process of identification or effect of meaning must proceed.

Therefore, contrary to what was perceived to be the common project of radical, independent, or avant-garde cinema in the 1960s and 1970s—namely, the destruction of narrative and visual pleasure (a project in which feminist filmmakers and critics participated enthusiastically, producing both film texts and textual readings which, together, articulated the feminist critique of representation that was to shape most of film theory as we now have it); contrary to that stoic prescription to destroy all pleasure in the text, I proposed, feminist work in film should be not anti-narrative or anti-Oedipal but quite the opposite. It should be narrative and Oedipal with a vengeance, working, as it were, with and against narrative in order to represent not just a female desire which Hollywood, in the best tradition of Western literature and iconography, has classically represented as the doomed power of the fetish (a fetish empowered for the benefit of men and doomed to disempower women); but working, instead, to represent the duplicity of the Oedipal scenario itself and the specific contradiction of the female subject in it.

I now want to suggest that plot, narrative (i.e. the growth and flowing of plot into story across the narrative layering of events, actantial functions, and discursive registers), and narrativity (the effective functioning of narrative on and with the reader/spectator to produce a subject of reading or a subject of vision)—in short, all the ingredients of the pleasure of the text—are mechanisms of coherence. Which is not to say solely mechanisms of closure, traps in which the subject is totally and necessarily contained, for closure is only an effect of particular narrative strategies (those of the so-called classical cinema, for example, or of Barthes's 'readerly text', a notion which his own reading, however, has belied); and particular narrative strategies, moreover, whose effectivity in producing closure is not universal or atemporal but historically and semiotically specific—I mean specific with regard to the history of cultural forms, media, genres, and spectatorship or context of reception.

Thus, to our contemporary eyes, even the texts of classical narrative cinema display, as feminist critics have repeatedly shown, the very gaps and paradoxes that the operation of narrative is meant to cover up; paradoxes which now can be seen to be at once the figure of repression and 'of the repression of the very functioning of repression', as Shoshana Felman pointed out of a non-filmic classic text, a Balzac novella, in her well-known essay 'Rereading Femininity' quite some time ago.[3] If it now can be said, not only of Balzac but also of the classical narrative text *tout court*, that the text 'opens up an ironic space which articulates the force of the question of femininity', it is because of Felman's rereading, Barthes's rereading, and the feminist rereadings and rewritings (I would like to say, remakes) of classical narrative films.

Here, then, I want to explore how narrative and narrativity, because of their capacity to inscribe desire and to direct, sustain, or undercut identification (in all the senses of the term), are mechanisms to be employed strategically and tactically in the effort to construct other forms of coherence, to shift the terms of representation, to produce the conditions of representability of another—and gendered—social subject. Obviously, therefore, much is at stake in narrative, in a poetics of narrative. Our suspicion is more than justified, but so is our attraction.

The terms *narrative* and *poetics*, especially when juxtaposed in 'narrative poetics', evoke the presence or the phantom of an 'anterior discourse', as Todorov used the phrase, à propos of Bakhtin's notion of intertextual polyvalence as a characteristic register of poetic (or literary) discourse.[4] They evoke the phantom of, precisely, *that* discourse: structuralist poetics, the systematic study of literary language in its most intimate quality—literaturnost, literariness—and specificity, the totality of its verbal structures; and hence, as concerns narrative, the vicissitudes of that basic model of structural analysis developed in the 1960s, out of Propp and Lévi-Strauss, by the contributors to the now legendary issue of *Communications* 8, and its further adventures in the somewhat narrower straits of contemporary narratology. (As you see, I can't resist the temptation to make a story. The attraction is evident. But . . . is the suspicion also justified?)

The program of structuralist poetics, with its detailed discussion of narrative syntax, as Peter Brooks remarks in his introduction to the Minnesota English edition of Todorov's *Poetics*, aims 'to *decompose* literary discourse into its component parts, and to study the *logic* of the possible significant combinations of parts'.[5] Brooks is very careful in choosing that word *decompose*, careful lest it should bear any resemblance to another word, which a less astute writer might have let slip incautiously in the sentence: the word *deconstruct*. For *deconstruct* is indeed a word 'already inhabited', as Bakhtin would say, by the thought of others—others not wholly sympathetic to the project of structural poetics.

I am referring to Paul de Man's critique of literary semiotics and its 'use of grammatical (especially syntactical) structures conjointly with rhetorical structures, without apparent awareness of a possible discrepancy between them'.[6] 'Todorov, who calls one of his books a *Grammar of the Decameron*,' wrote de Man with just a touch of sarcasm, may rightly think of his work as 'the elaboration of a systematic grammar of literary modes, genres, and also of literary figures' (pp. 6–7). However, if the relationship of grammar and logic is one of mutual and 'unsubverted' support, de Man argued, it is not so of the relationship between grammar and rhetoric. To study tropes and figures as a mere subset of syntactical relations is to assume a continuity between grammar and rhetoric which is in fact a discontinuity, a tension, even a contradiction.

He illustrated this point by analyzing a glaring case of what seems to be convergence, but is actually discontinuity, between grammatical and rhetorical structures: the rhetorical question, the very instance of a figure that is conveyed by means of a syntactical device. The contradiction there, de Man observed, is that 'grammar allows us to ask the question, but the sentence by means of which we ask it may deny the very possibility of asking' (p. 10). Thus, in effect, barring the intervention of an extratextual intention (which neither de Man nor Todorov would consider germane to his own enterprise), 'rhetoric radically suspends logic and opens up vertiginous possibilities of referential aberration'.[7]

But de Man's project for rhetorical deconstruction (the deconstructive reading of rhetorical figures and patterns in search of a negative truth) is also, in its way, constructive. The 'vertiginous possibilities of referential aberrations' must not be yielded to (again I cannot help hearing a loud intertextual intrusion: Hitchcock's film *Vertigo*, with its entirely made-up, constructed, filmic, illusionistic, non-referential image of the stairwell);[8] nor, on the other hand, will indetermination, absolute undecidability among readings, serve literature any better. A certain kind of coherence will be necessary, to replace the structural coherence of grammatical models and narrative logic, and one perhaps that will stand to logic and grammar in a relationship of 'subverted' support. De Man would find that in the notion of an 'allegory of reading', a coherence as formal and as internal to the text as is the linguistic-semiological notion of poetics, a coherence by which not only can the extratextual, 'the authority of the reference', be kept at a distance, but 'the entire question of meaning can be bracketed' (p. 5). Now, this bracketing of the question of meaning, which deconstruction and narratology have in common as a shared methodological, nay, epistemological, presupposition, is not yet altogether a moot or uncontested claim. Fredric Jameson, for one, arguing for narrative and, beyond that, for literature as 'a socially symbolic act', is not averse to calling his own readings of texts 'so many *interpretations*' and to defining the critical project of his *Political Unconscious* as 'the construction of a new *hermeneutics*'.[9] All that, of course, by way of taking a position, announcing a polemic, against precisely the poststructuralist program and its misconceived critique of all interpretive activity as necessarily totalizing, teleological, or historicist.

Meaning, for Jameson, does exist and constitutes a perfectly legitimate object of study on our part; all the more so, in fact, since it informs the operations of the political unconscious as they construct the master narratives, the political allegories, of both literature *and* criticism in any historical period. 'Master narratives', he writes, 'have inscribed themselves in the texts as well as in our thinking about them; such *allegorical narrative signifieds* are a persistent dimension of literary and cultural texts precisely because they reflect a fundamental dimension of our collective thinking and our collective fantasies about history and reality' (p. 34; emphasis added).

Once meaning is posed as a pertinent question (the 'allegorical narrative *signifieds*', he stresses; and note, too, if you will, the interesting intertextual return of the term *allegory* here), the relation of meaning to the referent needs be addressed; and Jameson does, acknowledging his debt to Althusser, in a statement which strongly resonates in my mind, with the Eco of *A Theory of Semiotics*, where Eco's own debt to Peirce is also properly acknowledged. Jameson writes:

> History is *not* a text, not a narrative, master or otherwise, but . . . , as an absent cause, it is inaccessible to us except in textual form, and . . . our approach to it and to the Real itself [capital *R* in *Real*, signaling that this is Lacan's term] necessarily passes through its prior textualization, its narrativization in the political unconscious.[10]

In this sense, then, interpretation can be seen as a rewriting of the text intended to show how the text itself is 'the rewriting or restructuration of a prior historical or ideological *subtext*', which the process of interpretation (re)constructs as the symbolic resolution of determinate contradictions in the Real. In such a way, for Jameson, the critical or aesthetic act 'always entertains some active relationship with the Real . . . draw[ing] the Real into its own texture' (p. 81).

The Peircean cast of this definition is apparent. A rewriting of a rewriting of a prior subtext that can be reconstructed only after the fact is a generational series very similar to Peirce's series: interpretant, sign, object, and ground.[11] And, interestingly enough, it is to Peirce that de Man appeals to provide, jointly with Nietzsche and Saussure, the philosophical foundation of semiotics as rhetoric (rather than grammar or logic); notably, Peirce's definition of 'pure rhetoric' (elsewhere called semiosis) as the process by which the interpretant of a sign produces not meaning but another sign, another interpretant, 'and so on, *ad infinitum*'.[12] Therefore, were it not for the important emphasis on the connection, however mediated, between text and world—an emphasis also definitely present in Peirce's notion of semiosis, as remarked by Eco, and apparently retained by Jameson—it might be tempting to see the latter's project of an 'immanent hermeneutics' as an allegory of writing, a theory of the practice of ideological deconstruction.

But another, somewhat unexpected, factor precludes such a reading: the coherence of Jameson's model is to be found less in deconstructive negativity than in the thick of the enemy camp, so to speak: in the structural logic of Greimas's semiotic rectangle, which Jameson reappropriates for dialectical negation as the 'locus and model of ideological closure': 'Seen in this way, the semiotic rectangle becomes a vital instrument for exploring the semantic and ideological intricacies of the text . . . because it maps the limits of a specific ideological consciousness and marks the conceptual points beyond which that consciousness cannot go' (p. 47). In other words, the structured semantic investments of a given text, which may be schematized by Greimas's rectangle, are taken by Jameson as symptomatic of the terms of an ideological system implicit in the logic of the narrative but 'unrealized' in the surface of the text, and so can be used to render manifest what the text does not say, hides, or 'represses'.

If proof be wanted that the rectangle doesn't lie, one could interrogate it, as does Christine Brooke-Rose in the lead essay of a recent issue of *Poetics Today*, on a matter of general competence: sexual relations. The rectangle, in its wisdom, provides three answers, i.e. conjures up three models or sets of oppositions, contraries, permutations, etc.: a social model, an economic model, and a 'personal' one. In all three cases the ideological system implicit in the logic of the narratives considered is one so familiar that it makes Brooke-Rose 'laugh out loud': for it is none other than 'the old double standard', which, she puns, 'lingua in sheer semiotic cheek, is made explicit as an "elementary structure of significance".'[13]

For some of us, that is too obvious to be funny. But I have wanted to cite the incident as an nth version of the story of a woman who, innocent of the past ten years of feminist critique around the notion of woman as sign, and quite on her own, venturing into the wilds of semiotics, discovers an inconsistence in Lévi-Strauss and begins to suspect that semiotics is 'a peculiarly reactionary discipline'.[14] Which, of course, it isn't—peculiarly, that is. But this nth version of the story shows that the suspicion (of semiotics, of narrative, and of the wisdom of the rectangle) *was* justified. As for the attraction. . . .

Let me propose quite plainly (I am aware of the risk) that the attraction is in the possibility, glimpsed if not assured, to make up one's story, the possibility to speak as subject of discourse, which also means to be listened to, to be granted authorship and author-ity over the story. Not that women have not been writing stories for several hundred years, or telling stories for much longer than that, but they have done so with little or no authority, with severe constraints as to genre, medium, and address, and mostly, in someone else's phrase, after great pain. Yet, Yvonne Rainer suggests, the urgency of narrative may even increase with one's work becoming more consciously and explicitly feminist.

But why would feminists, even more than women (the distinction is not easy to make but perhaps all the more important), want authority and authorship when those notions are admittedly outmoded, patriarchal and ethically compromised? Exactly. That is the cause of the suspicion. What we have for an answer to this question, then, is a paradox which is not one—that is to say, we have a contradiction. Of that contradiction, only feminism provides a critical understanding: not femaleness (the *fact* of being female), not femininity (as a positionality of desire, a narrative trope, a figure of style), but feminism, which is a critical reading of culture, a political interpretation of the social text and of the social subject, and a rewriting of our culture's 'master narratives'.

It is feminism that has, first, articulated the paradox of woman as both object and sign, at once captive and absent on the scene of Western representation; and it is feminism that now proposes—

although it must be said, there is more controversy on this issue than consensus—that what we thought to be a paradox, a seeming contradiction, is in effect a real contradiction, and, I will go so far as to say, an irreconcilable one. What that means is that I may speak, to be sure, but insofar as I speak I don't speak as a woman, but rather as a speaker (and when I do, I naturally take advantage of the podium). I also may read and write, but not as a woman, for men too have written 'as woman'—Nietzsche, Artaud, Lautréamont, even Joyce apparently did—and others nowadays, all honorable men, are 'reading as a woman'.

Then, when I look at the movies, film theorists try to tell me that the gaze is male, the camera eye is masculine, and so my look is also not a woman's. But I don't believe them anymore, because now I think I know what it is to look at a film as a woman. I do because certain films, by Yvonne Rainer, Chantal Akerman, Lizzie Borden, Sally Potter, and others, have shown it to me; they have somehow managed to inscribe in the film my woman's look—next to, side by side, together with, my other (cinematic) look. I shall come back to that. For now, let me rephrase the notion of contradiction, again quite plainly.

Feminism has produced, at least for feminists, a political-personal consciousness of gender as an ideological construct which defines the social subject; in thus en-gendering the subject, and in en-gendering the subject as political, feminism understands the female subject as one that, unlike Althusser's or Jameson's or Eco's, is not either 'in ideology' or outside ideology (e.g. in science), but rather is at once inside and outside the ideology of gender, or, as I have used the terms, is at once woman and women. In other words, woman is inside the rectangle, women are outside; the female subject of feminism is in both places at once. *That* is the contradiction.

Prompted by the feminist discourse on gender and representation, and by their own commitment to feminism (a discourse and a commitment which do not always go hand in hand), some contemporary filmmakers have begun a project to develop the means, conceptual and formal, to represent that contradiction itself, the contradiction which I see as constitutive of the female subject of feminism: to speak, like Cassandra, a discourse that elides woman as speaker-subject, and hence will not be heard by most; to tell stories resisting the drift of narrativization (the operation of narrative closure, or the 'family plot', as Hitchcock had occasion to call it); to make films against the plot that frames woman as narrative image, object, and ground of cinematic representation. In short, to reread, rewrite, remake all cultural narratives striving to construct another form of coherence, one that is, alas, founded on contradiction.

To that end, the mere reversal of the terms of narrative—heroine instead of hero, but they get married in the end anyway—will not do, although, as Charlotte Brontë more than intimates and as Jake says to Brett at the close of Hemingway's *The Sun Also Rises*, 'Isn't it pretty to think so?' But the other, if more sophisticated, kind of reversal will also not do; I am referring to anti-narrative programs promoting notions of *jouissance* (Kristeva, Barthes), libidinal dispersal (Lyotard), unbounded *différance* (Derrida), or the undifferentiated affectivity of a subject free of identification and (self-)representation (Deleuze).

What has come to mind, as I try to put into words something that will not fit, like the sense of a double, self-contradictory coherence, is the figure that I teased out a while ago from de Man's discussion of the relation between grammar and rhetoric: the oxymoron of a 'subverted support'. The relation of women to woman, as well as the female subject's relation to narrative (cinema), seems to me to be graspable in that contradictory, mutually subversive, and yet necessary or coexisting relationship of grammar and rhetoric in the figure of the rhetorical question, whereby one instigates the question, but the terms (the sentence) in which we ask the question may deny, as de Man wrote, 'the very possibility of asking'. For this reason I have dwelt at some length on the notions of rereading and rewriting in de Man and Jameson respectively: they may serve to convey, in terms already known and by analogy, if you will, my effort to articulate the form of a particular coherence which I see delineated in feminist critical writing and in feminist cinema. I hasten to specify that the phrase 'feminist cinema' is a notation for a process rather than an aesthetic or typological category: the notation for a process of reinterpretation and retextualization of cultural images and narratives whose strategies of coherence engage the spectator's identification through narrative and visual pleasure and yet succeed in drawing 'the Real' into the film's texture.

Having addressed thus far more general questions of narrative poetics, I must now sketch out something of the context in which the film-theoretical concern with narrative has developed, less in the direction of a narratology than toward a more ambitious or far-reaching theory of cultural process, linking social technologies (such as cinema) to the production of subjectivity in spectatorship. In this sense, the question of a poetics of film narrative splits into two intersecting lines of inquiry. On the one hand, there is the theoretical hypothesis of narrativity in cinema as a twofold operation, a production of meaning effects which work, I suggest, both in the manner of a grammar and in the manner of a rhetoric; a hypothesis cast widely across contemporary critical discourses from semiotics to feminism and from psychoanalysis to the theory of ideology.

On the other hand, a poetics of film narrative comprises the analysis of the film text and an account of the specific formal and generic problems addressed by filmmakers and critics as they grapple with expressive strategies ranging from the anti-narrative, abstract, or structural-materialist films of the 1950s and 1960s to the metanarrative experiments of the past decade (just in the United States, films such as *Blood Simple*, *Eating Raoul*, *Stranger Than Paradise*, *Variety*, *The Purple Rose of Cairo*—films that confront or engage narrative, unlike those of a De Palma, whose metanarrativity is unabashedly a box-office gimmick, an advertisement for itself). To the metanarrative category may be allocated, as well, those independent films that in shop talk are called theoretical films—films made explicitly to illustrate, reflect on, or re-present (I'm thinking here of Michael Snow) issues and terms of the theoretical discourse on cinema; and finally, the films to which I alluded earlier with the phrase 'feminist cinema', suggesting that in their work with and against narrative, such films employ strategies of what I call a double or self-subverting coherence.

Eventually, my own narrative will rejoin, coming full circle, the statement by Yvonne Rainer I quoted at the beginning of this essay—a statement of poetics, in fact: an individual artist's view of her own artistic process and concern with aesthetic form. I will suggest that this notion of poetics, discredited in formalist and functionalist days but perhaps on its way to renewed appreciation in these postmodern times, may offer artists and theorists something more interesting than the intentional fallacy of phallocentric criticism.

Now, then, to provide something of a context, one should say that the nexus of cinema, narrative, and semiotics may be initially located, like the broader question of cinematic signification—cinema as a system of signs and codes in the early years of semiotics (or semiology, as it was then called) in the mid-1960s. Thereafter, with the shifting emphasis on cinema as a signifying practice and cinema as semiotic production or productivity, the issue of narrative, or, better, narrativity, would also be reformulated.

The European debate around cinematic articulation, which developed in the context of the Mostra del Nuovo Cinema in Pesaro

(Italy), and the various stances taken by Eco, Pasolini, Metz, and Barthes on the question 'Is cinema a language?', are by now part of the legend of the semiotics of the cinema—a legend I need not retell in this setting.[15] Peter Wollen's influential book *Signs and Meanings in the Cinema*, which introduced semiology into Anglo-American film studies in 1969, did not yet single out the issue of narrative as one especially important or troublesome to cinema, although it was a central one in semiology—and had been so since Lévi-Strauss's arguments for the structural analysis of myth and the English translation of Propp's *Morphology of the Folktale* in 1958. The latter was a veritable milestone, a seminal work that prompted a flurry of research culminating in the 1966 issue of *Communications* devoted to 'The Structural Analysis of Narrative', edited by Roland Barthes, and including practically all the subgenres and prominent figures of narratology—people such as Greimas, Todorov, Bremond, Genette, Eco, and Metz.

Metz's contribution to this volume, a paper he first presented at the Pesaro film festival the same year, proposed the notion of a cinematic syntax ('la grande syntagmatique du film narratif') made up of six types of larger units or syntagms (e.g. the scene, the shot, parallel montage, 'autonomous' shots such as inserts, etc.).[16] It was this kind of inquiry into the ways of narrative organization specific to the medium that, some ten years later, captured the attention of film scholars in North America and caused them to become interested in semiology and structuralism, and thus to begin to follow the work of the film journal *Screen*, which by the mid-1970s was performing the role of mediator between French thought and British film culture.

But something had happened to semiology and structuralism in those ten years, which, as you have surely reckoned, included 1968 and 1970. What had happened to semiology and structuralism on their way across the Channel and the Atlantic is that they ran into psychoanalysis and feminism; and much as it was for Oedipus after the encounter with the Sphinx, this encounter forever changed the story of cinema. Thus, the next major step in the theory of narrative cinema after 'la grande syntagmatique' occurred in 1975–76 with the publication of three essays in *Screen*: a partial translation of Metz's *The Imaginary Signifier*, Laura Mulvey's 'Visual Pleasure and Narrative Cinema', and Stephen Heath's 'Narrative Space'. At this time, both the feminist critique of representation and psychoanalysis, or certain epistemological assumptions derived thereof, became established at the center of film narrative theory.

As Judith Mayne states in her rich and illuminating review of feminist film theory and criticism since the late 1960s, women's cinema has been shaped by the conjuncture of three major forces: the women's movement, independent filmmaking, and academic film studies. 'It is only a slight exaggeration to say that most feminist film theory . . . of the last decade has been a response, implicit or explicit, to the issues raised in Laura Mulvey's article: the centrality of the look, cinema as spectacle and narrative, psychoanalysis as a critical tool.'[17] The year 1966, besides the *Communications* issue on the structural analysis of narrative, had also seen the publication of Jacques Lacan's *Écrits.* Thus, it was hardly coincidental, though not a little surprising at the time, that Barthes's introduction to a volume concerned with the logic of narrative possibilities ended with the now-famous statement: 'It may be significant that it is at the same moment (around the age of three) that the little human "invents" at once sentence, narrative, and the Oedipus.'[18]

Once suggested, the connection between narrative and the Oedipus, or desire and narrative, appeared to be incontestable and opened up the likelihood that such a relationship might be akin to that of desire and language. And that evoked, on the scene of narrative and film theory, the uncanny presence of the subject: its constitution and ideological interpellation (as Althusser had called it) in the relations of meaning, in the symbolic and the imaginary, in cinema and in the film text. The nexus narrative/subjectivity thus came to the forefront of film theory, displacing the problematic of a cinematic language or narrative syntax. Two quotes from the essays by Mulvey and Heath referred to earlier, published in 1975 and 1976 respectively, will give an idea of the new cast of the film-theoretical question. Of cinematic codes, Mulvey writes:

> Playing on the tension between film as controlling the dimension of time (editing, narrative) and film as controlling the dimension of space (changes in distance, editing), cinematic codes create a gaze, a world, and an object, thereby producing an illusion cut to the measure of desire. . . . Going far beyond highlighting a woman's to-be-looked-at-ness, cinema builds the way she is to be looked at into the spectacle itself.[19]

And Heath:

> The film poses an image, not immediate or neutral, but posed, framed and centered. Perspective-system images bind the spectator in place, the suturing central position that is the sense of the image, that sets its scene (in place, the spectator completes the image as its subject). Film too, but it also moves in all sorts of ways and directions, flows with energies, is potentially a veritable

> festival of affects. Placed, that movement is all the value of film in its development and exploitation: reproduction of life and the engagement of the spectator in the process of that reproduction as articulation of coherence. What moves in film, finally, is the spectator, immobile in front of the screen. Film is the regulation of that movement, the individual as subject held in a shifting and placing of desire, energy, contradiction, in a perpetual re-totalization of the imaginary.[20]

Even beyond cinema, in the mainstream of semiotic studies since the mid-1970s, especially thanks to Umberto Eco's reading of Peirce, semiotic theory has favored a dynamic, processual view of signification as a working of the codes, a production of meaning which involves a subject in a social field. The object of narrative and of film-narrative theory, redefined accordingly, would be not narrative but narrativity, not so much the structure of narrative (its component units and their relations) as its work and effects; it would be less the formulation of a logic, a grammar, or a rhetoric of narrative per se—fundamental as the latter has been to our knowledge of cinema and to the establishment of film criticism as a humanistic discipline on a par with literary criticism, the obvious references here being Seymour Chatman's *Story and Discourse* and its literary antecedent, Wayne Booth's *The Rhetoric of Fiction*; and it would be less the description of a rhetoric of film narrative than the understanding of narrativity as the structuring and destructuring, even destructive, processes at work in the textual and semiotic relations of spectatorship.

The notion of spectatorship is most important at the present stage of film theory in its questioning of cinema as a social technology, a system of representation massively involved in the (re)production of social subjects. The notion of spectatorship, which seeks to define and to articulate that productive relation of the technology to the spectator-subject, is also pivotal to my discussion of the poetics of film narrative, to which I now turn in the next and last section of this essay. One, and not the least, reason why spectatorship is pivotal to what I have called a feminist cinema is that its concern with address (whom the film addresses, to whom it speaks, what and for whom it seeks to represent, whom it represents) translates into a conscious effort to address the spectator as female, regardless of the gender of the viewers; and that is what allows the film to draw into its discursive texture something of that 'Real' which is the untheorized experience of women.

In her statement of poetics, Yvonne Rainer outlines three phases or moments of a process of filmic inscription of 'feminine experience', a process which she calls an 'evolution'; but I would underplay the strictly chronological connotation of the word *evolution* and stress instead the sense of a dialectical developmental relationship between those three moments, as it indeed appears to be the case in Rainer's own work. Significantly, the three phases go from 'description' to 'speculation'.

The first is the 'description of individual feminine experience floating free of both social context and narrative hierarchy'. This, I would gloss, is the early and more formally experimental phase of a cinema of women which was aesthetically connected to avant-garde film and to performance art. Rainer herself came to film as a choreographer performer and her first film in 1972 was entitled *Lives of Performers.* But one also thinks of Sally Potter and Valie Export, for example, performance artists whose first films, *Thriller* and *Invisible Adversaries* respectively, clearly show that connection; while the relation to the Anglo-American avant-garde and, in Europe, to Godard is also apparent in Laura Mulvey and Peter Wollen's early films *Penthesilea* and *Riddles of the Sphinx*, or Chantal Akerman's *Je Tu Il Elle* and *News from Home*, Bette Gordon's *Empty Suitcases*, Marjorie Keller's *Misconception*, and of course Rainer's own *Film about a Woman Who* (1974), which had as counterpart a live performance entitled *This Is the Story of a Woman Who* (staged in 1973).

Writing about this film in 1977, Ruby Rich observed that 'while Rainer does not consider herself a feminist, while feminism is never the central issue in one of her films, her work is central to feminism'.[21] That is so, Rich stated, arguing against the accusation of formalism that was leveled at Rainer's film from the antiformalist and antitheoretical component of the women's movement, because 'Rainer's work on the frontier of form' helps women in the struggle against the oppressive mythology of romantic humanism by exposing its hidden agendas in cinematic representation. The two projects of early feminist filmmaking were, on one front, the formal-theoretical experimentation with cinematic codes, narrative frames, point of view and image construction, sound-image displacements, etc., in an attempt to alter or invent new terms of vision; and, on the other front, what Rich called the educational function of agitational or autobiographical filmmaking, which made women visible on the screen by documenting political demonstrations or portraying women's daily, real-life activities in the 'pre-aesthetic' sphere, as Silvia Bovenschen called it, of domestic life. In retrospect, both of these projects were equally important, and mutually supportive, in the development of feminism and feminist cinema. But at that time, up to the mid-1970s, they were seen in opposition to each other: the aesthetically radical, anti-narrative, and usually, if not necessarily, anti-feminist, vs. the politically radical, this latter, usually narrative (biographical or documentary) and, yes, definitely feminist.[22]

Something of this dichotomy is suggested in Rainer's own view of the second phase of women's cinema, characterized by 'descriptions of individiual feminine experience placed in radical juxtaposition against historical events'. That is certainly the case of her *Journeys from Berlin/1971*, as well as Helke Sander's *Redupers* (The All-Around Reduced Personality), the collectively made *Sigmund Freud's Dora* and *Song of the Shirt*, or even *Thriller* and *Riddles of the Sphinx* if among the radically juxtaposed historical events we can include, as I would, the experience of European Maoism as represented by the *Tel Quel* group or, in the Anglo-American context, the beginning of a sociopolitical discourse on pornography, and the coming of age of independent cinema's reflection on its own practices and political effectivity.

Yet again, speaking of *Journeys from Berlin* (1980), Kaja Silverman emphasizes how the formal originality of Rainer's experimentation with the disjunction of image and sound, and in particular the detachment or 'disembodiment' of the female voice on the soundtrack from the image of the female body on the screen, has not only aesthetic but also strong political implications:

> *Journeys from Berlin/71* makes clearer than any of the other films precisely what is at stake in this disassociation of sound and image: the freeing-up of the female voice from its obsessive and indeed exclusive reference to the female body, a reference which turns woman—in representation *and in fact*—back upon herself, in a negative and finally self-consuming narcissism.[23]

However, in spite of the critical insight, or foresight, of feminists such as Rich and Silverman, and certainly others as well, the two projects of early feminist cinema were thought to be mutually incompatible, as I said: the political demands of a consciousness-raising or educational cinema and the need to document women's lives in the private and public spheres appeared to be at odds with an individual artist's concern with aesthetic process and the formal or theoretical project to construct a new cinematic language and a new poetics of film.[24] These two film practices continued side by side but remained as radically distinct in feminist politics as the personal and the political stood in radical juxtaposition up there on the screen.

But now we come to the third phase of 'explicitly feminist speculations about feminine experience', the phase that Rainer sees characterized by an overt and even programmatic return to narrative, and which in her own work corresponds to *The Man Who Envied Women* (1985). Although the elements of narrative, however threadbare or in skeletal form, were present all along throughout the three phases (and not mistakenly Ruby Rich already noted a 'serious revitalization of melodrama' in *Film about a Woman Who*),[25] the emphasis on narrativity with regard to the more recent film is correlated to the words *explicitly feminist speculations.*

I said earlier that I intend to bring back and reappropriate the older notion of poetics as an artist's own articulation of her or his artistic project and process. I believe, and have argued elsewhere, that this notion is especially relevant to the understanding of feminist cinema because its project is by definition critical and self-critical, since feminist cinema has developed in a constant and unavoidable connection with feminist theory and practice, or criticism and politics, if you prefer, where the distinctive trait, the specificity, of feminism as a political-personal interpretation of the social text consists in what we call the practice of self-consciousness, that particular kind of ideological analysis which begins from and always refers back to the experience of gender and its construction of subjectivity. Moreover, the older notion of poetics seems especially relevant to the work of a 'writerly' filmmaker such as Rainer, who *writes* her films much in the sense in which a critic such as Roland Barthes or Virginia Woolf, or a philosopher such as Irigaray or Derrida, might be said to *write* an essay.

In a recent article in the *Independent*, Rainer makes several observations about TMWEW (*The Man Who Envied Women*) which I would like to quote and comment on:

> In many ways, TMWEW lies outside traditional narrative cinema. There is no plot, for instance, and although the voice of the (absent) female protagonist can be construed as a narrator, this voice departs from convention by refusing to push a story forward or . . . tie up the various strands. In the struggle for the film's truth this equivocal, invisible heroine is not always the victor. Consequently, in relation to the social issues broached within the film, the question of an externally imposed, predetermined and determining coherence looms very large for some. If the process of identification with the trajectory of fictional characters is thwarted, we look for opportunities to identify with an extra-diegetic author or ultimate voice 'behind' the film, if not the camera. . . . Rather than repositioning ourselves as spectators in response to

> cues that indicate we are being multivocally *addressed* and not just worked on by the filmic text, we still attempt to locate a singular author or wait for a conclusive outcome. The Master's Voice Syndrome all over again. And why not? Why else do we go to see narrative cinema than to be confirmed and reinforced in our most atavistic and oedipal mind-sets?[26]

Having first located the spectator (whom she specifies as gendered) in the clutches of narrativity, a prey to the Oedipal logic of desire, to the pull of identification, to the attempt, even though thwarted, to find a coherence and a truth, Rainer then recalls an instance of her own spectatorship, as a 10-year-old girl watching a Hollywood film, and her intense response of pleasure and anger, identification and subsequent secondarization (in Freud's term): in short, the making of a coherence for the self which is not only imaginary but profoundly cleft, inherently contradictory.

While this childhood movie-going memory had already surfaced many years earlier in the text of *Film about a Woman Who*, it had remained unanalyzed, simply recorded in the text, and its subjective effects only obscurely felt, until the writing of this essay where, not coincidentally, Rainer discusses the narrative strategies consciously deployed in her latest, 'explicitly feminist', film. These are precisely strategies of coherence, but based on contradiction and 'poetic ambiguity', formally complex strategies such as: have two actors play the male protagonist, represent the female protagonist not as narrative image but as the narrating voice; disrupt the glossy surface and homogeneous look of 'professional cinematography by means of optically degenerated shots', refilming, blown-up super 8 and video transfers; play off and contrast different authorial voices; play on 'incongruous juxtapositions of modes of address: recitation, reading, "real" or spontaneous speech, printed text, quoted texts, *et al.*, all in the same film'. If narrativity is disrupted, yet narrative is present and its seduction thematized in several seduction scenes which, again not coincidentally, are to do with theory and a dream sequence which Rainer calls an 'oedipal extravaganza'. Or, as she says, 'if I'm going to make a movie about Oedipus, i.e., Eddy and Edy Pussy Foot, I'm going to have to subject him to some calculated narrative screw-ups. It's elementary, dear Eddy: play with signifiers of desire.'[27]

However, you may object, this formal disruption of narrative is hardly news in avant-garde cinema for at least the past ten years. Please explain more fully the connection between these not uncommon narrative strategies and feminist cinema. Okay. Let me point out, first, that the usual view of the political or aesthetic import of subverting narrative, that is to say, of anti-narrative or abstract film practices, is to decenter the individualist or bourgeois subject, to work against or to destroy the coherence of narrativity which both constructs and confirms the coherence of that subject in its imaginary unity. This project does not usually include the questioning of sexual difference or the decentering of the masculinity, and even less the whiteness of the bourgeois subject. Second, if the Western bourgeois spectator-subject is understood, in keeping with the ideology of humanism, as simply human, that is to say, male and white, no less so are both the spectator addressed by radical (non-feminist) avant-garde film practices, and the deluded, divided, or diffuse subject of poststructuralist and anti-humanist discourse. For this latter subject is envisioned as non-gendered—gender being precisely an effect of delusion, an imaginary construct, nothing to do with the Real; which is to say, once again, that the subject is still (usually) white, and male in the last instance.

Feminist cinema, on the contrary, unlike other contemporary avant-garde, poststructuralist, or anti-humanist practices, begins from an understanding of spectatorship as gendered (as distinguishable, at the very least, in relation to sexual difference and its experience of gender), and then essays to fashion narrative strategies, points of identification, and places of the look that may address, engage, and construct the spectator as gendered subject; and most recently, as in Lizzie Borden's *Born in Flames*, as a subject constructed across racial as well as sexual differences. Hence the effort to devise strategies of a subverted coherence which, in the representation of women, are necessarily also self-subverting. For example, the reversal of penis envy in Rainer's film, ostensibly about a man who envied women but actually another 'film about a woman who', is a grammatical kind of reversal, a strategy of subversion of narrative syntax. But that is concurrent with another strategy, this time a rhetorical strategy, which questions or undermines the terms of the prior reversal, for in the end this is a film about *a-woman* who. . . . As Trisha's voice-over says toward the end of the film, opening up a whole new phase of women's cinema,

> I can't live without men, but I can live without a man. I've had this thought before, but this time the idea is not colored by stigma or despair or finality. I know there will sometimes be excruciating sadness. But I also know something is different now. Something in the direction of unwomanliness. Not a new woman, not non-woman or misanthropist or anti-woman, and not non-practicing lesbian. Maybe unwoman is also the wrong term. A-woman is closer. A-womanly. A-womanliness.[28]

To conclude, this is a film that problematizes woman's representability, both her representability as image and her status as narrator and as subject. She cannot be seen, her speech is not authorized or self-consistent, it is embodied in different voices; her narration is not authoritative, it doesn't reach climax or resolution, it doesn't produce a true confession or even a story. And yet, at the same time, the film insists that she is there, her presence inscribed figurally through metonymic effects of voice, other images (film images, video images, photographic images, dream images), and discourses (domestic, public, agitational, sexual, and theoretical). In other words, grammatically or logically, 'she' is not there, but rhetorically *she is* there: the absent Trisha's femaleness is clearly foregrounded, as is the maleness of Jack Deller, husband and theorist, for gender is very much at issue and not only overlays the personal and the political, the sexual and the social, but also specifically grounds the very possibility of meaning, of constructing an interpretation of the various cultural texts displayed in the film, and of producing an understanding of the determinate contradictions that the film concurrently locates in the real and in the text of cinema.

It is precisely in that space of contradiction, in the double and self-subverting coherence of its narrative grammar and figural ambiguities, that the film addresses me, spectator, *as a*(-)*woman*; that it solicits and inscribes my (un)womanly look and gendered subjectivity in what I might call *a recognition of misrecognition*; that is to say, in the personal-political contradictions of my own history of a-womanness.

This film does not move me along, bound in the regulated coherence of a master plot, to the closure of a framed narrative image of Woman as spectacle and object of a controlling gaze—my (master's) gaze. Nor does it, however, repel my woman's gaze, such as it is, or my feminist understanding of the female subject's history of a-womanness, contradiction, and self-subverting coherence. Instead, the film constructs the filmic terms, the filmic conditions of possibility, for women spectators to be asking the question, even as it denies the certainty of an answer. In deconstructing narrative space, the film constructs a critical space in which I am addressed, precisely, as a woman and a-woman.

The fact that, if I speak these words, *a woman* and *a-woman*, those who hear them cannot tell the difference (just as Archie Bunker couldn't in de Man's example of the rhetorical question), may perhaps convey two points I've tried to make: first, the potential of employing grammar and rhetoric in mutually subverting support, in support of subversive narrative practices; and second, the contradiction in which I find myself, as I speak, and which I am at pains to articulate here in writing.

Notes

Written as an address to the Sixth Annual Conference in the Humanities organized by James Phelan at the Ohio State University in April 1986 on the theme 'Narrative Poetics.' Revised and entitled 'Strategies of Coherence: The Poetics of Film Narrative' for inclusion in *Reading Narrative: Form, Ethics, Ideology*, edited by James Phelan from that conference.

1. Yvonne Rainer, 'More Kicking and Screaming from the Narrative Front/ Backwater', *Wide Angle*, 7: 1–2 (1985), 8.
2. Teresa de Lauretis, *Alice Doesn't: Feminism, Semiotics, Cinema* (Bloomington: Indiana University Press, 1984), 79.
3. Shoshana Felman, 'Rereading Femininity', *Yale French Studies*, 62 (1981), 44.
4. Tzvetan Todorov, *Introduction to Poetics*, trans. Richard Howard (Minneapolis: University of Minnesota Press, 1981), 23.
5. Ibid., p. xiv; emphasis added.
6. Paul de Man, 'Semiology and Rhetoric', in *Allegories of Reading* (New Haven and London: Yale University Press, 1979), 6.
7. Ibid. 10.
8. Hitchcock recounts with relish how that image came to be: 'I always remember one night at the Chelsea Arts Ball at Albert Hall in London when I got terribly drunk and I had the sensation that everything was going far away from me. I tried to get that into *Rebecca*, but they couldn't do it. The viewpoint must be fixed, you see, while the perspective is changed as it stretches lengthwise. I thought about the problem for fifteen years. By the time we got to *Vertigo*, we solved it by using the dolly and zoom simultaneously. I asked how much it would cost, and they told me it would cost fifty thousand dollars. When I asked why, they said, "Because to put the camera at the top of the stairs we have to have a big apparatus to lift it, counterweight it, and hold it up in space". I said, "There are no characters in this scene; it's simply a viewpoint. Why can't we make a miniature of the stairway and lay it on its side, then take our shot by pulling away from it? We can use a tracking shot and a zoom flat on the ground." So that's the way we did it, and it only cost us nineteen thousand dollars'(François Truffaut, *Hitchcock* (New York: Simon & Schuster, 1967), 187).
9. Fredric Jameson, *The Political Unconscious: Narrative as a Socially Symbolic Act* (Ithaca, NY: Cornell University Press, 1981), 21.
10. Ibid. 35. On the relation of textuality to 'the Real', Eco writes: 'There is sign production because there are empirical subjects which display labor in order to physically produce expressions, to correlate them to content, to segment content, and so on. But semiotics is entitled to recognize these subjects only insofar as they manifest themselves through sign-functions, producing sign-functions, criticizing other sign-functions and restructuring the pre-existing

sign-functions. By accepting this limit, semiotics fully avoids any risk of idealism. On the contrary semiotics recognizes as the only testable subject matter of its discourse the social existence of the universe of signification, as it was revealed by the physical testability of interpretants—which are, to reinforce this point for the last time, *material expressions*' (Umberto Eco, *A Theory of Semiotics* (Bloomington: Indiana University Press, 1976), 317.

11. See my reading of Peirce through Eco in *Alice Doesn't*, 172–75.
12. De Man, *Allegories of Reading*, 9. The words *ad infinitum*, emphasized by de Man, mark the exact point where his interpretation of Peirce and of semiosis differs from Eco's. See note 11 above.
13. Christine Brooke-Rose, 'Woman as a Semiotic Object', *Poetics Today*, 6: 1–2 (1985), 10.
14. Ibid. 19. Brooke-Rose seems unaware of the extensive work done in this area by feminist critics such as Elizabeth Cowie, 'Woman as Sign', *m/f*, 1 (1978); Gayle Rubin, 'The Traffic in Women: Notes on the "Political Economy" of Sex', in *Toward an Anthropology of Women*, ed. Rayna R. Reiter (New York: Monthly Review Press, 1975); and my own critique of semiotics in *Alice Doesn't*, to name but a few.
15. An account may be found in *Alice Doesn't*, 40–44.
16. Christian Metz, 'La Grande Syntagmatique du film narratif', *Communications*, 8 (1966), 120–24.
17. Judith Mayne, 'Feminist Film Theory and Criticism', *Signs*, 11: 1 (Autumn 1985), 83.
18. Roland Barthes, 'Introduction to the Structural Analysis of Narratives', in *Image–Music–Text*, trans. Stephen Heath (New York: Hill and Wang, 1977), 124.
19. Laura Mulvey, 'Visual Pleasure and Narrative Cinema', *Screen*, 16: 3 (Autumn 1975), 17.
20. Stephen Heath, 'Narrative Space', now in *Questions of Cinema* (Bloomington: Indiana University Press, 1981), 53.
21. B. Ruby Rich, 'The Films of Yvonne Rainer', *Chrysalis*, 2 (1977), 126.
22. The placing of radical feminist artistic practice in opposition to aesthetically radical or avant-garde practices was (and to some extent still is) more marked in the Anglo-American context than, say, in France or Italy; yet the other opposition, the perception of female experience and subjectivity as incommensurable with the discourse of history, was (and to some extent still is) common to Western feminism. For a comprehensive overview of these and other issues, see 'Feminist Film Criticism: An Introduction', in *Re-vision: Essays in Feminist Film Criticism*, ed. Mary Ann Doane, Patricia Mellencamp, and Linda Williams (Frederick, Md.: University Publications of America and the American Film Institute, 1984), 1–17; and Mayne, 'Feminist Film Theory and Criticism', 81–100.
23. Kaja Silverman, 'Dis-embodying the Female Voice', in Doane, Mellencamp, and Williams, *Re-vision: Essays in Feminist Film Criticism*, 137; emphasis added.
24. See Laura Mulvey, 'Feminism, Film, and the Avant-Garde', *Framework*, 10 (Spring 1979), 3–10.
25. Rich, 'The Films of Yvonne Rainer', 119.
26. Yvonne Rainer, 'Some Ruminations around Cinematic Antidotes to the

Oedipal Net(les) while Playing with De Lauraedipus Mulvey, or, He May Be Off Screen, but. . . .', *Independent*, April 1986, 22.

27. Ibid. 25.
28. Yvonne Rainer, *The Man Who Envied Women*, Filmscript, 58; also cited in Helen Demichiel, 'Rainer's Manhattan', *Afterimage*, December 1985, 19. There is a sense in which Trisha's contorted, and painful effort to express a female identity for which no current word or established visual form will do goes cautiously in the direction of Monique Wittig's much blunter statement, 'Lesbians are not women' ('The Straight Mind,' *Feminist Issues*, 1 (Summer 1980), 110). But the feeling that such is 'the direction of unwomanliness' where feminism at its best does take one is my own personal feeling, not, obviously, Yvonne Rainer's—or at least not yet.

15 The Orthopsychic Subject: Film Theory and the Reception of Lacan

Joan Copjec*

Through his appearance in *Television*, Lacan parodies the image of himself—of his teaching—that we have, to a large extent, received and accepted. Standing alone behind his desk, hands now supporting him as he leans assertively forward, now thrown upward in some emphatic gesture, Lacan stares directly out at us, as he speaks in a voice that none would call smooth of '*quelque chose, n'est-ce pas?*' This '*quelque chose*' is, of course, never made specific, never revealed, and so it comes to stand for a fact or a system of facts that is known, but not by us. This image recalls the one presented to Tabard by the principal in Vigo's *Zero for Conduct*. It is the product of the childish, paranoid notion that all our private thoughts and actions are spied on by and visible within a public world represented by parental figures. In appearing to us, then, by means of the 'mass media',[1] Lacan seems to confirm what we may call our 'televisual' fear—that we are perfectly, completely visible to a gaze that observes us from afar (*tele* meaning both 'distant' and [from *telos*] 'complete').[2] That this proffered image is parodic, however, is almost surely to be missed, so strong are our misperceptions of Lacan. And, so, the significance of the words with which he opens his address and by which he immediately calls attention to his self-parody: 'I always speak the truth. Not the whole truth, because there's no way to say it all. Saying the whole truth is materially impossible; words fail. Yet it's through this very impossibility that the truth holds onto the real.'[3]—the significance of these words may also be missed, as they have been generally in our theories of representation, the most sophisticated example of which is film theory.

Let me first, in a kind of establishing shot, summarize what I take to be the central misconception of film theory: believing itself to be

* Joan Copjec, 'The Delirium of Clinical Perfection' from *Oxford Literary Review*, vol. 8, 1–2 (1986), special edition on 'Sexual Difference' edited by Robert Young, reprinted by permission of *Oxford Literary Review* and the author.

following Lacan, it conceives the screen as mirror;[4] in doing so, however, it operates in ignorance of, and at the expense of, Lacan's more radical insight, whereby the mirror is conceived as screen.

THE SCREEN AS MIRROR

This misconception is at the base of film theory's formulation of two concepts—the apparatus and the gaze—and of their interrelation. One of the clearest and most succinct descriptions of this interrelation—and I must state here that it is *because* of its clarity, because of the way it responsibly and explicitly articulates assumptions endemic to film theory, that I cite this description, not to impugn it or its authors particularly—is provided by the editors of *Re-vision*, a collection of essays by feminists on film. Although its focus is the special situation of the female spectator, the description outlines the general relations among the terms *gaze*, *apparatus*, and *subject* as they are stated by film theory. After quoting a passage from Foucault's *Discipline and Punish* in which Bentham's architectural plan for the panopticon is laid out, the *Re-vision* editors make the following claim:

> The dissociation of the see/being seen dyad [which the panoptic arrangement of the central tower and annular arrangement ensures] and the sense of permanent visibility seem perfectly to describe the condition not only of the inmate in Bentham's prison but of the woman as well. For defined in terms of her visibility, she carries her own Panopticon with her wherever she goes, her self-image a function of her being for another. . . . . The subjectivity assigned to femininity within patriarchal systems is inevitably bound up with the structure of the look and the localization of the eye as authority.[5]

The panoptic gaze defines *perfectly* the situation of the woman under patriarchy: that is, it is the very image of the structure that obliges the woman to monitor herself with a patriarchal eye. This structure thereby guarantees that even her innermost desire will always be not a transgression but rather an implantation of the law, that even the 'process of theorizing her own untenable situation' can only reflect back to her 'as in a mirror' her subjugation to the gaze.

The panoptic gaze defines, then, the *perfect*, that is, the total visibility of the woman under patriarchy, of any subject under any social order, that is to say, of any subject at all. For the very condition and substance of the subject's subjectivity is his or her subjectivation by the law of the society that produces that subject. One becomes visible—not only to others but also to oneself—only through (by seeing through) the categories constructed by a specific, historically defined society. These categories of visibility are categories of knowledge.

The perfection of vision and knowledge can only be procured at the expense of invisibility and nonknowledge. According to the logic of the panoptic apparatus, these last do not and (in an important sense) cannot exist. One might summarize this logic—thereby revealing it to be more questionable than it is normally taken to be—by stating it thus: since all knowledge (or visibility) is produced by society (that is, all that it is possible to know comes not from reality but from socially constructed categories of implementable thought), since *all* knowledge is produced, *only* knowledge (or visibility) is produced, or *all* that is produced is knowledge (visible). This is too glaring a non sequitur—the *then* clauses are too obviously not necessary consequences of the *if* clauses—for it ever to be statable as such. And yet this lack of logical consequence is precisely what must be at work and what must go unobserved in the founding of the seeing/being seen dyad that figures the comprehension of the subject by the laws that rule over its construction.

Here—one can already imagine the defensive protestations—I have overstated my argument—there *is* a measure of indetermination available even to the panoptic argument. This indetermination is provided for by the fact that the subject is constructed not by one monolithic discourse but by a multitude of different discourses. What cannot be determined in advance are the articulations that may result from the chance encounter—sometimes on the site of the subject—of these various discourses. A subject of a legal discourse may find itself in conflict with itself as a subject of a religious discourse. The negotiation of this conflict may produce a solution that was anticipated by neither of the contributing discourses. Some film theorists have underlined this part of Foucault's work in an attempt to locate possible sources of resistance to institutional forms of power, to clear a space for a feminist cinema, for example.[6] I would argue, however, that this simple atomization and multiplication of subject positions and this *partes extra partes* description of conflict does not lead to a radical undermining of knowledge or power. Not only is it the case that at each stage what is *produced* is conceived in Foucauldian theory to be a *determinate* thing or position, but, in addition, knowledge and power are conceived as the overall effect of the *relations among* the various conflicting positions and discourses. Differences do not threaten panoptic power; they feed it.

This is quite different from the Lacanian argument, which states that that which is produced by a signifying system can never be determinate. Conflict in this case does not result from the clash between two different positions but from the fact that no position defines a resolute identity. Nonknowledge or invisibility is not registered as the wavering and negotiations between two certainties, two meanings or positions, but as the undermining of every certainty, the incompleteness of every meaning and position.[7] Incapable of articulating this more radical understanding of nonknowledge, the panoptic argument is ultimately *resistant to resistance*, unable to conceive of a discourse that would refuse rather than refuel power.

My purpose here is not simply to point out the crucial differences between Foucault's theory and Lacan's but also to explain how the two theories have failed to be perceived *as* different—how a psychoanalytically informed film theory came to see itself as expressible in Foucauldian terms, despite the fact that these very terms aimed at dispensing with psychoanalysis as a method of explanation. In Foucault's work the techniques of disciplinary power (of the construction of the subject) are conceived as capable of 'materially penetrat[ing] the body in depth without depending even on the mediation of the subject's own representations. If power takes hold on the body, this isn't through its having first to be interiorized in people's consciousness.'[8] For Foucault, the conscious and the unconscious are categories constructed by psychoanalysis and other discourses (philosophy, literature, law, etc.): like other socially constructed categories, they provide a means of rendering the subject visible, governable, trackable. They are categories through which the modern subject is apprehended and apprehends itself *rather than* (as psychoanalysis maintains) processes of apprehension; they are not processes that engage or are engaged by social discourses (film texts, for example). What the *Re-vision* editors force us to confront is the fact that in film theory these radical differences have largely gone unnoticed or have been nearly annulled. Thus, though the gaze is conceived as a metapsychological concept central to the description of the subject's psychic engagement with the cinematic apparatus, the concept, as we shall see, is formulated in a way that makes any psychical engagement redundant.

My argument is that film theory operated a kind of 'Foucauldization' of Lacanian theory; an early misreading of Lacan turned him into a 'spendthrift' Foucault—one who wasted a bit too much theoretical energy on such notions as the antithetical meaning of words, or repression, or the unconscious. It is the perceived frugality of Foucault (about which we will have more to say later), every bit as much as the recent and widely proclaimed interest in history, that has guaranteed Foucault's ascendancy over Lacan in the academy.

It was through the concept of the apparatus—the economic, technical, ideological institution—of cinema that the break between contemporary film theory and its past was effected.[9] This break meant that cinematic representation was considered to be not a clear or distorted reflection of a prior and external reality but one among many social discourses that helped to construct reality and the spectatorial subject. As is well known, the concept of the apparatus was not original to film theory but was imported from epistemological studies of science. The actual term *dispositif* (apparatus) used in film theory is borrowed from Gaston Bachelard, who employed it to counter the reigning philosophy of phenomenology. Bachelard proposed instead the study of 'phenomeno-*technology*,' believing that phenomena are not given to us directly by an independent reality but are, rather, constructed (cf. the Greek *technē*, 'produced by a regular method of making rather than found in nature') by a range of practices and techniques that define the field of historical truth. The objects of science are materializable concepts, not natural phenomena.

Even though it borrows his term and the concept it names, film theory does not locate its beginnings in the work of Bachelard but rather in that of one of his students, Louis Althusser.[10] (This history is by now relatively familiar, but since a number of significant points have been overlooked or misinterpreted, it is necessary to retrace some of the details.) Althusser was judged to have advanced and corrected the theory of Bachelard in a way that foregrounded the *subject* of science. Now, although he had argued that the scientific subject was formed in and by the field of science, Bachelard had also maintained that the subject was never *fully* formed in this way. One of the reasons for this merely partial success, he theorized, was an obstacle that impeded the subject's development; this obstacle he called the imaginary. But the problem with this imaginary, as Althusser later pointed out, was that it was itself largely untheorized and was thus (that is, almost by default) accepted by Bachelard as a *given*, as external and prior to rather than as an *effect* of historical determinations. The scientific subject was split, then, between two modes of thought: one governed by historically determined scientific forms, the other by forms that were eternal, spontaneous, and almost purely mythical.[11]

Althusser rethought the category of the imaginary, making it a part of the process of the historical construction of the subject. The imaginary came to name a process necessary to—rather than an impediment—of the ideological founding of the subject: the imaginary provided the form of the subject's lived relation to society. Through this relation the subject was brought to accept as its own, to recognize itself in, the representations of the social order.

This last statement of Althusser's position is important for our concerns here because it is also a statement of the basic position of film theory as it was developed in the 1970s, in France and in England by Jean-Louis Baudry, Christian Metz, Jean-Louis Comolli, Stephen Heath, and others. In sum, the screen is a mirror. The representations produced by the institution of cinema, the images presented on the screen, are accepted by the subject as its own.[12] There is, admittedly, an ambiguity in the notion of the subject's 'own image'; it can refer either to an image *of* the subject or an image *belonging to* the subject. Both references are intended by film theory. Whether that which is represented is specularized as an image of the subject's own body or as the subject's image of someone or something else, what remains crucial is the attribution to the image of what Lacan (not film theory, which has never, it seems to me, adequately accounted for the ambiguity) calls 'that belong to me aspect so reminiscent of property'.[13] It is this aspect that allows the subject to see in any representation not only a reflection of itself but a reflection of itself as master of all it surveys. The imaginary relation produces the subject as master of the image. This insight led to film theory's reconception of film's characteristic 'impression of reality'.[14] No longer conceived as dependent on a relation of verisimilitude between the image and the real referent, this impression was henceforth attributed to a relation of adequation between the image and the spectator. In other words, the impression of reality results from the fact that the subject takes the image as a full and sufficient representation of itself and its world; the subject is satisfied that it has been adequately reflected on the screen. The 'reality effect' and the 'subject effect' both name the same constructed impression: that the image makes the subject fully visible to itself.

The imaginary relation is defined as literally a relation of recognition. The subject reconceptualizes as its own concepts already constructed by the Other. Sometimes the reconstruction of representation is thought to take place secondarily rather than directly, after there has been a primary recognition of the subject as a 'pure act of perception'. This is, as we all know, Metz's scenario.[15] The subject first recognizes itself by identifying with the gaze and then recognizes the images on the screen. Now, *what* exactly is the gaze, in this context? Why does it emerge in this way from the theory of the apparatus? What does it add—or subtract—from Bachelard's theory, where it does not figure as a term?[16] All these questions will have to be confronted more fully in due course; for now we must begin with the observation that this ideal point can be nothing but *the signified of the image*, the point from which the image *makes sense* to the subject. In taking up its position at this point, the subject sees itself as *supplying* the image with sense. Regardless of whether one or two stages are posited, the gaze is always the point from which identification is conceived by film theory to take place. And because the gaze is always conceptualized as an analogue of that geometrical point of Renaissance perspective at which the picture becomes fully, undistortedly visible, the gaze always retains within film theory the sense of being that point at which sense and being coincide. The subject comes into being by identifying with the image's signified. Sense *founds* the subject—*that* is the ultimate point of the film-theoretical and Foucauldian concepts of the gaze.

The imaginary relation is not, however, merely a relation of knowledge, of sense and recognition; it is also a relation of love guaranteed by knowledge. The image seems not only perfectly to represent the subject, it seems also to be an image of the subject's perfection. An unexceptional definition of narcissism appears to support this relation: the subject falls in love with its own image as the image of its ideal self. *Except* narcissism becomes in this account the structure that instruments the *harmonious* relation between self and social order (since the subject is made to snuggle happily into the space carved out for it), whereas in the psychoanalytic account the subject's narcissistic relation to the self is seen to *conflict with and disrupt* other social relations. I am attempting to pinpoint here no minor point of disagreement between psychoanalysis and the panoptic argument: the opposition between the unbinding force of narcissism and the binding force of social relations is one of the defining tenets of psychoanalysis. It is nevertheless true that Freud himself often ran into difficulty trying to maintain the distinction and that many, from Jung on, have found it easier to merge the two forces into a libidinal monism.[17] But easier is not better; to disregard the distinction is not only to destroy psychoanalysis but also to court determinism.

Why is the representation of the relation of the subject to the social necessarily an imaginary one? This question, posed by Paul Hirst, should have launched a serious critique of film theory.[18] That it did not is attributable, in part, to the fact that the question was perceived to be fundamentally a question about the content of the concept of the imaginary. With only a slightly different emphasis, the question can be seen to ask how the imaginary came to bear, almost exclusively, the burden of the construction of the subject—despite the fact that we always speak of the 'symbolic' construction of the subject. One way of answering this is to note that in much contemporary theory the symbolic is itself structured like the imaginary, like Althusser's version of the imaginary. And thus Hirst's criticisms are aimed at our conception of the symbolic construction of the subject, in general. That this is so is made explicit once again by the *frugality of Foucault*, who exposes to us not only the content but also the emptiness of some of our concepts. For Foucault successfully demonstrates that the conception of the symbolic on which he (and, implicitly, others) relies makes the imaginary unnecessary.

...

What is the difference, then, between Foucault's version and psychoanalysis's version of the law/desire relation? Simply this: while Foucault conceives desire not only as an *effect* but also, as I have pointedly remarked, as a *realization* of the law, *psychoanalysis teaches us that the conflation of effect and realization is an error.*

...

Psychoanalysis denies the preposterous proposition that society is founded on desire—the desire for incest, let us say once again. Surely, it argues, it is the *repression* of this desire that founds society. The law does not construct a subject who simply and unequivocably has a desire, but one who *rejects* its desire, wants not to desire it. The subject is thus conceived as split from its desire, and desire itself is conceived as something—precisely—unrealized; it does not actualize what the law makes possible. Nor is desire committed to realization, barring any external hindrance. For the internal dialectic that makes the being of the subject dependent on the *negation* of its desire turns desire into a self-hindering process.

Foucault's definition of the law as positive and nonrepressive implies both that the law is (1) unconditional, that it *must* be obeyed, since only that which it allows can come into existence—*being is*, by definition, *obedience*—and that it is (2) unconditioned, since nothing, that is, no desire, precedes the law; there is no cause of the law and we must not therefore seek behind the law for its reasons. Law does not exist in order to repress desire.

. . .

Again: the claims of conscience are used to refute the experience of conscience. This paradox located by Freud will, of course, not appear as such to those who do not ascribe the claims *to* conscience. And yet something of the paradox *is* manifest in Foucault's description of panoptic power and film theory's description of the relation between the apparatus and the gaze. In both cases the model of self-surveillance implicitly recalls the psychoanalytic model of moral conscience even as the resemblance is being disavowed. The image of self-surveillance, of self-correction, is both required to construct the subject and made redundant by the fact that the subject thus constructed is, by definition, absolutely upright, completely correct. The inevitability and completeness of its success renders the orthopedic gesture of surveillance unnecessary. The subject is and can only be inculpable. The relation between apparatus and gaze creates only the mirage of psychoanalysis. There is, in fact, no psychoanalytic subject in sight.

ORTHOPSYCHISM

How, then, to derive a properly psychoanalytic—that is, a split—subject from the premise that this subject is the effect rather than the cause of the social order? Before turning, finally, to Lacan's solution, it will be necessary to pause to review one extraordinary chapter from Bachelard—chapter 4 of *Le rationalisme appliqué*, titled 'La surveillance intellectuelle de soi'[19]—where we will find some arguments that have been overlooked in more recent theorizations of the apparatus.[20]

Although Bachelard pioneered the theory of the institutional construction of the field of science, he also (as we have already said) persistently argued that the protocols of science never fully saturated, nor provided the content of, this field. The obstacle of the imaginary is only *one* of the reasons given for this. Besides this purely negative resistance *to* the scientific, there is also a positive condition *of* the scientific itself that prevented such a reduction from taking place. Both these reasons together guarantee that the concepts of science are never mere realizations of possibilities historically allowed and scientific thought is never simply habit, the regulated retracing of possible paths already laid out in advance.

. . .

Bachelard's chapter ends up celebrating a kind of euphoria of free thought. As a result of its orthopsychic relation to itself, that is, before an image that it *doubts*, the scientific subject is jubilant. Not because its image, its world, its thought reflects its own perfection, but because the subject is thus allowed to imagine that they are all *perfectible*. It is this sense of the perfectibility of things that liberates thought from the totally determining constraints of the social order. Thought is conceived to police, and not merely be policed by, the social/scientific order, and the paranoia of the 'Cassandra complex' (Bachelard's designation for the childish belief that everything is already known in advance, by one's parents, say) is thereby dispelled.

. . .

This scenario of surveillance—of the 'joy of surveillance'—is consciously delineated in relation to Freud's notion of moral conscience. But Bachelard opposes his notion to the 'pessimism' of that of Freud, who, of course, saw moral conscience as cruel and punishing. In Bachelard, surveillance, in seeming to offer the subject a pardon, is construed as primarily a positive or benign force. Bachelard, then, too, like Foucault and film theory, recalls and yet disavows the psychoanalytic model of moral conscience—however differently. Bachelard's orthopsychism, which is informed in the end by a psychologistic argument, cannot really be accepted by film theory as an alternative to panopticonism. Although Bachelard argues that a certain invisibility shelters the subject from what we might call (in the panoptic, not in the Lacanian sense) 'the gaze' of the institutional apparatus, the subject is nevertheless characterized by an exact legibility on another level. The Bachelardian subject may not locate *in its image* a full and upright being that it jubilantly (but wrongly) takes itself to be, but this subject does locate *in the process of scrutinizing* this image the joyous prospect of righting itself. Film theory's correct subject is here replaced by a self-correcting one.

Yet this detour through orthopsychism has not led only to a dead end. What we have forcibly been led to consider is the question of deception, of the suspicion of deception that must *necessarily* be raised if we are to understand the cinematic apparatus as a *signifying* apparatus, which places the subject in an external relationship to itself. Once the permanent possibility of deception is admitted (rather than disregarded, as it is by the theory of the panoptic apparatus), the concept of the gaze undergoes a radical change. For, where in the panoptic apparatus the gaze marks the subject's *visibility*, in Lacan's theory it marks the subject's *culpability*. The gaze stands watch over the *inculpation*—the faulting and splitting—of the subject by the apparatus.

THE MIRROR AS SCREEN

Film theory introduced the subject into its study, and thereby incorporated Lacanian psychoanalysis, primarily by means of 'The mirror stage as formative of the function of the "I."' It is to this essay that theorists made reference as they formulated their arguments about the subject's narcissistic relation to the film and about that relationship's dependence on 'the gaze'. While it is true that the mirror-phase essay does describe the child's narcissistic relation to its mirror image, it is, nevertheless, *not* in this essay but in Seminar XI that Lacan himself formulates *his* concept of the gaze. Here, particularly in those sessions collected under the heading 'Of the Gaze as *Object Petit a*', Lacan *reformulates* his earlier mirror-phase essay and paints a picture very different from the one painted by film theory.

Lacan tells his tale of the relation of the subject to its world in the form of a humorously recondite story about a sardine can. The story is told as a kind of mock Hegelian epic, a send-up of the broadly expansive Hegelian epic form by a deliberately 'little story' that takes place in a 'small boat' in a 'small port' and includes a single named character, 'Petit-Jean'. The entire overt plot consists in the sighting of a 'small can'. A truly short story of the object small a; the proof and sole guarantee of that alterity of the Other which Hegel's sweeping tale, in overlooking, denies.

. . .

What is it that is at stake here? Plainly, ultimately, it is 'I'—I, the subject, that takes shape in this revised version of the mirror stage. As if to underline the fact that it is the I that is the point of the discussion, Lacan tells a personal story. It is he, in fact, who is the first-person of the narrative; this portrait of the analyst as a young man is his own. The cameo role in Seminar XI prepares us, then, for the starring role Lacan plays as the narcissistic 'televanalyst' in *Television*. 'What is at stake in both cases,' Lacan says in *Television* about his performance both there and in his seminars, in general, 'is a gaze: a gaze to which, in neither case, do I address myself, but in the name of which I speak.'[21] What is he saying here about the relation between the I and the gaze?

The gaze is that which 'determines' the I in the visible; it is 'the instrument through which . . . [the] I [is] *photo-graphed*.'[22] This might be taken to confirm the coincidence of the Foucauldian and Lacanian positions, to indicate that, in both, the gaze determines the complete *visibility* of the I, the mapping of the I on a perceptual grid. Hence the disciplinary monitoring of the subject. But this coincidence can only be produced by a precipitous, 'snapshot' reading of Lacan, one that fails to notice the hyphen that splits the term *photo-graph*—into *photo*, 'light', and *graph*, among other things, a fragment of the Lacanian phrase 'graph of desire'—as it splits the subject that it describes.

Photo. One thing is certain: light does not enter these seminars in a straight line, through the laws of optics. Because, as he says, the geometric laws of the propagation of light map space only, and *not* vision, Lacan does not theorize the visual field in terms of these laws. Thus, the legitimate construction can*not* figure for him—as it *does* for film theory—the relation of the spectator to the screen. And these seminars cannot be used, as they are used by film theory, to support the argument that the cinematic apparatus, in direct line with the camera obscura, by recreating the space and ideology of Renaissance perspective, produces a centered and transcendent subject.[23]

This argument is critiqued in the seminars on the gaze as Lacan makes clear why the speaking subject *cannot* ever be totally trapped in the imaginary. Lacan claims, rather, that 'I am not simply that punctiform being located at the geometral point from which the perspective is grasped.'[24] Now, film theory, of course, has always claimed that the cinematic apparatus functions *ideologically* to produce a subject that *mis-recognizes* itself as source and center of the represented world. But although this claim might seem to imply agreement with Lacan, to suggest, too, that the subject is *not* the punctiform being that Renaissance perspective would have us believe it is, film theory's notion of misrecognition turns out to be different from Lacan's in important ways. Despite the fact that the term *misrecognition* implies an error on the subject's part, a failure properly to recognize its true relation to the visible world, the process by which the subject is installed in its position of misrecognition operates without the hint of failure. The subject unerringly assumes the position the perspectival construction bids it to take. Erased from the process of construction, the negative force of error emerges later as a charge directed at the subject. But from where does it come? Film theory has described only the construction of this position of misrecognition. Though it implies that there is another *actual*, nonpunctiform position, film theory has never been able to describe the construction of *this* position.

In Lacan's description, misrecognition retains its negative force in the process of construction. As a result, the process is conceived no longer as a purely positive one but rather as one with an internal dialectic. Lacan does not take the single triangle that geometrical perspective draws as an accurate description of its own operation. Instead he *re*diagrams this operation using, instead, *two interpenetrating* triangles. Thus he represents both the way the science of optics understands the emission of light *and* the way its straight lines become refracted, diffused (the way they acquire the 'ambiguity of a jewel') once we take into account the way the signifier itself interferes with this figuring. The second triangle cuts through the first, marking the elision or negation that is part of the process of construction. The second triangle diagrams the subject's mistaken belief that there is something behind the space set out by the first. It is this mistaken belief (this misrecognition) that causes the subject to *disbelieve* even those representations shaped according to the scientific laws of optics. The Lacanian subject, who may doubt the accuracy of even its most 'scientific representation', is submitted to a *superegoic* law that is radically different from the optical laws to which the film theoretical subject is submitted.

Graph. Semiotics, not optics, is the science that enlightens for us the structure of the visual domain. Because it alone is capable of lending things sense, the signifier alone makes vision possible. There is and can be no brute vision, no vision totally independent of language. Painting, drawing, all forms of picture making, then, are fundamentally graphic arts. And because signifiers are material, that is, because they are opaque rather than translucent, refer to other signifiers rather than directly to a signified, the field of vision is neither clear nor easily traversable. It is instead ambiguous and treacherous, full of traps. Lacan's Seminar XI refers constantly, but ambiguously, to these traps.

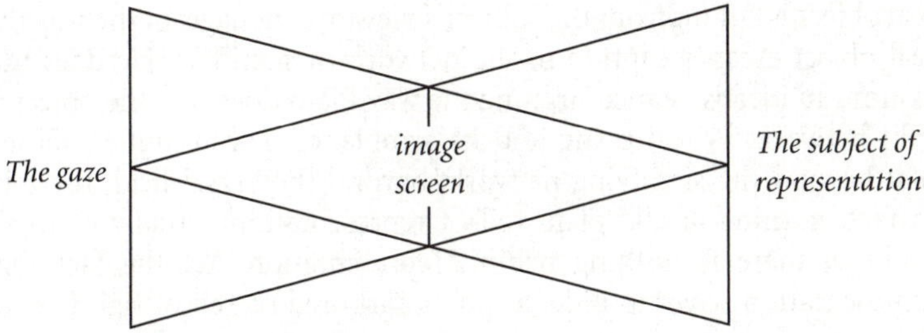

When Lacan says that the subject is trapped in the imaginary, he means that the subject can imagine nothing outside it; the imaginary cannot itself provide the means that would allow the subject to transcend it. When he says, on the other hand, that a painting, or any other representation, is a 'trap for the gaze', we understand this phrase as echoing the expression 'to trap one's attention'. That is, the representation *attracts* the gaze, induces us to imagine a gaze outside the field of representation. It is this second sense of trapping, whereby representation appears to generate its own beyond (to generate, we might say recalling Lacan's diagram, the *second* triangle, which the science of optics neglects to consider) that prevents the subject from ever being trapped in the imaginary. Where the Foucauldian and the film-theoretical positions always tend to trap the subject in representation (an idealist failing), to conceive of language as constructing the prison walls of the subject's being, Lacan argues that the subject sees these walls as *trompe l'oeil*, and is thus constructed by something *beyond* them.

For beyond everything that is displayed to the subject, the question is asked, 'What is being concealed from me? What in this graphic space does not show, does not stop *not* writing itself?' This point at which something appears to be *in*visible, this point at which something appears to be missing from representation, some meaning left unrevealed, is the point of the Lacanian gaze. It marks the *absence* of a signified; it is an *unoccupiable* point, not, as film theory claims, because it figures an unrealizable ideal but because it indicates an impossible real. In the former case, one would expect to find at the point of the gaze a signified, but here the signifier is absent—and so is the subject. The subject, in short, cannot be located or locate itself at the point of the gaze, since this point marks, on the contrary, its very annihilation. At the moment the gaze is discerned, the image, the entire visual field, takes on a terrifying alterity. It loses its 'belong-to-me aspect' and suddenly assumes the function of a screen.

Lacan is certainly *not* offering an agnostic description of the way the real object is cut off from the subject's view by language, of the way the real object escapes capture in the network of signifiers. He does not assume an idealist stance, arguing the way Plato does that the object is split between its real being and its semblance. Lacan argues, rather, that beyond the signifying network, beyond the visual field, there is, in fact, nothing at all.[25] The veil of representation actually conceals nothing; there is nothing behind representation. Yet the fact that representation *seems* to hide, to put an arbored screen of signifiers in front of something hidden beneath, is not treated by Lacan as a simple error that the subject can undo; nor is this deceptiveness of language treated as something that undoes the subject, deconstructs its identity by menacing its boundaries. Rather, language's opacity is taken as the very *cause* of the subject's being, that is, its desire, or want-to-be. The fact that it is materially impossible to say the whole truth—that truth always backs away from language, that words always fall short of their goal—*founds* the subject. Contrary to the idealist position that makes *form* the cause of being, Lacan locates the cause of being in the *informe*: the *unformed* (that which has no signified, no significant shape in the visual field) and the *inquiry* (the question posed to representation's presumed reticence). The subject is the effect of the impossibility of seeing what is lacking in the representation, what the subject, therefore, wants to see. The gaze, the object-cause of desire, is the object-cause of the subject of desire in the field of the visible. In other words, it is what the subject does not see and not simply what it sees that founds it.

It should be clear by now how different this description is from that offered by film theory. In film theory, the gaze is located 'in front of' the image, as its signified, the point of maximal meaning or sum of all that appears in the image *and* the point that 'gives' meaning. The subject is, then, thought to identify with and thus, in a sense, to *coincide with* the gaze. In Lacan, on the other hand, the gaze is located 'behind' the image, as that which fails to appear in it and thus as that which makes all its meanings suspect. And the subject, instead of coinciding with or identifying with the gaze, is rather *cut off from* it. Lacan does not ask you to think of the gaze as belonging to an Other who cares about what or where you are, who pries, keeps tabs on your whereabouts, and takes note of all your steps and missteps, as the panoptic gaze is said to do. When you encounter the gaze of the Other, you meet not a seeing eye but a blind one. The gaze is not clear or penetrating, not filled with knowledge or recognition; it is clouded over and turned back on itself, absorbed in its own enjoyment. The horrible truth, revealed to Lacan by Petit-Jean, is that *the gaze does not see you.* So, if you are looking for confirmation of the truth of your being or the clarity of your vision, you are on your own; the gaze of the Other is not confirming; it will not validate you.

Now, the subject instituted by the Lacanian gaze does not come into being as the realization of a possibility opened up by the law of the Other. It is rather an impossibility that is crucial to the constitution of the subject—the impossibility, precisely, of any ultimate confirmation from the Other. The subject emerges, as a result, as a desiring being, that is to say, an effect of the law but certainly not a realization of it, since desire as such can never be conceived as a realization. Desire fills no possibility but seeks after an impossibility; this makes desire always, constitutionally, contentless.

Narcissism, too, takes on a different meaning in Lacan, one more in accord with Freud's own. Since something always appears to be missing from any representation, narcissism *cannot* consist in finding satisfaction in one's own visual image. It must, rather, consist in the belief that one's own being exceeds the imperfections of its image. Narcissism, then, seeks the self beyond the self-image, with which the subject constantly finds fault and in which it constantly fails to recognize itself. What one loves in one's image is something *more* than the image ('in you more than you').[26] Thus is narcissism the source of the malevolence with which the subject regards its image, the aggressivity it unleashes on all its own representations.[27] And thus does the subject come into being as a transgression of, rather than in conformity to, the law. It is not the law, but the fault in the law—the desire that the law cannot ultimately conceal—that is assumed by the subject as its own. The subject, in taking up the burden of the law's guilt, goes beyond the law.

. . .

The effect of representation is the suspicion that some reality is being camouflaged, that we are being deceived as to the exact nature of some thing-in-itself that lies behind representation. In response to such a representation, against such a background of deception, the subject's own being breaks up between its unconscious being and its conscious semblance. At war both with its world and with itself, the subject becomes guilty of the very deceit it suspects. This can hardly, however, be called mimicry, in the old sense, since nothing is being mimed

In sum, the conflictual nature of Lacan's culpable subject sets it worlds apart from the stable subject of film theory. But neither does the Lacanian subject resemble that of Bachelard. For while in Bachelard orthopsychism—in providing an opportunity for the correction of thought's imperfections—allows the subject to wander from its moorings, constantly to drift from one position to another, in Lacan 'orthopsychism'[28]—one wishes to retain the term in order to indicate the subject's fundamental dependence on the faults it finds in representation and in itself—grounds the subject. The desire that it precipitates *transfixes* the subject, albeit in a conflictual place, so that all the subject's visions and revisions, all its fantasies, merely circumnavigate the absence that anchors the subject and impedes its progress.

Notes

1. In *The Four Fundamental Concepts of Psycho-Analysis*, ed. Jacques-Alain Miller, trans. Alan Sheridan (London: The Hogarth Press and the Institute of Psycho-Analysis, 1977), 274, Lacan speaks of the 'phantasies' of the 'mass media', as he very quickly suggests a critique of the familiar notion of 'the society of the spectacle'. This notion is replaced in Lacan by what might be called 'the society of [formed from] the nonspecularizable.'
2. *Liddell and Scott's Greek-English Lexicon*, 1906; all translations of ancient Greek terms are from this source.
3. Jacques Lacan, *Television/A Challenge to the Psychoanalytic Establishment*, ed. Joan Copjec, trans. Denis Hollier, Rosalind Krauss, and Annette Michelson, (New York: W. W. Norton, 1990), 3.
4. Mary Ann Doane points out that it is our very fascination with the model of the screen as mirror that has made it resistant to those theoretical objections that she herself makes ('Misrecognition and Identity', *Ciné-Tracts*, 11 (Fall 1980), 28).
5. Mary Ann Doane, Patricia Mellencamp, and Linda Williams (eds.), *Re-vision* (Los Angeles: The American Film Institute, 1984), 14. The introduction to this very useful collection of essays also attempts to detail some of the historical shifts in feminist theories of representation; I am only attempting to argue the need for one more shift, this time away from the panoptic model of cinema.
6. See, especially, Teresa de Lauretis, *Technologies of Gender* (Bloomington: Indiana University Press, 1987).
7. F. S. Cohen, in 'What is a question?' makes this important distinction clearly: 'Indetermination or doubt is not, as is often maintained, a wavering between different certainties, but the grasping of an incomplete form' (*The Monist*, 38 (1929), 354 n. 4).
8. Michel Foucault, *Power/Knowledge*, ed. Colin Gordon (New York: Pantheon, 1986), 186. The interview with Lucette Finas in which this statement occurs was also published in *Michel Foucault: Power, Truth, Strategy*, ed. Meaghan Morris and Paul Patton (Sydney: Feral Publications, 1979). The statement is quoted and emphasized in Mark Cousins and Athar Hussain's excellent book *Michel Foucault* (New York: St Martin's Press, 1984), 244.
9. Although some might claim that it was the introduction of the linguistic model into film studies that initiated the break, it can be more accurately argued that the break was precipitated by a shift in the linguistic model itself—from an exclusive emphasis on the relation between signifiers to an emphasis on the relation between signifiers and the subject, their signifying effect. That is, it was not until the *rhetorical* aspect of language was made visible—*by means of the concept of the apparatus*—that the field of film studies was definitively reformed. I am arguing, however, that once this shift was made, some of the sophistications introduced by semiology were, unfortunately, forgotten.

   To define a *break* (rather than a continuity) between what is often referred to as 'two stages', or the first and second semiology, is analogous to defining a break between Freud's first and second concept of transference. It was only with the second, the privileging of the analyst/analysand relationship, that psychoanalysis (properly speaking) was begun. Biography rather than theory is the source of the demand for the continuity of these concepts.

10. The best discussion of the relations between Bachelard and Althusser can be found in Etienne Balibar, 'From Bachelard to Althusser: the concept of "epistemological break"', *Economy and Society*, 5: 4 (November 1976), 385–411.
11. This image of the scientist discontinuous with him- or herself can be given a precise figuration, the alchemical image of the Melusines: creatures composed partially of inferior, fossilelike forms that reach back into the distant past (the imaginary) and partially of superior, energetic (scientific) activity. In *The Poetics of Space* (Boston: Beacon Press, 1969), 109, Bachelard, whose notion of the unconscious is more Jungian than Freudian, refers to this image from Jung's *Psychology and Alchemy.*
12. The one reservation Metz has to the otherwise operative analogy between mirror and screen is that, at the cinema, 'the spectator is absent from the screen: contrary to the child in the mirror' (Christian Metz, *The Imaginary Signifier* (Bloomington: Indiana University Press, 1982), 48). Jacqueline Rose clarified the error implied in this reservation by pointing out that 'the phenomenon of transitivism demonstrates that the subject's mirror identification can be with another child', that one always locates *one's own image in another* and thus the imaginary identification does not depend on a literal mirror ('The Imaginary', in *Sexuality in the Field of Vision* (London: Verso, 1986), 196). What is most often forgotten, however, is the corollary of this fact: one always locates *the other in one's own image.* The effect of *this* fact on the constitution of the subject is Lacan's fundamental concern.
13. Lacan, *The Four Fundamental Concepts*, 81.
14. It was Jean-Louis Baudry who first formulated this definition of the impression of reality. See his second apparatus essay, 'The Apparatus', in *Camera Obscura*, 1 (Fall 1976), esp. 118–119.
15. Metz's two-stage scenario is critiqued by Geoffrey Nowell-Smith in 'A Note on History/Discourse' (*Edinburgh* '76, 26–32); and by Mary Ann Doane in 'Misrecognition and Identity'.
16. I have elsewhere referred to the gaze as 'metempsychotic': although it is a concept abhorrent to feminist reason, the target of constant theoretical sallies, the gaze continues to reemerge, to be reincorporated, as an assumption of one film analysis after another. The argument I am making is that it is because we have not properly determined what the gaze is, whence it has emerged, that we have been unable to eliminate it. It is generally argued that the gaze is dependent on psychoanalytic structures of voyeurism and fetishism, presumed to be male. I am claiming instead that the gaze arises out of *linguistic* assumptions and that these assumptions, in turn, shape (and appear to be naturalized by) the psychoanalytic concepts.
17. Mikkel Borch-Jacobsen's interesting book, *The Freudian Subject* (Stanford, Calif.: Stanford University Press, 1988) grapples with this *necessary* distinction—with results very different from Lacan's.
18. Paul Hirst, 'Althusser's Theory of Ideology', *Economy and Society*, 5: 4 (November 1976), 385–411.

19. In order to dissociate his concept of science from that of idealism, conventionalism, and formalism, Bachelard formulated the concept of 'applied rationalism': a scientific concept must integrate within itself the conditions of its realization. (It is on the basis of this injunction that Heisenberg could dismiss as illegitimate any talk of an electron's location that could not also propose an experimental method of locating it.) And in order to dissociate his concept of science from that of the positivists, empiricists, and realists, Bachelard formulated the concept of 'technical materialism': the instruments and the protocols of scientific experiments must be theoretically formulated. The system of checks and balances according to which these two imperatives operate is what Bachelard normally means by *orthopsychism*. He extends the notion in *Le rationalisme appliqué*, however, to include the formation of the scientific subject.
20. Gaston Bachelard, *Le rationalisme appliqué* (Paris: Presses Universitaires de France, 1949), 65–81.
21. Lacan, *Television*, 7.
22. Lacan, *The Four Fundamental Concepts*, 106.
23. See especially Jean-Louis Baudry, 'Ideological Effects of the Basic Cinematographic Apparatus' (first published in French in *Cinéthique*, 7–8 (1970) and, in English, in *Film Quarterly*, 28 (Winter 1974–1975)) and Jean-Louis Comolli, 'Technique and Ideology: Camera, Perspective, Depth of Field' (first published in French in *Cahiers du cinéma*, 229, 230, 231, and 233 (1970–1971) and circulated in English translation as a British Film Institute off-print). This historical continuity has been taken for granted by film theory generally. For a history of the *non*continuity between Renaissance techniques of observation and our own, see Jonathan Crary, *Techniques of the Observer.* (Cambridge, Mass.: The MIT Press, 1990). In this book, Crary differentiates the camera obscura from the physiological models of vision that succeeded it. Lacan, in his seminars on the gaze, refers to both these models as they are represented by the science of optics and the philosophy of phenomenology. He exhibits them as two 'ways of being wrong about this function of the subject in the domain of the spectacle.'
24. Lacan, *The Four Fundamental Concepts*, 96.
25. The questions Moustapha Safouan poses to Lacan during Seminar XI (*The Four Fundamental Concepts*, 103) force him to be quite clear on this point: 'Beyond appearance there is nothing in itself, there is the gaze.'
26. This is the title given to the last session of the seminar published as *The Four Fundamental Concepts.* Although the 'you' of the title refers to the analyst, it can refer just as easily to the ideal image in the mirror.
27. Jacqueline Rose's 'Paranoia and the Film System' (*Screen*, 17: 4 (Winter 1976–1977)) is a forceful critique (directed specifically at Raymond Bellour's analyses of Hitchcock, but also at a range of film-theoretical assumptions) of that notion of the cinema that sees it as a successful resolution of conflict and refusal of difference. Rose reminds us that cinema, as 'technique of the imaginary' (Metz), necessarily unleashes a conflict, an aggressivity, that is irresolvable. While I am, for the most part, in agreement with this important essay, I am arguing here that aggressivity is *not* dependent on the shot-countershot structure. It is not the reversibility of the look but the unreturned look, the look that will not turn the subject into a fully observable being, that

Phase III. Race, Sexuality, and Postmodernism in Feminist Film Theory

Introductory Notes

If postmodernism comes first in this section, it is because I see the important issues around race and psychoanalysis—foregrounded in the late 1980s—as emerging partly from ongoing debates in feminist film theory about links between postmodernism and feminism. Given the modernist origins of feminist film theory in Britain and North America, it is perhaps not surprising that feminist film scholars were somewhat slow to engage with debates about postmodernism ongoing in literary and art criticism at least since Jean-François Lyotard's pioneering *The Postmodern Condition* (translated in 1984) and Fredric Jameson's influential 1984 essay on 'Postmodernism, or the Cultural Logic of Late Capitalism'. Debates, when they emerged, centred on whether or not feminism anticipated postmodernism in its critique of patriarchal culture (which is what Australian Meaghan Morris argues, as I note below), or whether postmodernism spelled the death knell of feminism.

Some feminists, myself included, thought it best to explore these questions, and postmodern aesthetic strategies' links to feminism, in a television form, the Music Video, with obvious postmodern characteristics, rather than in the apparently modernist filmic apparatus (see 'Further Reading' for this section). I could not, ultimately, include Australian Barbara Creed's essay to open this section, so let me discuss it briefly. The essay includes a lucid overview of debates about feminism and postmodernism, first in relation to Alice Jardine and literary feminism, then in regard to familiar male art critics, such as Craig Owens and Hal Foster, as well as philosophers and Marxists like Lyotard and Jameson mentioned above. Creed discusses both Alice Jardine's and Craig Owens's uses of Lyotard's theory of the collapse of totalizing 'Great Narratives' which, Creed reminds us, 'have been used to legitimate the quest for knowledge and the importance of scientific research'. Owens, meanwhile, argues that not only is there a narrative crisis but one of representation as well. The modernist concept of the art object as separate from the artist and the social world—while in some sense linked to that world if no longer mimetically (see classic essays in Phase I)—also began to fail in the latter quarter of this century. Creed notes that film feminists like Laura Mulvey had raised questions about a narrative crisis, albeit one different from that of Lyotard. Yet both agree 'that there is a crisis of narrative which has shaken the credibility of the major institutions in the West'. The subject of both the grand narratives and of representation, signifying practices, had hitherto been the white male: in Jardine's words, quoted by Creed, 'delegitimation, experienced as a crisis, is the loss of the paternal fiction, the West's heritage and guarantee . . .'.[1]

The last sections of Creed's essay take up Jardine's notion that 'the "feminine" signifies, not woman herself, but those "spaces" which could be said to conceptualize the master narrative's own "non-knowledge," that area over which the narrative has lost control. That is the unknown, the terrifying, the monstrous—everything which is not held in place by concepts such as Man, Truth, Meaning'.[2] We can see an interesting re-valuing of a female absence first articulated by both Claire Johnston and Laura Mulvey within modernist theoretical frames. Whereas the modernist deplores the absence of woman in patriarchal signifying practices, the postmodern feminist sees a potential in the very 'spaces' that the master's narrative does not consciously recognize but that reveal themselves where the narrative loses control. Woman is present, then, in male narratives, albeit indirectly. The influence of Jacques Derrida and deconstruction may be seen in Creed's and Jardine's formulations here.

Creed turns to the sci-fi horror film to explore how the body of woman is being used to investigate new possibilities for the body as a site of resistance and also to reveal the postmodern uncertainties about the future. Creed is careful to keep the tension between 'feminism' and 'postmodernism' so as to avoid creating yet one more totalizing theory, be it that of either of these terms. She suggests feminists follow Lyotard's recommendation to favour the 'short narratives' which 'the master discourses have attempted to suppress in order to validate their own positions'.[3]

To highlight the developing postmodern concepts of 'hybridity' and 'hybrid' identities, I start this section by reprinting the dense interview of Vietnamese–American film-maker Trinh T. Minh-Ha by Nancy Chen. A large number of important issues are taken up in this interview—issues to do with who can speak for whom, questions about the ability to 'know' the Other, problems of feminism and the 'personal' versus the 'political'. Trinh's postmodern cinematic strategies are investigated, challenged, debated, and objections to, and pleasures in, her images raised and discussed especially in relation to Trinh' s 1991 film on China, *Shoot for the Contents.* The question of the audience Trinh conceptualizes while making her films is interesting to juxtapose to the thread of feminist preoccupation with the 'spectator' evident throughout this volume, and returned to in selections that follow here. As a film-maker, Trinh has quite different ideas about the spectator than theorists have. She attempts to 'inscribe' the viewer 'in the way the film is scripted and shot. Through a number of creative strategies, this process is made visible and audible to the audience who is thus solicited to interact and to retrace it in viewing the film' (p. 335). Trinh notes that she asks all in the audience 'actually to put together "their own film" from the film they have seen—the film maker's intention cannot account for all the readings that they have mediated to their realities' (p. 335).

Arguably, postmodern concepts opened up theoretical space for new research on race and gender in feminist film theory. As Lola Young has pointed out (see 'Further Reading' this section), black scholars and others have long been researching the problems and issues of African Americans and black British peoples within history, sociology, political science, economics, and other social science disciplines. The humanities were somewhat slow to undertake such work, and when they did, it tended to focus on stereotypes rather than on exploring theoretical bases for racism. Once it became clear that the West's grand narratives and signifying practices were devised to keep the white male in place as Subject, room emerged to work on spaces where varied minorities and women could speak and begin to develop positions for themselves, theoretically, socially, and in images.

The following four essays address important issues regarding psychoanalysis and race that, again arguably, were opened up as postmodern theories about *grand recits* and master narratives made possible investigating the degree to which psychoanalysis was yet another 'master narrative' helping to keep the white male subject in His place, and the degree to which psychoanalysis was indispensable in understanding racist processes themselves. As in patriarchal signifying practices, psychoanalysis could be viewed as a discourse in which both women and peoples of colour are present if in 'spaces' where the discourse gets out of control; or in ways that the discourse cannot control, to put it a bit differently.

Each of the four essays uses a different method and takes up a different position vis-à-vis race and psychoanalysis. Jane Gaines, one of the first in North America to challenge white feminist film theory's neglect of issues of race, argues that 'a theory of the text and its spectator, based on the psychoanalytic concept of sexual difference, is unequipped to deal with a film which is about racial difference and sexuality' (p. 336). Gaines rehearses some of the critiques of Phase I theories already noted in the Phase II selections above, only now she argues that 'the Freudian–Lacanian scenario can eclipse the scenario of race–gender relations in Afro-American history, since the two accounts of sexuality are fundamentally incongruous' (p. 337). Gaines tries out a psychoanalytic reading of the film *Mahogany*, starring Diana Ross, to make her point. The danger for Gaines is that when we use a psychoanalytic model to explain black family relations, we force an erroneous universalization and inadvertently reaffirm white middle-class norms (p. 337). Her method involves turning to history and African-American literature to explain why psychoanalysis is incongruous to the black situation. Gaines argues that since a different social and political history—that of slavery—lies behind the construction of black male and female sexuality in the USA, the determining patriarchal scenario of white feminists has to be overridden. In concluding, she returns to the feminist 'double-bind' which was the focus of essays in Phase I: the universalizing tendency of Freud and Lacan, and the focus on change at the level of language that has led to turning history into discourse. Claiming controversially that psychoanalysis is antithetical to Marxism, Gaines also states that this theory has left no room for 'the real historical subject' who is nevertheless implicated when this theory is used.

Claire Pajaczkowska and Lola Young use an opposite strategy in their essay that follows Gaines's. Rather than seeing psychoanalysis as incongruous with black psychic life, they ask what a psychoanalytic perspective might contribute to an understanding of racism. Noting 'the long history which unites psychoanalysis and antiracist struggle' (p. 356), they usefully introduce a series of psychoanalytic concepts—trauma, the unconscious, identification, denial, and the Oedipus complex—in order to show their usefulness in accounting for white brutality to indigenous peoples in colonialism, for 'whiteness as an absent center', and finally, for certain jeopardized black identities. Their analysis of Neil Jordan's film *Mona Lisa* illuminates its destructive use of stereotypes because it represents 'dependency as intolerable, as excremental, and because it projects this onto working class,

Black and feminine identities' (p. 364). The following study of Toni Morrison's novel *Beloved* argues for the need to disentangle the pain of the past, including all the unspeakable experiences of black peoples, through a kind of psychoanalytic 'talking cure', before it is possible to engage the future. Slavery's radical destablizing resulted in 'the undermining and fragmentation of cultural self identity both for those who underwent the process of dispersal and disruption and for their descendants' (p. 367). The disturbing aspects of the past need to be confronted without sentimentalism and nostalgia, as in Morrison's novel. The piece ends with a useful coda about difficulties of teaching a text like *Beloved* in England.

I refer readers to an essay by Michele Wallace, 'Multiculturalism and Oppositionality' (listed in 'Further Reading' to this section but not included here), because it too reaffirms the usefulness of psychoanalysis in multicultural criticism through analysing three instances of multicultural programming in New York City, along with study of Yvonne Rainer's film, *Privilege*. Wallace responds to critiques of 'the eurocentric prioritization of sexual difference' (much like Gaines's objections) by rejecting the idea of simply prioritizing other kinds of difference to the exclusion of gender. Rather, she says, we need to theorize 'sexuality, the body and gender from other cultural perspectives' (p. 7). Rejecting Freudian, Lacanian, and Foucaultian discourses would return us 'to the pragmatics of race and class' and the old problem of 'a reductive social realism hamstringing critical analysis' (p. 7). However, Wallace regrets the 'almost total lack of theoretical discourse that relates "race" to gender and sexuality' (p. 7). Frantz Fanon's point that the colonizing enterprise constructs the very desires of the colonized, struck Wallace. Later on, after critiquing feminist theory's refusal to challenge racial/cultural apartheid, Wallace nevertheless stands unwilling 'to cede sexual difference to white women' since 'sexual difference is something that women of color, poor women, and gay women share with white, middle-class women' (p. 8). After arguing that people of colour need to be engaged in critical theorizing practices around multiculturalism, Wallace proceeds (controversially, to my mind) to critique Yvonne Rainer's *Privilege* because the film maker 'shows no concrete interest in having the women of color themselves theorize race, or class, or gender'. (Readers may return to Teresa de Lauretis's very different discussion of another Rainer film in her essay in Phase II or look at Kaplan's chapter on the film listed in 'Further Reading'.) Wallace similarly critiques the New Contemporary Museum's *Decade Show*, ostensibly about the need for provisional rather than fixed identities, for its failure to confront material realities and differences between subjects as these are implicated by vastly different speaking locations.[4]

Pratibha Parmar, an Asian-British video- and film-maker, meanwhile, takes up Wallace's challenge to people of colour to undertake their own theorizing as critics and artists. In this piece, Parmar develops a 'theoretical framework for discussing the cultural and political significance of black arts in postcolonial Britain' (p. 376). Speaking from a position of resisting the marginalization imposed on her as both lesbian and Asian by 'an England that is intensely xenophobic and insular', Parmar and her community have been seeking to locate themselves 'not in any one community but in the spaces between . . . different communities' (p. 376–7). Not afraid to risk many of the essentializing dangers pointed out by Claire Johnston and Eileen McGarry (see 'Further Reading' for Phase I essays), Parmar states that her aim as a video- and film-maker is to create 'images of ourselves as women, as people of color and as lesbians and gays; images that evoke passionate stirrings and that enable us to construct ourselves in our complexities'. She continues to note that 'As a lesbian I have searched in vain for images of lesbians of colour on the screen but I quickly realized that they exist only in our imagination . . ' (p. 378). Parmar began therefore to compile a repertoire of images of the lives of lesbians of colour. Later in the essay, Parmar notes the limitations of merely oppositional images and discourses as these tend to homogenize people of colour who, in fact, have many differences amongst themselves. New work in Cultural Studies spurred black feminists to critique identity politics in their writings and cultural productions. Parmar ends by noting her concern as a film-maker 'to challenge the normalizing and universalizing tendencies within the predominantly white lesbian and gay communities', and to assert the diversity of racial and cultural identities within gay/lesbian categories. Her current 'hybrid' aesthetic practices (as for example in her videos, *Khush* and *Bhangra Jig*) embody, she says, 'these postmodernist times' in which we 'construct our sense of selves through the hybridity of cultural practices . . .' (p. 382). Readers will here note echoes of Trinh's comments in the interview discussed above.

I end Phase III essays with Teresa de Lauretis's dense and carefully argued essay on 'Sexual Indifference and Lesbian Representation', later incorporated into her pioneering volume, *The Practice of Love*, because it pulls together many themes advanced in Phase III and, at the same time, looks back to essays in prior sections. Like others in this section, de Lauretis notes how the 'first emphasis on sexual difference as gender (woman's difference from man) has rightly come under attack for obscuring other differences in women's psycho social oppression' (p. 384). She goes on to stress the way in which, in its emphasis on sexual difference, feminist film theory opened up a critical space through which women could address themselves to women. Interestingly, de Lauretis introduces right away a parallel between the paradox of 'sexual *difference* (women are, or want, something different from men) and of sexual *indifference* (women are, or want, the same as men)', and that of racist and class-biased practices, 'where social difference is also . . . social indifference' (p. 384–385).

De Lauretis moves the reader through a useful analysis of sexual indifference as pointed out by Luce Irigaray in Freud, and then as David Halperin implicitly conveys it in his study of Greek philosophers. De Lauretis points out the intimate relationship of sexual and social indifference in Western culture for centuries—a link that 'has served to bolster colonial conquest and racist violence'—before turning to examine lesbian representation on the basis of the framework she so carefully has established. It is the conditions of possibility for lesbian representation that de Lauretis examines as she explores diverse attempts lesbian writers and artists have deployed in their struggle with 'the obdurate relation of reference to meaning, of flesh to language' (p. 386).

I leave the reader to engage with de Lauretis's fascinating readings, only pausing to note her inclusion of women of colour from Audre Lorde to Cherríe Moraga in her readings and her care to sort through the black/white and gay/straight divide in these contexts. Towards the end of the essay, de Lauretis reminds the reader of how important has been the question of address, 'of who produces cultural representations and for whom . . . and of who receives them and in what contexts' (p. 395) in feminism in general. In the visual arts, of course, and especially in women's cinema, the issue of spectatorship has loomed large, and here de Lauretis takes up some of the questions about lesbian spectatorship discussed in 1977 by Caroline Sheldon, and later by Mayne and Parmar in this and earlier sections. In addressing the specific context of lesbianism, de Lauretis returns to issues similar to those she and others addressed earlier in relation to the heterosexual female spectator: de Lauretis questions if a lesbian performance can so easily 'imply a spectator that is not the generic, universal male . . . but lesbian', as Kate Davy had suggested. De Lauretis argues that the most difficult task is that of 'defining an autonomous form of female sexuality and desire in the wake of a tradition still Platonic . . .' (p. 397–8). Perhaps more possible is 'devising strategies of representation which will, in turn, alter the standard of vision, the frame of reference of visibility, of *what can be seen*' (p. 398). And it is to examples of women's cinema and performance art that take up this challenge that the rest of the essay is devoted.

Notes

1. Barbara Creed, 'From Here to Modernity: Feminism and Postmodernism', *Screen*, 28:2 (1987), 50, 52, 56.
2 Ibid. 59.
3 Ibid. 67.
4. Michele Wallace, 'Multiculturalism and Oppositionality', *After image* (A publication of the Visual Studies Workshop), 19: 3 (October 1991), 7, 8.

16 Speaking Nearby

Trinh T. Minh-Ha and Nancy N. Chen*

Nancy N. Chen: *One of the most important questions for myself deals with the personal. In your latest film* SHOOT FOR THE CONTENTS *Clairmonte Moore refers to himself as 'a member of the residual class' which is a euphemism for 'living underground, for living outside the norm, and for living outside of the status quo'. Then another character Dewi refers to having the 'pull' of being here and there. I think that this reflects on the personal and I would like to ask how your family background or personal experience has influenced your work.*

Trinh T. Minh-Ha: Although the ideology of 'starting from the source' has always proved to be very limiting, I would take that question into consideration since the speaking or interviewing subject is never apolitical, and such a question coming from you may be quite differently nuanced. There is not much, in the kind of education we receive here in the West, that emphasizes or even recognizes the importance of constantly having contact with what is actually within ourselves, or of understanding a structure from within ourselves out. The tendency is always to relate to a situation or to an object as if it is only outside of oneself. Whereas elsewhere, in Vietnam, or in other Asian and African cultures for example, one often learns to 'know the world inwardly', so that the deeper we go into ourselves, the wider we go into society. For me, this is where the challenge lies in terms of materializing a reality, because the personal is not naturally political, and every personal story is not necessarily political.

In talking about the personal, it is always difficult to draw that fine line between what is merely individualistic and what may be relevant to a wider number of people. Nothing is *given* in the process of

* Trinh T. Minh-Ha and Nancy N. Chen, 'Speaking Nearby' from *Visualizing Theory* edited by Lucien Taylor (Routledge, 1994), reprinted by permission of the authors.

Trinh T. Minh-Ha, Director

understanding the 'social' of our daily lives. So every single work I come up with is yet another attempt to inscribe this constant flow from the inside out and outside in. The interview with Clairmonte in SHOOT FOR THE CONTENTS is certainly a good example to start with. His role in the film is both politically and personally significant. In locating himself, Clairmonte has partly contributed to situating the place from which the film speaks. The way a number of viewers reacted to his presence in the film has confirmed what I thought might happen when I was working on it. Usually in a work on China, people do not expect the voice of knowledge to be other than that of an insider—here a Chinese—or that of an institutionalized authority—a scholar whose expertise on China would immediately give him or her the license to speak about such and such culture, and whose superimposed name and title on the screen serve to validate what he or she has to say. No such signpost is used in SHOOT; Clairmonte, who among all the interviewees discusses Chinese politics most directly, is of African rather than Chinese descent; and furthermore, there is no immediate urge to present him as someone who 'speaks as . . .' What you have is the voice of a person who little by little comes to situate himself through the diverse social and political positions he assumes, as well as through his analysis of himself and of the media in the States. So when Clairmonte designates himself literally and figuratively as being from a residual class, this not only refers to the place from which he analyzes China—which is not that of an expert about whom he has spoken jokingly, but more let's say that of an ordinary person who is well versed in politics. The designation, as you've pointed out, also reflects back on my own situation: I have been making films on Africa from a hybrid site where the meeting of several cultures (on non-Western ground) and the notions of outsider and insider (Asian and Third World in the context of Africa) need to be re-read.

This is where you talk about the intersubjective situation in your writings.

Right. I have dealt with this hybridity in my previous films quite differently, but the place from which Clairmonte speaks in SHOOT is indirectly linked to the place from which I spoke in relation to Africa. Just as it is bothersome to see a member of the Third World talking about (the representation of) another Third World culture—instead of minding our own business (*laughter*) as we have been herded to—it is also bothersome for a number of viewers who had seen SHOOT, to have to deal with Clairmonte's presence in it. And of course, the question never comes out straight; it always comes out obliquely like: 'Why the Black man in the film? Has this been thought out?' Or, in the form of assumptions such as: 'Is he a professor at Berkeley?' 'Is he teaching African Studies or Sociology?'

In some ways those questions indicate there's a need for authenticity. My question about Clairmonte concerns what he said about identity and I think that the issue of identity runs throughout all of your work. You've often talked about hyphenated peoples and I'm interested if in any way that notion stems from your personal experience. Have you felt that people have tried to push you, to be a Vietnamese-American or Asian-American, or woman-filmmaker? All of these different categories is what Clairmonte points out to. In your works and writings you distinctly push away that tendency. I think you are quite right in pointing out earlier that there is a very strong tendency to begin with a psychological sketch like 'What are your primary influences . . .' (laughter) *I would be very interested in learning about your particular experiences in Vietnam. Could you talk more about that?*

I will. But again, for having been asked this question many times, especially in interviews for newspapers, I would link here the problematization of identity in my work with what the first chapter of *Woman, Native, Other* opened on: the dilemma, especially in the context of women, of having one's work explained (or brought to closure) through one's personality and particular attributes. In such a highly individualistic society as the one we belong to here, it is very comforting for a reader to consume difference as a commodity by starting with the personal difference in culture or background, which is the best way to escape the issues of power, knowledge and subjectivity raised.

My past in Vietnam does not just belong to me. And since the Vietnamese communities, whether here in the US or there in Vietnam, are not abstract entities, I can only speak while learning to keep silent, for the risk of jeopardizing someone's reputation and right to speech is always present. Suffice it to say that I come from a large family, in which three different political factions existed. These political tendencies were not always freely assumed, they were bound to circumstances as in the case of the family members who remained in Hanoi (where I was born) and those who were compelled to move to Saigon (where I grew up). The third faction comprised those involved with the National Liberation Front in the South. This is why the dualistic divide between pro- and anti-communists has always appeared to me as a simplistic product of the rivalry between (what once were) the two superpowers. It can never even come close to the complexity of the Vietnam reality. All three factions had suffered under the regime to which they belong, and all three had, at one time or another, been the scapegoat of specific political moments. As a family however, we love each other dearly despite the absurd situations in which we found ourselves divided. This is a stance that many viewers have recognized in SURNAME VIET GIVEN NAME NAM, but hopefully it is one that they will also see in the treatment of Mao as a figure and in the multiple play between Left and Right, or Right and Wrong in SHOOT.

How I came to study in the States still strikes me today as a miracle. The dozen of letters I blindly sent out to a number of universities to seek admission into work-study programs . . . It was like throwing a bottle to the sea. As an 'international student', I was put in contact with all other foreign students, as well as with 'minority' students who were often isolated from the mainstream of Euro-American students. It was hardly surprising then that the works of African American poets and playwrights should be the first to really move and impress me. By the sheer fact that I was with an international community, I was

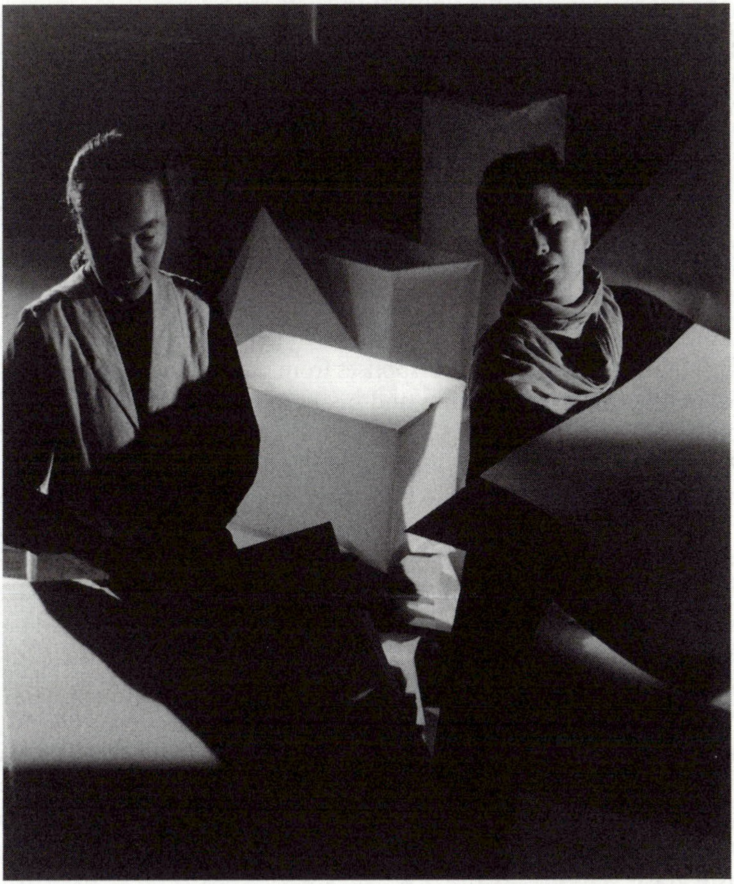

SHOOT FOR THE CONTENT 102 mins. Colour Film by Trinh T. Minh-Ha, 1992

introduced to a range of diverse cultures. So the kind of education I got in such an environment (more from outside than inside the classroom) would not have been as rich if I had stayed in Vietnam or if I had been born in the States. Some of my best friends there, and later on at the University of Illinois were Haitians, Senegalese and Kenyans. Thanks to these encounters, I subsequently decided to go to Senegal to live and teach.

In all your works, but particularly your writings on anthropology, ethnography and ethnographic films, there's a critique of the standard, the center of rationality, the center of TRUTH. I think that critique is also shared by many anthropologists, especially those in the post-structuralist tradition. Do you think that there is more possibility in ethnography if people use these tools? What do you think would be possible with reflexivity or with multivocality?

Anthropology is just one site of discussion among others in my work. I know that a number of people tend to focus obsessively on this site. But such a focus on anthropology despite the fact that the arguments advanced involve more than one occupied territory, discipline, profession and culture seems above all to tell us where the stakes are the highest. Although angry responses from professionals and academics of other fields to my films and books are intermittently expected, most of the masked outraged reactions do tend to come from Euro-American anthropologists and cultural experts. This, of course, is hardly surprising. They are so busy defending the discipline, the institution and the specialized knowledge it produces that what they have to say on works like mine only tells us about themselves and the interests at issue. I am reminded here of a conference panel years ago in which the discussion on one of my previous films was carried out with the participation of three Euro-American anthropologists. Time and again they tried to wrap up the session with dismissive judgements, but the audience would not let go of the discussion. After over an hour of intense arguments, during which a number of people in the audience voiced their disapproval of the anthropologists' responses, one woman was so exasperated and distressed, that she simply said to them: 'the more you speak, the further you dig your own grave.'

If we take the critical work in Reassemblage for example, it is quite clear that it is not simply aimed at the anthropologist, but also at the missionary, the Peace Corps volunteer, the tourist, and last but not least at myself as onlooker. In my writing and filmmaking, it has always been important for me to carry out critical work in such a way that there is room for people to reflect on their own struggle and to use the tools offered so as to further it on their own terms. Such a work is radically incapable of prescription. Hence, these tools are sometimes also appropriated and turned against the very filmmaker or writer, which is a risk I am willing to take. I have, indeed, put myself in a situation where I cannot criticize without taking away the secure ground on which I stand. All this is being said because your question, although steered in a slightly different direction, does remind me indirectly of another question which I often get under varying forms: at a panel discussion in Edinburgh on Third Cinema for example, after two hours of interaction with the audience, and of lectures by panelists, including myself, someone came to me and said in response to my paper: 'Oh, but then anthropology is still possible!' I took it both as a constructive statement and a misinterpretation. A constructive statement, because only a critical work developed to the limits or effected on the limits (here, of anthropology) has the potential to trigger such a question as: 'Is anthropology still a possible project?' And a misinterpretation, because this is not just a question geared toward anthropology, but one that involves all of us from the diverse fields of social sciences, humanities and arts.

Whether reflexivity and multivocality contribute anything to ethnography or not would have to depend on the way they are practiced. It seems quite evident that the critique I made of anthropology is not new; many have done it before and many are doing it now. But what remains unique to each enterprise are not so much the objects as the relationships drawn between them. So the question remains: how? How is reflexivity understood and materialized? If it is reduced to a form of mere breast-beating or of self-criticism for further improvement, it certainly does not lead us very far. I have written more at length on this question elsewhere ('Documentary Is/Not a Name', *October*, No. 52, 1990) and to simplify a complex issue, I would just say here that if the tools are dealt with only so as to further the production of anthropological knowledge, or to find a better solution for anthropology as a discipline, then what is achieved is either a refinement in the pseudo-science of appropriating Otherness or a mere stir within the same frame. But if the project is carried out precisely at that limit where anthropology could be abolished in what it tries to institutionalize, then nobody here is on safe ground. Multivocality, for example, is not necessarily a solution to the problems of centralized and hierarchical knowledge when it is practiced accumulatively—by juxtaposing voices that continue to speak within identified boundaries. Like the much abused concept of multiculturalism, multivocality here could also lead to the bland 'melting-pot' type of attitude, in which 'multi' means 'no'—no voice—or is used only to better mask the Voice—that very place from where meaning is put together. On the other hand, multivocality can open up to a non-identifiable ground where boundaries are always undone, at the same time as they are accordingly assumed. Working at the borderline of what is and what no longer is anthropology one also knows that if one crosses that border, if one can depart from where one is, one can also return to it more freely, without attachment to the norms generated on one side or the other. So the work effected would constantly question both its interiority and its exteriority to the frame of anthropology.

This goes back to your previous point that being within is also being without, being inside and outside. I think this answers my next question which is about how if naming, identifying and defining are problematic how does one go about practicing? I think that you are saying that it also opens up a space being right on that boundary. I would now like to turn from theory to filmmaking practice. Your writing has often been compared to performance art. Could you say that this is also true of your filmmaking as well as in the four films that you have made so far?

I like the thought that my texts are being viewed as performance art (*laughter*). I think it is very adequate. Viewers have varied widely in their approaches to my films. Again, because of the way these films are made, how the viewers enter them tells us acutely how they situate themselves. The films have often been compared to musical compositions and appreciated by people in performance, architecture, dance or poetry for example. So I think there is something to be said about the filmmaking process. Although I have never consciously taken inspiration from any specific art while I write, shoot or edit a film, for me, the process of making a film comes very close to those of composing music and of writing poetry. When one is not *just* trying to capture an object, to explain a cultural event, or to inform for the sake of information; when one refuses to commodify knowledge, one necessarily disengages oneself from the mainstream ideology of communication, whose linear and transparent use of language and the media reduces these to a mere vehicle of ideas. Thus, every time one puts forth an image, a word, a sound or a silence, these are never instruments simply called upon to serve a story or a message. They have a set of meanings, a function, and a rhythm of their own within the world that each film builds anew. This can be viewed as being characteristic of the way poets use words and composers use sounds.

Here I'll have to make clear that through the notion of 'poetic language', I am certainly not referring to the poetic as the site for the consolidation of a subjectivity, or as an estheticized practice of language. Rather, I am referring to the fact that language is fundamentally reflexive, and only in poetic language can one deal with meaning in a revolutionary way. For the nature of poetry is to offer meaning in such

Shoot for the Content 102 mins. Colour Film by Trinh T. Minh-Ha, 1992

a way that it can never end with what is said or shown, destabilizing thereby the speaking subject and exposing the fiction of all rationalization. Roland Barthes astutely summed up this situation when he remarked that 'the real antonym of the "poetic" is not the prosaic, but the stereotyped'. Such a statement is all the more perceptive as the stereotyped is not a false representation, but rather, an arrested representation of a changing reality. So to avoid merely falling into this pervasive world of the stereotyped and the clichéd, filmmaking has all to gain when conceived as a performance that engages as well as questions (its own) language. However, since the ideology of what constitutes 'clarity' and 'accessibility' continues to be largely taken for granted, poetic practice can be 'difficult' to a number of viewers, because in mainstream films and media our ability to play with meanings other than the literal ones that pervade our visual and aural environment is rarely solicited. Everything has to be packaged for consumption.

With regard to your films you've always been able to show that even what one sees with one's eyes, as you say in your books, is not necessarily the truth. My next question concerns Laura Mulvey's comment on language where any tool can be used for dominance as well as empowerment. Do you think that this is also true of poetic approaches to film?

Oh yes. This is what I have just tried to say in clarifying what is meant by the 'poetic' in a context that does not lend itself easily to classification. As numerous feminist works of the last two decades have shown, it is illusory to think that women can remain outside of the patriarchal system of language. The question is, as I mentioned earlier, how to engage poetical language without simply turning it into an estheticized, subjectivist product, hence allowing it to be classified. Language is at the same time a site for empowerment and a site for enslavement. And it is particularly enslaving when its workings remain invisible. Now, how one does bring that out in a film, for example, is precisely what I have tried to do in SURNAME VIET GIVEN NAME NAM. This is an aspect of the film that highly differentiates it, let's say, from REASSEMBLAGE. If in the latter the space of language and meaning is constantly interrupted or effaced by the gaps of non-senses, absences and silences; in SURNAME VIET, this space is featured manifestly as presences—albeit presences positioned in the context of a critical politics of interview and translation.

Viewers who take for granted the workings of language and remain insensitive to their very visible treatment in SURNAME VIET, also tend to obscure the struggle of women and their difficult relation to the symbolic contract. Hence, as expected, these viewers' readings are likely to fall within the dualist confine of a pro- or anti-communist rationale. Whereas, what is important is not only what the women say but what site of language they occupy (or do not occupy) in their struggle. With this also comes the play between the oral and the written, the sung and the said, the rehearsed and the non-rehearsed, and the different uses of English as well as of Vietnamese. So, if instead of reading the film conventionally from the point of view of content and subject matter, one reads it in terms of language plurality, comparing the diverse speeches—including those translated and reenacted from the responses by women in Vietnam, and those retrieved 'authentically' on the site from the women in the States about their own lives—then one may find oneself radically shifting ground in one's reading. The play effected between literal and non-literal languages can be infinite and the two should not be mutually exclusive of each other. Everything I criticize in one film can be taken up again and used *differently* in another film. There is no need to censor ourselves in what we can do.

I'm also intrigued by your works where you mention 'talking nearby instead of talking about'—this is one of the techniques you mention to 'make visible the invisible'. How might indirect language do precisely that?

This link is nicely done; especially between 'speaking nearby' and indirect language. In other words, a speaking that does not objectify, does not point to an object as if it is distant from the speaking subject or absent from the speaking place. A speaking that reflects on itself and can come very close to a subject without, however, seizing or claiming it. A speaking in brief, whose closures are only moments of transition opening up to other possible moments of transition—these are forms of indirectness well understood by anyone in tune with poetic language. Every element constructed in a film refers to the world around it, while having at the same time a life of its own. And this life is precisely what is lacking when one uses word, image, or sound just as an instrument of thought. To say therefore that one prefers not to speak about but rather to speak nearby, is a great challenge. Because actually, this is not just a technique or a statement to be made verbally. It is an attitude in life, a way of positioning oneself in

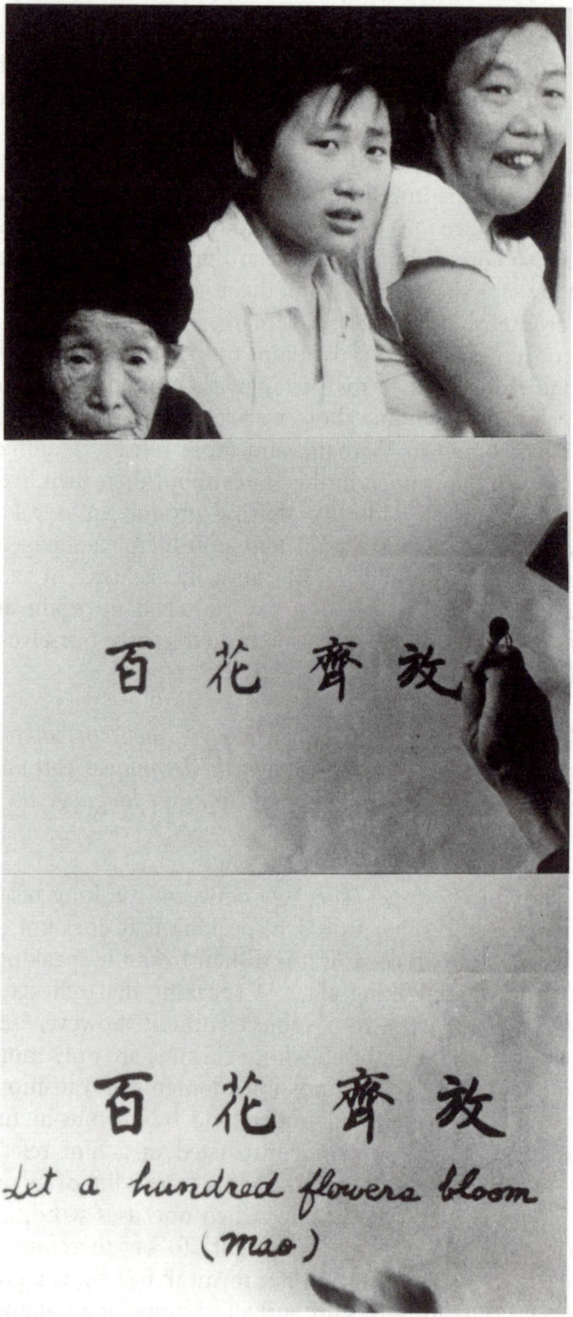

百花齊放
百花齊放
Let a hundred flowers bloom
(mao)

SHOOT FOR THE CONTENT 102 mins. Colour Film by Trinh T. Minh-Ha, 1992

relation to the world. Thus, the challenge is to materialize it in all aspects of the film—verbally, musically, visually. That challenge is renewed with every work I realize, whether filmic or written.

The term of the issue raised is, of course, much broader than the questions generated by any of the specific work I've completed (such as REASSEMBLAGE, in which the speaking about and speaking nearby serve as a point of departure for a cultural and cinematic reflection). Truth never yields itself in anything said or shown. One cannot just point a camera at it to catch it: the very effort to do so will kill it. It is worth quoting here again Walter Benjamin for whom, 'nothing is poorer than a truth expressed as it was thought'. Truth can only be approached indirectly if one does not want to lose it and find oneself hanging on to a dead, empty skin. Even when the indirect has to take refuge in the very figures of the direct, it continues to defy the closure of a direct reading. This is a form of indirectness that I have to deal with in SURNAME VIET, but even more so in SHOOT. Because here, there is necessarily, among others, a layered play between political discourse and poetical language, or between the direct role of men and the indirect role of women.

That leads me to some questions that I had about your latest film because you choose Mao as a political figure and he is also one who plays with language. There is a quote in the film: 'Mao ruled through the power of rhymes and proverbs.' I think this is a very apt statement about the scope of the film. I'm curious as to 'Why China?' You mentioned before about how your next project or your next film is a rupture from the previous one. So was going to China just a complete change from SURNAME VIET*?*

It's not quite a rupture. I don't see it that way. Nor do I see one film as being better than another; there is no linear progress in my filmic work. There is probably only a way of raising questions differently from different angles in different contexts. The rupture I mentioned earlier has more to do with my general educational background. So why China? One can say that there is no more an answer to this question than to: 'Why Africa?' which I often get, and 'Why Vietnam?' (*laughter*), which I like to also ask in return. Indeed, when people inquire matter-of-factly about my next film in Vietnam, I cannot help but ask 'why Vietnam?' Why do I have to focus on Vietnam? And this leads us back to a statement I made earlier, concerning the way marginalized peoples are herded to mind their own business. So that the area, the 'homeland' in which they are allowed to work remains heavily marked, whereas the areas in which Euro-Americans' activities are deployed can go on unmarked. One is here confined to one's own culture, ethnicity, sexuality and gender. And that's often the only way for insiders within the marked boundaries to make themselves heard or to gain approval.

This being said, China is a very important step in my personal itinerary, even though the quest into Chinese culture has, in fact, more to do with the relation between the two cultures—Vietnamese and Chinese—than with anything strictly personal. The Vietnamese people are no exception when it comes to nationalism. Our language is equipped with numerous daily expressions that are extremely pejorative toward our neighbors, especially toward Chinese people. But Vietnam was the site where the Chinese and Indian cultures met, hence what is known as the Vietnamese culture certainly owes much from the crossing of these two ancient civilizations.

Every work I have realized was designed to transform my own consciousness. If I went to Africa to dive into a culture that was mostly unknown to me then, I went to China mainly because I was curious as to how I could depart from what I knew of Her. The prejudices that the Vietnamese carry vis-à-vis the Chinese are certainly historical and political. The past domination of Vietnam by China and the antagonistic relationship nurtured between the two nations (this relationship has only been normalized some months ago) have been weighing so heavily on the Vietnamese psyche that very often Vietnamese identity would be defined in contradistinction to everything thought to be Chinese. And yet it merits looking a bit harder at the Vietnamese culture—at its music, to mention a most explicit example—to realize how much it has inherited from both China and India. It is not an easy task to deny their influences, even when people need to reject them in order to move on. An anecdote whose humor proved to be double-edged was that, during my stay in China, I quickly learned to restrain myself from telling people that I was originally from Vietnam—unless someone really wanted to know (precisely because of the high tension between the two countries at the time). The local intellectuals, however, seemed to be much more open vis-à-vis Vietnam as they did not think of Her as an enemy country but rather, as a neighbor or 'a brother.' This, to the point that one of them even told me reassuringly in a conversation. 'Well you know it's alright that you are from Vietnam; after all, She is a province of China.' (*laughter*)

So it reifies that power relationship . . .

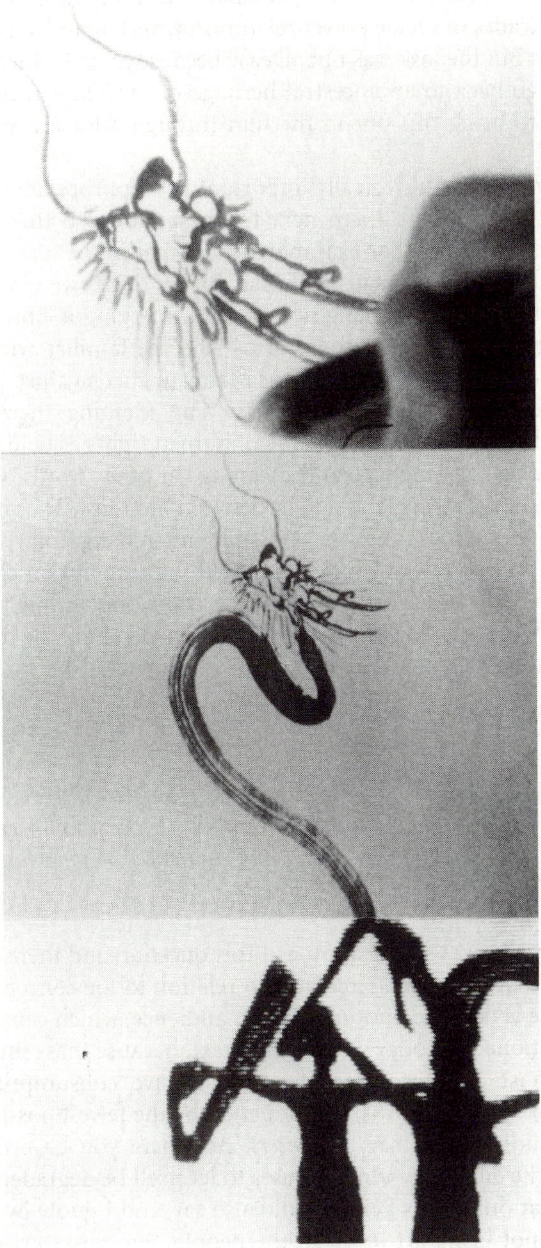

Shoot for the Content 102 mins. Colour Film by Trinh T. Minh-Ha, 1992

Yes, right . . . (*laughter*). On a personal level, I did want to go further than the facades of such a power relationship and to understand China differently. But the task was not all easy because to go further here also meant to go back to an ancestral heritage of the Vietnamese culture. I've tried to bring this out in the film through a look at politics via the arts.

Sometimes, it is strategically important to reappropriate the stereotypes and to juxtapose them next to one another so that they may cancel each other out. For example the fact that in the film, the 'Great Man' can be both Confucius and Mao, makes these two giants' teachings at time sillily interchangeable. Such a merging is both amusing and extremely ironical for those of us who are familiar with China's history and the relentless campaigns Mao launched against all vestiges of Confucianism in Chinese society. The merging therefore also exposes all wars fought in the name of human rights as being first and foremost a war of language and meaning. In other words, what Mao called 'the verbal struggle' is a fight between 'fictions'. The coexistence of opposite realities and the possible interchangeability of their fictions is precisely what I have attempted to bring out on all levels of the film, verbally as well as cinematically. If the only feeling the viewer retains of SHOOT is that of a negative void, then I think the film would just be falling flat on what it tries to do; it would be incapable of provoking the kind of vexed, as well as elated and excited reactions it has so far.

You mention the viewer quite often, and in another interview you once said that audience-making is the responsibility of the filmmaker. Can you talk about who your viewers are, what audience, or for whom are you making a film, if such a purpose exists?

There are many ways to approach this question and there are many languages that have been circulated in relation to the concept of audience. There is the dated notion of mass audience, which can no longer go unquestioned in today's critical context, because mass implies first and foremost active commodification, passive consumption. Mass production, in other words, is production by the fewest possible number, as Gandhi would say (*laughter*). And here you have this other notion of the audience, which refuses to let itself be degraded through standardization. For, as Lenin would also say, and I quote by memory, 'one does not bring art *down* to the people, one raises art *up* to the people.' Such an approach would avoid the levelling out of differences implied in the concept of the 'mass' which defines the people as an anonymous aggregate of individuals incapable of really thinking for themselves, incapable of being challenged in their frame of thought, and hence incapable of understanding the product if information is not packaged for effortless and immediate consumption. They are the ones who are easily 'spoken for' as being also smart consumers whose growing sophisticated needs require that the entertainment market produce yet faster goods and more effectual throwaways in the name of better service. Here, the problem is not that such a description of the audience is false, but that its reductive rationale reinforces the ideology in power.

The question 'for whom does one write?' or 'for whom does one make a film?' was extremely useful some thirty years ago, in the 60s. It has had its historical moment, as it was then linked to the compelling notion of 'engaged art'. Thanks to it, the demystification of the creative act has almost become an accepted fact: the writer or the artist is bound to look critically at the relations of production and can no longer indulge in the notion of 'pure creativity'. But thanks to it also, the notion of audience today has been pushed much further in its complexities, so that simply knowing for whom you make a film is no longer sufficient. Such a targeting of audience, which has the potential to change radically the way one writes or makes a film, often proves to be no more than a common marketing tool in the process of commodification. Hence, instead of talking about 'the audience', theorists would generally rather talk about 'the spectator' or 'the viewer'. Today also, many of us have come to realize that power relationships are not simply to be found in the evident locations of power—here, in the establishments that hold the means of production—but that they also circulate among and within ourselves because the way we write and make films is the way we position ourselves socially and politically. Form and content cannot be separated.

Furthermore, in the context of 'alternative', 'experimental' films, to know or *not* to know whom you are making a film for can both leave you trapped in a form of escapism: you declare that you don't care about audience; you are simply content with the circulation of your work among friends and a number of marginalized workers like yourself; and you continue to protect yourself by remaining safely within identified limits. Whereas I think each film one makes is a bottle thrown into the sea. The fact that you always work on the very limits of the known and unknown audiences, you are bound to modify these limits whose demarcation changes each time and remains unpredictable to you. This is the context in which I said that the filmmaker is responsible for building his or her audience.

So of importance today, is to make a film in which the viewer—whether visually present or not—is inscribed in the way the film is scripted and shot. Through a number of creative strategies, this process is made visible and audible to the audience who is thus solicited to interact and to retrace it in viewing the film. Anybody can make REASSEMBLAGE for example. The part that cannot be imitated, taught, or repeated is the relationship one develops with the tools that define one's activities and oneself as filmmaker. That part is irreducible and unique to each worker, but the part that could be opened up to the viewer is the 'unsutured' process of meaning production. With this, we'll need to ask what accessibility means: a work in which the creative process is offered to the viewer? Or a work in which high production values see to it that the packaging of information and of fiction stories remain mystifying to the non-connoisseur audience—many of whom still believe that you have to hold several millions in your hand in order to make a feature of real appeal to the wide number?

You've answered on many levels but your last point draws attention to the state of independent art and experimental film here in the US. Could you comment on your experience with or interactions with those who try to categorize your work as documentary, as ethnographic, as avant-garde feminist, as independent? Could you talk about the process of independent filmmaking instead of more mainstream films?

Independent filmmaking for me is not simply a question of producing so-called 'low-budget' films outside the funding networks of Hollywood. It has more to do with a radical difference in understanding filmmaking. Here, once a film is completed, you're not really done with it, rather, you're starting another journey with it. You cannot focus solely on the creative process and leave the responsibilities of fundraising and distribution to someone else (even if you work with a producer and a distributor). You are as much involved in the pre- and the post- than in the production stage itself. Once your film is released you may have to travel with it and the direct contact you have with the public does impact the way you'll be making your next film. Not at all in the sense that you serve the needs of the audience, which is what the mainstream has always claimed to do, but rather in the sense of a mutual challenge: you challenge each other in your assumptions and expectations. So for example, the fact that a number of viewers react negatively to certain choices you have made or to the direction you have taken does not necessarily lead you to renounce them for the next time. On the contrary, precisely because of such reactions you may want to persist and come back to them yet in different ways.

In my case, the contact also allows me to live out the demystification of *intention* in filmmaking. With the kind of interaction I solicit from the viewers—asking each of them actually to put together 'their own film' from the film they have seen—the filmmaker's intention cannot account for all the readings that they have mediated to their realities. Thereby, the process of independent filmmaking entails a different relationship of creating and receiving, hence of production and exhibition. Since it is no easy task to build one's audiences, the process remains a constant struggle, albeit one which I am quite happy to carry on. Viewers also need to assume their responsibilities by looking critically at the representative place from which they voice their opinions on the film. Ironically enough, those who inquire about the audience of my films often seem to think that they and their immediate peers are the only people who get to see the film and can understand it. What their questions say in essence is: We are your audience. Is that all that you have as an audience? (*laughter*). If that is the case, then I think that none of us independent filmmakers would continue to make films. For me, interacting with the viewers of our films is part of independent filmmaking. The more acutely we feel the changes in our audiences, the more it demands from us as filmmakers. Therefore, while our close involvement in the processes of fundraising and distribution often proves to be frustrating, we also realize that this mutual challenge between the work and the film public, or between the creative gesture and the cinematic apparatus is precisely what keeps independent filmmaking alive.

17 White Privilege and Looking Relations: Race and Gender in Feminist Film Theory

Jane Gaines*

This article was originally conceived as a challenge to the paradigm which dominated feminist film theory in Britain and the US for roughly ten years. Because that paradigm, significantly introduced and developed in *Screen*, has since lost its exclusive position in the field, some of the heatedness of the original essay no longer seems necessary. And yet, since the juxtaposition of psychoanalytic theory and the image of the black woman in history still produces friction, some of the contention is necessarily retained in what follows. Fortunately, laments about the dearth of theoretical work by black feminists are already starting to sound dated, since in the US we have begun to see the publication of important literary criticism, coinciding with a major effort to reprint the neglected writings of nineteenth-century Afro-American women.[1] Other feminist film critics, in the year that this article was first delivered as a talk, remarked about the gap in the field produced by the absence of a perspective on women of colour.[2] Although there is somewhat more work being done on Asian, Hispanic and Afro-American women, and we are beginning to hear from black feminists who have started to work in film and television studies, feminist film theory itself has not, as yet, shown signs of the anticipated transformation.[3]

What I want to do here is to show how a theory of the text and its spectator, based on the psychoanalytic concept of sexual difference, is unequipped to deal with a film which is about racial difference and sexuality. The Diana Ross star-vehicle *Mahogany* (directed by Berry Gordy, 1975) immediately suggests a psychoanalytic approach because the narrative is organised around the connections between voyeurism and photographic acts, and because it exemplifies the classical cinema

* Jane Gaines, 'White Privilege and Looking Relations: Race and Gender in Feminist Film Theory' from *Screen*, Vol. 29, no 4 (1988), reprinted by permission of John Logie Baird Centre and the author.

which has been so fully theorised in Lacanian terms. But as I will argue, the psychoanalytic model works to block out considerations which assume a different configuration, so that, for instance, the Freudian-Lacanian scenario can eclipse the scenario of race–gender relations in Afro-American history, since the two accounts of sexuality are fundamentally incongruous. The danger here is that when we use a psychoanalytic model to explain black family relations, we force an erroneous universalisation and inadvertently reaffirm white middle-class norms.

By taking gender as its starting point in the analysis of oppression, feminist theory helps to reinforce white middle-class values, and to the extent that it works to keep women from seeing other structures of oppression, it functions ideologically. In this regard, bell hooks criticises a feminism which seems unable to think of women's oppression in terms other than gender:

> Feminist analyses of woman's lot tend to focus exclusively on gender and do not provide a solid foundation on which to construct feminist theory. They reflect the dominant tendency in Western patriarchal minds to mystify women's reality by insisting that gender is the sole determinant of woman's fate.[4]

Gender analysis rather exclusively illuminates the condition of white middle-class women, hooks says, and its centrality in feminist theory suggests that those women who have constructed this theory have been ignorant of the way women in different racial groups and social classes *experience* oppression. Many of us would not dispute this. But exactly how should the feminist who does not want to be racist in her work respond to this criticism? In one of the few considerations of this delicate dilemma, Marilyn Frye, in her essay 'On Being White', urges us *not* to do what middle-class feminists have historically done: to assume responsibility for everyone. To take it upon oneself to rewrite feminist theory so that it encompasses our differences is another exercise of racial privilege, she says, and therefore all that one can do with conscience, is to undertake the study of our own 'determined ignorance'.[5] One can begin to learn about the people whose history cannot be imagined from a position of privilege. My argument then takes two different turns. One of these juxtaposes black feminist theory with those aspects of feminist theory which have a tendency to function as normative; the other juxtaposes people's history with the discourses of representation, in order to ask the even more difficult question of how we can grasp the interacting levels of the social formation.

I

I recall from graduate school in the late 1970s the voice of feminist film theory as I first heard it—firm in its insistence on attention to cinematic language, and strict in its prohibition against comparisons between actuality and text. This voice of feminist film theory I always heard as a British-accented female voice, and over and over again I heard it reminding me that feminists could only analyse the ideological through its encoding in the conventions of editing and the mechanics of the motion-picture machine. This was the point in the history of the field when there were only two texts which had earned the distinction of 'feminist film theory' (as opposed to criticism), and in the US we were very aware that they came out of British Marxism: Claire Johnston's 'Women's Cinema as Counter-Cinema', and Laura Mulvey's 'Visual Pleasure and Narrative Cinema', which has probably been reprinted more times than any other academic essay in English in a ten-year time span.[6] In retrospect, we understand that the apparent intransigence of the theory of cinema as patriarchal discourse, as it developed out of these essays, is the legacy of the Althusserian theory of the subject. While it is clear from the point of view of Marxist feminism that the psychoanalytic version of the construction of the subject was a welcome supplement to classical Marxism, what was gained with a theory of the social individual was at the cost of losing the theory of social antagonism.

The ramifications for feminism would be different on the American side of the Atlantic. The theory of the subject as constituted in language, imported into US academic circles, could swell to the point where it seemed to be able to account for all oppression, expression and socio-sexual functioning in history. The enormously complicated developments through which European Marxists saw a need for enlarging the capacity of the theory of ideology were lost in translation, so that in the US what we heard was that 'Representation reproduces the patriarchal order'. Stuart Hall has described this tendency, in both discourse theory and Lacanian psychoanalysis, as the opposite of the economism which these theories intended to modify – 'a reduction upward rather than downward'. What transpires in such movements to correct economism is that, as he says, 'the metaphor of x operates like y is reduced to x = y.'[7]

This would happen with a vengeance in the US university scene where the theory of classical cinema as patriarchal discourse would appear at first quite alone and recently divorced from larger Marxist debates. On campuses where students could not hope to acquire any background in political economy, a film course introduction to the analysis of subjectivity and cinema might well be the only exposure to Marxist theory in an entire college career. We must now wonder, however, if the relatively easy assimilation of *Screen* theory into studies in the US had something to do with the way the radical potential of the theory was quieted through the very psychoanalytic terminology it employed. We further need to consider the warm reception given to high feminist film theory in women's studies circles in terms of the new respectability of academic feminism in the US, surely signalled by Peter Brooks' statement that 'Anyone worth his salt in literary criticism today has to become something of a feminist.'[8]

Within film and television studies in the US, the last three years have seen a break with the theory of representation which, it appears, had gripped us for so long. The new feminist strategies which engage with, modify or abandon the stubborn notion that we are simultaneously positioned in language and ideology, are too numerous to detail. In the US, as in Britain, one of the most influential challenges to this theory posed the question of our reconstitution at different historical moments. How could the formative moment of one's entry into language be the one condition overriding all other determining conditions of social existence? This question would become especially pertinent as theoretical interest shifted from the text which produced subjects to the subjects who produced texts; the 'real historical subject' became the escape route through which theorists abandoned a text weighted down with impossible expectations.

II

In the US, lesbian feminists raised the first objections to the way in which film theory explained the operation of the classic realist text in terms of tensions between masculinity and femininity. The understanding of spectatorial pleasure in classical cinema as inherently male drew an especially sharp response from critics who argued that this theory cancelled the lesbian spectator whose viewing pleasure could never be construed as anything like male voyeurism. Positing a lesbian spectator would significantly change the trajectory of the gaze. It might even lead us to see how the eroticised star body might be not just the object, but what I would term the visual objective of another female gaze within the film's diegesis—a gaze with which the viewer might identify; following this argument, Marilyn Monroe and Jane Russell in *Gentlemen Prefer Blondes* are 'only for each other's eyes'.[9] Two influential studies building on the lesbian reading of *Gentlemen Prefer Blondes* suggested that the lesbian reception of *Personal Best* held a key to challenging the account of cinema as producing patriarchal subject positions—since lesbian viewers, at least, were subverting dominant meanings and confounding textual structures.[10]

Consistently, lesbians have charged that cultural theory posed in psychoanalytic terms is unable to conceive of desire or explain pleasure without reference to the binary oppositions male/female. This is the function of what Monique Wittig calls the heterosexual assumption, or the 'straight mind', that unacknowledged structure not only built into Lacanian psychoanalysis, but underlying the basic divisions of Western culture; organising all knowledge, yet escaping any close examination.[11] Male/female is a powerful, but sometimes blinding construct. And it is difficult to see that the paradigm which we embraced so quickly in our first lessons in feminism may have been standing in the way of our further education.

The male/female opposition, seemingly so fundamental to feminism, may actually lock us into modes of analysis which will continually misinterpret the position of many women. Thus it is that women of colour, like lesbians, an afterthought in feminist analysis, remain unassimilated by this problematic. Feminist anthologies consistently include articles on black female and lesbian perspectives as illustration of the liberality and inclusiveness of feminism; however, the very concept of 'different perspectives', while validating distinctness and maintaining woman as common denominator, still places the categories of race and sexual preference in theoretical limbo. Our political etiquette is correct, but our theory is not so perfect.

In Marxist feminist analysis, the factors of race and sexual preference have remained loose ends; as categories of oppression they fit somewhat awkwardly into a model based on class relations in capitalist society. Although some gay historians see a relationship between the rise of capitalism and the creation of the social homosexual, only with a very generous notion of sexual hierarchies—such as the one Gayle Rubin has suggested—can sexual oppression (as distinct from gender oppression) be located within a framework based on class.[12] Race has folded into Marxist models more neatly than sexual preference, but the orthodox formulation which understands racial conflict as class struggle, is still unsatisfactory to Marxist feminists who want to know exactly how gender intersects with race. The oppression of *women* of colour remains incompletely grasped by the classical Marxist paradigm.

Just as the Marxist model based on class has obscured the function of gender, the feminist model based on the male/female division under patriarchy has obscured the function of race. The dominant feminist paradigm actually encourages us not to think in terms of any oppression other than male dominance and female subordination. Thus it is that feminists and lesbians, says Barbara Smith, seem '. . . blinded to the implications of any womanhood that is not white womanhood . . .'.[13] For purposes of analysis, black feminists agree that class is as significant as race; however, if these feminists hesitate to emphasise gender as a factor, it is in deference to the way black women describe their experience, for it is clear that Afro-American women have historically formulated identity and political allegiance in terms of race rather than gender or class.[14] Feminism, however, seems not to have heard the statements of women of colour who say that they experience oppression first in relation to race rather than gender, and that for them exploitation can be personified by a white female.[15] Even more difficult for feminist theory to digest is black female identification with the black male. On this point, black feminists diverge from white feminists, in repeatedly reminding us that they do not necessarily see the black male as patriarchal antagonist, but feel instead that their racial oppression is 'shared' with men.[16] In the most comprehensive analysis of all, black lesbian feminists have described race, class and gender oppression as an 'interlocking' synthesis in the lives of black women.[17]

The point here is not to rank the structures of oppression in a way that implies the need for black women to choose between solidarity with men or solidarity with women, between race or gender as the basis for a political strategy. At issue is the question of the fundamental antagonism which has been so relevant for Marxist feminist theory. Where we have foregrounded one antagonism in our analysis, we have misunderstood another, and this is most dramatically illustrated in applying the notion of patriarchy. Feminists have not been absolutely certain what they mean by patriarchy: alternately it has referred to either father-right or domination of women; but what is consistent about the use of the concept is the rigidity of the structure it describes.[18] Patriarchy is incompatible with Marxism where it is used trans-historically without qualification, and where it becomes the source from which all other oppressions are tributary, as in the radical feminist theory of patriarchal order, which sees oppression in all forms and through all ages as derived from the male/female division.[19] This deterministic model, which Sheila Rowbotham says functions like a 'feminist base-superstructure', has the disadvantage of leaving us with no sense of movement, or no idea of how women have acted to change their condition, especially in comparison with the fluidity of the Marxist conception of class.[20]

The radical feminist notion of absolute patriarchy has also one-sidedly portrayed the oppression of women through an analogy with slavery, and since this theory has identified woman as man's savage or repressed Other it competes with theories of racial difference which understand the black as the 'unassimilable Other'.[21] Finally, the notion of patriarchy is most obtuse when it disregards the position white women occupy over black men as well as black women.[22] In order to rectify this tendency in feminism, black feminists refer to 'racial patriarchy', which is based on an analysis of the white patriarch/master in US history, and his dominance over the black male as well as the black female.[23]

III

I want now to reconsider the connotations of sexual looking, with reference to a film in which racial difference structures a hierarchy of access to the female image. In *Mahogany*, her follow-up to *Lady Sings The Blues*, Diana Ross plays an aspiring fashion designer who dreams of pulling herself up and out of her Chicago South Side neighbourhood by means of a high-powered career. During the day, Tracy Chambers is assistant to the modelling supervisor for a large department store. At night she attends design school, where the instructor reprimands her for sketching a cocktail dress instead of completing the assignment, the first suggestion of the exotic irrelevance of her fantasy career. She loses her job, but the famous fashion photographer Sean McEvoy (Anthony Perkins) discovers her as a model and whisks her off to Rome. There, Tracy finally realises her ambition to become a designer, when a wealthy Italian admirer gives her a business of her own. After the grand show unveiling her first collection of clothes, she returns to Chicago and is reunited with community organiser Brian Walker (Billy Dee Williams), whose political career is a counterpoint to Tracy's modelling career.

With its long fashion photography montage sequences temporarily interrupting the narrative, *Mahogany* invites a reading based on the alternation between narrative and woman-as-spectacle as theorised by Laura Mulvey in 'Visual Pleasure and Narrative Cinema'. To the allure of pure spectacle these sequences add the fascination of masquerade and transformation. Effected with wigs and make-up colours, the transformations are a play on and against 'darkness'; Diana Ross is a high-tech Egyptian queen, a pale mediaeval princess, a turbaned Asiatic, a body-painted blue nymph. As her body colour is powdered over or washed out in bright light, and as her long-haired wigs blow around her face, she becomes suddenly 'white'.

Contemporary motion pictures never seem to exhaust the narrative possibilities associated with the camera-as-deadly-weapon metaphor; *Mahogany* adds to this the sadomasochistic connotations of high fashion photography with reference to the mid-seventies work of Guy Bourdin and Helmut Newton, linked to the tradition of 'attraction by shock'.[24] The montage sequences chronicling Tracy's career, from perfume ads to high fashion magazine covers, equate the photographic act with humiliation and violation. Camera zoom and freeze-frame effects translate directly into aggression, as in the sequence in which Sean pushes Tracy into a fountain and her dripping image solidifies into an Italian Revlon advertisement. Finally, the motif of stopping-the-action-as-aggression is equated with the supreme violation: attempted murder. Pressing his favourite model to her expressive limits, Sean drives her off an expressway ramp. Since this brutality escalates after the scene in which he fails with Tracy in bed, the film represents her punishment as a direct consequence of his impotence.

With its classic castration threat scenario, its connection between voyeurism and sadism, and its reference to fetishisation—as seen in Sean's photographic shrine to the models he has abused—*Mahogany* is the perfect complement to a psychoanalytic analysis of classical Hollywood's visual pleasure. The film further provides material for such an analysis by producing its own 'proof' that there is only an incremental difference between voyeurism (fashion photography) and sadism (murder). The black and white photographic blow-ups of Tracy salvaged from the death car seem undeniable evidence of the fine line between looking and killing, or, held at another angle, between advertising imagery and pornography.

This, then, is to suggest the kind of evidence in the film which would support an analysis of it as patriarchal discourse, in its use of the female image as fetish to assuage castration anxiety, and through its rich offering of views to please the male spectator. There's even an inescapable suggestion of voyeurism as pathology, since the gaze is that of the actor whose star persona is fatally haunted by the protagonist of *Psycho.* To explain the ideological function of the film in terms of the construction of male pleasure, however, is to 'aid and abet' the film's other ideological project. In following the line of analysis I have outlined, one is apt to step into an ideological signifying trap set up by the chain of meanings that lead away from seeing the film in terms of racial conflict. Because there are so many connotative paths—photographer exploits model, madman assaults woman, voyeur attempts murder—we may not immediately see white man as aggressor against black woman. Other strategies encourage the viewer to forget or not notice racial issues. For instance, the narrative removes Tracy from racially polarised Chicago to Rome, where the brown Afro-American woman with Caucasian features is added to the collection of a photographer who names his subjects after prized objects or their qualities. Losing her black community identity, Tracy becomes Mahogany, acquiring the darkness, richness and value the name connotes; that is, her blackness becomes commodified.

Mahogany functions ideologically for black viewers in the traditional Marxist sense, that is, in the way the film obscures the class nature of social antagonisms. This has certain implications for working-class black viewers, who would gain most from seeing the relationship between race, gender and class oppression. Further, *Mahogany* has the same trouble with representing black femaleness that the wider culture has had historically; a black female is either all woman and tinted black, or mostly black and scarcely woman. These two expectations correspond with the two worlds and two struggles which structure the film: the struggle over the sexual objectification of Tracy's body in the face of commercial exploitation, and the struggle of the black community in the face of class exploitation. But the film identifies this antagonism as the hostility between fashion and politics, embodied respectively by Tracy and Brian, and it is through them that it organises conflict and, eventually, reconciliation. Intensifying this conflict between characters, the film contrasts 'politics' and 'fashion' in one daring homage to the aesthetic of 'attraction by shock'; Sean arranges his models symmetrically on the back stairwell of a run-down Chicago apartment building and uses the confused tenants and street people as props. Flamboyant excess, the residue of capital, is juxtaposed with a kind of dumbfounded poverty. For a moment, the scene figures the synthesis of gender, class and race, but the political glimpse is fleeting. Forced together as a consequence of the avant-garde's socially irresponsible quest for a new outrage, the political antagonisms are suspended—temporarily immobilised as the subjects pose.

The connection between gender, class and race oppression is also denied as the ghetto photography session's analogy between commercial exploitation and race/class exploitation merely registers on the screen as visual incongruity. Visual discrepancy, which, as I have argued, is used for aesthetic effect, also makes it difficult to grasp the confluence of race, class and gender oppression in the image of Tracy Chambers. The character's class background magically becomes decor in the film—it neither radicalises her nor drags her down: instead it sets her off. Diana Ross is alternately weighed down by the glamour iconography of commercial modelling or stripped to a black body. But the *haute couture* iconography ultimately dominates the film. Since race is decorative and class does not reveal itself to the eye, Tracy can only be seen as exploited in terms of her role as a model.

If the film plays down race, it does not do so just to accommodate white audiences. In worshipping the success of the black cult star and combining this with Diana Ross's own dream-come-true—a chance to design all of the costumes in her own film *Mahogany* hawks the philosophy of black enterprise and social aspiration. Here it does not matter where you come from, what you should be asking yourself, in the words of the theme song, is 'Where are you going, do you know?' Race, then, should be seen as any other obstacle—to be transcended through diligent work and dedication to a goal. Supporting the film's self-help philosophy is the related story of Diana Ross's 'discovery' as a skinny teenager singing in a Baptist Church in Detroit. With *Mahogany*, Motown president and founder Berry Gordy (who fired Tony Richardson and took over the film's direction) helps Diana Ross to make something of herself again, just as he helped so many aspiring recording artists, by coaching them in money management and social decorum in his talent school.[25]

The phenomenon of Motown Industries is less a comment on the popularity of the self-help philosophy than a verification of the discrepancy between the opportunity formula and the social existence of black Americans. Ironically, black capitalism's one big success thrives on the impossibility of black enterprise: soul entertainment as compensation and release sells because capitalism cannot deliver well-being to all.[26] Black music and performance, despite the homogenisation of the original forms, represents a utopian aspiration for black Americans, as well as for white suburbanites. Simon Frith describes the need supplied by rock fantasy:

> Black music had a radical, rebellious edge: it carried a sense of possibility denied in the labor market; it suggested a comradeship, a sensuality, a grace and joy and energy lacking in work . . . the power of rock fantasy rests, precisely on utopianism.[27]

Given that popular culture can accommodate the possibility of both containment and resistance in what Stuart Hall calls its 'double movement', I want to turn to the ways *Mahogany* can be seen to move in the other direction.[28]

Racial conflict looms or recedes in this film rather like the perceptual trick in which, depending on the angle of view, one swirling pattern or the other pops out at the viewer. Some perceptual ambiguity, for instance, is built into the confrontation between black and white, as in the scene in which Sean lures Brian into a struggle over an unloaded weapon. The outcome, in which Sean, characterised as a harmless eccentric, manipulates Brian into pulling the trigger, could be read as confirming the racist conception that blacks who possess street reflexes are murderous aggressors. *Ebony* magazine, the black equivalent of *Life* magazine in the US, however, features a promotional still of the scene (representing Brian holding a gun over Sean), with a caption describing how Brian is tricked but still wins the fight.[29] Just as viewers choose the winners of such ambiguous conflicts, they may also choose to inhabit 'looking' structures. The studies of lesbian readership already cited show that subcultural groups can interpret popular forms to their advantage, even without invitation from the text. Certainly more work needs to be done with the positioning of the audience around the category of race, considering, for instance, the social prohibitions against the black man's sexual glance, the interracial intermingling of male 'looks', and other visual taboos related to sanctions against interracial sexuality, but these are beyond the scope of this article.

One of the original tenets of contemporary feminist film theory—that the (male) spectator possesses the female indirectly through the eyes of the male protagonist (his screen surrogate)—is problematised here by the less privileged black male gaze. Racial hierarchies of access to the female image also relate to other scenarios which are unknown by psychoanalytic categories. Considering the racial categories which psychoanalysis does not recognise, then, we see that the white male photographer monopolises the classic patriarchal look controlling the view of the female body, and that the black male protagonist's look is either repudiated or frustrated. The sumptuous image of Diana Ross is made available to the spectator via the white male character (Sean) but *not* through the look of the black male character (Brian). In the sequence in which Tracy and Brian first meet outside her apartment building, his 'look' is renounced. In each of the three shots of Tracy from Brian's point of view, she turns from him, walking out of his sight and away from the sound of his voice as he shouts at her through a megaphone. The relationship between the male and female protagonist is negotiated around Brian's bullhorn, emblem of his charismatic black leadership, through which he tries to reach both the black woman and his constituents. Both visual and audio control is thus denied the black male, and the failure of his voice is consistently associated with Tracy's publicity image in the white world. The discovery by Brian's aides of the Mahogany advertisement for Revlon in *Newsweek* coincides with the report that the Gallup polls show the black candidate trailing in the election. Later, the film cuts from the *Harper's Bazaar* cover featuring Mahogany to Brian's limping campaign where the sound of his voice magnified through a microphone is intermittently drowned out by a passing train as he makes his futile pitch to white factory workers. The manifest goal of the film, the reconciliation of the black heterosexual couple, is thwarted by the commercial appropriation of her image, but, in addition, its highly-mediated form threatens the black political struggle.

IV

For black feminists, history seems to be the key to understanding black female sexuality. 'The construction of the sexual self of the Afro-American woman,' says Rennie Simson, 'has its roots in the days of slavery.'[30] Looking at this construction over time reveals a pattern of patriarchal phases and female sexual adjustments that has no equivalent in the history of white women in the US. In the first phase, characterised by the dominance of the white master during the period of slavery, black men and women were equal by default. To have allowed the black male any power over the black woman would have threatened the power balance of the slave system. Thus, as Angela Davis explains social control in the slave community, 'The man slave could not be the unquestioned superior within the "family" or community, for there was no such thing as the "family" provided among the Slaves.'[31] The legacy of this phase has involved both the rejection of the pedestal the white female has occupied, as well as the heritage of retaliation against white male abuse. If the strategy for racial survival was resistance during the first phase, it was accommodation during the next. During Reconstruction, the black family, modelled after the white bourgeois household, was constituted defensively in an effort to preserve the race.[32] Black women yielded to their men in deference to a tradition that promised respectability and safety. Re-evaluating this history, black feminists point out that, during Reconstruction, the black male, following the example of the white patriarch, 'learned' to dominate. Poet Audre Lorde, for instance, sees sexism in black communities as not original to them, but as a plague that has struck.[33] One of the most telling manifestations of the difference between the operation of patriarchy in the lives of black as opposed to white women is the way this is worked out *at the level of language* in the formal conventions organising the short stories and novels of Afro-American women. Particularly in the work of early writers such as Harriet E. Wilson, Frances E. W. Harper, and Pauline Hopkins, the black father is completely missing and, as Hazel Carby says, 'The absent space in fiction by black women confirms this denial of patriarcal power to black men'[34]. The position consistently taken by black feminists, that patriarchy was originally foreign to the Afro-American community and was introduced into it historically, then, represents a significant break with feminist theories which see patriarchal power invested equally in all men throughout history, and patriarchal form as colour blind.

Black history also adds another dimension to the concept of 'rape', which has emerged as the favoured metaphor for defining women's jeopardy in the second wave of feminism, replacing 'prostitution', which articulated women's fears in the nineteenth century.[35] The charge of rape, conjuring up a historical connection with lynching, is inextricably connected in North American history with the myth of the black man as archetypal rapist. We can never again use the concept of 'rape' quite so abstractly in its generic or metaphorical sense, after we have considered the way 'white' or 'black' has historically modified, or shall we say 'inflamed', the act and the term. During slavery, white male abuse of black women was a symbolic blow to black manhood, understood as rape only within the black community. With the increase in the sexual violation of black women during Reconstruction, the act of rape began to reveal its fuller political implications.

After emancipation, the rape of black women was a 'message' to black men, which, according to one historian, could be seen as 'a reaction to the effort of the freedman to assume the role of patriarch, able to provide for and protect his family'.[36] Simultaneous with the actual violation of black women, the empty charge of rape hurled at the black man clouded the real issue of black (male) enfranchisement, by creating a smokescreen through the incendiary issue of interracial sexuality. Writing at the turn of the century, black novelist Pauline Hopkins unmasked the alibis for lynching in *Contending Forces:*

> Lynching was instituted to crush the manhood of the enfranchised black. Rape is the crime which appeals most strongly to the heart of the home life . . . The men who created the mulatto race, who recruit its ranks year after year by the very means which they invoked lynch law to suppress, bewailing the sorrows of violated womanhood![37]

Here is a sexual scenario to rival the Oedipal myth; the black woman sexually violated by the white man, but the fact of her rape repressed and displaced on to the virginal white woman, and thus used symbolically as the justification for the actual castration of the black man. It is against this historical scenario that we should place the symbolic castration that is the penalty of sexual looking—a penalty that must surely diminish in comparison with the very real threat of actual castration that such looking would once have carried with it.

V

Quite simply, then, there are structures relevant to any interpretation of *Mahogany* which override the patriarchal scenario feminists have theorised as formally determining. From Afro-American history, we should recall the white male's appropriation of the black woman's body which weakened the black male and undermined the community. From Afro-American literature, we should also consider the scenario of the talented and beautiful mulatta who 'passes' in white culture, but decides to return to black society.[38] The mulatta suggests the rich possibilities of a theory of black female representation which takes account of 'passing' as an eroticising alternation and a peculiar play on difference, as well as a sign of the double consciousness of those women who can be seen as either black or white at the same time as they may see themselves as both races at once. Further, we need to reconsider the woman's picture narrative convention—the career renounced in favour of the man—in the context of black history. Tracy's choice recapitulates black aspiration and the white middle-class model which equates stable family life with respectability, but her decision is significantly different from the white heroine's capitulation since it favours black community cooperation over acceptance by white society. Finally, one of the most difficult questions raised by Afro-American history and literature has to do with interracial hetero-sexuality and sexual 'looking'. *Mahogany* suggests that, since a black male character is not allowed the position of control occupied by a white male character, race could be a factor in the construction of cinematic language. More work on looking and racial taboos might determine whether or not mainstream cinema can offer the male spectator the pleasure of looking at a white female character via the gaze of a black male character. Framing the question of male privilege and viewing pleasure as the 'right to look' may help us to rethink film theory along more materialist lines, considering, for instance, how some groups have historically had the licence to 'look' openly while other groups have 'looked' illicitly.[39] In other words, does the psychoanalytic model allow us to consider the prohibitions against homosexuality and miscegenation?

Feminists who use psychoanalytic theory have been careful to point out that 'looking' positions do not correlate with social groups, and that ideological positioning is placement in a representational system which has no one-to-one correspondence with social experience. This, of course, keeps the levels of the social ensemble hopelessly separate. While I would not want to argue that form is ideologically neutral, I would suggest that we have overemphasised the ideological function of 'signifying practice' at the expense of considering other ideological implications of the conflicting meanings in the text. Or, as Terry Lovell puts it:

> . . . while interpretation depends on analysis of the work's signifying practice, assessment of its meanings from the point of view of its validity, or of its ideology, depends on comparison between those structures of meaning and their object of reference, through the mediation of another type of discourse.[40]

The impetus behind Marxist criticism, whether we want to admit it or not, is to make comparisons between social reality as we live it and ideology as it does not correspond to that reality. This we attempt to do knowing full well (having learned from post-structuralism), the futility of looking for real relations which are completely outside ideology in either the present or in history. And we probably need to turn this critique on the emerging notion of the 'days of slavery' as the key to black female sexuality, in order to avoid the temptation of using it as some searing truth which, held up to the bloated discourses of patriarchy, had the power to make them finally groan and shrivel.

Thus, while I am still willing to argue, as I did in the earlier version of this article, that we can see the *Mahogany* narrative as a metaphor of the search for black female sexuality, I see something else in hindsight. I would describe this as the temptation in an emerging black feminist criticism, much like an earlier tendency in lesbian criticism, to place sexuality safely out of patriarchal bounds by declaring it outside culture, by furtively hiding it in subcultural enclaves where it can remain 'its essential self', protected from the meaning-making mainstream culture. *Mahogany*, then, is finally about the mythical existence of something elusive yet potent. We know it through what white men do to secure it, and what black men are without it. It is the ultimate object of desire to the photographer-connoisseur of women who dies trying to record its 'trace' on film. It is known by degree—whatever is most wild and enigmatic, whatever cannot be conquered or subdued—the last frontier of female sexuality. Although it is undetectable to the advertising men who can only analyse physical attributes, it is immediately perceptible to a lesbian (Gavina herself, the owner of the Italian advertising agency), who uses it to promote the most intangible and subjective of commodities—perfume.[41] Contrary to the suggestion that black female sexuality might still remain in excess of culture, and hence unfathomed and uncodified, it is worked over again and again in mainstream culture because of its apparent elusiveness, and in this context it is rather like bottled scent which is often thought to convey its essence to everyone but the person wearing it.

To return to my main point, as feminists have theorised women's sexuality, they have universalised from the particular experience of white women, thus effecting what Hortense Spillers has called a 'deadly metonymy'.[42] While white feminists theorise the female image in terms of objectification, fetishisation and symbolic absence, their black counterparts describe the body as the site of symbolic resistance and the 'paradox of non-being', a reference to the period in Afro-American history when black female did not signify 'woman'.[43] What strikes me still in this comparison is the stubbornness of the terms of feminist discourse analysis which has not been able to deal, for instance, with what it has meant historically to be designated as not-human, and how black women, whose bodies were legally not their own, fought against treatment based on this determination. Further, feminist analysis of culture as patriarchal cannot conceive of any connection between the female image and class or racial exploitation which includes the male. Historically, black men and women, although not equally endangered, have been simultaneously implicated in incidents of interracial brutality. During two different periods of Afro-American history, sexual assault, '. . . symbolic of the effort to conquer the resistance the black woman could unloose', was a warning to the entire black community.[44] If, as feminists have argued, women's sexuality evokes an unconscious terror in men, then black women's sexuality represents a special threat to white patriarchy; the possibility of its eruption stands for the aspirations of the black race as a whole.

My frustration with the feminist voice that insists on change *at the level of language* is that this position can only deal with the historical situation described above by turning it into discourse, and even as I write this, acutely aware as I am of the theoretical prohibitions against mixing representational issues with historical ones, I feel the pressure to transpose people's struggles into more discursively manageable terms. However, a theory of ideology which separates the levels of the social formation, in such a way that it is not only inappropriate but theoretically impossible to introduce the category of history into the analysis, cannot be justified with Marxism. This has been argued elsewhere by others, among them Stuart Hall, who finds the 'universalist tendency' found in both Freud and Lacan responsible for this impossibility. The incompatibility between Marxism and psychoanalytic theory is insurmountable at this time, he argues, because 'the concepts elaborated by Freud (and reworked by Lacan) cannot, *in their in-general and universalist form*, enter the theoretical space of historical materialism'.[45] In discussions within feminist film theory, it has often seemed the other way round—that historical materialism could not enter the space theorised by discourse analysis drawing on psychoanalytic concepts. Sealed off as it is (in theory), this analysis may not comprehend the category of the real historical subject, but its use will always have implications *for* that subject.

Notes

1. Mary Helen Washington, *Invented Lives: Narratives of Black Women, 1860–1960* (New York: Doubleday, 1987); Hazel Carby, *Reconstructing Womanhood: The Emergence of the Afro-American Woman Novelist* (New York: Oxford University Press, 1987); Valerie Smith, *Self-Discovery and Authority in Afro-American Narrative* (Cambridge, Mass.: Harvard University Press, 1987);

Henry Louis Gates, Jr (ed.), *The Schomburg Library of Nineteenth-Century Black Women Writers*, vols. 1–30 (New York: Oxford University Press, 1988).

2. Judith Mayne, 'Feminist Film Theory and Criticism', *Signs*, 11: 1 (Autumn 1985), 99; Teresa de Lauretis, 'Rethinking Women's Cinema: Aesthetics and Feminist Theory', *New German Critique*, 34 (Winter, 1985), reprinted in Teresa de Lauretis, *Technologies of Gender* (Bloomington: Indiana University Press, 1987), 138–139.
3. For an example of the new work in film and television by black feminist critics, see Jacqueline Bobo, '"The Color Purple": Black Women as Cultural Readers', and Alile Sharon Larkin, 'Black Women Filmmakers Defining Ourselves: Feminism in Our Own Voice', in Diedre Pribram (ed.), *Female Spectators: Looking at Film and Television* (London and New York: Verso, 1988).
4. bell hooks, *Feminist Theory: From Margin to Center* (Boston: South End Press, 1984), 12.
5. Marilyn Frye, *The Politics of Reality* (Trumansburg, New York: The Crossing Press, 1984), 113, 118.
6. Claire Johnston, 'Women's Cinema as Counter-Cinema', in Claire Johnston (ed.), *Notes on Women's Cinema* (London: Society for Education in Film and Television, 1973), reprinted in Patricia Erens (ed.), *Sexual Stratagems* (New York: Horizon, 1979), Bill Nichols (ed.), *Movies and Methods* (Berkeley and Los Angeles, University of California Press, 1976); Laura Mulvey, 'Visual Pleasure and Narrative Cinema', *Screen*, 16: 3 (Autumn, 1975), reprinted in Karyn Kay and Gerald Peary (eds.), *Women and Cinema* (New York: Dutton, 1977); Tony Bennett, et al. (eds.), *Popular Film and Television* (London: British Film Institute, 1981); Brian Wallis (ed.), *Art After Modernism: Rethinking Representation* (New York: The New Museum of Contemporary Art, 1984); Gerald Mast and Marshall Cohen (eds.), *Film Theory and Criticism*, 3rd edn. (New York: Oxford, 1985); Bill Nichols (ed.), *Movies and Methods II* (University of California Press, 1985).
7. Stuart Hall, 'On Postmodernism and Articulation: An Interview', *Journal of Communication Inquiry* 10: 2 (Summer, 1986), 57.
8. As quoted in Annette Kolodny, 'Respectability is Eroding the Revolutionary Potential of Feminist Criticism', *The Chronicle of Higher Education*, 4 May 1988, A 52.
9. Lucie Arbuthnot and Gail Seneca, 'Pre-Text and Text in "Gentlemen Prefer Blondes"', *Film Reader*, 5 (Winter, 1981), 13–23.
10. Chris Straayer, '"Personal Best": Lesbian/Feminist Audience', *Jump Cut* 29 (February, 1984), 40–44; Elizabeth Ellsworth, 'Illicit Pleasures: Feminist Spectators and "Personal Best"', *Wide Angle*, 8: 2 (1986), 46–56.
11. Monique Wittig, 'The Straight Mind', *Feminist Issues*, Summer 1980, 107–111.
12. Gayle Rubin, 'Thinking Sex: Notes for a Radical Theory of the Politics of Sexuality', in Carol Vance (ed.), *Pleasure and Danger* (Boston and London: Routledge & Kegan Paul, 1984), 307.
13. Barbara Smith, 'Towards a Black Feminist Criticism', in Elaine Showalter (ed.), *The New Feminist Criticism* (New York: Pantheon, 1985), 169.
14. Bonnie Thornton Dill, 'Race, Class, and Gender: Prospects for an All-Inclusive Sisterhood', *Feminist Studies*, 9: (Spring, 1983), 134; for a slightly different version of this essay see '"On the Hem of Life": Race, Class, and the Prospects for Sisterhood', in Amy Swerdlow and Hanna Lessinger (eds.), *Class, Race, and*

Sex: *The Dynamics of Control* (Boston: Hall, 1983); Margaret Simons, 'Racism and Feminism: A Schism in the Sisterhood', *Feminist Studies*, 5: 2 (Summer, 1979), 392.

15. Adrienne Rich, in *On Lies, Secrets, and Silence* (New York: Norton, 1979), 302–303, notes that while blacks link their experience of racism with the white woman, this is still patriarchal racism working through her. It is possible, she says, that 'a black first grader, or that child's mother, or a black patient in a hospital, or a family on welfare, may experience racism most directly in the person of a white woman, who stands for those service professions through which white male supremacist society controls the mother, the child, the family, and all of us. It is *her* racism, yes, but a racism learned in the same patriarchal school which taught her that women are unimportant or unequal, not to be trusted with power, where she learned to mistrust and fear her own impulses for rebellion; to become an instrument.'
16. Gloria Joseph, 'The Incompatible Menage à Trois: Marxism, Feminism and Racism', in Lydia Sargent (ed.), *Women and Revolution* (Boston: South End Press, 1981), 96; The Combahee River Collective in 'Combahee River Collective Statement', in Barbara Smith (ed.), *Home Girls* (New York: Kitchen Table Press, 1983), 275, compares their alliance with black men with the negative identification white women have with white men: 'Our situation as Black people necessitates that we have solidarity around the fact of race, which white women of course do not need to have with white men, unless it is their negative solidarity as racial oppressors. We struggle together with Black men against racism, while we struggle with Black men about sexism.'
17. Combahee River Collective, ibid. 272.
18. Michèle Barrett, *Women's Oppression Today* (London: Verso, 1980), 15.
19. For a comparison between radical feminism, liberal feminism, Marxist and socialist feminism, see Alison Jaggar, *Feminist Politics and Human Nature* (Sussex: The Harvester Press, 1985).
20. Sheila Rowbotham, 'The Trouble with Patriarchy', in Raphael Samuel (ed.), *People's History and Socialist Theory* (London and Boston: Routledge & Kegan Paul, 1981), 365.
21. Frantz Fanon, *Black Skin, White Masks*, trans. Charles Lam Markmann (Paris: 1952; reprinted New York: Grove Press, 1967), 161.
22. Margaret Simons, 'Racism and Feminism', op. cit., 387.
23. Barbara Omolade, 'Hearts of Darkness', in Ann Snitow, Christine Stansell, and Sharon Thompson (eds.), *Powers of Desire* (New York: Monthly Review Press, 1983), 352.
24. Nancy Hall-Duncan, *The History of Fashion Photography* (New York: Alpine Books, 1979), 196.
25. Stephen Birmingham, *Certain People* (Boston and Toronto: Little, Brown, 1977), 262–263.
26. Manning Marable, in *How Capitalism Underdeveloped Black America* (Boston: South End Press, 1983), 157, lists Motown Industries as the largest grossing black-owned corporation in the US which did 64.8 million dollars in business in 1979.
27. Simon Frith, *Sound Effects* (New York: Pantheon, 1981), 264.
28. Stuart Hall, 'Notes on Deconstructing "The Popular"', in *People's History and Socialist Theory*, 228.

29. 'Spectacular New Film for Diana Ross: "Mahogany"', *Ebony*, October 1975, 146.
30. Rennie Simpson, 'The Afro-American Female: The Historical Context of the Construction of Sexual Identity', in *Powers of Desire*, op. cit., 230.
31. Angela Davis, 'The Black Woman's Role in the Community of Slaves', *The Black Scholar*, December 1971, 5–6.
32. Barbara Omolade, 'Hearts of Darkness', op. cit., 352.
33. Gloria Joseph, 'The Incompatible Ménage à Trois', op. cit., 99; Audre Lorde, *Sister Outsider* (Trumansburg, New York: The Crossing Press, 1984), 119, says: 'Because of the continuous battle against racial erasure that Black women and Black men share, some Black women still refuse to recognize that we are also oppressed as women, and that sexual hostility against Black women is practiced not only by the white racist society, but implemented within our Black communities as well. It is a disease striking the heart of Black nationhood, and silence will not make it disappear.'
34. Hazel Carby, '"On the Threshold of Woman's Era": Lynching, Empire, and Sexuality in Black Feminist Theory', *Critical Inquiry*, 12: 1 (Autumn, 1985), 276; Harriet E. Wilson, *Our Nig* (1859; reprinted New York: Random House, 1983); Frances E. W. Harper, *Iola Leroy, or Shadows Uplifted* (1892; reprinted New York: Oxford University Press, 1988); Pauline E. Hopkins, *Contending Forces* (1900; reprinted Oxford University Press, 1988).
35. Linda Gordon and Ellen DuBois, 'Seeking Ecstasy on the Battlefield: Danger and Pleasure in Nineteenth Century Feminist Sexual Thought', *Feminist Review*, 13 (Spring, 1983), 43.
36. Jacquelyn Dowd Hall, '"The Mind That Burns in Each Body": Women, Rape, and Racial Violence', in *Powers of Desire*, op. cit., 332: see also Jacquelyn Dowd Hall, *The Revolt Against Chivalry* (New York: Columbia University Press, 1979); Angela Davis, *Women, Race and Class* (New York: Random House, 1983), chapter 11.
37. As quoted in Hazel Carby, *Reconstructing Womanhood*, op. cit., 275.
38. See, for instance, Jessie Fauset, *There is Confusion* (New York: Boni and Liveright, 1924), and *Plum Bun* (1928; reprinted New York: Routledge & Kegan Paul, 1983); Nella Larsen, *Quicksand* (1928) and *Passing* (1929), reprinted New Brunswick: Rutgers University Press, 1986.
39. Fredric Jameson in 'Pleasure: A Political Issue', *Formations of Pleasure* (Boston and London: Routledge & Kegan Paul, 1983), 7, interprets Mulvey's connection between viewing pleasure and male power as the conferral of a 'right to look'. He does not take this further, but I find the term suggestive and at the same time potentially volatile.
40. Terry Lovell, *Pictures of Reality* (London: British Film Institute, 1980), 90.
41. Richard Dyer, 'Mahogany', in Charlotte Brunsdon (ed.), *Films for Women* (London: British Film Institute, 1986), 135, suggested this first about Gavina.
42. Hortense J. Spillers, 'Interstices: A Small Drama of Words', in Carol Vance (ed.), *Pleasure and Danger*, op. cit., 78.
43. Ibid. 77.
44. Angela Davis, 'The Black Woman's Role in the Community of Slaves', op. cit., 11.
45. Stuart Hall, 'Debate: Psychology, Ideology and the Human Subject', *Ideology and Consciousness*, October 1977, 118–119.

18 Racism, Representation, Psychoanalysis

Claire Pajaczkowska and Lola Young*

What might a psychoanalytic perspective contribute to an understanding of racism? Far from explaining it away as an individual pathology, the psychoanalytic emphasis on the complex and often painful transactions between the psychic and social can reveal how deeply racism permeates not only the institutions of a post-colonial society like Britain, but also the ways in which we experience ourselves and others. Nowhere is this more evident than in Frantz Fanon's pioneering studies of the emotional dynamics of negrophobia and its effects on the Black subject. In that spirit, this article examines the way in which our ordinary identities are mediated through symbolic categories that are themselves profoundly racialized. We look in particular at the complex systems of representation embodied in two popular texts, the British film *Mona Lisa* and Toni Morrison's Pulitzer Prize-winning novel *Beloved*. We have selected these because of the contrast they offer. One is a film that uses destructive stereotypes, the other a novel that traces and counteracts the damage caused by such stereotypes. We are thus responding to Fanon's call for a psychoanalysis of racism that both deconstructs negrophobia and contributes to the affirmation and celebration of autonomous Black culture.

There is a long history which unites psychoanalysis and antiracist struggle. It has been suggested that psychoanalysis was forged from the cumulative wit of hundreds of generations of Jewish survivors of persecution and diaspora, and that the systematic understanding of the psyche was initially the need to understand the oppressor, to anticipate the next blow, in order to deflect it and continue with self realization. The insights of psychoanalysis have, to some extent, become part of

* Clare Pajaczkowska and Lola Young, 'Racism, Representation and Psychoanalysis' from *'Race', Culture and Difference* edited by J. Donald and A. Rattansi (Sage, 1992), reprinted by permission of the authors.

twentieth-century common sense, but it remains to be fully integrated into this generation of antiracist struggle.

We begin by introducing some key psychoanalytic concepts that are valuable in analysing texts and the ways in which they interact with cultural forms to produce a subjective sense of self, or identity, for the spectator or reader. We suggest what light these concepts might cast on one of the most important, but least examined, features of racism: that is, ordinary white identity. We then offer our analyses of *Mona Lisa* and *Beloved*.

As it is part of our argument that a psychoanalytic perspective makes it possible to draw on intuition, experience and memory in a critical account of racism, we should perhaps acknowledge our own investment in this project. This article has developed from joint teaching over a number of years, particularly teaching a course 'Representing Other Cultures', as part of an undergraduate course in Cultural History. The section on *Mona Lisa* is written by Claire Pajaczkowska that on *Beloved* by Lola Young. The latter especially draws on the way the book interacts with the reader's own intuition, experience and memory in an attempt to acknowledge the usually implicit personal investment in theoretical work.

PSYCHOANALYTIC CONCEPTS

The starting point of our analysis is that the capacity for racism is based on innate human characteristics, but that this capacity is not necessarily activated by society in a destructive way. Although racism exists as a subjective structure it also exists as an objective reality, produced by the history of imperialism, colonialism and exploitation. How, then, do subjective structures influence objective reality, and, conversely, how do external structures become part of our inner reality? How does history interact with memory to produce our sense of personal, familial, group, institutional, national and international identity? Because culture is an intermediate space, in which we find the subjective and objective realities of memory and history represented in the form of narratives and dramas, it is both fascinating and instructive to analyse. In order to link narrative scenarios to their symbolic and historic meanings we have drawn especially on a number of psychoanalytic concepts.

Trauma

The first concept is that of trauma; originally derived from the Greek word meaning 'wound' or 'injury' but defined analytically as 'an event in the subject's life defined by its intensity, by the subject's inability to respond adequately to it, and by the upheaval and long-lasting effects that it brings about in psychical organisation' (Laplanche and Pontalis 1988: 465). This psychoanalytic account of trauma shows that unless experiences can be symbolized in a way that is both subjectively and objectively true, the human subject is deprived of its fundamental link with others. The human subject loses the community of communication, and deprivation of this link creates a loss comparable in scale to the emotional loss of an infant separated from its mother. The sense of identity of a Black person trying to recover her history and culture within the combination of White narcissism and denial that passes for 'history' in most post-colonial societies, is one that will necessarily contain the 'trauma' of an intense life event for which the culture provides no symbolic equivalents and to which the subject is therefore unable to respond adequately. What is a history without representation? What is the identity of a person for whom reading and writing were illegal, the family illegal as was the case under slavery? Is not such deprivation in fact a theft? The trauma of slavery is evident in the realization that although its reality must be represented, in order to become real, the reality of its dehumanization of Black people is one for which there are no adequate words.

Trauma is a concept which depends, for its meaning, on several other concepts central to the psychoanalytic explanation of life, and before turning to the more detailed textual analysis of the film and the novel four of these will be introduced.

The Unconscious

The concept most fundamental to psychoanalysis is that of the unconscious mind. The existence of an unconscious mind is a hypothesis proposed by Freud in the late nineteenth century to account for patterns which he saw emerging across symptoms, dreams, fantasies and memories, common to both 'pathological' and 'normal' behaviour. He understood the unconscious mind to be a highly structured form of subjective reality, analogous in logic to the emotional world of infants and children, which continues to be active in adult life. In textual analysis the existence of the unconscious is discovered in the patterns underlying texts' narrative, imagery, vocabulary, characters and symbols. In ideology the unconscious mind is evident in the meanings and values attributed to human differences and is especially evident in the meanings racism attributes to physical and visual difference.

Identification

Identification is a process which may be conscious or unconscious, comprising the processes of introjection, projection and judgement, and through which people are able to find the links of identity and difference amongst themselves. The emotional process of identification has physiological precursors in the development of infants. Thus the introjection of meanings, symbols, images or concepts of another person is based on what was once a physical process of 'taking in' food, warmth, love. Projection of oneself onto other people or concepts is also based on their physical expulsions and rejections. Both introjection and projection are central parts of healthy identity, are innate characteristics of the human subject, but both can be misused for the purposes of defence. In racism these processes are used to maintain violently exploitative structures of identity. Film and literature employ the viewer/reader's identification, providing characters and situations which are introjected and become part of the reader's imaginative world. Similarly, the reader projects onto the text, either its characters or its scenario, aspects of his or her own experience, fantasy or memory which brings the texts 'to life' or endows them with meaning.

Denial

Another concept linked to the unconscious and identification is that of denial or disavowal. The mechanism of projection, when employed as a defense, can serve to protect the subject from knowledge of its own ambivalence. In order to deny knowledge of its own ruthlessness and aggression the subject has to maintain the fiction that 'foreigners are dirty' or that 'black men are violent'. Often sexuality is combined with aggression, and also experienced as 'dirty', in which case thoughts will be doubly denied or disavowed and will become projected onto whichever screen or scapegoat is socially condoned. Denial is a powerful emotional defence against acknowledging painful, distressing or troubling knowledge. It is also the widespread reaction of most White people when asked to consider the reality of racism. This is an attitude described by the American writer James Baldwin as the 'sin of ignorance', or simply not wanting to know. What most people do not want to know about is their own capacity for aggression, whether this is expressed in the form of violence or indifference, and the knowledge thus remains unconscious, so that much racism, for example, is enacted in the guise of virtue. The emotional state produced by denial is one of blankness, and the role of blankness in sustaining White identity as normal and as 'undefined' will be discussed in greater detail below.

The Oedipus Complex

Named after the protagonist of the Greek tragic myth, the Oedipus complex refers to the persistence of infantile reality within the adult unconscious. The small child becomes passionately attached, desirous and possessive of the parent of the opposite sex and ambivalently attached to the parent of the same sex. The desire and aggression cannot be satisfied, the small child cannot 'win', and the impossibility of the triangular structure results in the child's realization of his own helplessness, the difference between the generations and some degree of self-consciousness. In adults this predicament exists only as an aspect of unconscious mental life, or in a symbolic form in narratives or drama. Psychoanalysts and structuralist literary critics note the similarity between narrative structure and Oedipal structure; some have suggested that these are equivalent with the textual form reflecting an external, cultural version of the subjective Oedipal form. We have noted how racist ideology weaves fantasies of sexuality and power and how these find expression in dramas, narratives and imagery.

WHITENESS AS AN ABSENT CENTRE

The analytic concepts described above make it possible to articulate the absent centre of White identity. The identity of White culture is 'absent' in a number of senses, both political and subjective. Within European history descriptions of Whiteness are absent due to denial of imperialism, and this leaves a blank in the place of knowledge of the destructive effects of wielding power. An identity based on power never has to develop consciousness of itself as responsible, it has no sense of its limits except as these are perceived in opposition to others.

The blankness of the identity of empire covers an ambivalence which is often unconscious, and which, consequently, can most readily be perceived in the representations it creates of the colonial 'other'; representations which are projections of the 'split off' parts of the self. If we take three aspects of 'ordinary' identity in our culture, those of being White, being middle class and being male, we find processes which maintain this identity as a cultural norm, an absence, a negativity, with the power to define itself only in terms of what it designates its opposites. If Whiteness is assumed, in European culture, to be an identity without boundaries, without definition, without question, what will happen when this identity becomes defined in terms of its historical determinants and in terms of its subjective limits? If White identity is dependent on comparisons between itself and its others, it thereby lacks integrity; and much of White identity is contradictory, fragmented, disintegrated, projecting itself onto series of imaginary dramas, narratives, scenarios. The White and middle class male ego, shored up in its power to define what is real, for itself, will tend to characterize any threatening, negative, unreasonable attributes as Black, working class or feminine elements or characteristics. Why is White identity so resistant to self-awareness and what is its missing content? Catherine Hall's (1989 and 1991) historical research on British, White, male, middle-class identity in the second half of the nineteenth century is especially useful here. Her detailed study of the British Colonial presence in Australia and Jamaica shows how the brutal, often sadistic, politics of colonial administrators were based on the ideology of middle-class masculinity of the time. According to that ideology men were supposed, above all else, to be independent. It was a highly idealized and fictional version of independence, held to be a personal virtue and moral goal throughout these men's education, that led to the ruthless control, exploitation and punishment of all perceived occurrences of dependence, especially the imaginary dependence of others. The characteristics of dependence were typically attributed, by colonial administrators, to the indigenous peoples. The literature and imagery of that time are replete with examples of fantasies of indolence and greed; of natives waiting passively to be fed, without effort, by bountiful nature, fantasies of uncontrolled sexuality and fecundity. All of these fantasies bore no relation to the actual predicament of the indigenous peoples, but formed what can now be recognized as the disowned, 'split off' or disavowed aspects of the 'independent' man's self-identity. The colonists' inability to differentiate between their projection and their real predicament resulted from the blankness at the centre of White identity and concealed the extremely sadistic means habitually employed to suppress and control rebellion.

Different historical accounts of the causes of imperialism, slavery and racism accord different kinds of determinacy to ideological processes. There are many reasons why the middle classes of mid-nineteenth century Britain might want to deny their dependency. As a class they were economically dependent on the surplus value produced by waged labour, a dependency that was systematically misrepresented to assuage their guilt. Also the middle class often emulated their idea of aristocracy, along with having an ambivalent envy of the parasitic wealth of this class. Men may well have envied the social and economic parasitism of middle-class femininity, despite the Victorians' idealization of 'home' life. These factors are historically specific, but since this ideology of the overvaluation of independence seems still to be current in contemporary definitions of masculinity it is useful to explore the significance of its subjective components.

In the place of negativity, the blankness or absence of self-reflection, let's put the concept of narcissism or excessive self-regard to the exclusion of external reality. Narcissism can often be used as a defence against feelings of helplessness, the traumatic loss of self-regard. Joan Rivière, a psychoanalyst writing in 1937, maintained that any blow to adult narcissism is emotionally evocative of earliest traumas of life such as the loss of infantile omnipotence, traumas that are forgotten or repressed into the unconscious. 'Psychoanalysis can trace this anxiety of dependence back through countless situations to the very early one experienced by us all in babyhood . . . A baby at the breast is actually completely dependent on someone else, but has no fear of this.' When the immature ego experiences frustration of the immediate satisfaction of its needs it reacts with overwhelming anger, loss and threatened destruction. 'It is our first experience of something like death, a recognition of the non-existence of something, of an overwhelming loss, both in ourselves and in others as it seems' (Rivière and Klein 1937: 8). The infantile response to separation indicates the intensity and power of the sensations and emotions at stake in the adult unconscious. Because the infantile experience is repressed it will exist as an unconscious memory of threat, and it is the intensity of the pressure exerted by this memory that lies beneath the blankness identified as the absent centre of White identity. Overlaid onto the primary narcissistic wound are the other threats of loss of identity, control, status, power, belonging, safety, decorum; ego losses which threaten traditional identities of gender, class, ethnicity and nation. We have described the process of projection as one of the psychic mechanisms fundamental to racism, and can now further note that unless the primary experience of dependence is recognized as a subjective reality, as part of the self, the anxiety and threat it represents for the ego will continue to be projected outwards onto other people, classes, genders, races, nations in a way that will tend to be destructive.

It has been suggested (Glasser 1985: 409) that men tend to project their sexuality onto the idea of women, that is, that men tend to experience their sexuality as something external to themselves. This is possibly because mental mechanisms are to some extent based on bodily processes, and the external male sexual organs, with their involuntary and hence alarming changes, symbolize sexual response as occurring 'outside' the self and its control. Western culture has further exacerbated this mental capacity by evolving representations which tend to depict women as sexual objects thereby disabling men from integrating their own sexuality, and facilitating their location of sexuality in the image or idea of woman.

As we have noted, representations of anger and aggression tend to be projected onto Black people. The fear of loss of individuality is projected onto the idea of the 'masses', so that the working class becomes a mirror reflecting disowned envy and discontent. These projections leave White, middle-class, male identity as one of safety, power, control, independence and contentment, perhaps smug or self-righteous. Yet this is an illusory identity because it is actually highly dependent on its others to shore up its sense of security, to reflect back the disowned parts of itself as inferior, contemptible, dependent, frightened or threatening, perhaps excremental. The illusory identity needs narratives constantly to reaffirm its fictitious centrality. This is what is meant by the 'androcentrism' and 'ethnocentrism' of cultural forms where emotional and intellectual distortions are created in order to shore up the narcissistic illusion of the centrality of White, masculine, middle-class identity.

MONA LISA

An audience at the cinema is also projecting aspects of itself onto characters and predicaments in the narrative of the film. This is part of the process of identification described above; and as Laura Mulvey has analysed (Mulvey 1975), the audience is in a state of heightened narcissism where both desire and sadism are displaced, leaving an emptiness in the viewing subject with a consequent craving for the action and passion represented in the narrative. The film *Mona Lisa* is a vehicle for the split off aspects of a White and middle-class identity. Its title refers to the popular concept of culture, Leonardo's masterpiece, the painting that people feel they ought to admire or revere whether it has any meaning for them or not. The title also refers to a popular song, the soundtrack of the film, which laments the enigmatic appeal of the idea of woman for man. The film's narrative revolves around the enigma of a young Black woman, Simone, who is chauffeured to her assignments as a call girl by an ineffectual working-class criminal, George. In the film it is the enigma of Simone's sexuality that is investigated, controlled, possessed and finally destroyed. George needs to discover whatever it is that she does behind closed doors. Mystery was unbearable for the man and was transformed, through narrative, into mastery.

. . .

Eventually the narrative reaches its climax and the tantalizing underworld of desire and fear destroys itself in an orgiastic frenzy of voyeurism, a chase with guns, violence, and an Oedipal parricide. Simone 'disappears' from reality, last seen framed in the rear view mirror of George's car. Was she a figment of his imagination? An image he conjured up from memory and fantasy while driving his car, a masturbation fantasy? A part of his identity? George never has to resolve this problem because the film simply annihilates the underworld, returns us to an autumnal park scene with naturalistic lighting where George has been reunited with his daughter and his pal, and restored to his rightful place in the world as a car mechanic. The concluding triangle erases the existence of the Black people central to the narrative, and offers a 'post-feminist' world which has destroyed any need for the role of wife and mother.

The film represents a dramatic enactment of the kinds of fantasies an Oedipal boy uses to attack all forms of maturity and integrity, but especially the idea of woman. Simone represents the 'bad' mother who could not be possessed or controlled by the son, whose sexuality is a threatening enigma to him, who seems to have betrayed him and is therefore blackened by being equated with the son's sexualized hatred. The narrative represents an Oedipal journey in which action results from the desire to avenge seven years' imprisonment for an unspecified crime for which the victim feels himself to have been wrongly accused. The action consists of an investigation into the sexuality of a woman and detection of what it is that men and women do behind closed doors. The desire to know conclusively and the desire to retrieve a lost child lead to a spectacular drama choreographing all forms of perverse, infantile sexuality, and climaxing in a parricidal murder. This sequence parallels Freud's description of human psycho-sexual development. Infantile sexuality leads to the Oedipus complex, an impossible desire to possess the mother, a burning curiosity about the secrets of the parents' reproductive power, the desire to see every-thing and to know everything. The impossibility of this predicament reactivates other losses, such as the loss of infantile omnipotence and the loss of the breast described above by Joan Rivière, giving rise to anger and immense frustration. Repression of both incestuous and parricidal wishes take place and with this a recognition of the father as authority (represented in the film by the court case), the capacity for conscience, guilt and concern, the superego. This is followed by seven years or so of latency (the prison years) and the onset of adolescent sexuality which reactivates the unconscious Oedipal predicament (the drama between Simone and George). Unconscious guilt is experienced as a vague feeling of discomfort, threat, anxiety or danger, reflected in the film's visual style and in its investigative narrative.

...

Despite the film's self-consciously anti-naturalistic style, and the many references to other fiction genres, the pastiche of *film noir* and the detective thriller, the narrative and the visual style work to reinforce contemporary ideologies of white, middle-class masculinity which are deeply destructive in undermining the recognition of responsibility, and which deny the need to work together for social change based on interdependence and respect.

MEMORY, HISTORY AND *BELOVED*

This account is a meditation on Toni Morrison's *Beloved* which uses the text to ask questions about history, to think about some teaching issues, and to try to ascertain what benefits might be gained through an acknowledgement of a relationship between our theoretical work and personal circumstances. Both the form and the terms in which *Beloved* is expressed and the emphasis given to remembering and speaking the unspeakable past as a means of understanding and progressing forward from the often overwhelming present, evoke certain psychoanalytic concepts such as the notion of the 'talking cure'.

Beloved is set in the period after the American Civil War (1861–1865) known as the Reconstruction. The action starts in Cincinnati and returns through flashbacks to events which occurred at the ironically named 'Sweet Home' plantation in Mississippi. After an absence of 18 years one of the ex-'Sweet Home' boys, Paul D, intervenes in the female household which is comprised of Sethe and her youngest daughter Denver, and the ghost of Sethe's eldest daughter, named Beloved. The narrative is concerned with the reasons why Beloved's life was tragically cut short, and tells of how she returns as a young adult, her ghost having been ejected forcibly from 124 (Bluestone Road) by Paul D.

By assembling the fragments of their individual and collective memories, Sethe, Paul D—who becomes Sethe's lover—Baby Suggs, Beloved's grandmother, and Denver, Beloved's younger sister, come to understand and to articulate the events and emotions experienced in the past. It is these past conditions which inform the way they experience the present and suggest possibilities for working at the future.

Morrison writes of Sethe's main preoccupation as being that of 're-memory'. The act of 're-memory' entails the piecing together of fragments of memory, myth and facts to form a coherent account of experiences previously denied in one way or another. These 're-memories' are temporally fluid, merging past with present and are a conscious act of reclamation.

> Some things you forget. Other things you never do . . . If a house burns down, it's gone, but the place—the picture of it stays, and not just in my re-memory, but out there in the world. What I remember is a picture floating out there outside my head. I mean, even if I don't think it, even if I die, the picture of what I did, or knew or saw is still out there. Right in the place where it happened. (Morrison 1987: 36)

The first time I read *Beloved*, I was in the USA, south of the Mason-Dixon line in Virginia. The geographical and emotional position I occupied contributed another dimension to my reading and comprehension. I could 'see' my forebears labouring in the cotton fields, singing their scathing attacks on their slave-owners. I thought of those of us who—like Sethe—are unable to identify our mothers, have experienced fractured childhoods or have been unwillingly separated from our parents for various reasons. I felt I could begin to understand the meaning and significance of 're-memory' and its bearing on our world-views. The heritage of the struggle for freedom and human rights, and to reclaim the past is fundamental to the evolution of Black cultures not only in the USA but throughout the African diaspora.

I'd bought the book months before I read it. In fact, I had actively avoided reading it because at that moment in my personal history, having just experienced a devastating loss which echoed other episodes of dispossession and distress, I didn't feel I would be capable of dealing with what I thought would be yet more emotional devastation, centred around loss and deprivation. When I did come to read the book, it was not just the actual narrative or my identification with Sethe and her daughters Denver and Beloved which I found so demanding, it was also having to recognize my complicity in erasing sections of my memory in order to survive. It is precisely that strategy which Sethe uses, that of recognizing that the 'future was a matter of keeping the past at bay' (p. 42). Personal and collective survival is based on the repression of the memory of past events which resurface, sometimes through madness. It seems self-evident that we cannot engage with the future before we have disentangled the past. Deprivation, humiliation, the 'middle passage',[1] slavery; all such experiences are unspeakable and the text acknowledges that but it also suggests ways in which these events may be articulated.

A sense of being located historically and socially is fundamental to a sense of belonging and participating in the creative processes of a particular culture. If cultural belonging-ness resides in those discourses which call upon collective memory, then with a lack of access to the elements of that memory, along with a sense of dislocation comes a feeling of loss of cultural cohesion.

Slavery radically destabilized Africa and resulted in the undermining and fragmentation of cultural self identity both for those who underwent the process of dispersal and disruption and for their descendants. Black people are frequently in the position of having to piece together distorted fragments of the past and of past selves in order to re-create a self-determined picture of individual and collective cultural identities. Reclamation of the past through 're-membering' is considered to be virtually a moral obligation by some African-Americans since the official histories have failed to document and acknowledge the meanings of the experiences of their ancestors.

. . .

So with Black women's experiences not foregrounded in narratives of slavery written by Black men and also denied a place in 'White' accounts of history, how are Black women to relate to history? By drawing attention to the circumstances under which Sethe makes her escape, Toni Morrison gives women's experience of slavery a voice and, most importantly, a language through Sethe. Sethe is an active historical agent as opposed to a passive victim or an absence. In making these comments, the intention is not to disparage those remarkable acts of heroism and courage that Black men carried out against extremely oppressive odds. The issue being raised is that there is another facet to the incompleteness of documentation about this period.

Sethe's—Denver's and Beloved's—re-telling of their narratives is an affirmation of their 'selves' in opposition to a world designed to obliterate all traces of self-determined being. Sethe is pregnant with her fourth child when she is subjected to a humiliating ordeal by Schoolteacher's sons just before she makes her escape as they suck milk from her breasts. Surviving a beating from Schoolteacher—the new owner of 'Sweet Home'—Sethe almost dies during her escape as she gives birth to Denver, named after the 'whitegirl' who assisted in the delivery in a rickety boat.

There is a conscious evocation and a reaffirmation of the power and heritage of African folk memory through the use of the supernatural and the uncanny, and the merging of fantasy, myth and history to form 'magical realism'. The use of the supernatural as a normal part of everyday life alongside the historical accounts of slavery is a departure from the literary tradition of much early writing although the naturalizing of the supernatural is part of an African-American oral heritage and has its beginnings in various African cultural traditions.

...

For the sake of the (separate) survival of both Blacks and Whites, White Americans have had to undergo a process of re-construction which refers not only to the economic, social and cultural sphere but also to the realm of the psyche. Whites have had to re-construct the reality of their past taking into account the distortions, self-deception and denials that constitute many European versions of 'history'. In order to maintain the self-deception and claim validity for certain interpretations of historical events, distortions in the accounts of the past and disavowal of the implications of their forebears' involvement in slavery have typified literary, dramatic and cinematic renderings of the period, certainly in American popular culture.

The invisible White presence is at once clearly defined and less than significant in *Beloved*. The most important feature of 'race' dealt with is not the relationship of Black slaves to their White owners: it is the relationships within the community and how the community deals with the problems laid at their doorsteps. Individual Whites are in one sense peripheral. Whites frequently attempt to make Blacks invisible in cultural production by ignoring or subordinating presence through crass stereotyping. This is reflected in the limited range of characterizations offered through cultural products and is self-evident on studying particular texts. White American reconstruction writers in particular portrayed a constant stream of brutal rapists, tragic 'mulattos' and sexually promiscuous Blacks, and it is against this backdrop that African-American writers work.

The process of projection as described in the introduction to this article is recognized in *Beloved* and is described as White people getting rid of their negative feelings about themselves by discharging their anger with themselves onto Blacks. According to Laplanche and Pontalis, 'Projection emerges . . . as the primal means of defence against those endogenous excitations whose intensity makes them too unpleasurable: the subject projects these outside so as to be able to flee from them (e.g., phobic avoidance) and protect himself from them . . . the subject now finds himself obliged to believe completely in something that is henceforth subject to the laws of external reality' (Laplanche and Pontalis 1988: 352).

As previously indicated, however, the act of disavowal affects and—in part at least—determines 'external reality' since facets of that reality are denied. Through an analysis of the recurring stereotypes mentioned above, it is possible to identify a cycle whereby (White) anxiety and guilt is apparently resolved through projection and denial and disavowal of the reality of a traumatizing realization. The emotional flow is from anxiety to denial to projection: then to distortion upon which enactment is based and from there, there is further denial. This cycle is important politically because the enactment phase involves the mechanics of individual, institutional and state racisms.

As the institution of slavery necessitated sustained inhumanity towards fellow human beings—requiring the ruthless and violent subordination of Blacks—slaves had to be viewed as non-humans, as property, so that it was then acceptable to ill-treat them. As James Baldwin has pointed out, White people's own inhumanity was projected onto Blacks and this misrecognition of what constituted brutality was enacted through master–slave relations, determined by slave-holders. However, such acts are not without cost to the oppressor. Since Blacks were—and still are—a living reminder of the horrors perpetrated in the name of economic development, civilization or whatever, many Whites were horrified and disgusted by Blacks. Of course this set of ideas regarding Blacks' status as human beings is wholly inconsistent with notions of reason, the logic of 'Enlightenment' and so on, and that is why the representations in White cultural products are distorted to fit the scheme: the distortion has then to be defended through repetition and elaboration (Baldwin 1988: 3). Since guilt underpins White anxiety about Blacks, many Whites know and fear that their status in society—in the world—is partially due to their capacity to brutalize people for their own advantage. Even non-racist Whites benefit from the fact of their Whiteness at the expense of Blacks. So our disproportionately low presence in historical representations and mainstream culture should not be surprising: it is a part of the enactment phase of the cycle referred to previously.

Frantz Fanon asserted that 'race' and sex need to be considered in conjunction with each other since many of the anxieties that Whites have about Blacks are of a sexual nature. The lascivious, sexually debased Black is the distorted representation which allowed the continued sexual abuse of female slaves and the lynching and castration of male slaves. Bred like animals, subjected to abuse and forbidden to marry and to form stable, long-term relationships, the attempts to control Black fertility and sexuality were the reflection of Whites' attempts to regulate their own sexuality according to the socio-sexual morality of the time. The idealization of White female sexual purity and the valorization of 'masculine' characteristics such as courage, autonomous action and independence fed into the repression of sexuality in favour of a celebration of 'masculinity' and 'femininity'. A classic example of the alleged threat posed by Black male hypersexuality to White American femininity can be found in D. W. Griffith's film *The Birth of a Nation* (1915). A more contemporary British example appears in *Mona Lisa*, in the character of Anderson (Clarke Peters). The brute male negro unable to control his excessive sexual energy is characterized as a pimp who preys on White schoolgirls, plying them with drugs and beating them up when they inevitably fail to satisfy him.

...

Beloved, though, is not judgmental: neither Sethe's infanticide nor White people's behaviour are condemned. In the introduction to *The*

Mother Daughter Plot: Narrative, Psychoanalysis, Feminism, Marianne Hirsch says, 'The novel contains more than judgement: it contains the stories that precede and follow judgement, the stories that form and surround the relationship of mother and daughter during slavery and in post-abolition times' (Hirsch 1989: 7).

A fabrication woven from fear, anxiety, fantasy and myth formed the backcloth for the initial encounter between Europeans and Africans. This was not conducive to the production of an open, equitable relationship. However, despite the denials, distortions and disruptions which characterized our dispersal, in the same way that Sethe constructs herself from the fragments of memory and re-memory that become available to her, so may peoples of a diaspora manage to achieve authority over the re-creation of the self after the many attempts to destroy it. The identification within the text of the necessity to rebuild the past from fragments and the idea of 're-memory' has particular resonance in the context of a desire on the part of many people to see the past through a sentimentalized haze. Although much of what she writes generally advocates a rootedness in the past and a reference to origins and traditions, Morrison's work is not based on a nostalgia for the past. The issue is one of how useful to any of us is a history which denies its more disturbing aspects.

Implications for Teaching

I would now like to pose some questions related to teaching which uses *Beloved* as a focus and to indicate some of the difficulties raised by working on this text in a British context. In particular, the way in which slavery has been dealt with in the teaching of British history is characterized by a lack of emphasis on Britain's involvement in the slave trade and the absence of information about how Africans resisted slavery and struggled to abolish it both in this country and in the Caribbean. In terms of how slavery is approached in literature, in films and on television, again we are identifying an absence rather than a negative presence. If it is dealt with at all in cultural products, the standard manner of describing the actuality of slavery is to re-present the condition of enslavement in the ways in which it is conventionally expressed through the educational system.

In this country at any rate, Africa's loss and the enslavement of the sixty million to whom *Beloved* is dedicated has been enshrined in a mythology which seeks to purify the actions of the pro-slavery plantocracy and, to some extent, justify the prolonged brutality. Some of the unimaginably terrible conditions during the 'middle passage' of the triangular slave trade are illustrated in various school texts and isolated vicious incidents are described. However, this does not invalidate my main contention. The semiotician Roland Barthes describes a process of 'inoculation' whereby a limited number of inhumane actions are admitted by the perpetrators: this 'immunizes the contents of the collective imagination by means of a small inoculation of acknowledged evil; one thus protects it against the risk of a generalized subversion' (Barthes 1973: 42).

One of the results of this selective approach to this period of history has been that generations of children, Black and White, have been led to believe in a series of misrepresentative narratives masquerading as objective historical fact. These narratives indict the actions of *other* nations and invoke Britain as being the country that fought *against* slavery, *against* the barbarity of Europeans and Americans, rather than being prime instigators, responsible for more than half of the international trade in human beings during the period between 1791 and 1806 (Fryer 1984).

If this collective historical amnesia and national disavowal typifies British accounts of slavery, how are we to relate to Morrison's belief that modern history begins with slavery? A way of avoiding the crucial issues about guilt and responsibility, and the acts of denial implicit in that question, is to answer that Morrison's consciousness is determined by, and culturally and historically specific to, the African-American situation. It is clear that whatever the temporal and cultural specificity of Morrison's *Beloved*, her narrative also corresponds to current national and international features of 'race'. As anyone who is aware of events in continental Europe realizes, there are a number of potentially depressing features on the current 'race relations' landscape.[2] Another issue is that with many White academics there is a sense of a lack of knowledge of, or engagement with, what might be termed Black experience. Given this reluctance, one question might be: is there a correlation between how much Whites know of Black people's experiences and how much they can become involved with what the text has to offer? A related issue is whether or not White people might read the text differently from Black readers.

If there are small numbers of Black students in a group, those students can become the uncomfortable focus of the course-work in which the class is immersed. In fact, they may—and I have experienced this myself both as lecturer and student in predominantly White gatherings—come to embody the text for White people in the group.

There is a moment in which skin colour becomes both an accusation and a judgement. It can also be a mystification; a way of saying 'you can't know it in the same way that I live it'. Through an approach which encourages students to identify for themselves the resonances of *Beloved* with their own histories and present lives, it is possible to have fruitful intra-cultural dialogue and hopefully an inter-cultural one as well.

The point of raising these issues in terms of Black readers and White readers is not to homogenize or to deny intra-group differences but to suggest broad areas for further examination. I am not suggesting that there are definitive answers to these questions and I would like to point out that the questions are problematic in themselves. The reluctance of many White academics to actively support and encourage what amounts to a less ethnocentric, more diverse approach to developing curricula, has been likened to the reluctance of the early venture capitalists to travel inland from the Guinea coast. They are not yet ready it seems—for a number of reasons—to venture into the interior of the 'dark continent'. Perhaps a crucial question would be: is it possible for White academics to venture into the interior without colonizing it?

Notes

1. The 'middle passage' refers to the transfer of slaves from Africa to the Caribbean across the Atlantic Ocean. This is probably one of the least documented aspects of the slave-trade but what is clear is that the conditions on board the ships involved in the trade were appalling. The death rate of slaves in transit over a period of a 100 years (between 1680 and 1780), averaged one in eight. Slaves were herded together, kept in spaces not big enough for them to sit up, systematically flogged, virtually starved and thrown overboard if weak or sickly.
2. For instance, in Britain there is the apparent demise of antiracist movements, the slow process of systemic change in institutions, the lack of significant progress in educational achievement and so on. In France, there are politicians who are elected on openly racist platforms. In Germany, officially there is no such thing as 'racism', only 'hostility towards foreigners'. I am not pointing out these events in order to spread a paralysis of the will through despair but to indicate the relevance of *Beloved* for us all.

References

Baldwin, J. (1988). 'A talk to teachers', in R. Simonson, and S. Walker, (eds.), *The Graywolf Annual For Multicultural Literacy*. Minnesota: Graywolf Press.
Barthes, R. (1973). *Mythologies*. London: Paladin.

Ellison, R. (1972). *Invisible Man.* New York: Plume.

Fryer, P. (1984). *Staying Power: The History of Black People in Britain.* London: Pluto Press.

Glasser, M. (1985). 'The weak spot: observations on male sexuality'. *International Journal of Psychoanalysis*, 66.

Hall, C. (1989). 'The economy of intellectual prestige: Thomas Carlyle, John Stuart Mill and the case of Governor Eyre'. *Cultural Critique*, 12 (Spring).

—— (1991). 'Missing stories: gender and ethnicity in England in the 1830s and '40s', in L. Grossberg, C. Nelson, and P. Treitler, (eds.), *Cultural Studies Now and in the Future.* London: Routledge.

Hirsch, M. (1989). *The Mother Daughter Plot: Narrative, Psychoanalysis, Feminism.* Indianapolis: Indiana University Press.

Laplanche, J., and Pontalis, J. B. (1988). *The Language of Psychoanalysis.* London: Karnac.

Morrison, T. (1987). *Beloved.* New York: Plume.

Mulvey, L. (1975). 'Visual pleasure and narrative cinema'. *Screen*, 16 (3).

—— (1989). 'Visual pleasure and narrative cinema', in *Visual and Other Pleasures.* London: Macmillan.

Rivière, J., and Klein, M. (1937). *Love, Hate and Reparation.* London: Hogarth.

19 That Moment of Emergence

Pratibha Parmar*

> To be a lesbian means engaging in a complex, often treacherous, system of cultural identities, representations and institutions, and a history of sexual regulation. . . . Being a lesbian tests the meanings of sexual identity in ways that evoke intense, sometimes violent, social disapproval, while being straight is taken for granted as a neutral position from which gay folks deviate.
>
> (Martha Gever)[1]

> For me being a lesbian is not only a fight against homophobia and the kind of homophobia we face everyday, but it's also a fight against the system that creates that . . . a class system as well as a system that is imperialist. It's a system that's responsible for the incidences of racism that all of my family and all of the people I know of Asian and African descent have had to go through in all of the Western countries, and I think its critical that we come together and bring all these experiences together and actually reach beyond ourselves. . . .
>
> (Punam Khosla)[2]

To be an artist, a lesbian and a woman of color engaged in mapping out our visual imaginations is both exciting and exhausting. The creative upsurge in black women and women of color's cultural production in Britain has not been given the spotlight and visibility that it deserves. Women of color have been organizing and creating communities which have inspired a new sense of collective identity, and it is only through our own efforts that we have ensured against our erasure as artists and cultural producers.

I don't think that this is because of a mere oversight or even

* Pratibha Parmar, 'That Moment of Emergence', © Pratibha Parmar 1993, from *Queer Looks: Perspectives on Lesbian and Gay Film and Video* edited by Martha Gever, Pratibha Parmar and John Greyson (Routledge, 1993), reprinted by permission of the author.

deliberate conspiracy. I think it is much more to do with the persistence of a fantasy of what constitutes an authentic national culture, a fantasy which posits what and who is English. The dominance of the ideology of English ethnicity, although deeply ingrained in the cultural canons of British society and arts institutions, is and has been challenged by black artists and cultural producers through our work. We have been changing the very heart of what constitutes Englishness by recoding it with our diasporan sensibilities. Our ancestral as well as personal experiences of migration, dispersal, and dislocation give us an acute sense of the limitations of national identities. Some of us claim an English as well as a British identity, and in so doing transform the very terrain of Englishness and expose the ruptures in the discourses of white supremacy. The fact that British national culture is heterogeneous and ethnically differentiated is something that still needs hammering home to those who are persistent in their view that to be black and British is an anachronism. Our visual outpourings are our referents for our 'imagined communities' and utopian visions, which we seek to articulate and live and work towards.

By reflecting on my own working practices as a filmmaker and video artist, and in unfolding my personal and historical context, I hope to be able to contribute to the ongoing development of a general theoretical framework for discussing the cultural and political significance of black arts in postcolonial Britain.[3] It is a framework which differs from previous forms of cultural critiques because of the ways in which it seeks to centralize the black subjectivity and our experiences of difference. The more we assert our own identities as historically marginalized groups, the more we expose the tyranny of a so-called center. I came into making videos and films from a background in political activism and cultural practice, and not from film school or art school. As an Asian woman I have never considered myself as somebody's 'other', nor have I seen myself as 'marginal' to an ubiquitous, unchanging, monolithic 'center'. But since my arrival in England in the mid-1960s, it has been a constant challenge and struggle to defy those institutions and cultural canons which seek repeatedly to make me believe that because of my visible difference as an Asian woman I am an 'other' and therefore 'marginal'.

There is a particular history that informs the thematic concerns of my work as much as my aesthetic sensibilities. That history is about a forced migration to an England that is intensely xenophobic and insular, an England that is so infused with outdated notions of itself as the Mother Country for its ex-colonial subjects that it refuses to look at the ashes of its own images as a decaying nation, let alone a long-dead empire.

When my family, like many other Indian families, arrived in Britain in the mid-sixties, anti-black feelings were running high and 'Paki-bashing' was a popular sport amongst white youths. It was in the school playground that I first encountered myself as an undesirable alien, objectified in the frame of 'otherness'. All those of us perceived as 'marginal', 'peripheral', and the 'other' know what it is like to be defined by someone else's reality and often someone else's psychosis.

> We can read ourselves against another people's pattern, but since it is not ours . . . we emerge as its effects, its errata, its counternarratives. Whenever we try to narrate ourselves, we appear as dislocations in their discourse.
>
> (Edward Said)[4]

I do not speak from a position of marginalization but more crucially from the resistance to that marginalization. As a filmmaker, it is important for me to reflect upon the process through which I constantly negotiate the borderlines between shifting territories . . . between the margin and the center . . . between inclusion and exclusion . . . between visibility and invisibility. For example, as lesbians and gays of color, we have had to constantly negotiate and challenge the racism of the white gay community, and at the same time confront the homophobia of communities of color.

What we have been seeing in recent years is the development of a new politics of difference which states that we are not interested in defining ourselves in relation to someone else or something else, nor are we simply articulating our cultural and sexual differences. This is not a unique position, but one that is shared by many cultural activists and critics on both sides of the Atlantic. We are creating a sense of ourselves and our place within different and sometimes contradictory communities, not simply in relation to . . . not in opposition to . . . nor in reversal to . . . nor as a corrective to . . . but in and for ourselves. Precisely because of our lived experiences of racism and homophobia, we locate ourselves not within any one community but in the spaces between these different communities.

Toni Morrison was once asked why she wrote the books that she did, and she replied that these were the books she wanted to read. In some ways, the reason why I make the films and videos that I do is also because they are the kinds of films and videos I would like to see: films and videos that engage with the creation of images of ourselves as women, as people of color and as lesbians and gays; images that evoke passionate stirrings and that enable us to construct ourselves in our complexities. I am also interested in making work that documents our stories and celebrates and validates our existence to ourselves and our communities. As a lesbian I have searched in vain for images of lesbians of color on the screen but I very quickly realized that they exist only in my own imagination, so one of my aims as a filmmaker is to begin to compile that repertoire of images of ourselves. The joy, the passion and desire embodied in our lives is as important to highlight and nourish as are the struggles against racism and homophobia. Desire for me is expressed sexually, but also in a need to re-create communities which are affirming and strengthening.

Experiences of migration and displacement, and the need to make organic links between race and sexuality, guide my desire to create works that throw up the contradictions of being 'queer' and Asian. Images of Asian women in the British media have their root in the heyday of the British empire. The commonsense racist ideas about Asian women's sexuality have been determined by racist patriarchal ideologies. On the one hand, we are seen as sexually erotic and exotic creatures full of oriental promise, and on the other as sari-clad women who are dominated by their men, as oppressed wives or mothers breeding prolifically and colonizing the British landscape.

The idea that many of us have our own self-defined sexuality is seen as subversive and threatening by the dominant white society in which we live, as well as by the majority of the Asian community. Within our communities our existence as lesbians and gays continues to be denied or is dismissed as a by-product of corrupting Western influences. In fact many of us are internal exiles within our own communities. This is despite the fact that there is an ancient history of homosexuality in India pre-dating the Western history of homosexuality. This history is only now being uncovered by Indian lesbian and gay historians.

Unique to the British context has been the use of the word 'black', which was mobilized as a political definition for peoples of African, Asian, and Afro-Caribbean descent. As different ethnic groups use 'people of color' in North America, so in Britain a political alliance was formed using the word black. This united us in a fragile alliance against racism, since we experienced British institutional racism in very similar ways. However, in recent years this strategic use has lost its currency as questions of ethnic difference and national identities begin to take primacy.

The mid-1980s have seen a new generation of video artists and filmmakers emerging from the different black communities in Britain. This growth of independent film and video cultures has shown that there are many of us working not only to challenge harmful images but also to construct a whole new language of visual representation. Instead of allowing our marginality to impose a silence on us, we are actively engaged in making videos and films that have begun to redefine and recast notions of 'mainstream', 'difference', and 'otherness'.

It is important to create and proclaim assertive and empowering images which question and unsettle the dominant discourses of representation of people who are not white, male, and heterosexual, but it is equally important to move beyond the merely oppositional. Interrupting the discourses of dominant media with a strong counterdiscourse or corrective is sometimes necessary and has been an effective strategy used by some black filmmakers in Britain, particularly in the early 1970s. But one of the dangers with this has been the way in which perceptions of the black communities as a homogeneous group have been reinforced. Differences of class, culture, ethnicity, sexuality, and gender became subjugated, and the black communities were represented as an undifferentiated mass. Diversity, the multiplicity of our histories, experiences, and identities were reduced to 'typical' and 'representative' stereotypes.

My personal and political history of involvement in the antiracist movement in the mid-1970s, in feminism, and in lesbian and gay initiatives has given me the grounding for my work in film and video in many fundamental ways.

The development of cultural studies in the mid-1980s has been an important theoretical influence on my work as a filmmaker, and on the work of many other black filmmakers. As a postgraduate student at the Centre for Contemporary Cultural Studies at the University of Birmingham in the early 1980s, I was involved with a group of students in writing and publishing the book, *The Empire Strikes Back: Race and Racism in 70s Britain.*[5] Our project was to examine the everyday lived experiences of black British people as culture. We developed critiques of the paradigms of race relations which had consistently pathologized black cultures and communities. We also critiqued white feminist theory and practice which did not acknowledge or grapple with the power dynamics around race and class. We rejected their Eurocentric bias and put forward our own analysis. We were the new generation that saw ourselves as both black and British, and, unlike the dominant communities, we did not see a contradiction between these two terms. Our alternative discourse around issues of race, gender, national identity, sexual identity, and culture marked a turning point. We, the children of postcolonial migrant citizens, were indeed striking back with no punches pulled.

As one of the founding members of the first black lesbian group in Britain in 1984, it was invigorating finally to find a community of lesbians of color where we could talk about our common experiences of racism and isolation within the white lesbian and feminist community, as well as share cultural similarities and a sense of integration. The collective empowerment that came as a result of this coming together was also crucial for our political visibility. The key point here was that my experiences as a woman, as a lesbian, and as an Asian person were not compartmentalized or seen as mutually exclusive; instead it was the ways in which I/we located ourselves within and between these differing subjectivities that gave us a sense of integration. This was against the duality that was constantly being either self-imposed or externally imposed upon us, so that the much-asked question of whether we were going to prioritize our race over our sexuality was made redundant. This claim to an integrated identity was a strategic claim inasmuch as many of us found political empowerment in a collective group identity and a heightening of our consciousness. Of course, in due course many of us also realized that 'there is no real me to return to, no whole self that synthesizes the woman, the woman of color, and the (writer or the artist or the lesbian). There are, instead, diverse recognitions of self through difference, and unfinished, contingent, arbitrary closures that make possible both politics and identity.'[6]

It was only in the late 1980s that a rigorous critique of an 'identity politics' was initiated, attempting to prioritize or create hierarchies of oppression. This revealed some extremely useful and positive insights, namely, that it is the constant negotiating between these identities that provides the framework for our cultural and political practice. Secondly, identities are not fixed in time and space, but what is valuable is the multiplicity of our experiences as lesbians of color, as women and as black people. June Jordan, the black American poet, writer, and political activist, has said, 'We should try to measure each other on the basis of what we do for each other rather than on the basis of who we are.'[7]

Indeed, some of the insights about the fluctuating nature of identities and a critique of identity politics have been pioneered and initiated by black feminists and feminists of color, and subsequently incorporated into writings on black cultural production.[8]

The choices I have made about what themes or issues to highlight in my work have also been about timing, funding, and how particular political moments have thrown up urgent issues. For example, I made the video *ReFraming AIDS* in the summer of 1987, when there were concerted and massive attacks both at the local and national level against lesbian and gay rights in Britain. This was at a time when the first government media campaign on AIDS fuelled existing antigay prejudices by representing AIDS as a gay plague. The antigay blacklash was vehement, and through the video I wanted to create a space where different lesbians and gays could talk about the content of that backlash, for instance showing how black lesbians and gay men were being affected specifically around immigration and policing, and how AIDS was being used to further restrict the entry of black people into the country. By intercutting the government media ads with images and voices from the lesbian and gay communities, I also attempted to subvert the dominant images of the disease by linking ideas about racial difference, social difference, and sexuality in an historical context. The filmmaker Stuart Marshall was instrumental in allowing me to make these historical connections within the video.

One of the responses to my making *ReFraming AIDS* was that of surprise. What was I, an Asian lesbian, doing making a video about AIDS that did not have just black women's voices, but also the voices of black and white men? Why had I dared to cross the boundaries of race and gender? Underlying this criticism was the idea that, as an Asian lesbian filmmaker, my territory should be proscribed and limited to my very specific identities, and to my 'own' communities.

It is such experiences that have reinforced my criticism of an essentialist identity politics as being divisive, exclusionary, and retrogressive. I would assert that our territories should be as broad as we choose. Without doubt we still need categories of self-enunciation, but we need them in a political and theoretical discourse on identity which gives us the space for the diversity of our imaginations and visions.

While it is crucial to acknowledge Stuart Hall's valuable insight that 'it is important to recognize that we all speak from a particular place, out of particular experiences, histories and cultures,' for me it is equally important that we are not constrained and contained by those positions . . . by fixed identity tags . . . that we do not get caught up in an essentialist 'bantustan'[9] that decrees that you do not cross boundaries of your experiences. Such prescriptive thinking can be both creatively and politically stultifying.

One of my concerns as a filmmaker is to challenge the normalizing and universalizing tendencies within the predominantly white lesbian and gay communities—to assert the diversity of cultural and racial identities within the umbrella category of gay and lesbian. There is a need also to redefine 'community', and just as there isn't a homogeneous black community, similarly there isn't a monolithic lesbian and gay community.

In my video *Memory Pictures*, and my films *Flesh and Paper* and *Khush*, I interrogate Asian gay and lesbian identities in ways which point to the complexities that we occupy as lesbians and gays of color. I explore our histories of diaspora, the memories of migration and upheaval, the search for an integration of our many selves, and the celebration of 'us', our differences, and our eroticisms.

It is a condition of these postmodernist times that we all live heterogeneous realities, constructing our sense of selves through the hybridity of cultural practices, and this is inevitably reflected in the aesthetic form employed in my work. The form itself needs to be interrogated as much as the content, and by using a combination of styles and narratives—for instance, documentary realism, poetry, dramatic reconstructions, experimental, autobiographical—I attempt to enunciate the nuances of our subjectivities in my work. Furthermore, the influences of the mass media and popular culture inevitably find their way into the work in a self-conscious way. The four-minute video, *Bhangra Jig*, commissioned by Channel Four as a 'television intervention' piece to celebrate Glasgow as the cultural capital of Europe for 1991, borrows unashamedly from advertising codes and pop promos.

In the film *Khush*, which I made for Channel Four's lesbian and gay series *Out on Tuesday*, one of my strategies was to use a diverse range of visual modes. So, for instance, my reworking of a classical dance sequence from an old Indian popular film utilizes the strategy of disrupting the given heterosexual codes. In the original film, the female dancer's act is intercut with a male gaze, but for *Khush* I re-edited this sequence and took out the male gaze. I reused this sequence with scenarios of two Asian women watching and enjoying this dance. The gaze and the spectator became inverted. Clearly, postmodernist interest in reworking available material gives us an opportunity to use strategies of appropriation as an assault on racism, sexism, and homophobia. It is these politicized appropriations of dominant codes and signifying systems which give us powerful weapons in the struggle for empowerment.

This hybrid aesthetic, as it has come to be known, works with and against the 'tools of the master' because these are tools which we, as cultural activists and artists, have appropriated and reformulated with our diasporic imaginations. In *Bhangra Jig* this was precisely my aim: to allude to Glasgow's history as the second biggest city of the British empire, as reflected in the city's architectural signs and symbols. At the same time I juxtapose against these memories of colonial carnage the vibrancy of our cultures of resistance: Bhangra music and dance as signifying practices of Asian youth culture, crossovers of reggae, soul, and traditional agrarian Indian music and dance. For *Bhangra Jig* to be shown several times within one week on British TV (known for its history of stereotyping and the invisibility of self-determined imagery of Asian people) not only disrupts dominant ideas of European culture but also offers new meanings of what constitutes national cultures and identities.

Just as much as I distance myself from any notion of an essentialist lesbian or black aesthetic, so, too, do I reject the idea that I am forever relegated to the confines of an outsider looking in. Lesbians of color around the world are asserting our visions through film and video, and our creative efforts can only but grow in the twenty-first century as the map continues to be redrawn with our imaginations.

Notes

1. Martha Gever, 'The Names We Give Ourselves', in Russell Ferguson et al. (eds.), *Out There: Marginalization and Contemporary Cultures* (Cambridge/ New York: MIT Press and the New Museum of Contemporary Art, 1990), 191.
2. Punam Khosla, speaking in the film *Khush*, by Pratibha Parmar, made for Channel Four's lesbian and gay series *Out on Tuesday*, 1991.
3. See the writings of Stuart Hall, Paul Gilroy, Kobena Mercer, Lubaina Himid, and the journal *Third Text*.
4. Edward Said, *After the Last Sky: Palestinian Lives* (New York: Pantheon, 1986).
5. Centre for Contemporary Cultural Studies, *The Empire Strikes Back: Race and Racism in 70s Britain* (London: Hutchinson, 1982).
6. 'Woman, Native, Other: Pratibha Parmar Interviews Trinh T. Minh-Ha,' *Feminist Review*, no. 36 (Autumn, 1990), 73.
7. Pratibha Parmar, 'Other Kinds of Dreams: An Interview with June Jordan', *Feminist Review*, no. 31 (Spring, 1989), 63.
8. See Barbara Christian, 'The Race for Theory', *Feminist Studies*, 4: 1 (1988); S. Grewal et al. (eds.), *Charting the Journey: Writings by Black and Third World Women* (London: Sheba Feminist Publishers, 1987); Pratibha Parmar, 'Black Feminism: The Politics of Articulation', in Jonathan Rutherford (ed.), *Identity: Community, Culture, Difference* (London: Lawrence and Wishart, 1990), 101–126.
9. I thank Trinh T. Minh-Ha for voicing this very apt analogy.

20 Sexual Indifference and Lesbian Representation

Teresa de Lauretis*

If it were not Lesbian, this text would make no sense

(Nicole Brossard, *L'Amèr*)

There is a sense in which lesbian identity could be assumed, spoken, and articulated conceptually as political through feminism—and, current debates to wit, *against* feminism; in particular through and against the feminist critique of the Western discourse on love and sexuality, and therefore, to begin with, the rereading of psychoanalysis as a theory of sexuality and sexual difference. If the first feminist emphasis on sexual difference as gender (woman's difference from man) has rightly come under attack for obscuring the effects of other differences in women's psychosocial oppression, nevertheless that emphasis on sexual difference did open up a critical space—a conceptual, representational, and erotic space—in which women could address themselves to women. And in the very act of assuming and speaking from the position of subject, a woman could concurrently recognize women as subjects *and* as objects of female desire.

It is in such a space, hard-won and daily threatened by social disapprobation, censure, and denial, a space of contradiction requiring constant reaffirmation and painful renegotiation, that the very notion of sexual difference could then be put into question, and its limitations be assessed, both *vis-à-vis* the claims of other, not strictly sexual, differences, and with regard to sexuality itself. It thus appears that 'sexual difference' is the term of a conceptual paradox corresponding to what is in effect a real contradiction in women's lives: the term, at once, of a sexual *difference* (women are, or want, something different from men) and of a sexual *indifference* (women are, or want, the same as men).

* Teresa de Lauretis, 'Sexual Indifference and Lesbian Representation' from *Theatre Journal*, vol. 40 no.2 (May 1988), pp. 155–177, © The Johns Hopkins University Press 1988, reprinted by permission of the publisher, The Johns Hopkins University Press and the author.

And it seems to me that the racist and class-biased practices legitimated in the notion of 'separate but equal' reveal a very similar paradox in the liberal ideology of pluralism, where social difference is also, at the same time, social indifference.

The psychoanalytic discourse on female sexuality, wrote Luce Irigaray in 1975, outlining the terms of what here I will call sexual (in)difference, tells 'that *the feminine occurs only within models and laws devised by male subjects.* Which implies that there are not really two sexes, but only one. A single practice and representation of the sexual.'[1] Within the conceptual frame of that *sexual indifference*, female desire for the self-same, an other female self, cannot be recognized. 'That a woman might desire a woman "like" herself, someone of the "same" sex, that she might also have auto- and homosexual appetites, is simply incomprehensible' in the phallic regime of an asserted sexual difference between man and woman which is predicated on the contrary, on a complete indifference for the 'other' sex, woman's. Consequently, Irigaray continues, Freud was at a loss with his homosexual female patients, and his analyses of them were really about male homosexuality. 'The object choice of the homosexual woman is [understood to be] determined by a *masculine* desire and tropism'—that is, precisely, the turn of so-called sexual difference into sexual indifference, a single practice and representation of the sexual.

> So there will be no female homosexuality, just a hommo-sexuality in which woman will be involved in the process of specularizing the phallus, begged to maintain the desire for the same that man has, and will ensure at the same time, elsewhere and in complementary and contradictory fashion, the perpetuation in the couple of the pole of 'matter.'[2]

With the term *hommo-sexuality* [*hommo-sexualité*]—at times also written *hom(m)osexuality* [*hom(m)osexualité*]—Irigaray puns on the French word for man, *homme*, from the Latin *homo* (meaning 'man'), and the Greek *homo* (meaning 'same'). In taking up her distinction between homosexuality (or homo-sexuality) and 'hommosexuality' (or 'hom(m)osexuality'), I want to remark the conceptual distance between the former term, homosexuality, by which I mean lesbian (or gay) sexuality, and the diacritically marked hommo-sexuality, which is the term of sexual indifference, the term (in fact) of heterosexuality; I want to re-mark both the incommensurable distance between them and the conceptual ambiguity that is conveyed by the two almost identical acoustic images. Another paradox—or is it perhaps the same?

. . .

Pardon me, I must be going!

(Djuna Barnes, *The Ladies Almanack*)

Lesbian representation, or rather, its condition of possibility, depends on separating out the two contrary undertows that constitute the paradox of sexual (in)difference, on isolating but maintaining the two senses of homosexuality and hommo-sexuality. Thus the critical effort to dislodge the erotic from the discourse of gender, with its indissoluble knot of sexuality and reproduction, is concurrent and interdependent with a rethinking of what, in most cultural discourses and sociosexual practices, is still, nevertheless, a gendered sexuality. In the pages that follow, I will attempt to work through these paradoxes by considering how lesbian writers and artists have sought variously to escape gender, to deny it, transcend it, or perform it in excess, and to inscribe the erotic in cryptic, allegorical, realistic, camp, or other modes of representation, pursuing diverse strategies of writing and of reading the intransitive and yet obdurate relation of reference to meaning, of flesh to language.

Gertrude Stein, for example, 'encrypted' her experience of the body in obscure coding, her 'somagrams' are neither sexually explicit or conventionally erotic, nor 'radically visceral or visual', Catharine Stimpson argues.[3] Stein's effort was, rather, to develop a distinguished 'anti-language' in which to describe sexual activity, her 'delight in the female body' (38) or her ambivalence about it, as an abstract though intimate relationship where 'the body fuses with writing itself' (36), an act 'at once richly pleasurable and violent' (38). But if Stein does belong to the history of women writers, claims Stimpson, who also claims her for the history of lesbian writers, it is not because she wrote out of femaleness 'as an elemental condition, inseparable from the body' (40), the way some radical feminist critics would like to think; nor because her writing sprung from a preoedipal, maternal body, as others would have it. Her language was not 'female' but quite the contrary, 'as genderless as an atom of platinum' (42), and strove to obliterate the boundaries of gender identity.

Djuna Barnes's *Nightwood*, which Stimpson calls a 'parable of damnation,'[4] is read by others as an affirmation of inversion as homosexual difference. In her 'Writing Toward *Nightwood*: Djuna Barnes's Seduction Stories', Carolyn Allen reads Barnes's 'little girl' stories as sketches or earlier trials of the sustained meditation on inversion that was to yield in the novel the most suggestive portrait of the invert, the third sex.

> In that portrait we recognize the boy in the girl, the girl in the Prince, not a mixing of gendered behaviors, but the creation of a new gender, 'neither one and half the other' . . . . In their love of the same sex [Matthew, Nora, and Robin] admire their non-conformity, their sexual difference from the rest of the world.[5]

That difference, which for the lesbian includes a relation to the self-same ('a woman is yourself caught as you turn in panic; on her mouth you kiss your own,' says Nora), also includes her relation to the child, the 'ambivalence about mothering one's lover', the difficult and inescapable ties of female sexuality with nurture and with violence. In this light, Allen suggests, may we read Barnes's personal denial of lesbianism and her aloofness from female admirers as a refusal to accept and to live by the homophobic categories promoted by sexology: man and woman, with their respective deviant forms, the effeminate man and the mannish woman—a refusal that in the terms of my argument could be seen as a rejection of the hommo-sexual categories of gender, a refusal of sexual (in)difference.

Thus the highly metaphoric, oblique, allusive language of Barnes's fiction, her 'heavily embedded and often appositional' syntax, her use of the passive voice, indirect style, and interior monologue techniques in narrative descriptions, which Allen admirably analyzes in another essay, are motivated less by the modernist's pleasure in formal experimentation than by her resistance to what *Nightwood* both thematizes and demonstrates, the failure of language to represent, grasp, and convey her subjects: 'The violation [of reader's expectation] and the appositional structure permit Barnes to suggest that the naming power of language is insufficient to make Nora's love for Robin perceivable to the reader.'[6]

> 'Dr Knox,' Edward began, 'my problem this week is chiefly concerning restrooms.'
>
> (Judy Grahn, 'The Psychoanalysis of Edward the Dyke')

Ironically, since one way of escaping gender is to so disguise erotic and sexual experience as to suppress any representation of its specificity, another avenue of escape leads the lesbian writer fully to embrace gender, if by replacing femaleness with masculinity, as in the case of Stephen Gordon in *The Well of Loneliness*, and so risk to collapse lesbian homosexuality into hommo-sexuality. However, representation is related to experience by codes that change historically and, significantly, reach in both directions: the writer struggles to inscribe experience in historically available forms of representation, the reader accedes to representation through her own historical and experiential context; each reading is a rewriting of the text, each writing a rereading of (one's) experience The contrasting readings of Radclyffe Hall's novel by lesbian feminist critics show that each critic reads from a particular position, experiential but also historically available to her, and, moreover, a position chosen, or even politically assumed, from the spectrum of contemporary discourses on the relationship of feminism to lesbianism. The contrast of interpretations also shows to what extent the paradox of sexual (in)difference operates as a semiotic mechanism to produce contradictory meaning effects.

The point of contention in the reception of a novel that by general agreement was the single most popular representation of lesbianism in fiction, from its obscenity trial in 1928 to the 1970s, is the figure of its protagonist Stephen Gordon, the 'mythic mannish lesbian' of the title of Esther Newton's essay, and the prototype of her more recent incarnation, the working-class butch.[7] Newton's impassioned defense of the novel rests on the significance of that figure for lesbian self-definition, not only in the 1920s and 1930s, when the social gains in gender independence attained by the New Woman were being reappropriated via sexological discourses within the institutional practices of heterosexuality, but also in the 1970s and 1980s, when female sexuality has been redefined by a women's movement 'that swears it is the enemy of traditional gender categories and yet validates lesbianism as the ultimate form of femaleness' (558).

Newton argues historically, taking into account the then available discourses on sexuality which asserted that 'normal' women had at best a reactive heterosexual desire, while female sexual deviancy articulated itself in ascending categories of inversion marked by increasing masculinization, from deviant—but rectifiable—sexual orientation (or 'homosexuality' proper, for Havelock Ellis) to congenital inversion. Gender crossing was at once a symptom and a sign of sexual degeneracy.[8] In the terms of the cultural representations available to the novelist, since there was no image of female sexual desire apart from the male, Newton asks, 'Just how was Hall to make the woman-loving New Woman a sexual being? . . . To become avowedly sexual, the New Woman had to enter the male world, either as a heterosexual on male terms (a flapper) or as—or with—a lesbian in male body drag (a butch)' (572–73). Gender reversal in the mannish lesbian, then, was not merely a claim to male social privilege or a sad pretense to male sexual behavior, but represented what may be called, in Foucault's phrase, a 'reverse discourse': an assertion of sexual agency and feelings, but autonomous from men, a reclaiming of erotic drives directed toward women, of a desire for women that is not to be confused with woman identification.

While other lesbian critics of *The Well of Loneliness* read it as an espousal of Ellis's views, couched in religious romantic imagery and marred by a self-defeating pessimism, aristocratic self-pity, and inevitable damnation, what Newton reads in Stephen Gordon and in Radclyffe Hall's text is the unsuccessful attempt to represent a female desire not determined by 'masculine tropism', in Irigaray's words, or, in my own, a female desire not hommo-sexual but homosexual. If Radclyffe Hall herself could not envision homosexuality as part of an autonomous female sexuality (a notion that has emerged much later, with the feminist critique of patriarchy as phallic symbolic order), and if she therefore did not succeed in escaping the hommo-sexual categories of gender ('Unlike Orlando, Stephen is trapped in history; she cannot declare gender an irrelevant game,' as Newton remarks [570]), nevertheless the figure of the mannish female invert continues to stand as the representation of lesbian desire against both the discourse of hommo-sexuality and the feminist account of lesbianism as woman identification. The context of Newton's reading is the current debate on the relationship of lesbianism to feminism and the reassertion, on the one hand, of the historical and political importance of gender roles (e.g. butch–femme) in lesbian self-definition and representation, and on the other, of the demand for a separate understanding of sex and gender as distinct areas of social practice.

The latter issue has been pushed to the top of the theoretical agenda by the polarization of opinions around the two adverse and widely popularized positions on the issue of pornography taken by Women Against Pornography (WAP) and by S/M lesbians (Samois). In 'Thinking Sex,' a revision of her earlier and very influential 'The Traffic in Women', Gayle Rubin wants to challenge the assumption that feminism can contribute very much to a theory of sexuality, for 'feminist thought simply lacks angles of vision which can encompass the social organization of sexuality.'[9] While acknowledging some (though hardly enough) diversity among feminists on the issue of sex, and praising 'pro-sex' feminists such as 'lesbian sadomasochists and butch–femme dykes', adherents of 'classic radical feminism', and 'unapologetic heterosexuals' for not conforming to 'movement standards of purity' (303), Rubin nonetheless believes that a 'theory and politics specific to sexuality' must be developed apart from the theory of gender oppression, that is feminism. Thus she goes back over her earlier feminist critique of Lacan and Lévi-Strauss and readjusts the angle of vision:

'The Traffic in Women' was inspired by the literature on kin-based systems of social organization. It appeared to me at the time that gender and desire were systematically intertwined in such social formations. This may or may not be an accurate assessment of the relationship between sex and gender *in tribal organizations.* But it is surely not an adequate formulation for sexuality *in Western industrial societies.* (307, emphasis added)

In spite of Rubin's rhetorical emphasis (which I underscore graphically in the above passage), her earlier article also had to do with gender and sexuality in Western industrial societies, where indeed Rubin and several other feminists were articulating the critique of a theory of symbolic signification that elaborated the very notion of desire (from psychoanalysis) in relation to gender as symbolic construct (from anthropology)—a critique that has been crucial to the development of feminist theory. But whereas 'The Traffic in Women' (a title directly borrowed from Emma Goldman) was focused on women, here her interest has shifted toward a non-gendered notion of sexuality concerned, in Foucault's terms 'with the sensations of the body, the quality of pleasures, and the nature of impressions'.[10]

Accordingly, the specificity of either female or lesbian eroticism is no longer a question to be asked in 'Thinking Sex', where the term 'homosexual' is used to refer to both women and men (thus sliding inexorably, it seems, into its uncanny hommo-sexual double), and which concludes by advocating a politics of 'theoretical as well as sexual puralism' (309). At the opposite pole of the debate, Catharine MacKinnon argues:

If heterosexuality is the dominant gendered form of sexuality in a society where gender oppresses women through sex, sexuality and heterosexuality are essentially the same thing. This does not erase homosexuality, it merely means that sexuality in that form may be no less gendered.[11]

I suggest that, despite or possibly because of their stark mutual opposition and common reductivism, both Rubin and MacKinnon collapse the tension of ambiguity, the semantic duplicity, that I have tried to sort out in the two terms homosexual and hommo-sexual, and thus remain caught in the paradox of sexual (in)difference even as they both, undoubtedly, very much want to escape it, one by denying gender, the other by categorically asserting it. As it was, in another sense, with Radclyffe Hall, Newton's suggestive reading notwithstanding. I will return to her suggestions later on.

> A theory in the flesh.
>
> (Cherríe Moraga, *This Bridge Called My Back*)

It is certain, however, as Rubin notes, that 'lesbians are *also* oppressed as queers and perverts' (308, emphasis added), not only as women; and it is equally certain that some lesbians are also oppressed as queers and perverts, and *also* as women of color. What cannot be elided in a politically responsible theory of sexuality, of gender, or of culture is the critical value of that 'also', which is neither simply additive nor exclusive but signals the nexus, the mode of operation of *interlocking* systems of gender, sexual, racial, class, and other, more local categories of social stratification.[12] Just a few lines from *Zami*, Audre Lorde's 'biomythography', will make the point, better than I can.

> But the fact of our Blackness was an issue that Felicia and I talked about only between ourselves. Even Muriel seemed to believe that as lesbians, we were all outsiders and all equal in our outsiderhood. 'We're all niggers,' she used to say, and I hated to hear her say it. It was wishful thinking based on little fact; the ways in which it was true languished in the shadow of those many ways in which it would always be false.
>
> It was hard enough to be Black, to be Black and female, to be Black, female, and gay. To be Black, female, gay, and out of the closet in a white environment, even to the extent of dancing in the Bagatelle, was considered by many Black lesbians to be simply suicidal. And if you were fool enough to do it, you'd better come on so tough that nobody messed with you. I often felt put down by their sophistication, their clothes, their manners, their cars, and their femmes.[13]

If the black/white divide is even less permeable than the gay/straight one, it does not alone suffice to self-definition: 'Being Black dykes together was not enough. We were different. . . . Self-preservation warned some of us that we could not afford to settle for one easy definition, one narrow individuation of self' (226). Neither race nor gender nor homosexual difference alone can constitute individual identity or the basis for a theory and a politics of social change. What Lorde suggests is a more complex image of the psycho-socio-sexual subject ('our place was the very house of difference rather than the security of any one particular difference') which does not deny gender or sex but transcends them. Read together with the writings of other lesbians of color or those committed to antiracism, Lorde's image of the house of difference points to a conception of community not pluralistic but at once global and local—global in its inclusive and macro-political strategies, and local in its specific, micro-political practices.

I want to propose that, among the latter, not the least is the practice of writing, particularly in that form which the *québecoise* feminist writer Nicole Brossard has called '*une fiction théorique*', fiction/theory: a formally experimental, critical and lyrical, autobiographical and theoretically conscious, practice of writing-in-the-feminine that crosses genre boundaries (poetry and prose, verbal and visual modes, narrative and cultural criticism), and instates new correlations between signs and meanings, inciting other discursive mediations between the symbolic and the real, language and flesh.[14] And for all its specific cultural, historical, and linguistic variation—say between francophone and anglophone contemporary Canadian writers, or between writers such as Gloria Anzaldúa, Michelle Cliff, Cherríe Moraga, Joanna Russ, Monique Wittig, or even the Virginia Woolf of *Three Guineas* and *A Room of One's Own*—the concept of fiction/theory does make the transfer across borderlines and covers a significant range of practices of lesbian (self-)representation.

> Lesbians are not women.
>
> (Monique Wittig, 'The Straight Mind')

In a superb essay tracing the intertextual weave of a lesbian imagination throughout French literature, the kind of essay that changes the landscape of both literature and reading irreversibly, Elaine Marks proposes that to undomesticate the female body one must dare reinscribe it in excess—as excess—in provocative counterimages sufficiently outrageous, passionate, verbally violent and formally complex to both destroy the male discourse on love and redesign the universe.[15] The undomesticated female body that was first *concretely* imaged in Sappho's poetry ('she is suggesting equivalences between the physical symptoms of desire and the physical symptoms of death, not between Eros and Thanatos,' Marks writes [372]) has been read and effectively recontained within the male poetic tradition—with the very move described by Halperin above—as phallic or maternal body. Thereafter, Marks states, no 'sufficiently challenging counterimages' were produced in French literature until the advent of feminism and the writing of a lesbian feminist, Monique Wittig.

'Only the women's movement', concurred the writer in her preface to the 1975 English edition of *The Lesbian Body*, 'has proved capable of producing lesbian texts in a context of total rupture with masculine culture, texts written by women exclusively for women, careless of male approval.'[16] If there is reason to believe that Wittig would no longer accept the designation lesbian-feminist in the 1980s (her latest published novel in English, *Across the Acheron*, more than suggests as much), Marks's critical assessment of *The Lesbian Body* remains, to my way of seeing, correct:

> In *Le corps lesbien* Monique Wittig has created, through the incessant use of hyperbole and a refusal to employ traditional body codes, images sufficiently blatant to withstand reabsorption into male literary culture. . . . The J/e of *Le corps lesbien* is the most powerful lesbian in literature because as a lesbian-feminist she reexamines and redesigns the universe. (375–76)

Like Djuna Barnes's, Wittig's struggle is with language, to transcend gender. Barnes, as Wittig reads her, succeeds in 'universalizing the feminine' because she 'cancels out the genders by making them obsolete. I find it necessary to suppress them. That is the point of view of a lesbian.'[17] And indeed, from the impersonal *on* [one] in *L'Opoponax*, to the feminine plural *elles* [they] replacing the generic masculine *ils* [they] in *Les guérillères*, to the divided, linguistically impossible *j/e* [*I*], lover and writing subject of *The Lesbian Body*, Wittig's personal pronouns work to 'lesbianize' language as impudently as her recastings of both classical and Christian myth and Western literary genres (the Homeric heroes and Christ, *The Divine Comedy* and *Don Quixote*, the epic, the lyric, the *Bildungsroman*, the encyclopaedic dictionary) do to literary history.[18] What will not do, for her purposes, is a 'feminine writing' [*écriture féminine*] which, for Wittig, is no more than 'the naturalizing metaphor of the brutal political fact of the domination of women' (63) and so complicit in the reproduction of femininity and of the female body as Nature.

Thus, as I read it, it is in the garbage dump of femininity, 'In this dark adored adorned gehenna,' that the odyssey of Wittig's *j/e-tu* in *The Lesbian Body* begins: 'Fais tes adieux m/a trés belle,' 'say your farewells m/y very beautiful . . . strong . . . indomitable . . . learned . . . ferocious . . . gentle . . best beloved to what they call affection tenderness or gracious abandon. No one is unaware of what takes place here, it has no name as yet.'[19] Here where?—in this book, this journey into the body of Western culture, this season in hell. And what takes place here?—the dismemberment and slow decomposition of the *female* body limb by limb, organ by organ, secretion by secretion. No one will be able to stand the sight of it, no one will come to aid in this awesome, excruciating and exhilarating labor of love: dis-membering and re-membering, reconstituting the body in a new erotic economy, relearning to know it ('it has no name as yet') by another semiotics, reinscribing it with invert/inward desire, rewriting it otherwise, other-wise: a *lesbian* body.

The project, the conceptual originality and radical import of Wittig's lesbian as subject of a 'cognitive practice' that enables the reconceptualization of the social and of knowledge itself from a position eccentric to the heterosexual institution, are all there in the first page of *Le corps lesbien*.[20] A 'subjective cognitive practice' and a practice of writing as consciousness of contradiction ('the language you speak is made up of words that are killing you,' she wrote in *Les guérillères*); a consciousness of writing, living, feeling, and desiring in the noncoincidence of experience and language, in the interstices of representation, 'in the intervals that your masters have not been able to fill with their words of proprietors.'[21] Thus, the struggle with language to rewrite the body beyond its precoded, conventional representations is not and cannot be a reappropriation of the female body as it is, domesticated, maternal, oedipally or preoedipally en-gendered, but is a struggle to transcend both gender and 'sex' and re-create the body other-wise: to see it perhaps as monstrous, or grotesque, or mortal, or violent, and certainly also sexual, but with a material and sensual specificity that will resist phallic idealization and render it accessible to women in another sociosexual economy. In short, if it were not lesbian, this body would make no sense.

> Replacing the Lacanian slash with a lesbian bar.
>
> (Sue-Ellen Case, 'Towards a Butch–Femme Aesthetic')

At first sight, the reader of *The Lesbian Body* might find in its linguistically impossible subject pronoun several theoretically possible valences that go from the more conservative (the slash in *j/e* represents the division of the Lacanian subject) to the less conservative (*j/e* can be expressed by writing but not by speech, representing Derridean *différance*), and to the radical feminist ('*j/e* is the symbol of the lived, rending experience which is *m/y* writing, of this cutting in two which throughout literature is the exercise of a language which does not constitute m/e as subject,' as Wittig is reported to have said in Margaret Crosland's introduction to the Beacon paperback edition I own). Another reader, especially if a reader of science fiction, might think of Joanna Russ's brilliant lesbian-feminist novel, *The Female Man*, whose protagonist is a female genotype articulated across four spacetime probabilities in four characters whose names all begin with J—Janet, Jeannine, Jael, Joanna—and whose sociosexual practices cover the spectrum from celibacy and 'politically correct' monogamy to live toys and the 1970s equivalent of s/m.[22] What Wittig actually said in one of her essays in the 1980s is perhaps even more extreme:

> The bar in the j/e of *The Lesbian Body* is a sign of excess. A sign that helps to imagine an excess of 'I,' an 'I' exalted. 'I' has become so powerful in *The Lesbian Body* that it can attack the order of heterosexuality in texts and assault the so-called love, the heroes of love, and lesbianize them, lesbianize the symbols, lesbianize the gods and the goddesses, lesbianize the men and the women. This 'I' can be destroyed in the attempt and resuscitated. Nothing resists this 'I' (or this *tu* [you], which is its name, its love), which spreads itself in the whole world of the book, like a lava flow that nothing can stop.[23]

Excess, an exaltation of the 'I' through costume, performance, *mise-en-scène*, irony, and utter manipulation of appearance, is what Sue-Ellen Case sees in the discourse of camp. If it is deplorable that the lesbian working-class bar culture of the 1950s 'went into the feminist closet' during the 1970s, when organizations such as the Daughters of Bilitis encouraged lesbian identification with the more legitimate feminist dress codes and upwardly mobile lifestyles, writes Case, 'yet the closet, or the bars, with their hothouse atmosphere [have] given us camp—the style, the discourse, the *mise-en-scène* of butch–femme roles.' In these roles, 'recuperating the space of seduction,'

> the butch–femme couple inhabit the subject position together. . . . These are not split subjects, suffering the torments of dominant ideology. They are coupled ones that do not impale themselves on the poles of sexual difference or metaphysical values, but constantly seduce the sign system, through flirtation and inconstancy into the light fondle of artifice, replacing the Lacanian slash with a lesbian bar.[24]

The question of address, of who produces cultural representations and for whom (in any medium, genre, or semiotic system, from writing to performance), and of who receives them and in what contexts, has been a major concern of feminism and other critical theories of cultural marginality. In the visual arts, that concern has focused on the notion of spectatorship, which has been central to the feminist critique of representation and the production of different images of difference, for example in women's cinema.[25] Recent work in both film and performance theory has been elaborating the film-theoretical notion of spectatorship with regard to what may be the specific relations of homosexual subjectivity, in several directions. Elizabeth Ellsworth, for one, surveying the reception of *Personal Best* (1982), a commercial man-made film about a lesbian relationship between athletes, found that lesbian feminist reviews of the film adopted interpretive strategies which rejected or altered the meaning carried by conventional (Hollywood) codes of narrative representation. For example, they redefined who was the film's protagonist or 'object of desire', ignored the sections focused on heterosexual romance, disregarded the actual ending and speculated, instead, on a possible extratextual future for the characters beyond the ending. Moreover, 'some reviewers named and illicitly eroticized moments of the film's "inadvertent lesbian verisimilitude" [in Patrice Donnelly's performance] . . . codes of body language, facial expression, use of voice, structuring and expression of desire and assertion of strength in the face of male domination and prerogative.'[26]

While recognizing limits to this 'oppositional appropriation' of dominant representation, Ellsworth argues that the struggle over interpretation is a constitutive process for marginal subjectivities, as well as an important form of resistance. But when the marginal community is directly addressed, in the context of out-lesbian performance such as the WOW Cafe or the Split Britches productions, the appropriation seems to have no limits, to be directly 'subversive', to yield not merely a site of interpretive work and resistance but a representation that requires no interpretive effort and is immediately, univocally legible, signalling 'the creation of new imagery, new metaphors, and new conventions that can be read, or given new meaning, by a very specific spectator.'[27]

The assumption behind this view, as stated by Kate Davy, is that such lesbian performance 'undercut[s] the heterosexual model by implying a spectator that is not the generic, universal male, not the cultural construction "woman" but lesbian—a subject defined in terms of sexual similarity . . . whose desire lies outside the fundamental model or underpinnings of sexual difference' (47). Somehow, this seems too easy a solution to the problem of spectatorship, and even less convincing as a representation of 'lesbian desire'. For, if sexual similarity could so unproblematically replace sexual difference, why would the new lesbian theatre need to insist on gender, if only as 'the residue of sexual difference' that is, as Davy herself insists, worn in the 'stance, gesture, movement, mannerisms, voice, and dress' (48) of the butch–femme play? Why would lesbian camp be taken up in theatrical performance, as Case suggests, to recuperate that space of seduction which historically has been the lesbian bar, and the Left Bank salon before it—spaces of daily-life performance, masquerade, cross-dressing, and practices constitutive of both community and subjectivity?

In an essay on 'The Dynamics of Desire' in performance and pornography, Jill Dolan asserts that the reappropriation of pornography in lesbian magazines ('a visual space meant at least theoretically to be free of male subordination') offers 'liberative fantasies' and 'representations of one kind of sexuality based in lesbian desire', adding that the 'male forms' of pornographic representation 'acquire new meanings when they are used to communicate desire for readers of a different gender and sexual orientation'.[28] Again, as in Davy, the question of lesbian desire is begged; and again the ways in which the new context would produce new meanings or 'disrupt traditional meanings' (173) appear to be dependent on the presumption of a unified lesbian viewer/reader, gifted with undivided and non-contradictory subjectivity, and every bit as generalized and universal as the female spectator both Dolan and Davy impute (and rightly so) to the anti-pornography feminist performance art. For, if all lesbians had one and the same definition of 'lesbian desire' there would hardly be any debate among us, or any struggle over interpretations of cultural images, especially the ones we produce.

What is meant by a term so crucial to the specificity and originality claimed for these performances and strategies of representation, is not an inappropriate question, then. When she addresses it at the end of her essay, Dolan writes. 'Desire is not necessarily a fixed, male-owned commodity, but can be exchanged, with a much different meaning, between women' (173). Unless it can be taken as the ultimate camp representation, this notion of lesbian desire as commodity exchange is rather disturbing. For, unfortunately—or fortunately, as the case may be—commodity exchange does have the same meaning 'between women' as between men, by definition—that is, by Marx's definition of the structure of capital. And so, if the 'aesthetic differences between cultural feminist and lesbian performance art' are to be determined by the presence or absence of pornography, and to depend on a 'new meaning' of commodity exchange, it is no wonder that we seem unable to get it off (our backs) even as we attempt to take it on.

> The king does not count lesbians.
>
> (Marilyn Frye, *The Politics of Reality*)

The difficulty in defining an autonomous form of female sexuality and desire in the wake of a cultural tradition still Platonic, still grounded in sexual (in)difference, still caught in the tropism of hommo-sexuality, is not to be overlooked or wilfully bypassed. It is perhaps even greater than the difficulty in devising strategies of representation which will, in turn, alter the standard of vision, the frame of reference of visibility, of *what can be seen.* For, undoubtedly, that is the project of lesbian performance, theatre and film, a project that has already achieved a significant measure of success, not only at the WOW Cafe but also, to mention just a few examples, in Cherríe Moraga's *teatro, Giving Up the Ghost* (1986), Sally Potter's film *The Gold Diggers* (1983), or Sheila McLaughlin's *She Must Be Seeing Things* (1987). My point here is that redefining the conditions of vision, as well as the modes of representing, cannot be predicated on a single, undivided identity of performer and audience (whether as 'lesbians' or 'women' or 'people of color' or any other single category constructed in opposition to its dominant other, 'heterosexual women', 'men', 'whites', and so forth).

Consider Marilyn Frye's suggestive Brechtian parable about our culture's conceptual reality ('phallocratic reality') as a conventional stage play, where the actors—those committed to the performance/maintenance of the Play, 'the phallocratic loyalists'—visibly occupy the foreground, while stagehands—who provide the necessary labor and framework for the material (re)production of the Play—remain invisible in the background. What happens, she speculates, when the stagehands (women, feminists) begin thinking of themselves as actors and try to participate visibly in the performance, attracting attention to their activities and their own role in the play? The loyalists cannot conceive that anyone in the audience may see or focus their attention on the stagehands' projects in the background, and thus become 'disloyal' to the Play, or, as Adrienne Rich has put it, 'disloyal to civilization',[29] Well, Frye suggests, there are some people in the audience who do see what the conceptual system of heterosexuality, the Play's performance, attempts to keep invisible. These are lesbian people, who can see it because their own reality is not represented or even surmised in the Play, and who therefore reorient their attention toward the background, the spaces, activities and figures of women elided by the performance. But 'attention is a kind of passion' that 'fixes and directs the application of one's physical and emotional work':

> If the lesbian sees the women, the woman may see the lesbian seeing her. With this, there is a flowering of possibilities. The woman, feeling herself seen, may learn that she *can be* seen; she may also be able to know that a woman can see, that is, can author perception. . . . The lesbian's seeing undercuts the mechanism by which the production and constant reproduction of heterosexuality for women was to be rendered *automatic. (172)*

And this is where we are now, as the critical reconsideration of lesbian history past and present is doing for feminist theory what Pirandello, Brecht, and others did for the bourgeois theatre conventions, and avant-garde filmmakers have done for Hollywood cinema; the latter, however, have not just disappeared, much as one would wish they had. So, too, have the conventions of seeing, and the relations of desire and meaning in spectatorship, remained partially anchored or contained by a frame of visibility that is still heterosexual, or hommo-sexual, and just as persistently color blind.

For instance, what are the 'things' the Black/Latina protagonist of McLaughlin's film imagines seeing, in her jealous fantasies about her white lover (although she does not 'really' see them), if not those very images which our cultural imaginary and the whole history of cinema have constructed as the visible, what can *be seen*, and eroticized? The originality of *She Must Be Seeing Things* is in its representing *the question of* lesbian desire in these terms, as it engages the contradictions and complicities that have emerged subculturally, in both discourses and practices, through the feminist-lesbian debates on sex-radical imagery as a political issue of representation, as well as real life. It may be interestingly contrasted with a formally conventional film like Donna Deitch's *Desert Hearts* (1986), where heterosexuality remains off screen, in the diegetic background (in the character's past), but is actively present nonetheless in the spectatorial expectations set up by the genre (the love story) and the visual pleasure procured by conventional casting, cinematic narrative procedures, and commercial distribution. In sum, one film works *with and against* the institutions of heterosexuality and cinema, the other works *with* them. A similar point could be made about certain films with respect to the novels they derive from, such as *The Color Purple* or *Kiss of the Spider Woman*, where the critical and formal work of the novels against the social and sexual indifference built into the institution of heterosexuality is altogether suppressed and rendered invisible by the films' compliance with the apparatus of commercial cinema and its institutional drive to, precisely, commodity exchange.

So what *can* be seen? Even in feminist film theory, the current 'impasse regarding female spectatorship is related to the blind spot of lesbianism,' Patricia White suggests in her reading of Ulrike Ottinger's film *Madame X: An Absolute Ruler* (1977).[30] That film, she argues, on the contrary, displaces the assumption 'that feminism finds its audience "naturally"' (95); it does so by addressing the female spectator through specific scenarios and 'figures of spectatorial desire' and 'trans-sex identification', through figures of transvestism and masquerade. And the position the film thus constructs for its spectator is not one of essential femininity or impossible masculinization (as proposed by Mary Ann Doane and Laura Mulvey, respectively), but rather a position of marginality or 'deviance' *vis-à-vis* the normative heterosexual frame of vision.[31]

Once again, what *can* be seen? 'When I go into a store, people see a black person and only incidentally a woman,' writes Jewelle Gomez, a writer of science fiction and author of at least one vampire story about a black lesbian blues singer named Gilda. 'In an Upper West Side apartment building late at night when a white woman refuses to get on an elevator with me, it's because I am black. She sees a mugger as described on the late night news, not another woman as nervous to be out alone as she is.'[32] If my suspicion that social and sexual indifference are never far behind one from the other is not just an effect of paranoia, it is quite possible that, in the second setting, the elevator at night, what a white woman sees superimposed on the black image of the mugger is the male image of the dyke, and both of these together are what prevents the white woman from seeing the other one like herself. Nevertheless, Gomez points out, 'I can pass as straight, if by some bizarre turn of events I should want to . . . but I cannot pass as white in this society.' Clearly, the very issue of passing, across any boundary of social division, is related quite closely to the frame of vision and the conditions of representation.

'Passing demands quiet. And from that quiet—silence,' writes Michelle Cliff.[33] It is 'a dual masquerade—passing straight/passing lesbian [that] enervates and contributes to speechlessness—to speak might be to reveal.'[34] However, and paradoxically again, speechlessness can only be overcome, and her 'journey into speech' begin, by 'claiming an identity they taught me to despise'; that is, by passing black 'against a history of forced fluency', a history of passing white.[35] The dual masquerade, her writing suggests, is at once the condition of speechlessness and of overcoming speechlessness, for the latter occurs by recognizing and representing the division in the self, the difference and the displacement from which any identity that needs to be claimed derives, and hence can be claimed only, in Lorde's words, as 'the very house of difference'.

Those divisions and displacements in history, memory, and desire are the 'ghost' that Moraga's characters want to but cannot altogether give up. The division of the Chicana lesbian Marisa/Corky from the Mexican Amalia, whose desire cannot be redefined outside the heterosexual imaginary of her culture, is also the division of Marisa/Corky from herself, the split produced in the girl Corky by sexual and social indifference, and by her internalization of a notion of hommo-sexuality which Marisa now lives as a wound, an infinite distance between her female body and her desire for women. If 'the realization of shared oppression on the basis of being women and Chicanas holds the promise of a community of Chicanas, both lesbians and heterosexual,' Yvonne Yarbro-Bejarano states, nevertheless 'the structure of the play does not move neatly from pain to promise,' and the divisions within them remain unresolved.[36] The character Marisa, however, I would add, has moved away from the hommo-sexuality of Corky (her younger self at age 11 and 17); and with the ambiguous character of Amalia, who loved a man almost as if he were a woman and who can love Marisa only when she (Amalia) is no longer one, the play itself has moved away from any simple opposition of 'lesbian' to 'heterosexual' and into the conceptual and experiential continuum of a female, Chicana subjectivity from where the question of lesbian desire must finally be posed. The play ends with that question—which is at once its outcome and its achievement, its *éxito*.

> What to do with the feminine invert?
>
> (Esther Newton, 'The Mythic Mannish Lesbian')

Surveying the classic literature on inversion, Newton notes that Radclyffe Hall's 'vision of lesbianism as sexual difference and as masculinity', and her 'conviction that sexual desire must be male', both assented to and sought to counter the sociomedical discourses of the early twentieth century. 'The notion of a feminine lesbian contradicted the congenital theory that many homosexuals in Hall's era espoused to counter the demands that they undergo punishing "therapies" (575). Perhaps that counter-demand led the novelist further to reduce the typology of female inversion (initially put forth by Krafft-Ebing as comprised of four types, then reduced to three by Havelock Ellis) to two: the invert and the 'normal' woman who misguidedly falls in love with her. Hence the novel's emphasis on Stephen, while her lover Mary is a 'forgettable and inconsistent' character who in the end gets turned over to a man. However, unlike Mary, Radclyffe Hall's real-life lover Una Troubridge 'did not go back to heterosexuality even when Hall, late in her life, took a second lover', Newton points out. Una would then represent what *The Well of Loneliness* elided, the third type of female invert, and the most troublesome for Ellis: the 'womanly' women 'to whom the actively inverted woman is most attracted. These women differ in the first place from normal or average women in that. . . they seem to possess a genuine, though not precisely sexual, preference for women over men.'[37] Therefore, Newton concludes, 'Mary's real story has yet to be told' (575), and a footnote after this sentence refers us to 'two impressive beginnings' of what could be Mary's real story, told from the perspective of a self-identified, contemporary femme.[38]

The discourses, demands, and counter-demands that inform lesbian identity and representation in the 1980s are more diverse and socially heterogeneous than those of the first half of the century. They include, most notably, the political concepts of oppression and agency developed in the struggles of social movements such as the women's movement, the gay liberation movement, and Third World feminism, as well as an awareness of the importance of developing a theory of sexuality that takes into account the working of unconscious processes in the construction of female subjectivity. But, as I have tried to argue, the discourses, demands, and counter-demands that inform lesbian representation are still unwittingly caught in the paradox of socio-sexual (in)difference, often unable to think homosexuality and hommo-sexuality at once separately *and* together. Even today, in most representational contexts, Mary would be either passing lesbian or passing straight, her (homo)sexuality being in the last instance what cannot be seen. Unless, as Newton and others suggest, she enter the frame of vision *as or with* a lesbian in male body drag.[39]

Notes

1. Luce Irigaray, '*Cosí fan tutti*', in *This Sex Which Is Not One*, trans. Catherine Porter (Ithaca, NY: Cornell University Press, 1985), 86. The phrase 'sexual

indifference' actually appeared in Luce Irigaray, *Speculum of the Other Woman* [1974], trans. Gillian C. Gill (Ithaca, NY: Cornell University Press, 1985), 28.

2. Irigaray, *Speculum*, 101–103.
3. Catharine R. Stimpson, 'The Somagrams of Gertrude Stein', in *The Female Body in Western Culture: Contemporary Perspectives*, ed. Susan Suleiman (Cambridge, Masss.: Harvard University Press, 1986), 34.
4. Catharine R. Stimpson, 'Zero Degree Deviancy: The Lesbian Novel in English', *Critical Inquiry*, 8: 2 (1981), 369.
5. Carolyn Allen, 'Writing Toward *Nightwood:* Djuna Barnes's Seduction Stories', forthcoming in *Silence and Power: A Reevaluation of Djuna Barnes*, ed. M. L. Broe (Carbondale: Southern Illinois University Press, 1987).
6. Carolyn Allen, '"Dressing the Unknowable in the Garments of the Known": The Style of Djuna Barnes' *Nightwood*', in *Women's Language and Style*, ed. Butturft and Epstein (Akron: L&S Books, 1978), 116.
7. Esther Newton, 'The Mythic Mannish Lesbian: Radclyffe Hall and the New Woman', *Signs*, 9: 4 (1984), 557–575. See also Madeline Davis and Elizabeth Lapovsky Kennedy, 'Oral History and the Study of Sexuality in the Lesbian Community: Buffalo, New York, 1940–1960', *Feminist Studies*, 12: 1 (1986), 7–26; and Joan Nestle, 'Butch–Fem Relationships: Sexual Courage in the 1950s', *Heresies*, 12 (l981), 21–24, now reprinted in Joan Nestle, *A Restricted Country* (Ithaca, NY: Firebrand Books, 1987), 100–109.
8. See the discussion of Krafft-Ebing, Ellis, and others in George Chauncey, Jr., 'From Sexual Inversion to Homosexuality: Medicine and the Changing Conceptualization of Female Deviance', *Salmagundi*, 58–59 (1982–83), 114–146, and in Carroll Smith-Rosenberg, 'The New Woman as Androgyne', in *Disorderly Conduct: Visions of Gender in Victorian America* (New York: Oxford University Press, 1985), 245–349.
9. Gayle Rubin, 'Thinking Sex: Notes for a Radical Theory of the Politics of Sexuality', in *Pleasure and Danger: Exploring Female Sexuality*, ed. Carole S. Vance (Boston: Routledge & Kegan Paul, 1984), 309; 'The Traffic in Women: Notes on the "Political Economy" of Sex', in *Toward an Anthropology of Women*, ed. Rayna R. Reiter (New York: Monthly Review Press, 1975), 157–210. On the feminist 'sex wars' of the 1970s and 1980s, see B. Ruby Rich, 'Feminism and Sexuality in the 1980s', *Feminist Studies*, 12: 3 (1986), 525–561. On the relationship of feminism to lesbianism, see also Wendy Clark, 'The Dyke, the Feminist and the Devil', in *Sexuality: A Reader*, ed. *Feminist Review* (London: Virago, 1987), 201–215.
10. Michel Foucault, *The History of Sexuality* (New York: Pantheon, 1978), 106, cited by Rubin, 'Thinking Sex', 307. For a critical reading of the relevance and limitations of Foucault's views with regard to female sexuality, see Biddy Martin, 'Feminism, Criticism, and Foucault', *New German Critique, 27* (1982), 3–30, and Teresa de Lauretis, *Technologies of Gender: Essays on Theory, Film, and Fiction* (Bloomington: Indiana University Press, 1987), chapters 1 and 2.
11. Catharine A MacKinnon, *Feminism Unmodified: Discourses on Life and Law* (Cambridge, Mass.: Harvard University Press, 1987), 60.
12. 'Combahee River Collective, 'A Black Feminist Statement', in *This Bridge Called My Back: Writings by Radical Women of Color*, ed. Cherríe Moraga and Gloria Anzaldúa (New York: Kitchen Table: Women of Color Press, 1983), 210.

13. Audre Lorde, *Zami: A New Spelling of My Name* (Trumansburg, New York: The Crossing Press, 1982), 203 and 224.
14. 'Writing. It's work. Changing the relationship with language . . . Women's fictions raise theoretical issues: women's theorizing appears as/in fiction. Women's writing disturbs our usual understanding of the terms fiction and theory which assign value to discourses . . . Fiction/theory has been the dominant mode of feminist writing in Québec for more than a decade,' states Barbara Godard for the editorial collective of *Tessera*, no. 3, a Canadian feminist, dual-language publication that has appeared annually as a special issue of an already established magazine ('Fiction/Theory: Editorial', *Canadian Fiction Magazine*, 57 (1986), 3–4). See Nicole Brossard, *L'Amèr ou Le Chapitre effrité* (Montréal: Quinze, 1977), and *These Our Mothers Or: The Disintegrating Chapter*, trans. Barbara Godard (Toronto: Coach House, 1983). On Brossard and other Canadian writers of fiction/theory, see Shirley Neuman, 'Importing Difference', and other essays in *A Mazing Space: Writing Canadian Women Writing*, ed. Shirley Neuman and Smaro Kamboureli (Edmonton: Longspoon Press and NeWest Press, 1986).
15. Elaine Marks, 'Lesbian Intertextuality', in *Homosexualities and French Literature*, ed. George Stambolian and Elaine Marks (Ithaca, NY: Cornell University Press, 1979), 353–377.
16. Monique Wittig, *The Lesbian Body*, trans. David LeVay (New York: William Morrow, 1975), 9, cited by Marks, 373.
17. Monique Wittig. 'The Point of View: Universal or Particular', *Feminist Issues*, 3: 2 (1983), 64.
18. See Hélène Vivienne Wenzel, 'The Text as Body/Politics: An Appreciation of Monique Wittig's Writings in Context', *Feminist Studies*, 7: 2 (1981), 264–287, and Namascar Shaktini, 'Displacing the Phallic Subject: Wittig's Lesbian Writing', *Signs*, 8: 1 (1982), 29–44, who writes: 'Wittig's reorganization of metaphor around the lesbian body represents an epistemological shift from what seemed until recently the absolute, central metaphor—the phallus' (29).
19. Monique Wittig, *Le corps lesbien* (Paris: Minuit, 1973), 7. I have revised the English translation that appears in *The Lesbian Body*, 15.
20. The concept of 'subjective, cognitive practice' is elaborated in Wittig, 'One Is Not Born a Woman', *Feminist Issues*, 1: 2 (1981), 47–54. I discuss it at some length in my 'Eccentric Subjects', forthcoming in *Poetics Today.*
21. Monique Wittig *Les Guérillères*, trans. David LeVay (Boston: Beacon Press, 1985), 114.
22. Joanna Russ, *The Female Man* (New York: Bantam, 1975). See also Catherine L. McClenahan, 'Textual Politics: The Uses of Imagination in Joanna Russ's *The Female Man*', *Transactions of the Wisconsin Academy of Sciences, Arts and Letters* 70 (1982), 114–125.
23. Monique Wittig, 'The Mark of Gender', *Feminist Issues, 5: 2* (1985), 71.
24. Sue-Ellen Case, 'Towards a Butch–Femme Aesthetic', in *Feminist Perspectives on Contemporary Women's Drama*, ed. Lynda Hart (Ann Arbor: University of Michigan Press, forthcoming). The butch–femme couple, like Wittig's *j/e–tu* and like the s/m lesbian couple—all of whom, in their respective self-definitions, are one the name and the love of the other—propose a dual subject that brings to mind again Irigaray's *This Sex Which Is Not One*, though they all would adamantly deny the latter's suggestion that a non-phallic eroti-

cism may be traced to the preoedipal relation to the mother. One has to wonder, however, whether the denial has more to do with the committedly heterosexual bias of neo-Freudian psychoanalysis and object relations theory, with their inability to work through the paradox of sexual (in)difference on which they are founded but perhaps not destined to, or with our rejection of the maternal body which phallic representation has utterly alienated from women's love, from our desire for the self-same, by colonizing it as the 'dark continent' and so rendering it at once powerless and inaccessible to us and to all 'others'.

25. See, for example, Judith Mayne, 'The Woman at the Keyhole: Women's Cinema and Feminist Criticism', and B. Ruby Rich, 'From Repressive Tolerance to Erotic Liberation: *Maedchen in Uniform*', in *Re-vision: Essays in Feminist Film Criticism*, ed. Mary Ann Doane, Patricia Mellencamp and Linda Williams (Frederick, Md.: University Publications of America and the American Film Institute, 1984), 49–66 and 100–130; and Teresa de Lauretis, 'Rethinking Women's Cinema: Aesthetics and Feminist Theory', in *Technologies of Gender*, 127–148.
26. Elizabeth Ellsworth, 'Illicit Pleasures: Feminist Spectators and Personal Best', *Wide Angle*, 8: 2 (1986), 54.
27. Kate Davy, 'Constructing the Spectator: Reception, Context, and Address in Lesbian Performance', *Performing Arts Journal*, 10: 2 (1986), 49.
28. Jill Dolan, 'The Dynamics of Desire: Sexuality and Gender in Pornography and Performance', *Theatre Journal*, 39: 2 (1987), 171.
29. 'To Be and Be Seen', Marilyn Frye, *The Politics of Reality: Essays in Feminist Theory* (Trumansburg, New York: The Crossing Press, 1983), 166–173; Adrienne Rich, 'Disloyal to Civilization: Feminism, Racism, Gynephobia', in *On Lies, Secrets, and Silence: Selected Prose 1966–1978* (New York: Norton, 1979), 275–310.
30. Patricia White, 'Madame X of the China Seas', *Screen*, 28: 4 (1987), 82.
31. The two essays discussed are Mary Ann Doane, 'Film and the Masquerade: Theorising the Female Spectator,' *Screen* 23: 3–4 (1982), 74–87 and Laura Mulvey, 'Afterthoughts on "Visual Pleasure and Narrative Cinema" Inspired by *Duel in the Sun*', *Framework*, 15/16/17 (1981), 12–15. Another interesting discussion of the notion of masquerade in lesbian representation may be found in Sue-Ellen Case, 'Toward a Butch–Femme Aesthetic'.
32. Jewelle Gomez, 'Repeat After Me: We Are Different. We Are the Same', *Review of Law and Social Change*, 14: 4 (1986), 939. Her vampire story is 'No Day Too Long', in *Worlds Apart: An Anthology of Lesbian and Gay Science Fiction and Fantasy*, ed. Camilla Decarnin, Eric Garber, and Lyn Paleo (Boston: Alyson Publications, 1986), 215–223.
33. 'Passing', in Michelle Cliff, *The Land of Look Behind* (Ithaca, NY: Firebrand Books, 1985), 22.
34. Michelle Cliff, 'Notes on Speechlessness', *Sinister Wisdom*, 5 (1978), 7.
35. Michelle Cliff, 'A Journey into Speech' and 'Claiming an Identity They Taught Me to Despise', both in *The Land of Look Behind*, 11–17 and 40–47; see also her novel *No Telephone to Heaven* (New York: E. P. Dutton, 1987).
36. Yvonne Yarbro-Bejarano, 'Cherríe Moraga's *Giving up the Ghost:* The Representation of Female Desire', *Third Woman*, 3: 1–2 (1986), 118–119. See also

Cherríe Moraga, *Giving Up the Ghost: Teatro in Two Acts* (Los Angeles: West End Press, 1986).

37. Havelock Ellis, 'Sexual Inversion in Women', *Alienist and Neurologist*, 16 (1895), 141–158, cited by Newton, 'The Mythic Mannish Lesbian', 567.
38. Joan Nestle, 'Butch–Fem Relationships' (see note 7 above) and Amber Hollibaugh and Cherríe Moraga, 'What We're Rollin' Around in Bed With', both in *Heresies*, 12 (1981), 21–24 and 58–62.
39. For many of the ideas developed in this essay, I am indebted to the other participants of the student-directed seminar on Lesbian History and Theory sponsored by the Board in Studies in History of Consciousness at the University of California, Santa Cruz in Fall 1987. For support of various kinds, personal and professional, I thank Kirstie McClure, Donna Haraway, and Michael Cowan, Dean of Humanities and Arts.

Phase IV. Spectatorship, Ethnicity, and Melodrama

Introductory Notes

In this final section, I have collected essays that pertain to ethnicity and melodrama. Significantly, one finds scholars dealing with these topics returning to spectatorship. Mary Ann Doane's 1982 essay importantly furthered arguments begun in her essay in Phase I by adding to Mulvey's binary of passivity/activity aligned with female/male in cinema that of proximity and distance in regard to the image. I begin with this essay because it seems to me to open up space precisely for feminists to theorize female spectatorship differently—which begins to happen in the essays that follow.

Agreeing with Noel Burch and Christian Metz, Doane argues that for the male, the distance 'between the film and the spectator must be maintained, even measured' (p. 422). However, for the female spectator, in Doane's now famous formulation, 'there is a certain over-presence of the image—she *is* the image.' This results in a certain narcissism: As Doane puts it, 'the female look demands a becoming' (p. 423). Doane elaborates this position through examining so-called 'new French Feminisms', Freudian theories and Joan Riviere's concept of the female masquerade. In this latter phenomenon, the woman by her excess of femininity manufactures 'a lack in the form of a certain distance between oneself and one's image' (p. 000). In the latter half of the essay, Doane proceeds to elaborate what it might mean to 'masquerade' as a spectator through an examination of photographer Doisineau's picture 'Un Regard Oblique'. Doane concludes that there are only two possible positions for the female spectator—the masochism of over-identification with the image or the narcissism involved in becoming one's own object of desire. Masquerade is an effective strategy because it enables the female spectator to create a distance from the image in which it is manipulable. Doane objects to theories of repression because they lack power: women need to elaborate a theory of female spectatorship so as to dislocate the one male culture has constructed for them.

Annette Kuhn's 1984 intervention usefully highlights various problems in the work on female spectatorship in television soap operas and women's film melodramas. After noting the differing generic features between soap operas and melodramas, Kuhn outlines the three problems her essay will address, namely the problem of gendered spectatorship itself; secondly, the linked issue of the spectator conceived as universal or within an historical specificity; finally, the relationship between TV or film texts and their social historical and institutional contexts, which other essays in this volume have also aimed to address within the modernist problematic.

In regard to the first two problems, while she recognizes the difference between film and television critics of melodrama and soap opera respectively, Kuhn sees both groups as reducing the spectator and the audience to one another. This happens largely because the psychoanalytic theories which have been used 'offer little scope for theorizing subjectivity in its cultural or historical specificity' (p. 440). The universalism/specificity split is most evident in 'the gulf between textual analysis and contextual inquiry' (p. 440). Completely different methods are used in each type of analysis. Kuhn cites the case of Pam Cook's study of Gainsborough melodramas as both exemplary in trying to heal this gulf, but also failing in its aims.

In her final section, Kuhn usefully elaborates the different disciplinary methods needed to look at spectators or at audiences. Since there is often little discussion of the disciplinary base for different critical methods, Kuhn's essay is important in this regard. The method of study taken up by textual critics coming out of literary studies has produced the spectator largely as a subject constituted in signification. Kuhn argues that the model 'disregards the broader social implications of film going or televiewing . . . The social audience emphasizes the status of cinema and television as social and economic institutions' (p. 443). Scholars in TV studies are more likely to take up questions of a female *audience*, since TV theory 'has until fairly recently existed under the sociological rubric of media studies . . .' (p. 445).

Kuhn concludes by calling for more theorizing of the continuity between women as textual spectators and their status as social audience. This in turn suggests dealing with texts in their contexts. Further, such distinctions need also to inform debates about feminists producing film or video, since 'questions of context and reception are always paramount' here (p. 448).

Jackie Stacey's 1987 essay, 'Desperately Seeking Difference', proceeds to build on those of both Mary Ann Doane and Annette Kuhn. Stacey picks up on the relatively neglected homosexual pleasures of female spectatorship which had been discussed by Caroline Sheldon in 1977, by Lucy Arbuthnot and Gail Seneca in 1981, Chris Straayer in 1986, by Elizabeth Ellsworth also in 1986, and in de Lauretis' essay in Phase III here (see 'Further Reading' to Phase I and this phase). So, it is not quite the case that 'homosexual pleasures of female spectatorship' had been 'ignored completely' by 1987. Stacey uses arguments from D. N. Rodowick (see Phase II essays) as well as from Mary Ann Doane and Annette Kuhn. She considers the two possibilities offered by these critics as alternatives to Mulvey's thesis (masculine identification or absence): the film text can be read and enjoyed from different gendered positions or, despite the masculine apparatus, spectators can respond differently to the visual pleasures of the text. For Stacey, both alternatives end up with the feminist film theory double-bind I noted in discussing Phase I essays—namely 'how to argue for a feminine specificity without falling into the trap of biological essentialism' (p. 454).

In order to develop a more contradictory model of spectatorship, Stacey examines two narrative films 'which develop around one woman's obsession with another woman' (p. 456), namely, *All About Eve* and *Desperately Seeking Susan.* Stacey concludes in the first case that Eve engages in active looking within the diegesis and this 'articulation of feminine desire is foregrounded at several points in the narrative' (p. 459). But while Eve is punished for acting on her desires, in the second case, Roberta (played by Rosanna Arquette) 'acts upon her desires . . . and eventually her initiatives are rewarded with the realization of her desires' (p. 460). Stacey points out that the difference which pushes the narrative forward in this film is not sexual difference but the difference between two women. She concludes that it is this focus on difference that prevents the female spectator from having to choose between either desire or identification—the usual binary of feminist film criticism.

If the female homosexual spectator had been relatively neglected, how much truer has this been of the black female spectator. Very little has been theorized about this spectator, and Jacqueline Bobo sets out to remedy this gap. I could not ultimately include any selection from Bobo's important *Black Women as Cultural Readers*, but readers should study this volume. Bobo analyses black women as audience, especially their responses to Spielberg's *The Color Purple* and Julie Dash's *Daughters of the Dust.* The audience response supports Bobo's sense of the importance of black women as cultural producers, creating images of themselves 'different from those continually reproduced in traditional works'. A contrast between a scene repeated in the two famous versions of *Imitation of Life* and Julie Dash's comment on the scene in *Daughters of the Dust* nicely makes the point. Bobo's interviews of black women giving their responses to *Daughters of the Dust* rebutt critic's denigration of the film and reveal the film's importance to a community of black women interpreters.[1]

Bobo uses this term advisedly: she points to Toni Morrison's concept of shared familiarity, an 'instant intimacy' between the reader and the novel through a secret that is to be shared'. Bobo believes that *Daughters of the Dust* created precisely that 'instant intimacy' that was shared between black women in an interpretive framework 'as cultural producers, critics and audience members'. This interpretive community at once provides a foundation for continued cultural production and 'can help form progressive and effective coalitions' with the aim of transforming black women's consciousness and awareness of their historical situation.[2]

Bobo's brief reading of repeated scenes in the two versions *of Imitation of Life* suggests the importance of work on black cultural readings of these melodramas, as of treatment of melodramas in national and ethnic cinemas other than Hollywood. In the essays that follow, I provide an idea of work that has been done in 'classic' essays and by scholars doing later research in different ethnic and methodological contexts. My early, polemical 1983 essay on King Vidor's 1937 melodrama, *Stella Dallas*, is reprinted here partly because of its rather obscure site of publication, a feminist journal *Heresies*, now out of print, but also because it marks a particular moment in the North American Women's Movement which can be read through its discourse. Also, after Linda Williams developed a different position on the film, our work became the object of a fruitful debate in *Cinema Journal* (1984–1985: see 'Further Reading') between Williams and myself as well as several other feminist critics on melodrama, female spectatorship, and the feminist 'double-bind' that has been a theme throughout this volume. Briefly put, I argued (deliberately polemically) first that *Stella Dallas* opened up possibilities for feminists to focus on the mother not from the daughter position but looking at mothers' subjectivities—or at what patriarchal discourse about those subjectivities might be; and then went on to show how the narrative process in *Stella Dallas* ends up punishing Stella for resisting the Mother position she is asked to fulfil, and also for her protesting the expected motherly propriety by her eccentric dress. I claimed that Stella was forced to become 'mother-as-spectator'—a metaphor elaborated in the film through analogies to literal cinematic spectatorship. By implication, I suggested that female spectators of the film are invited to accept Stella's renunciation of her daughter and her place in her daughter's life so that the child can become part of the patriarchal upper-class world movies have made so desirable. Stella literally makes herself absent. In later work, I complicate this analysis and develop sub-categories of women's melodramas to distinguish different kinds of address (see 'Further Reading').

In her dense, useful essay, which includes reference to Laura Mulvey, Claire Johnston's and Mary Ann Doane's classic positions in feminist film theory discussed in Phase I essays, Williams focuses on what happens when a female 'look' is made a central feature of a narrative. What happens, Williams asks, 'when the look of desire articulates a rather different visual economy of mother–daughter possession and dispossession?' (p. 481). Critiquing classic positions, Williams argues that what is needed 'is a theoretical and practical recognition of the ways in which women actually do speak to one another within patriarchy' (p. 483) One of the spaces in which the critic may locate women who (in Christine Gledhill's words) 'out of their socially constructed differences as women, can and do resist', is the woman's melodrama—the genre which 'has historically addressed female audiences about issues of primary concern to women' (p. 484). After detouring through some of Freud's theories together with those of North American and French feminists, Williams turns to *Stella Dallas* to make her argument that women's melodramas have reading positions which demand a certain female competence, and that this competence comes from how women take on their identities under patriarchy. Briefly, Williams argues that 'like the ideal mother of soaps', we identify 'with *all* the conflicting points of view' which a film like *Stella Dallas* in fact offers (p. 494). Female viewers, for Williams, resist in the only ways they can, that is 'by struggling with the contradictions inherent in these images of ourselves and our situation' (p. 494).

Extending work on Hollywood melodrama to other national cinemas has been an important 1990s' development. In the following essay, Ana M. López examines women and melodrama in Mexican cinema. López distinguishes three 'master narratives' of Mexican society relevant to her study of melodrama, namely those of religion, nationalism, and modernization. Here, López introduces categories rarely dealt with in relation to the Hollywood film, showing how specific contexts for cinema require their own perspectives. In Mexico, since questions of individual identity are 'complicated by a colonial heritage that defines woman . . . as the origin of *national* identity', such categories are central. López shows how the social functions of melodrama are impacted upon by Mexico's colonial heritage, and how the Revolution further 'problematized the position of women in Mexico' (p. 508), rendering them 'a terrain to be traversed in the quest for male identity'. In her central section, López shows how melodramas addressed pressing contradictions and desires within Mexican society, and she isolated three principal conflicts that are dealt with: namely, 'the clash between old . . . values and modern . . . life, the crisis of male identity . . . and the instability of female identity' in the passage from the old to the new. These conflicts are played out in the private sphere of the home and the public one of the nightclub.

In her study of films set in the home, López finds relevant the categories of the 'maternal melodrama' (serving patriarchal needs) and the 'woman's film', addressing female spectators, that I developed earlier. In several of the male-centred maternal melodramas, the archetypal good mother is set against the haughty independent woman 'as passionate and devilish as the mothers are asexual and saintly' (p. 513). Turning to the public Night Club setting, López discusses the few Mexican melodramas that were structured around woman's identity and presented from a female point of view. She provides examples of stars playing the innocent fallen woman who sang professionally in stories told from the central character's point of view. The so-called *rumberas* are more sordid and present excessively sexual women. López however explains the complex image of the prostitute as 'emblem of desire, necessary evil and mother of the nation' (p. 517). The *rumbera* is not simple resisting film, but rather, with its suffering mother, yet one more fantasy.

I could not include Yanmei Wei's study of femininity in Zhang Yimou's family melodrama, so let me say a bit about it here. Wei's essay interestingly focuses specifically on the role of music in producing the powerful emotional effect of Zhang's melodramas on spectators. Like López, Wei's method involves linking family melodrama's concerns to larger national and cultural struggles, rather than focusing mainly on psychoanalytic processes as often in North American and European feminist scholarship. In her case, Wei links the dominance of family melodrama in Chinese cinema since its inception to the central role that the family has always played in Chinese cultural struggle and transformation. In *Raise the Red Lantern*, Wei shows how the family becomes so highly ritualized as to be like Theatre, and paradoxically the women have to turn to play-acting to survive the 'inhuman life-theater'. Wei shows how the heroine's repressed desires 'are signified by the flute music, while the non-diegetic female choir sings out her growing awareness of her situation'. In the rest of the essay, Wei teases out the complex and contradictory meanings of the flute—at once the instrument of sorrow for men and women, and a phallic symbol displacing erotic desire—and also those of the female choir. Wei argues that Zhang deliberately avoids the voyeuristic male gaze of feminist film theory by refusing shots of lovemaking. Meanwhile, the melancholy tune sung by the choir 'instructs the viewer, now deprived of the pleasure of looking, to identify with the female character'. While Wei appreciates these aspects of *Raise the Red Lantern*, when she contrasts its use of music to that in Zhang's earlier film, *Red Sorghum*, she has to conclude that Zhang keeps intact the linking of masculinity with power and virility, and of femininity with powerlessness. The treatment of women is sympathetic in *Raise the Red Lantern*, and does allow the female spectator to actively identify with the heroine; nevertheless, the association of joy and optimism with masculinity, and of being burdened and helpless with femininity, remains troubling.[3]

Tania Modleski's 'Three Men and Baby M' returns us to Hollywood cinema but continues the project of exploring images of masculinity. Focusing on the American remake of the French *Three Men and a Cradle*, this essays examines the new phenomenon of films about men taking over the mothering role. Modleski's thick psychoanalytic close reading points out the film's blatant theme of male envy of women while at the same time displaying male fear and disgust of women. She also points out the pedophilic aspects of both the French and American versions, since women are infantilized and the baby sexualized, as also the linking of the baby with feces, in classical Freudian manner. In the last section of the essay, Modleski compares *Three Men and Baby M* with John Ford's *Three Godfathers* in order to establish the heroes' regressive rejection of the symbolic father and refusal of castration. But if the film is situated firmly in the pre-Oedipal, Modleski notes, this does not engage 'a utopian celebration of the maternal' (p. 530). Rather it reflects male encroachment into the mother's traditional domain. Modleski warns against feminists unthinkingly endorsing 'men's need to nurture' (p. 531), because instead of undermining patriarchy, they may be shoring it up. It is possible,

Modleski concludes, that men may participate in childbearing so as to make women more marginal than ever.

Let me include in these 'Notes' a brief discussion of new work by Christine Gledhill which once again I could not reprint. Taking a very different approach to reading melodrama than any of the last three essays, in her essay 'Women Reading Men', Gledhill nevertheless continues the focus on masculinity. Returning to the assumption that 'woman is image' while 'men' remain men, she investigates the possibility that 'man' may be 'image' as well. Noting that the human body in cinema operates on two levels, as we have seen throughout this volume—that is, in reference to the social world but also 'metaphorically, symbolically and mythically', Gledhill sees this as true for male as it is for female bodies, for black as for white bodies, and indeed for all peoples. Her premiss is that culture needs to be taken in an active sense 'as constant negotiation, process, fantasising work'. She is interested in 'the processes of gender negotiation made possible in the fantasizing activity represented by popular texts and their engagement by female audiences'. She proceeds to exemplify her framework through discussion of the three heroes in *The Deer Hunter.* Gledhill uses melodrama theory, and her wide knowledge of classical film melodramas, to construct a series of broad mythic male archetypes—such as Romantic Hero, New Man, Older Man, Villain, Wounded Man, etc.—that correspond to the more frequently discussed female ones. She works some of these through in relation first to early melodramas and then shows the contradictions and negotiations that have to take place as the link between gendered bodies and moral values is strained as women try to maintain social virtue while also emancipating themselves in the twentieth century. Gledhill's example of new negotiations required as male archetypes seek renewal is Clint Eastwood's films. Gledhill concludes that her use of the melodramatic aesthetic as a model for reading conflict between male and female figures 'enables us to understand the relation between ideology and popular culture as a mutual dynamic rather than a series of ideological distortions suggested by a focus on representation'. In taking films as cultural products rather than critics' texts, Gledhill argues, we can see male protagonists in terms of 'the possibilities of projection and introjection which they offer' female spectators.[4]

I end this section and the book with a late essay by Laura Mulvey, whose pioneering 1975 text has woven itself like a thread through the essays in the volume. In this excerpt from her essay on Ousmane

Sembene's *Xala*, Mulvey continues feminist film theory's interest in masculinity and its 'troubles', perhaps signalling this as a significant new focus in feminist film studies. Mulvey both celebrates African cinema and takes the opportunity to work through different levels and modes of fetishism as a theoretical concept, as a theme throughout *Xala*, and as a set of practices. She shows how Sembene 'weaves a series of reflections on fetishism across the film', exploring its structure, i.e. 'surrender of knowledge to belief', in both the individual and as 'distortions of value and attributions of inappropriate meaning may also be shared by social groups in a kind of collective fantasy' (p. 540). Mulvey argues that cinema itself may be 'fetishistic', in the sense of appropriating objects, turning them into images and wrapping them in connotations that are collectively understood. Mulvey will argue that Sembene makes exquisite use of the language of cinema, 'its hieroglyphic or pictographic possibilities', to create 'a text which is about the meanings of objects as symptoms' (p. 541). She shows that 'the form of the film engages the spectators' ability to read the signs that emanate from colonialism and its neo-colonialist offspring' (p. 541). Of particular value in this essay is Mulvey's addressing the similarities and differences between Marx's and Freud's concepts of fetishism, and her demonstration that, while Sembene's use of fetishism is not 'an exact theoretical working through of Marxist or Freudian concepts . . . his use is *Marxist* and *Freudian*' (p. 550).

Notes

1. Jacqueline Bobo, *Black Women as Cultural Readers* (New York: Columbia University Press, 1995), 46–50.
2. Ibid. 59, 60.
3. Yanmei Wei, 'Music and Femininity in Zhang Yimou's Family Melodrama', *Cine Action* (1997), 22, 24, 26.
4. Christine Gledhill, 'Women Reading Men' in Pat Kirkham and Janet Thumin (eds.), *Me Jane: Masculinity, Movies and Women* (New York: St Martin's Press, 1995), 75, 76, 77, and 91.

21 Film and the Masquerade: Theorising the Female Spectator

Mary Ann Doane*

I. HEADS IN HIEROGLYPHIC BONNETS

In his lecture on 'Femininity', Freud forcefully inscribes the absence of the female spectator of theory in his notorious statement, '. . . to those of you who are women this will not apply—you are yourselves the problem . . .'[1] Simultaneous with this exclusion operated upon the female members of his audience, he invokes, as a rather strange prop, a poem by Heine. Introduced by Freud's claim concerning the importance and elusiveness of his topic—'Throughout history people have knocked their heads against the riddle of the nature of femininity . . .'—are four lines of Heine's poem:

> Heads in hieroglyphic bonnets,
> Heads in turbans and black birettas,
> Heads in wigs and thousand other
> Wretched, sweating heads of humans . . .[2]

The effects of the appeal to this poem are subject to the work of over-determination Freud isolated in the text of the dream. The sheer proliferation of heads and hats (and hence, through a metonymic slippage, minds), which are presumed to have confronted this intimidating riddle before Freud, confers on his discourse the weight of an intellectual history, of a tradition of interrogation. Furthermore, the image of hieroglyphics strengthens the association made between femininity and the enigmatic, the undecipherable, that which is 'other'. And yet Freud practices a slight deception here, concealing what is elided by removing the lines from their context, castrating, as it were, the stanza. For the question over which Heine's heads brood is

* Mary Ann Doane, 'Film and the Masquerade: Theorising the Female Spectator' from *Screen*, vol. 23 no.3/4 (1982), reprinted by permission of John Logie Baird Centre and the author.

not the same as Freud's—it is not 'What is Woman?', but instead, '... what signifies Man?' The quote is taken from the seventh section (entitled 'Questions') of the second cycle of *The North Sea*. The full stanza, presented as the words of 'a young man,/ His breast full of sorrow, his head full of doubt', reads as follows:

> O solve me the riddle of life,
> The teasingly time-old riddle,
> Over which many heads already have brooded,
> Heads in hats of hieroglyphics,
> Turbaned heads and heads in black skull-caps,
> Heads in perrukes and a thousand other
> Poor, perspiring human heads—
> Tell me, what signifies Man?
> Whence does he come? Whither does he go?
> Who lives up there upon golden stars?[3]

The question in Freud's text is thus a disguise and a displacement of that other question, which in the pre-text is both humanistic and theological. The claim to investigate an otherness is a pretense, haunted by the mirror-effect by means of which the question of the woman reflects only the man's own ontological doubts. Yet what interests me most in this intertextual mis-representation is that the riddle of femininity is initiated from the beginning in Freud's text as a question in masquerade. But I will return to the issue of masquerade later.

More pertinently, as far as the cinema is concerned, it is not accidental that Freud's eviction of the female spectator/auditor is co-present with the invocation of a hieroglyphic language. The woman, the enigma, the hieroglyphic, the picture, the image—the metonymic chain connects with another: the cinema, the theatre of pictures, a writing in images of the woman but not *for* her. For she *is* the problem. The semantic valence attributed to a hieroglyphic language is two-edged. In fact, there is a sense in which the term is inhabited by a contradiction. On the one hand, the hieroglyphic is summoned, particularly when it merges with a discourse on the woman, to connote an indecipherable language, a signifying system which denies its own function by failing to signify anything to the uninitiated, to those who do not hold the key. In this sense, the hieroglyphic, like the woman, harbours a mystery, an inaccessible though desirable otherness. On the other hand, the hieroglyphic is the most readable of languages. Its immediacy, its accessibility are functions of its status as a *pictorial* language, a writing in images. For the image is theorised in terms of a certain *closeness*, the lack of a distance or gap between sign and referent. Given its iconic characteristics, the relationship between signifier and signified is understood as less arbitrary in imagistic systems of representation than in language 'proper'. The intimacy of signifier and signified in the iconic sign negates the distance which defines phonetic language. And it is the absence of this crucial distance or gap which also, simultaneously, specifies both the hieroglyphic and the female. This is precisely why Freud evicted the woman from his lecture on femininity. Too close to herself, entangled in her own enigma, she could not step back, could not achieve the necessary distance of a second look.[4]

Thus, while the hieroglyphic is an indecipherable or at least enigmatic language, it is also and at the same time potentially the most universally understandable, comprehensible, appropriable of signs.[5] And the woman shares this contradictory status. But it is here that the analogy slips. For hieroglyphic languages are *not* perfectly iconic. They would not achieve the status of languages if they were—due to what Todorov and Ducrot refer to as a certain non-generalisability of the iconic sign:

> Now it is the impossibility of generalizing this principle of representation that has introduced even into fundamentally morphemographic writing systems such as Chinese, Egyptian, and Sumerian, the phonographic principle. We might almost conclude that every logography [the graphic system of language notation] grows out of *the impossibility of a generalized iconic representation*; proper nouns and abstract notions (including inflections) are then the ones that will be noted phonetically.[6]

The iconic system of representation is inherently deficient—it cannot disengage itself from the 'real', from the concrete; it lacks the gap necessary for generalisability (for Saussure, this is the idea that, 'Signs which are arbitrary realise better than others the ideal of the semiotic process.'). The woman, too, is defined by such an insufficiency. My insistence upon the congruence between certain theories of the image and theories of femininity is an attempt to dissect the *episteme* which assigns to the woman a special place in cinematic representation while denying her access to that system.

The cinematic apparatus inherits a theory of the image which is not conceived outside of sexual specifications. And historically, there has always been a certain imbrication of the cinematic image and the representation of the woman. The woman's relation to the camera and the scopic regime is quite different from that of the male. As Noël Burch points out, the early silent cinema, through its insistent inscription of scenarios of voyeurism, conceives of its spectator's viewing pleasure in terms of that of the Peeping Tom, behind the screen, reduplicating the spectator's position in relation to the woman as screen.[7] Spectatorial desire, in contemporary film theory, is generally delineated as either voyeurism or fetishism, as precisely a pleasure in seeing what is prohibited in relation to the female body. The image orchestrates a gaze, a limit, and its pleasurable transgression. The woman's beauty, her very desirability, becomes a function of certain practices of imaging—framing, lighting, camera movement, angle. She is thus, as Laura Mulvey has pointed out, more closely associated with the surface of the image than its illusory depths, its constructed 3-dimensional space which the man is destined to inhabit and hence control.[8] In *Now Voyager*, for instance, a single image signals the momentous transformation of the Bette Davis character from ugly spinster aunt to glamorous single woman. Charles Affron describes the specifically cinematic aspect of this operation as a 'stroke of genius':

> The radical shadow bisecting the face in white/dark/white strata creates a visual phenomenon quite distinct from the makeup transformation of lipstick and plucked eyebrows. . . . This shot does not reveal what we commonly call acting, especially after the most recent exhibition of that activity, but the sense of face belongs to a plastique pertinent to the camera. The viewer is allowed a different perceptual referent, a chance to come down from the nerve-jarring, first sequence and to use his eyes anew.[9]

A 'plastique pertinent to the camera' constitutes the woman not only as the image of desire but as the desirous image—one which the devoted cinéphile can cherish and embrace. To 'have' the cinema is, in some sense, to 'have' the woman. But *Now Voyager* is, in Affron's terms, a 'tear-jerker', in others, a 'woman's picture', i.e. a film purportedly produced for a female audience. What, then, of the female spectator? What can one say about her desire in relation to this process of imaging? It would seem that what the cinematic institution has in common with Freud's gesture is the eviction of the female spectator from a discourse purportedly about her (the cinema, psychoanalysis)—one which, in fact, narrativises her again and again.

II. A LASS BUT NOT A LACK

Theories of female spectatorship are thus rare, and when they are produced, seem inevitably to confront certain blockages in conceptualisation. The difficulties in thinking female spectatorship demand consideration. After all, even if it is admitted that the woman is frequently the object of the voyeuristic or fetishistic gaze in the cinema, what is there to prevent her from reversing the relation and appropriating the gaze for her own pleasure? Precisely the fact that the reversal itself remains locked within the same logic. The male striptease, the gigolo—both inevitably signify the mechanism of reversal itself, constituting themselves as aberrations whose acknowledgment simply reinforces the dominant system of aligning sexual difference with a subject/object dichotomy. And an essential attribute of that dominant system is the matching of male subjectivity with the agency of the look.

The supportive binary opposition at work here is not only that utilised by Laura Mulvey—an opposition between passivity and activity, but perhaps more importantly, an opposition between proximity and distance in relation to the image.[10] It is in this sense that the very logic behind the structure of the gaze demands a sexual division. While the distance between image and signified (or even referent) is theorised as minimal, if not non-existent, that between the film and the spectator must be maintained, even measured. One need only think of Noël Burch's mapping of spectatorship as a perfect distance from the screen (two times the width of the image)—a point in space from which the filmic discourse is most accessible.[11]

But the most explicit representation of this opposition between proximity and distance is contained in Christian Metz's analysis of voyeuristic desire in terms of a kind of social hierarchy of the senses: 'It is no accident that the main socially acceptable arts are based on the senses at a distance, and that those which depend on the senses of contact are often regarded as "minor" arts (= culinary arts, art of perfumes, etc.).'[12] The voyeur, according to Metz, must maintain a distance between himself and the image—the cinéphile *needs* the gap which represents for him the very distance between desire and its object. In this sense, voyeurism is theorised as a type of meta-desire:

> If it is true of all desire that it depends on the infinite pursuit of its absent object, voyeuristic desire, along with certain forms of sadism, is the only

desire whose principle of distance symbolically and spatially evokes this fundamental rent.[13]

Yet even this status as meta-desire does not fully characterise the cinema for it is a feature shared by other arts as well (painting, theatre, opera, etc.). Metz thus adds another reinscription of this necessary distance. What specifies the cinema is a further re-duplication of the lack which prompts desire. The cinema is characterised by an illusory sensory plenitude (there is 'so much to see') and yet haunted by the absence of those very objects which are there to be seen. Absence is an absolute and irrecoverable distance. In other words, Noël Burch is quite right in aligning spectatorial desire with a certain spatial configuration. The viewer must not sit either too close or too far from the screen. The result of both would be the same—he would lose the image of his desire.

It is precisely this opposition between proximity and distance, control of the image and its loss, which locates the possibilities of spectatorship within the problematic of sexual difference. For the female spectator there is a certain over-presence of the image—she *is* the image. Given the closeness of this relationship, the female spectator's desire can be described only in terms of a kind of narcissism—the female look demands a becoming. It thus appears to negate the very distance or gap specified by Metz and Burch as the essential precondition for voyeurism. From this perspective, it is important to note the constant recurrence of the motif of proximity in feminist theories (especially those labelled 'new French feminisms') which purport to describe a feminine specificity. For Luce Irigaray, female anatomy is readable as a constant relation of the self to itself, as an autoeroticism based on the embrace of the two lips which allow the woman to touch herself without mediation. Furthermore, the very notion of property, and hence possession of something which can be constituted as other, is antithetical to the woman: '*Nearness* however, is not foreign to woman, a nearness so close that any identification of one or the other, and therefore any form of property, is impossible. Woman enjoys a closeness with the other that is *so near she cannot possess it any more than she can possess herself*.' Or, in the case of female madness or delirium, '. . . women do not manage to articulate their madness: they suffer it directly in their body . . .'.[15] The distance necessary to detach the signifiers of madness from the body in the construction of even a discourse which exceeds the boundaries of sense is lacking. In the words of Hélène Cixous, 'More so than men who are coaxed toward social success, toward sublimation, women are body.'[16]

This theme of the overwhelming presence-to-itself of the female body is elaborated by Sarah Kofman and Michèle Montrelay as well. Kofman describes how Freudian psychoanalysis outlines a scenario whereby the subject's passage from the mother to the father is simultaneous with a passage from the senses to reason, nostalgia for the mother henceforth signifying a longing for a different positioning in relation to the sensory or the somatic, and the degree of civilization measured by the very distance from the body.[17] Similarly, Montrelay argues that while the male has the possibility of displacing the first object of desire (the mother), the female must become that object of desire:

> Recovering herself as maternal body (and also as phallus), the woman can no longer repress, 'lose;' the first stake of representation. . . . From now on, anxiety, tied to the presence of this body, can only be insistent, continuous. This body, so close, which she has to occupy, is an object in excess which must be 'lost,' that is to say, repressed, in order to be symbolised.[18]

This body so close, so excessive, prevents the woman from assuming a position similar to the man's in relation to signifying systems. For she is haunted by the loss of a loss, the lack of that lack so essential for the realisation of the ideals of semiotic systems.

Female specificity is thus theorised in terms of spatial proximity. In opposition to this 'closeness' to the body, a spatial distance in the male's relation to his body rapidly becomes a temporal distance in the service of knowledge. This is presented quite explicitly in Freud's analysis of the construction of the 'subject supposed to know'. The knowledge involved here is a knowledge of sexual difference as it is organised in relation to the structure of the look, turning on the visibility of the penis. For the little girl in Freud's description seeing and knowing are simultaneous—there is no temporal gap between them. In 'Some Psychological Consequences of the Anatomical Distinction Between the Sexes', Freud claims that the girl, upon seeing the penis for the first time, 'makes her judgement and her decision in a flash. She has seen it and knows that she is without it and wants to have it.'[19] In the lecture on 'Femininity' Freud repeats this gesture, merging perception and intellection: 'They [girls] at once notice the difference and, it must be admitted, its significance too.'[20]

The little boy, on the other hand, does not share this immediacy of understanding. When he first sees the woman's genitals he 'begins by showing irresolution and lack of interest; he sees nothing or disowns what he has seen, he softens it down or looks about for expedients for bringing it into line with his expectations'.[21] A second event, the threat of castration, is necessary to prompt a rereading of the image, endowing it with a meaning in relation to the boy's own subjectivity. It is in the distance between the look and the threat that the boy's relation to knowledge of sexual difference is formulated. The boy, unlike the girl in Freud's description, is capable of a re-vision of earlier events, a retrospective understanding which invests the events with a significance which is in no way linked to an immediacy of sight. This gap between the visible and the knowable, the very possibility of disowning what is seen, prepares the ground for fetishism. In a sense, the male spectator is destined to be a fetishist, balancing knowledge and belief.

The female, on the other hand, must find it extremely difficult, if not impossible, to assume the position of fetishist. That body which is so close continually reminds her of the castration which cannot be 'fetishised away'. The lack of a distance between seeing and understanding, the mode of judging 'in a flash', is conducive to what might be termed as 'over-identification' with the image. The association of tears and 'wet wasted afternoons' (in Molly Haskell's words)[22] with genres specified as feminine (the soap opera, the 'woman's picture') points very precisely to this type of over-identification, this abolition of a distance, in short, this inability to fetishise. The woman is constructed differently in relation to processes of looking. For Irigaray, this dichotomy between distance and proximity is described as the fact that:

> The masculine can partly look at itself, speculate about itself, represent itself and describe itself for what it is, whilst the feminine can try to speak to itself through a new language, but cannot describe itself from outside or in formal terms, except by identifying itself with the masculine, thus by losing itself.[23]

Irigaray goes even further: the woman always has a problematic relation to the visible, to form, to structures of seeing. She is much more comfortable with, closer to, the sense of touch.

The pervasiveness, in theories of the feminine, of descriptions of such a claustrophobic closeness, a deficiency in relation to structures of seeing and the visible, must clearly have consequences for attempts to theorise female spectatorship. And, in fact, the result is a tendency to view the female spectator as the site of an oscillation between a feminine position and a masculine position, invoking the metaphor of the transvestite. Given the structures of cinematic narrative, the woman who identifies with a female character must adopt a passive or masochistic position, while identification with the active hero necessarily entails an acceptance of what Laura Mulvey refers to as a certain 'masculinisation' of spectatorship.

> . . . as desire is given cultural materiality in a text, for women (from childhood onwards) trans-sex identification is a *habit* that very easily becomes *second Nature.* However, this Nature does not sit easily and shifts restlessly in its borrowed transvestite clothes.[24]

The transvestite wears clothes which signify a different sexuality, a sexuality which, for the woman, allows a mastery over the image and the very possibility of attaching the gaze to desire. Clothes make the man, as they say. Perhaps this explains the ease with which women can slip into male clothing. As both Freud and Cixous point out, the woman seems to be *more* bisexual than the man. A scene from Cukor's *Adam's Rib* graphically demonstrates this ease of female transvestism. As Katherine Hepburn asks the jury to imagine the sex role reversal of the three major characters involved in the case, there are three dissolves linking each of the characters successively to shots in which they are dressed in the clothes of the opposite sex. What characterises the sequence is the marked facility of the transformation of the two women into men in contradistinction to a certain resistance in the case of the man. The acceptability of the female reversal is quite distinctly opposed to the male reversal which seems capable of representation only in terms of farce. Male transvestism is an occasion for laughter; female transvestism only another occasion for desire.

Thus, while the male is locked into sexual identity, the female can at least pretend that she is other—in fact, sexual mobility would seem to be a distinguishing feature of femininity in its cultural construction. Hence, transvestism would be fully recuperable. The idea seems to be this: it is understandable that women would want to be men, for everyone wants to be elsewhere than in the feminine position. What is not understandable within the given terms is why a woman might flaunt her femininity, produce herself as an excess of femininity, in other words, foreground the masquerade. Masquerade is not as recuperable as transvestism precisely because it constitutes an acknowledgement that it is femininity itself which is constructed as mask—as the decorative layer which conceals a non-identity. For Joan Riviere, the first to theorise the concept, the masquerade of femininity is a kind of reaction-formation against the woman's trans-sex identification, her transvestism. After assuming the position of the subject of discourse rather than its object, the intellectual woman whom Riviere analyses felt compelled to compensate for this theft of masculinity by over-doing the gestures of feminine flirtation.

> Womanliness therefore could be assumed and worn as a mask, both to hide the possession of masculinity and to avert the reprisals expected if she was found to possess it—much as a thief will turn out his pockets and ask to be searched to prove that he has not the stolen goods. The reader may now ask how I define womanliness or where I draw the line between genuine womanliness and the masquerade. My suggestion is not, however, that there is any such difference; whether radical or superficial, they are the same thing.[25]

The masquerade, in flaunting femininity, holds it at a distance. Womanliness is a mask which can be worn or removed. The masquerade's resistance to patriarchal positioning would therefore lie in its denial of the production of femininity as closeness, as presence-to-itself, as, precisely, imagistic. The transvestite adopts the sexuality of the other—the woman becomes a man in order to attain the necessary distance from the image. Masquerade, on the other hand, involves a realignment of femininity, the recovery, or more accurately, simulation, of the missing gap or distance. To masquerade is to manufacture a lack in the form of a certain distance between oneself and one's image. If, as Moustafa Safouan points out, '. . . to wish to include in oneself as an object the cause of the desire of the Other is a formula for the structure of hysteria',[26] then masquerade is anti-hysterical for it works to effect a separation between the cause of desire and oneself. In Montrelay's words, 'the woman uses her own body as a disguise.'[27]

The very fact that we can speak of a woman 'using' her sex or 'using' her body for particular gains is highly significant—it is not that a man cannot use his body in this way but that he doesn't have to. The masquerade doubles representation; it is constituted by a hyperbolisation of the accoutrements of femininity. *A propos* of a recent performance by Marlene Dietrich, Sylvia Bovenschen claims, '. . . we are watching a woman demonstrate the representation of a woman's body.'[28] This type of masquerade, an excess of femininity, is aligned with the *femme fatale* and, as Montrelay explains, is necessarily regarded by men as evil incarnate: 'It is this evil which scandalises whenever woman plays out her sex in order to evade the word and the law. Each time she subverts a law or a word which relies on the predominantly masculine structure of the look.'[29] By destabilising the image, the masquerade confounds this masculine structure of the look. It effects a defamiliarisation of female iconography. Nevertheless, the preceding account simply specifies masquerade as a type of representation which carries a threat, disarticulating male systems of viewing. Yet, it specifies nothing with respect to female spectatorship. What might it mean to masquerade as spectator? To assume the mask in order to see in a different way?

III. 'MEN SELDOM MAKE PASSES AT GIRLS WHO WEAR GLASSES'

The first scene in *Now Voyager* depicts the Bette Davis character as repressed, unattractive and undesirable or, in her own words, as the spinster aunt of the family. ('Every family has one.') She has heavy eye brows, keeps her hair bound tightly in a bun, and wears glasses, a drab dress and heavy shoes. By the time of the shot discussed earlier, signalling her transformation into beauty, the glasses have disappeared, along with the other signifiers of unattractiveness. Between these two moments there is a scene in which the doctor who cures her actually confiscates her glasses (as a part of the cure). The woman who wears glasses constitutes one of the most intense visual clichés of the cinema. The image is a heavily marked condensation of motifs concerned with repressed sexuality, knowledge, visability and vision, intellectuality, and desire. The woman with glasses signifies simultaneously intellectuality and undesirability; but the moment she removes her glasses (a moment which, it seems, must almost always be *shown* and which is itself linked with a certain sensual quality), she is transformed into spectacle, the very picture of desire. Now, it must be remembered that the cliché is a heavily loaded moment of signification, a social knot of meaning. It is characterised by an effect of ease and naturalness. Yet, the cliché has a binding power so strong that it indicates a precise moment of ideological danger or threat—in this case, the woman's appropriation of the gaze. Glasses worn by a woman in the cinema do not generally signify a deficiency in seeing but an active looking, or even simply the fact of seeing as opposed to being seen. The intellectual woman looks and analyses, and in usurping the gaze she poses a threat to an entire system of representation. It is as if the woman had forcefully moved to the other side of the specular. The overdetermination of the image of the woman with glasses, its status as a cliché, is a crucial aspect of the cinematic alignment of structures of seeing and being seen with sexual difference. The cliché, in assuming an immediacy of understanding, acts as a mechanism for the naturalisation of sexual difference.

But the figure of the woman with glasses is only an extreme moment of a more generalised logic. There is always a certain excessiveness, a difficulty associated with women who appropriate the gaze, who insist upon looking. Linda Williams has demonstrated how, in the genre of the horror film, the woman's active looking is ultimately punished. And what she sees, the monster, is only a mirror of herself—both woman and monster are freakish in their difference—defined by either 'too much' or 'too little'.[30] Just as the dominant narrative cinema repetitively inscribes scenarios of voyeurism, internalising or narrativising the film-spectator relationship (in films like *Psycho, Rear Window, Peeping Tom*), taboos in seeing are insistently formulated in relation to the female spectator as well. The man with binoculars is countered by the woman with glasses. The gaze must be dissociated from mastery. In *Leave Her to Heaven* (John Stahl, 1945), the female protagonist's (Gene Tierney's) excessive desire and over-possessiveness are signalled from the very beginning of the film by her intense and sustained stare at the major male character, a stranger she first encounters on a train. The discomfort her look causes is graphically depicted. The Gene Tierney character is ultimately revealed to be the epitome of evil—killing her husband's crippled younger brother, her unborn child and ultimately herself in an attempt to brand her cousin as a murderess in order to insure her husband's future fidelity. In *Humoresque* (Jean Negulesco, 1946), Joan Crawford's problematic status is a result of her continual attempts to assume the position of spectator—fixing John Garfield with her gaze. Her transformation from spectator to spectacle is signified repetitively by the gesture of removing her glasses. Rosa, the character played by Bette Davis in *Beyond the Forest* (King Vidor, 1949) walks to the station every day simply to *watch* the train departing for Chicago. Her fascination with the train is a fascination with its phallic power to transport her to 'another place'. This character is also specified as having a 'good eye'—she can shoot, both pool and guns. In all three films the woman is constructed as the site of an excessive and dangerous desire. This desire mobilises extreme efforts of containment and unveils the sadistic aspect of narrative. In all three films the woman dies. As Claire Johnston points out, death is the 'location of all impossible signs',[31] and the films demonstrate that the woman as subject of the gaze is clearly an impossible sign. There is a perverse rewriting of this logic of the gaze in *Dark Victory* (Edmund Goulding, 1939), where the woman's story achieves heroic and tragic proportions not only in blindness, but in a blindness which mimes sight—when the woman pretends to be able to see.

IV. OUT OF THE CINEMA AND INTO THE STREETS: THE CENSORSHIP OF THE FEMALE GAZE

This process of narrativising the negation of the female gaze in the classical Hollywood cinema finds its perfect encapsulation in a still photograph taken in 1948 by Robert Doisneau, '*Un Regard Oblique*'. Just as the Hollywood narratives discussed above purport to centre a female protagonist, the photograph appears to give a certain prominence to a woman's look. Yet, both the title of the photograph and its organisation of space indicate that the real site of scopophiliac power is on the margins of the frame. The man is not centred; in fact, he occupies a very narrow space on the extreme right of the picture.

'*Un Regard Oblique*': a dirty joke at the expense of the woman's look.

Nevertheless, it is his gaze which defines the problematic of the photograph; it is his gaze which effectively erases that of the woman. Indeed, as subject of the gaze, the woman looks intently. But not only is the object of her look concealed from the spectator, her gaze is encased by the two poles defining the masculine axis of vision. Fascinated by nothing visible—a blankness or void for the spectator—unanchored by a 'sight' (there is nothing 'proper' to her vision—save, perhaps, the mirror), the female gaze is left free-floating, vulnerable to subjection. The faint reflection in the shop window of only the frame of the picture at which she is looking serves merely to rearticulate, *en abŷme*, the emptiness of her gaze, the absence of her desire in representation.

On the other hand, the object of the male gaze is fully present, *there* for the spectator. The fetishistic representation of the nude female body, fully in view, insures a masculinisation of the spectatorial position. The woman's look is literally outside the triangle which traces a complicity between the man, the nude, and the spectator. The feminine presence in the photograph, despite a diegetic centring of the female subject of the gaze, is taken over by the picture as object. And, as if to doubly 'frame' her in the act of looking, the painting situates its female figure as a spectator (although it is not clear whether she is looking at herself in a mirror or peering through a door or window). While this drama of seeing is played out at the surface of the photograph, its deep space is activated by several young boys, out-of-focus, in front of a belt shop. The opposition out-of-focus/in-focus reinforces the supposed clarity accorded to the representation of the woman's 'non-vision'. Furthermore, since this out-of-focus area constitutes the precise literal centre of the image, it also demonstrates how the photograph makes figurative the operation of centring—draining the actual centre point of significance in order to deposit meaning on the margins. The male gaze is centred, in control—although it is exercised from the periphery.

The spectator's pleasure is thus produced through the framing/negation of the female gaze. The woman is there as the butt of a joke—a 'dirty joke' which, as Freud has demonstrated, is always constructed at the expense of a woman. In order for a dirty joke to emerge in its specificity in Freud's description, the object of desire—the woman—must be absent and a third person (another man) must be present as witness to the joke—'so that gradually, in place of the woman, the onlooker, now the listener, becomes the person to whom the smut is addressed . . .'.[32] The terms of the photograph's address as joke once again insure a masculinisation of the place of the spectator. The operation of the dirty joke is also inextricably linked by Freud to scopophilia and the exposure of the female body':

> Smut is like an exposure of the sexually different person to whom it is directed. By the utterance of the obscene words it compels the person who is assailed to imagine the part of the body or the procedure in question and shows her that the assailant is himself imagining it. It cannot be doubted that the desire to see what is sexual exposed is the original motive of smut.[33]

From this perspective, the photograph lays bare the very mechanics of the joke through its depiction of sexual exposure and a surreptitious act of seeing (and desiring). Freud's description of the joke-work appears to constitute a perfect analysis of the photograph's orchestration of the gaze. There is a 'voice-off' of the photographic discourse, however—a component of the image which is beyond the frame of this little scenario of voyeurism. On the far left-hand side of the photograph, behind the wall holding the painting of the nude, is the barely detectable painting of a woman imaged differently, in darkness—*out of sight* for the male, blocked by his fetish. Yet, to point to this almost invisible alternative in imaging is also only to reveal once again the analyst's own perpetual desire to find a not-seen that might break the hold of representation. Or to laugh last.

There is a sense in which the photograph's delineation of a sexual politics of looking is almost uncanny. But, to counteract the very possibility of such a perception, the language of the art critic effects a naturalisation of this joke on the woman. The art-critical reception of the picture emphasizes a natural but at the same time 'imaginative' relation between photography and life, ultimately subordinating any formal relations to a referential ground: 'Doisneau's lines move from right to left, directed by the man's glance; the woman's gaze creates a line of energy like a hole in space.... The creation of these relationships from life itself is imagination in photography.'[34] 'Life itself', then, presents the material for an 'artistic' organisation of vision along the lines of sexual difference. Furthermore, the critic would have us believe that chance events and arbitrary clicks of the shutter cannot be the agents of a generalised sexism because they are particular, unique—'Keitesz and Doisneau depend entirely upon our recognition that they were present at the instant of the unique intersection of events.'[35] Realism seems always to reside in the streets and, indeed, the out-of-focus boy across the street, at the centre of the photograph, appears to act as a guarantee of the 'chance' nature of the event, its arbitrariness, in short—its realism. Thus, in the discourse of the art critic the photograph, in capturing a moment, does not construct it; the camera finds a naturally given series of subject and object positions. What the critic does not consider are the conditions of reception of photography as an art form, its situation within a much larger network of representation. What is it that makes the photograph not only readable but pleasurable—at the expense of the woman? The critic does not ask what makes the photograph a negotiable item in a market of signification.

V. THE MISSING LOOK

The photograph displays insistently, in microcosm, the structure of the cinematic inscription of a sexual differentiation in modes of looking. Its process of framing the female gaze repeats that of the cinematic narratives described above, from *Leave Her to Heaven* to *Dark Victory.* Films play out scenarios of looking in order to outline the terms of their own understanding. And given the divergence between masculine and feminine scenarios, those terms would seem to be explicitly negotiated as markers of sexual difference. Both the theory of the image and its apparatus, the cinema, produce a position for the female spectator—a position which is ultimately untenable because it lacks the attribute of distance so necessary for an adequate reading of the image. The entire elaboration of femininity as a closeness, a nearness, as present-to-itself is not the definition of an essence but the delineation of a *place* culturally assigned to the woman. Above and beyond a simple adoption of the masculine position in relation to the cinematic sign, the female spectator is given two options: the masochism of over-identification or the narcissism entailed in becoming one's own object of desire, in assuming the image in the most radical way. The effectivity of masquerade lies precisely in its potential to manufacture a distance from the image, to generate a problematic within which the image is manipulable, producible, and readable by the woman. Doisneau's photograph is not readable by the female spectator—it can give her pleasure only in masochism. In order to 'get' the joke, she must once again assume the position of transvestite.

It is quite tempting to foreclose entirely the possibility of female spectatorship, to repeat at the level of theory the gesture of the photograph, given the history of a cinema which relies so heavily on voyeurism, fetishism, and identification with an ego ideal conceivable only in masculine terms. And, in fact, there has been a tendency to theorise femininity and hence the feminine gaze as repressed, and in its repression somehow irretrievable, the enigma constituted by Freud's question. Yet, as Michel Foucault has demonstrated, the repressive hypothesis on its own entails a very limited and simplistic notion of the working of power.[36] The 'no' of the father, the prohibition, is its only technique. In theories of repression there is no sense of the productiveness and positivity of power. Femininity is produced very precisely as a position within a network of power relations. And the growing insistence upon the elaboration of a theory of female spectatorship is indicative of the crucial necessity of understanding that position in order to dislocate it.

Notes

This article is an expanded version of a paper presented at a symposium on recent film theory at Yale University, February 1982, organised by Miriam Hansen and Donald Crafton.

1. Sigmund Freud, 'Femininity', *The Standard Edition of the Complete Psychological Words of Sigmund Freud*, ed James Strachey (London: The Hogarth Press and the Institute of Psycho-analysis, 1964), 113.
2. This is the translation given in a footnote in *The Standard Edition*, 113.
3. Heinrich Heine, *The North Sea*, trans. Vernon Watkins (New York: New Direction Books, 1951), 77.
4. In other words, the woman can never ask her own ontological question. The absurdity of such a situation within traditional discursive conventions can be demonstrated by substituting a 'young woman' for the 'young man' of Heine's poem.
5. As Oswald Ducrot and Tzvetan Todorov point out in *Encyclopedic Dictionary of the Sciences of Language*, trans. Catherine Porter (Baltimore and London: Johns Hopkins University Press, 1979), 195, the potentially universal understandability of the hieroglyphic is highly theoretical and can only be thought as the unattainable ideal of an imagistic system: 'It is important of course not to exaggerate either the resemblance of the image with the object—the design is stylized very rapidly—or the 'natural' and 'universal' character of the signs: Sumerian, Chinese, Egyptian and Hittite hieroglyphics for the same object have nothing in common.'
6. Ibid. 194. Emphasis mine.
7. See Noël Burch's film, *Correction Please, or How We Got Into Pictures.*
8. Laura Mulvey, 'Visual Pleasure and Narrative Cinema', *Screen*, 16: 3 (Autumn 1975), 12–13.
9. Charles Affron, *Star Acting: Gish, Garbo, Davis* (New York: E P Dutton, 1977), 281–282.
10. This argument focuses on the image to the exclusion of any consideration of the soundtrack primarily because it is the process of imaging which seems to

constitute the major difficulty in theorising female spectatorship. The image is also popularly understood as metonymic signifier for the cinema as a whole and for good reason: historically, sound has been subordinate to the image within the dominant classical system. For more on the image/sound distinction in relation to sexual difference see my article, 'The Voice in the Cinema: The Articulation of Body and Space', *Yale French Studies*, 60, 33–50.

11. Noël Burch, *Theory of Film Practice*, trans. Helen R Lane (New York and Washington: Praeger Publishers, 1973), 35.
12. Christian Metz, 'The Imaginary Signifier', *Screen*, 16: 2 (Summer 1975), 60.
13. Ibid. 61.
14. Luce Irigaray, 'This Sex Which Is Not One', *New French Feminisms*, ed. Elaine Marks and Isabelle de Courtivron (Amherst: The University of Massachusetts Press, 1980), 104–105.
15. Irigaray, 'Women's Exile', *Ideology and Consciousness*, 1 (May 1977), 74.
16. Hélène Cixous, 'The Laugh of the Medusa', *New French Feminisms*, 257.
17. Sarah Kofman, 'Ex: The Woman's Enigma', *Enclitic*, 4: 2 (Fall 1980), 20.
18. Michèle Montrelay, 'Inquiry into Femininity', *m/f*, 1 (1978), 91–92.
19. Freud, 'Some Psychological Consequences of the Anatomical Distinction between the Sexes', *Sexuality and the Psychology of Love*, ed. Philip Rieff (New York: Collier Books, 1963), 187–188.
20. Freud, 'Femininity', op. cit., 125.
21. Freud, 'Some Psychological Consequences . . .', op. cit., 187.
22. Molly Haskell, *From Reverence to Rape* (Baltimore: Penguin Books, 1974), 154.
23. Irigaray, 'Women's Exile', op. cit., 65.
24. Mulvey, 'Afterthoughts . . . inspired by Duel in the Sun', *Framework* (Summer 1981), 13.
25. Joan Riviere, 'Womanliness as a Masquerade', *Psychoanalysis and Female Sexuality*, ed. Hendrik M Ruitenbeek (New Haven: College and University Press, 1966), 213. My analysis of the concept of masquerade differs markedly from that of Luce Irigaray. See *Ce sexe qui n'en est pas un* (Paris: Les Éditions de Minuit, 1977), 131–132. It also diverges to a great extent from the very important analysis of masquerade presented by Claire Johnston in 'Femininity and the Masquerade: Anne of the Indies', *Jacques Tourneur* (London: British Film Institute, 1975), 36–44. I am indebted to her for the reference to Riviere's article.
26. Moustafa Safouan, 'Is the Oedipus Complex Universal?', *m/f*, 5–6 (1981), 84–85.
27. Montrelay, op. cit., 93.
28. Silvia Bovenschen, 'Is There a Feminine Aesthetic?', *New German Critique*, 10 (Winter 1977), 129.
29. Montrelay, op. cit., 93.
30. Linda Williams, 'When the Woman Looks . . .', in *Re-vision: Feminist Essays in Film Analysis*, ed. Mary Ann Doane, Pat Mellencamp and Linda Williams, forthcoming.
31. Johnston, op. cit., 40.
32. Freud, *Jokes and Their Relation to the Unconscious*, trans. James Strachey (New York: W W Norton & Company, Inc, 1960), 99.
33. Ibid. 98.

22 Women's Genres

Annette Kuhn*

I

Television soap opera and film melodrama, popular narrative forms aimed at female audiences, are currently attracting a good deal of critical and theoretical attention. Not surprisingly, most of the work on these 'gynocentric' genres is informed by various strands of feminist thought on visual representation. Less obviously, perhaps, such work has also prompted a series of questions which relate to representation and cultural production in a more wide-ranging and thoroughgoing manner than a specifically feminist interest might suggest. Not only are film melodrama (and more particularly its subtype the 'woman's picture') and soap opera directed at female audiences, they are also actually enjoyed by millions of women. What is it that sets these genres apart from representations which possess a less gender-specific mass appeal?

One of the defining generic features of the woman's picture as a textual system is its construction of narratives motivated by female desire and processes of spectator identification governed by female point-of-view. Soap opera constructs woman-centred narratives and identifications, too, but it differs textually from its cinematic counterpart in certain other respects: not only do soaps never end, but their beginnings are soon lost sight of. And whereas in the woman's picture the narrative process is characteristically governed by the enigma-retardation-resolution structure which marks the classic narrative, soap opera narratives propose

> competing and intertwining plot lines introduced as the serial progresses. Each plot . . . develops at a different pace, thus preventing any clear resolution

* Annette Kuhn, 'Women's Genres' from *Screen*, vol. 25 no.1 (1984), reprinted by permission of John Logie Baird Centre and the author.

of conflict. The completion of one story generally leads into others, and ongoing plots often incorporate parts of semi-resolved conflicts.[1]

Recent work on soap opera and melodrama has drawn on existing theories, methods and perspectives in the study of film and television, including the structural analysis of narratives, textual semiotics and psychoanalysis, audience research, and the political economy of cultural institutions. At the same time, though, some of this work has exposed the limitations of existing approaches, and in consequence been forced if not actually to abandon them, at least to challenge their characteristic problematics. Indeed, it may be contended that the most significant developments in film and TV theory in general are currently taking place precisely within such areas of feminist concern as critical work on soap opera and melodrama.

In examining some of this work, I shall begin by looking at three areas in which particularly pertinent questions are being directed at theories of representation and cultural production. These are, firstly, the problem of gendered spectatorship; secondly, questions concerning the universalism as against the historical specificity of conceptualisations of gendered spectatorship; and thirdly, the relationship between film and television texts and their social, historical and institutional contexts. Each of these concerns articulates in particular ways with what seems to me the central issue here—the question of the audience, or audiences, for certain types of cinematic and televisual representation.

II

Film theory's appropriation to its own project of Freudian and post-Freudian psychoanalysis places the question of the relationship between text and spectator firmly on the agenda. Given the preoccupation of psychoanalysis with sexuality and gender, a move from conceptualising the spectator as a homogeneous and androgynous effect of textual operations[2] to regarding her or him as a gendered subject constituted in representation seems in retrospect inevitable. At the same time, the interests of feminist film theory and film theory in general converge at this point in a shared concern with sexual difference. Psychoanalytic accounts of the formation of gendered subjectivity raise the question, if only indirectly, of representation and feminine subjectivity. This in turn permits the spectator to be considered as a gendered subject position, masculine or feminine: and theoretical work on soap opera and the woman's picture may take this as a starting point for its inquiry into spectator–text relations. Do these 'gynocentric' forms address, or construct, a female or a feminine spectator? If so, how?

On the question of film melodrama, Laura Mulvey, commenting on King Vidor's *Duel in the Sun*,[3] argues that when, as in this film, a woman is at the centre of the narrative, the question of female desire structures the hermeneutic: 'what does *she* want?' This, says Mulvey, does not guarantee the constitution of the spectator as feminine so much as it implies a contradictory, and in the final instance impossible, 'phantasy of masculinisation' for the female spectator. This is in line with the author's earlier suggestion that cinema spectatorship involves masculine identification for spectators of either gender.[4] If cinema does thus construct a masculine subject, there can be no unproblematic feminine subject position for any spectator. Pam Cook, on the other hand, writing about a group of melodramas produced during the 1940s at the Gainsborough Studios, evinces greater optimism about the possibility of a feminine subject of classic cinema. She does acknowledge, though, that in a patriarchal society female desire and female point-of-view are highly contradictory, even if they have the potential to subvert culturally dominant modes of spectator–text relation. The characteristic 'excess' of the woman's melodrama, for example, is explained by Cook in terms of the genre's tendency to '[pose] problems for itself which it can scarcely contain.'[5]

Writers on TV soap opera tend to take views on gender and spectatorship rather different from those advanced by film theorists. Tania Modleski, for example, argues with regard to soaps that their characteristic narrative patterns, their foregrounding of 'female' skills in dealing with personal and domestic crises, and the capacity of their programme formats and scheduling to key into the rhythms of women's work in the home, all address a female spectator. Furthermore, she goes as far as to argue that the textual processes of soaps are in some respects similar to those of certain 'feminine' texts which speak to a decentred subject, and so are 'not altogether at odds with . . . feminist aesthetics'.[6] Modleski's view is that soaps not only address female spectators, but in so doing construct feminine subject positions which transcend patriarchal modes of subjectivity.

Different though their respective approaches and conclusions might be, however, Mulvey, Cook and Modleski are all interested in the problem of gendered spectatorship. The fact, too, that this common concern is informed by a shared interest in assessing the progressive or transformative potential of soaps and melodramas is significant in light of the broad appeal of both genres to the mass audiences of women at which they are aimed.

But what precisely does it mean to say that certain representations are aimed at a female audience? However well theorised they may be, existing conceptualisations of gendered spectatorship are unable to deal with this question. This is because spectator and audience are distinct concepts which cannot—as they frequently are—be reduced to one another. Although I shall be considering some of its consequences more fully below (in part III), it is important to note a further problem for film and television theory, posed in this case by the distinction between spectator and audience. Critical work on the woman's picture and on soap opera has necessarily, and most productively, emphasised the question of gendered spectatorship. In doing this, film theory in particular has taken on board a conceptualisation of the spectator derived from psychoanalytic accounts of the formation of human subjectivity.

Such accounts, however, have been widely criticised for their universalism. Beyond, perhaps, associating certain variants of the Oedipus complex with family forms characteristic of a patriarchal society and offering a theory of the construction of gender, psychoanalysis seems to offer little scope for theorising subjectivity in its cultural or historical specificity. Although in relation to the specific issues of spectatorship and representation there may, as I shall argue, be a way around this apparent impasse, virtually all film and TV theory—its feminist variants included—is marked by the dualism of universalism and specificity.

Nowhere is this more evident than in the gulf between textual analysis and contextual inquiry. Each is done according to different rules and procedures, distinct methods of investigation and theoretical perspectives. In bringing to the fore the question of spectator–text relations, theories deriving from psychoanalysis may claim—to the extent that the spectatorial apparatus is held to be coterminous with the cinematic or televisual institution—to address the relationship between text and context. But as soon as any attempt is made to combine textual analysis with analysis of the concrete social, historical and institutional conditions of production and reception of texts, it becomes clear that the context of the spectator/subject of psychoanalytic theory is rather different from the context of production and reception constructed by conjunctural analyses of cultural institutions.

The disparity between these two 'contexts' structures Pam Cook's article on the Gainsborough melodrama, which sets out to combine an analysis of the characteristic textual operations and modes of address of a genre with an examination of the historical conditions of a particular expression of it. Gainsborough melodrama, says Cook, emerges from a complex of determinants, including certain features of the British film industry of the 1940s, the nature of the female cinema audience in the post-World War II period, and the textual characteristics of the woman's picture itself.[7] While Cook is correct in pointing to the various levels of determination at work in this instance, her lengthy preliminary discussion of spectator–text relations and the woman's picture rather outbalances her subsequent investigation of the social and industrial contexts of the Gainsborough melodrama. The fact, too, that analysis of the woman's picture in terms of its interpellation of a female/feminine spectator is simply placed alongside a conjunctural analysis tends to vitiate any attempt to reconcile the two approaches, and so to deal with the broader issue of universalism as against historical specificity. But although the initial problem remains, Cook's article constitutes an important intervention in the debate because, in tackling the text-context split head-on, it necessarily exposes a key weakness of current film theory.

In work on television soap opera as opposed to film melodrama, the dualism of text and context manifests itself rather differently, if only because—unlike film theory—theoretical work on television has tended to emphasise the determining character of the contextual level, particularly the structure and organisation of television institutions. Since this has often been at the expense of attention to the operation of TV texts, television theory may perhaps be regarded as innovative in the extent to which it attempts to deal specifically with texts as well as contexts. Some feminist critical work has in fact already begun to address the question of TV as text, though always with characteristic emphasis on the issue of gendered spectatorship. This emphasis constitutes a common concern of work on both TV soaps and the woman's picture, but a point of contact between text and context in either medium emerges only when the concept of social audience is considered in distinction from that of spectator.

III

Each term—spectator and social audience—presupposes a different set of relations to representations and to the contexts in which they are received. Looking at spectators and at audiences demands different methodologies and theoretical frameworks, distinct discourses which construct distinct subjectivities and social relations. The *spectator*, for example, is a subject constituted in signification, interpellated by the film or TV text. This does not necessarily mean that the spectator is merely an effect of the text, however, because modes of subjectivity which also operate outside spectator–text relations in film or TV are activated in the relationship between spectators and texts.

This model of the spectator/subject is useful in correcting more deterministic communication models which might, say, pose the spectator not as actively constructing meaning but simply as a receiver and decoder of preconstituted 'messages'. In emphasising spectatorship as a set of psychic relations and focusing on the relationship between spectator and text, however, such a model does disregard the broader social implications of filmgoing or televiewing. It is the social act of going to the cinema, for instance, that makes the individual cinemagoer part of an audience. Viewing television may involve social relations rather different from filmgoing, but in its own ways TV does depend on individual viewers being part of an audience, even if its members are never in one place at the same time. A group of people seated in a single auditorium looking at a film, or scattered across thousands of homes watching the same television programme, is a *social audience.* The concept of social audience, as against that of spectator, emphasises the status of cinema and television as social and economic institutions.

Constructed by discursive practices both of cinema and TV and of social science, the social audience is a group of people who buy tickets at the box office, or who switch on their TV sets; people who can be surveyed, counted and categorised according to age, sex and socio-economic status.[8] The cost of a cinema ticket or TV licence fee, or a readiness to tolerate commercial breaks, earns audiences the right to look at films and TV programmes, and so to be spectators. Social audiences become spectators in the moment they engage in the processes and pleasures of meaning-making attendant on watching a film or TV programme. The anticipated pleasure of spectatorship is perhaps a necessary condition of existence of audiences. In taking part in the social act of consuming representations, a group of spectators becomes a social audience.

The consumer of representations as audience member and spectator is involved in a particular kind of psychic and social relationship: at this point, a conceptualisation of the cinematic or televisual apparatus as a regime of pleasure intersects with sociological and economic understandings of film and TV as institutions. Because each term describes a distinct set of relationships, though, it is important not to conflate social audience with spectators. At the same time, since each is necessary to the other, it is equally important to remain aware of the points of continuity between the two sets of relations.

These conceptualisations of spectator and social audience have particular implications when it comes to a consideration of popular 'gynocentric' forms such as soap opera and melodrama. Most obviously, perhaps, these centre on the issue of gender, which prompts again the question: what does 'aimed at a female audience' mean? What exactly is being signalled in this reference to a gendered audience? Are women to be understood as a subgroup of the social audience, distinguishable through discourses which construct *a priori* gender categories? Or does the reference to a female audience allude rather to gendered spectatorship, to sexual difference constructed in relations between spectators and texts? Most likely, it condenses the two meanings; but an examination of the distinction between them may nevertheless be illuminating in relation to the broader theoretical issues of texts, contexts, social audiences and spectators.

The notion of a female social audience, certainly as it is constructed in the discursive practices through which it is investigated, presupposes a group of individuals already formed as female. For the sociologist interested in such matters as gender and lifestyles, certain people bring a pre-existent femaleness to their viewing of film and TV. For the business executive interested in selling commodities, TV programmes and films are marketed to individuals already constructed as female. Both, however, are interested in the same kind of woman. On one level, then, soap operas and women's melodramas address themselves to a social audience of women. But they may at the same time be regarded as speaking to a female, or a feminine, spectator. If soaps and melodramas inscribe femininity in their address, women—as well as being already formed *for* such representations—are in a sense also formed *by* them.

In making this point, however, I intend no reduction of femaleness to femininity: on the contrary, I would hold to a distinction between femaleness as social gender and femininity as subject position. For example, it is possible for a female spectator to be addressed, as it were, 'in the masculine', and the converse is presumably also true. Nevertheless, in a culturally pervasive operation of ideology, femininity is routinely identified with femaleness and masculinity with maleness. Thus, for example, an address 'in the feminine' may be regarded in ideological terms as privileging, if not necessitating, a socially constructed female gender identity.

The constitutive character of both the woman's picture and the soap opera has in fact been noted by a number of feminist commentators. Tania Modleski, for instance, suggests that the characteristic narrative structures and textual operations of soap operas both address the viewer as an 'ideal mother'—ever-understanding, ever-tolerant of the weaknesses and foibles of others—and also posit states of expectation and passivity as pleasurable: 'the narrative, by placing ever more complex obstacles between desire and fulfilment, makes anticipation of an end an end in itself'.[9] In our culture, tolerance and passivity are regarded as feminine attributes, and consequently as qualities proper in women but not in men.

Charlotte Brunsdon extends Modleski's line of argument to the extra-textual level: in constructing its viewers as competent within the ideological and moral frameworks of marriage and family life, soap opera, she implies, addresses both a feminine spectator and female audience.[10] Pointing to the centrality of intuition and emotion in the construction of the woman's point-of-view, Pam Cook regards the construction of a feminine spectator as a highly problematic and contradictory process: so that in the film melodrama's construction of female point-of-view, the validity of femininity as a subject position is necessarily laid open to question.[11]

This divergence on the question of gendered spectatorship within feminist theory is significant.. Does it perhaps indicate fundamental differences between film and television in the spectator–text relations privileged by each? Do soaps and melodramas really construct different relations of gendered spectatorship, with melodrama constructing contradictory identifications in ways that soap opera does not? Or do these different positions on spectatorship rather signal an unevenness of theoretical development—or, to put it less teleologically, reflect the different intellectual histories and epistemological groundings of film theory and television theory?

Any differences in the spectator–text relations proposed respectively by soap opera and by film melodrama must be contingent to some extent on more general disparities in address between television and cinema. Thus film spectatorship, it may be argued, involves the pleasures evoked by looking in a more pristine way than does watching television. Whereas in classic cinema the concentration and involvement proposed by structures of the look, identification and point-of-view tend to be paramount, television spectatorship is more likely to be characterised by distraction and diversion.[12] This would suggest that each medium constructs sexual difference through spectatorship in rather different ways: cinema through the look and spectacle, and television—perhaps less evidently—through a capacity to insert its flow, its characteristic modes of address, and the textual operations of different kinds of programmes into the rhythms and routines of domestic activities and sexual divisions of labour in the household at various times of day.

It would be a mistake, however, simply to equate current thinking on spectator–text relations in each medium. This is not only because theoretical work on spectatorship as it is defined here is newer and perhaps not so developed for television as it has been for cinema, but also because conceptualisations of spectatorship in film theory and TV theory emerge from quite distinct perspectives. When feminist writers on soap opera and on film melodrama discuss spectatorship, therefore, they are usually talking about different things. This has partly to do with the different intellectual histories and methodological groundings of theoretical work on film and on television. Whereas most TV theory has until fairly recently existed under the sociological rubric of media studies, film theory has on the whole been based in the criticism-oriented tradition of literary studies. In consequence, while the one tends to privilege contexts over texts, the other usually privileges texts over contexts.

However, some recent critical work on soap opera, notably work produced within a cultural studies context, does attempt a *rapprochement* of text and context. Charlotte Brunsdon, writing about the British soap opera *Crossroads*, draws a distinction between subject positions proposed by texts and a 'social subject' who may or may not take up these positions.[13] In considering the interplay of 'social reader and social text', Brunsdon attempts to come to terms with problems posed by the universalism of the psychoanalytic model of the spectator/subject as against the descriptiveness and limited analytical scope of studies of specific instances and conjunctures. In taking up the instance of soap opera, then, one of Brunsdon's broader objectives is to resolve the dualism of text and context.

'Successful' spectatorship of a soap like *Crossroads*, it is argued, demands a certain cultural capital: familiarity with the plots and characters of a particular serial as well as with soap opera as a genre. It also demands wider cultural competence, especially in the codes of conduct of personal and family life. For Brunsdon, then, the spectator addressed by soap opera is constructed within culture rather than by representation. This, however, would indicate that such a spectator, a 'social subject', might—rather than being a subject in process of gender positioning—belong after all to a social audience already divided by gender.

The 'social subject' of this cultural model produces meaning by decoding messages or communications, an activity which is always socially situated.[14] Thus although such a model may move some way towards reconciling text and context, the balance of Brunsdon's argument remains weighted in favour of context: spectator–text relations are apparently regarded virtually as an effect of socio-cultural contexts. Is there a way in which spectator/subjects of film and television texts can be thought in a historically specific manner, or indeed a way for the social audience to be rescued from social/historical determinism?

Although none of the feminist criticism of soap opera and melodrama reviewed here has come up with any solution to these problems, it all attempts, in some degree and with greater or lesser success, to engage with them. Brunsdon's essay possibly comes closest to an answer, paradoxically because its very failure to resolve the dualism which ordains that spectators are constructed by texts while audiences have their place in contexts begins to hint at a way around the problem. Although the hybrid 'social subject' may turn out to be more a social audience member than a spectator, this concept does suggest that a move into theories of discourse could prove to be productive.

Both spectators and social audience may accordingly be regarded as discursive constructs. Representations, contexts, audiences and spectators would then be seen as a series of interconnected social discourses, certain discourses possessing greater constitutive authority at specific moments than others. Such a model permits relative autonomy for the operations of texts, readings and contexts, and also allows for contradictions, oppositional readings and varying degrees of discursive authority. Since the state of a discursive formation is not constant, it can be apprehended only by means of inquiry into specific instances or conjunctures. In attempting to deal with the text–context split and to address the relationship between spectators and social audiences, therefore, theories of representation may have to come to terms with discursive formations of the social, cultural and textual.

IV

One of the impulses generating feminist critical and theoretical work on soap opera and the woman's picture is a desire to examine genres which are popular, and popular in particular with women. The assumption is usually that such popularity has to do mainly with the social audience: TV soaps attract large numbers of viewers, many of them women, and in its heyday the woman's picture also drew in a mass female audience. But when the nature of this appeal is sought in the texts themselves or in relations between spectators and texts, the argument becomes rather more complex. In what specific ways do soaps and melodramas address or construct female/feminine spectators?

To some extent, they offer the spectator a position of mastery: this is certainly true as regards the hermeneutic of the melodrama's classic narrative, though perhaps less obviously so in relation to the soap's infinite process of narrativity. At the same time, they also place the spectator in a masochistic position of either—in the case of the woman's picture—identifying with a female character's renunciation or, as in soap opera, forever anticipating an endlessly held-off resolution. Culturally speaking, this combination of mastery and masochism in the reading competence constructed by soaps and melodramas suggests an interplay of masculine and feminine subject positions. Culturally dominant codes inscribe the masculine, while the feminine bespeaks a 'return of the repressed' in the form of codes which may well transgress culturally dominant subject positions, though only at the expense of proposing a position of subjection for the spectator.

At the same time, it is sometimes argued on behalf of both soap opera and film melodrama that in a society whose representations of itself are governed by the masculine, these genres at least raise the possibility of female desire and female point-of-view. Pam Cook advances such a view in relation to the woman's picture, for example.[15] But how is the oppositional potential of this to be assessed? Tania Modleski suggests that soap opera is 'in the vanguard not just of TV art but of all popular narrative art'.[16] But such a statement begs the question: under what circumstances can popular narrative art itself be regarded as transgressive? Because texts do not operate in isolation from contexts, any answer to these questions must take into account the ways in which popular narratives are read, the conditions under which they are produced and consumed, and the ends to which they are appropriated. As most feminist writing on soap opera and the woman's melodrama implies, there is ample space in the articulation of these various instances for contradiction and for struggles over meaning.

The popularity of television soap opera and film melodrama with women raises the question of how it is that sizeable audiences of women relate to these representations and the institutional practices of which they form part. It provokes, too, a consideration of the continuity between women's interpellation as spectators and their status as a social audience. In turn, the distinction between social audience and spectator/subject, and attempts to explore the relationship between the two, are part of a broader theoretical endeavour: to deal in tandem with texts and contexts. The distinction between social audience and spectator must also inform debates and practices around cultural production, in which questions of context and reception are always paramount. For anyone interested in feminist cultural politics, such considerations will necessarily inform any assessment of the place and the political usefulness of popular genres aimed at, and consumed by, mass audiences of women.

Notes

1. Muriel G Cantor and Suzanne Pingree, *The Soap Opera* (Beverley Hills, Calif.: Sage Publications), 1983, 22. Here 'soap opera' refers to daytime (US) or early evening (UK) serials . . . not prime-time serials like *Dallas* and *Dynasty*.
2. See Jean-Louis Baudry, 'Ideological Effects of the Basic Cinematographic Apparatus', *Film Quarterly* 28: 2 (1974–5), 39–47; Christian Metz, 'The Imaginary Signifier', *Screen*, 16: 2 (Summer 1975), 14–76.
3. Laura Mulvey, 'Afterthoughts on "Visual Pleasure and Narrative Cinema"', *Framework*, nos. 15/16/17 (1981), 12–15.
4. Laura Mulvey, 'Visual Pleasure and Narrative Cinema', *Screen*, 16: 3 (Autumn 1975), 6–18.
5. Pam Cook, 'Melodrama and the Women's Picture', in Sue Aspinall and Robert Murphy (eds.), *Gainsborough Melodrama* (London: BFI, 1983), 17.
6. Tania Modleski, *Loving with a Vengeance: Mass Produced Fantasies for Women* (Hamden, Conn.: The Shoe String Press, 1982), 105. See also Tania Modleski, 'The Search for Tomorrow in Today's Soap Operas', *Film Quarterly*, 33: 1 (1979), 12–21.

7. Cook, op. cit.
8. Methods and findings of social science research on the social audience for American daytime soap operas are discussed in Cantor and Pingree, op. cit., chapter 7.
9. Modleski, *Loving with a Vengeance*, op. cit., 88.
10. Charlotte Brunsdon, 'Crossroads: Notes on Soap Opera', *Screen*, 22: 4 (1981), 32–37.
11. Cook, op. cit., 19.
12. John Ellis, *Visible Fictions* (London: Routledge and Kegan Paul, 1982).
13. Brunsdon, op. cit., 32.
14. A similar model is also adopted by Dorothy Hobson in *Crossroads: The Drama of a Soap Opera* (London: Methuen, 1982).
15. Cook, op. cit. E Ann Kaplan takes a contrary position in 'Theories of Melodrama: a Feminist Perspective', *Women and Performance: A Journal of Feminist Theory*, 1: 1 (1983), 40–48.
16. Modleski, *Loving with a Vengeance*, op. cit., 87.

23 Desperately Seeking Difference

Jackie Stacey*

During the last decade feminist critics have developed an analysis of the constructions of sexual difference in dominant narrative cinema, drawing on psychoanalytic and post-structuralist theory. One of the main indictments of Hollywood film has been its passive positioning of the woman as sexual spectacle, as there 'to be looked at', and the active positioning of male protagonist as bearer of the look. This pleasure has been identified as one of the central structures of dominant cinema, constructed in accordance with masculine desire. The question which has then arisen is that of the pleasure of the woman spectator. While this issue has hardly been addressed, the specifically homosexual pleasures of female spectatorship have been ignored completely. This article will attempt to suggest some of the theoretical reasons for this neglect.

THEORIES OF FEMININE SPECTATORSHIP: MASCULINISATION, MASOCHISM OR MARGINALITY

Laura Mulvey's 'Visual Pleasure and Narrative Cinema'[1] has been the springboard for much feminist film criticism during the last decade. Using psychoanalytic theory, Mulvey argued that the visual pleasures of Hollywood cinema are based on voyeuristic and fetishistic forms of looking. Because of the ways these looks are structured, the spectator necessarily identifies with the male protagonist in the narrative, and thus with his objectification of the female figure via the male gaze. The construction of woman as spectacle is built into the apparatus of dominant cinema, and the spectator

* Jackie Stacey, 'Desperately Seeking Difference' from *Screen*, vol. 28 no.1 (1987), reprinted by permission of John Logie Baird Centre and the author.

position which is produced by the film narrative is necessarily a masculine one.

Mulvey maintained that visual pleasure in narrative film is built around two contradictory processes: the first involves objectification of the image and the second identification with it. The first process depends upon 'direct scopophilic contact with the female form displayed for [the spectator's] enjoyment'[2] and the spectator's look here is active and feels powerful. This form of pleasure requires the separation of the 'erotic identity of the subject from the object on the screen'.[3] This 'distance' between spectator and screen contributes to the voyeuristic pleasure of looking in on a private world. The second form of pleasure depends upon the opposite process, an identification with the image on the screen 'developed through narcissism and the constitution of the ego'.[4] The process of identification in the cinema, Mulvey argued, like the process of objectification, is structured by the narrative. It offers the spectator the pleasurable identification with the main male protagonist, and through him the power to indirectly possess the female character displayed as sexual object for his pleasure. The look of the male character moves the narrative forward and identification with it thus implies a sense of sharing in the power of his active look.

Two absences in Mulvey's argument have subsequently been addressed in film criticism. The first raises the question of the male figure as erotic object,[5] the second that of the feminine subject in the narrative, and, more specifically in relation to this article, women's active desire and the sexual aims of women in the audience in relationship to the female protagonist on the screen. As David Rodowick points out:

> her discussion of the female figure is restricted only to its function as masculine object-choice. In this manner, the place of the masculine is discussed as both the subject and object of the gaze: and the feminine is discussed only as an object which structures the masculine look according to its active (voyeuristic) and passive (fetishistic) forms. So where is the place of the feminine subject in this scenario?[6]

There are several possible ways of filling this theoretical gap. One would use a detailed textual analysis to demonstrate that different gendered spectator positions are produced by the film text, contradicting the unified masculine model of spectatorship. This would at least provide some space for an account of the feminine subject in the film text and in the cinema audience. The relationship of spectators to these feminine and masculine positions would then need to be explored further: do women necessarily take up a feminine and men a masculine spectator position?

Alternatively, we could accept a theory of the masculinisation of the spectator at a textual level, but argue that spectators bring different subjectivities to the film according to sexual difference,[7] and therefore respond differently to the visual pleasures offered in the text. I want to elaborate these two possibilities briefly, before moving on to discuss a third which offers a more flexible or mobile model of spectatorship and cinematic pleasure.

The first possibility is, then, arguing that the film text can be read and enjoyed from different gendered positions. This problematises the monolithic model of Hollywood cinema as an 'anthropomorphic male machine'[8] producing unified and masculinised spectators. It offers an explanation of women's pleasure in narrative cinema based on different processes of spectatorship, according to sexual difference. What this 'difference' signifies, however, in terms of cinematic pleasure, is highly contestable.

Raymond Bellour has explored the way the look is organised to create filmic discourse through detailed analyses of the system of enunciation in Hitchcock's work.[9] The mechanisms for eliminating the threat of sexual difference represented by the figure of the woman, he argues, are built into the apparatus of the cinema. Woman's desire only appears on the screen to be punished and controlled by assimilation to the desire of the male character. Bellour insists upon the masochistic nature of the woman spectator's pleasure in Hollywood film.

> I think that a woman can love, accept, and give positive value to these films only from her own masochism, and from a certain sadism that she can exercise in return on the masculine subject, within a system loaded with traps.[10]

Bellour, then, provides an account of the feminine subject and women's spectatorship which offers a different position from the masculine one set up by Mulvey. However, he fixes these positions within a rigid dichotomy which assumes a biologically determined equivalence between male/female and the masculine/feminine, sadistic/masochistic positions he believes to be set up by the cinematic apparatus. The apparatus here is seen as determining, controlling the meaning produced by a film text unproblematically.

> . . . the resulting picture of the classical cinema is even more totalistic and deterministic than Mulvey's. Bellour sees it as a logically consistant, complete and closed system.[11]

The problem here is that Bellour's analysis, like those of many structural functionalists, leaves no room for subjectivity. The spectator is presumed to be an already fully constituted subject and is fixed by the text to a predetermined gender identification. There is no space for subjectivity to be seen as a process in which identification and object choice may be shifting, contradictory or precarious.

A second challenge to the model of the masculinised spectator set up by Mulvey's 1975 essay comes from the work of Mary Ann Doane. She draws on Freud's account of asymmetry in the development of masculinity and femininity to argue that women's pleasures are not motivated by fetishistic and voyeuristic drives:

> For the female spectator there is a certain over-presence of the image—she *is* the image. Given the closeness of this relationship, the female spectator's desire can be described only in terms of a kind of narcissism—the female look demands a becoming. It thus appears to negate the very distance or gap specified . . . as the essential precondition for voyeurism.[12]

Feminist critics have frequently challenged the assumption that fetishism functions for women in the same way that it is supposed to for men. Doane argues that the girl's understanding of the meaning of sexual difference occurs simultaneously with seeing the boy's genitals; the split between seeing and knowing, which enables the boy to disown the difference which is necessary for fetishism, does not occur in girls:

> It is in the distance between the look and the threat that the boy's relation to the knowledge of sexual difference is formulated. The boy, unlike the girl in Freud's description, is capable of a re-vision. . . . This gap between the visible and the knowable, the very possibility of disowning what is seen, prepares the ground for fetishism.[13]

This argument is useful in challenging the hegemony of the cinema apparatus and in offering an account of visual pleasure which is neither based on a phallic model, nor on the determinacy of the text. It allows for an account of women's potential resistance to the dominant masculine spectator position. However, it also sets women outside the problematic pleasures of looking in the cinema, as if women do not have to negotiate within patriarchal regimes. As Doane herself has pointed out:

> The feminist theorist is thus confronted with something of a double bind: she can continue to analyse and interpret various instances of the repression of woman, of her radical absence in the discourses of men—a pose which

necessitates remaining within that very problematic herself, repeating its terms; or she can attempt to delineate a feminine specificity, always risking a recapitulation of patriarchal constructions and a naturalization of 'woman'.[14]

In fact, this is a very familiar problem in feminist theory: how to argue for a feminine specificity without falling into the trap of biological essentialism. If we do argue that women differ from men in their relation to visual constructions of femininity, then further questions are generated for feminist film theory: do all women have the same relationship to images of themselves? Is there only one feminine spectator position? How do we account for diversity, contradiction or resistance within this category of feminine spectatorship?

The problem here is one which arises in relation to all cultural systems in which women have been defined as 'other' within patriarchal discourses: how can we express the extent of women's oppression without denying femininity any room to manoeuvre (Mulvey 1975), defining women as complete victims of patriarchy (Bellour 1979), or as totally other to it (Doane 1982)? Within the theories discussed so far, the female spectator is offered only the three rather frustrating options of masculinisation, masochism or marginality.

TOWARDS A MORE CONTRADICTORY MODEL OF SPECTATORSHIP

A different avenue of exploration would require a more complex and contradictory model of the relay of looks on the screen and between the audience and the diegetic characters.

It might be better, as Barthes suggests, neither to destroy difference nor to valorize it, but to multiply and disperse differences, to move towards a world where differences would not be synonymous with exclusion.[15]

In her 1981 'Afterthoughts' on visual pleasure, Mulvey addresses many of the problems raised so far. In an attempt to develop a more 'mobile' position for the female spectator in the cinema, she turns to Freud's theories of the difficulties of attaining heterosexual femininity.[16] Required, unlike men, to relinquish the phallic activity and female object of infancy, women are argued to oscillate between masculine and feminine identifications. To demonstrate this oscillation between positions, Mulvey cites Pearl Chavez's ambivalence in *Duel in the Sun*, the splitting of her desire (to be Jesse's 'lady' or Lewt's tomboy lover), a splitting which also extends to the female spectator. Mulvey's revision is important for two reasons: it displaces the notions of the fixity of spectator positions produced by the text, and it focuses on the gaps and contradictions within patriarchal signification, thus opening up crucial questions of resistance and diversity. However, Mulvey maintains that fantasies of action 'can only find expression . . . through the metaphor of masculinity'. In order to identify with active desire, the female spectator must assume an (uncomfortably) masculine position: '. . . the female spectator's phantasy of masculinisation is always to some extent at cross purposes with itself, restless in its transvestite clothes'.[17]

OPPRESSIVE DICHOTOMIES

Psychoanalytic accounts which theorise identification and object choice within a framework of linked binary oppositions (masculinity/femininity: activity/passivity) necessarily masculinise female homosexuality. Mary Ann Doan's reading of the first scene in the film *Caught* demonstrates the limitations of this psychoanalytic binarism perfectly.

> The woman's sexuality, as spectator, must undergo a constant process of transformation. She must look, as if she were a man with the phallic power of the gaze, at a woman who would attract that gaze, in order to be that woman. . . . The convolutions involved here are analogous to those described by Julia Kristeva as 'the double or triple twists of what we commonly call female homosexuality': 'I am looking, as a man would, for a woman'; or else, 'I submit myself, as if I were a man who thought he was a woman, to a woman who thinks she is a man.'[18]

Convolutions indeed. This insistence upon a gendered dualism of sexual desire maps homosexuality onto an assumed antithesis of masculinity and femininity. Such an assumption precludes a description of homosexual positionality without resorting to the manoeuvres cited by Doane. In arguing for a more complex model of cinematic spectatorship, I am suggesting that we need to separate gender identification from sexuality, too often conflated in the name of sexual difference.

In films where the woman is represented as sexual spectacle for the masculine gaze of the diegetic and the cinematic spectator, an identification with a masculine heterosexual desire is invited. The spectator's response can vary across a wide spectrum between outright acceptance and refusal. It has proved crucial for feminist film theorists to explore these variations. How might a woman's look at another woman, both within the diegesis and between spectator and character, compare with that of the male spectator?

This article considers the pleasures of two narrative films which develop around one woman's obsession with another woman, *All About Eve* (directed by Joseph Mankiewicz, 1950) and *Desperately Seeking Susan* (directed by Susan Seidelman, 1984). I shall argue that these films offer particular pleasures to the women in the audience which cannot simply be reduced to a masculine heterosexual equivalent. In so doing I am not claiming these films as 'lesbian films',[19] but rather using them to examine certain possibilities of pleasure.

I want to explore the representation of forms of desire and identification in these films in order to consider their implications for the pleasures of female spectatorship. My focus is on the relations between women on the screen, and between these representations and the women in the audience. Interestingly, the fascinations which structure both narratives are precisely about difference—forms of otherness between women characters which are not merely reducible to sexual difference, so often seen as the sole producer of desire itself.

THE INSCRIPTION OF ACTIVE FEMININE DESIRE

In *Alice Doesn't*, Teresa de Lauretis explores the function of the classic masculine Oedipal trajectory in dominant narrative. The subjects which motivate the narrative along the logic of the 'Oedipus', she argues, are necessarily masculine:

> However varied the conditions of the presence of the narrative form in fictional genres, rituals or social discourses, its movement seems to be that of a passage, a transformation predicated on the figure of the hero, a mythical subject . . . the *single* figure of the hero who crosses the boundary and penetrates the other space. In so doing, the hero, the mythical subject, is constructed as a human being and as male; he is the active principle of culture, the establisher of distinction, the creator of differences. Female is what is not susceptible to transformation, to life or death;[20]

De Lauretis then proceeds to outline the significance of this division between masculine and feminine within the textual narrative in terms of spectatorship.

> Therefore, to say that narrative is the production of Oedipus is to say that each reader—male or female—is constrained and defined within the two positions of a sexual difference thus conceived: male-hero-human, on the side of the subject; the female-obstacle-boundary-space, on the other.[21]

As de Lauretis herself acknowledges later in the chapter, this analysis leaves little space for either the question of the feminine subject in the narrative, or the pleasures of desire and identification of the women in the audience. In order to explore these questions more concretely, I want to discuss two texts—one a Hollywood production of 1950, the other a recent US 'independent'—whose central narrative concern is that of female desire. Both *All About Eve* and *Desperately Seeking Susan* have female protagonists whose desires and identifications move the narratives forward. In de Lauretis's terms, these texts construct not only a feminine object or desire in the narrative, but also a feminine subject of that desire.

All about Eve is particularly well suited to an analysis of these questions, as it is precisely about the pleasures and dangers of spectatorship for women. One of its central themes is the construction and reproduction of feminine identities, and the activity of looking is highlighted as an important part of these processes. The narrative concerns two women, a Broadway star and her most adoring spectator, Eve. In its course, we witness the transformation of Eve Butler (Anne Baxter) from spectator to star herself. The pleasures of spectatorship are emphasised by Eve's loyal attendance at every one of Margot Channing's (Bette Davis) performances. Its dangers are also made explicit as an intense rivalry develops between them. Eve emerges as a greedy and ambitious competitor, and Margot steps down from stardom into marriage, finally enabling her protegée to replace her as 'actress of the year' in a part written originally for Margot.

Eve's journey to stardom could be seen as the feminine equivalent to the masculine Oedipal trajectory described by de Lauretis above. Freud's later descriptions of the feminine Oedipal journey[22] contradict his previous symmetrical model wherein the girl's first love object is her father, as the boy's is his mother. In his later arguments, Freud also posited the mother as the girl's first love object. Her path to heterosexuality is therefore difficult and complex, since it requires her not only to relinquish her first object, like the boy, but to transform both its gender (female to male) and the aim (active to passive) directed at it. Up to this point, active desire towards another woman is an experience of all women, and its re-enactment in *All About Eve* may constitute one of the pleasures of spectatorship for the female viewer.

Eve is constantly referred to as innocent and childlike in the first half of the film and her transformation involves a process of maturation, of becoming a more confident adult. First she is passionately attached to Margot, but then she shifts her affection to Margot's lover Bill, attempting unsuccessfully to seduce him. Twice in the film she is shown interrupting their intimacy: during their farewell at the airport and then during their fierce argument about Margot's jealousy, shortly before Bill's welcome-home party. Eve's third object of desire, whom she actively pursues, is the married playwright, Lloyd Richards, husband to Margot's best friend. In both cases the stability of the older heterosexual couples, Margot and Bill, Karen and Lloyd, are threatened by the presence of the younger woman who completes the Oedipal triangle. Eve is finally punished for her desires by the patriarchal power of the aptly named Addison de Wit, who proves to be one step ahead of her manipulations.

The binary opposition between masculinity and femininity offers a limited framework for the discussion of Eve's fascination with Margot, which is articulated actively through an interplay of desire and identification during the film. In many ways, Margot is Eve's idealised object of desire. She follows Margot from city to city, never missing any of her performances. Her devotion to her favourite Broadway star is stressed at the very start of the film.

KAREN. But there are hundreds of plays on Broadway. . . .
EVE. Not with Margot Channing in them!

Margot is moved by Eve's representation of her 'tragic' past, and flattered by her adoration, so she decides to 'adopt' her.

MARGOT (*voice over*). We moved Eve's few pitiful possessions into my apartment. . . . Eve became my sister, mother, lawyer, friend, psychiatrist and cop. The honeymoon was on!

Eve acts upon her desire to become more like her ideal. She begins to wear Margot's cast-off clothes, appearing in Margot's bedroom one morning in her old black suit. Birdie, Margot's personal assistant, responds suspiciously to Eve's behaviour.

MARGOT. She thinks only of me.

BIRDIE. She thinks only *about* you—like she's studying you—like you was a book, or a play, or a set of blueprints—how you walk, talk, eat, think, sleep.

MARGOT. I'm sure that's very flattering, Birdie, and I'm sure there's nothing wrong with it.

The construction of Bette Davis as the desirable feminine ideal in this narrative has a double significance here. As well as being a 'great star' for Eve, she is clearly the same for the cinema audience. The film offers the fictional fulfilment of the spectator's dreams as well as Eve's, to be a star like Bette Davis, like Margot. Thus the identifications and desires or Eve, to some extent, narrativise a traditional pleasure of female spectatorship.

Margot is not only a star, she is also an extremely powerful woman who intimidates most of the male characters in the film. Her quick wit and disdain for conventional politeness, together with her flare for drama offstage as much as on, make her an attractive figure for Eve, an 'idealistic dreamy-eyed kid', as Bill describes her. It is this *difference* between the two women which motivates Eve, but which Eve also threatens. In trying to 'become as much like her ideal as possible', Eve almost replaces Margot in both her public and her private lives. She places a call to Bill on Margot's behalf, and captures his attention when he is on his way upstairs to see Margot before his coming home party. Margot begins to feel dispensible.

MARGOT. I could die right now and nobody would be confused. My inventory is all in shape and the merchandise all put away.

Yet even dressed in Margot's costume, having taken her role in the evening's performance, Eve cannot supplant her in the eyes of Bill, who rejects her attempt at seduction. The difference between the two women is repeatedly stressed and complete identification proves impossible.

All About Eve offers some unusual pleasures for a Hollywood film, since the active desire of a female character is articulated through looking at the female star. It is by watching Margot perform on the stage that Eve becomes intoxicated with her idol. The significance of active looking in the articulation of feminine desire is foregrounded at various points in the narrative. In one scene, we see Eve's devoted spectatorship in progress during one of Margot's performances. Eve watches Margot from the wings of the stage, and Margot bows to the applause of her audience. In the next scene the roles are reversed, and

Margot discovers Eve on the empty stage bowing to an imaginary audience. Eve is holding up Margot's costume to sample the pleasures of stardom for herself. This process is then echoed in the closing scene of the film with Eve, now a Broadway star herself, and the newly introduced Phoebe, an adoring schoolgirl fan. The final shot shows Phoebe, having covertly donned Eve's bejewelled evening cloak, holding Eve's award and gazing at her reflection in the mirror. The reflected image, infinitely multiplied in the triptych of the glass, creates a spectacle of stardom that is the film's final shot, suggesting a perpetual regeneration of intra-feminine fascinations through the pleasure of looking.

THE DESIRE TO BE DESPERATE

Like *All About Eve, Desperately Seeking Susan* concerns a woman's obsession with another woman. But instead of being punished for acting upon her desires, like Eve, Roberta (Rosanna Arquette) acts upon her desires, if in a rather more haphazard way, and eventually her initiatives are rewarded with the realisation of her desires. Despite her classic feminine behaviour, forgetful, clumsy, unpunctual and indecisive, she succeeds in her quest to find Susan (Madonna).

Even at the very beginning of the film, when suburban housewife Roberta is represented at her most dependent and childlike, her actions propel the narrative movement. Having developed her own fantasy narrative about Susan by reading the personal advertisements, Roberta acts upon her desire to be 'desperate' and becomes entangled in Susan's life. She anonymously attends the romantic reunion of Susan and Jim, and then pursues Susan through the streets of Manhattan. When she loses sight of her quarry in a second-hand shop, she purchases the jacket which Susan has just exchanged. The key found in its pocket provides an excuse for direct contact, and Roberta uses the personals to initiate another meeting.

Not only is the narrative propelled structurally by Roberta's desire, but almost all the spectator sees of Susan at the beginning of the film is revealed through Roberta's fantasy. The narrativisation of her desires positions her as the central figure for spectator identification: through her desire we seek, and see, Susan. Thus, in the opening scenes, Susan is introduced by name when Roberta reads the personals aloud from under the dryer in the beauty salon. Immediately following Roberta's declaration 'I wish I was desperate', there is a cut to the first shot of Susan.

The cuts from the Glass' party to Susan's arrival in New York City work to the same effect. Repelled by her husband's TV commercial for his bathroom wares, Roberta leaves her guests and moves towards the window, as the ad's voice-over promises 'At Gary's Oasis, all your fantasies can come true.' Confronted with her own image in the reflection, she pushes it away by opening the window and looking out longingly onto Manhattan's skyline. The ensuing series of cuts between Roberta and the bridge across the river to the city link her desiring gaze to Susan's arrival there via the same bridge.

At certain points within *Desperately Seeking Susan*, Roberta explicitly becomes the bearer of the look. The best illustration of this transgression of traditional gender positionalities occurs in the scene in which she first catches sight of Susan. The shot sequence begins with Jim seeing Susan and is immediately followed with Roberta seeing her. It is, however, Roberta's point of view which is offered for the spectator's identification. Her look is specified by the use of the payslot telescope through which Roberta, and the spectator, see Susan.

In accordance with classic narrative cinema, the object of fascination in *Desperately Seeking Susan* is a woman—typically, a woman coded as a sexual spectacle. As a star Madonna's image is saturated in sexuality. In many ways she represents the 1980s 'assertive style' of heterosexual spectacle, inviting masculine consumption. This is certainly emphasised by shots of Susan which reference classic pornographic poses and camera angles; for example, the shot of Susan lying on Roberta's bed reading her diary, which shows Susan lying on her back, wearing only a vest and a pair of shorts over her suspenders and lacy tights. (Although one could argue that the very next shot, from Susan's point of view, showing Gary upside down, subverts the conventional pornographic codes.) My aim is not to deny these meanings in *Desperately Seeking Susan*, in order to claim it as a 'progressive text', but to point to cinematic pleasures which may be available to the spectator *in addition* to those previously analysed by feminist film theory. Indeed, I believe such a project can only attempt to work within the highly contradictory constructions of femininity in mainstream films.

Susan is represented as puzzling and enigmatic to the protagonist, and to the spectator. The desire propelling the narrative is partly a desire to become more like her, but also a desire to know her, and to solve the riddle of her femininity. The protagonist begins to fulfil this desire by following the stranger, gathering clues about her identity and her life, such as her jacket, which, in turn, produces three other clues, a key, a photograph and a telephone number. The construction of her femininity as a riddle is emphasised by the series of intrigues and misunderstandings surrounding Susan's identity. The film partly relies on typical devices drawn from the mystery genre in constructing the protagonist's, and thus the spectator's, knowledge of Susan through a series of clues and coincidences. Thus, in some ways, Susan is positioned as the classic feminine enigma; she is, however, investigated by another woman.

One line of analysis might simply see Roberta as taking up the position of the masculine protagonist in expressing a desire to be 'desperate', which, after all, can be seen as identifying with Jim's position in relation to Susan, that of active desiring masculinity. Further legitimation for this reading could be seen in Jim's response to Roberta's advertisement to Susan in the personals. He automatically assumes it has been placed there by another man, perhaps a rival. How can we understand the construction of the female protagonist as the agent and articulator of desire for another woman in the narrative within existing psychoanalytic theories of sexual difference? The limitations of a dichotomy which offers only two significant categories for understanding the complex interplay of gender, sexual aim and object choice, is clearly demonstrated here.

DIFFERENCE AND DESIRE BETWEEN WOMEN

The difference which produces the narrative desire in *Desperately Seeking Susan* is not sexual difference, but the difference between two women in the film. It is the difference between suburban marriage and street credibility. Two sequences contrast the characters using smoking as a signifier of difference. The first occurs in Battery Park, where Roberta behaves awkwardly in the unfamiliar territory of public space. She is shown sitting on a park bench, knees tightly clenched, looking around nervously for Susan. Jim asks her for a light, to which she timidly replies that she does not smoke. The ensuing cut shows Susan, signalled by Jim's shout of recognition. Susan is sitting on the boat rail, striking a match on the bottom of her raised boot to light a cigarette.

Smoking is used again to emphasise difference in a subsequent sequence. This time, Roberta, having by now lost her memory and believing she may be Susan, lights a cigarette from Susan's box. Predictably, she chokes on the smoke, with the unfamiliarity of an adolescent novice. The next cut shows us Susan, in prison for attempting to skip her cab fare, taking a light from the prison matron and blowing the smoke defiantly straight back into her face. The contrast in their smoking ability is only one signifier of the characters' very different femininities. Roberta is represented as young, inexperienced and asexual, while Susan's behaviour and appearance are coded as sexually confident and provocative. Rhyming sequences are used to emphasise their differences even after Roberta has taken on her new identity as Susan. She ends up in the same prison cell, but her childlike acquiescence to authority contrasts with Susan's defiance of the law.

Susan transgresses conventional forms of feminine behaviour by appropriating public space for herself. She turns the public lavatory into her own private bathroom, drying her armpits with the hand blower, and changing her clothes in front of the mirror above the washbasins as if in her own bedroom. In the streets, Susan challenges the patronising offer of a free newspaper from a passerby by dropping the whole pile at his feet and taking only the top copy for herself. In contrast to Susan's supreme public confidence, Roberta is only capable in her own middle class privacy. Arriving home after her day of city adventures, she manages to synchronise with a televised cooking show, catching up on its dinner preparations with confident dexterity in her familiar domestic environment.

As soon as Roberta becomes entangled in Susan's world, her respectable sexuality is thrown into question. First she is assumed to be having an affair, then she is arrested for suspected prostitution, and finally Gary asks her if she is a lesbian. When the two photographs of Roberta, one as a bride and one as a suspected prostitute, are laid down side by side at the police station, her apparent transformation from virgin to whore shocks her husband. The ironic effect of these largely misplaced accusations about Roberta's sexuality works partly in relation to Susan, who is represented as the epitome of opposition to acceptable bourgeois feminine sexuality. She avoids commitment, dependency or permanence in her relationships with men, and happily takes their money, while maintaining an intimate friendship with the woman who works at the Magic Box.

Roberta's desire is finally rewarded when she meets Susan in an almost farcical chase scene at that club during the chaotic film finale. Gary finds Roberta, Des finds 'Susan' (Roberta), Jim finds Susan, the villain finds the jewels (the earrings which Susan innocently pocketed earlier in the film), Susan and Roberta catch the villain, and Susan and Roberta find each other. . . . The last shot of the film is a front-page photograph of the two women hand in hand, triumphantly waving their reward cheque in return for the recovery of the priceless Nefertiti earrings. In the end, both women find what they were searching for throughout the narrative: Roberta has found Susan, and Susan has found enough money to finance many future escapades.

Roberta's desire to become more like her ideal—a more pleasingly coordinated, complete and attractive feminine image[23]—is offered temporary narrative fulfilment. However, the pleasures of this feminine desire cannot be collapsed into simple identification, since difference and otherness are continuously played upon, even when Roberta 'becomes' her idealised object. Both *Desperately Seeking Susan* and *All About Eve* tempt the woman spectator with the fictional fulfilment of becoming an ideal feminine other, while denying complete transformation by insisting upon differences between women. The rigid distinction between *either* desire *or* identification, so characteristic of psychoanalytic film theory, fails to address the construction of desires which involve a specific interplay of both processes.

Notes

I would like to thank Sarah Franklin, Richard Dyer, Alison Light, Chris Healey and the Women Thesis Writers Group in Birmingham for their inspiration, support and helpful comments during the writing of this article.

1. Laura Mulvey, 'Visual Pleasure and Narrative Cinema', *Screen*, 16: 3 (Autumn 1975), 6–18.
2. Ibid. 13.
3. Ibid. 10.
4. Ibid.
5. There have been several attempts to fill this theoretical gap and provide analyses of masculinity as sexual spectacle: see Richard Dyer, 'Don't Look Now—The Male Pin-Up', *Screen*, 23: 3/4 (September–October 1982); Steve Neale, 'Masculinity as Spectacle', *Screen*, 24: 6 (November–December 1983); and Andy Medhurst, 'Can Chaps Be Pin-Ups?', *Ten*, 8: 17 (1985).
6. David Rodowick, 'The Difficulty of Difference', *Wide Angle*, 5: 1 (1982), 8.
7. Mary Ann Doane. 'Film and the Masquerade: Theorising the Female Spectator', *Screen*, 23: 3/4 (September–October 1982), 74–87.
8. Constance Penley, 'Feminism, Film Theory and the Bachelor Machines', *m/f*, 10 (1985), 39–56.
9. *Enunciator*: 'the term . . . marks both the person who possesses the right to speak within the film, and the source (instance) towards which the series of

representations is logically channelled back,' Raymond Bellour, 'Hitchcock the Enunciator', *Camera Obscura*, 2 (1977), 94.

10. Raymond Bellour, 'Psychosis, Neurosis, Perversion', *Camera Obscura*, 3/4 (1979), 97.
11. Janet Bergstrom, 'Enunciation and Sexual Difference', *Camera Obscura*, 3/4 (1979), 57. See also Janet Bergstrom, 'Alternation, Segmentation, Hypnosis: An Interview with Raymond Bellour', *Camera Obscura*, 3/4 (1979).
12. Mary Ann Doane, 'Film and the Masquerade', op. cit., 78.
13. Ibid. 80.
14. Mary Ann Doane, Patricia Mellencamp, and Linda Williams, 'Feminist Film Criticism: An Introduction', in Mary Ann Doane, Patricia Mellencamp, and Linda Williams (eds.), *Re-Vision* (Frederick, Md.: American Film Institute, 1984), 9.
15. Ibid. 14.
16. Laura Mulvey, 'Afterthoughts on "Visual Pleasure and Narrative Cinema" . . . Inspired by "Duel in the Sun" ', *Framework*, 15/16/17 (1981), 12–15.
17. Ibid. 15.
18. Mary Ann Doane citing Julia Kristeva, *About Chinese Women*, in 'Caught and Rebecca: The Inscription of Femininity as Absence', *Enclitic*, 5: 2/6: 1 (Fall 1981/Spring 1982), 77.
19. For a discussion of films which might be included under this category, see Caroline Sheldon, 'Lesbians and Film; Some Thoughts', in Richard Dyer (ed.), *Gays and Film* (New York: Zoetrope, revised edition 1984).
20. Teresa de Lauretis, *Alice Doesn't: Feminism, Semiotics and the Cinema* (London: Macmillan, 1984), 113, 119.
21. Ibid. 121.
22. See, for example, Sigmund Freud, 'Some Psychical Consequences of the Anatomical Distinction between the Sexes' (1925) in *On Sexuality*, Pelican Freud Library, vol. 7 (Harmondsworth, 1977), 331–343.

24 The Case of the Missing Mother: Maternal Issues in Vidor's *Stella Dallas*

E. Ann Kaplan*

For complex reasons, feminists have focused on the Mother largely from the daughter position. When I first joined a consciousness-raising group in 1969, we dealt with Mothering only in terms of our own relationships to our mothers, and this despite the fact that a few of us in the group already had children. As a graduate student and mother of a 1-year-old girl, I badly needed to talk about issues of career versus Motherhood, about how having the child affected my marriage, about the conflict between my needs and the baby's needs; but for some reason, I felt that these were unacceptable issues.

I think this was because at that time feminism was very much a movement of daughters. The very attractiveness of feminism was that it provided an arena for separation from oppressive closeness with the Mother; feminism was in part a reaction against our mothers who had tried to inculcate the patriarchal 'feminine' in us, much to our anger. This made it difficult for us to identify with Mothering and to look from the position of the Mother.

Unwittingly, then, we repeated the patriarchal omission of the Mother. From a psychoanalytic point of view, we remained locked in ambivalence toward the Mother, at once still deeply tied to her while striving for an apparently unattainable autonomy. Paradoxically, our complex Oedipal struggles prevented us from seeing the Mother's oppression (although we had no such problems in other areas), and resulted in our assigning the Mother, in her heterosexual, familial setting, to an absence and silence analogous to the male relegation of her to the periphery.

Traditional psychoanalysis, as an extension of patriarchy, has omit-

* E. Ann Kaplan, 'The Case of the Missing Mother: Patriarchy and the Maternal in Vidor's *Stella Dallas*' from *Heresies*, vol. 4 no. 4 (1983), reprinted by permission of the author.

ted the Mother, except when she is considered from the child's point of view. Since patriarchy is constructed according to the male unconscious feminists grew up in a society that repressed the Mother. Patriarchy chose, rather, to foreground woman's status as *castrated*, as lacking, since this construction benefits patriarchy. If the phallus defines everything, legitimacy is granted to the subordination of women. Feminists have been rebellious about this second construction of ourselves as *castrated*, but have only recently begun to react strongly against the construction of the Mother as marginal.

This reaction began in the mid-1970s with the ground-breaking books about motherhood by Adrienne Rich, Dorothy Dinnerstein, and Jane Lazarre.[1] Rich and Dinnerstein exposed the repression of the Mother, and analyzed the reasons for it, showing both psychoanalytic and socio-economic causes. Building on Melanie Klein's and Simone de Beauvoir's ideas, Dinnerstein described the early childhood experience as one of total dependency on a Mother who is not distinguished from the self (she is 'good' when present, 'bad' when absent). This, together with the Mother's assimilation to natural processes through her reproductive function, results in her split cultural designation and representation.

Rich shows in numerous ways how the Mother is either idealized, as in the myths of the nurturing, ever-present but self-abnegating figure, or disparaged, as in the corollary myth of the sadistic, neglectful Mother who puts her needs first. The Mother as a complex person in her own right, with multiple roles to fill and conflicting needs and desires, is absent from patriarchal representations. Silenced by patriarchal structures that have no room for her, the Mother-figure, despite her actual psychological importance, has been allotted to the margins, put in a position limited to that of spectator.

These constructions contributed to feminists' negative attitude toward Mothering in the early days of the movement. We were afraid not only of becoming like our own mothers, but also of falling into one or the other of the mythic paradigms, should we have children. Put on the defensive, feminists rationalized their fears and anger, focusing on the destructiveness of the nuclear family as an institution, and seeing the Mother as an agent of the patriarchal establishment. We were unable then to see that the Mother was as much a victim of patriarchy as ourselves, constructed as she is by a whole series of discourses—psychoanalytic, political, and economic.

The Hollywood cinema is as responsible as anything for perpetuating the useless patriarchal myths. Relatively few Hollywood films make the Mother central, relegating her, rather, to the periphery of a narrative focused on a husband, son, or daughter. The dominant paradigms are similar to those found in literature and mythology throughout Western culture, and may be outlined quite simply:

1. The Good Mother, who is all-nurturing and self-abnegating—the 'Angel in the House'. Totally invested in husband and children, she lives only through them, and is marginal to the narrative.[2]

2. The Bad Mother or Witch—the underside to the first myth. Sadistic, hurtful, and jealous, she refuses the self-abnegating role, demanding her own life. Because of her 'evil' behavior, this Mother often takes control of the narrative, but she is punished for her violation of the desired patriarchal ideal, the Good Mother.[3]

3. The Heroic Mother, who suffers and endures for the sake of husband and children. A development of the first Mother, she shares her saintly qualities, but is more central to the action. Yet, unlike the second Mother, she acts not to satisfy herself but for the good of the family.[4]

4. The Silly, Weak, or Vain Mother. Found most often in comedies, she is ridiculed by husband and children alike, and generally scorned and disparaged.[5]

As these limited paradigms show, Hollywood has failed to address the complex issues that surround Mothering in capitalism. Each paradigm is assigned a moral position in a hierarchy that facilitates the smooth functioning of the system. The desirable paradigm purposely presents the Mother from the position of child or husband, since to place the camera in the Mother's position would raise the possibility of her having needs and desires of her own. If the Mother reveals her desire, she is characterized as the Bad Mother (sadistic, monstrous), much as the single woman who expresses sexual desire is seen as destructive.

It is significant that Hollywood Mothers are rarely single and rarely combine Mothering with work. Stahl's and Sirk's versions of *Imitation of Life* are exceptions (although in other ways the Mother figures reflect the myths). Often, as in *Mildred Pierce*, the Mother is punished for trying to combine work and Mothering. Narratives that do focus on the Mother usually take that focus because she resists her proper place. The work of the film is to reinscribe the Mother in the position patriarchy desires for her and, in so doing, teach the female audience the dangers of stepping out of the given position. *Stella Dallas* is a clear example: the film 'teaches' Stella her 'correct' position, bringing her from resistance to conformity with the dominant, desired myth.

How could she—oh how could she have become a part of the picture on the screen, while her mother was still in the audience, out there, in the dark, looking on?

This quotation is taken from the 1923 novel *Stella Dallas*, by Olive Higgins. It shows how the cinema had already, by 1923, become a metaphor for the oppositions of reality and illusion, poverty and wealth. Within the film *Stella Dallas*, we find the poor on the outside (Laurel's mother, Stella) and the rich on the inside (Laurel and the Morrisons). This mimics, as it were, the situation of the cinema spectator, who is increasingly subjected to a screen filled with rich people in luxurious studio sets.

But it is not simply that the 1937 version of *Stella Dallas* makes Stella the working-class spectator, looking in on the upper-class world of Stephen Dallas and the Morrison family. She is excluded not only as a working-class woman, but also as the Mother. Ben Brewster notes that the 1923 novel moves Laurel 'decisively into the world of Helen Morrison, shifting its point of identification to Laurel's mother, Stella Dallas, who abolishes herself as visible to her daughter so as to be able to contemplate her in that world.'[6] It is the process by which Stella Dallas makes herself literally Mother-as-spectator that interests me, for it symbolizes the position that the Mother is most often given in patriarchal culture, regardless of which paradigm is used.

Stella is actually a complex mixture of a number of the Mother paradigms. She tries to resist the position as Mother that patriarchal marriage, within the film, seeks to put her in—thus, for a moment, exposing that position. First, she literally objects to Mothering because of the personal sacrifices involved; then, she protests by expressing herself freely in her eccentric style of dress. The film punishes her for both forms of resistance by turning her into a 'spectacle' produced by the upper class' disapproving gaze, a gaze the audience is made to share through the camera work and editing.

The process by which Stella is brought from resistance to passive observer highlights the way the Mother is constructed as marginal or absent in patriarchy. As the film opens, we see Stella carefully preparing herself to be the object of Stephen Dallas' gaze; she self-consciousiy creates the image of the sweet, innocent but serious girl as she stands in the garden of her humble dwelling pretending to read a book. Despite all her efforts to be visible, her would-be lover fails to notice her. The cinema spectator, seeing that Stephen is as much someone *with* class as Stella is without it, realizes that Stella is overlooked because she is working class.

Stella's plan to escape from her background is understandable, given the place her mother occupies within the family. This gaunt and haggard figure slaves away at sink and stove in the rear of the frame, all but invisible on a first viewing. She only moves into the frame to berate Stella for refusing to give her brother the lunch he wants. 'What do you want to upset him for? What would I do without him?' she asks, betraying her economic and psychological dependence on this young man, not yet ground down (as is her husband) by toil at the mill. As Stella narcissistically appraises her own fresh beauty in the kitchen's dismal mirror, she is inspired to take her brother his lunch after all, hoping to meet Stephen Dallas, whom she now knows is a runaway millionaire.

Stella's 'performance' at the mill office, where Stephen has settled down to a lonely lunch, is again self-conscious. But this time her flawless acting wins her what she wants. Dressed as a virginal young lady, she gazes adoringly up at Stephen instead of following the directions he is giving her—an attention that surprises but flatters the heart-sick man.

Shortly after this, we find Stephen and Stella at the movies. A shot of upper-class men and women dancing on a screen, filmed from the perspective of the theater audience, is followed by a front shot of Stella and Stephen. He munches disinterestedly on popcorn while she snuggles up to him, intensely involved in the film. This scene confirms that Stella has been acting 'as if in the movie,' performing with Stephen according to codes learned through watching films. We see how films indeed do 'teach' us about the life we should desire and about how to *respond* to movies. As the film ends, Stella is weeping; and as women watching Stella watching the screen, we are both offered a model of how *we* should respond to films and given insight into the mechanisms of cinematic voyeurism and identification. Stella, the working-class spectator, is outside the rich world on the screen, offered as spectacle for her emulation and envy. 'I want to be like the women in the movies,' Stella says to Stephen on their way home.

Meanwhile, Stella and Stephen themselves become objects of the envious, voyeuristic gaze of some passersby when they embrace outside the cinema. The women watching are now 'on the outside', while Stella is beginning her brief sojourn 'inside' the rich world she envied on screen. Thus, to the basic audience-screen situation of the *Stella*

Dallas film itself, Vidor has added two levels: Stella and Stephen in the movie house, and Stella and Stephen as 'spectacle' for the street 'audience'. Stella will herself create yet another spectator-screen experience (one that is indeed foreshadowed in the movie scene here), when she becomes 'spectator' to the screen/scene of her daughter's luxurious wedding in the Morrison household at the end of the film. Stella has made her daughter into a 'movie star' through whom she can live vicariously.

This is only possible through Motherhood as constructed in patriarchy, and thus Stella's own mothering is central to her trajectory. It is fitting that the movie scene cuts directly to Stella's haggard mother laboring in her kitchen the following morning. Her victimization is underscored by her total fear of Stella's father, who is yelling loudly. Both the mother and son are terrified that the father will discover that Stella has not come home. Indeed, the father angrily ejects his daughter from his house—until her smiling arrival, already wed to Stephen Dallas, mitigates all sins.

This is the last we see of Stella's family. For all intents and purposes the working-class family is eliminated on Stella's entrance into Stephen Dallas' upper-class world—it is made as invisible in filmic terms as it is culturally. What Stella has to contend with are her remaining working-class desires, attitudes, and behaviors, which the film sees ambiguously as either ineradicable (which would involve an uncharacteristic class determinism), or as deliberately retained by Stella. Women are socialized to be flexible precisely so that they can marry into a higher class, taking their family up a notch as they do so. We have seen that Stella is aware of how she *should* behave. ('I want to be with you,' she tells Stephen after seeing the movie, 'I want to be like you. I want to be like all the people you've been around.') But Stella resists this change once she has won her upper-class man, which makes her at once a more interesting and a more tragic heroine. Given the structures that bind her, she has more sense of self than is ultimately good for her.

It is both Stella's (brief) resistance to Mothering and her resistance to adapting to upper-class mores that for a moment expose the construction of Mothering in patriarchy and at the same time necessitate her being *taught* her proper construction. Stella first violates patriarchal code when, arriving home with her baby, she manifests not delight but impatience with her new role, demanding that she and Stephen go dancing that very night. Next, she violates the codes by wearing a garish dress and behaving independently at the club, leaving their table to dance with a stranger, Mr. Munn (who is from the wrong set), and going to sit at Munn's table.

This behavior is immediately 'placed' for the spectator when the camera takes Stephen's point of view on the scene, although it could as easily have stuck with Stella's perspective and shown the stuffiness of the upper class. Staying with Stephen, who has now collected their coats and is waiting by the dance floor, the camera exposes Stella's vigorous dancing and loud behavior as 'unseemly'. At home, Stephen begs Stella to 'see reason', in other words, to conform to his class. He does not take kindly to Stella's round reply ('How about you doing some adapting?'), and when he asks her to move to New York because of his business she refuses on account of 'just beginning to get into the right things' (which the spectator already knows are the *wrong* things from Stephen's perspective).

The following scene shows even more clearly how the film wrenches Stella's point of view away from the audience, forcing us to look at Stella through Stephen's eyes. As a Mother, Stella is no longer permitted to control her actions, or to be the camera's eye (as she was in the scenes before her marriage and Motherhood). The scene with Laurel as a baby opens with the camera still in Stella's point of view. We see her with her maid, feeding and delighting in her baby. Munn and his friends drop by, and a spontaneous little party develops. Everyone is having fun, Laurel included. Suddenly Stephen arrives, and the camera shifts to his perspective. The entire scene changes in an instant from a harmless gathering to a distasteful brawl, rendering Stella a neglectful Mother. The camera cuts to the stubbed-out cigarettes in Laurel's food bowl, to the half-empty liquor glasses, to the half-drunk, unshapely men; we get Stephen's eye moving around the room. Laurel begins to cry at her father's shouting, as the friends hurriedly and shamefacedly slip away. Stella has become the 'object', and judged from Stephen's supposedly superior morality, is found to be lacking in Motherliness.

These scenes initiate a pattern through which Stella is made into a 'spectacle' (in a negative sense) both within the film story and for the cinema spectator. It is the first step on the way to her learning her 'correct' place as 'spectator', as *absent* Mother (as she gradually realizes through the upper-class judgments of her that she is an embarrassment to her child). The second step is for both audience and Stella to validate the alternative model of the upper-class Morrison family, set up over and against Stella. The lower-class Stella and the cinema audience thus become the admiring spectators of the Morrison's perfect lifestyle. Other figures are brought in to provide further negative judgments of Stella as Mother. For example, Stella does not take Laurel to cultural events, so the schoolteacher has to do this: Stella then behaves loudly in public with an ill-mannered man, where she is seen by the teacher. Moreover, Laurel's peers indicate disapproval of Stella by refusing to attend Laurel's party, and later on her upper-class friends at the hotel laugh outright at Stella's appearance. By implicating us—the cinema specator—in this process of rejection, we are made to accede to the 'rightness' of Stella's renunciation of her daughter, and thus made to agree with Stella's position as absent Mother.

Once the lacks in Stella's Mothering have been established from the upper-class perspective (which is synonymous with patriarchy's construction of the ideal Mother), we are shown this 'Ideal' in the concrete form of Helen Morrison. Refined, calm, and decorous, devoted to her home and children, she embodies the all-nurturing, self-effacing Mother. She is a saintly figure, worshipped by Laurel because she gives the child everything she needs and asks nothing in return (she is even tender toward Stella, for whom she shows 'pity' without being condescending). Modern viewers may find

Having installed her daughter in middle-class life, framed as in the movies, Stella leaves tearful but triumphant.

these scenes embarrassingly crude in their idealization of upper-class life, but within the film's narrative this is obviously the desired world: the happy realm where all Oedipal conflicts are effaced and family members exude perfect harmony. The contrast with Stella's world could not be more dramatic; it reveals her total lack of refinement.

But if unmannerliness were the sum of Stella's faults, patriarchy would not be as threatened by her as it evidently is, nor demand such a drastic restitution as the renunciation of her child. What is behind this demand for such an extreme sacrifice on Stella's part? What has she really done to violate patriarchy's conception of the Mother?

The clue to answering this question lies in her initial *resistance* to Mothering, for 'selfish' reasons, and her subsequent enthusiastic embracing of Motherhood. The refusal and then the avid assumption of the role are linked from a patriarchal point of view through the same 'fault', namely that Stella is interested in *pleasing herself.* She refuses Mothering when she does not see anything in it for her, when it seems only to stand in the way of fun; but she takes it up avidly once she realizes that it can give her pleasure, and can add more to her life than the stuffy Stephen can! Shortly after Stephen has left, Stella says, 'I thought people were crazy to have kids right away. But I'm crazy about her. Who wouldn't be?' And later on, talking on the train to Munn (who would clearly like a fully sexual relationship with her), Stella remarks. 'Laurel uses up all the feelings I have; I don't have any for anyone else.'

In getting so much pleasure for herself out of Laurel, Stella violates the patriarchal myth of the self-abnegating Mother, who is supposed to be completely devoted and nurturing but not satisfy any of her needs through the relationship with her child. She is somehow supposed to keep herself apart while giving everything to the child: she is certainly not supposed to prefer the child to the husband, since this kind of bonding threatens patriarchy.

That Laurel returns Stella's passion only compounds the problem: the film portrays Laurel as devoted to her mother to an unhealthy degree, as caring too much, or more than is good for her. In contrast to the worshipful stance that Laurel has toward Mrs. Morrison, her love for her own mother is physical, tender, and selfless. For instance, on one occasion Stella's crassness offends the child deeply (she nearly puts face cream all over Laurel's lovely picture of Mrs. Morrison), but Laurel forgives her and tenderly brushes her hair. Most remarkable is the train sequence, where Laurel overhears her friends ridiculing her mother. Hurt for her mother (not for herself), she creeps down into Stella's bunk and kisses her tenderly, snuggling up to her under the covers. Finally, of course, Laurel is almost ready to give up her own chance for the pleasures of the Morrison family and upper-class life when she realizes why Stella wanted to let the Morrisons have her. It takes Stella's trick to make Laurel stay (and I'll come back to this 'trick' in a moment).

The very mutuality of this Mother–daughter relationship makes it even more threatening and in need of disruption than, for example, the one-sided dedication to the daughter in *Mildred Pierce.* That film highlights the dangerous narcissism of a love like Mildred's (where the investment in the child is tantamount to merging, to abandoning the boundaries altogether). This love must be punished not only because it excludes men (as does Stella's relationship to Laurel), but also because of the threat that deep female-to-female bonding poses in patriarchy. Veda's negative bonding (she is tied through hatred) offers a kind of protection for patriarchy: it ensures that Mildred's love will be destructive and self-defeating.

In contrast, *Stella Dallas* in the end provides an example of Mother love that is properly curtailed and subordinated to what patriarchy considers best for the child. In renouncing Laurel, Stella is only doing what the Good Mother should do, according to the film's ideology. By first making Stella into a 'spectacle' (i.e. by applying an external standard to her actions and values), the film 'educates' Stella into her 'correct' position of Mother-as-spectator, Mother as absent.

Stella's entry into the Morrison household at once summarizes her prior 'unfitness' and represents her readiness to succumb to the persistent demands that have been made on her throughout the film. In this amazing scene, shot from the butler's perspective, she is still a 'spectacle' viewed from the upper-class position: she stands, more ridiculously clad than ever, on the threshold of the huge mansion, her figure eclipsed by the luxurious surroundings that overwhelm her with awe and admiration. It is the lower-class stance, as Stella gawks *from the outside* at the way the rich live.

Incongruous within the house, Stella must be literally pushed outside—but of her own volition. The decorous, idealized Morrison family could not be seen depriving Stella of her child (remember: Mrs. Morrison is represented as tender toward Stella), so Stella must do it herself. Paradoxically, the only method she can conceive of, once she realizes Laurel's unwavering commitment to her, is by pretending to step outside of her Mother role. 'A woman wants to be something else besides a mother,' she tells a crestfallen Laurel, who has left the Morrisons to be at home with her. Ironically, through these deceptive words, Stella is binding herself into the prescribed Mother role; her self-sacrificing 'trick'—her pretense that she is weary of Mothering—is the only way she can achieve her required place as 'spectator', relinquishing the central place she had illicitly occupied.

Structured as a 'screen' within the screen, the final sequence of Laurel's wedding literalizes Stella's position as the Mother-spectator. We recall the previous movie scene (Stephen and Stella looking at the romantic upper-class couples on the screen) as Stella stands outside the window of the Morrison house, looking in on her daughter's wedding, unseen by Laurel. Stella stares from the outside at the upper-class 'ideal' world inside. And as spectators in the cinema, identifying with the camera, (and thus with Stella's gaze), we learn what it is to be a Mother in patriarchy—it is to renounce, to be on the outside, and to take pleasure in this positioning. Stella's triumphant look as she turns away from the window to the camera assures us she is satisfied to be reduced to spectator. Her desires for herself no longer count, merged as they are with those of her daughter. While the cinema spectator feels a certain sadness in Stella's position, she also identifies with Laurel and with her attainment of what we have all been socialized to desire—romantic marriage into the upper class. We thus accede to the necessity for Stella's sacrifice.

With *Stella Dallas*, we begin to see why the Mother has so rarely occupied the center of the narrative: for how can the *spectator* be subject, at least in the sense of controlling the action? The Mother can only be subject to the degree that she resists her culturally prescribed positioning, as Stella does at first. It is Stella's *resistance* that sets the narrative in motion, and provides the opportunity to teach her as well as the spectator the Mother's 'correct' place.

Given the prevalence of the Mother-as-spectator myth, it is not surprising that feminists have had trouble dealing with the Mother as subject. An analysis of the psychoanalytic barriers to 'seeing' the Mother needs to be accompanied by an analysis of cultural myths that define the Good Mother as absent, and the Bad Mother as present but resisting. We have suppressed too long our anger at our mothers because of the apparently anti-woman stance this leads to. We need to work through our anger so that we can understand how the patriarchal construction of the Mother has made her position an untenable one.

Unfortunately, today's representations of the Mother are not much better than that in *Stella Dallas*, made in 1937. Ironically, the mass media response to the recent women's movement has led to numerous representations of the nurturing *Father*, as well as a splitting of the female image into old-style Mothers and new-style efficient career women. *Kramer Versus Kramer* established the basic model for the 1980s: the wife leaves her husband to become a successful career woman, willingly abandoning her child to pursue her own needs. The husband steps into the gap she leaves and develops a close, loving relationship to his son, at some cost to his career—which he willingly shoulders. If the wife, like Stella, is reduced to a 'spectator' (she returns to peek in on her child's doings), it is ultimately because she is also (albeit in a very different way) a Bad Mother. Meanwhile, the husband pals up with a solid, old-style earth Mother who lives in his apartment building, just so that we know how far his wife has strayed. Cold, angular career women, often sexually aggressive, have come to dominate the popular media while Fathers are becoming nurturing. (*The World According to Garp* is another recent example.) And there are also plenty of sadistic Mothers around (e.g. *Mommie Dearest*).

Thus, the entire structure of sex-role stereotyping remains intact. The only change is that men can now acquire previously forbidden 'feminine' qualities. But career women immediately lose their warm qualities, so that even if they do combine mothering and career, they cannot be Good Mothers. It is depressing that the popular media have only been able to respond to the women's movement in terms of what it has opened up for *men*. It is up to feminists to redefine the position of the Mother as participant, initiator of action—as subject in her own right, capable of a life with many dimensions.

Notes

1. See Adrienne Rich, *Of Woman Born: Motherhood as Experience and Institution* (New York: Norton, 1976); Dorothy Dinnerstein, *The Mermaid and the Minotaur* (New York: Harper & Row, 1977); Jane Lazarre, *The Mother-Knot* (New York: McGraw-Hill, 1976).
2. Examples of films embodying this myth are: *A Fool There Was* (1914), *Meet Me in St. Louis* (1944), *Christopher Strong* (1933), *Our Daily Bread* (1937), *The River* (1950), *The Searchers* (1956).
3. Examples are: *Craig's Wife* (1936), *Little Foxes* (1941), *Now Voyager* (1942), *Marnie* (1966); most recently: *Mommie Dearest* (1981), *Frances* (1982).
4. Examples are: Griffith's films, *The Blot* (1921), *Imitation of Life* (1934, 1959: the black Mother in both versions), *Stella Dallas* (1937), *The Southerner* (1945), *Mildred Pierce* (1946), *The Best Years of Our Lives (1946).*

25 Something Else Besides a Mother

Stella Dallas *and the Maternal Melodrama*

Linda Williams*

The device of devaluing and debasing the actual figure of the mother while sanctifying the institution of motherhood is typical of the 'woman's film' in general and the sub-genre of the maternal melodrama in particular.[1] In these films it is quite remarkable how frequently the self-sacrificing mother must make her sacrifice that of the connection to her children—either for her or their own good.

With respect to the mother–daughter aspect of this relation, Simone de Beauvoir noted long ago that because of the patriarchal devaluation of women in general, a mother frequently attempts to use her daughter to compensate for her own supposed inferiority by making 'a superior creature out of one whom she regards as her double'.[2] Clearly, the unparalleled closeness and similarity of mother to daughter sets up a situation of significant mirroring that is most apparent in these films. One effect of this mirroring is that although the mother gains a kind of vicarious superiority by association with a superior daughter, she inevitably begins to feel inadequate to so superior a being and thus, in the end, to feel inferior. Embroiled in a relationship that is so close, mother and daughter nevertheless seem destined to lose one another through this very closeness.

Much recent writing on women's literature and psychology has focused on the problematic of the mother–daughter relationship as a paradigm of a woman's ambivalent relationship to herself.[3] In *Of Woman Born* Adrienne Rich writes, 'The loss of the daughter to the mother, mother to the daughter, is the essential female tragedy. We acknowledge Lear (father–daughter split), Hamlet (son and mother), and Oedipus (son and mother) as great embodiments of the human

* Linda Williams, 'Something Else Besides a Mother' *Stella Dallas* and the Maternal Melodrama' from *Cinema Journal*, vol. 24 no. 1 (1985). Reprinted with permission of the author.

tragedy, but there is no presently enduring recognition of mother–daughter passion and rapture.' No tragic, high culture equivalent perhaps. But Rich is not entirely correct when she goes on to say that 'this cathexis between mother and daughter—essential, distorted, misused—is the great unwritten story.'[4]

If this *tragic* story remains unwritten, it is because tragedy has always been assumed to be universal; speaking for and to a supposedly universal 'mankind', it has not been able to speak for and to womankind. But melodrama is a form that does not pretend to speak universally. It is clearly addressed to a particular bourgeois class and often—in works as diverse as *Pamela, Uncle Tom's Cabin*, or the 'woman's film—to the particular gender of woman.[5]

. . .

Much recent feminist film criticism has divided filmic narrative into male and female forms: 'male' linear, action-packed narratives that encourage identification with predominantly male characters who 'master' their environment; and 'female' less linear narratives encouraging identification with passive, suffering heroines.[6] No doubt part of the enormous popularity of *Mildred Pierce* among feminist film critics lies with the fact that it illustrates the failure of the female subject (the film's misguided, long-suffering mother-hero who is overly infatuated with her daughter) to articulate her own point of view, even when her own voice-over introduces subjective flashbacks.[7] *Mildred Pierce* has been an important film for feminists precisely because its 'male' film noir style offers such a blatant subversion of the mother's attempt to tell the story of her relationship to her daughter.

The failure of *Mildred Pierce* to offer either its female subject or its female viewer her own understanding of the film's narrative has made it a fascinating example of the way films can construct patriarchal subject-positions that subvert their ostensible subject matter. More to the point of the mother–daughter relation, however, is a film like *Stella Dallas*, which has recently begun to receive attention as a central work in the growing criticism of the melodrama in general and maternal melodrama in particular.[8] Certainly the popularity of the original novel, of the 1925 (Henry King) and 1937 (King Vidor) film versions, and finally of the later long-running radio soap opera, suggests the special endurance of this mother–daughter love story across three decades of female audiences. But it is in its film versions in particular, especially the King Vidor version starring Barbara Stanwyck, that we encounter an interesting test case for many recent theories of the cinematic presentation of female subjectivity and the female spectator.

Since so much of what has come to be called the classical narrative cinema concerns male subjects whose vision defines and circumscribes female objects, the mere existence in *Stella Dallas* of a female 'look' as a central feature of the narrative is worthy of special scrutiny. Just what is different about the visual economy of such a film? What happens when a mother and daughter, who are so closely identified that the usual distinctions between subject and object do not apply, take one another as their primary objects of desire? What happens, in other words, when the look of desire articulates a rather different visual economy of mother–daughter possession and dispossession? What happens, finally, when the significant viewer of such a drama is also a woman? To fully answer these questions we must make a detour through some recent psychoanalytic thought on female subject formation and its relation to feminist film theory. We will then be in a better position to unravel the mother–daughter knot of this particular film. So for the time being we will abandon *Stella Dallas* to her forlorn place in the rain, gazing at her daughter through the big picture window—the enigma of the female look at, and in, the movies.

FEMINIST FILM THEORY AND THEORIES OF MOTHERHOOD

Much recent feminist film theory and criticism has been devoted to the description and analysis of Oedipal scenarios in which, as Laura Mulvey has written, woman is a passive image and man the active bearer of the look.[9] The major impetus of these forms of feminist criticism has been less concerned with the existence of female stereotypes than with their ideological, psychological, and textual means of production. To Claire Johnston, the very fact of the iconic representation of the cinematic image guarantees that women will be reduced to objects of an erotic male gaze. Johnston concludes that 'woman as woman' cannot be represented at all within the dominant representational economy.[10] A primary reason for this conclusion is the hypothesis that the visual encounter with the female body produces in the male spectator a constant need to be reassured of his own bodily unity.

It is as if the male image producer and consumer can never get past the disturbing fact of sexual difference and so constantly produces and consumes images of women designed to reassure himself of his threatened unity. In this and other ways, feminist film theory has appropriated some key concepts from Lacanian psychoanalysis in order to explain why subjectivity always seems to be the province of the male.

According to Lacan, through the recognition of the sexual difference of a female 'other' who lacks the phallus that is the symbol of patriarchal privilege, the child gains entry into the symbolic order of human culture. This culture then produces narratives which repress the figure of lack that the mother—former figure of plenitude—has become. Given this situation, the question for woman becomes, as Christine Gledhill puts it: '*Can women speak, and can images of women speak for women?*'[11] Laura Mulvey's answer, and the answer of much feminist criticism, would seem to be negative:

> Woman's desire is subjected to her image as bearer of the bleeding wound, she can exist only in relation to castration and cannot transcend it. She turns her child into the signifier of her own desire to possess a penis (the condition, she imagines, of entry into the symbolic). Either she must gracefully give way to the word, the Name of the Father and the Law, or else struggle to keep her child down with her in the half-light of the imaginary. Woman then stands in patriarchal culture as signifier for the male other, bound by a symbolic order in which man can live out his phantasies and obsessions through linguistic command by imposing them on the silent image of woman still tied to her place as bearer of meaning, not maker of meaning.[12]

This description of the 'visual pleasure of narrative cinema' delineates two avenues of escape which function to relieve the male viewer of the threat of the woman's image. Mulvey's now-familiar sketch of these two primary forms of mastery by which the male unconscious overcomes the threat of an encounter with the female body is aligned with two perverse pleasures associated with the male—the sadistic mastery of voyeurism and the more benign disavowal of fetishism. Both are ways of not-seeing, of either keeping a safe distance from, or misrecognising what there is to see of, the womans' difference.

The purpose of Mulvey's analysis is to get 'nearer to the roots' of women's oppression in order to break with those codes that cannot produce female subjectivity. Her ultimate goal is thus an avant-garde film-making practice that will break with the voyeurism and fetishism of the narrative cinema so as to 'free the look of the camera into its materiality in space and time', and the 'look of the audience into dialectics, passionate detachment'.[13] To Mulvey, only the radical destruction of the major forms of narrative pleasure so bound up in looking at women as objects can offer hope for a cinema that will be able to represent not woman as difference but differences of women.

It has often been remarked that what is missing from Mulvey's influential analysis of visual pleasure in cinematic narrative is any discussion of the position of the female viewing subject. Although many feminist works of film criticism have pointed to this absence, very few have ventured to fill it.[14] It is an understandably easier task to reject 'dominant' or 'institutional' modes of representation altogether than to discover within these existing modes glimpses of a more 'authentic' (the term itself is indeed problematic) female subjectivity. And yet I believe that this latter is a more fruitful avenue of approach, not only as a means of identifying what pleasure there is for women spectators within the classical narrative cinema, but also as a means of developing new representational strategies that will more fully speak to women audiences. For such speech must begin in a language, that, however circumscribed within patriarchal ideology, will be recognised and understood by women. In this way, new feminist films can learn to build upon the pleasures of recognition that exist within filmic modes already familiar to women.

Instead of destroying the cinematic codes that have placed women as objects of spectacle at their centre, what is needed, and has already begun to occur, is a theoretical and practical recognition of the ways in which women actually do speak to one another within patriarchy. Christine Gledhill, for example, makes a convincing case against the tendency of much semiotic and psychoanalytic feminist film criticism to blame realist representation for an ideological complicity with the suppression of semiotic difference. Such reasoning tends to believe that the simple rejection of the forms of realist representation will perform the revolutionary act of making the viewer aware of how images are produced. Gledhill argues that this awareness is not enough: the social construction of reality and of women cannot be defined in terms of signifying practice alone. 'If a radical ideology such as feminism is to be defined as a means of providing a framework for political action, one must finally put one's finger on the scales, enter some kind of realist epistemology.'[15]

But what kind? Any attempt to construct heroines as strong and powerful leaves us vulnerable, as Gledhill notes, to the charge of male identification:

> However we try to cast our potential feminine identifications, all available positions are already constructed from the place of the patriarchal other so as

to repress our 'real' difference. Thus the unspoken remains unknown, and the speakable reproduces what we know, patriarchal reality.[16]

One way out of the dilemma is 'the location of those spaces in which women, out of their socially constructed differences as women, can and do resist'.[17] These include discourses produced primarily for and (often, but not always) by women and which address the contradictions that women encounter under patriarchy: women's advice columns, magazine fiction, soap operas, and melodramatic 'women's films'. All are places where women speak to one another in languages that grow out of their specific social roles—as mothers, housekeepers, caretakers of all sorts.[18]

Gledhill's assertion that discourses about the social, economic, and emotional concerns of women are consumed by predominantly female audiences could be complemented by the further assertion that *some* of these discourses are also differently inscribed to necessitate a very different, female reading. This is what I hope to show with respect to *Stella Dallas.* My argument, then, is not only that some maternal melodramas have historically addressed female audiences about issues of primary concern to women, but that these melodramas also have reading positions structured into their texts that demand a female reading competence This competence derives from the different way women take on their identities under patriarchy and is a direct result of the social fact of female mothering. It is thus with a view to applying the significance of the social construction of female identity to the female positions constructed by the maternal melodrama that I offer the following cursory summary of recent feminist theories of female identity and motherhood.

While Freud was forced, at least in his later writing, to abandon a theory of parallel male and female development and to acknowledge the greater importance of the girl's pre-Oedipal connection to her mother, he could only view such a situation as a deviation from the path of 'normal' (e.g. male heterosexual) separation and individuation.[19] The result was a theory that left women in an apparent state of regressive connection to their mothers.

What Freud viewed as a regrettable lack in a girl's self development, feminist theories now view with less disparagement. However else they may differ over the consequences of female mothering, most agree that it allows women not only to remain in connection with their first love objects but to extend the model of this connectedness to all other relations with the world.[20]

In *The Reproduction of Mothering* the American sociologist Nancy Chodorow attempts to account for the fact that 'women, as mothers, produce daughters with mothering capacities and the desire to mother'.[21] She shows that neither biology nor intentional role training can explain the social organisation of gender roles that consign women to the private sphere of home and family, and men to the public sphere that has permitted them dominance. The desire and ability to mother is produced, along with masculinity and femininity, within a division of labour that has already placed women in the position of primary caretakers. Superimposed on this division of labour are the two 'Oedipal asymmetries'[22] that Freud acknowledged: that girls enter the triangular Oedipal relation later than boys: that girls have a greater continuity of pre-Oedipal symbiotic connection to the mother.

In other words, girls never entirely break with their original relationship to their mothers, because their sexual identities as women do not depend upon such a break. Boys, however, must break with their primary identification with their mothers in order to become male identified. This means that boys define themselves as males negatively, by differentiation from their primary caretaker who (in a culture that has traditionally valued women as mothers first, workers second) is female.

The boy separates from his mother to identify with his father and take on a masculine identity of greater autonomy. The girl, on the other hand, takes on her identity as a woman in a positive process of becoming like, not different from, her mother. Although she must ultimately transfer her primary object choice to her father first and then to men in general if she is to become a heterosexual woman, she still never breaks with the original bond to her mother in the same way the boy does. She merely *adds* her love for her father, and finally her love for a man (if she becomes heterosexual) to her original relation to her mother. This means that a boy develops his masculine gender identification in the *absence* of a continuous and ongoing relationship with his father, while a girl develops her feminine gender identity in the *presence* of an ongoing relationship with the specific person of her mother.

In other words, the masculine subject position is based on a rejection of a connection to the mother and the adoption of a gender role identified with a cultural stereotype, while the female subject position identifies with a specific mother. Women's relatedness and men's denial of relatedness are in turn appropriate to the social division of their roles in our culture: to the man's role as producer outside the home and the woman's role as reproducer inside it.[23]

Chodorow's analysis of the connectedness of the mother–daughter bond has pointed the way to a new value placed on the multiple and continuous female identity capable of fluidly shifting between the identity of mother and daughter.[24] Unlike Freud, she does not assume that the separation and autonomy of the male identification process is a norm from which women deviate. She assumes, rather, that the current social arrangement of exclusive female mothering has prepared men to participate in a world of often alienated work, with a limited ability to achieve intimacy.[25]

Thus Chodorow and others[26] have questioned the very standards of unity and autonomy by which human identity has typically been measured. And they have done so without recourse to a biologically determined essence of femaleness.[27]

Like Nancy Chodorow, the French feminist psychoanalyst Luce Irigaray turns to the problems of Freud's original attempt to sketch identical stages of development for both male and female. In *Speculum de l'autre femme* Irigaray echoes Chodorow's concern with 'Oedipal asymmetries'. But what Irigaray emphasises is the *visual* nature of Freud's scenario—the fact that sexual difference is originally perceived as an absence of the male genitalia rather than the presence of female genitalia. In a chapter entitled 'Blind Spot for an old Dream of Symmetry' the 'blind spot' consists of a male vision trapped in an 'Oedipal destiny' that cannot *see* woman's sex and can thus only represent it in terms of the masculine subject's own original complementary other: the mother.[28]

'Woman' is represented within this system as either the all-powerful (phallic) mother of the child's pre-Oedipal imaginary or as the unempowered (castrated) mother of its post-Oedipal symbolic. What is left out of such a system of representation is the whole of woman's pleasure—a pleasure that cannot be measured in phallic terms.

But what Freud devalued and repressed in the female body, Irigaray and other French feminists engaged in 'writing the female body' in an *écritire féminine*,[29] are determined to emphasise. In *Ce sexe qui n'en est pas un* (This sex which is not one) Irigaray celebrates the multiple and diffuse pleasures of a female body and a female sex that is not just one thing, but several, But when forced to enter into the 'dominant scopic economy' of visual pleasure she is immediately relegated, as Mulvey has also pointed out with respect to film, to the passive position of 'the beautiful object'[30]

Irigaray's admittedly utopian[31] solution to the problem of how women can come to represent themselves to themselves is nevertheless important. For if women cannot establish the connection between their bodies and language, they risk either having to forego all speaking of the body—in a familiar puritanical repression of an excessive female sexuality—or they risk an essentialist celebration of a purely biological determination. Irigaray thus proposes a community of women relating to and speaking to one another outside the constraints of a masculine language that reduces everything to its own need for unity and identity—a 'female homosexuality' opposed to the reigning 'male homosexuality' that currently governs the relations between both men and men, and men and women.[32]

A 'female homosexual economy' would thus challenge the dominant order and make it possible for woman to represent herself to herself. This suggests an argument similar to that of Adrienne Rich in her article 'Compulsory Heterosexuality and Lesbian Existence'. Rich argues that lesbianism is an important alternative to the male economy of dominance. Whether or not a woman's sexual preferences are actually homosexual, the mere fact of 'lesbian existence' proves that it is possible to resist the dominating values of the male coloniser with a more nurturing and empathic relationship similar to mothering.[33] The female body is as necessary to Rich as it is to Irigaray as the place to begin.

Adrienne Rich's critique of psychoanalysis is based on the notion that its fundamental patriarchal premises foreclose the envisioning of relationships between women outside of patriarchy. Irigaray's recourse to the female body ironically echoes Rich's own but it is constructed from *within* psychoanalytic theory. The importance of both is not simply that they see lesbianism as a refuge from an oppressive phallic economy—although it certainly is that for many women—but that it is a theoretical way out of the bind of the unrepresented, and unrepresentable, female body.

The excitement generated when women get together, when they go to the market together 'to profit from their own value, to talk to each other, to desire each other', is not to be underestimated.[34] For only by learning to recognise and then to represent a difference that is not different to other women, can women begin to see themselves. The trick, however, is not to stop there; woman's recognition of herself in the bodies of other women is only a necessary first step to an understanding of the interaction of body and psyche, and the distance that separates them.[35]

Perhaps the most valuable attempt to understand this interaction is Julia Kristeva's work on the maternal body and pre-Oedipal sexuality. Like Irigaray, Kristeva attempts to speak the pre-Oedipal relations of woman to woman. But unlike Irigaray, she does so with the knowledge that such speech is never entirely authentic, never entirely free of the phallic influence of symbolic language. In other words, she stresses the necessity of positing a place from which women can speak themselves, all the while recognising that such places do not exist. That is, it cannot be conceived or represented outside of the symbolic language which defines women negatively.[36]

Thus, what Kristeva proposes is a self-conscious dialectic between two imperfect forms of language. The first is what she calls the 'emiotic': a pre-verbal, maternal language of rhythm, tone and colour linked to the body contact with the mother before the child is differentiated by entrance into the symbolic. The second is the 'symbolic' proper, characterised by logic, syntax, and a phallocratic abstraction.[37] According to Kristeva, all human subjects articulate themselves through the interaction of these two modes. The value of this conception is that we no longer find ourselves locked into an investigation of different sexual *identities*, but are freed rather into an investigation of *sexual differentiations*—subject positions that are associated with maternal or paternal functions.

Speaking from the mother's position, Kristeva shows that maternity is characterised by division. The mother is possessed of an internal heterogeneity beyond her control:

> Cells fuse, split and proliferate; volumes grow, tissues stretch, and body fluids change rhythm, speeding up or slowing down. Within the body, growing as a graft, indomitable, there is an other. And no one is present, within that simultaneously dual and alien space, to signify what is going on. 'It happens, but I'm not here.'[38]

But even as she speaks from this space of the mother, Kristeva notes that it is vacant, that there is no unified subject present there. Yet she speaks anyway, consciously recognising the patriarchal illusion of the all-powerful and whole phallic mother. For Kristeva it is the dialectic of two inadequate and incomplete sexually *differentiated* subject positions that is important. The dialectic between a maternal body that is too diffuse, contradictory, and polymorphous to be represented and a paternal body that is channelled and repressed into a single representable significance makes it possible for woman to be represented at all.

So, as Jane Gallop notes, women are not so essentially and

exclusively body that they must remain eternally unrepresentable.[39] But the dialectic between that which is pure body and therefore escapes representation and that which is a finished and fixed representation makes possible a different kind of representation that escapes the rigidity of fixed identity. With this notion of a dialetic between the maternal unrepresentable and the paternal already-represented we can begin to look for a way out of the theoretical blind of the representation of women in film and at the way female spectators are likely to read *Stella Dallas* and its ambivalent scene.

'SOMETHING ELSE BESIDES A MOTHER'

. . .

One basic conflict of *Stella Dallas* comes to revolve around the *excessive presence* of Stella's body and dress. She increasingly flaunts an exaggeratedly feminine presence that the offended community prefers not to see. (Barbara Stanwyck's own excessive performance contributes to this effect. I can think of no other film star of the period so willing to exceed both the bounds of good taste and sex appeal in a single performance.) But the more ruffles, feathers, furs, and clanking jewellery that Stella dons, the more she emphasises her pathetic inadequacy.

Her strategy can only backfire in the eyes of an upper-class restraint that values a streamlined and sleek ideal of femininity. To these eyes Stella is a travesty, an overdone masquerade of what it means to be a woman.[40] At the fancy hotel to which Stella and Laurel repair for their one fling at upper-class life together, a young college man exclaims at the sight of Stella, 'That's not a woman, that's a Christmas tree!' Stella, however, could never understand such a backward economy, just as she cannot understand her upper-class husband's attempts to lessen the abrasive impact of her presence by correcting her English and toning down her dress. She counters his efforts with the defiant claim, 'I've always been known to have stacks of style'!

'Style' is the war paint she applies more thickly with each new assault on her legitimacy as a woman and a mother. One particularly affecting scene shows her sitting before the mirror of her dressing table as Laurel tells her of the 'natural' elegance and beauty of Helen Morrison, the woman who has replaced Stella in Stephen's affections. Stella's only response is to apply more cold cream. When she accidentally gets cold cream on Laurel's photo of the ideal Mrs Morrison, Laurel becomes upset and runs off to clean it. What is most moving in the scene is the emotional complicity of Laurel, who soon realises the extent to which her description has hurt her mother, and silently turns to the task of applying more peroxide to Stella's hair. The scene ends with mother and daughter before the mirror tacitly relating to one another through the medium of the feminine mask—each putting on a good face for the other, just as they did at the birthday party.

'Stacks of style', layers of make-up, clothes, and jewellery—these are, of course, the typical accoutrements of the fetishised woman. Yet such fetishisation seems out of place in a 'woman's film' addressed to a predominantly female audience. More typically, the woman's film's preoccupation with a victimised and suffering womanhood has tended, as Mary Ann Doane has shown, to repress and hystericise women's bodies in a medical discourse of the afflicted or in the paranoia of the uncanny.[41]

We might ask, then, what effect a fetishised female image has in the context of a film 'addressed' and 'possessed by' women? Certainly this is one situation in which the woman's body does not seem likely to pose the threat of castration—since the significant viewers of (and within) the film are all female. In psychoanalytic terms, the fetish is that which disavows or compensates for the woman's lack of a penis. As we have seen above, for the male viewer the successful fetish deflects attention away from what is 'really' lacking by calling attention to (over-valuing) other aspects of woman's difference. But at the same time it also inscribes the woman in a 'masquerade of femininity'[42] that forever revolves around her 'lack'. Thus, at the extreme, the entire female body becomes a fetish substitute for the phallus she doesn't possess. The beautiful (successfully fetishised) woman thus represents an eternal essence of biologically determined femininity constructed from the point of view, so to speak, of the phallus.

In *Stella Dallas*, however, the fetishisation of Stanwyck's Stella is unsuccessful; the masquerade of femininity is all too obvious; and the significant point of view on all this is female. For example, at the fancy hotel where Stella makes a 'Christmas tree' spectacle of herself she is as oblivious as ever to the shocking effect of her appearance. But Laurel experiences the shame of her friends' scorn. The scene in which Laurel experiences this shame is a grotesque parody of Stella's fondest dream of being like all the glamorous people in the movies. Stella has put all of her energy and resources into becoming this glamorous image. But incapacitated by a cold, as she once was by pregnancy, she must remain off-scene as Laurel makes a favourable impression. When she finally makes her grand entrance on the scene, Stella is spied by Laurel and her friends in a large mirror over a soda fountain. The mirror functions as the framed screen that reflects the parody of the image of glamour to which Stella once aspired. Unwilling to acknowledge their relation, Laurel runs out. Later, she insists that they leave. On the train home, Stella overhears Laurel's friends joking about the vulgar Mrs Dallas. It is then that she decides to send Laurel to live with Stephen and Mrs Morrison and to give Laurel up for her own good. What is significant, however, is that Stella overhears the conversation at the same time Laurel does—they are in upper and lower berths of the train, each hoping that the other is asleep, each pretending to be asleep to the other. So Stella does not just experience her own humiliation; she sees for the first time the travesty she has become by sharing in her daughter's humiliation.

By seeing herself through her daughter's eyes, Stella also sees something more. For the first time Stella sees the reality of her social situation from the vantage point of her daughter's understanding, but increasingly upper-class, system of values: that she is a struggling, uneducated woman doing the best she can with the resources at her disposal. And it is *this* vision, through her daughter's sympathetic, mothering eyes—eyes that perceive, understand, and forgive the social graces Stella lacks—that determines her to perform the masquerade that will alienate Laurel forever by proving to her what the patriarchy has claimed to know all along: that it is not possible to combine womanly desire with motherly duty.

It is at this point that Stella claims, falsely, to want to be 'something else besides a mother'. The irony is not only that by now there is really nothing else she wants to be, but also that in pretending this to Laurel she must act out a painful parody of her fetishised self. She thus resurrects the persona of the 'good-times' woman she used to want to be (but never entirely was) only to convince Laurel that she is an unworthy mother. In other words, she proves her very worthiness to be a mother (her desire for her daughter's material and social welfare) by acting out a patently false scenario of narcissistic self-absorption—she pretends to ignore Laurel while lounging about in a negligee, smoking a cigarette, listening to jazz, and reading a magazine called 'Love'.

In this scene the conventional image of the fetishised woman is given a peculiar, even parodic, twist. For where the conventional masquerade of femininity can be read as an attempt to cover up supposedly biological 'lacks' with a compensatory excess of connotatively feminine gestures, clothes, and accoutrements, here fetishisation functions as a blatantly pathetic disavowal of much more pressing social lacks—of money, education, and power. The spectacle Stella stages for Laurel's eyes thus displaces the real social and economic causes of her presumed inadequacy as a mother onto a pretended desire for fulfilment as a woman—to be 'something else besides a mother'.

At the beginning of the film Stella pretended a maternal concern she did not really possess (in bringing lunch to her brother in order to flirt with Stephen) in order to find a better home. Now she pretends a lack of the same concern in order to send Laurel to a better home. Both roles are patently false. And though neither allows us to view the 'authentic' woman beneath the mask, the succession of roles ending in the final transcendent self-effacement of the window scene—in which Stella forsakes all her masks in order to become the anonymous spectator of her daughter's role as bride—permits a glimpse at the social and economic realities that have produced such roles. Stella's real offence, in the eyes of the community that so ruthlessly ostracises her, is to have attempted to play both roles at once.

Are we to conclude, then, that the film simply punishes her for these untimely resistances to her proper role? E. Ann Kaplan has argued that such is the case, and that throughout the film Stella's point of view is undercut by those of the upper-class community—Stephen, or the snooty townspeople—who disapprove of her behaviour. Kaplan notes, for example, that a scene may begin from Stella's point of view but shift, as in the case of an impromptu party with Ed Munn, to the more judgmental point of view of Stephen halfway through.[43]

I would counter, however, that these multiple, often conflicting, points of view—including Laurel's failure to see through her mother's act—prevent such a monolithic view of the female subject. Kaplan argues, for example, that the film punishes Stella for her resistances to a properly patriarchal view of motherhood by turning her first into a spectacle for a disapproving upper-class gaze and then finally into a mere spectator, locked outside the action in the final window scene that ends the film.[44]

Certainly this final scene functions to efface Stella even as it glorifies her sacrificial act of motherly love. Self-exiled from the world into which her daughter is marrying, Stella loses both her daughter and her (formerly fetishised) self to become an abstract (and absent) ideal of motherly sacrifice. Significantly, Stella appears in this scene for the first time stripped of the exaggerated marks of femininity—the excessive make-up, furs, feathers, clanking jewellery, and ruffled dresses—that have been the weapons of her defiant assertions that a woman *can* be 'something else besides a mother'.

It would be possible to stop here and take this ending as Hollywood's last word on the mother, as evidence of her ultimate unrepresentability in any but patriarchal terms. Certainly if we only remember Stella as she appears here at the end of the film, as Val in French's *The Women's Room* remembers her, then we see her only at the moment when she becomes representable in terms of a 'phallic economy' that idealises the woman as mother and in so doing, as Irigaray argues, represses everything else about her. But although the final moment of the film 'resolves' the contradiction of Stella's attempt to be a woman *and* a mother by eradicating both, the 108 minutes leading up to this moment present the heroic attempt to live out the contradiction.[45] It seems likely, then, that a female spectator would be inclined to view even this ending as she has the rest of the film: from a variety of different subject positions. In other words, the female spectator tends to identify with contradiction itself—with contradictions located at the heart of the socially constructed roles of daughter, wife *and* mother—rather than with the single person of the mother.

In this connection the role of Helen Morrison, the upper-class widowed mother whom Stephen will be free to marry with Stella out of the way, takes on special importance. Helen is everything Stella is not: genteel, discreet, self-effacing, and sympathetic with everyone's problems—including Stella's. She is, for example, the only person in the film to see through Stella's ruse of alienating Laurel. And it is she who, knowing Stella's finer instincts, leaves open the drapes that permit Stella's vision of Laurel's marriage inside her elegant home.

In writing about the narrative form of daytime soap operas, Tania Modleski has noted that the predominantly female viewers of soaps do not identify with a main controlling figure the way viewers of more classic forms of narrative identify. The very form of soap opera encourages identification with multiple points of view. At one moment, female viewers identify with a woman united with her lover, at the next with the sufferings of her rival. While the effect of identifying with a single controlling protagonist is to make the spectator feel empowered, the effect of multiple identification in the diffused soap opera is to divest the spectator of power, but to increase empathy. 'The subject/spectator of soaps, it could be said, is constituted as a sort of ideal mother: a person who possesses greater wisdom than all her children, whose sympathy is large enough to encompass the conflicting claims of her family (she identifies with them all), and who has no demands or claims of her own (she identifies with no character exclusively).'[46]

In *Stella Dallas* Helen is clearly the representative of this idealised, empathic but powerless mother. E. Ann Kaplan has argued that female spectators learn from Helen Morrison's example that such is the proper role of the mother; that Stella has up until now illicitly hogged the screen. By the time Stella has made her sacrifice and become the mere spectator of her daughter's apotheosis, her joy in her daughter's success assures us, in Kaplan's words, of her satisfaction in being reduced to spectator. . . . 'While the cinema spectator feels a certain sadness in Stella's position, we also identify with Laurel and with her attainment of what we have all been socialised to desire; that is, romantic marriage into the upper class. We thus accede to the necessity for Stella's sacrifice.'[47]

But do we? As Kaplan herself notes, the female spectator is identified with a variety of conflicting points of view as in the TV soap opera: Stella, Laurel, Helen and Stephen cannot resolve their conflicts without someone getting hurt. Laurel loses her mother and visibly suffers from this loss; Stella loses her daughter and her identity; Helen wins Stephen but powerlessly suffers for everyone including herself (when Stella had refused to divorce Stephen). Only Stephen is entirely free from suffering at the end, but this is precisely because he is characteristically oblivious to the sufferings of others. For the film's ending to be perceived as entirely without problem, we would have to identify with this least sensitive and, therefore, least sympathetic point of view.

Instead, we identify, like the ideal mother viewer of soaps, with *all* the conflicting points of view. Because Helen is herself such a mother, she becomes an important, but not an exclusive, focus of spectatorial identification. She becomes, for example, the significant witness of Stella's sacrifice. Her one action in the entire film is to leave open the curtains—an act that helps put Stella in the same passive and powerless position of spectating that Helen is in herself. But if this relegation to the position of spectator outside the action resolves the narrative, it is a resolution not satisfactory to any of its female protagonists.

Thus, where Kaplan sees the ending of *Stella Dallas* as satisfying patriarchal demands for the repression of the active and involved aspects of the mother's role, and as teaching female spectators to take their dubious pleasures from this empathic position outside the action, I would argue that the ending is too multiply identified, too dialectical in Julia Kristeva's sense of the struggle between maternal and paternal forms of language, to encourage such a response. Certainly the film has constructed concluding images of motherhood—first the high-toned Helen and finally a toned-down Stella—for the greater power and convenience of the father. But because the father's own spectatorial empathy is so lacking—Stephen is here much as he was with Stella at the movies, present but not identified himself—*we* cannot see it that way. We see instead the contradictions between what the patriarchal resolution of the film asks us to see—the mother 'in her place' as spectator, abdicating her former position *in* the scene—and what we as empathic, identifying female spectators can't help but feel—the loss of mother to daughter and daughter to mother.

This double vision seems typical of the experience of most female spectators at the movies. One explanation for it, we might recall, is Nancy Chodorow's theory that female identity is formed through a process of double identification. The girl identifies with her primary love object—her mother—and then, without ever dropping the first identification, with her father. According to Chodorow, the woman's sense of self is based upon a continuity of relationship that ultimately prepares her for the empathic, identifying role of the mother. Unlike the male who must constantly differentiate himself from his original object of identification in order to take on a male identity, the woman's ability to identify with a variety of different subject positions makes her a very different kind of spectator.

Feminist film theorists have tended to view this multiple identificatory power of the female spectator with some misgiving. In an article on the female spectator, Mary Ann Doane has suggested that when the female spectator looks at the cinematic image of a woman, she is faced with two main possibilities: she can either over-identify (as in the masochistic dramas typical of the woman's film) with the woman on the screen and thus lose herself in the image by taking this woman as her own narcissistic object of desire; or she can temporarily identify with the position of the masculine voyeur and subject this same woman to a controlling gaze that insists on the distance and difference between them.[48] In this case she becomes, as Laura Mulvey notes, a temporary transvestite.[49] Either way, according to Doane, she loses herself.

Doane argues that the only way a female spectator can keep from losing herself in this over-identification is by negotiating a distance from the image of her like—by reading this image as a sign as opposed to an iconic image that requires no reading. When the woman spectator regards a female body enveloped in an exaggerated masquerade of femininity, she encounters a sign that requires such a reading. We have seen that throughout a good part of *Stella Dallas* this is what Stella does with respect to her own body. For Doane, then, one way out of the dilemma of female over-identification with the image on the screen is for this image to act out a masquerade of femininity that manufactures a distance between spectator and image, to 'generate a problematic within which the image is manipulable, producible, and readable by women'.[50]

In other words, Doane thinks that female spectators need to borrow some of the distance and separation from the image that male spectators experience. She suggests that numerous avant-garde practices of distanciation can produce this necessary distance. This puts us back to Mulvey's argument that narrative pleasure must be destroyed by avant-garde practices. I would argue instead that this manufacturing of distance, this female voyeurism-with-a-difference, is an aspect of *every* female spectator's gaze at the image of her like. For rather than adopting either the distance and mastery of the masculine voyeur or the over-identification of Doane's woman who loses herself in the image, the female spectator is in a constant state of juggling all positions at once.

Ruby Rich has written that women experience films much more dialectically than men. 'Brecht once described the exile as the ultimate dialectician in that the exile lives the tension of two different cultures. That's precisely the sense in which the woman spectator is an equally inevitable dialectician.'[51] The female spectator's look is thus a dialectic of two (in themselves) inadequate and incomplete (sexually and socially) differentiated subject positions. Just as Julia Kristeva has shown that it is the dialectic of a maternal body that is channelled and repressed into a single, univocal significance that makes it possible for women to be represented at all, so does a similar dialectic inform female spectatorship when a female point of view is genuinely inscribed in the text.

We have seen in *Stella Dallas* how the mediation of the mother and daughter's look at one another radically alters the representation of them both. We have also seen that the viewer cannot choose a single 'main controlling' point of identification but must alternate between a number of conflicting points of view, none of which can be satisfactorily reconciled. But the window scene at the end of the film would certainly seem to be the moment when all the above contradictions collapse into a single patriarchal vision of the mother as pure spectator (divested of her excessive bodily presence) and the daughter as the (now properly fetishised) object of vision. Although it is true that this ending, by separating mother and daughter, places each within a visual economy that defines them from the perspective of patriarchy, the female spectator's own look at each of them does not acquiesce in such a phallic visual economy of voyeurism and fetishism.

For in looking at Stella's own look at her daughter through a window that strongly resembles a movie screen,[52] the female spectator does not see and believe the same way Stella does. In this final scene, Stella is no different than the naïve spectator she was when, as a young woman, she went to the movies with Stephen. In order to justify her sacrifice, she must *believe* in the reality of the cinematic illusion she sees: bride and groom kneeling before the priest, proud father looking on. We, however, *know* the artifice and suffering behind it—Laurel's disappointment that her mother has not attended the wedding; Helen's manipulation of the scene that affords Stella her glimpse; Stella's own earlier manipulation of Laurel's view of her 'bad' motherhood. So when we look at Stella looking at the glamorous and artificial 'movie' of her daughter's life, we cannot, like Stella, naïvely believe in the reality of the happy ending, any more than we believe in the reality of the silent movements and hackneyed gestures of the glamorous movie Stella once saw.

Because the female spectator has seen the cost to both Laurel and Stella of the daughter's having entered the frame, of having become the properly fetishised image of womanhood, she cannot, like Stella, believe in happiness for either. She knows better because she has seen what each has had to give up to assume these final roles. But isn't it just such a balance of knowledge and belief (of the fetishist's contradictory phrase 'I know very well but just the same . . .')[53] that has characterised the sophisticated juggling act of the ideal cinematic spectator?

The psychoanalytic model of cinematic pleasure has been based on the phenomenon of fetishistic disavowal: the contradictory gesture of *believing* in an illusion (the cinematic image, the female penis) and yet *knowing* that it is an illusion, an imaginary signifier. This model sets up a situation in which the woman becomes a kind of failed fetishist: lacking a penis she lacks the biological foundation to engage in the sophisticated game of juggling presence and absence in cinematic representation; hence her presumed over-identification, her lack of the knowledge of illusion[54] and the resulting one, two, and three handkerchief movies. But the female spectator of *Stella Dallas* finds herself balancing a very different kind of knowledge and belief than the mere existence or non-existence of the female phallus. She *knows* that women can find no genuine form of representation under patriarchal structures of voyeuristic or fetishistic viewing, because she has seen Stella lose herself as a woman and as a mother. But at the same time she *believes* that women exist outside this phallic economy, because she has glimpsed moments of resistance in which two women have been able to represent themselves to themselves through the mediation of their own gazes.

This is a very different form of disavowal. It is both a *knowing* recognition of the limitations of woman's representation in patriarchal language and a contrary *belief* in the illusion of a pre-Oedipal space between women free of the mastery and control of the male look. The contradiction is as compelling for the woman as for the male fetishist, even more so because it is not based on the presence or absence of an anatomical organ, but on the dialectic of the woman's socially constructed position under patriarchy.

It is in a very different sense, then, that the psychoanalytic concepts of voyeurism and fetishism can inform a feminist theory of cinematic spectatorship—not as inscribing woman totally on the side of the passive object who is merely seen, as Mulvey and others have so influentially argued, but by examining the contradictions that animate women's very active and fragmented ways of seeing.

I would not go so far as to argue that these contradictions operate for the female viewer in every film about relations between women. But the point of focusing on a film that both addresses female audiences and contains important structures of viewing *between* women is to suggest that it does not take a radical and consciously feminist break with patriarchal ideology to represent the contradictory aspects of the woman's position under patriarchy. It does not even take the ironic distancing devices of, for example, the Sirkian melodrama to generate the kind of active, critical response that sees the work of ideology in the film. Laura Mulvey has written that the ironic endings of Sirkian melodrama are progressive in their defiance of unity and closure:

> It is as though the fact of having a female point of view dominating the narrative produces an excess which precludes satisfaction. If the melodrama offers a fantasy escape for the identifying women in the audience, the illusion is so strongly marked by recognisable, real and familiar traps that the escape is closer to a daydream than a fairy story. The few Hollywood films made with a female audience in mind evoke contradictions rather than reconciliation, with

the alternative to mute surrender to society's overt pressure lying in defeat by its unconscious laws.[55]

Although Mulvey here speaks primarily of the ironic Sirkian melodrama, her description of the contradictions encountered by the female spectator apply in a slightly different way to the very un-ironic *Stella Dallas*. I would argue that *Stella Dallas* is a progressive film not because it defies both unity and closure, but because the definitive closure of its ending produces no parallel unity in its spectator. And because the film has constructed its spectator in a female subject position locked into a primary identification with another female subject, it is possible for this spectator to impose her own radical feminist reading on the film. Without such female subject positions inscribed within the text, the stereotypical self-sacrificing mother character would flatten into the mere maternal essences of so many motherly figures for melodrama.

Stella Dallas is a classic maternal melodrama played with a very straight face. Its ambivalences and contradictions are not cultivated with the intention of revealing the work of patriarchal ideology within it. But like any melodrama that offers a modicum of realism yet conforms to the 'reconciliation of the irreconciliable' proper to the genre,[56] it must necessarily produce, when dealing with conflicts among women, a 'shock of recognition'.

. . .

Female spectators resist the only way we can by struggling with the contradictions inherent in these images of ourselves and our situation. It is a terrible underestimation of the female viewer to presume that she is wholly seduced by a naïve belief in these masochistic images, that she has allowed these images to put her in her place the way the films themselves put their women characters in their place.

It seems, then, that Adrienne Rich's eloquent plea for works that can embody the 'essential female tragedy' of mother–daughter passion, rapture, and loss is misguided but only with respect to the mode of tragedy. I hope to have begun to show that this loss finds expression under patriarchy in the 'distorted' and 'misused' cathexes of the maternal melodrama. For unlike tragedy melodrama does not reconcile its audience to an inevitable suffering. Rather than raging against a fate that the audience has learned to accept, the female hero often accepts a fate that the audience at least partially questions.

The divided female spectator identifies with the woman whose very triumph is often in her own victimisation, but she also criticises the price of a transcendent 'eradication' which the victim-hero must pay. Thus, although melodrama's impulse towards the just 'happy ending' usually places the woman hero in a final position of subordination, the 'lesson' for female audiences is certainly not to become similarly eradicated themselves. For all its masochism, for all its frequent devaluation of the individual person of the mother (as opposed to the abstract ideal of motherhood), the maternal melodrama presents a recognisable picture of woman's ambivalent position under patriarchy that has been an important source of realistic reflections of women's lives. This may be why the most effective feminist films of recent years have been those works—like Sally Potter's *Thriller*, Michelle Citron's *Daughter Rite*, Chantal Akerman's *Jeanne Dielman . . .* , and even Jacques Rivette's *Céline and Julie Go Boating*—that work *within and against* the expectations of female self-sacrifice experienced in maternal melodrama.

Notes

1. An interesting and comprehensive introduction to this sub-genre can be found in Christian Viviani's 'Who is Without Sin? The Maternal Melodrama in American Film, 1930–1939', in Christine Gledhill (ed.), *Home is Where the Heart Is: Studies in Melodrama and the Woman's Film* (London: BFI, 1987), 83–99.

   B. Ruby Rich and I have also briefly discussed the genre of these sacrificial maternal melodramas in our efforts to identify the context of Michelle Citron's avant-garde feminist film, *Daughter Rite.* Citron's film is in many ways the flip side to the maternal melodrama, articulating the daughter's confused anger and love at the mother's sacrificial stance. 'The Right of Re-Vision: Michelle Citron's *Daughter Rite*', *Film Quarterly*, 35: 1 (Fall 1981), 17–22
2. *The Second Sex*, trans. H. M. Parshley (New York Bantam, 1961), 488–9.
3. An excellent introduction to this rapidly growing area of study is Marianne Hirsch's review essay, 'Mothers and Daughters', *Signs: Journal of Women in Culture and Society*, 7: 1 (1981), 200–22. See also Judith Kegan Gardiner, 'On Female Identity and Writing by Women', *Critical Inquiry*, 8: 2 (Winter 1981), 347–61.
4. *Of Woman Born* (New York: Bantam, 1977), 240, 226.
5. Martha Vicinus, writing about the nineteenth-century melodrama, suggests that melodrama's 'appropriate' endings offer 'a temporary reconciliation of the irreconcilable'. The concern is typically not with what is possible or actual but what is desirable. 'Helpless and Unfriended: Nineteenth-Century Domestic Melodrama', *New Literary History*, 13: 1 (Autumn 1981), 132. Peter Brooks emphasises a similar quality of wish-fulfilment in melodrama, even arguing that psychoanalysis offers a systematic realisation of the basic aesthetics of the genre: 'If psychoanalysis has become the nearest modern equivalent of religion in that it is a vehicle for the cure of souls, melodrama

is a way station toward this status, a first indication of how conflict, enactment, and cure must be conceived in a secularised world', (p. 202).

6. Most prominent among these are Claire Johnston's 'Women's Cinema as Counter Cinema', in *Notes on Women's Cinema*, ed. Claire Johnston, *Screen*, Pamphlet 2 (SEPT: 1972); and Laura Mulvey's 'Visual Pleasure and Narrative Cinema', *Screen*, 16: 3 (Autumn 1975), 6–18
7. The list of feminist work on this film is impressive. It includes: Pam Cook, 'Duplicity in Mildred Pierce', in *Women in Film Noir*, ed. E. Ann Kaplan (London: BFI, 1978), 68–82; Molly Haskell, *From Reverence to Rape: The Treatment of Women in the Movies* (New York: Holt, Rinehart and Winston, 1973), 175–80; Annette Kuhn, *Women's Pictures: Feminism and Cinema* (London Routledge and Kegan Paul, 1982), 28–35; Joyce Nelson, '*Mildred Pierce* Reconsidered', *Film Reader*, 2 (January 1977), 65–70 and Janet Walker, 'Feminist Critical Practice: Female Discourse in *Mildred Pierce*', *Film Reader*, 5 (1982), 164–71.
8. Molly Haskell only gave the film brief mention in her chapter on 'The Woman's Film', *From Reverence to Rape: The Treatment of Women in the Movies* (New York: Holt, Rinehart and Winston, 1973), 153–88. Since then the film has been discussed by Christian Viviani (see note 1); Charles Affron in *Cinema and Sentiment* (Chicago: University of Chicago Press, 1983), 74–6; Ben Brewster, 'A Scene at the Movies', *Screen*, 23: 2 (July–August 1982), 4–5; and E. Ann Kaplan, 'Theories of Melodrama: A Feminist Perspective', *Women and Performance: A Journal of Feminist Theory*, 1: 1 (Spring/Summer 1983), 40–48. Kaplan also has a longer article on the film, 'The Case of the Missing Mother: Maternal Issues in Vidor's *Stella Dallas*', *Heresies*, 16 (1983), 81–5. Laura Mulvey also mentions the film briefly in her 'Afterthoughts on "Visual Pleasure and Narrative Cinema" Inspired by *Duel in the Sun* (King Vidor, 1946)', *Framework*, 15/16/17 (Summer 1981), 12–15—but only in the context of Vidor's much more male-oriented western. Thus, although *Stella Dallas* keeps coming up in the context of discussions of melodrama, sentiment, motherhood, and female spectatorship, it has not been given the full scrutiny it deserves, except by Kaplan, many of whose arguments I challenge in the present work.
9. Mulvey, 11. See also most of the essays in *Re-vision: Essays in Feminist Film Criticism*, ed. Mary Ann Doane, Patricia Mellencamp, and Linda Williams (Frederick: University Publications of America, Inc., 1984).
10. Claire Johnston, for example, writes, 'Despite the enormous emphasis placed on women as spectacle in the cinema, woman as woman is largely absent.' 'Woman's Cinema as Counter-Cinema', *Notes on Women's, Cinema*, 26.
11. Christine Gledhill, 'Developments in Feminist Film Criticism', *Re-vision: Essays in Feminist Film Criticism*, 31. Originally published in *Quarterly Review of Film Studies*, 3: 4 (1978), 457–93.
12. Mulvey, 7.
13. Mulvey, 7, 18.
14. The few feminists who have begun this difficult but important work are: Mary Ann Doane, 'Film and the Masquerade: Theorizing the Female Spectator', *Screen*, 23: 3–4 (Sept–Oct. 1982), 74–87; Gertrud Koch, 'Why Women Go to the Movies', *Jump Cut*, 27 (July 1982), trans. Marc Silberman, 51–3; Judith Mayne 'The Woman at the Keyhole: Women's Cinema and Feminist

Criticism', *Re-vision: Essays in Feminist Film Criticism*, 44–66; and Mulvey herself in 'Afterthoughts on "Visual Pleasure and Narrative Cinema" Inspired by *Duel in the Sun* (King Vidor, 1946)', *Framework*, 15/16/17 (Summer 1981), 12–15; B. Ruby Rich, in Michelle Citron et al., 'Women and Film: A Discussion of Feminist Aesthetics', *New German Critique*, 13 (1978), 77–107; and Tania Modleski, *Loving with a Vengeance: Mass Produced Fantasies for Women* (Hamden, Conn.: Archon Books, 1982). Since I wrote this article, two important new books on women and film have appeared. Both take considerable account of the processes by which the female spectator identifies with screen images. They are: E. Ann Kaplan's *Women and Film: Both Sides of the Camera* (New York: Methuen, 1983); and Teresa de Lauretis' *Alice Doesn't: Feminism, Semiotics, Cinema* (Bloomington: Indiana University Press, 1984).

15. Gledhill, 41.
16. Gledhill, 37.
17. Gledhill, 42.
18. Gledhill, 44–5.
19. Freud begins this shift in the 1925 essay, 'Some Psychological Consequences of the Anatomical Distinction between the Sexes', *Standard Edition of the Complete Psychological Works* (Hogarth Press, 1953–74), vol. 19. He continues it in the 1931 essay 'Female Sexuality', vol, 21.
20. Marianne Hirsch's review essay, 'Mothers and Daughters', *Signs: Journal of Women in Culture and Society*, 7: 1 (Autumn 1981) 200–22, offers an excellent summary of the diverse strands of the continuing re-appraisal of the mother–daughter relation. Hirsch examines theories of this relation in Anglo-American and neo-Freudian object relations psychology (Chodorow, Miller, Dinnerstein), in Jungian myth criticism, and in the French feminist theories developing out of structuralism, post-structuralism, and Lacanian psychoanalysis. A recent study of how female connectedness affects female moral development is Carol Gilligan's *In a Different Voice* (Cambridge Mass.: Harvard Univ. Press, 1982).
21. Chodorow, *The Reproduction of Mothering: Psychoanalysis and the Sociology of Gender* (Berkeley: University of California Press, 1978), 7.
22. 'Oedipal asymmetries' is Chodorow's term, 7.
23. Chodorow, 178.
24. Marianne Hirsch surveys the importance of this point in her review essay 'Mothers and Daughters', 209. So, too, does Judith Kegan Gardiner in 'On Female Identity and Writing by Women', *Critical Inquiry: Writing and Sexual Difference*, 8: 2 (Winter 1981), 347–61
25. Chodorow, 188.
26. These others include: Dorothy Dinnerstein, *The Mermaid and the Minotaur: Sexual Arrangements and the Human Malaise* (New York: Harper and Row, 1976); Jessie Bernard, *The Future of Motherhood* (New York: Dial Press, 1974); and Jean Baker Miller, *Toward a New Psychology of Women* (Boston: Beacon Press, 1976).
27. This is the real advance of Chodorow's theories over those of an earlier generation of feminist psychoanalysts. Karen Horney, for example, found it necessary, as both Juliet Mitchell and Jane Gallop point out, to resort to generalising statements of women's essential, biologically determined nature, thus leaving no possibility for change. Horney, 'On the Genesis of the Castra-

tion Complex in Women', *International Journal of Psycho-Analysis*, 5 (1924), 50–65.

28. Paris: Editions de Minuit, 1974.
29. Other French feminists involved in this 'feminine writing' are Hélène Cixous, Monique Wittig, Julia Kristeva and Michèle Montrelay. A critical introduction to these writers can be found in Ann Rosalind Jones, 'Writing the Body: Toward an Understanding of L'Ecriture féminine' and Helene Vivienne Wenzel's 'The Text as Body/Politics: An Appreciation of Monique Wittig's Writings in Context', both in *Feminist Studies*, 7: 2 (Summer 1981), 247–87.
30. 'Ce sexe qui n'en est pas un', trans. Claudia Reeder, *New French Feminisms*, ed. Elaine Marks and Isabelle de Courtivron (Amherst: University of Mass. Press, 1980), 100 –1.
31. Anglo-American feminists have thus been critical of the new French feminists for two different reasons: American feminists have criticised an essentialism that would seem to preclude change (see, for example, the essay by Jones referred to in note 29); British feminists have criticised their apparent failure to account for the way the female body is mediated by language (see, for example, Beverly Brown and Parveen Adams, 'The Feminine Body and Feminist Politics', *m/f*, 3 (1979), 35–50).
32. Irigaray, 106–7.
33. Rich, *Signs*, 5: 4 (Summer 1980), 631–60.
34. Irigaray, 110.
35. Mary Ann Doane, 'Womans' Stake: Filming the Female Body', October, 17 (Summer 1981), 30.
36. Kristeva's work has been translated in two volumes. *Desire in Language: A Semiotic Approach to Literature and Art*, trans. Thomas Gora, Alice Jardine, Leon S. Roudiez (New York: Columbia University Press, 1980); and *About Chinese Women*, trans. Anita Barrows (New York: Horizon Books, 1977).
37. Alice Jardine, 'Theories of the Feminine: Kristeva', *enclitic*, 4: 2 (Fall 1980) 13.
38. Kristeva, 'Motherhood According to Giovanni Bellini', in *Desire in Language*, 237–70.
39. Jane Gallop, 'The Phallic Mother: Freudian Analysis', in *The Daughter's Seduction: Feminism and Psychoanalysis* (Ithaca, NY: Cornell University Press, 1982), 113–31.
40. Ann Kaplan emphasises this 'wrenching' of the filmic point of view away from Stella and towards the upper-class values and perspectives of Stephen and the townspeople. 'The Case of the Missing Mother', 83.
41. Doane, 'The Woman's Film: Possession and Address', in Gledhill (ed.), *Home is Where the Heart Is*, 283–298.
42. The term—originally used by Joan Rivière—is employed in Mary Ann Doane, 'Film and the Masquerade: Theorising the Female Spectator', *Screen*, 23: 34 (September/October 1982), 74–87.
43. Ann Kaplan, 'The Case of the Missing Mother', 83.
44. Ibid.
45. Molly Haskell notes this tendency of women audiences to come away with a memory of heroic revolt, rather than the defeat with which so many films end, in her pioneering study *From Reverence to Rape: The Treatment of Women in the Movies* (New York: Holt, Rinehart and Winston, 1973), 31.
46. Modleski, 'The Search for Tomorrow in Today's Soap Opera: Notes on a

Feminine Narrative Form', *Film Quarterly*, 33: 1 (Fall 1979), 14. A longer version of this article can be found in Modleski's book *Loving with a Vengeance: Mass Produced Fantasies for Women* (Hamden, Conn.: Archon Books, 1982), 85–109.

47. Kaplan, 'Theories of Melodrama', 46.
48. Doane, 'Film and the Masquerade', 87.
49. Mulvey, 'Afterthoughts on "Visual Pleasure and Narrative Cinema" Inspired by *Duel in the Sun* (King Vidor, 1946)', 13.
50. Doane, 87.
51. Ruby Rich, in Michelle Citron et al., 'Women and Film: A Discussion of Feminist Aesthetics', *New German Critique*, 13 (1978), 87. Although Rich goes on to suggest that this dialectic is an either/or choice—'to identify either with Marilyn Monroe or with the man behind me hitting the back of my seat with his knees'—I think the more proper sense of the word would be to construe it as a continuous conflict and tension that informs female viewing and which in many cases does not allow the choice of one or the other.
52. Ben Brewster has cited the many cinematic references of the original novel as an indication of just how effective as an appeal to reality the cinematic illusion has become. 'A Scene at the Movies', *Screen*, 23: 2 (July–August 1983), 4–5.
53. Freud's theory that the little boy believes in the maternal phallus even after he knows better because he has seen evidence that it does not exist has been characterised by Octave Mannoni as a contradictory statement that both asserts and denies the mother's castration. In this 'Je sais bien mais quand mème' (I know very well but just the same), the 'just the same' is the fetish disavowal. Mannoni, *Clefs pour l'imaginaire* (Paris: Seuil, 1969), 9–30. Christian Metz later applied this fetishistic structure to the institution of the cinema as the creator of believable fictions of perceptually real human beings who are nevertheless absent from the scene. Thus the cinema aims all of its technical prowess at the disavowal of the lack on which its 'imaginary signifier' is based. *The Imaginary Signifier: Psychoanalysis and the Cinema*, trans. Celia Britton, Annwyl Williams, Ben Brewster, and Alfred Guzzetti (Bloomington Indiana: Indiana University Press, 1982), 69–76.
54. Doane, 'Film and the Masquerade', 80–1
55. Mulvey, 'Notes on Sirk and Melodrama' (Reprinted in this anthology, 75–79).
56. Vicinus, 132.

26 Tears and Desire: Women and Melodrama in the 'Old' Mexican Cinema

Ana M. López*

The melodrama has been a crucial site for the interrogation of many of the categories utilized for the contemporary study of the cinema and for debates over questions of genre, narration, ideology, subjectivity, and representation.[1] Above all, however, film melodrama has been one of the most important areas for the development of feminist film criticism. Long considered a 'feminine' mode because of its insistent attention to the domestic sphere and related emotional issues, the melodrama—especially that subset of the genre known as the 'woman's film' and ostensibly addressed to female audiences—has proven to be a productive area for the investigation of the representation of women, female subjectivity, and desire, gendered critical categories, and the role of women as cultural producers and consumers.[2] Emerging in the context of the 1960s–1970s rediscovery and reassessment of the classical Hollywood cinema and the 1970s–1980s boom in feminist scholarship, this investigation of the melodramatic mode was limited, until very recently, to the study of the Hollywood melodrama and its relationship to US society, ideology, and patriarchy. However, recent studies exploring the historical and international inscription of women and melodramatic representation (in cinemas as diverse as German Weimar films, French films of the 1920s and 1930s, the *bourekas* films of 1970s Israeli cinema, and the commercial 1950s Hindi cinema)[3] have begun to delineate the complex lines of historical and cultural affiliations that link and differentiate the social functions of the melodramatic in specific moments of Western and non-Western societies. Above all, the investigation of the gendering of subjects in melodramatic representation in non-US societies has forced scholars to confront

* Ana M. Lopez, 'Tears and Desire: Women and Melodrama in the "Old" Mexican Cinema' from *Multiple Voices in Feminist Criticism* edited by D. Carson, L. Dittmar and J. Welsch (University of Minnesota Press, 1993), reprinted by permission of the author.

conflicting, historically specific claims of national, ethnic, and gender identity.

Within this context, I want to explore the placement of women in Mexican film melodramas of the 1940s and 1950s and its relationship to Mexican society. Rather than present a content-based description of the 'types' of women represented (virgins/mothers versus whores, for example) or summarize clichéd plot resolutions,[4] I am concerned with the interrelations among patriarchal Mexican society, women's place in Mexican culture and national identity, and film production and consumption. Emphasizing the different articulations of gender and subjectivity in a society formed by colonization and marked by a history of violence and discontinuity, I attempt to link the history of the classical Mexican cinema melodrama with Mexican society, to trace the inscription of the melodramatic alongside the social positioning of women, and to highlight moments when conflicting voices and needs visibly erupt into the cinematic and social spheres.

THE MELODRAMA AND THE LATIN AMERICAN CINEMA

As has been extensively detailed elsewhere, the melodrama, along with music and comedy, became synonymous with the cinema in Latin America after the introduction of sound.[5] Taking advantage of Hollywood's temporary inability to satisfy the linguistic needs of the Latin-American market, local producers used the new technology to exploit national characteristics. Argentina took on the tango and its melodramatic lyrics and developed the tango melodrama genre in the early 1930s. Similarly, Mexico made the melodrama a central genre of the sound cinema after the success of *Santa* (1931, Antonio Moreno), an adaptation of a well-known melodramatic novel by Federico Gamboa about an innocent provincial girl forced into urban prostitution and redeemed only in death.[6]

Furthermore, the rapid establishment of a specific Latin-American star system heavily dependent on radio and popular musical entertainers gave rise to melodramas with at least one or two musical performances to heighten a film's 'entertainment value'. Starring singers-turned-actors, narratives about entertainers sprinkled with performances became *de rigueur*. Thus Libertad Lamarque's suffering mothers always also sang, Pedro Infante could weep over his little black child with the popular song 'Angelitos Negros' ('Little Black

Angels') in the film of the same title, and Ninón Sevilla could vent her sexual anger and frustration dancing wild rumbas in the *cabaretera* (brothel) films of the 1950s. In these and other films, the narrative stoppage usually generated by performances was reinvested with emotion, so that melodramatic pathos emerged in the moment of performance itself (through gesture, sentiment, interactions with the audience within the film, or simply music choice). And in a film such as *Amor en las Sombras* (*Love in the Shadows*, 1959, Tito Davison), which featured ten complete performances in less than two hours' screen time, music and song rather than dramatic action propel the narrative.

Despite this diversity, however, two basic melodramatic tendencies developed between 1930 and 1960: family melodramas that focused on the problems of love, sexuality, and parenting, and epic melodramas that reworked national history, especially the events of the Mexican Revolution. Although the two categories are somewhat fluid, with some family melodramas taking place in the context of the Revolution and its aftermath, I shall be concerned primarily with the operations of the former. The revolutionary melodramas are perhaps as significant for the development of a gendered 'Mexican' consciousness as the family ones, but I am interested in analyzing the cinematic positioning of women within the Mexican domestic sphere, and the ideological operations of the family melodramas provide us with privileged access to that realm. Set in quintessential domestic spaces (homes or similar places) that, as Laura Mulvey says, 'can hold a drama in claustrophobic intensity and represent . . . the passions and antagonisms that lie behind it,'[7] the family melodramas map the repressions and contradictions of interiority and interior spaces—the home and unconscious—with more urgency than is possible within the cathartic large-scale action of revolutionary dramas.

THE MELODRAMA, WOMEN, AND MEXICO

The melodramatic is deeply embedded in Mexican and Hispanic culture and intersects with the three master narratives of Mexican society: religion, nationalism, and modernization. First of all, Hispanic culture carries the burden of its Christianity, which, as Susan Sontag argues in *Against Interpretation*, is already melodramatic—rather than tragic—in structure and intention. In Christianity, as Sontag says, 'every crucifixion must be topped by a resurrection,' an optimism inimical to the pessimism of tragedy.[8] Furthermore, the staples of the family melodrama—sin and suffering abnegation—are essential components of the Christian tradition: sin allows for passion and, although it must always be punished, passion, after all, justifies life.

Perhaps most significantly, the melodrama always addresses questions of individual (gendered) identity within patriarchal culture and the heart of Mexico's definition as a nation. In Mexico, questions of individual identity are complicated by a colonial heritage that defines woman—and her alleged instability and unreliability—as the origin of *national* identity. The Mexican nation is defined, on the one hand, by Catholicism and the Virgin Guadalupe, the Virgin Mother and patron saint, and, on the other, by the *Chingada*, the national betrayal of Doña Marina– also known as La Malinche or Malintzin Tenepal—the Aztec princess who submitted to Cortez and handed her people over to the conquistadores.[9] As Cherríe Moraga succinctly puts it,

> Malinche fucked the white man who conquered the Indian peoples of Mexico and destroyed their culture. Ever since, brown men have been accusing her of betraying her race, and over the centuries continue to blame her entire sex for this 'transgression'.[10]

Raped, defiled, and abused, Malintzin/Malinche is the violated mother of modern Mexico, *la chingada*—the fucked one—or *la vendida*—the sellout. As Octavio Paz explains in *The Labyrinths of Solitude*, Malinche's 'sons' (*sic*), the Mexican people, are 'the sons of La Chingada, the fruits of a rape, a farce.[11] Thus the origins of the nation are located at a site—the violated mother—that is simultaneously an altar of veneration and the place of an original shame. The victim of a rape, Malinche/La Chingada, mother of the nation, carries the guilt of her victimization. Deeply marked by this 'otherness', Mexican national identity rejects and celebrates its feminine origins while gender identity, in general, is problematized even further. To be Malinche—a woman—is to be a traitor, the great whore-mother of a bastard race. The melodramatic became the privileged place for the symbolic re-enactment of this drama of identification and the only place where female desire—and the utopian dream of its realization—could be glimpsed.

Mexico's colonial heritage—first Spanish and most recently North American—also affects the social functions of the melodrama. Colonialism always implies a crisis of identity for the colonial subject, caught between the impulse to imitate the colonizer and the desire for an always displaced autonomy. Like Caliban in Shakespeare's *Tempest*, the colonized must use the colonizer's 'words'—the imported cinematic apparatus—and learn the colonizer's language before he or she can even think of articulating his or her own speech: 'You taught me language and my profit on't is I know how to curse.' Just as in Brazil the parodic *chanchada* genre can be seen as a response to the impossibility of thinking of a national cinema without considering the Hollywood cinema as well as Brazil's own underdevelopment, in Mexico, melodrama's excess explicitly defies the Hollywood dominant:

> Since there can be no nostalgic return to pre-colonial purity, no unproblematic recovery of national origins undefiled by alien influences, the artist in the dominated culture cannot ignore the foreign presence but must rather swallow it and recycle it to national ends.[12]

As Carlos Monsiváis has said, 'If competition with North America is impossible artistically or technically, the only defense is excess, the absence of limits of the melodrama.'[13] Thus the melodrama's exaggerated signification and hyperbole—its emphasis on anaphoric events pointing to other implied, absent meanings or origins—become, in the Mexican case, a way of cinematically working through the problematic of an underdeveloped national cinema.

The melodrama is also formally and practically linked with the specific trajectory of Mexican national identity and the significance of the Revolution for the nation-building project. If we agree with Peter Brooks that the melodrama is 'a fictional system for making sense of experience as a semantic field of force' that 'comes into being in a world where the traditional imperatives of truth and ethics have been violently thrown into question,'[14] then we should not be surprised by the cultural currency of the melodrama in post-Revolutionary Mexico. In the midst of the great social upheavals of this period, the country seemed ungovernable and the city an unruly mecca: the Revolution changed the nature of public life, mobilized the masses, shook up the structures of the family without changing its roots and, as Monsiváis says, 'served as the inevitable mirror where the country recognized its physiognomy'. The Revolution may not have 'invented' the Mexican nation, but 'its vigor, for the first time, lent legendary characteristics to the masses that sustained it.'[15] In other words, the Revolution created a new class—the new urban poor soon to be a working class—whose willpower, roughness, and illiteracy became insistently visible in the formerly feudal national landscape.

The Revolution also further problematized the position of women in Mexico. Women had fought alongside the men and had followed the troops cooking, healing, and providing emotional and physical solace, either as legitimate wives, lovers, or paid companions. Known generally as *soldaderas*, these women formed the backbone of an incipient feminist movement that emerged after the Revolution. Yet as Jean Franco argues in *Plotting Women*,

> The Revolution with its promise of social transformation encouraged a Messianic spirit that transformed mere human beings into supermen and constituted a discourse that associated virility with social transformation in a way that marginalized women at the very moment when they were, supposedly, liberated.[16]

Precisely when the nation created itself anew under the aegis of Revolutionary mythology and its male superhero redeemers, women were, once again, relegated to the background, and in cultural production—especially in national epic allegories—represented as a terrain to be traversed in the quest for male identity. Simultaneously, while the new secular state ostensibly promoted women's emancipation to combat Catholicism and its alleged counterrevolutionary ideology,[17] Mexico found itself caught in the wheels of capitalist modernization.

The new class created by the Revolution—an increasingly mobile, urban, migratory class of male and female workers—was entertained by the popular theater (*teatro frívolo* or *género chico*) before it found the cinema, but after the coming of sound, Spanish-language movies became the principal discursive tool for social mapping. While the *género chico* and its carnivalesque ribaldry[18] attracted a socially but not sexually mixed audience, the cinema was family entertainment and, by design and by commercial imperatives, broader based. By the late 1930s and through the 1940s and 1950s, the national cinema granted access not only to entertainment, but also to vital behaviors and attitudes: 'One didn't go to the cinema to dream, but to learn.'[19] There was not much room here for the carnivalesque celebration that continued to take place in the *teatro frívolo*: the cinema helped transmit new habits and reiterated codes of behaviour, providing the new nation with the common bases and collective ties necessary for national unity. In fact, the cinema helped make a new post-Revolutionary middle class viable.

If it is indeed true, as Monsiváis says, that film melodramas served this kind of socializing function, what exactly were the lessons they taught women? How did the melodrama mediate the post-Revolutionary crisis of national and gendered identity and its subsequent institutionalization? Rather than blindly enforce or teach unambiguous high moral values, stable codes of behaviour, or obedience to the patriarchal order, the family melodramas staged specific dramas of identity that often complicated straightforward ideological identification for men *and* women without precluding accommodation. However, the melodrama's contradictory play of identifications constituted neither false communication nor a simple lesson imposed upon the people from above. Rather, these films addressed pressing contradictions and desires within Mexican society. And even when their narrative work suggests utter complicity with the work of the Law, the emotional excesses set loose and the multiple desires detonated are not easily recuperated.

The narratives of the Mexican family melodrama deal with three principal conflicts: the clash between old (feudal, *porfirian*) values and modern (industrialized, urban) life, the crisis of male identity that emerges as a result of this clash, and the instability of female identity that at once guarantees and threatens the passage from the old to the new. These conflicts are played out in two distinct physical and psychic spaces—the home, a private sphere valorized and sanctified by the Law, and the nightclub, a barely tolerated social space as liminal as the home is central. Only marginally acceptable, the nightclub is nevertheless the part of the patriarchal public sphere where the personal—and issues of female subjectivity, emotion, identity, and desire—finds its most complex articulation in the Mexican melodrama.

THE HOME: MOTHERS, FAMILIES, AND THEIR OTHERS

Although Mexican patriarchal values insist on the sanctity of the traditional home (as an extension of the 'fatherland' blessed by God), the extended families in them are rarely well adjusted precisely because of the rigidity of the fathers' law and in spite of the saintliness of the mothers. In Mexico, the family as an institution has a contradictory symbolic status as a site for the crystallization of tensions between traditional patriarchal values (especially the cult of machismo) and modernizing tendencies and, as a source of maternal support and nurturing the secular state could not replace.[20] This ambivalence is clearly evidenced in the deployment of the Mexican cinema's so-called mother obsession. Although it is undoubtedly true that the Mexican melodrama's fascination with saintly mother figures can be traced to the deeply conservative social impulses of the post-Revolutionary middle classes, who countered their insecurity over the legitimacy of their status with aggressive nationalism and an obsessive attachment to traditional values, how this mother obsession is worked out in the melodrama complicates any assessment of the politics and social mapping of such representations.

Director Juan Orol and the actress Sara García created the archetypal mother of the Mexican melodrama in *Madre Querida* (*Dear Mother*, 1935), the heart-wrenching story of a young boy who goes to a reformatory for arson and whose mother dies of grief precisely on the tenth of May (Mother's Day in Mexico). Over the next decades, García played suffering, self-sacrificing mothers in countless films such as *No Basta ser Madre* (*It's Not Enough to Be a Mother*, 1937), *Mi Madrecita* (*My Little Mother*, 1940), and *Madre Adorada* (*Beloved Mother*, 1948). However, despite their self-acknowledged narrative focus on mothers and their positioning of the mother as the central ideological tool for social and moral cohesion, these and other films ostensibly glorifying mothers as repositories of conservative family values were clearly maternal melodramas rather than women's films. This distinction, invoked by E. Ann Kaplan in her discussion of Hollywood 1920s and 1930s melodramas,[21] is significant for Mexican cinema, because it helps to distinguish between films that focus on male oedipal dramas and films that more self-consciously address female spectators. Indeed, one could argue that despite their focus on mothers, these family melodramas are patriarchal rather than maternal because they attempt to preserve patriarchal values over the sanctity of the mother. In attempting to reinforce the patriarchy their narrative logic breaks down: the moral crisis created in these films revolves around the fathers' identity and not the mothers', whose position is never put into question.

In *Cuando los hijos se van* (*When the Children Go Away*, 1941, Juan Bustillo Orol), for example, a rigid provincial family is torn asunder by the father's (Fernando Soler) inability to see the true characters of his sons or to recognize their mother's (Sara García) more sensitive assessment of their characters. Influenced by the 'bad' son, the father banishes the 'good' son to the city, while the mother, with her unerring maternal instinct, never doubts his integrity and is ultimately proven right by the narrative: the banished son returns a popular radio star and saves the family from a bankruptcy engineered by his sibling. Despite the narrative's obvious privileging of the mother's sight, the film attempts to shore up a patriarchal family structure threatened not only by the patriarch's inability to see, but by the other world lying outside the patriarch's control: Mexico City, emblem of modernization and progress, and the modern and highly pleasurable world outside the family. The film attempts to idealize the family as a unit whose preservation is worth all sacrifices, even death, but its suggestion that the familial crisis is caused by the father's blindness and irrational rigidity, especially when compared to the mother's unerring instinct, puts in question the very patriarchal principle it seeks to assert.

Mothers may have a guaranteed place in the home as pillars of strength, tolerance, and self abnegation—in other words, as Oedipal illusions—but outside the home they are prey to the male desires that the Mexican home and family disavow. As a foil to the mother's righteous suffering and masochistic respect for the Law, men, especially father figures, are self-indulgent and unable to obey the moral order. It is their desire—unleashed because of maternal asexuality— that most threatens and disturbs the stability of the family and its women. While denying desire within the family, outside it is a compelling and at times controlling force. Thus a variant of the family melodrama focuses on the impossible attraction of 'other' women: the 'bad' mothers (*las malas*), the vamps, the mistresses.

While Sara García portrayed the archetypal good mother, María Félix depicted her opposite, the *mala mujer* (bad woman): the haughty, independent woman, as passionate and devilish as the mothers are asexual and saintly. The titles of Félix's films clearly reveal her star persona: *Doña Bárbara* (Fernando de Fuentes, 1943), *La Mujer de Todos* (*Everyone's Woman*, Julio Bracho, 1946), *La Devoradora* (*The Devourer*, Fernando de Fuentes, 1946), *Doña Diabla* (Tito Davison, 1949). *Doña Bárbara*, her third film, most clearly defined this persona.[22] After being brutally raped as a young girl, Bárbara becomes a rich independent landowner—la Doña—who enjoys despoiling and humiliating others, especially men. She exults in her power and discards lovers and even her own daughter easily, exhibiting neither pity nor shame and relishing her hatred. Despite her power, Bárbara, like most of Félix's characters, is simply the vampiresque flip side of the saintly mothers of the family melodramas. Easily classified as antifamily melodramas insofar as they reject the surface accoutrements of the patriarchal family, ultimately her films forcefully reinscribe the need for the standard family. Despite titles focusing on the female character, Félix's films are male-centered narratives, where the specular pleasure lies with the woman (and her masquerades of masculinity), but the narrative remains with a male protagonist. Even in *Doña Bárbara*, the principal narrative agent is Santos Luzardo, a young man (Julián Soler) who challenges la Doña's power when he refuses her seduction. The film is more concerned with how he defeats Bárbara than with Bárbara's point of view or her downfall. Bárbara remains unknowable, an enigma given a sociological raison d'être—the rape—and the face of a goddess, but whose subjectivity and desires remain unknown. As a star, Félix could not embody female desire, for she was an ambivalent icon, as unknowable, cold, and pitiless as the mother figure was full of abnegation and tears.[23] Her presence is simply an echo of the dangers of desire for men rather than its realization for women.

WOMAN'S DESIRE ON THE MARGINS OF THE HOME

In general, only two kinds of Mexican melodramas were structured around woman's identity and presented from a female point of view: the fallen-but-redeemed-by-motherhood women's films and the *cabaretera* subgenre. Each type also had its prototypical female star: whereas the former films most often starred Dolores del Rio or, somewhat later, Libertad Lamarque, two stars whose characters suffered copiously for their meager sins and relished child obsessions without equal, the latter were epitomized by the sexy *rumberas* portrayed by Cuban actress Ninón Sevilla. Since neither Lamarque nor Sevilla are Mexican, the relative independence achieved by Lamarque's characters and the sexual wantonness of Sevilla's could be distanced as foreign otherness even when the actresses portrayed Mexican women. However, Mexican-born del Rio began her career in Hollywood, and, unlike the other two, was always considered a great actress, the *grande dame* of the Mexican cinema, whose face would acquire mythical status as *the* archetype of the moral and physical perfection of the indigenous woman.

Lamarque, singer and Argentine stage and movie star, acquired a tango-inspired star persona after successfully competing for screen time with singing idol Jorge Negrete in Luis Buñuel's *Gran Casion* (1946). Neither matriarchal mother, vampish other, nor a symbol of indigenous purity, Lamarque was most often a prototypically innocent fallen woman who also sang professionally. In *Soledad* (*Solitude*, Tito Davison, 1948), for example, Lamarque plays a young orphaned servant (Argentine!) tricked into a false marriage by the family heir, made pregnant, and abandoned but finally successful as an entertainer.

Despite their innocence, however, Lamarque's characters fall uneasily into the prevailing stereotypes of the Mexican cinema. In her best films, where she portrays entertainers with tragic pasts or fates, the need to position her simultaneously in relation to family life and to public life as a performer complicates the affirmation of standard social structures and woman's position vis-à-vis the private and public spheres. Her status as a respectable performer—and the incumbent independence of a salary, relationships outside the domestic sphere, and the adoring gaze of diegetic audiences—destabilizes her identity as a hopeless mother. Thus *Soledad* is unable to sustain the figurative melodramatic signification of its initial scenes (for example, prefiguring the falsity of the wedding ceremony via ominous mise-en-scènes and the *coup de theatre* of a candle blown out by violent wind when the couple first embrace) and depends increasingly on Soledad's voice rather than her silence to unravel its melodrama. Told from her point of view and, by film's end, literally dependent on her voice, the melodrama of *Soledad* ends appropriately with her long lost daughter's anguished cry of recognition: 'Mother!' But by now Soledad is far more than 'just a mother' and remains an outstanding model of self-sufficiency.

THE CABARET: *RUMBERAS* AND FEMALE DESIRE

Whereas Lamarque's characters are usually tricked or forced by circumstances into successful careers as singers while all they really want to be is wives and mothers, Ninón Sevilla and other *cabareteras* (María Antonieta Pons, Leticia Palma, and Meche Barba) present a different problematic. Much more sordid, their fates and entertainment activities project a virulent form of desire onto the screen. Nowhere else have screen women been so sexual, so wilful, so excessive, so able to express their anger at their fate through vengeance. As François Truffaut (under the pseudonym Robert Lacheney) wrote in *Cahiers du cinéma* in 1954,

> From now on we must take note of Ninón Sevilla, no matter how little we may be concerned with feminine gestures on the screen or elsewhere. From her inflamed look to her fiery mouth, everything is heightened in Ninón (her forehead, her lashes, her nose, her upper lip, her throat, her voice) . . . Like so

many missed arrows, [she is an] oblique challenge to bourgeois, Catholic, and all other moralities.[24]

Albeit uneasily, Lamarque's sophisticated performers could be narratively recuperated within an expanded domestic sphere, but Sevilla's excessively gendered gestures engaged melodramatic tropes beyond the point of hyperbole. Thus with Sevilla, the performative excess of the 'musical/performance melodrama' readies its zenith and the boundary between performance and melodrama disappears entirely.

. . .

In Mexico, the prostitute as emblem of desire, necessary evil, and mother of the nation (Malinche/Malintzin) has a prominent place in national cutural history. Prostitution might indeed be the oldest profession everywhere, but rarely have prostitutes been the preferred subject of so many popular culture texts as in Mexico. What we see in the *cabaretera* films of the late 1940s and 1950s is the culmination of a complex process in which the figure of the prostitute—albeit cloaked with the shameful aura of Malinche—became the site of a serious challenge to the *porfirian* moral order and an emblem of modernity.

Officially regulated and socially shunned, the post-Revolutionary prostitute and her spaces—the brothel, assignation house, and cabaret—had a distinct social function: they offered men a place to escape from the burdens of home and saintly wives and to engage in uninhibited conversations and the ambivalent pleasures of the flesh. Mexican culture always celebrated the myth of the prostitute, but in the 1920s the prostitute also assumed a different iconic status in the wildly popular romantic visions of singer-composer Agustín Lara. Idealized and simultaneously romantic and perverse, the prostitute of Lara's songs was not pitied for falling from grace. Lara's popular songs embodied a fatalistic worship of the 'fallen woman' as the only possible source of pleasure for modern man.[25] Though at first considered scandalous (and prohibited in schools by the Mexican Ministry of Public Education), Lara's audacious songs were quickly absorbed as a new popular culture idiom, the exaltation of the Lost Woman.[26]

By the late 1940s,[27] the cinema had completely assumed Lara's vision of the prostitute as an object of self-serving worship and his songs were the central dramatic impulse propelling the action of many *cabaretera* films. Thus, for example, *Aventurera* is clearly inspired by a song of the same title (sung by Pedro Vargas in the film):[28]

Sell your love expensively, adventuress
Put the price of grief on your past
And he who wants the honey from your mouth
Must pay with diamonds for your sin
Since the infamy of your destiny
Withered your admirable spring
Make your road less difficult,
Sell your love dearly, adventuress

Lara's songs idealized woman as a purchasable receptacle for man's physical needs—the ultimate commodity for modern Mexican society—but also invested her with the power of her sexuality: to sell at will, to name her price, to choose her victim. Nevertheless, as Monsiváis says, his songs also made the object of pleasure, once used, abstract:

> The deified prostitute protects the familiar one, exalts the patriarchy, and even moves the real prostitute herself to tears, granting a homey warmth to its evocation of exploited lives.[29]

In literature, in the songs of Agustín Lara and others, and finally in the cinema, the prostitute and the nightlife of which she is an emblem became an anti-utopian paradigm for modern life. The exaltation of female desire and sin and of the nightlife of clubs and cabarets clearly symbolized Mexico's new (post-World War II) cosmopolitanism and the first waves of developmentalism. The *cabaretera* films were the first decisive cinematic break with *porfirian* morality. Idealized, independent, and extravagantly sexual, the exotic *rumbera* was a social fantasy, but one through which *other* subjectivities could be envisioned, other psychosexual/social identities forged.

But the *rumbera* is not a simple model of resistance. When analyzed as part of a specific process of neurotic determinations[30] and in the context of the suffering mother, the emerging image of female subjectivity is deeply contradictory and without an easy resolution. In fact, it is a fantasy. As Ninón Sevilla with much self-awareness explains to her lover in the *cabaretera* film *Mulata* (Gilberto Martínez Solares, 1953), the impossible challenge of female identity is the insecurity of 'never knowing whether a man has loved me or desired me'. Not that one is necessarily preferable to the other—she can be either the wife *or* the sexual object—but that Mexican society insists that they are mutually exclusive.

Notes

Research for this essay was made possible, in part, by grants from the Mellon Foundation and the Roger Thayer Stone Center for Latin American Studies at Tulane University. Parts of this essay have appeared in 'Celluloid Tears: Melodrama in the "Old" Mexican Cinema', *Iris*, 13 (Summer 1991), and in *Mediating Two Worlds*, ed. Ana López, John King, and Manuel Alvarado (London: British Film Institute, 1992).

1. See, for example, Christine Gledhill, 'The Melodramatic Field: An Investigation' in *Home is Where the Heart Is: Studies in Melodrama and the Woman's Film*, ed. Christine Gledhill (London: British Film Institute, 1987), 5–39; Robert Lang, *American Film Melodrama: Griffith, Vidor, Minnelli* (Princeton: Princeton University Press, 1989); and Rick Altman, 'Dickens, Griffith, and Film Theory Today', *South Atlantic Quarterly*, 88 (Spring 1989): 321–59.
2. See, for example, the essays collected in Christine Gledhill (ed.), *Home is Where the Heart Is*, and Mary Ann Doane, *The Desire to Desire: The Woman's Film of the 1940s* (Bloomington: Indiana University Press, 1987).
3. Patrice Petro, *Joyless Streets: Women and Melodramatic Representation in Weimar Germany* (Princeton: Princeton University Press, 1989); Maureen Turim, 'French Melodrama: Theory of a Specific History', *Theater Journal*, 39 (October 1987); Ginnette Vincendeau, 'Melodramatic Realism: On Some French Women's Films in the 1930s', *Screen*, 30 (Summer 1989); Ella Shohat, *Israeli Cinema: East/West and the Politics of Representation* (Austin: University of Texas Press, 1989); Ravi Vasudevan, 'The Melodramatic Mode and the commercial Hindi Cinema', *Screen*, 30 (Summer 1989).
4. For this kind of analysis, see Carl J. Mora, 'Feminine Images in Mexican Cinema: The Family Melodrama; Sara García, "The Mother of Mexico" and the Prostitute', *Studies in Latin American Popular Culture*, 4 (1985), 228–35.
5. This period of the Latin-American cinema has generated much solid historical/archival research. For Mexico, see especially Emilio García Riera, *Historia Documental del Cine Mexicano*, 10 vols. to date (Mexico City: Ediciones Era, 1969), and Moises Viñas (ed.), *Historia del Cine Mexicano* (Mexico City: UNAM/UNESCO, 1987). In English, see Carl J. Mora, *Mexican Cinema: Reflections of a Society, 1896–1980* (Berkeley: University of California Press, 1982). For a succinct and well-informed comparative historical analysis of this period in English, see John King, *Magical Reels: A History of Cinema in Latin America* (London: Verso, 1990).
6. Although the Mexican cinema would not take off on an industrial scale until the 1936 international success of the *comedia ranchera* (ranch comedy) *Allá en el Rancho Grande* (*Out on the Big Ranch*, Fernando de Fuentes), melodramatic films were a staple from the 1930s through the 1960s. Aided by US wartime policies, (and US resentment of Argentina's neutrality), the Mexican cinema thrived during the war and immediate postwar periods, producing 124 films in 1950, the majority of which were melodramas. I am using the term *melodrama* here loosely, for the Mexican cinema (and other Latin American cinemas, especially Brazil's and its *chanchadas*) proved extraordinarily adept at generic mixing. I use the word *melodramatic* in its broadest sense, as a structuring principle of expectations and conventions against

which individual films establish their uniqueness as singular products, while recognizing that the term has a different currency in Latin America than in the United States or Europe.

7. Laura Mulvey, 'Melodrama in and out of the Home', in *High Theory/Low Culture*, ed. Colin MacCabe (New York: St Martin's Press, 1986), 95
8. Susan Sontag, 'Death of Tragedy', *Against Interpretation* (New York: Dell, 1966), 132–39.
9. An Aztec legend claimed that Quetzalcoatl, a feathered serpent god, would come from the East to redeem his people on a given day of the Aztec calendar, which, coincidentally, was the same day (21 April 1519) that Cortez and his men (fitting the description of Quetzalcoatl) landed in Vera Cruz. Thus Malintzin Tenepal became Cortez's translator, strategic advisor, and eventually mistress, believing that she was saving her people. This is how recent scholarship has reinterpreted the 400-year-old legacy of female betrayal, the founding moment of the Mexican nation. See Nancy Alarcón, 'Chicana's Feminist Literature: A Re-Vision Through Malintzin/or Malintzin: Putting Flesh Back on the Object', in *This Bridge Called My Back: Writings by Radical Women of Color*, ed. Cherrié Moraga and Gloria Anzaldúa (New York: Kitchen Table: Women of Color Press, 1983).
10. Cherrié Moraga, 'From a Long Line of Vendidas: Chicanas and Feminism', in *Feminist Studies/Critical Studies*, ed. Teresa de Lauretis (Bloomington: Indiana University Press, 1986), 174–75.
11. Octavio Paz, *The Labyrinths of Solitude: Life and Thought in Mexico* (New York: Grove Press, 1961), 85.
12. João Luiz Vieira and Robert Stam, 'Parody and Marginality: The Case of Brazilian Cinema', *Framework*, 28, (1985), reprinted in *The Media Reader*, ed Manuel Alvarado and John O. Thompson (London: British Film Institute, 1990), 96.
13. Carlos Monsiváis, 'Reir Llorando (Notas Sobre la Cultura Popular Urbana)', in *Politica Cultural del Estado Mexicano*, ed. Moises Ladrón de Guevara (Mexico City: Ed. GEFE/SEP, 1982), 70.
14. Peter Brooks, *The Melodramatic Imagination* (New Haven: Yale University Press, 1976), xiii, 14–15.
15. Monsiváis 'Reir Llorando', 27.
16. Jean Franco, *Plotting Women: Gender and Representation in Mexico* (New York: Columbia University Press, 1989), 102.
17. However, women did not win the right to vote in national elections until 1953.
18. The *género chico*, or *teatro frívolo*, was a vaudevillelike theatrical genre that developed in neighbourhood playhouses and tents. While the bourgeois theater staged classical melodramas from Spain and France that outlined the parameters of decent behavior and exalted heightened sensibilities in perfect Academic Spanish, the *género chico* thrived with popular characters and satire. Carnivalesque in the Bakhtinian sense, it included in its repertory taboo words and gestures and popular speech while exalting the grotesque and demanding a constant interaction between players and audience. See Ruth S. Lamb, *Mexican Theater of the Twentieth Century* (Claremont, Calif.: Ocelot Press, 1975), and Manuel Manón, *Historia del Teatro Popular de Mexico* (Mexico City: Editorial Cultura, 1932).

19. Carlos Monsiváis, 'El Cine Nacional', in *Historia General de Mexico*, vol. 4 (Mexico City: El Colegio de Mexico, 1976), 446.
20. See Jean Franco, 'The Incorporation of Women: A Comparison of North American and Mexican Popular Narrative', *Studies in Entertainment: Critical Approaches to Mass Culture*, ed. Tania Modleski (Bloomington: Indiana University Press, 1986).
21. E. Ann Kaplan. 'Mothering, Feminism, and Representation: The Maternal in Melodrama and the Woman's Film 1910–40', in *Home is Where the Heart Is*, 123–29.
22. For an extensive analysis of Mariá Félix's career and star persona, see Paco Ignacio Taíbo, *María Félix: 47 Pasos por el Cine* (Mexico City: Joaquín Mortiz/Planeta, 1985).
23. See Carlos Monsiváis, 'Crónica de Sociales: María Félix en dos tiempos', in *Escenas de Pudor y Liviandad* (Mexico City: Grijalbo, 1981), 161–68.
24. Robert Lacheney, *Cahiers du cinéma*, 30 (1954); cited by Emilio Garcia Riera, *Historia Documental del Cine Mexicano*, vol. 4, 132–34, and Jorge Ayala Blanco, *La Aventura del Cine Mexicano* (Mexico City: Ediciones Era, 1968), 144–45.
25. 'The Perverted One'

    To you, life of my soul, perverted woman whom I love
    To you, ungrateful woman
    To you, who makes me suffer and makes me cry
    I consecrate my life to you, product of evil and innocence
    All of my life is yours, woman
    I want you, even if they call you perverted.

26. As Eduardo Galeano summarizes it in *Century of the Wind*, 'Lara exalts the Lost woman, in whose eyes are seen sun-drunk palm trees; he beseeches Love from the Decadent One, in whose pupils boredom spreads like a peacock's tail; he dreams of the sumptuous bed of the silky-skinned Courtesan; with sublime ecstasy he deposits roses at the feet of the Sinful One and covers the Shameful Whore with incense and jewels in exchange for the honey of her mouth' (New York: Pantheon, 1988), 110.
27. As Jorge Ayala Blanco indicates, in a few months between 1947 and 1948 alone, precisely coinciding with the Mario Rodríguez Alemán *sexenio*, over twelve *cabaretera* films were produced. See *La Aventura del Cine Mexicano*, 137.
28. The Lara song 'Aventurera' had already been featured in the 1946 María Félix film *La Devoradora* (Fernando de Fuentes). At the time, Lara and Félix were enjoying a much-publicized, albeit short-lived, marriage, and he ostensibly wrote the song explicitly for her.
29. Carlos Monsiváis, *Amor Perdido* (Mexico City: Ediciones Era, 1977), 60.
30. John Hill. *Sex, Class and Realism: British Cinema 1956–1963* (London: British Film Institute, 1986).

27 Three Men and Baby M

Tania Modleski*

While some of the films in the current boom of baby boom movies suggest that woman's primary role is to be a mother, others show men taking over this role. The enormously popular French film, *Three Men and a Cradle*, and the American remake, *Three Men and a Baby*, which are about an infant named Mary who is left on the doorstep of the infant's father and his two male housemates, are interesting manifestations of the concern about father's rights that has intensified with the controversy over surrogate motherhood. Indeed, what we might call the American 'Baby M' film could be seen as the 'theory' of contemporary fathering, while surrogate motherhood is, or at least seemed for a time to be, the practice. This is a practice that involves, as Katha Pollitt has argued, women signing away one of the rights that, until the twentieth century, they rarely possessed: 'the right to legal custody of their children'.[1] It is in *this* historical context, in which women's rights as mothers have been virtually nonexistent, that a film like *Three Men and a Baby* must be seen, rather than being considered the product of a historically unprecedented, feminist-inspired, and altogether contemporary reconceptualization of the paternal role. To be sure, although *Three Men and a Baby* does its utmost to invest desire in the humorous and sentimental vision of a collective male fatherhood, it is a relatively benign version of a father's rights scenario, since it does in fact 'make room for Mommy' at the very end of the film. Nevertheless, by keeping the mother from the audience's sight until this point, the film effectively de-realizes her—just as, in Pollitt's argument, the term 'surrogate mother' renders the woman's role 'as notional as possible', thereby suggesting that since the (biological) mother is the surrogate, the father must be 'the real thing' (683). Moreover, even though the men in the film do ultimately incorporate

* Tania Modleski, 'Three Men and Baby M' from *Camera Obscura*, vol. 17 (May 1988), pp. 71–81, © Tania Modleski 1988, reprinted by permission of the publisher, The Johns Hopkins University Press and the author.

the mother, her return is experienced by the audience as an unfair intrusion and the men's inclusion of her in their ménage a generous (if also pragmatic) gesture.

Even in some of its small details the film surreally evokes, while comically displacing, paternal anxieties about men's relatively minimal role in the process of conception, a role that the very language used in the Baby M case worked to expand. For example, it employs a comic gag involving that infamous do-it-yourself inseminator: a turkey baster. In the men's initial fumbling attempts to give the baby a bath, they use the baster to squirt water at her vaginal and anal areas so as to avoid touching 'where the poop was'. As this image suggests, the film's popularity may in part be attributed to the way it arouses and contains, in a highly condensed manner, a whole host of male fears not only about fathering, but about female sexuality itself. I would like to look at some of these fears as well as to situate the film within the context of an older myth, embodied in John Ford's 1948 film *Three Godfathers*, a story which has been filmed so many times, it is impossible to escape the conclusion that it touches on some very powerful cultural themes. The fact that Ford's film involves a male child, however, will give us an opportunity to analyze how different the stakes are when the sex of the child is female.

The most striking aspect of *Three Men and a Baby*, on first viewing, is the explicitness with which the film reveals men's desire to usurp women's procreative function. In the scene where the three men, having become unwittingly involved with drug dealers, attempt to capture the criminals for the police, the baby's father, Jack (Ted Danson), disguises himself as a pregnant woman. We first see him in a long shot side view walking down the dark street, and then the camera switches to a frontal view, as he opens up his coat to reveal little Mary being carried in a sling. The image is a disturbing and unsettling one, reminiscent of those medieval icons of the virgin whose body opens up to display scenes of the holy family. Later, after Mary has been taken away by her mother and the men are mourning the baby's loss, Jack puts a pillow under his sweater and poses in front of a mirror. What are we to make of such scenes? It would appear that 'womb envy' and male hysteria are no longer latent thematics to be teased out by the psychoanalytically-oriented feminist critic; such envy *is* the manifest content of the film. Are we to conclude that, *pace* Freud, femininity in man is no longer something to be denied and repressed, no longer the object of 'normal' male 'contempt', but rather a condition that man desires for himself? Are men now prepared openly to avow their bisexuality?

There are two points to be made here: first, that envy of woman can coexist with castration anxiety and with the profoundest misogyny—that men can want to *be* women and still hate and fear them—and, second, that this envy is in fact concomitant with a fear of feminization, even though existing in logical contradiction to it, so that male identification with woman is hedged about with many varieties of 'masculine protest'.

Indeed, the pedophilic aspects of both the French and American versions of the film point to a kind of revulsion on the part of the men to mature womanhood. That Walt Disney should produce, and audiences receive as 'heartwarming', a film laden with jokes about a female baby as an adequate object of sexual desire for three aging bachelors (for example, when Jack takes a shower with her) is perhaps not surprising, but it is certainly disturbing, given statistics which show female children to be the chief victims of sexual abuse and males to comprise the overwhelming majority of perpetrators. In both films the men lose interest in sleeping around after Mary becomes part of their lives—a development we're clearly supposed to approve, since it shows the men learning to commit to someone. (As the theme song has it, 'Something happened, baby, in my life/The minute I saw you/All the others faded from my life/The minute I saw you'.) The fact that this someone is less than a year old, the fact that, as regards the rest of the sex, the men have thrown out the woman with the bath water—ie. in giving up philandering, they virtually give up interest in women—may perhaps be easily overlooked. Indeed, the ending of the French film points to the kind of comic inversion at the heart of both films, suggesting the infantilization of woman and the sexualization of babyhood that is part of the film wish. At the end of that film, the mother, exhausted from trying to care for the baby alone, is shown *asleep in her baby's crib*, while the baby, walking for the first time, advances toward the camera, and is caught in a freeze frame—a device that, originating in the French New Wave, has become a cliché of film and television, but is entirely appropriate to the pedophilic impulse to freeze the life process so that the object will not outgrow the desire. Even the baby's name, 'Mary', points to this reversal of mother/child roles since 'Mary', Christianity's mythical mother, becomes Mary the magical foundling—and it also, in a related ideological inversion, expresses a *male* desire to undergo virgin birth, to dispense with the Woman's part in conception altogether.

It is clear that in this film fear of woman, along with the castration anxiety her sight provokes, are not less pronounced than in older classical narrative film, but are, in fact, rather more so. In the film's opening sequence, Peter (played by Tom Selleck, whose TV character, Magnum, is also part of a trio of male buddies) is being given a birthday party, during which many jokes are made about the men's prowess (or lack of it) with women. Michael (Steve Guttenberg), carrying a video camera, conducts a mock interview with Rebecca, the woman with whom Peter has an 'open' relationship, and he asks her why she finds Peter attractive. She responds that he has an 'amazing . . .' and substitutes a knee in the groin for the word. The anxiety about castration, conjured up everywhere in the text, is even projected onto the mise-en-scène: in the hallway the walls are painted with pictures of chorus girls whose legs are high in the air, their genital areas emphasized by a lamp which hangs on a level with their crotches. During the party, Peter disappears from the heterosexual scene and is found in his room with a group of men who are watching video tapes of him playing basketball; Rebecca persuades him to rejoin the party only with great difficulty. When the baby arrives, interestingly enough after the birthday party, this event elicits a hysterical reaction from Michael and Peter (Jack, the father, is out of the country). While Peter runs in his jogging clothes to buy food and diapers, Michael is left to care for the baby, and he tries desperately to entertain it so it will stop crying, at one point pulling open his shirt to show the baby a hairy chest, at another turning on the television, and then turning it off again quickly when Dr. Ruth appears on the screen saying, 'Women are wondering, are they having orgasms; men are worried about their penises.' The comic anxiety about bodies, the urge to put masculinity on display (Michael's hairy chest; Peter/Tom Selleck's muscular arms and legs, the famous 'thighs and whiskers')[2] are provoked by the arrival of this tiny incarnation of sexual difference, and build up to a gag in which the men try to diaper the baby, emitting sounds of disgust because she has 'doodled', while the camera in some shockingly voyeuristic shots focuses on the baby's genitals. The confusion between genitality and anality exhibited here in the conflict between sound and image are symptomatic of the psychosexual dynamics of the text as a whole—a confusion, which, as we shall see, amounts to a regression to a childhood fantasy that denies what Freud calls 'the clear-cut distinction between anal and genital processes' insisted upon in adult sexuality.[3]

In fact, one of the main sources of the film's humor lies in its play on the meanings of the word shit. When Jack goes away, he asks his housemates to receive a package that he has agreed to hold for a friend, and when the baby arrives, the men mistakenly believe her to be the package. They are so preoccupied by the baby that when the real package, containing heroin, arrives, it goes unnoticed. A few days later, two men come by to pick up the heroin, and they converse with Michael at cross purposes about 'the shit'. Michael says, 'there's been shit all over this place for days,' and the men ask, 'Well, did you put the shit back?' The film becomes virtually obsessed with the fact of shit: a policeman's horse 'befouls' the sidewalk in front of the house; Michael plants the heroin in the baby's diaper, and the head of the narcotic's squad assumes when he holds her that she needs to be changed; the heroin is subsequently hidden in the 'garbage pail with the other dirty diapers'; and, finally, the three men almost fail in their efforts to entrap the criminals because Jack goes back to the car at a crucial moment to change the baby, who has once again 'doodled'.

The equation of feces with baby (the baby mistaken for the 'shit', the heroine for the heroin), which is *the* central joke of the film is, as we know from Freud, a common fantasy dating from childhood; the child first views the feces as a 'gift' and later they 'come to acquire the meaning of "baby"—for babies, according to one of the sexual theories of children, are acquired by eating and are born through the bowels'.[4] The 'cloacal theory', which is at least as old as Dante (according to a traditional mythology, the devil gives birth to babies by shitting them out), is particularly suited to facilitate the fantasy, expressed so forthrightly in the film, of male usurpation of women's reproductive function. We might even speculate that the necessity of relinquishing anal eroticism and its attendant fantasies results in a feeling of deprivation that aggravates male envy of women for possessing certain pleasures and privileges (few and equivocal as they may be) denied to men. As Lou Andreas Salomé, whom Freud cites, points out, 'From that time on, what is "anal" remains the symbol of everything that is to be repudiated and excluded from life'. And this is so because 'the prohibition against getting pleasure from anal activity and its products is the first occasion on which the infant has a glimpse of an environment hostile to his instinctual impulses, on which he learns to separate his own entity, from this alien one and on which he carries out the first "repression" of his possibilities for pleasure'.[5] As this passage helps us to understand, however—and this point cannot be stressed enough at a time when feminists are increasingly becoming preoccupied with masculinity (as this volume attests), searching for ways to displace the primacy of castration in film theory and in psychoanalysis, and affirming as tacitly feminist the 'nonphallic' values of male subjectivity—the regressive fantasy involving babies and bowels in no way precludes castration anxiety but, on the contrary, exacerbates it: it is, in fact a prototype of it. 'Feces', 'child,' and 'penis', writes Freud, 'form a unity, an unconscious concept . . .—the concept, namely, of a little thing that can become separated from one's body'[6] (what Lacan calls *objet petit a*). Further, in his case history of the Wolf Man, Freud explicitly addresses himself to the question of how castration anxiety may coexist with 'an identification with women by means of the bowel'. Admitting that this state of affairs is a logical contradiction, Freud adds that this 'is not saying much', since the unconscious is in fact characterized by conflict and contradiction. Analyzing the Wolf Man, Freud shows how the identification actually *gives rise* to the dread; for not only does the substitution of the bowel for the womb fantasmatically empower men by enabling them to appropriate women's reproductive function, but, in being associated with the female genitalia, the bowel itself comes to signify castration—'the necessary condition of femininity'.[7]

Given that the baby in the film signifies castration in an overdetermined way—both because of her genitals and because, as 'shit', she is psychically associated with the male desire to become woman—she not surprisingly is made into the comically fetishized object of disavowal, and is masculinized in a variety of ways. For example, when Peter, the architect, takes the baby on the construction site of one of his jobs, she wears a little pink hardhat that later becomes the object over which he mourns after Mary's mother takes her away. At another point, he reads to her in a tender, soothing voice an account of a bloody boxing match from the newspaper. He says to Michael, who, it will be remembered, did *not* allow Mary to listen to Dr. Ruth talking about women's orgasms, that it's not 'what you say but how you say it'.

Remarking further on the significance of the anal zone, the organ by which the Wolf Man fantasmatically achieved an identification with women, Freud tells us that this organ was also the means by which a 'passive homosexual attitude to men was able to express itself'.[8] We can speculate that the popularity of a film like *Three Men and a Baby* is partly attributable to its successful negotiation of homosocial desire—male bonding in this case being effected through the agency of a baby girl, rather than through the exchange of women, as has usually been the case. Father's rights, male appropriation of femininity, and male homoeroticism fuse perfectly in a film that nearly squeezes woman out of the picture altogether, just as the mother is squeezed to one side of the frame in the last shot of the film.

In this final shot, as the four push the baby stroller off screen, we are left facing the picture of the three men whose caricatures have been painted on the elevator doors. Only now, in addition to a picture of the mother painted in on one side, a picture of the baby has been added, exactly at crotch level of the men. We are presented with a perfect image of disavowal: the baby, whose arrival had given rise to the men's feminine identification and whose genitals had signified castration anxiety and induced hysteria, is equated with the endangered penises. All of those little objects which may be separated from the body are, the image assures us, intact. In the 1980s version of 'Superman', he is the one who 'has it all'—penis *and* baby: in fact, the perfect penis-baby.

That the men have gotten away with something, have, indeed, subverted the law, is suggested by the film's criminal subplot, involving the heroin package. Given that the men are involved in an 'unlawful', 'unnatural' appropriation of femininity, it is highly significant that the package containing an illegal substance arrives at the same time as the baby and is confused with it. The narcotics officer assigned to the case is revealed to be a family man and at one point he asks to hold the baby, whose diaper is loaded with heroin. While Michael tries to refuse, Peter, unaware of the presence of the incriminating diaper, forces Michael to hand the baby over to the inspector. Later, the men manage to appease the law by entrapping the real criminals—a plot which, as we have seen, actually involves the baby's father dressing up as a pregnant woman. When the police arrive on the scene, the narcotics officer thanks the men and then asks again to hold the baby, but at this point the men triumphantly refuse, each saying 'no' in turn. Unlike the trajectory of many older Hollywood films, which involves the heroes' accepting the father and the castration he represents, in this film the men ultimately reject paternal authority and the castration he represents: in short, they refuse to grow up.

Three Men and a Baby is a profoundly regressive film on many levels. On the psychic level, as I have tried to demonstrate by analyzing the central joke as if it were a highly condensed, overdetermined dream image, it involves a regression to the anal stage. On the social and narrative levels, it involves a desire to reject the symbolic father and to refuse castration. This Peter Pan fantasy (*about* a man named Peter, and brought to us by Walt Disney) even incorporates a kind of

Wendy figure at the end, a woman who is not (or not any longer) the object of any man's desire but part of the group which gets to play perpetually with the baby. (There is even a scene in which Peter tastes the milk from the nipple of the bottle, and then pours it into his coffee.) That mass art involves 'the infantilizing of culture' has been remarked upon often—by Ariel Dorfman, for example, who points not only to the adult values that are projected onto children and their culture but to 'the infantilization that the mass media seem to radiate onto adults'.[9] Long before Dorfman, T. W. Adorno noted the same process of infantilization when he analyzed the lyrics of popular songs, but Adorno could not have anticipated the latest postmodern twist to the process given by the film, in which song lyrics addressed to one's 'baby' would *literally* refer to a baby ('Little baby want to hold you tight/ I don't ever want to say goodnight'), though retaining, of course, the sexual charge they have gained from years of metaphoricity.[10]

It becomes apparent that the film is centered around a paradox: in order for the men to be the kind of fathers they want to be (fathers who also take on the role of mothers, of nurturers), the men actually have to deny the father who represents the law (though, as we have seen, not without hedging their bets). In this respect it is interesting to compare the film to its antecedent, John Ford's *Three Godfathers*, which deals with three outlaws who inherit a male baby from a woman they encounter in the desert while they are hiding out. Shortly before dying, the woman names the baby Robert William Pedro Hightower, after the three men (John Wayne is Robert Hightower, a name whose phallic connotations scarcely require commentary). From the moment they receive the baby, the men are reformed characters, and their sole mission is to get him out of the desert and into New Jerusalem (the film draws explicitly on the myth of the Christ child), a journey in which they find themselves increasingly guided by the Bible. Two of the men—William and Pedro—die in the course of the journey, but come back as ghosts to encourage Hightower when he is on the verge of succumbing to exhaustion.

Preoccupied with sacrifice, redemption and the scriptural law of the father, *Three Godfathers* suggests precisely how the narrative dramatically shifts when the baby is male and Oedipus is at stake. But even in this film there are moments of narrative instability and turbulence, provoked, I would argue, by the very fact that the men are in some sense taking over the role of the mother, and hence in danger of being 'unmanned'. Many of the film's jokes are related to the men's inability to perform certain 'naturally' feminine tasks, like breast-feeding. The sense of uneasiness instigated by the film's very premise may also be detected in the other main source of humor in the film, which has to do with the problem of names. Early in the film, the men encounter the town marshall (Ward Bond), on whose shingle is written the name 'B. Sweet.' Hightower laughs uproariously at this name, and then laughs again when he discovers that Sweet's wife calls her husband by the feminine name of Pearly, although Sweet calls *himself* Buck. Later the joke is on Hightower, when at his trial, the judge reveals his middle name to be Marmaduke. Finally, throughout the middle part of the film, a running gag has the men arguing about the baby's name: Hightower keeps referring to him as 'Little Robert,' whereupon the second man insists, 'Robert *William*,' and the third, 'Robert William *Pedro*'. (We might compare *Three Men and a Baby*'s use of the generic female name 'Mary'). This is a film, then, that is obsessed with the idea of passing on the name of the 'father'—a concern that obviously could be expressed only in relation to a male child—while at the same time revealing through its comical play with names an insecurity about masculine identity and a discomfort with the close homosocial relationship of the three men whose 'marriage' is suggested by the composite name given the son.

One moment of *Three Godfathers* is particularly notable for the hysteria of its comedy: when the men are first learning to care for the baby, they read in a book that its body should be rubbed with oil. In a rather lengthy closeup Hightower's hand is shown greasing the baby's backsides, while the men's laughter fills the soundtrack, its prolonged hilarity far exceeding the response justified by the image. The sight of an exposed, naked and vulnerable body in the midst of the repressive world of Ford's west provokes this hysterical reaction because it would seem to violate several strong taboos—taboos relating to pedophilia, homosexuality, and even sensuality itself, i.e. the very intimate pleasure of the parent's bodily contact with the child. According to one of the most famous articles on John Ford, the landmark essay 'John Ford's *Young Mr. Lincoln*' written by the *Cahiers du Cinéma* collective, such moments of comedy in Ford's films are signs 'of a constant disorder of the universe', a disorder which subverts the 'castrating action' of the Ideal Law, and are thus to be affirmed precisely because they point to a desire capable of undermining the patriarchal order.[11]

It would appear that now, in the 1980s, we have precisely the (fully comic) film the *Cahiers* editors might have approved, a film that rescues the father from his repressive, castrating function and admits his desire for the child. It is important, of course, to recognize that such an illicit desire may be most easily embodied in the genre of comedy, which facilitates disavowal by allowing us to deny the seriousness of its concerns. Thus, comedy, as the realm of the carnivalesque, has always permitted a certain freedom of expression in relation to our collective anxieties, fears, and wishes (a fact that is often ignored by auteurist critics who tend to neglect issues of genre—thus, for instance, Howard Hawks's comedies are considered unique for their inversions of the all-male world of adventure films; Pee-wee Herman and Jerry Lewis are viewed as exemplary male hysterics; etc.). Nevertheless, despite the notorious problems inherent in claims for the subversiveness of comedy as a genre, feminists themselves have found the realm of comedy and carnival to be an important arena both for the working out of utopian desire and for ideological and psychical subversions of the dominant regime. Critics like Juliet Mitchell and Laura Mulvey, drawing on the work of Julia Kristeva (the latter indebted to Mikhail Bakhtin), have discussed the relation of carnival to the preoedipal—the traditional province of the maternal—and the way it semiotically disrupts the symbolic order, challenging norms, hierarchies, and established systems.[12] In some ways *Three Men and a Baby*, with it's carnivalesque defiance of psychic and social categories (related to gender, age, etc.), its refusal to renounce the pleasures proscribed by the symbolic order, seems to confirm the insights of these theorists. But while the film may indeed be said to situate itself in the preoedipal, it is clearly very far from engaging in a utopian celebration of the maternal; on the contrary, it constitutes a flagrant encroachment of the (ever multiplying) fathers onto the mother's traditional domain.

The desire expressed by the film for what we might see as a kind of preoedipal father/child relation corresponds, interestingly, to a development in contemporary critical theory. A recent lecture on Oedipus Rex with which feminist film theorist Laura Mulvey toured the United States, drew on the work of Marie Balmary, whose *Psychoanalyzing Psychoanalysis* searches for a profounder understanding of the lessons Oedipus Rex holds for psychoanalysis and finds the key in the story of Laius, father of Oedipus (see especially Balmary's chapter rather ominously entitled 'Oedipus Has Still More to Teach Us').[13] Mulvey expressed the desire to use Balmary's insights to find a way of importing the father into the preoedipal relation, a move that has in fact already been theorized by Julia Kristeva. In the first chapter of her book *Tales of Love*, Kristeva waxes lyrical about the concept of 'imaginary paternity', speaking of 'a warm but dazzling, domesticated paternity', one that while it guarantees the subject's entry into an Oedipal disposition, 'can also be playful and sublimational'. Kristeva writes eloquently of the desire for such an entity:

> Maintaining against the winds and high tides of our modern civilization the requirement of a stern father who, through his Name, brings about separation, judgment, and identity, constitutes a necessity, a more or less pious wish. But we can only note that jarring such sternness, far from leaving us orphaned or inexorably psychotic, reveals multiple and varied destinies for paternity—notably archaic, imaginary paternity.[14]

One might note that in the Baby M case a similar desire to jar such 'sternness' led many feminists to support Mr. Stern himself, and to reject the claims of the biological mother of the child, Mary Beth Whitehead. Women like Mary Gordon in her essay in *Ms.* magazine wrote compellingly about men's need to nurture—an argument that, as Janice Doane and Devon Hodges point out, ironically allied her with both nature and the symbolic order—with, that is, 'a judge who argues in favor of men's driving need to procreate'.[15]

While the desire to find alternatives to harsh notions of phallic paternity is entirely understandable, feminists need to be very clear about whether in endorsing these alternatives they are undermining patriarchal structures or, on the contrary, shoring up patriarchy against its ruins—in this case, ironically, by relocating it *in* the ruins of a more ancient civilization. Freud, it will be recalled, likened the discovery of the girl's preoedipal relation with the mother to the discovery in archaeology of an older civilization buried beneath a more modern one.[16] Now, along with the mother, Kristeva would place an 'archaic father' who 'introduces the Third Party as a condition of psychic life, to the extent that it is a loving life (34)'. Although woman in Kristeva's scheme still has a place (which would seem, however, to be dispensable since Kristeva says this father is the same as both parents), it is a very traditional one—the place of the female whose desire for the male Other initiates the child into 'the loving life'. Yet we can see from *Three Men and a Baby* that this place can be occupied by men on behalf of themselves and each other. Indeed, the men in the film show themselves to be continually preoccupied with, desirous of, the image of themselves *as* fathers: in a swimming pool, surrounded by mothers and babies, they take pictures of themselves playing with Mary, and when the child is taken away, one of them whiles away the lonely hours looking at videotapes of himself and the baby.

Nevertheless, while optional, women are not altogether absent from the picture; rather, they serve further to legitimate and guarantee the men's appropriation of the maternal. In a montage showing the men performing various activities with their baby, they are surrounded by women who are charmed not just, it would appear, by the baby herself but by this 'warm' and 'dazzling' incarnation of one of the 'varied destinies' of paternity. In short, the women occupy a role similar to that taken up by Kristeva—and consistent with the one she herself theorizes: that of the woman who so desires the father, desires to save the father (from himself, as it were) that she authorizes the widening of the patriarchal sphere and underwrites the diminishment of her function within this sphere.

Such is also the role of the female audience of the film. Although, as I have tried to show, the film is entirely preoccupied with male fantasies and fears, it seems clear that the women in the audience are as amused and deeply touched by the film as men are—probably more so. No doubt the reasons for this appeal are complex. In my experience of different audiences, much of the laughter at the beginning of the film was aimed at the men for the incompetence they displayed in dealing with the child, although by the end, the pathos of the situation had clearly overwhelmed all other response. No doubt, too, the film speaks to a legitimate desire on the part of women for men to become more involved in interpersonal relationships, to be more nurturant as individuals, and to assume greater responsibility for childcare. At the same time, it suggests the limits and problems of this aspect of the feminist agenda. Some years ago, both Dorothy Dinnerstein and Nancy Chodorow wrote forcefully of the need for men to contribute more extensively to parenting arrangements—a development which they believed would lead to the psychic and social recognition of women as full human beings. However, *Three Men and a Baby* demonstrates the insufficiency of this solution to the problem of misogyny: it is possible, the film shows, for men to respond to the feminist demand for their increased participation in childrearing in such a way as to make women more marginal than ever. In the final analysis, the effect of films like *Three Men and a Baby* and *Three Men and a Cradle* and of television programs like *My Two Dads* (about a girl who lives with two men, either of whom could be her father) and *Full House* (about three men and *three* little girls) is simply to give men more options than they already have in patriarchy: they can be real fathers, 'imaginary' fathers, godfathers, *and* in the older sense of the term, surrogate mothers. The fact that in every one of these cases the children reared exclusively by men are female suggests that the daughters are being seduced *away* from feminism and into a world where they may become so 'dazzled' by the proliferating varieties of paternity that they are unable to see whose interests are really being served.

Notes

1. Katha Pollitt, 'The Strange Case of Baby M', *The Nation* (23 May 1987), 683.
2. 'Thighs and Whiskers–The Fascination of "Magnum, p.i."' is the title of an article by Sandy Flitterman, in *Screen* 26: 2 (March–April 1985), 42–59.
3. Sigmund Freud, *Three Essays on the Theory of Sexuality*, trans. James Strachey (New York: Basic Books, 1962), 53 n.
4. Freud, *Three Essays*, 52.
5. Freud, *Three Essays*, 53 n.
6. Sigmund Freud, From 'History of an Infantile Neurosis' (New York: Collier Books, 1963), 275.
7. Freud, 'History of an Infantile Neurosis', 268. Obviously, to point out what some feminists seem to be losing sight of—that we still live in a phallocentric culture, where castration is very much at stake for men—is not to say that men do in fact *possess* the phallus.
8. Freud, 'History of an Infantile Neurosis', 268.
9. Ariel Dorfman, 'The Infantilizing of Culture', in *American Media and Mass Culture: Left Perspectives*, ed. Donald Lazere (Berkeley: University of California Press, 1987), 149. See Dorfman's *The Empire's Old Clothes: What the Lone Ranger, Babar, and Other Innocent Heroes Do to Our Minds* (New York: Pantheon Books, 1983).
10. Theodor W. Adorno (with the assistance of George Simpson), 'On Popular Music', *Studies in Philosophy and Social Science*, 9: 1 (1941), 17–48.
11. Editors of *Cahiers du Cinéma*, 'John Ford's *Young Mr. Lincoln*', in *Movies and Methods*, ed. Bill Nichols (Berkeley: University of California Press, 1976), 526.
12. Laura Mulvey, 'Changes', *Discourse*, 7 (Spring 1985), 11–30. Juliet Mitchell, 'Psycho-analysis: Child Development and Femininity', *Women the Longest Revolution: Essays in Feminism, Literature and Psycho-analysis* (London: Virago, 1984), 291. For an interesting feminist analysis of carnival, see Mary Russo, 'Female Grotesques: Carnival and Theory', *Feminist Studies/Critical Studies*, ed. Teresa de Lauretis (Bloomington: Indiana University Press, 1986), 213–229.
13. Marie Balmary, *Psychoanalyzing Psychoanalysis: Freud and the Hidden Fault of the Father*, trans. Ned Lukacher (Baltimore: The Johns Hopkins University Press, 1982), 7–24.

14. Julia Kristeva, *Tales of Love*, trans. Leon S. Roudiez (New York: Columbia University Press, 1987), 46.
15. Mary Gordon, '"Baby M"—New Questions about Biology and Destiny', *Ms.* (June 1987), 25–28. Janice Doane and Devon Hodges, 'The Baby M Case: A Risky Business', forthcoming in *Differences: A Journal of Feminist Cultural Studies.*
16. Sigmund Freud, 'Female Sexuality', *Standard Edition of the Complete Psychological Works*, trans. James Strachey (London: Hogarth Press), vol. 21.

28 The Carapace that Failed: Ousmane Sembene's *Xala*

Laura Mulvey*

> The film language of Xala can be constructed on the model of an African poetic form called 'sem-enna-worq' which literally means 'wax and gold'. The term refers to the 'lost wax' process in which a goldsmith creates a wax form, casts a clay mold around it, then drains out the wax and pours in pure molten gold to form the valued object. Applied to poetics, the concept acknowledges two levels of interpretation, distinct in theory and representation. Such poetic form aims to attain maximum ideas with minimum words. 'Wax' refers to the most obvious and superficial meaning, whereas the 'gold' embedded in the art work offers the 'true' meaning, which may be inaccessible unless one understands the nuances of folk culture.
>
> (Teshome H. Gabriel)[1]

This quotation illustrates the intense interest that recent African cinema holds for any film theory concerned with the 'hieroglyphic' tradition, and potential, of cinema. The catch-all phrase 'hieroglyph' is useful in that it evokes three processes: a code of composition, the encapsulation, that is, of an idea in an image at a stage just prior to writing; a mode of address that asks an audience to apply their ability to decipher the poetics of the 'screen script'; and, finally, the work of criticism as a means of articulating the poetics that an audience recognises but leaves implicit. My critical perspective cannot include the 'nuances of folk culture' or, indeed, other important aspects of African culture and history but attempts to present *Xala*'s significance for film theory beyond its immediate cultural context. While as a critic I would like to fulfil the third deciphering function, that of 'articulation', my critical process does not aspire to go beyond making explicit the first

* Laura Mulvey, 'The Carapace That Failed: Ousmane Sembene's *Xala*' from *Fetishism and Curiosity* by Laura Mulvey (Third Text, 1991), reprinted by permission of the publisher and the author.

two hieroglyphic processes, that is the 'screen script' and its mode of address to an audience. African cinema should no longer be seen as a 'developing' cinema. It has already made an original and significant contribution to contemporary cinema and its cumulative history and aesthetics.

The germinal ground in which the African cinema developed in the post-colonial period was the francophone sub-Sahara, above all Senegal and Mali, and first of all with Ousmane Sembene. Geographically, this area has its own cultural traditions dating back to the old Mande empire founded by Sundiata in the 11th century, and revived in resistance to French colonialism as the Dyula Revolution led by Samoury Toure in the late 19th century. It was not until independence in 1960, when the French were abandoning most of their African colonies in the hope of holding on to Algeria, that the conditions for an African cinema came into being. Sembene's work, first as a writer, then as a film-maker, crosses the 1960 divide and is also divided by it. During the 1950s, he had made his name as an African writer, writing, of course, in French. His first novel, *Le Docker noir* (1956), was written while he was working in the docks and as a union organiser in Marseille. *Les Bouts de bois de Dieu* was published in 1960 (after a number of others) based on his experiences during the famous 1947–8 strike on the Bamako–Dakar railway. Then, in 1961, immediately after Senegal achieved independence, he went to the Soviet Union to study at the Moscow Film School and his first short film, *Borom Sarret*, was shown at the Tours film festival in 1963. *La Noire de . . .*, released in 1966, was the first full-length feature from the sub-Sahara.

Sembene's novels were written during the period in which African poets, novelists, Marxist theorists and intellectuals in Paris were grouped around the journal *Présence Africaine.* Sembene was critical of the *négritude*[2] movement with which they were identified. He considered the concept to be irrelevant to the popular resistance that grew into the independence movement, and he identified himself with, and was part of, the anti-colonial struggle in Senegal rather than intellectual circles in Paris. While he wrote novels in French during the colonial period, the cinema offered Sembene a means of contact with popular traditions and his films are directed towards the cultural needs of the ordinary people, who had no access either to the French language or to traditions of written culture:

> Often the worker or the peasant don't have time to pause on the details of their daily lives; they live them and do not have time to tie them down. The

film-maker though, can link one detail to another to put a story together. There is no longer a traditional storyteller in our days and I think the cinema can replace him.[3]

This last observation is characteristic of Sembene's commitment to promoting and transforming traditional culture, to using the technological developments of Western society in the interests of African culture. Sembene was more interested in finding a dialectical relationship between the two cultures than in an uncritical nostalgia for pre-colonial pure Africanness. This position is underlined by his background as a worker and his Marxism.

The cinema can speak across the divisions created by oral tradition and written language and is, therefore, a perfect mechanism for a cultural dialectic. It can perpetuate an oral cultural tradition as the spoken language plays a major role in cinema; and it can bring oral traditions into the modernity of the post-colonial. Sembene himself was the son of a fisherman and self-educated into French literacy. His own Wolof language, like the Mandinke, had no written equivalent. In the social structure of the Mande tradition, the task of maintaining and creating oral culture devolved onto a specific social grouping, the *griots*, dependent on the nobility in pre-colonial times. They functioned as the repository of historical memory, traditionally that of the kings and their families, and as creators, among other things, of poetry and music. African culture has had to negotiate a contemporary *modus vivendi* between writing in French, its own traditional oral forms and the facts of post-colonial cultural life. While the figure of the *griot* may evoke the oral culture of the pre-colonial past, he (and, sometimes, she) spoke primarily to an elite. The cinema economically and politically had to address a mass audience in post-colonial Africa.

In *Xala* the question of language is at the political centre of the drama. The economic division between the indigenous entrepreneurial elite and the impoverished people is reflected in a division between French and Wolof. The elite use French exclusively to communicate among themselves and as their official language. They speak Wolof only across class and gender lines and treat it as inferior and archaic. In the novel *Xala*, which Sembene wrote up from his script while searching for funds for the film, the young people on the Left have developed a written equivalent for Wolof and are publishing a journal in their native language for the first time. In the film, Sembene sets up a parallel between two figures who are quite marginal to the story but significant for its politics. One is a young student selling the new journal; the other is a peasant, robbed of his village's savings which he had brought to town to buy seed. Both get caught in the police round-up of beggars that forms the film's central tableau, and become integrated into the beggar community. Any moves by the people towards cultural and economic advance and self-sufficiency are dashed in the polarisation between the entrepreneurial elite and the underclass it creates.

Although the cinema has often been evoked as a continuation of the *griot* tradition, there are important points of difference besides those of class. The oral tradition of the *griot* was based on verbal language as such. The cinema sets up a dialectic between what is said and what is shown. One can undercut, or play off, the other. In *Xala*, Sembene uses the language of cinema to create a poetics of politics. He gives visibility to the forms, as opposed to the content, of social contradiction and then, through the forms, illuminates the content. He forges links between underlying structures, or formations, and the symptoms they produce on the surface, stamped, as it were, onto everyday existence, across all classes. This is an aesthetic that depends on making visible those aspects of economic and political structure that are either invisible or repressed in articulated language. It is a cinema of what cannot be said. Underlying structures mark the lives of the ruling elite as well as the people, and as the story unfolds signs and symptoms signal an insistent return of the repressed. The repression is both political, of the people by the ruling elite, and psychoanalytic, of the ruling elite by their relation to Frenchness, its consequent phobias and fetishisms. The two spheres become increasingly interlinked throughout the film. While Sembene's analysis of signs is always historical and, in the last resort, materialist, he also acknowledges the place of sexuality and the structure of the psyche in the symptomology of neo-colonialism. There are shades of Frantz Fanon's *Black Skin, White Masks.*

Xala is set in Senegal after independence when the presence of the colonial power is concealed behind a façade of self-government. The story's premise is that independence politics had become inextricably compromised with colonial financial structures. The opening, pre-credit, sequence of *Xala* shows a crowd celebrating as a group of African businessmen expel the French from the Chamber of Commerce and take control of their own economy. The people in the crowd are depicted in such a way as to evoke 'Africanness', with bare breasts, dancing and drums. These connotative images never appear again in the film; (thereafter the characters' clothes and appearance are appropriate for the Islamic sub-Sahara). The businessmen are dressed in loose shirts and trousers made out of 'African'- type materials. They appear at the top of the steps, ejecting a few objects that evoke the colonising culture (including a bust of Marie-Antoinette). The camera is placed at the bottom of the steps. As the men turn to go into the building, the camera dips slightly to change its angle and the steps suddenly resemble a stage on which a performance has just taken place. When the camera joins the men back in the Chamber, they are dressed in the dark European business suits that they will wear for the rest of the film. While the crowds still celebrate, a posse of police arrive and, under the command of one of the recently expelled Frenchmen, push the people back from the central space in front of the Chambre de Commerce, literally enacting the process of domination and repression. The other two Frenchmen then enter the Chambre and place an attaché case in front of each African businessman. Each case is full of money. The two men step backwards with the silent subservience they maintain, as 'advisers', for the rest of the film. The sequence closes as El Hadji Abdou Kader Beye invites his colleagues to the party celebrating his marriage to a third wife. All the speeches are in French.

I have chosen the word 'carapace' to evoke the central poetic and politcal themes in *Xala* in order to convey an image of vulnerable flesh covered by a protecting shell. The carapace doubles as a mask behind which the ruling elite camouflages itself, adopting the clothes, language and behaviour of its former colonial masters. The carapace also evokes the social structure of neo-colonialism. The entrepreneurial bourgeoisie live the life of an upper crust, floating and parasitical on the lives of the people. In *Xala* the carapace conceals not simply vulnerable flesh, but flesh that is wounded by class exploitation. Whereas a scab indicates that a wound has developed its own organic means of protection, the carapace of neo-colonialism denies and disavows the wound and prevents healing. The elite encase themselves in expensive Western cars, while the beggars' bodies are crippled by deformed or missing limbs. Concealed corruption at the top of the social hierarchy manifests itself on the wounded bodies of the dispossessed. During the film, the gap between the two groups, the beggars and the elite, narrows until the final scene which brings them together. The central character is El Hadji, a member of the entrepreneurial elite, who finds he is impotent when he marries his third wife. A tension then runs through the film between the vulnerability of his body, his failed erection, on one side and, on the other, his outward carapace made up of European props. In the end, his sexual vulnerability has brought him to realise that the carapace has failed and he exposes his own body, naked and covered in spit, to the beggars' ritual of humiliation and salvation.

During a climactic scene just before the end of the film, El Hadji is being hounded out of the Chamber of Commerce by his equally corrupt colleagues. His most vindictive antagonist seizes his attaché case, and opens it to find it empty except for the magic object with which El Hadji had attempted to ward off the curse of impotence, the *xala*, that has afflicted him. His enemy holds it up for public ridicule. El Hadji seizes it and waves it defiantly in the faces of the others, shouting: 'This is the true fetish, not the fetishism of technology.' At this moment, Sembene brings into the open the theoretical theme of his film, that is the different discourses of fetishism. Up until that point, these different discourses had been woven into the story implicitly, creating the complex semiotic system that makes special demands on the spectator's reading powers. Suddenly the three strands are condensed together in one object. The object acts simultaneously as a signifier of religious belief that pre-dates Islam and colonialism, as a signifier, in the context of the story, of El Hadji's sexual impotence, and it is enclosed, concealed, in the attaché case, a key signifier of financial corruption and the commodity fetishism that corruption breeds.

Sembene weaves a series of reflections on fetishism across the film. As something in which are invested a meaning and a value beyond or beside its actual meaning and value, a fetish demands the willing surrender of knowledge to belief. The fetishist overrates his object, and ignoring the commonsense value attributed to it by society, secretly attaches mysterious powers to it. But, however intensely invested, this secret belief is vulnerable, acknowledging, even more secretly, what it simultaneously disavows. For an individual, the fetish object may be invested with private magical or sexual significance, but distortions of value and attributions of inappropriate meaning may also be shared by social groups in a kind of collective fantasy. The fetish thus acts, either individually or collectively, as a sign, signalling the intervention of fantasy into the normal course of the reality principle. And the intervention of fantasy signals a point of anxiety which cannot face the possibility of knowledge, and in the process of avoiding it, erects a belief in an object that, in turn, denies knowledge of its actual value. While supporting the suspension of disbelief, the fetish also materialises the unspeakable, the disavowed, the repressed.

The cinema, too, appropriates objects, turns them into images and wraps them in connotations and resonances that are either collectively understood, or acquire specific significance within the context of a particular story. Sembene makes use of the language of cinema, its hieroglyphic or pictographic possibilities, and creates a text which is about the meaning of objects and objects as symptoms. His use of cinematic rhetoric is the key to *Xala*. The form of the film engages the spectators' ability to read the signs that emanate from colonialism and its neo-colonialist offspring. And, because the film shows an African ruling elite accepting and appropriating the fetishisms of European capitalism, it allows a double reading. As a comedy of fetishistic manners *Xala* uses signs, objects and the rhetoric of cinema to allow its audience direct engagement with, and access to solving, the enigmas represented on the screen. But *Xala* also sets off a kind of chain reaction of theoretical reflections on fetishism, linking together otherwise diverse ideas, and highlighting the age-old function of fetishism as a conduit for the to and fro of cultural and economic exchange between Europe and Africa.

I

There is a double temporality hidden in Sembene's use of the discourses of fetishism in *Xala*. Behind, or beside, the thematic strands of the story, lies another extra-diegetic, history. This history, quite appropriately, is not visible in the film. But any consideration of fetishism in Senegal today raises 'ghosts' from the past. These are reminders that the word first came into existence in the proto-colonial exchanges, beginning in the mid-15th century, between Portuguese merchant traders and the inhabitants of the West African coast, part of which is now Senegal. Sembene depicts an entrepreneurial, pre-capitalist economy in contemporary Senegal and the film is about the function, within that economy, of fetishised objects as signifiers of unequal exchange. The attention of anyone interested in the history of the concept of fetishism is drawn to its origins in that earlier period of pre-capitalist, mercantile, economic exchange.

Before analysing the theme of fetishism in the film itself, I would like to use it as an excuse to raise some of these ghosts and make some introductory points about the history of the concept of fetishism.

. . .

The recent revival of interest in the origins of the term 'fetishism' has drawn attention to its conceptual contribution to the European polarisation between primitive and civilised thought and consequent moral and intellectual justifications for imperialism. In other words, the concept of fetishism cannot be dismissed because of its compromised place in exploitative exchange and imperialist ethnography. On the contrary, the concept and its history can throw light on the 'enormous misunderstandings' between Europe and Africa.

William Pietz has discussed the origins of both the word and the concept in a series of articles in the journal *Res.*[4] He shows how the word emerged in the encounter between West African and European Christian cultures in the 16th and 17th centuries. It was a 'novel word that appeared as a response to an unprecedented type of situation'[5] of relations between 'cultures so radically different as to be mutually incomprehensible'.[6] Pietz argues that the term bears witness to its own history. To reject the term completely, as purely and simply a relic of colonialism and imperialist anthropology, is to ignore its historical specificity and the cultural implications that go with it. Pietz demonstrates that fetishism is a debased derivation of the Portuguese *feticio*, which means witchcraft, in turn derived from the Latin *facticium* which means artificial, something made up to look like something else. *Feticio* was applied by the Portuguese wholesale to beliefs and practices which they neither could nor would interpret, but encountered in their commercial relations. In the pidgin of middlemen who settled in West Africa and became *soi-disant* experts on native customs, the word became *fetisso*. Pietz notes: 'It brought a wide array of African objects and practices under a category that, for all its misrepresentation of cultural facts enabled the formation of more or less non-coercive commercial relations between members of bewilderingly different cultures.'[7]

. . .

The concept of the fetish provided an antinomy for the rational thought of the Enlightenment. It gives a new form and historic twist to the long-standing and familiar spirit/body and abstraction/materiality polarisations. It coincides with the iconoclastic purification of Christianity from the trappings of idolatrous Catholicism, in which a return to the Old Testament and the precedent of the Jewish, monotheistic rejection of Egyptian iconology was influential. Pietz emphasises that the coming into being of the concept of the fetish was necessarily in conjunction with 'the emergent articulation of the ideology of the commodity form'.[8] W. J. Mitchell points out: 'If Adam Smith is Moses he is also Martin Luther.'[9] It was this discourse of fetishism ('the mist-enveloped regions of the religious world') that Marx turned back onto his own society and that Freud used to define the furthest limits of the psyche's credulity. Both analogies gave the concept of the fetish a new pertinence, turning it away from its anthropological roots towards questions of signification. The fetish raises questions of meaning quite apart from its constructed antinomy with abstraction. It epitomises the human ability to project value onto a material object, repress the fact that the projection has taken place, and then interpret the object as the autonomous source of that value. The process becomes invisible; as the object acquires exchange value, its historical specificity drops into obscurity. The enigma, then, challenges the historian or analyst. The fetish is a sign rather than an idea and it can be analysed semiologically rather than philosophically. This process is central to *Xala*.

II

After the credits the film proper opens with El Hadji collecting his two other wives to go to the party. The elder, Adja Awa Astou, is traditional and religious. In the interview cited earlier Sembene says 'He got his first wife before becoming a somebody.' The second, Oumi N'Doye, is Westernised and mercenary. Sembene says 'Along with his economic and social development, he takes a second who corresponds, so to speak, to a second historical phase.' Awa's daughter Rama, who stands up to her father throughout the film, synthesises progressive elements in both African and Western cultures. She has posters of Amilcar Cabral and Charlie Chaplin in her room; she dresses in African style and rides a motor scooter; she is a student at the university and will only speak Wolof. N'gone, El Hadji's new wife, is dressed for a Western white wedding and her face is covered with a bridal veil. Sembene says: 'The third, his daughter's age but without her mind, is only there for his self-esteem.' Then, on the wedding night, El Hadji finds he is impotent. During the rest of the film he tries to work out who could have cursed him and visits two *marabouts* to find a cure. His financial affairs unravel, unable to sustain the cost of three households and the lavish wedding, until he is finally expelled from the Chamber of Commerce.

The central enigma in *Xala* cannot be deciphered until the very last scene, when the beggars, who at the beginning of the film are marginal to the story but gradually come to occupy its centre, invade El Hadji's house. Then the different clues that have been signalled by Sembene throughout the film fall into place and complete the picture. El Hadji does not function as a knowing narrator and the only character with whom the spectator is given any identification, personally and ideologically, is Rama, who plays only a small, though important, part in the film. El Hadji is a didactic hero. He is made into an example, rather as Brecht makes an example out of Mother Courage. He only engages sympathy through the disaster he has brought on himself, and, like a tragic hero of the cathartic theatre, he is stripped literally to nakedness. On a more significant level, he cannot command the narration because he is unable to understand his own history and the audience are thus deprived of the safety and security of a hero who will guide them through events, and provide them with an appropriate moral perspective. And the spectator realises, at the end, that the film itself has held the clues to the enigma of El Hadji's *xala*, and these linked images and figurations can, retrospectively, be deciphered. Sembene's use of cinema demands a spectator who is actively engaged with reading and interpreting the sounds and images unrolling on the screen.

. . .

In *Xala* the visual coding of ideas is even more marked and further emphasised by the absence of a surrogate narrator. This mode of cinematic address is perfectly suited to the film's subject matter: fetishism. El Hadji and his colleagues have lost touch with their own history and society through adopting Frenchness as a sign of superior class position. There is an unbridgeable gap between the elite's own origins, their present masquerade of Westernised commodity culture and the condition of the people. The gap is demonstrated by the elite's use of French rather than Wolof, and safeguarded by a fetishisation of European objects. These things, for instance El Hadji's Mercedes, are the literal materials of the carapace, his defence against political and economic reality, and the outward manifestations of a corruption that sucks the life blood of the people. When the Mercedes is repossessed, Modu, the chauffeur, carries a wooden stool as he guides his employer along the street. The stool is like a shrunken or wizened version of the proud object of display. It is a trace of, or a memorial to, the Mercedes and its meaning for El Hadji. Because Modu has been so closely identified with the car and its welfare, his presence links the two objects ironically together. Sembene consistently links people with things, things substitute for people or for each other, things acquire associations and resonances that weave like threads of meaning through the film. At the same time, he raises the issue of substitution and exchange in a social and economic sphere. The *marabout* who cures El Hadji's *xala*, Sereen Mada, restores it when the cheque that El Hadji gave him in payment is bounced by the bank.

As the members of the Chamber of Commerce arrive at El Hadji's wedding party, the camera is positioned so that, as each man walks past, his attaché case is framed in close-up. On the outside, the attaché case is emblematic of the power of the international business community, but inside, as only the audience can know, is the secret evidence of corruption and collaboration with the old colonial masters. While seeming to be signs of power and authority, the attaché cases represent the real impotence of the entrepreneurial elite in relation to neo-colonialism. Once the film has established these associations, the image of the attaché case evokes them whenever it appears. So that when El Hadji walks dejectedly away, carrying his attaché case, from N'gone's house after his failed wedding night, he seems to be bowed down with a double impotence. And, in his final confrontation with his colleagues, his case is empty apart from the fetish given him by the phoney *marabout*. The failed fetish is found in the place formerly occupied by the colonialists' banknotes..

Although the particular discourse of sexuality, on which Freud's theory of fetishism depends, cannot be imposed carelessly on another culture, Sembene's juxtaposition of the psycho-sexual with the socio-economic is explicit. He uses the sexual as the point of fissure, or weakness, in the system of economic fetishism. El Hadji's impotence is a symptom of something else, a sign of the eruption of the unconscious onto the body itself. In Freud, the fetish enables the psyche to live with castration anxiety; it contributes to the ego's mechanisms of defence; it conceals the truth that the conscious mind represses. When the fetish fails to function effectively, the symptoms it holds in check start to surface. In *Xala*, the fragile carapace collapses under pressure from class politics and economics but these pressures are expressed through, and latch onto, sexuality and work on the body's vulnerability to the psyche. For Sembene, class politics determine over and above sexuality. Sexuality plays its part in the drama as the site of the symptom, the first sign of a return of the repressed. In his representation of repression, Sembene makes full use of the *double entendre* that can condense its political and psychoanalytic connotations.

The morning after the wedding El Hadji's secretary opens his shop. Modu delivers El Hadji in the Mercedes. El Hadji asks his secretary to telephone the President of the Chamber of Commerce who comes over to see him at once. Interspersed and separate from these events, the beggars are slowly collecting and taking up their usual positions outside in the street. As the local women empty their slops into the drain outside the shop, the secretary runs out with her disinfectant spray to ward off infection. As El Hadji's car appears, so do the beggars and their music; as the President's car appears, so do the cripples. In the back office, El Hadji tells the President about the *xala*. The President reacts with horror saying 'Who? Who could have done this to you?' At that moment the beggars' music drifts into the room. El Hadji gets up from his chair without answering and goes through to the front office and closes the window. He asks the President to call the police and remove this 'human refuse', adding that 'it's bad for tourism'. The police arrive, and under the direction of their French commander, load the beggars and cripples into a lorry and drive them out of town. They are left miles away, in the middle of nowhere, and start their slow, painful, trek back into town.

When watching this scene, the spectator cannot but be conscious of a figuration of 'repression'. The President orders that the beggars be removed from sight and from consciousness. And their return then figures a 'return of the repressed'. To the mutilated limbs of the cripples is now added a baton wound on the head of the boy who guides the blind man and whom Modu employs to clean the car. The repression is both physical and social, and the bodies of the beggars are symptoms of social and economic injustice. But this scene also contains a clue to the enigma, to the source of the *xala*, to its source in El Hadji's social and historical position. This other, psychic, dimension is not revealed until the final scene in the film. El Hadji's fall is complete: Oumi has left him, N'gone's Badyen (her father's sister) has repudiated the marriage, his cheque to the *marabout* had bounced so the *xala* has returned, his bank has refused to extend his loans, and his colleagues have voted unanimously to expel him from the Chamber of Commerce for embezzling 30 tons of rice destined for the country people. As Modu takes him to Awa's house, he tells El Hadji that the blind man can cure the *xala*. The scene builds up to the final revelation as the beggars invade the house under the blind man's leadership. While some of the beggars loot the kitchen, the blind man sits in judgment. He says to El Hadji:

'Do you recognise me? . . . Our story goes back a long way.' He tells how El Hadji had taken his clan's land. 'What I have become is your fault. You appropriated our inheritance. You falsified our names and we were expropriated. I was thrown in prison. I am of the Beye family. Now I will get my revenge. I arranged your *xala.* If you want to be a man you will undress nude in front of everyone. We will spit on you.'.

It was this first act of expropriation that had set El Hadji on the road to wards entrepreneurial success and had taken him from the country to the town, away from loyalty to family and towards individualism, from traditional modes of inheritance towards falsified written legal documents, away from the continuity of his own history and into a charade of Frenchness. His failure to recognise the beggar indicates that he had covered his tracks by 'forgetting'. But when the President asked who had cursed him, his response was to shut out the sound of the beggar's song. This gesture signified both an acknowledgment of the truth and the need, quickly, to re-enact its repression.

During the final scene with the beggars, the tailor's dummy with N'gone's wedding veil, returned contemptuously to El Hadji by the Badyen, stands clearly visible in the corner. The presence of these objects sets off a chain of associations that run back through the film as the links between them begin to emerge. N'gone acts as a pivot between the two fetishistic systems: the economic and the sexual. She is woman as commodity, woman as fetish and woman as consumer of commodities. This sphere of capitalist consumption has been traditionally the province of women; Luce Irigaray, in her essay 'Women on the Market', traces the development from the anthropological exchange of women to the emergence of women as both consumers and consumed in modern, urban society. N'gone's marriage to El Hadji was based on exchange. At the wedding his gifts are displayed including, most prominently, a car key. The car, which stands decked out with ribbons outside the gate of the villa on the back of a truck, is El Hadji's present to her in exchange for her virginity. As he leaves the villa after his unconsummated wedding night, he stops by the car and touches it mournfully, so that it seems to substitute for N'gone's unattainable sexuality. The car's fetishistic quality, its elevation out of ordinary use, the ribbons, are displaced onto her figure. She is first seen concealed behind her wedding veil, packaged like a valuable commodity, and she speaks only once throughout the film. To emphasise this 'thingness' and 'to-be-looked-at-ness', Sembene places her next to a large, nude but tasteful, photograph of her as the Badyen prepares her for her wedding night. As she is undressed and her wedding veil placed on the tailor's dummy, the camera pans up from her naked back to her body in the photograph. In a later scene the same camera movement reiterates this juxtaposition.

N'gone's fetishised erotic appearance contrasts with Oumi's immediate, vital, demanding and corporeal sexuality. N'gone is image and commodity and, half concealed behind the wedding veil, she evokes the double nature of commodity fetishism. The commodity, to circulate and realise the capital invested in it, must seduce its consumer and, in its very seductiveness, its 'packagedness', disguise the secret of its origins. That is, the inherent unglamorousness of the production process should be invisible and, most of all, class relations, the extraction of surplus value, must be concealed by seductive surface. N'gone's image as fetish evokes the processes of veiling, disguise and substitution necessary to commodity fetishism and it is perhaps significant that when El Hadji, temporarily cured of his *xala* by Sereen Mada, goes triumphantly to his new bride she has her period and is 'not available'. Her perfect surface is tarnished by menstrual blood. Although the depiction of N'gone suggests links with the appearance and circulation of the commodity under capitalism, the story is taking place in a non-industrialised and 'underdeveloped' country. The money El Hadji needed to acquire her as commodity, in the specific economic conditions of neo-colonialism, came from financial corruption and exploitative entrepreneurial capitalism. He paid for the wedding and N'gone's gifts by embezzling and illegally selling the quota of rice intended for the country people. The secret corruption is displaced onto the little car that N'gone will receive in exchange for her virginity; the car's fetishistic qualities are displaced onto N'gone for whom a photograph and a tailor's dummy become substitutes and metaphors.

Marx evolved his theory of commodity fetishism in the process of developing his theory of value. The problem Marx perceived to be at stake in the theory of value is connected to the question of visibility and invisibility of labour power and of value. Here the question of materiality and abstraction returns, in the context of a capitalist system of thought that Marx can show to be deeply imbricated with fetishism, its phobic other. W. J. Mitchell says: 'Marx's turning the rhetoric of iconoclasm on its principal users was a brilliant tactical manoeuvre; given nineteenth-century Europe's obsession with primitive, oriental, "fetishistic" cultures that were the prime object of imperialist expansion, one can hardly imagine a more effective rhetorical move.'[10]

Marx identified commodity fetishism as emerging out of the gap between a belief in the commodity as its own autochthonous source of value and knowledge of its true source in human labour. This gap is finally papered over and disguised under capitalism, as the labour market necessary for mass industrial production can only function by transforming individual labour power into abstract and generalised wage labour. The commodity's glamour, verging into sex appeal, seals these complicated processes into a fixation on seeing, believing and not understanding.

Money, the means of expression of value as a symbolic equivalent, is comparable, Marx said, to language. The disavowal characteristic of fetishism is due to misunderstandings of the complex stages inherent in an abstract, symbolic system and the political need to disavow the worker's labour power as source of the commodity's value. Just as a religious believer refuses to accept the human origin of his object (either physical or abstract) of worship, so capitalism refuses to accept that value originates in the labour of the working class. The more abstract the process, the more utterly fundamental is the denial of human origin. While belief in a fetish may be obviously a disavowal of its intractable materiality, belief in an abstract god creates a gap between man and spirit that is harder to materialise. 'A commodity is therefore a mysterious thing, because in it, the social character of men's labour appears to them as an objective character stamped on the product of that labour.'[11] It was at this point that Marx evoked, in his famous phrase, 'the mist-enveloped regions of the religious world' where 'the productions of the human brain appear as independent beings endowed with life and entering into relations both with one another and the human race'. Then

> value does not stalk about with a label describing what it is. It is value that converts every product into a social hieroglyphic . . . The determination of the magnitude of value by labour time is therefore a secret, hidden in the apparent fluctuations of the relative values of commodities . . . it is the ultimate money form of the world of commodities that actually conceals instead of disclosing the social character of private labour and the social relations between the individual producers.[12]

The hieroglyph of value is like a *trompe-l'oeil.* It appears on the surface to be intrinsic to its commodity but, with a move to another perspective, from the visible to the theoretical, its structure may be made accessible to knowledge. The commodity thus seals its enigmatic self-sufficiency behind a masquerade, a surface that disavows both the structure of value and its origin in working-class labour. Instead it is inscribed with a different kind of semiotic, one that is directed towards the market place, which further disguises, or papers over, the semiotic that originated in its production. Baudrillard argues in 'The Political

Economy of the Sign' that increasingly in the consumer societies of advanced capitalism, both the object form (use value) and the commodity form (exchange value) are transfigured into sign value. This is partly the function of advertising, which is expert in the creation of sign values, weaving an intricate web of connotation, as Roland Barthes describes in his analysis of the Panzani advertisement in the essay 'The Rhetoric of the Image'. Baudrillard then argues that spending, or perhaps one should say 'shopping', elevates the commodity form into sign value, so that the economic is then transfigured into sign systems, and economic power becomes visibly transmuted into the trappings of social privilege. Consumer objects can then create needs in advance of the consumer's awareness of a need, bearing out Marx's point that 'production not only produces goods but it produces people to consume them and corresponding needs.'

The circulation of European commodities, in a society of the kind depicted in *Xala*, caricatures and exaggerates the commodity fetishism inherent in capitalism. Rather than representing an enigma that may be deciphered, politically and theoretically, to reveal its place in the historical and economic order of things, the commodity's ties with history have been effectively severed. The chain of displacements that construct the concept of value is attenuated to the point that all connection with the source of value is irredeemably lost in the movement from capitalism to colonialism. Floating freely outside First World economy, the gulf between luxury objects monopolised by a Third World elite and the labour power of the working class in the producing country seems vast. Belief in the commodity's supposedly self-generated value does not demand the process of disavowal it depends on at home so that it can live out its myth as an object of cult. In *Xala*, Sembene uses the neo-colonial economy to show the capitalist commodity 'superfetishised'. Modu, for instance, only puts imported bottled water into the Mercedes. These things take on pure 'sign value' (as Baudrillard would put it). However, the objects enable another process of disavowal. Sembene suggests that these fetishised objects seal the repression of history and of class and colonial politics under the rhetoric of nationhood. His use of the concept of fetishism is not an exact theoretical working through of the Marxist or Freudian concepts of fetishism, however; his use is *Marxist* and *Freudian.* The interest of the film lies in its inextricable intermeshing of the two.

In its final images, *Xala*'s class and psychoanalytic themes are suddenly polarised into a new pattern. Sembene invokes horror of the body and its materiality through the desperate and degraded condition of the beggars and cripples. As El Hadji is denounced by the blind man, their wounds and their missing limbs demonstrate the political fact that financial corruption and profit are manifested on the bodies of the poor. The Western objects that the entrepreneurial elite fetishise inflict not impotence but castration on those they impoverish. The wounded body, the source of horror in the Freudian concept of castration anxiety, returns in the wounded bodies of the beggars and the hunger of the peasants. These bodies break through the barriers maintained by the French language and symbolised, for instance, by El Hadji's cult of Evian water. The otherness of Africa which horrified Europeans is perpetuated in colonialism's real horror of the ordinary people, and grotesquely more so, in the irresponsible greed of the new ruling class.

For Freud, the site of castration anxiety is the mother's body. For Julia Kristeva, the mother's body is the site of abjection. The child's relation to its mother was a time of boundarilessness and a time when the body and its fluids were not a source of disgust. For Kristeva, the ego defines itself by a demarcation of its limits through mastering its waste and separating itself from those of the mother. It establishes itself as an individual, in its oneness. This concept of individualism is, it has been extensively argued, a crucial basis for the ideology of entrepreneurial capitalism. And, as has also been extensively argued, the residue of disgust, bodily waste, is the matter of ritual. In the last moments of *Xala*, the beggars take their revenge on El Hadji in a role reversal of power and humiliation. As El Hadji stands naked in front of his wife and daughter, the beggars crowd around and spit on him. This is the price that the blind man exacts for lifting the *xala*. And as the scene seems to continue beyond endurance, the film ends with a freeze-frame.

Sembene's film opens with the theatre of politics, moves through a ceremonial celebration of marriage, closes with a ritual of rebirth. The prophylactic rituals of fetishised manhood fail, both financially and sexually. Teshome Gabriel says: 'The spitting on El Hadji helps reincorporate him into the people's fold. In other words, the ritual becomes a folk method of purgation which makes El Hadji a literal incarnation of all members of the class or group that spit on him and consequently reintegrates him into folk society'.[13]

In submitting to the body, and to everything that fetishism disavows, psychic and political, El Hadji signals a lifting of amnesia and an acceptance of history. The freeze-frame resurrects a man, whole through community, stripped of the trappings of colonialism and fetishised individualism.

Teshome Gabriel draws attention to a scene between El Hadji and Rama in which words, emblems and the film image weave an intricate pattern of meanings at different levels of visibility:

Before Rama stands up to walk out of the frame Sembene makes us take note, once again, of the map of Africa behind her. We notice too that the colour of the map reflects the exact same colours of Rama's traditional boubou, native costume—blue, purple, green and yellow —and it is not divided into boundaries and states. It denotes pan-Africanism:

El Hadji: My child, do you need anything? (He searches in his wallet.)
Rama: Just my mother's happiness. (She walks out of frame as the camera lingers on the map.)

What Sembene is saying here is quite direct and no longer inaccessible. On one level Rama shows concern for her mother . . . On another level . . . her concern becomes not only her maternal mother but 'Mother Africa'. This notion carries an extended meaning when we observe the shot of El Hadji—to his side we see a huge colonial map of Africa. The 'wax' and the 'gold' are posited jointly by a single instance of composition. Two realities fight to command the frame, but finally the 'gold' meaning leaps out and breaks the boundaries of the screen.[14]

Notes

1. Teshome H. Gabriel, '*Xala:* Cinema of Wax and Gold', in Peter Stevens (ed.), *Jump Cut: Hollywood, Politics and Counter Culture* (Toronto: Between the Lines, 1985), 335.
2. Noureddine Ghai says: 'The concept of "negritude" was developed by a group of French-speaking black intellectuals studying in Paris in the 1930s and 1940s, among them Leopold Senghor, later to be the first president of Senegal after . . . colonial rule. It denoted a view of black people as particularly gifted in the art of immediate living, of sensual experience, of physical skill and prowess, all of which belonged to them by birth right. It was an attempt at the time to combat the racist view of African civilisation as a null quantity, and the ideology that French colonial rule was providing otherwise worthless, culture-less beings with the opportunity to assimilate themselves to French culture . . . Sembene is one of the many later African writers who have criticised the concept vigorously, among other things for underpinning the view that the European contribution to global culture is technological and rational, while Africa can remain in acute economic disarray because it is happy just "being".' 'An Interview with Ousmane Sembene', in J. Downing (ed.), *Film and Politics in the Third World* (Brooklyn: Autonomedia, 1987).
3. Ibid. 46.
4. William Pietz, 'The Problem of the Fetish', Part 1, *Res,* 9 (Spring 1985),

5–17; Part 2, *Res*, 13 (Spring 1987), 23–46; Part 3a, *Res*, 16 (Autumn 1988), 105–24 (Peabody Museum, Harvard University, Cambridge, Mass.).
5. W. Pietz, 'The Problem of the Fetish', Part 1, p. 6.
6. W. Pietz, 'The Problem of the Fetish', Part 2, p. 21.
7. Ibid. 23.
8. W. Pietz, 'The Problem of the Fetish', Part 1, p. 7.
9. W. J. Mitchell, *Iconology: Image, Text, Ideology* (Chicago: Chicago University Press, 1986).
10. Ibid. 200.
11. K. Marx, *Capital*, vol. 1, p. 72.
12. Ibid. 74–5.
13. T. Gabriel, '*Xala:* Cinema of Wax and Gold', 340.
14. Ibid.

Further Reading

Phase I. Pioneers and Classics: The Modernist Mode

ARBUTHNOT, LUCY, and SENECA, GAIL, 'Pre-Text and Text in *Gentlemen Prefer Blondes*', *Film Reader*, 5 (1982), 13–23.

BERGSTROM, JANET, 'The Avant-Garde: Histories and Theories', *Screen*, 19: 3 (Autumn 1978), 119–27.

BOVENSCHEN, SILVIA, 'Is there a Feminine Aesthetic?', *New German Critique*, 10 (Winter 1977), 111–37.

CLARK, VÉVÉ A., HODSON, MILLICENT, and NEIMAN, CATRINA, *The Legend of Maya Deren: A Documentary Biography and Collected Works* (New York: Anthology Film Archives, 1984).

COOK, PAM, and JOHNSTON, CLAIRE, 'The Place of Women in the Cinema of Raoul Walsh', in Bill Nichols (ed.), *Movies and Methods*, ii (Berkeley: University of California Press, 1985), 379–87.

CORNWELL, REGINA, 'Maya Deren and Germaine Dulac: Activists of the Avant-Garde', *Film Library Quarterly*, 5: 1 (Winter 1971–2), 29–38.

COWIE, ELIZABETH, 'Fantasia', *m/f*, 9 (1984), 70–105.

DE LAURETIS, TERESA, *Alice Doesn't: Feminisms, Semiotics, Cinema* (Bloomington: Indiana University Press, 1984).

FLITTERMAN-LEWIS, SANDY, *To Desire Differently: Feminism and the French Cinema* (Urbana and Chicago: University of Illinois Press, 1990).

—— 'Montage/Discourse: Germaine Dulac's *The Smiling Madame Beudet*', *Wide Angle*, 4: 3 (1980), 54–59.

—— and BARRY, JUDITH, 'Textual Strategies: The Politics of Art-Making', in Hilary Robinson (ed.), *Visibly Female: Feminism and Art Today* (London: Camden Press, 1987), 106–17.

GLEDHILL, CHRISTINE, 'Developments in Feminist Film Criticism', in Mary Ann Doane, Patricia Mellencamp, and Linda Williams (eds.), *Re-Vision: Essays in Feminist Film Criticism* (Frederick, Md.: University Publications of America, 1984), 18–48.

HASKELL, MOLLY, *From Reverence to Rape: The Treatment of Women in the Movies* (New York: Penguin, 1974).

HEATH, STEPHEN, 'Difference', *Screen*, 19: 3 (Autumn 1978), 50–127.

—— and MELLENCAMP, PATRICIA, (eds.), *Cinema and Language* (Frederick, Md.: University Publications of America in Association with The American Film Institute, 1983).

KAPLAN, E. ANN, 'Lois Weber, Early Cinema and Feminine Issues' (with reference to *The Blot* (1921), in E. Ann Kaplan, *Motherhood and Representation* (London and New York: Routledge, 1992), 132–8.

KUHN, ANNETTE (ed.), *Women in Film: An International Guide* (New York: Fawcette Columbine, 1991).

—— *Cinema, Censorship and Sexuality 1909–1925* (London and New York: Routledge, 1988).

MCGARRY, EILEEN, 'Documentary Realism and Women's Cinema', *Women and Film*, 2: 7 (1975), 50–9.

MAYNE, JUDITH, 'The Woman at the Keyhole: Women's Cinema and Feminist Criticism', in Mary Ann Doane, Patricia Mellencamp, and Linda Williams (eds.), *Re-Vision: Essays in Feminist Film Criticism* (Frederick, Md.: University Publications of America, 1984), 49–66

METZ, CHRISTIAN, *The Imaginary Signifer: Psychoanalysis and the Cinema.* trans. Celia Britton et al. (Bloomington: Indiana University Press, 1977).

ROMAN, LESLIE G., CHRISTIAN SMITH, LINDA, with ELLSWORTH, ELIZABETH, *Becoming Feminine: The Politics of Popular Culture* (London and Philadelphia: Palmer Press, 1988).

ROSEN, MARJORIE, *Popcorn Venus: Women, Movies and the American Dream* (New York: Coward McCann and Georghagen, 1973).

SCOTT, JOAN (ed.), *Feminism and History* (Oxford and New York: Oxford University Press, 1996).

SHELDON, CAROLINE, 'Lesbians and Film: Some Thoughts', Richard Dyer (ed.), *Gays and Film* (London: The British Film Institute, 1977), 5–26.

SILVERMAN, KAJA, *The Subject of Semiotics* (New York: Oxford University Press, 1983).

SNITOW, ANN, and STANSELL, CHRISTINE (eds.), *Powers of Desire* (New York: Monthly Review Press, 1983).

STAM, ROBERT, BURGOYNE, ROBERT, and FLITTERMAN-LEWIS, SANDY (eds.), *New Vocabularies in Film Semiotics* (London and New York: Routledge, 1992).

TRINH, T. MINH-HA, 'If Upon Leaving . . . A Conversation Piece' (with Leslie Thornton, Laleen Jayamanne), in R. Ferguson et al. (eds.), *Discourses: Conversations in Postmodern Art and Culture* (Cambridge, Mass.: MIT Press, 1990), 44–64.

Phase II. Critiques of Phase I Theories: New Methods

BRENNAN, TERESA, 'Introduction', *Between Feminism and Psychoanalysis* (London and New York: Routledge, 1989), 1–23.

BRUNO, GIULIANA, and NADOTTI, MARIA (eds.), *Off Screen: Women and Film in Italy* (London and New York: Routledge, 1988).

BRUNSDON, CHARLOTTE, *Films for Women* (London: British Film Institute, 1986).

CASE, SUE-ELLEN, 'Tracking the Vampire', *Differences*, 3: 2 (Summer 1991), 1–20.

Copjec, Joan, *Read my Desire* (Cambridge, Mass.: MIT Press, 1994).

De Lauretis, Teresa, 'Oedipus Interruptus', *Wide Angle*, 7: 1–2 1985), 34–40.

—— 'The Essence of the Triangle: Or Taking the Risk of Essentialism Seriously. Feminist Theory in Italy, the U.S. and Britain', in Naomi Schor (ed.), *The Essential Difference* (Bloomington: Indiana University Press, 1994).

—— *The Practice of Love: Lesbian Sexuality and Perverse Desire* (Bloomington: Indiana University Press, 1994).

Doane, Mary Ann, *The Desire to Desire* (Bloomington: Indiana University Press, 1987).

—— Mellencamp, Patricia, and Williams, Linda (eds.), *Re-Vision: Essays in Feminist Film Criticism* (Frederick, Md.: University Publications of America (in Association with The American Film Institute), 1984).

Erens, Patricia (ed.), *Sexual Stratagems: The World of Women in Film* (New York: Horizon Press, 1979).

Geraghty, Christine, 'Albert Finney: A Working-Class Hero', in P. Kirkham and J. Thumin (eds.), *Me Jane: Masculinity, Movies and Women* (London: Lawrence and Wishart, 1995), 62–72.

Gilroy, Paul, Parmar Pratibha, et al., (eds.), *The Empire Strikes Back: Race and Racism in the 1970s* (London: Hutchinson, in Association with the Centre for Contemporary Cultural Studies, University of Birmingham, 1982).

Gledhill, Christine, 'Women Reading Men', in P. Kirkham and J. Thumin (eds.), *Me Jane: Masculinity, Movies and Women* (New York: St Martin's Press, 1995), 73–93

hooks, bell, 'The Oppositional Gaze', in *Black Looks: Race and Representation* (Boston: South End Press, 1992), 115–32.

Jacobs, Lea, *The Wages of Sin: Censorship and the Fallen Woman Film 1928–1942* (Madison: University of Wisconsin Press, 1991).

Kaplan, E. Ann, 'Fanon, Trauma and Cinema', in Antony Alessandini (eds.), *Frantz Fanon: Critical Perspectives* (London and New York: Routledge, 1999), 146–58.

—— 'Body Politics: Menopause, Mastectomy and Cosmetic Surgery in Films by Rainer, Tom and Onwurah', in *Looking for the Other: Feminism, Film and the Imperial Gaze* (New York and London: Routledge, 1997), 256–91.

Kirkham, Pat, and Thumin, Janet, (eds.), *Me Jane: Masculinity, Movies and Women* (New York: St Martin's Press, 1995).

LeSage, Julia, 'The Human Subject—You, He, or Me? (Or the Case of the Missing Penis)', *Jump Cut: A Review of Contemporary Cinema*, 4 (Nov.–Dec. 1974), 26–7. Reprinted in *Screen*, 16: 2 (1975), 77–82, with Comment, 83–90.

—— 'Artful Racism, Artful Rape: Griffith's *Broken Blossoms*', *Jump Cut*, 26 (1981). Reprinted in Christine Gledhill (ed.), *Home is Where the Heart Is* (London: BFI, 1987), 235–54.

—— 'Subversive Fantasies: *Celine and Julie Go Boating*', *Jump Cut*, 23/4 (Spring 1981).
MULVEY, LAURA, 'Afterthoughts on "Visual Pleasure": Inspired by *Duel in the Sun*', *Framework*, 15–17 (Summer 1981), 12-15.
—— 'Changes', *Discourse*, 7 (1985), 11–20.
PENLEY, CONSTANCE (ed.), *Feminism and Film Theory* (London and New York: Routledge, 1988).
—— *The Future of an Illusion: Film, Feminism and Psychoanalysis* (Minneapolis: University of Minnesota Press, 1989).
PIETROPAOLO, LAURA, TESTAFERRI, ADA, (eds.), *Feminism in the Cinema* (Bloomington and Indianapolis: Indiana University Press, 1995).
ROSE, JAQUELINE, *Sexuality in the Field of Vision* (London: Verso, 1986).
STERN, LESLIE, 'Feminism and Cinema—Exchanges', *Screen*, 20: 3–4 (1979–80), 89–105.
THOMAS, DEBORAH, 'Psychoanalysis and Film Noir', in Ian Cameron (ed.), *The Book of Film Noir* (New York: Continuum, 1990), 71–87.
WHITE, PATRICIA, 'Female Spectator, Lesbian Spectre: *The Haunting*', Reprinted in E. Ann Kaplan (ed.) *Women in Film Noir*, new revised edition (London: BFI, 1998), 130–51.

Phase III. Race, Sexuality, and Postmodernism in Feminist Film Theory

Bad Object Choices (eds.), *How Do I Look? Queer Film and Video* (Seattle, Wash.: Bay Press, 1991).
BOBO, JACQUELINE, *Black Video and Filmmakers* (New York and London: Routledge, 1998).
BRUNO, GIULIANA, *Streetwalking on a Ruined Map: Cultural Theory and the City Films of Elvira Notari* (Princeton: Princeton University Press, 1993).
CASE, SUE-ELLEN, *The Domain-Matrix: Performing Lesbian at the End of Print Culture* (Bloomington: Indiana University Press, 1997).
CREED, BARBARA, 'From Here to Modernity: Feminism and Postmodernism', *Screen*, 28: 2 (1987), 47–68.
DENT, GINA (ed.), *Black Popular Culture*, A Project by Michele Wallace (Seattle, Wash.: Bay Press, 1992).
DOANE, MARY ANN, 'Dark Continents: Epistemologies of Racial and Sexual Difference in Psychoanalysis and the Cinema', from Mary Ann Douane (ed.), *Femmes Fatales* (New York: Routledge, 1991), 209–99.
DYER, RICHARD, *Stars* (London: BFI, 1980).
—— *White* (London and New York: Routledge, 1997).
FOSTER, HAL, *The Anti-Aesthetic* (Port Townsend Wash.: Bay Press, 1983).
FRIEDBERG, ANNE, *Window Shopping: Cinema and the Postmodern* (Berkeley: University of California Press, 1993).

GEVER, MARTHA, PARMAR, PRATIBHA, and GREYSON, JOHN (eds.), *Queer Looks: Perspectives on Lesbian and Gay Film and Video* (London and New York: Routledge, 1993).

HOOKS, BELL, *Black Looks: Race and Representation* (Boston: South End Press, 1992).

JAMESON, FREDRIC, *Postmodernism, or, the Cultural Logic of Late Capitalism* (Durham, NC.: Duke University Press, 1991).

KAPLAN, E. ANN, 'Feminism, Postmodernism and MTV', in E. Ann Kaplan (ed.), *Postmodernism and Its Discontents* (London: Verso, 1988), 30–44.

—— 'Problematising Cross-Cultural Analysis: The Case of Women in Recent Chinese Cinema', originally published in *Wide Angle*, 2: 11 (Spring 1989), 49–50. Reprinted in Chris Berry (ed.), *Perspectives on Chinese Cinema* (London: British Film Institute, 1991), 141–54.

—— 'The Couch-Affair: Gender and Race in the Hollywood Transference', *American Imago*, 50: 4 (Winter 1993), 481–514.

—— *Looking for the Other: Feminism, Film and the Imperial Gaze* (New York and London: Routledge 1997).

KUHN, ANNETTE, *Alien Zone: Cultural Theory and Contemporary Science Fiction Cinema* (London and New York: Verso, 1990).

LYOTARD, JEAN-FRANÇOIS, *The Postmodern Condition*, trans. Geoff Bennington and Brian Masumi (Manchester: Manchester University Press, 1979).

MEAGHAN, MORRIS, *The Pirate's Fiancée: Feminism, Reading, Postmodernism* (London and New York: Verso, 1988).

MERCK, MANDY (ed.), *The Sexual Subject: A Screen Reader in Sexuality* (London and New York: Routledge, 1992).

PARMAR, PRATIBHA, 'Black Feminism: The Politics of Articulation', in Jonathan Rutherford (ed.), *Identity, Community, Culture, Difference* (London: Lawrence and Wishart, 1990), 101–26.

SPENDER, DALE, *Nattering on the Net: Women, Power and Cyberspace* (London: Spinifex Press, 1996).

STABLES, KATE, 'The Postmodern Always Rings Twice: Constructing the *Femme Fatale* in 90s Cinema', in E. Ann Kaplan (ed.), *Women in Film Noir*, new revised edition (London: BFI, 1998), 164–82.

STAM, ROBERT, and SHOHAT, ELLA, *Unthinking Eurocentrism: Multiculturalism and the Media* (London and New York: Routledge, 1994).

STRAAYER, CHRIS, '*Femme Fatale* or Lesbian Femme: Bound in Sexual Difference', in E. Ann Kaplan (ed.), *Women in Film Noir*, new revised edition (London: BFI, 1998), 151–163.

TRINH, T. MINH-HA, 'The World as a Foreign Land', (1989), Reprinted in *When the Moon Waxes Red: Representation, Gender and Cultural Politics*, (New York and London: Routledge l991), 185–99.

WALLACE, MICHELE, 'Multiculturalism and Oppositionality', *Afterimage* (October 1991), 6–9.

YOUNG, LOLA, *Fear of the Dark: 'Race', Gender and Sexuality in Cinema* (London and New York: Routledge, 1995), 13–37.

Phase IV. Spectatorship, Ethnicity, and Melodrama

BOBO, JACQUELINE, 'Black Women as Interpretive Community,' (with reference to Julie Dash's *Daughters of the Dust*), in Jacqueline Bobo, *Black Women as Cultural Readers* (New York: Columbia University Press, 1995), 33–60.

BYARS, JACKIE, *All that Hollywood Allows: Re-reading Gender in 1950s Melodrama* (Chapel Hill: University of North Carolina Press, 1991).

CARSON, DIANE, DITTMAR, LINDA, and WELSCH, JANICE (eds.), *Multiple Voices in Feminist Film Criticism* (Minneapolis: University of Minnesota Press, 1993).

COOK, PAM, 'Melodrama and the Woman's Picture', in Sue Aspinall and Bob Murphy (eds.), *Gainsborough Melodrama*, Dossier No. 18 (London: British Film Institute, 1983).

DIAWARA, MANTHIA (ed.), *Black American Cinema: Aesthetics and Spectatorship* (New York and London: Routledge, 1993).

GLEDHILL, CHRISTINE (ed.), *Home is Where the Heart Is: Studies in Melodrama and the Woman's Film* (London: BFI 1987).

JACOBS, LEA, '*Now, Voyager:* Some Problems of Enunciation and Sexual Difference', *Camera Obscura*, 7 (1981), 89–110.

KAPLAN, E. ANN, 'Melodrama/Subjectivity/Ideology: Western Melodrama Theories and Their Relevance to Recent Chinese Cinema', reprinted in Wimal Dissanayeke (ed.), *Melodrama and Asian Cinema* (Cambridge: Cambridge University Press, 1993), 55–76.

—— 'Classical Hollywood Film and Melodrama', in John Hill and Pamela Church Gibson (eds.), *The Oxford Guide to Film Studies* (London; Oxford University Press, 1998), 272–288.

KIRSCHNER, SAM, and KIRSCHNER, DIANA ADILE (eds.), *Perspectives on Psychology and the Media* (Washington, DC: American Psychological Association, 1997).

MAYNE, JUDITH, *Cinema and Spectatorship* (London and New York: Routledge, 1993), 70–6.

PETRO, PATRICE, *Joyless Streets: Women and Melodramatic Representation in Weimar Germany* (Princeton: Princeton University Press, 1989).

STACEY, JACKIE, *Star Gazing: Hollywood Cinema and Female Spectatorship* (London and New York: Routledge, 1993), 19–48.

TRINH, T. MINH-HA, 'All-Owning Spectatorship', reprinted in *When the Moon Waxes Red* (London and New York: Routledge, 1991), 185–99.

YANMEI WEI, 'Music and Femininity in Zhang Yimou's Family Melodrama', *CineAction*, (1997), 18–27.

Index

Adam's Rib 426
Adams, Parveen 91, 94, 95
Adorno, Theodore W. 528
Affron, Charles 421
Akerman, Chantal 97, 278, 500
Alice Doesn't (de Lauretis) 266, 456–7
All About Eve 456, 457–60, 464
Allen, Carolyn 386–7
Althusser, Louis 70, 100, 102, 131, 141, 276, 291–2
The American Cinema (Sarris) 26, 139
Amor en las Sombras (Love in the Shadows) 507
'Anthony Mann: Looking at the Male' (Willemen) 258
'Approaching the Work of Dorothy Arzner' (Cook) 141
Arbuthnot, Lucie 123, 124
'Art as a Device' (Shklovsky) 144
Arzner, Dorothy 24, 30–1, 139–41, 142–8, 160–74, 177, 178
Aventura 516–17

Bacall, Lauren 40
Bachelard, Gaston 291, 295–6, 302
Bakhtin, Mikhail 267, 268
Baldwin, James 359–60, 369–70
Barba, Meche 515
Barnes, Djuna 386, 387, 393
Barry, Judith 130
Barrymore, John 243
Barthelmass, Richard 243
Barthes, Roland 23–4, 98, 147, 205, 244, 266, 273, 276, 326, 372, 550
Baudrillard, Jean 549–50
Baudry, Jean-Louis 217
Beauvoir, Simone de 479
Bellour, Raymond 186, 254, 452–3, 454
Beloved (Morrison) 356, 365–73
Benjamin, Walter 329
Berliner, Bernhard 207
Beyond the Forest 429
Bhangra Jig 382, 383
The Birth of a Nation 370
Blood and Sand 236, 238, 244
Bobo, Jacqueline 13, 411–12
Boetticher, Budd 40
Border Incident 258
Bourdin, Guy 343
Bovenschen, Silvia 278, 427
Bracho, Julio 513
Brennan, Teresa 8
British Film Institute (BFI) 165
Britton, Andrew 161–2
Brooke-Rose, Christine 270–1
Brooks, Peter 267–8, 339, 509
Brossard, Nicole 384, 392
Brown, Beverley 94, 95
Brunsdon, Charlotte 444, 445–6
Burch, Noël 421, 422, 423

Cahiers du cinéma 25, 515–16, 529
The Camera: Je/La Caméra: Eye 87–8
Capra, Frank 100–1
Carby, Hazel 348
Case, Sue-Ellen 394, 395, 397
Ce sexe qui n'est pas un (Irigaray) 486
Céline and Julie Go Boating 500
The Celluloid Closet (Russo) 162
Centre for Cultural Studies, Birmingham (CCS) 3, 9
Chasseguet-Smirgel, Janine 211, 212
A Child is Being Beaten (Freud) 126, 239
Chodorow, Nancy 132, 134, 211, 485–6, 495, 532
Christopher Strong 143, 145, 146, 161, 170–2
Citron, Michelle 500
Civilization and Its Discontents (Freud) 192, 194–5
Cixous, Hélène 423–4, 426
Clarke, Shirley 29
Cliff, Michelle 400
The Color Purple 399–400
Contending Forces (Hopkins) 349
Cook, Pam 41, 63, 73–4, 141, 142, 439–40, 441, 444, 447
Copjec, Joan 287–303
Corinne, Tee 162
Le corps lesbien see *The Lesbian Body* (Wittig)

Course in General Linguistics (Saussure) 56, 58–9
Coward, Rosalind 59
Cowie, Elizabeth 48–64
Craig's Wife 143, 145, 146–7, 168
Crawford, Joan 162
Creed, Barbara 12, 309
The Crisis of Political Modernism (Rodowick) 184
Crossroads 445–6
Cruze, James 140
Cuando los hijos se van (When the Children Go Away) 512–13

Dance, Girl, Dance 30, 144, 145, 146, 161, 168, 169, 170, 173–4, 177
Dark Victory 429–30
Dash, Julie 412
Daughter Rite 500
Daughters of Bilitis 395
Daughters of the Dust (Dash) 412
Davis, Angela 347–8
Davison, Tito 507, 514
Davy, Kate 396, 397
de Lauretis, Teresa 8–9, 10, 177, 231, 265–84, 384–402, 456–7
de Man, Paul 268–9, 270, 273
De Palma 274
Deitch, Donna 177, 399
del Rio, Dolores 514
Deleuze, Gilles 181, 183–4, 203–5, 206, 207–8, 210–11, 239, 273
Delon, Alain 256–7
Deren, Maya 164
Derrida, Jacques 273, 394
Desert Hearts 177, 399
Desperately Seeking Susan 177, 456, 457, 460–4
The Devil is a Woman 211
Dialogues (Deleuze and Parnet) 181–4
Dickes, Robert 216
Dietrich, Marlene 40, 43–4, 81, 159, 160, 162, 208–9, 211, 212
Dinnerstein, Dorothy 134, 467, 532
Disney, Walt 523, 527
Doane, Janice 531
Doane, Mary Ann 86–98, 126, 209, 219, 230, 231, 236, 418–34, 453–4, 455, 490, 495–6
'Documentary Realism and Women's Cinema' (McGarry) 6
Doisneau, Robert 430–3
Dolan, Jill 397
Doña Bárbara 514
Dorfman, Ariel 528
Double Indemnity 78, 80, 82
Douchet 44
'The Dread of Woman' (Horney) 121
'The Drive to Become Both Sexes' 218
Ducrot, Oswald 420
Duel in the Sun 228–9, 258, 439, 454
'The Dynamics of Desire' (Dolan) 397

Eagleton, Terry 131
Eastwood, Clint 256, 257
Eco, Umberto 269, 270, 277
Ecrits (Lacan) 60–1, 276
Eisenstein, S. M. 29
Elementary Structures of Kinship (Lévi-Strauss) 51–3
Ellis, Havelock 388, 389, 402
Ellis, John 59, 254–4, 261–2
Ellsworth, Elizabeth 396
The Empire Strikes Back: Race and Racism in 70s Britain 379
Enzensberger, Hans Magnus 28
Export, Valie 278

Fairbanks, Douglas 242
Fanon, Frantz 356, 370
Félix, María 513, 514
Felman, Shoshana 169, 267
The Female Man (Russ) 395
Fenichel, Otto 219
Film about a Woman Who 278, 280, 281
First Comes Courage 143, 147
Flesh and Paper 382
Flitterman, Sandy 130
Ford, John 26, 27, 142, 259, 522, 528, 529
Foucault, Michel 140–1, 212, 242, 289–90, 291, 294–5, 389, 390, 434
Franco, Jean 510
Frank, Alvan 217
French New Wave 523
Freud, Sigmund 37, 39, 106, 126, 188–95 *passim* 197–8, 206, 233, 234, 239, 240, 358, 418–19, 424–5, 431–2, 457–8, 484, 485, 526, 545
Friday, Nancy 126–7
Frith, Simon 346
Frye, Marilyn 337, 398, 399
Full House 533

Gabriel, Theshome H. 535, 551, 552
Gaines, Jane 336–52
Gainsborough Studios 439, 441
Gallop, Jane 488–9
Gamboa, Federico 506

Gandhi, Mohandas 332
Garbo, Greta 40, 159, 160, 162
García, Sara 512, 513
Gay Movement 253
Gentlemen Prefer Blondes 27, 123, 340
Geraghty, Christine 155
Gever, Martha 375
Gidal, Peter 87, 96
Giddis, Diane 69
Gilda 79, 80
Glasser, M. 363
Gledhill, Christine 13, 66–84, 151, 203, 416, 482, 483–4
Gomez, Jewelle 400
Gordon, Mary 531
Gordy, Berry 336, 345
Goulding, Edmund 429–30
Grahn, Judy 387
Griffiths, D. W. 370
Grundrisse (Marx) 187
Les guérillères (Wittig) 393, 394

Hall, Catharine 361
Hall, Radclyffe 387–9, 401–2
Hall, Stuart 338, 346, 352, 381
Halprin, Sarah 167
Hansen, Miriam 190–1, 226–45
Haraway, Donna 169
Harper, Frances E. W. 348
Hart, William S. 242
Haskell, Molly 40, 79, 425
Hawks, Howard 26, 27, 256, 530
Heath, Stephen 88–9, 124, 215, 275, 276–7
Heine, Heinrich 418–19
Hepburn, Katherine 159, 160, 170–1
Heston, Charlton 259
Hirsch, Marianne 371
Hirst, Paul 294
Hitchcock, Alfred 43, 44, 45, 141, 196, 197, 272
Hodges, Devon 531
Holden, William 260
Honor Among Lovers 143, 144, 145
hooks, bell 337
Hopkins, Pauline 348, 349
Horney, Karen 91, 121
Houston, Beverle 171
Hudson, Rock 263
Humoresque 86, 429

'Ideology and Ideological State Apparatuses' (Althusser) 100, 102
The Imaginary Signifier (Metz) 214, 275
'Instincts and their Vicissitudes' (Freud) 234
Irigaray, Luce 94–5, 175–6, 385, 389, 423, 425, 486–7, 493, 547
It's a Wonderful Life 100–17

Jacobson, Edith 220
Jameson, Fredric 269–70
Jardine, Alice 310
Jeanne Dielman 23 Quai du Commerce – 1080 Bruxelles 97, 98, 500
'John Ford's *Young Mr. Lincoln*' 529
Johnston, Claire 22–33, 41, 63, 73–4, 122, 139–48, 160–1, 169–70, 429, 481
Jordan, June 380
Journeys from Berlin/1971 279
Jump Cut 162
Jung, Carl 293

Kaplan, E. Ann 119–35, 230, 231, 466–77, 492, 494–5, 512
Kaplan, Nelly 24
Karpenstein, Christa 235
Kay, Karyn 139, 166
Kholstomer (Tolstoy) 144–5
Khosla, Punam 375
Khush 382
King, Henry 480
Kiss of the Spider Woman 399–400
Klute 66, 83
Kofman, Sarah 424
Kracauer, Siegfried 226
Kraft-Ebing, Richard 402
Kramer Versus Kramer 477
Kristeva, Julia 94, 95–6, 130, 135, 455, 488, 496, 530–1, 532, 551
Kristofferson, Kris 260
Kubie, Lawrence 218, 219
Kuhn, Annette 437–48

Labyrinths of Solitude, The (Paz) 508
Lacan, Jacques 38, 60–1, 90, 91, 119–20, 188–9, 287–8, 290–1, 292, 296–302, 482, 526
Lacheney, Robert *see* Truffaut, François
Lamarque, Libertad 514–15, 516
Laplanche, Jean 90, 96, 214, 358, 369
Lara, Agustín 516–17
Laura 79, 80
Lazarre, Jane 467
Leave Her to Heaven 429
Lenin, V. I. 23, 147, 332
Leone, Sergio 261, 262

LeSage, Julia 123, 124, 127
The Lesbian Body (Wittig) 393–4, 395
Lévi-Strauss, Claude 49–53, 59, 60, 62, 182
Loewald, Hans 211, 218
López, Ana M. 505–17
Lorde, Audre 348, 391–2, 401
Lovell, Terry 350
Lupino, Ida 31
Lyotard, Jean-François 209, 273

M'Uzan, Michael de 207
MacKinnon, Catharine 390
Madame X: An Absolute Ruler 400
Madre Querida (Dear Mother) 512
Mahogany 336–7, 342–7, 350, 351
Major Dundee 259–60
The Man Who Envied Women 280–3
The Man Who Shot Liberty Valance 259
Mangolte, Babette 87–8
Mankiewicz, Joseph 456
Mann, Anthony 258
Mannoni, Octave 167
Marks, Elaine 392–3
Martineau, Barbara 29
Marx, Karl 23, 28, 187, 548–9, 550
Masoch, Leopold von Sacher- 203, 204, 205, 214, 215
Masochism in Modern Man (Reik) 207
Masochism: An Interpretation of Coldness and Cruelty (Deleuze) 203
Mayne, Judith 159–78, 275–6
McCrea, Joel 259
McGarry, Eileen 6
McLaughlin, Sheila 398, 399
Melville 256
Memory Pictures, Pratibha Parmar 382
Merrily We Go To Hell 143, 144, 145, 146
Metz, Christian 124, 167, 205, 213–14, 236, 237, 275, 293, 422–3
Mildred Pierce 79, 468, 475, 480
Millett, Kate 29
Mitchell, Juliet 61–3, 530
Mitchell, W. J. 542, 548
Modleski, Tania 230, 439–40, 444, 447–8, 493–4, 521–33
Moment by Moment 128–9
Mona Lisa 356, 363–5, 370
Monroe, Marilyn 40, 123–4, 340
Monsieur Beaucaire 233–4, 244
Monsiváis, Carlos 509, 510, 517
Montrelay, Michèle 86, 92–4, 424, 427
Moore, Clairmonte 317, 318–19
Moraga, Cherríe 391, 398, 401, 508
Morocco 25, 43, 44, 159, 209, 212
Morphology of the Folktale (Propp) 275
Morrison, Toni 356, 366, 368, 377, 412
Mother Daughter Plot: Narrative, Psychoanalysis, Feminism, The 371–2
Motown Industries 345
'Multiculturalism and Oppositionality' (Wallace) 313
Mulvey, Laura 24–5, 34–47, 120–2, 124, 132, 184–99 *passim* 209, 213–14, 219, 253–63 *passim* 276, 363–4, 421, 426, 439–40, 450–1, 454–5, 482–3, 495, 498–9, 507, 530
Mulvey, Nancy 228–9, 233, 237, 535–52
My Brilliant Career 129
My Two Dads 533

Nana 143, 146
National Film Theatre 139
Neale, Steve 253–64
Negulesco, Jean 429
New Criticism 5
Newton, Esther 388, 389, 401–2
Newton, Helmut 343
Nietzsche, Friedrich 270, 272
Nightwood (Barnes) 386, 387
North by Northwest 254
The North Sea (Heine) 418–19
Northwestern Conference on Feminist Film Criticism 127
Not Wanted 31
Now Voyager 421, 428

Of Woman Born (Rich) 479
'On Being White' (Frye) 337
One Hundred and Twenty Days in Sodom (Sade) 204–5
Only Angels Have Wings 42
Orol, Juan 512
Ottinger, Ulrike 400
Out of the Past 78, 80–1
Out on Tuesday 382
Owens, Craig 309–10

Pajaczkowska, Claire 356–65
Pakula, Alan 83
Palma, Letitia 515
Panofsky, Erwin 22, 23
Parmar, Pratibha 375–83
Parnet, Claire 181–4
Pat Garrett and Billy the Kid 259, 260
Paz, Octavio 508
Peary, Gerald 139, 166
Peckinpah, Sam 259, 260
Peirce, Charles 269, 270

Personal Best 396
Pietz, William 542
'Place of Women in the Cinema of Raoul Walsh' (Cook and Johnston) 63
Plotting Women (Franco) 510
'The Political Economy of the Sign' (Baudrillard) 549–50
Political Unconscious (Jameson) 269
Pollitt, Katha 521
Pons, María Antonieta 515
Pontalis, J. B. 358, 369
The Postman Always Rings Twice 78, 81, 82
Potter, Sally 87, 98, 131–2, 278, 500
Présence Africaine 536
Propp, Vladimir 258, 275
Psychoanalysis and Feminism (Mitchell) 61–2
'Psychoanalysis and Film Noir' (Thomas) 157–8

Rainer, Yvonne 265, 271, 274, 277–8, 279, 280–1
Raise the Red Lantern 415
Le rationalisme appliqué (Bachelard) 295
Rear Window 44
Reassemblage 322, 329, 334
Red Sorghum 415
Redford, Robert 129, 232
ReFraming AIDS 381
Un Regard Oblique 430–3
Reik, Theodore 207
The Reproduction of Mothering (Chodorow) 485
Re-vision 288, 290
The Revolt of Mamie Stover 64
Rich, Adrienne 398, 467, 479–80, 487, 499
Rich, Ruby 123, 124, 278, 280, 496
Riddles of the Sphinx 88–9, 97, 132
Rivette, Jacques 500
Riviere, Joan 362, 426–7
Rodowick, David N. 181–99, 213, 257, 451
Ross, Diana 336, 342, 343, 345, 347
Rothman, Stephanie 24
Rowbotham, Sheila 342
Rubin, Gayle 340, 389–90, 391
Russ, Joanna 395
Russell, Jane 123–4, 340
Russell, Rosalind 166
Russo, Vito 162

Sacher-Masoch, Leopold von *see* Masoch, Leopold von Sacher-
Sade, Marquis de 204–5, 214
Safouan, Moustafa 427
Said, Edward 377
Salomé, Lou Andreas 525
Samois 389
Le Samourai 256
Sarris, Andrew 26, 139
Saturday Night and Sunday Morning 155
Saturday Night Fever 128, 263
Saussure, Ferdinand de 56, 58–9, 131, 270, 420
The Scarlet Empress 214
Schafer, Roy 207, 211
Scott, Joan 9
Screen 34, 275, 336, 339
Seidelman, Susan 177, 456
Sembene, Ousmane 536–8, 540–1, 543–4, 545, 547, 550–1
Seminar XI 297, 299
Seneca, Gail 123, 124
Sevilla, Ninón 514, 515, 516, 517
Shanghai Express 214
She Must Be Seeing Things 398, 399
The Sheik 238–9
Shklovsky, Victor 72, 144
Shoot for the Contents 317, 318–19, 329, 332
Sigmund Freud's Dora 125, 131, 132, 279
Signs and Meanings in the Cinema (Wollen) 275
Silverman, Kaja 100–17, 279
Simson, Rennie 347
Sirk, Douglas 142, 146, 263, 468
Smith, Barbara 341
Smith, Sharon 48
Snow, Michael 274
Socarides, Charles 216, 219
Soledad (Solitude) 514–15
The Song of the Sheikh 241
Sontag, Susan 507–8
Speculum de l'autre femme (Irigaray) 486
Spillers, Hortense 351
Split Britches 396
Stacey, Jackie 450–64
Stahl, John 429, 468
Stanwyck, Barbara 489
Stein, Gertrude 386
Stella Dallas 230, 468–77, 480–1, 489–93, 494–5, 496–9
Sternberg, Josef von 25, 43, 81, 122, 196–7, 208–9, 211, 212, 214, 262
Stewart, James 259
Stimpson, Catharine 386

Stoller, Robert 211
Structural Anthropology (Lévi-Strauss) 50, 53, 55, 57
Studlar, Gaylyn 203–20
Surname Viet Given Name Nam 320, 326–7, 329
Suter, Jacquelyn 161

Tales of Love (Kristeva) 530–1
Television 287, 297
'Thinking Sex' (Rubin) 389, 390
Thomas, Deborah 157–8
'Three Essays on the Theory of Sexuality' (Freud) 37, 239
Three Godfathers 522, 528
Three Men and a Baby 521–8, 530–3
Three Men and a Cradle 521, 532
Thriller 87, 98, 131–2, 500
T-Men 258
To Have and Have Not 40, 42
Todorov, Tzvetan 268, 420
Tolstoy, Leo 144–5, 147
Toure, Samoury 536
Tours film festival (1863) 536
'The Traffic in Women' (Rubin) 389, 390
Travolta, John 128–9, 232, 263
Trinh, T. Minh-Ha 317–35
Troubridge, Una 402
Truffaut, François (Robert Lacheney) 515–16

'Unrememberable and the Unforgettable: The Passive Primal Repression' (Frank) 217

Valentino, Rudolph 226–8, 231, 232, 233–6, 237–9, 240–5
Varda, Agnès 32
Vertigo 44, 45, 268
Vidor, King 429, 439, 470–1, 480
Visible Fictions (Ellis) 254–5
'Visual Pleasure and Narrative Cinema' (Mulvey) 275, 450
von Sternberg, Josef *see* Sternberg, Josef von

Walker, Alexander 242
Wallace, Michele 313–14
Wayne, John 259
Weber, Lois 30
Wei, Yanmei 414–15
The Well of Loneliness (Hall) 387–9, 402
West, Mae 25–6, 244
White, Patricia 400
The Wild Bunch 259, 260
Wild Party 143
Willemen, Paul 153, 258, 261
Williams, Linda 230, 241, 429, 479–500
Wilson, Harriet E. 348
Wittig, Monique 177, 340, 392, 393–5
Wolf Man 526
Wollen, Peter 26, 27, 29, 275
'The "Woman's Film": Possession and Address' (Doane) 126
Women Against Pornography 127–8, 130, 389
'Women on the Market' (Irigaray) 547
'Women Reading Men' (Gledhill) 3, 416
Women Who Loved Women (Corinne) 162
Women's Movement 139, 253
Wood, Robin 27, 209
The Work of Dorothy Arzner: Towards a Feminist Cinema (ed. Johnston) 165
WOW Café 396, 398
'Writing Toward *Nightwood*: Djuna Barnes's Seduction Stories' (Allen) 386–7
Wulff, M. 216

Xala 535, 537–41, 543–8, 550–1

Yarbro-Bejarano, Yvonne 401
'You Don't Know What You're Doing Do You, Mr. Jones?' (Mulvey) 24–5
Young, Lola 156–7, 311, 356–63, 365–73

Zami (Lorde) 391
Zilboorg, Gregory 219
Zucker, Carole 209

OXFORD READINGS IN FEMINISM

Series Editors: **Susan James** and **Teresa Brennan**

Oxford Readings in Feminism provide accessible, one-volume guides to the very best in contemporary feminist thinking, assessing its impact and importance in key areas of study.

Collected together by scholars of outstanding reputation in their field, the articles chosen represent the most important work on feminist issues, and concise, lively introductions to each volume crystallize the main line of debate in the field.

This engaging book brings together carefully selected essays on feminism and film which trace the major developments in theory, criticism, and practices of women and cinema from 1973 to the present day. *Feminism and Film* illuminates the powerful, if controversial, role feminist research has played in the emergence of Film Studies as a discipline during these years, and demonstrates a variety of methods of feminist film study. As well as a wide-ranging introduction by Kaplan, which sets her selection of essays in context, readers will find examples of social-role, psychoanalytic, structuralist, post-structuralist, gay and lesbian, postmodern, and postcolonial feminist film criticism. In bringing together the major theories in feminism and film, this book should provoke fruitful discussion and debate in the classroom and beyond.

E. Ann Kaplan is Professor of English and Director of the Humanities Institute, the State University of New York, Stony Brook.

Series cover design: the Senate

Logo inspired by Mary Kelly's '*Pecunia*'

OXFORD
UNIVERSITY PRESS

www.oup.com

ISBN 0-19-878234-9

9 780198 782346